INTERNATIONAL BIBLE LESSON COMMENTARY

FORMERLY TARBELL'S

The New Standard In
Biblical Exposition Based
On The International
Sunday School
Lessons (ISSL)

NexGen® is an imprint of
Cook Communications Ministries, Colorado Springs, CO 80918
Cook Communications, Paris, Ontario
Kingsway Communications, Eastbourne, England

THE KJV INTERNATIONAL BIBLE LESSON COMMENTARY

First printing, 2006
Printed in U.S.A.
1 2 3 4 5 6 7 8 9 10 Printing/Year 10 09 08 07 06

Editor: Daniel Lioy, Ph.D.
Product Development Manager: Karen Pickering
Cover Design: Ray Moore/Two Moore Design
Cover Photo: ©2000-2005 PhotoSpin, Inc.

ISBN: 0781443113

CONTENTS

SEPTEMBER, OCTOBER, NOVEMBER 2006
GOD'S LIVING COVENANT

UNIT I: IN COVENANT WITH GOD

UNIT II: GOD'S COVENANT WITH JUDGES AND KINGS

UNIT III: LIVING AS GOD'S COVENANTED PEOPLE

DECEMBER 2006, JANUARY, FEBRUARY 2007
JESUS CHRIST: A PORTRAIT OF GOD

UNIT I: CHRIST, THE IMAGE OF GOD

UNIT III: CHRIST GUIDES AND PROTECTS

Contents

■

March, April, May 2007
Our Community Now and in God's Future

■

June, July, August 2007
Committed to Doing Right

The York Academy in York, Pennsylvania, was chartered in 1787. It grew and eventually became the York College of Pennsylvania. For the next 140 years, however, this distinguished educational institution never graduated a student, although hundreds attended. The reason was that its founders believed that learning never stops!

The same may be said of us who are Christians. Our learning never stops. If we take our faith seriously, we will make learning God's Word a lifelong activity. After all, in the Greek New Testament the word rendered *disciple* means "learner." Discipleship implies a sincere and continuous effort on our part to learn more and more about the Messiah.

Although I have been teaching for over 25 years, I can testify that I still regard myself as a learner. The more I take the study of Scripture seriously, the more I learn. And the more I learn, the more I enjoy teaching. It's a never-ending cycle!

Occasionally, I talk with a teacher who claims to be bored or burned out. Usually, that teacher, I discover, has stopped learning. "I taught that Sunday school class for 15 years," one weary teacher groaned. "No, you haven't," replied a knowledgeable older friend. "You have taught that class for one year 15 times!"

Let this year be a learning experience for you as well as for your class. Let the Scriptures speak to you. Listen to the Spirit's message through those passages each week. Pray that your heart and mind may be opened.

Just as you would discipline yourself to learn more about your favorite hobby, discipline yourself as much as possible to learn more about the Good News through the Bible. Then approach your teaching each week with zest and expectancy. Discover that, as you find joy and meaning in learning about the Savior, your class members will also begin to become lifetime learners in the faith.

Your fellow learner at the feet of the Master Teacher,
Dan Lioy

USE *THE KJV INTERNATIONAL BIBLE LESSON COMMENTARY* WITH MATERIAL FROM THESE PUBLISHERS

Sunday school materials from the following denominations and publishers follow the International Sunday School Lesson outlines (sometimes known as the Uniform Series). Because *The KJV International Bible Lesson Commentary* (formerly *Tarbell's*) follows the same ISSL outlines, you can use *The KJV International Bible Lesson Commentary* as an excellent teacher resource to supplement the materials from these publishing houses.

Nondenominational:

Standard Publishing—*Adult*

Urban Ministries—*All ages*

Echoes Teacher's Commentary (Cook Communications Ministries) *Adult*

Denominational:

Advent Christian General Conference—*Adult*

American Baptist (Judson Press)—*Adult*

Church of God in Christ (Church of God in Christ Publishing House)—*Adult*

Church of Christ Holiness—*Adult*

Church of God (Warner Press)—*Adult*

Church of God by Faith—*Adult*

National Baptist Convention of America (Boyd)—*All ages*

National Primitive Baptist Convention—*Adult*

Progressive National Baptist Convention—*Adult*

Presbyterian Church (U.S.A.) (Bible Discovery Series—Presbyterian Publishing House or P.R.E.M.)—*Adult*

Union Gospel Press—*All ages*

United Holy Church of America—*Adult*

United Methodist Church (Cokesbury)—*All ages*

GOD'S COVENANT WITH NOAH

BACKGROUND SCRIPTURE: Genesis 9:1-17
DEVOTIONAL READING: Psalm 36:5-9

KEY VERSE: And I will remember my covenant, which is between me and you and every living creature of all flesh; and the waters shall no more become a flood to destroy all flesh. Genesis 9:15.

KING JAMES VERSION

GENESIS 9:1 And God blessed Noah and his sons, and said unto them, Be fruitful, and multiply, and replenish the earth. 2 And the fear of you and the dread of you shall be upon every beast of the earth, and upon every fowl of the air, upon all that moveth upon the earth, and upon all the fishes of the sea; into your hand are they delivered. 3 Every moving thing that liveth shall be meat for you; even as the green herb have I given you all things. 4 But flesh with the life thereof, which is the blood thereof, shall ye not eat. 5 And surely your blood of your lives will I require; at the hand of every beast will I require it, and at the hand of man; at the hand of every man's brother will I require the life of man.
6 Whoso sheddeth man's blood, by man shall his blood be shed: for in the image of God made he man. 7 And you, be ye fruitful, and multiply; bring forth abundantly in the earth, and multiply therein.

8 And God spake unto Noah, and to his sons with him, saying, 9 And I, behold, I establish my covenant with you, and with your seed after you; 10 And with every living creature that is with you, of the fowl, of the cattle, and of every beast of the earth with you; from all that go out of the ark, to every beast of the earth. 11 And I will establish my covenant with you; neither shall all flesh be cut off any more by the waters of a flood; neither shall there any more be a flood to destroy the earth.

12 And God said, This is the token of the covenant which I make between me and you and every living creature that is with you, for perpetual generations: 13 I do set my bow in the cloud, and it shall be for a token of a covenant between me and the earth. 14 And it shall come to pass, when I bring a cloud over the earth, that the bow shall be seen in the cloud: 15 And I will remember my covenant, which is between me and you and every living creature of all flesh; and the waters shall no more become a flood to destroy all flesh.

NEW REVISED STANDARD VERSION

GENESIS 9:1 God blessed Noah and his sons, and said to them, "Be fruitful and multiply, and fill the earth. 2 The fear and dread of you shall rest on every animal of the earth, and on every bird of the air, on everything that creeps on the ground, and on all the fish of the sea; into your hand they are delivered. 3 Every moving thing that lives shall be food for you; and just as I gave you the green plants, I give you everything.
4 Only, you shall not eat flesh with its life, that is, its blood. 5 For your own lifeblood I will surely require a reckoning: from every animal I will require it and from human beings, each one for the blood of another, I will require a reckoning for human life.

6 Whoever sheds the blood of a human,
    by a human shall that person's blood be shed;
for in his own image
    God made humankind.

7 And you, be fruitful and multiply, abound on the earth and multiply in it."

8 Then God said to Noah and to his sons with him, 9 "As for me, I am establishing my covenant with you and your descendants after you, 10 and with every living creature that is with you, the birds, the domestic animals, and every animal of the earth with you, as many as came out of the ark. 11 I establish my covenant with you, that never again shall all flesh be cut off by the waters of a flood, and never again shall there be a flood to destroy the earth." 12 God said, "This is the sign of the covenant that I make between me and you and every living creature that is with you, for all future generations: 13 I have set my bow in the clouds, and it shall be a sign of the covenant between me and the earth.
14 When I bring clouds over the earth and the bow is seen in the clouds, 15 I will remember my covenant that is between me and you and every living creature of all flesh; and the waters shall never again become a flood to destroy all flesh.

Monday, August 28	Psalm 36:5-9	*God Is Gracious*
Tuesday, August 29	Genesis 7:1-12	*Noah Enters the Ark*
Wednesday, August 30	Genesis 7:13-24	*The Flood Rages*
Thursday, August 31	Genesis 8:1-12	*The Water Subsides*
Friday, September 1	Genesis 8:13-22	*God Makes a Promise*
Saturday, September 2	Genesis 9:1-7	*God Instructs Noah*
Sunday, September 3	Genesis 9:8-17	*God Covenants with Noah*

BACKGROUND

Genesis is the book of beginnings. In this portion of Scripture we find the beginnings of the material universe, human life, human sin, divine judgment on human sin, covenant promises, and the Israelite tribes—to name just a few. Genesis provides a foundation for a great deal of what we can know about life and our Lord. Genesis is also part of the first five books forming a group of their own at the beginning of the Old Testament. Together, Genesis through Deuteronomy are usually called the "Torah" (meaning "law" or "teaching") or the "Pentateuch" (literally, "five-volumed [book]"). Genesis provides the background for the Exodus and wilderness settings of the other four books.

In terms of authorship, most Bible scholars credit Moses as the person responsible for the content of the Pentateuch, including Genesis. No less of an authority than the Messiah provided warrant for this view when He said to the Jewish authorities at the Jerusalem temple, *Did not Moses give you the law?* (John 7:19). Here *the law* refers evidently refers to the first five books of the Bible.

Furthermore, numerous times throughout the New Testament, Moses is credited as saying things found in *the law.* Despite the skepticism of some, it seems reasonable to maintain that Moses had the ability to write the Pentateuch. Acts 7:22 reveals that he received one of the best educations available in his day. His instruction would have included languages, history, and law. Whether Moses worked alone on the Pentateuch is open to debate. He could have had one or more assistants. In particular, someone else added Deuteronomy 34, which records the account of his death.

In terms of sources, Moses may have listened to oral accounts that had been passed down from generation to generation. As well, he had access to records that had been preserved by the Hebrew community in Egypt. There's also the possibility he had documents from the archives of Pharaoh. As Moses and possibly one or more assistants worked from these sources, the Spirit of God guided Moses to convey only what is true. At times his communication with the divine was immediate and direct (see Num. 12:8). This suggests that some of what appears in the Pentateuch could have come directly from divine revelation.

Moses lived 120 years. Most likely, he wrote all the Pentateuch in the last third of his life. It was during this time that he led the Israelites out of Egypt and governed them as they camped here and there on the Sinai Peninsula and in the Transjordan. During that period Moses would have time to compose a long and difficult literary work.

According to 1 Kings 6:1, work on the first temple began in the fourth year of King Solomon's reign and the 480th year after the Exodus. The fourth year of Solomon's reign is usually identified as 966 B.C. That means the Exodus must have taken place around the year 1446 B.C. And since Moses died at the end of the 40-year wilderness wandering period, he must have composed the Pentateuch during the period 1446–1406 B.C.

NOTES ON THE PRINTED TEXT

Hebrews 11 spotlights several examples of people from the opening chapters of Genesis who lived by faith, including Noah (see 11:7). His trust in and obedience to God is all the more noteworthy due to the rampant spread of human wickedness in Noah's day. Indeed, evil had increased to such a point that God was pained at His creation's moral condition. So He determined to destroy His creation; but He also planned to preserve Noah, who had found favor with God. In particular, God was pleased with Noah's righteousness, which was demonstrated by his obedient faith.

As an act of grace, God instructed Noah to build an ark that would preserve his family and a remnant of God's creation from the Flood that would destroy the earth (Gen. 6). When these preparations were complete, the waters began to cover the earth and do their destructive work (chap. 7). After the waters receded, Noah, his family, and the animals disembarked from the ark and began a new era in history. From here on out, the small band of people would repopulate areas devastated by the Flood (chap. 8).

It was appropriate, therefore, that God and the remnant of survivors mark the occasion by reaffirming their relationship. Noah offered burnt sacrifices. Then God spoke, making a promise, pronouncing a blessing, giving instructions, and establishing a covenant (8:20-21). Throughout history, God made several covenants with people. These agreements came at God's initiative, and He Himself fixed the terms and conditions (if any). In the case of the covenant made after the Flood, God established an unconditional covenant with all people and all animals. He would never again use water to destroy all life. People and animals don't have to do anything to ensure that God will keep this promise. Of His own mercy, He permits even the wicked to live on the earth as long as it lasts.

The burnt offerings Noah sacrificed were pleasing to God. The sacrifice showed Noah's devotion, which contrasted sharply with the spiritual rebellion of the people who had been killed by the Flood. The Lord promised never again to send such a flood upon the earth. He made that commitment in spite of humanity's evil tendencies. Though wickedness would again show itself on the earth, He would not send another such flood to destroy all life (8:22).

Next, the Lord blessed the survivors. He reminded them that His earlier command to have children and spread out across the earth was still in effect (9:1). He also reaffirmed human dominion over the animal kingdom (9:2). The people could use animals for their food. Some scholars take 9:3 to mean that before this time, vegetarianism had been the rule for people. Others, however, think people were always allowed to eat animals.

In light of the present permission to eat animals, and in light of the recent destruction of many lives, God took this opportunity to reaffirm the sanctity of life—both animal life and human life. While people could eat animal flesh, they were not to eat blood, since life is identified with blood. They would have to drain animal carcasses of blood before eating them (9:4). More importantly, human life was to be honored and guarded. God would demand an accounting from each animal and person who treated human life lightly. Since people are made in the image of God, God decreed that murder would receive the punishment of death (9:5-6). Lastly, God renewed His instructions for people to have children (9:7). Human life, which is sacred in God's eyes, was to be spread abroad throughout the earth.

Earlier, the Lord had decided never again to send a flood to destroy all life (8:21). As He wound up His speech with Noah, He solemnly confirmed that decision with a covenant. He enacted this agreement with Noah, his descendants, and with all living creatures, including the birds, the wild animals, and the domestic animals (9:8-11). The sign of the covenant was the rainbow (9:12-13). The bow in the clouds would function as a reminder to God that He should limit the damage any rainstorm could do. He would not allow the water to continue rising on the earth until all living things had died (9:14-15).

Some scholars believe that until this period in history there had never been a rainbow. Others believe that rainbows had always been appearing near rain clouds, but that after the Flood, God invested this beautiful arch of color in the sky with a new and special meaning. After the traumatic experience of the Flood, Noah's family needed the reassurance God gave them. Without it, every time rain began to fall, they would have wondered about the possibility of another flood. God reassured Noah's family about the future of the human race, which would consist of their descendants.

Although the text does not mention it, the rainbow can also function as a reminder to people. It can reassure us of God's goodness to all people, whether or not they worship and obey Him (see Jas. 1:17). God's goodness gives people an opportunity to repent and recognize what He has done for them. Sadly, few people recognize the significance of the rainbow when they see it. It means patience and mercy—for now. God's nature does not allow Him to delay judgment forever. If people do not respond to His goodness and His offer of salvation in Christ, they will receive the just punishment for their sins.

SUGGESTIONS TO TEACHERS

God saw that the earth needed a new start, and He gave it one. Granted, the Flood was not an easy way to begin again, but God's grace preserved all those who trusted Him. In a similar way, by grace through faith in Christ, we can realize new beginnings in all areas of life.

1. A NEW START FOR NOAH. What was it like for Noah to walk into a fresh, new world? It was as if an erasure had taken place and a fresh page had been inserted. This was an opportunity for Noah and his descendants to start over.

2. A NEW START FOR US. Imagine someone giving you a book containing a record of every word you had ever spoken, every deed you had ever done, and every thought you had ever entertained. And imagine that with the book you were handed an eraser and were told that you could wipe out any of the book's contents that you wished and that the actuality of the facts themselves would also disappear with the erasing. Of course, we can't erase our past. But we don't need to, for Jesus has done something much more effective. He makes it possible for God to forgive our past. In fact, Jesus begins a transformation process to make us what we could never become, no matter how much we tried.

3. A NEW HOPE FOR A BRIGHTER FUTURE. When we trust in Christ for salvation, we realize new beginnings in all areas of life. This is the basis for our hope in a brighter future. Jesus came to bring renewal where sin has caused harm and destruction. And though it may not always be an easy path to the fresh start we desire, the rainbow reminds us that God wants us to experience new beginnings, and He will take us there if we will trust Him.

FOR ADULTS

■ **TOPIC:** Finding Security

■ **QUESTIONS:** 1. What did God command Noah and his descendants to do? 2. After the Flood, what sort of authority did God give to humankind over the other creatures of the earth? 3. What would be the punishment for murdering another human being? 4. What was the nature of the covenant that God established with Noah and his descendants? 5. What might be the significance of the rainbow as a sign of God's covenant with Noah?

■ **ILLUSTRATIONS:**

Where Can Security Be Found? The 10th edition of the *Merriam Webster's Collegiate Dictionary* defines security as "freedom from danger" and "freedom from fear or anxiety." In the world of computers, a feeling of security is obtained when one's system is adequately defended from a host of malicious programs through the use of firewalls and antivirus software (among other things). Experts claim that having the most up-to-date products installed on one's computer can lead to a more secure operating system.

In the spiritual realm, freedom from anxiety as well as a myriad of unforeseen dangers can found through faith in Christ. Indeed, Scripture assures us that nothing can separate believers from His love (Rom. 8:38-39) and that He is able to protect them until the last day (1 Pet. 1:5). This means that when our faith is in Christ, we have nothing to fear.

A New Beginning. Operation Fresh Start is a government program designed to help individuals and communities make use of various resources so they can recover from a flood, earthquake, or other natural disaster. The aim is not just to reestablish things the way they were before the tragedy occurred. It is to create an opportunity for cities and towns to modernize, improve, and redesign their communities in ways that are truly stronger and better than ever.

There's a sense in which new life in Christ is like this. For example, Jesus doesn't just spiritually revamp us. He helps us to go beyond the brokenness in our lives to experience a new beginning. This is more than just overcoming our past. It is an opportunity for the focus and direction of our lives to be transformed through faith in Him.

Are You a One-Note Melody? In his book *Don't Park Here,* C. William Fisher reminds us that the transforming power of the risen Christ should be at work in all aspects of our lives, throughout our lives. He says that too many believers are like piano players who use only one or two "notes." Their testimonies to the power of God in their lives begin and end with "I was saved 40 years ago and I know I'm going to heaven."

Yet there are so many more melodies Christ wants to "play" in our lives, Fisher says. "Why, with all the rich, wide range of the keyboard of spiritual insight and truth, do so many Christians play only on one note? Why should we be content to be a dull monotone when God intends this life to be a rich, harmonious symphony?"

What a Difference! At our first meeting, Bobby sat uncomfortably on a very comfortable couch. Like so many before him—those with broken lives seeking counsel—he had come to me searching for the life preserver as he felt himself going down for the last time.

Bobby had been a professional soccer player with a promising career, but drugs, alcohol, and a steady stream of lies and deceit had finally brought him down. After losing his dream, a wife, and a young daughter, Bobby was now in danger of losing his freedom. At this moment, only the judge knew for sure.

As I shared the Gospel and the power of the risen Christ with Bobby, he immediately took hold of this life preserver from heaven. Bobby experienced a glorious conversion that day—plucked out of the kingdom of darkness and transplanted into the kingdom of God's Son.

It's exciting to see a genuine conversion lead a person to repentance, and then take him or her into the fullness of restitution. Bobby walked through circumstance after desperate circumstance—all the while seeing God's delivering power continuing to go before him.

Bobby hoped God would soften the hearts of several key people as he began to put his life back together again, and the Lord did. This young man knew firsthand that the same Spirit that had transformed other saints in the past had also changed him. That resurrection power of Christ is available for you as well.

■ **FOR YOUTH** ■ TOPIC: God's Promise to Noah
■ QUESTIONS: 1. In what way did God bless Noah and his descendants? 2. Why do you think God allowed people to eat animals as food? 3. In what way did God make it clear that human life was to be valued? 4. What is the significance of the rainbow? 5. What opportunities might God be giving you for a fresh start?

■ **ILLUSTRATIONS:**

A Fresh Start. Henry Grimes was an A-list jazz musician in the 1950s and '60s. He played with everyone from swing master Benny Goodman to free jazz saxophonist Albert Ayler. Then Grimes disappeared. For almost 40 years he lived a life of homeless shelters, day labor, and emotional isolation.

Suddenly, in 2003, Grimes was "rediscovered" in Los Angeles by a jazz fan and social worker, and soon he started getting job offers. Before long Grimes had a new contract with a small Swedish label that released some recordings he made in Europe in the summer of 2004.

You don't have to wait until the later years of your life to experience a fresh start. The best time is right now while you are still young. Let your faith in Christ be the basis for a brighter future filled with hope.

Changed Lives. In *Evidence That Demands a Verdict,* Josh McDowell lists a number of conversion testimonies of people from a wide variety of backgrounds. One is Christa Nitzschke, who had read a number of pagan philosophers. Through a girlfriend's help, however, Christa trusted in Jesus. "I committed my life to Him," Christa declared. Charlie Abero was a radical Marxist in India. Through a Christian speaker, Charlie heard a presentation that made much more sense to him than communism. "I became a Christian," he testified. "I have found purpose and meaning for my life."

These testimonies indicate that it is not enough to assent to the messiahship of Jesus. Even demons believe that there is one God and fear Him (Jas. 2:19), but they do not worship and obey Him. Correct information is insufficient. Belief entails an unswerving faith in Christ. Have you committed yourself to Jesus in this way, trusting Him for eternal life?

A Decision to Stay. Courtney discovered the campus life at her large state university had not proved to be as much fun she had expected. Most of her dorm mates drank heavily and several were weekend binge drinkers. A couple of girls on her floor did drugs. And several were sexually immoral.

Courtney found herself struggling to maintain the values she had received from her parents and her church. She privately had questions about the Bible and doubts about the person of Christ. Previously, Courtney's faith had not meant much to her. But in the crucible of dorm life, this sophomore found herself torn between going along with the pleasure-seeking values of her peers and the traditional ideas of her upbringing. The inner tug-of-war became increasingly difficult to endure.

One evening, while lying in bed and pondering her situation, Courtney found Galatians 2:20 coming to mind: *Nevertheless I live; yet not I, but Christ liveth in me.* The young adult was surprised that these words presented themselves to her, for she had not looked at a Bible or thought about Jesus much since leaving home. But the verse seemed to bring her a sense of calm and hope.

Over the next few days, Courtney found herself repeating the verse and considering the truth it revealed. Strangely, she became aware that the Lord seemed to be accompanying her. His Presence, to her surprise, seemed to confer stamina and stability to her pressure-filled daily life. Eventually, Courtney realized that the Savior was actually with her in her trials.

Courtney sought out the university chaplain and discovered a supportive community of friendly fellow Christians. At first, she was ready to move out of her dorm and find a residence with women who shared her faith in the resurrected Jesus. But as Courtney engaged in Bible study and discussion with her Christian friends, she sensed that the Lord wanted her to remain in her dorm as a witness for Him.

Courtney decided to stay in her old room, and her quiet testimony as a Christian won the respect of many of her peers. Several, in fact, privately came to her asking about her faith. When this happened, she would smile and share the Gospel!

GOD'S COVENANT WITH ABRAM

BACKGROUND SCRIPTURE: Genesis 17
DEVOTIONAL READING: Hebrews 6:13-20

2

KEY VERSE: Neither shall thy name any more be called Abram, but thy name shall be Abraham; for a father of many nations have I made thee. Genesis 17:5.

KING JAMES VERSION

GENESIS 17:1 And when Abram was ninety years old and nine, the LORD appeared to Abram, and said unto him, I am the Almighty God; walk before me, and be thou perfect. 2 And I will make my covenant between me and thee, and will multiply thee exceedingly. 3 And Abram fell on his face: and God talked with him, saying,

4 As for me, behold, my covenant is with thee, and thou shalt be a father of many nations. 5 Neither shall thy name any more be called Abram, but thy name shall be Abraham; for a father of many nations have I made thee. 6 And I will make thee exceeding fruitful, and I will make nations of thee, and kings shall come out of thee.

7 And I will establish my covenant between me and thee and thy seed after thee in their generations for an everlasting covenant, to be a God unto thee, and to thy seed after thee. 8 And I will give unto thee, and to thy seed after thee, the land wherein thou art a stranger, all the land of Canaan, for an everlasting possession; and I will be their God. . . .

15 And God said unto Abraham, As for Sarai thy wife, thou shalt not call her name Sarai, but Sarah shall her name be. 16 And I will bless her, and give thee a son also of her: yea, I will bless her, and she shall be a mother of nations; kings of people shall be of her. 17 Then Abraham fell upon his face, and laughed, and said in his heart, Shall a child be born unto him that is an hundred years old? and shall Sarah, that is ninety years old, bear? 18 And Abraham said unto God, O that Ishmael might live before thee! 19 And God said, Sarah thy wife shall bear thee a son indeed; and thou shalt call his name Isaac: and I will establish my covenant with him for an everlasting covenant, and with his seed after him. 20 And as for Ishmael, I have heard thee: Behold, I have blessed him, and will make him fruitful, and will multiply him exceedingly; twelve princes shall he beget, and I will make him a great nation. 21 But my covenant will I establish with Isaac, which Sarah shall bear unto thee at this set time in the next year. 22 And he left off talking with him, and God went up from Abraham.

NEW REVISED STANDARD VERSION

GENESIS 17:1 When Abram was ninety-nine years old, the LORD appeared to Abram, and said to him, "I am God Almighty; walk before me, and be blameless. 2 And I will make my covenant between me and you, and will make you exceedingly numerous." 3 Then Abram fell on his face; and God said to him, 4 "As for me, this is my covenant with you: You shall be the ancestor of a multitude of nations. 5 No longer shall your name be Abram, but your name shall be Abraham; for I have made you the ancestor of a multitude of nations. 6 I will make you exceedingly fruitful; and I will make nations of you, and kings shall come from you. 7 I will establish my covenant between me and you, and your offspring after you throughout their generations, for an everlasting covenant, to be God to you and to your offspring after you. 8 And I will give to you, and to your offspring after you, the land where you are now an alien, all the land of Canaan, for a perpetual holding; and I will be their God." . . .

15 God said to Abraham, "As for Sarai your wife, you shall not call her Sarai, but Sarah shall be her name. 16 I will bless her, and moreover I will give you a son by her. I will bless her, and she shall give rise to nations; kings of peoples shall come from her." 17 Then Abraham fell on his face and laughed, and said to himself, "Can a child be born to a man who is a hundred years old? Can Sarah, who is ninety years old, bear a child?" 18 And Abraham said to God, "O that Ishmael might live in your sight!" 19 God said, "No, but your wife Sarah shall bear you a son, and you shall name him Isaac. I will establish my covenant with him as an everlasting covenant for his offspring after him. 20 As for Ishmael, I have heard you; I will bless him and make him fruitful and exceedingly numerous; he shall be the father of twelve princes, and I will make him a great nation. 21 But my covenant I will establish with Isaac, whom Sarah shall bear to you at this season next year." 22 And when he had finished talking with him, God went up from Abraham.

Monday, September 4	Hebrews 6:13-20	*God's Promise Is Sure*
Tuesday, September 5	Hebrews 11:8-16	*Abraham Had Heroic Faith*
Wednesday, September 6	Genesis 15:1-8	*God's Promise to Abram*
Thursday, September 7	Genesis 15:12-21	*God Foretells Future Greatness*
Friday, September 8	Genesis 16:1-15	*God Blesses Hagar*
Saturday, September 9	Genesis 17:1-8	*God Covenants with Abraham*
Sunday, September 10	Genesis 17:15-22	*God Promises a Son*

BACKGROUND

At first glance it might appear that God originally called Terah from Ur in the land of the Chaldeans to go to Canaan, but other passages make it clear that God called Abram to leave his homeland (Gen. 15:7; Neh. 9:7; Acts 7:2-3). Ur was a highly civilized town in ancient Mesopotamia, known for its temple dedicated to the moon god Nanna. In fact, other biblical references tell us that Abram's family worshiped idols and other gods while in Ur (Josh. 24:2).

Abram began his journey to Canaan with his father, his wife, and a nephew named Lot. After traveling 600 miles north along the Fertile Crescent trade route, Abram's family arrived in Haran, where they stayed for a time, accumulating possessions and servants (Gen. 11:31; 12:5). Once Terah died, Abram continued his journey, obeying the message God had given him while in Ur.

God called Abram to leave everything that was significant to him: his culture, his relatives, and his family. God asked a 75-year-old man to leave the security of his homeland and set out for an unknown destination. In return, God promised to bless him in an unprecedented way. For instance, despite Abram's childlessness, God promised to make him a great nation with many descendants. God also pledged to give Abram honor and make him a source of blessing to others. Through Abram and his descendants, God would pour out great blessings for all humanity (12:1-3).

In response to God's call, Abram left Haran with his wife Sarai and his nephew lot to travel the 400 miles to Canaan. They took with them considerable possessions, slaves, and hired servants. Apart from God's revelation, Abram would not have left the security and wealth of his homeland. From a human perspective, residing in a comfortable house among friends and relatives outweighed the prospect of living in a tent as an alien in a far-off land. But when God called, Abram responded in faith, believing that God was able to do what He promised (12:4-5).

God honored Abram's faith and obedience. When he arrived at Shechem, the Lord appeared to him and promised to give the land of Canaan to his descendants. This is the first time, according to the text, that the Lord appeared to Abram since he left Ur, and the first time we know that God explicitly promised Canaan to the patriarch. In response to the Lord's appearance, Abram built an altar and offered sacrifices to the

Lord. This act showed that he believed God and was thankful for what He would do for him. At Bethel, Abram built another altar and again worshiped the Lord. Then he continued south to the deserts of the Negev, in the southernmost part of Canaan, where he apparently settled for a while (12:6-9).

In the years following Abram's initial encounter with God, the patriarch had to deal with a famine that prompted him to sojourn for a while in Egypt (Gen. 12:10-20). Then, while back in Canaan, the patriarch and Lot, his nephew, decided to part company (13:1-13). Once Lot had left, God appeared again to Abram. The patriarch was thinking about where he would live. So the Lord used this opportunity to repeat His promise that Abram's descendants would one day possess the whole of Canaan. An implication of this was that Abram should continue to live in Canaan (13:14-15).

The Lord also assured the patriarch that his offspring would be like the dust of the earth in number (13:16). That was quite a promise for a man who was over 75 and had no children. Next, the Lord invited Abram to walk through the land his descendants would occupy. The patriarch was to inspect the property that, in a sense, he already possessed—through God's promise (13:17). Presumably Abram did this. Then he settled for a while at Hebron. Close by was the town of Mamre, whose terebinth trees were probably used in Canaanite worship. It was near this center of false worship that Abram offered sacrifices to the true God (13:18).

Genesis 14 records that Abram defeated powerful armies from the East who captured Sodom and Gomorrah and took Lot and his family captive. Abram rescued Lot along with all the other people and goods taken from these cities. After this incident, the Lord visited the patriarch in a vision to reassure him and calm his fears. In particular, God pledged that a son of Abram, yet to be born, would become his heir. To further encourage the patriarch, the Lord led him out into the darkness of the night. Then, with a myriad of stars in view, God declared that Abram's offspring would be just as numerous. God saw that the patriarch believed Him and God honored Abram's faith (15:1-6).

NOTES ON THE PRINTED TEXT

After God's encounter with Abram recorded in Genesis 15, Abram had a son named Ishmael by Hagar, a servant of Sarai. For many years Abram thought that Ishmael, whose name means "God heard," was the heir the Lord promised him. When the patriarch was 99 years old, God appeared again to him after about 13 years of silence. The Lord encouraged Abram to walk before Him and be *perfect* (17:1) or blameless.

The Lord next declared His intent to confirm His covenant with the patriarch (17:2). In 15:18-21, God had ratified part of His pledge to Abram, namely, that his descendants would live in Canaan. Even so, the Lord had yet to guarantee explicitly the promise of numerous descendants and eternal possession of the land. These other aspects of the covenant are now in view.

The expression *fell on his face* (17:3) means either the patriarch dropped to his knees and placed his forehead on the ground or that he completely prostrated himself. In any case, Abram realized that he was in the presence of almighty God and thus responded in a reverential manner. As the patriarch worshiped, the Lord declared that part of His covenant included making His servant *a father of many nations* (17:4).

As Abram lay in the facedown posture of humility, God changed his name from *Abram* (17:5), which means "exalted father," to *Abraham*, which means "father of many." This change was appropriate because Abraham would be the father of multitudes through his yet-to-be-born son. Then, God once again listed the provisions of the covenant: Abraham would have many descendants who would possess the land of Canaan. God wound up this recital with the promise, *I will be their God* (17:8). The close relationship between God and Abraham would be mirrored by the relationship between God and Abraham's descendants.

Previously, Abraham had requested a sign confirming the covenant, and God had responded by sending a firepot and a blazing torch through the pieces of animals (see 15:17). This time, however, God asked for a sign. He told Abraham to be circumcised and to circumcise all the males of his household. This practice was to be repeated on all Abraham's male descendants as well as others in the covenant community (17:9-14).

Abraham was not the only person to get a name change. The Lord changed his wife's name too, from *Sarai* (17:15), which means "my princess," to *Sarah*, which means "a princess." The change emphasizes Sarah's role as the ancestress of royal figures. The Lord's blessing on Sarah included enabling her once barren womb to bear a son for the patriarch. Indeed, through this child Sarah would become a *mother of nations* (17:16); and kings of countries would be among her descendants.

When Abraham heard God say that Sarah would bear a son, he laughed (17:17). He believed that God would give him offspring, but he certainly didn't think the descendants would come through a son of Sarah's. He and she were both too old for children. A birth now seemed ridiculous. Abraham thought he had worked out a way for God's promises to be fulfilled: Ishmael would be his heir. So Abraham suggested this option to God (17:18).

The Lord declared that He would establish His covenant with Isaac and his descendants. Moreover, this covenant would be perpetual in nature (17:19). This did not mean that God had ignored Abraham's previous statement concerning Ishmael. Like his father, Ishmael would become the head of a great nation; and this nation would have 12 rulers (17:20; see 25:16).

Such statements notwithstanding, the Lord remained firm in His intent to make Isaac the recipient of the covenant promises. God revealed to Abraham that within a year Sarah would give birth to the child (17:21). The conversation then ended and the Lord left Abraham (vs. 22). While the manner in which God had appeared to the patriarch is debated, the certainty of His promises is clear.

SUGGESTIONS TO TEACHERS

We humans tend toward independence. It is difficult for us to place our future, our money, and our careers in the hands of anyone else. Within our control, the outcome may not be an incredible success, but at least it will be predictable and safe. However, God desires that we instead step into a wonderful world of adventure with Him at the controls.

1. ABRAHAM'S JOURNEY OF FAITH. God stretched Abraham's faith in many ways. The Lord told the patriarch that he would have a son. Moving to an unknown country was a risk, but the promise of having children as an old, childless couple was physically impossible. Even Abraham thought God needed help here. Rather than resting in God's promise, the patriarch began to create his own plan. Abraham heard and believed the Lord's promises, but he seemed to have difficulty shifting his mind from the natural to the supernatural. It was difficult for the patriarch to wait on the Lord and trust Him to accomplish His will in His way and in His time.

2. OUR JOURNEY OF FAITH. Are we any different than Abraham? God is stretching our faith, for example, when He asks us to watch our spouse suffer with cancer, or to forgive a drunken driver who killed our child or grandchild in a horrible accident. In the midst of such tragedies, the Lord wants us to trust His promise that He causes all things to work together for our eternal good (Rom. 8:28). How can we do that? It seems impossible!

3. OUR DECISION TO TRUST GOD—NO MATTER WHAT. The record of Scripture and of our own experiences in following God tell us that He seems to love the word "impossible." He most often does not work through our agenda, and we don't always see Him working in ways we understand. But He asks us to learn to trust His heart.

4. HANDS OFF! It can be hard to believe that God can do all things and is working even when we cannot see Him at work. So we "help" God work out His will. It's like a three-year-old helping his father paint the house. It may bring us satisfaction seeing our hand in the process. At best, however, it will be messy. At worst, it will have to be done all over again. Instead, we need to leave the painting to the Lord.

■ **TOPIC:** Trusting Promises

■ **QUESTIONS:** 1. Why did God tell Abraham that He is all-powerful? 2. What is significant about God changing the name of the patriarch and his wife? 3. What are the particulars of the covenant that God noted to Abraham? 4. In what way would God bless Ishmael and his descendants? 5. Why are we often reluctant to believe that God can do what He has promised?

■ **ILLUSTRATIONS:**

In God We Trust. In 1987, journalist Andrés Tapia suddenly realized his once-loving marriage was falling apart. Something was deeply troubling his wife, Lori, and he had no idea how to cope. "I never knew what I would find when I got home," he writes. "Sometimes she would be curled up in the fetal position in a corner of our apartment, her eyes reflecting a soul drained of hope. Frightened, I'd ask her what was wrong. No answer."

After much prayer, and Andrés' own unsuccessful attempts to help Lori shake her depression, the couple sought professional help. According to Andrés, after months of therapy, Lori learned that nearly all of her symptoms matched those of people who had been sexually abused as children. What followed were four difficult years of harsh memories, counseling, and continual dependence on God to heal Lori's emotions and their wounded marriage. For the Tapias, there were no pat answers or once-for-all solutions. "There are still days when Lori's depression shows up like an unwelcome visitor," Andrés admits. "But now Lori and I, with God's help, fight it out and move on."

None of us can know what trials and tests life will throw in our way. And few of us are so perfect that we never ask God "Why me?" or "What good can possibly come from this?" Yet, as this week's lesson dramatically shows, it is when we cling to God in these darkest times that our trust in Him can deepen into a powerful, sustaining faith.

Believing the Promise. In his book, *The Presence,* Bruce Larsen tells about a woman in one of his former congregations. Mrs. Chan was a tiny, energetic, and faith-filled woman. "Her daughter and son-in-law were on the verge of divorce. The problem, according to Mrs. Chan, was that her son-in-law was not a Christian. If he would just be converted, all would be well.

"She had been praying about this for some time and felt she had clear guidance. She planned to send the young man plane fare to Seattle. She would bring him to church, and he would give his life to Jesus. She was hoping he could then be baptized that very afternoon." Mrs. Chan spoke to one of her pastors about her plan. He tried to dissuade her, to help her see the foolishness of her plan. "God doesn't operate that way," the pastor told her. "You can't manipulate God or your son-in-law like that."

Mrs. Chan didn't listen to the pastor's advice. She sent the young man plane fare, and he worshiped with her the next Sunday. The invitation was issued at the end of the service for those who wanted to start the life of faith for the first time. The young man came forward and trusted in Jesus Christ for salvation. "He came, Reverend Larsen," Mrs. Chan said, beaming that Sunday, "and when you gave the invitation, he gave his life to God." Mrs. Chan was not at all surprised at the outcome.

"God spoke," Larsen writes. "Mrs. Chan acted, and her daughter's husband came into the kingdom."

Feeling Tested—and Testy. *How in the world did I get into this job?* you wonder. The interviews went well. The people seemed honest. God seemed to give you the go-ahead. But now you're facing grumpy coworkers, a manager who eats up good employees, and the most insensitive HR reps you can imagine. *Was this really God's job for me?* you wonder.

Now you're praying—long and hard. You get to work early and stay late. You complete assignments well in advance of deadlines. You keep a low profile. You keep praying. You remain faithful in the tasks God has given you. You don't trade insult for insult. And after a year passes, things suddenly change. Amazingly, four people who made your life miserable move along and move out. God has parted the waters and you can walk through (so to speak).

Perhaps you or someone you know is going through this sort of experience. If you or a loved one is feeling tested—and testy—ask God to renew your trust in Him. He will part the waters in His time and in His way.

| FOR YOUTH | ■ TOPIC: God's Promise to Abram
■ QUESTIONS: 1. What incentive did Abraham have to live uprightly in the Lord's presence? 2. In what way would Abraham be the ances- |

tor of many nations? 3. What was the nature of God's covenant to the patriarch? 4. Why did Abraham laugh at the news that Sarah would bear him a son? 5. What does it mean to believe that God can do what seems impossible in our lives?

■ ILLUSTRATIONS:

Trusting Faith. Spencer Morgan Rice, the minister of a church in Boston, once told about how early in his ministry he was serving a small congregation in the Los Angeles basin. The sexton of the church took as much interest in those who came to pray and meditate as he did the upkeep of the church. (A sexton is a church officer or employee who takes care of the congregational property and performs related duties.)

One man in particular attracted the attention of the sexton. This man dropped by the church briefly every day about noon. He would walk down the center aisle, stand at the chancel steps, and stare at the altar for a moment. Then he would leave.

After a few days, the sexton began to worry. The man was not well-dressed. He was not the cleanest. He did not always walk steadily. The sexton mentioned his concern to Rice, who suggested the sexton simply ask the man if there was anything the church could do for him. When the sexton asked, the man said, "No, thank you. I just come in every day and stand before the altar and say, 'Jesus, it's Jim.' It is not much of a prayer, I know, but I think God knows what I mean."

Months slipped by. The sexton never again mentioned their daily visitor. Then, one morning Rice got a call from the director of a home for aged men run by a local parish. The staff ministered to men broken by life. Rice tells the rest of the story this way:

> The director told me that Jim had been admitted, and I said I would be out to
> see him. The director met me at the door and said, "You know, Pastor Rice,

Jim has been here for two months. He went into the most cantankerous ward we have. Every staff member here has tried their best to bring some sense of joy and calm to that ward. We failed. Jim went into that ward and the place is transformed. It is a new place. I went to him two days ago and I asked, 'Jim, how is it that you have been able to bring such joy and such a sense of peace to these men?' And he said, 'Oh, it is because of my visitor.'" And the director said, "I know he didn't have any visitors. That chair hadn't been occupied the 60 days he has been here. So I said, 'Jim, what visitors? I've never seen a visitor.' And he said, 'Ma'am, every day at 12:00, He comes and stands at the foot of my bed and says that He's Jesus!'"

The God of the Impossible. When Pam Hughes chose to become a teacher, she knew she wanted to touch children's lives, just as her mother, who was also a schoolteacher, had. What Pam hadn't counted on was the fact that some children would seem so untouchable. "I had a student I'll call Gary whom I can only describe as obnoxious and obstinate. He was so much trouble, I thought I was being especially punished when I had to teach him for both sixth and seventh grade."

Pam had little faith that Gary would ever change. "But he surprised me," Pam says. "To my amazement, he changed when he realized I was truly trying to care for him, that I was trying to like him as a person. That insight made a real difference for our relationship and for him as a person. After he graduated, I ran into him at a mall, and he called out to me. We chatted for a while, and I was stunned. I was certain he'd be one of the kids who would walk the other way if he saw me coming."

Even as young people, many of us live with Garys every day—individuals we are sure will never change. We also see situations that look hopeless or impossible. We may know that God is all powerful enough to change any life, or any situation—but it's something else altogether to expect such changes. This week's lesson encourages us to accept the truth of God's almighty power to do in our lives and in the lives of our peers what seems impossible.

GOD'S COVENANT WITH ISRAEL

BACKGROUND SCRIPTURE: Exodus 19:1-6; 24:3-8
DEVOTIONAL READING: Psalm 119:33-40

KEY VERSE: And Moses came and told the people all the words of the LORD, and all the judgments: and all the people answered with one voice, and said, All the words which the LORD hath said will we do. Exodus 24:3.

3

KING JAMES VERSION

EXODUS 19:1 In the third month, when the children of Israel were gone forth out of the land of Egypt, the same day came they into the wilderness of Sinai. 2 For they were departed from Rephidim, and were come to the desert of Sinai, and had pitched in the wilderness; and there Israel camped before the mount. 3 And Moses went up unto God, and the LORD called unto him out of the mountain, saying, Thus shalt thou say to the house of Jacob, and tell the children of Israel; 4 Ye have seen what I did unto the Egyptians, and how I bare you on eagles' wings, and brought you unto myself. 5 Now therefore, if ye will obey my voice indeed, and keep my covenant, then ye shall be a peculiar treasure unto me above all people: for all the earth is mine: 6 And ye shall be unto me a kingdom of priests, and an holy nation. These are the words which thou shalt speak unto the children of Israel. . . .

24:3 And Moses came and told the people all the words of the LORD, and all the judgments: and all the people answered with one voice, and said, All the words which the LORD hath said will we do. 4 And Moses wrote all the words of the LORD, and rose up early in the morning, and builded an altar under the hill, and twelve pillars, according to the twelve tribes of Israel. 5 And he sent young men of the children of Israel, which offered burnt offerings, and sacrificed peace offerings of oxen unto the LORD. 6 And Moses took half of the blood, and put it in basons; and half of the blood he sprinkled on the altar. 7 And he took the book of the covenant, and read in the audience of the people: and they said, All that the LORD hath said will we do, and be obedient. 8 And Moses took the blood, and sprinkled it on the people, and said, Behold the blood of the covenant, which the LORD hath made with you concerning all these words.

NEW REVISED STANDARD VERSION

EXODUS 19:1 On the third new moon after the Israelites had gone out of the land of Egypt, on that very day, they came into the wilderness of Sinai. 2 They had journeyed from Rephidim, entered the wilderness of Sinai, and camped in the wilderness; Israel camped there in front of the mountain. 3 Then Moses went up to God; the LORD called to him from the mountain, saying, "Thus you shall say to the house of Jacob, and tell the Israelites: 4 You have seen what I did to the Egyptians, and how I bore you on eagles' wings and brought you to myself. 5 Now therefore, if you obey my voice and keep my covenant, you shall be my treasured possession out of all the peoples. Indeed, the whole earth is mine, 6 but you shall be for me a priestly kingdom and a holy nation. These are the words that you shall speak to the Israelites." . . .

24:3 Moses came and told the people all the words of the LORD and all the ordinances; and all the people answered with one voice, and said, "All the words that the LORD has spoken we will do." 4 And Moses wrote down all the words of the LORD. He rose early in the morning, and built an altar at the foot of the mountain, and set up twelve pillars, corresponding to the twelve tribes of Israel. 5 He sent young men of the people of Israel, who offered burnt offerings and sacrificed oxen as offerings of well-being to the LORD. 6 Moses took half of the blood and put it in basins, and half of the blood he dashed against the altar. 7 Then he took the book of the covenant, and read it in the hearing of the people; and they said, "All that the LORD has spoken we will do, and we will be obedient." 8 Moses took the blood and dashed it on the people, and said, "See the blood of the covenant that the LORD has made with you in accordance with all these words."

BACKGROUND

Exodus 15:22—18:27 provides details of the Hebrews' journey from the Red Sea crossing to Mount Sinai. The Hebrews reached God's mountain in the third month of their journey out of Egypt (Exod. 19:1). According to 3:1, Horeb was *the mountain of God*—a place where God spoke to Moses. Bible scholars have sought the answers to a couple of questions regarding Horeb: "Where is it?" and "What is its relationship to Mount Sinai?"

Many mountains on the Sinai Peninsula and in neighboring areas have been tentatively identified as Horeb. Ancient Christian tradition says Horeb is Jebel Sufsafeh, a rugged granite peak in the south-central Sinai. Some scholars think Horeb and Sinai are different names for the same peak. Others think Horeb was a mountain range and Sinai a particular peak within that range. But Christian tradition identifies Jebel Musa, a peak next to the traditional Horeb, as Sinai.

In any case, while the Israelites were encamped at the base of Mount Sinai, Moses climbed its slopes to speak with God. The Lord's speech to Moses in Exodus 20 is similar to a three-part pattern of ancient Near Eastern treaties made between a king and his subjects. In such a covenant, the people would pledge complete obedience to the king in return for his gracious mercy and care for them. The first two parts of the treaty would include an identification of the king and a historical prologue in which the king reminded the people of his care for them (20:1-2). The third part would be the conditions of the covenant that the people were agreeing to follow (20:3-17). Obeying the covenant would then bring blessings to the people.

The Bible never hides the fact that the group Moses led to Mount Sinai was a timid and undisciplined collection of nobodies. Regarded as the dregs of society by the powerful and important people in that age, the Israelites who reluctantly followed Moses appeared to be the least-promising material for God to mold into a nation. And their descendants acknowledged that the rag-tag crew of escapees from Egypt's labor camps could never make any claims of being stronger, more clever, or wiser than any other community. The one distinguishing feature about this group of people was that God had claimed them as His own. He had rescued them from the slave gangs, brought them safely across the Red Sea, and called them to be a nation that would serve Him.

In His judgment of Egypt, God brought 10 successive plagues upon the nation of the Nile. The 10 plagues were blood (7:17-24), frogs (7:25—8:15), gnats (8:16-19), flies (8:20-32), livestock disease (9:1-7), boils (9:8-12), hail (9:13-35), locusts (10:3-20), darkness (10:21-23), and the death of the firstborn (11:1-8; 12:21-30). Some Bible scholars think that the first nine plagues were natural phenomena in Egypt that were miraculous in their intensity and the timing of their occurrence. In this case God used natural means to achieve divine objectives. Others, however, see them more directly as supernatural (as blood, for example, taken literally).

The final plague, the death of the firstborn in Egypt, was unquestionably different. It was clearly outside the realm of the natural and normal experience of the Egyptians. But like the other plagues, it fell upon prince and peasant alike. This most devastating of the plagues reached even the family of Pharaoh himself. Interestingly, inscriptions have been discovered indicating that Thutmose IV, who succeeded Amenhotep II as pharaoh, was neither Amenhotep's firstborn son nor his heir apparent. If Amenhotep II was the pharaoh of the Exodus, these inscriptions would correlate with the biblical narrative.

NOTES ON THE PRINTED TEXT

Three months to the day that the Israelites had left the land of Egypt, they came to the desert of Sinai (Exod. 19:1). Bible scholars usually choose one of two dates for the Exodus, an early one or a late one. The earlier dating suggests that Exodus occurred around 1440 B.C., during Amenhotep II's reign (1450–1425). According to the other view, the event took place under the reign of Rameses II (1304–1237) in about 1280 B.C.

A straightforward, literal interpretation of 1 Kings 6:1 would demand the earlier date. Furthermore, some important archaeological evidence favors the earlier date. The stele of Pharaoh Merneptah (a large stone in his tomb that lists his military victories) suggests that the Israelites were firmly settled in Canaan when Merneptah's armies attacked them around 1230 B.C. Joshua's conquest of Canaan, the subsequent building of cities, and the settlement of the land would have taken a considerable length of time to accomplish, perhaps 150 years. If this view is correct, then the king of Egypt who oppressed the Israelites but died before the Exodus (Exod. 2:23) was Thutmose III, and his successor, Amenhotep II, was the pharaoh of the Exodus.

Other evidence favors a later Exodus, about 1280 B.C., with Rameses II as the pharaoh. The storage city built by the Hebrews, Rameses (1:11), was one of many massive building projects this pharaoh accomplished with slave labor. Also, this city became the capital of Egypt during the time of Rameses II instead of Thebes, which is far south along the Nile River. Since the Hebrews lived in the area near Rameses, Moses and Aaron would have had easy access to speak to Pharaoh and his court if he was at Rameses.

In either case, after the Hebrews left Egypt, they journeyed across the desert to Mount Sinai. When God had called Moses to lead His people, as a token sign of His promised presence (3:12), the Lord said that Moses and the people would worship at this mountain. When they arrived, Moses went up the mountain to receive the words of the Lord for the nation. The focus was the covenant God was about to establish with the Israelites, the descendants of Jacob (19:1-3).

Before giving the law, the Lord gave the people reasons to be holy. They themselves had seen how God had rescued them from bondage in Egypt. As young eagles are taught to fly while being carried on the wings of adult eagles, so God had lovingly carried His people out of danger into safety. Like an eagle caring for her young, the Lord had displayed His unfailing compassion for Israel (19:4).

Furthermore, if the people kept their covenant with God, they would be His *peculiar treasure* (19:5). In ancient times, such treasures represented the king's most valued property. The same word is used in 1 Chronicles 29:3 to refer to David's personal gold and silver he had reserved for the construction of the temple. The word denoted property that was extremely valuable to the owner, as Israel was in God's sight (Deut. 26:18).

The Hebrews became God's personal possession when He chose them and redeemed them from bondage in Egypt. He did not do it because of their goodness, but He loved them and was faithful to the promises given to Abraham, Isaac, and Jacob. The Lord promised to place great value on Israel and set her apart for a special purpose, if His people obeyed His law (Exod. 19:5).

God's plan was to make the Hebrews a *kingdom of priests, and an holy nation* (19:6). Like priests, the people would reveal the Lord's grace and mercy to the nations of the world. Also, like God, they would be unique and distinct in their behavior. By keeping the Lord's covenant and obeying His commandments, they would reflect His holy character to the Gentiles. The latter, in turn, would be drawn to the Lord by what they saw.

Exodus 20—23 details some of the ordinances, decrees, and stipulations of God's covenant with Israel, perhaps the most familiar of which would be the Ten Commandments. Then the Lord told Moses to descend Mount Sinai and have Aaron, Aaron's two sons (Nadab and Abihu, who were to have been the next high priests), and 70 elders of the people (who probably represented Jacob's descendants; see 1:5) to ascend Mount Sinai as a group. All of them except Moses were to remain somewhere partway up the mountain. Moses was to return to the top of the mountain to further consult with the Lord (24:1-2).

The preparations for this ascent are given in 24:3-8. In obedience to the Lord, Moses stated all God's declarations—including His ordinances and decisions on vital matters—to the people; and in response, the Israelites declared their unanimous resolve to heed the Lord's directives (24:3). Moses ended the episode by recording *all the words of the Lord* (24:4). Then early the next morning Moses built an altar at the foot of the mountain. He also arranged 12 pillars corresponding to Israel's 12 tribes. The standing stones complemented the altar to create a place of worship.

Since the Levitical priesthood had not yet been established, Moses sent many of the firstborn men of the Israelites to sacrifice young bulls as a sign that the people meant to worship God alone (24:5). The various offerings formally sealed the covenant and revealed that the Lord's acceptance of the Israelites was on the basis of atonement for sin.

Moses next placed half the blood from the animals into bowls, and later sprinkled it onto the people, symbolizing their oath to be obedient to God (24:6). Then, after the Israelites affirmed their intent to heed the stipulations of the covenant (24:7), Moses sprinkled the other half of the animals' blood on the altar, symbolizing God's forgiveness and His acceptance of the offering (24:8). In such a blood ritual, the two parties of a covenant were considered to be organically united into a sacred bond—of "one blood," as it were.

SUGGESTIONS TO TEACHERS

A minister related that in the course of going over wedding vows with prospective brides and grooms who are planning their marriage ceremonies, he tells them that the word "covenant" appears in the liturgy. But in asking them what the word means, he almost always gets a confused look or a vague reply. Few can give a definition that reflects the Bible's understanding of "covenant." You may want to kick off your lesson by asking the members of your class to relate what "covenant" means to them. (Don't be too dismayed at the ignorance of the Bible that some might show!)

1. REMINDER OF THE DIVINE DELIVERANCE. God established the covenant at Mount Sinai after He reminded the people how He had redeemed them from slavery in Egypt. Our covenanted relationship with the Lord stems from His gracious acts on our behalf, particularly His sacrificial love through Christ. We should respond by exclusively worshiping and serving the Lord.

2. REITERATION OF THE DIVINE DECISION. God called the Israelites to be a kingdom of priests and a holy nation. Have your students explain what these words should mean to God's people today (see 1 Pet. 2:9-10).

3. RESPONSE TO THE DIVINE DICTATES. Spend some time exploring with the students some of the ways in which God's ordinances and decrees apply to believers today.

4. RESPECT FOR THE DIVINE DEMANDS. Jesus said that loving God was the first commandment, and that the second was loving other people (Mark 12:29-31). Have your class members consider where their relationships with others might be frayed and what they can do to bring reconciliation.

■ **TOPIC:** Being Mutually Responsible

■ **QUESTIONS:** 1. In what way had the Lord rescued His people? 2. How could the Israelites become the Lord's treasured possession? 3. In what way was the covenant ratified? 4. What did the people pledge to do? 5. Why is it impossible to have an intimate relationship with the Lord without being obedient to His commands?

■ **ILLUSTRATIONS:**

Sermon in a Carving. While in a quaint old church outside Winchester, England, a visitor was studying a Bible resting on an old carved oak lectern. He had noticed that in nearly all old English churches, the lectern was shaped like an eagle. The pulpit in this sanctuary was also shaped like a huge eagle, except that the bird had the beak of a parrot. While examining the odd beak on the eagle, the visitor moreover noticed that a small heart was carved on the head of the eagle. The perplexed tourist asked the attendant why the lectern had the parrot's beak and the little carved heart.

"You must understand," stated the attendant, "that this ancient eagle was carved this way to remind everyone who reads the Holy Word to us not to do so mechanically like a parrot, but fervently from the heart." This reminds us that when we study God's covenant to His people, we must not merely mouth the words in parrot-like fashion, but read them from the heart!

Regulations for Our Own Safety and Survival. Tom Johnston flies his own airplane. He stressed that it was important for him to follow the regulations of the Federal Aviation Administration. He also believes that Christians must heed what the Lord commanded in Scripture.

"I have become aware of how much the air traffic control system is like God's presence with us. I do a good deal of my travel flying my own plane. So it is not surprising that I am thinking about flight safety!

"Whenever I make a flight, I have to prepare carefully. My preparation begins by checking my currency logs: that I have had my required periodic flight check and physical, that I have flown sufficient recent instrument approaches and flight hours without outside reference, and that my airplane and instruments have all had the required Federal Aviation Administration checks. Next, I prepare and file a flight plan of where I would like to go. Then I get a detailed weather briefing and do a careful preflight inspection of the plane. Sometimes this preparation to fly can take as much time as the flight itself!

"The air traffic control system itself is awesome. My aircraft is tracked all the way to my destination by a gigantic computer with the help of radar. A host of highly trained air traffic controllers direct my flight, warn me of other traffic, vector me around thunderstorms, alert me if I deviate from my assigned heading or altitude, and provide me with a sector of safe airspace. I am in constant radio contact with these controllers, and sometimes I talk with as many as twenty or thirty of them during the course of a trip. It is reassuring to have someone there to help me when I need it!

"All of my flight and the activity of the air traffic controllers are precisely and extensively codified by the Federal Aviation Administration. Rather than resent these regulations, I have come to value them. Each regulation has been carefully researched, tested, and evaluated for its primary purpose: to provide aircraft with a safe and reliable flying environment. I know that these regulations are also strictly enforced, and that if I fail to follow them, I am not only endangering my own safety and that of others, but I can be punished for the violation." (Thomas Johnston, *The Trinitarian,* Synod of the Trinity Newsletter, Winter 2004).

When we heed God's Word, we are ensuring our own spiritual safety and survival. However, when we spurn the Lord's commands, we flirt with spiritual disaster.

Mistaken Understanding. Tim Robbins, the film director who has produced several acclaimed movies, was interviewed at the Berlin Film Festival in 1996 about his motion picture entitled *Dead Man Walking.* When asked about the place of God and faith, this director mumbled, "I believe in . . . er . . . that there are people who live highly enlightened lives and who achieve a certain level of spirituality in connection with a force of goodness. And because these people have walked the earth, I believe that they have created God."

Nothing could be farther from what the Bible teaches! Scripture reveals that God created the universe and humankind, not the other way around. This means that He is the sovereign Lord and that people exist to worship and serve Him. They show their love for Him by obeying His Word and loving others. They can do so only in His power and wisdom. Their motivation is not to exalt themselves but rather to glorify the Lord.

FOR YOUTH

■ TOPIC: God's Promise to Israel

■ QUESTIONS: 1. What had the Lord done to set His people free from Egypt? 2. What does it mean that the Israelites were God's treasured possession? 3. In what sense would the people of the covenant be a priestly kingdom and a holy nation? 4. What was the intent of the various sacrifices offered on the altar Moses had constructed? 5. What should be our response to the marvelous ways the Lord has worked in our lives?

■ ILLUSTRATIONS:

Medium or the Message? In Cecil B. deMille's movie entitled *The Ten Commandments,* an arrow of fire circles and then strikes the rock beside Moses, searing ancient Hebrew letters into the stone. The fire gouges out the rock and carves it onto two slabs. Old Moses marches down the mountain carrying the two tablets in his hands, ready to share God's law with the Israelites.

Archaeologists continue to debate the exact shape and size of the stone tablets. Some think they were no more than 12 inches high, while others claim they were small clay slabs similar to those excavated throughout many Near Eastern sites. A few maintain that the tablets were stone slates on which the laws were scratched with a sharp tool.

More important than the material on which the Ten Commandments were inscribed is the message of God they contained. We learn that He wants us to love Him with our entire heart and that He wants us to love others unconditionally and sacrificially. When we do these things, our lives and those of others will be transformed in profound ways.

No-No's. Remember when you were a small child and headed for the stove. You were fascinated with the brilliant orange coils of the hot electric range. You wanted to pick up those coils, but your mother quickly thrust your hand away from the hot object. In your mind touching the stove became a "No! No!" That was the law of the family. There was no room for experimentation. The restriction was made to keep you from potential burn. Similarly, God has established His laws to keep you from experiencing potential spiritual tragedy.

Standards. Judith Martin (who is otherwise known as Miss Manners) receives lots of mail from young people. An eighth grader's letter was typical. The teenage girl asked for Judith's opinion on what is "socially acceptable" on and off school grounds. Martin wrote that the issue was not a question of manners but morals. There are standards of life, and these should be taught by parents.

Long before Judith Martin wrote about proper conduct, God gave Moses a set of moral standards for people to follow in life. Even today, the principles embodied in such biblical directives as the Ten Commandments are worth studying and heeding.

COVENANT RENEWED

BACKGROUND SCRIPTURE: Joshua 24
DEVOTIONAL READING: Psalm 51:1-12

KEY VERSE: And if it seem evil unto you to serve the LORD, choose you this day whom ye will serve. . . . but as for me and my house, we will serve the LORD. Joshua 24:15.

4

KING JAMES VERSION

JOSHUA 24:1 And Joshua gathered all the tribes of Israel to Shechem, and called for the elders of Israel, and for their heads, and for their judges, and for their officers; and they presented themselves before God. . . .
14 Now therefore fear the LORD, and serve him in sincerity and in truth: and put away the gods which your fathers served on the other side of the flood, and in Egypt; and serve ye the LORD.

15 And if it seem evil unto you to serve the LORD, choose you this day whom ye will serve; whether the gods which your fathers served that were on the other side of the flood, or the gods of the Amorites, in whose land ye dwell: but as for me and my house, we will serve the LORD. 16 And the people answered and said, God forbid that we should forsake the LORD, to serve other gods; 17 For the LORD our God, he it is that brought us up and our fathers out of the land of Egypt, from the house of bondage, and which did those great signs in our sight, and preserved us in all the way wherein we went, and among all the people through whom we passed: 18 And the LORD drave out from before us all the people, even the Amorites which dwelt in the land: therefore will we also serve the LORD; for he is our God. 19 And Joshua said unto the people, Ye cannot serve the LORD: for he is an holy God; he is a jealous God; he will not forgive your transgressions nor your sins. 20 If ye forsake the LORD, and serve strange gods, then he will turn and do you hurt, and consume you, after that he hath done you good. 21 And the people said unto Joshua, Nay; but we will serve the LORD. 22 And Joshua said unto the people, Ye are witnesses against yourselves that ye have chosen you the LORD, to serve him. And they said, We are witnesses. 23 Now therefore put away, said he, the strange gods which are among you, and incline your heart unto the LORD God of Israel. 24 And the people said unto Joshua, The LORD our God will we serve, and his voice will we obey.

NEW REVISED STANDARD VERSION

JOSHUA 24:1 Then Joshua gathered all the tribes of Israel to Shechem, and summoned the elders, the heads, the judges, and the officers of Israel; and they presented themselves before God. . . .
14 "Now therefore revere the LORD, and serve him in sincerity and in faithfulness; put away the gods that your ancestors served beyond the River and in Egypt, and serve the LORD. 15 Now if you are unwilling to serve the LORD, choose this day whom you will serve, whether the gods your ancestors served in the region beyond the River or the gods of the Amorites in whose land you are living; but as for me and my household, we will serve the LORD."

16 Then the people answered, "Far be it from us that we should forsake the LORD to serve other gods; 17 for it is the LORD our God who brought us and our ancestors up from the land of Egypt, out of the house of slavery, and who did those great signs in our sight. He protected us along all the way that we went, and among all the peoples through whom we passed; 18 and the LORD drove out before us all the peoples, the Amorites who lived in the land. Therefore we also will serve the LORD, for he is our God."

19 But Joshua said to the people, "You cannot serve the LORD, for he is a holy God. He is a jealous God; he will not forgive your transgressions or your sins. 20 If you forsake the LORD and serve foreign gods, then he will turn and do you harm, and consume you, after having done you good." 21 And the people said to Joshua, "No, we will serve the LORD!" 22 Then Joshua said to the people, "You are witnesses against yourselves that you have chosen the LORD, to serve him." And they said, "We are witnesses." 23 He said, "Then put away the foreign gods that are among you, and incline your hearts to the LORD, the God of Israel." 24 The people said to Joshua, "The LORD our God we will serve, and him we will obey."

HOME BIBLE READINGS

BACKGROUND

The Book of Joshua chronicles the conquest of Canaan that occurred between the fall of Jericho and Joshua's challenge to the people of Shechem to serve only the Lord. At the time of Israel's conquest, the superpowers of the Near East had lost their grip on the land of Canaan. The Hittites had gradually faded into oblivion. Neither Egypt nor Babylon could maintain a military presence in the region. Due to the absence of these military powers, what resulted was a series of city-states that maintained, at best, fragile alliances. The timing was perfect for Israel to enter and conquer the land.

This portion of Scripture can be divided into four literary sections. The first part deals with the Israelites' entrance into the promised land (1:1—5:12), while the second part concerns the people's conquest of Canaan (5:13—12:24). In this section, we learn that the Israelites first conducted a central campaign, then a southern campaign, and finally a northern campaign. These military successes were not due to Joshua's skill or the Israelites' prowess, but rather to God's intervention. In fact, His providence enabled Joshua to distribute the land among Israel's tribes. The third section of the book discusses this in detail (13—21).

Joshua was not only a great military commander but also a capable civil and spiritual leader. He knew that simply occupying Canaan was only part of the job. The Israelites, as the people of Yahweh, also had to wage a holy war against the ungodly inhabitants of the land. The Canaanites had become so steeped in iniquity that God would use the Israelites to spew them out of Palestine. Of course, Israel's conquest of Canaan would be in fulfillment of the covenant that the Lord had pledged to Abraham and his descendants.

Once the land had been conquered and divided up among Israel's tribes, it was necessary for God's people to build a nation there for themselves. The key to their success was their obedience to the Mosaic covenant. Just as God had been faithful to the Israelites, so too they needed to remain faithful to Him. Ultimately, their continued possession and prosperity in Canaan was dependent on their observance of the law.

Chapters 22 through 24 are the epilogue—and fourth section—of the book. Here we find Joshua, the nation's preeminent soldier-statesman, exhorting the Israelites to accept the challenge of following the Lord. The glory days of conquest were gone. But perhaps more important would be the challenge to remain faithful to God in the ordinary activities of life.

This would not be easy. After all, God's people would be surrounded by paganism. There would be a tremendous temptation on the part of the Israelites to adopt the thinking and practices of their ungodly neighbors. That's why the renewal of the covenant at Shechem was so pivotal in the life of the faith community. The ceremony was Joshua's last opportunity, before his death, to emphasize to the current generation of Israelites that following the Lord wholeheartedly was in their long-term best interests.

The Deuteronomic principle of "obey and be blessed, or disobey and be punished" is presented clearly throughout the book, both in principle and in practice. Israel's military victories and defeats paralleled the nation's spiritual condition. If the Israelites remained faithful to God's will, they defeated their enemies. If they compromised God's commands and fell into sin and rebellion, or if they failed to consult the Lord, they experienced humiliating defeats.

Through the conquest of Canaan, God also demonstrated to the Canaanite peoples exactly who He was. His miraculous demonstration of power over nature put the gods of the Canaanites to shame. Though He was compassionate, He showed that He would not tolerate evil forever. Apparently, God had extended the opportunity to repent to those who were about to be conquered. But so far as the Book of Joshua records, Rahab and her family were the only ones to accept God's offer.

NOTES ON THE PRINTED TEXT

Joshua had all the people and their representatives assemble *before God* (Josh. 24:1) for what would be an important covenant-affirming ceremony. Shechem was a historically significant place where God had promised the land of Canaan to Abraham (Gen. 12:6-7). After a brief review of God's faithfulness and provision through all they had experienced (Josh. 24:2-13), Joshua issued a determined call for wholehearted devotion to God.

Joshua described the attitude of God's servants as having a *fear* (24:14) of the Lord. This idea of fear is actually linked with obedience and reverence (Deut. 4:10; 5:29; 6:2, 13, 24). God is to be held in awe like no one and nothing else. He is the only *living God* (Josh. 3:10). Therefore, idols were worthless and must be *put away* (24:14). That Joshua even had to tell the people to throw away their idols attests to the strong magnetism of idolatry so pervasive in the land (Deut. 20:16-18). The gods of other peoples enticed worshipers because their veneration was so often built around promiscuous sexual relations. This was especially true of the Amorites, whose fertility cults included several sexually immoral practices.

Against this and other such practices, Joshua called on the people to choose whom they would serve (Josh. 24:15). Of course, he exhorted them to make the correct choice—serve the Lord *in sincerity and in truth* (24:14). It was a real choice because the alternatives were real and all around them. Abraham had chosen not to serve the idols of Ur beyond the Euphrates River. Likewise, Moses had refused to bow down to the false gods of Egypt. Instead, these people of faith committed to serving the one true God.

Tragically, the generation of Israelites whom God set free from Egypt had chosen not to be wholeheartedly devoted to the Lord. Instead, they worshiped a golden calf at Mount Sinai, a god much like the ones in Egypt. That was one of the reasons why those who had escaped Egypt died without seeing the promised land. When the people remembered those consequences, how could it possibly be *evil* (24:15) for them to serve the Lord? Joshua purposefully challenged their logic. Would their generation make the same poor choices as those before them, or like Joshua and his household would they choose instead to serve the Lord?

The people had one united response to Joshua's charge of idolatry: *God forbid* (24:16). The worst thing they could do in the face of all God had done for them would be to *serve other gods.* What audacity it would take to forsake the Lord for worthless idols! The gods of the land didn't save the people who worshiped them, such as the Amorites. It thus made no sense for Israel to bow before them. Indeed, it was the Lord who rescued His people from Egypt by performing mighty miracles. As the Israelites traveled through the wilderness, God protected them from their enemies (24:17). He even drove out the Amorites and other native peoples living in Canaan. Because Yahweh was Israel's God, the people pledged to worship and serve only Him (24:18).

Joshua told the people that despite what they had pledged, they were not able to *serve the Lord* (24:19). Joshua wanted to fully impress upon the people that their God was *holy* and *jealous*, especially in the sense that He wanted to protect them. He was an exacting God, not to be trifled with, presumed upon, or carelessly regarded. Far from wanting to deflate the zeal his call had evoked, Joshua wanted to properly ground it. God demanded continuous, single-minded devotion. He wasn't interested in riding their emotional tides, nor would He tolerate idolatrous flirtations or fads. Any *transgressions* committed by them would be a willful casting aside of His authority. Yet all sin is willful, and a holy and jealous God would not treat any of their *sins* lightly. Forsaking Him was certainly more costly than it ever would be to serve Him (24:20).

The stakes were severe, since the people would be entering into a covenant that allowed no room for superficial whims. However, they were determined to be nothing like the unfaithful generation that preceded them (24:21). Joshua responded by saying that they were witnesses to their own commitment, and the people agreed (24:22). Thus, if they ever drifted away from the Lord, their own words would condemn them.

Then the Israelite leader told the people to let their lives bear fruit in keeping with their commitment. Specifically, he wanted them to throw away the idols that remained in their tents. This action would back up their apparent change in attitude. Joshua wanted them to *incline [their] heart unto the LORD* (24:23) completely. As before, the people restated their commitment to God (24:24).

Joshua was the last central authority figure in Israel until the monarchy began in about 1050 B.C. He had initiated the process of the Israelites' conquest; individual tribes were to conquer and settle the rest of the land on their own. Thus, by bringing the people of Israel into the promised land, God fulfilled His promise to Abraham. But once they had arrived, the ability to remain in the land depended on their willingness to obey His law and be true to His covenant. Upon Joshua's death, however, Israel entered into the period of the judges, and the people seemed to lose their vision for the possession of the land. They entered into a cycle of rebellion, oppression, repentance, and eventual deliverance.

SUGGESTIONS TO TEACHERS

Life demands making choices. Some are relatively insignificant. Whether you have orange juice or grapefruit juice for breakfast, or wear the blue suit or the gray one are not momentous decisions. But deciding whether to make a lifetime commitment in marriage to a person, or choosing a career path that will not be as financially rewarding as other jobs—these are the choices that are major. Encourage the members of your class to relate some of the toughest decisions they have faced in their lives and to explain why these were so hard to make. In light of this week's lesson, help them to consider how God calls His people to make the big decisions in the context of the biggest choice of all, namely, to put the Lord first by trusting and obeying Him.

1. CHART. Joshua reminded the Israelites of what God had done for them in the past. A good point in making the right choices in life is to recall the Lord's mighty acts in the past, both those recorded in Scripture and those remembered in one's personal life.

2. CHALLENGE. Joshua challenged the people to make a conscious, public declaration of their loyalty to God. Regardless of what we, as believers, think, say, or do, everyday we are faced with the challenge of consciously deciding to serve the Lord exclusively. Discuss with your students what the most important challenges are that God has presented to them.

3. CHANGE. Choosing to worship and serve God means forsaking all the idols prevalent today in society. List the following items on a chalkboard, overhead, or sheet of newsprint: knowledge, success, popularity, money, pleasure, power, physical attractiveness, and consumerism. Then explain that these are just some of the many "idols" that people in our society typically worship. Discuss with the class how difficult it is to replace these things with exclusive devotion to the Lord.

4. CHARGE. Joshua called upon a new generation of Israelites to renew their pledge to worship and serve the Lord. As Christians, we do the same each time we gather together to observe the Lord's Supper. Remind your students about the New Covenant that we have through faith in Christ.

■ TOPIC: Making Life's Choices

■ QUESTIONS: 1. Why did Joshua urge the Israelites to obey the Lord? 2. How difficult do you think it was for the Israelites to worship the Lord exclusively? 3. Why was it important for the Israelites to remember that the Lord had rescued them from slavery in Egypt? 4. Why did Joshua urge the Israelites to put aside the foreign gods worshiped by their ancestors? 5. Why is it important for us to worship and serve the Lord today?

■ ILLUSTRATIONS:

From Klan to Christ. Aaron Daniels came home from a conference of Promise Keepers in Birmingham, Alabama, in May 1997, determined to make some different choices. For starters, he burned his Ku Klux Klan (KKK) robe. He announced that he would no longer use racial epithets in his home or anywhere else. Daniels also began to pray, asking the Lord to help him choose to live a new life.

The 34-year-old TV cable lineman had grown to hate African Americans in high school. Daniels had also started taking drugs. Eventually flunking out of school, he drifted to New Mexico to live with a sister and her husband. Daniels married in 1988, but divorced his wife two years later. In 1991, he was invited to the KKK, and found a focus for his simmering hatred. By 1993, Daniels had risen to be the second-in-command in two counties for the Klan. He then was elevated to Grand Dragon. When his bosses found out about his Klan involvement, they demanded that he choose between the Klan or his job. Daniels reluctantly quit the Klan.

Daniels remarried, and then was introduced to Promise Keepers by his father, Dan Daniels. But Aaron wanted no part of Promise Keepers or the Christian faith. He was furious when he read an article in a Promise Keepers' magazine sent by his father that criticized the KKK. Finally, Aaron reluctantly accompanied his father to the Birmingham conference in May 1997. But Aaron only went to please his father.

The message given that day hit Aaron hard. God changed the thinking of this former Grand Dragon when Dr. Raleigh Washington preached on racial reconciliation. Aaron, weeping, found himself hugging the African American man beside him. Since the conference, Daniels' new life in Christ has involved making serious choices, including regular church attendance and introducing other men to Promise Keepers.

A Return to Childhood Roots. The StoryCorps oral history project recounts the decision made by Barb Fuller-Curry to return to her childhood roots. She grew up on a farm in Whiteside County, Illinois, where her parents took turns working the fields in order to make ends meet. At the time, Curry thought little about the sacrifices her mother and father made.

When she became an adult, Curry moved away to raise her own family. Then, four decades later, she returned to her childhood farm to care for her ailing mother, who passed away in 2005. Today Curry lives in the house her parents built. This is her way of honoring the life choices her parents made so that she could have a better and brighter future.

<table>
<tr><td>■ FOR YOUTH</td><td>■ TOPIC: Making the Right Choice
■ QUESTIONS: 1. Where did Joshua present his challenge to the people? 2. What did Joshua tell the people they should do? 3. What choices did the people have? 4. What reasons did the Israelites give for choosing to serve God? 5. What are the consequences if we refuse to allow the Lord to be the center of our lives?</td></tr>
</table>

■ **ILLUSTRATIONS:**

A Profound Change. *A Christmas Carol* is a novella written by Charles Dickens that became an instant success after first being published in 1843. The story is about an old and bitter miser, Ebenezer Scrooge, who undergoes a profound change of attitude.

On Christmas Eve, Scrooge is visited by the ghost of his deceased business partner, Jacob Marley. Marley, who in life was as miserly as Scrooge, is condemned to an eternity of carrying a heavy chain, which he forged in life, and being unable to interfere for the good of humankind, which he would never have thought to do in life. The reason for Marley's visit is to give Scrooge an opportunity to change his ways.

Scrooge is skeptical of what he has seen and heard, but during the course of the night, he is visited by spirits of "Christmas Past," "Christmas Present," and "Christmas Yet to Come." The ghosts show Scrooge scenes from his life to help him recognize that the decisions he made up to that point were selfish and self-centered. In the end, Scrooge changes his life and reverts to the generous, kindhearted person he was in his youth.

Throughout the years God gives you, there will be all sorts of decisions you will have to make. Some of these will be minor, while others will be major. Be sure that your life choices—whether big or small—are the right ones. When all is said and done, strive to ensure that your decisions are characterized by sensitivity, kindness, and generosity toward others.

Lure of Gold. On a Philadelphia stage, the Master of Ceremonies leaned on a glittering gold bowl. Behind the pounding beat of rock music, Dick Clark, the guest host, stood beside Miss Pennsylvania on the blinking stage covered with neon strips and bright blue lights. The star-studded extravaganza was part of the Pennsylvania Lottery.

But not everyone was excited. Tony Milillo, President of the Council on Compulsive Gambling of Pennsylvania, was unhappy with the gold curtains, canned applause, and hype. He not only worried about the effects on the compulsive gamblers, but also on the youth who live in his state.

Milillo noted that teenagers are warned not to smoke, take drugs, or engage in pre-marital sex. But they are told that games of chance, which feed on a person's greedy desire for money, are acceptable. He also pointed out that as daily drawings lose their appeal, the state has turned to other gimmicks, especially instant tickets, which appeal to teenagers and help them become addicted to gambling.

The love of money is just one kind of "idol" that can enslave teens, even those who are Christians. Adolescents within the community of faith should make the Lord the exclusive object of their devotion.

No Fear: A Barna Survey indicated that half of the population becomes annoyed when a stranger tries to share his or her religious beliefs with the listener. However, when a family member, close friend, or trusted associate does the same, the listener is not annoyed and often expresses interest and gratitude.

Joshua had no fear about telling others that he trusted and served the Lord. He even challenged others to live exclusively for God. Does fear prevent you from sharing your faith with others?

GOD SENDS JUDGES

BACKGROUND SCRIPTURE: Judges 2:11-23
DEVOTIONAL READING: Deuteronomy 6:4-9

KEY VERSE: Nevertheless the LORD raised up judges, which delivered them out of the hand of those that spoiled them. Judges 2:16.

KING JAMES VERSION

JUDGES 2:16 Nevertheless the LORD raised up judges, which delivered them out of the hand of those that spoiled them. 17 And yet they would not hearken unto their judges, but they went a whoring after other gods, and bowed themselves unto them: they turned quickly out of the way which their fathers walked in, obeying the commandments of the LORD; but they did not so. 18 And when the LORD raised them up judges, then the LORD was with the judge, and delivered them out of the hand of their enemies all the days of the judge: for it repented the LORD because of their groanings by reason of them that oppressed them and vexed them. 19 And it came to pass, when the judge was dead, that they returned, and corrupted themselves more than their fathers, in following other gods to serve them, and to bow down unto them; they ceased not from their own doings, nor from their stubborn way. 20 And the anger of the LORD was hot against Israel; and he said, Because that this people hath transgressed my covenant which I commanded their fathers, and have not hearkened unto my voice; 21 I also will not henceforth drive out any from before them of the nations which Joshua left when he died: 22 That through them I may prove Israel, whether they will keep the way of the LORD to walk therein, as their fathers did keep it, or not. 23 Therefore the LORD left those nations, without driving them out hastily; neither delivered he them into the hand of Joshua.

NEW REVISED STANDARD VERSION

JUDGES 2:16 Then the LORD raised up judges, who delivered them out of the power of those who plundered them. 17 Yet they did not listen even to their judges; for they lusted after other gods and bowed down to them. They soon turned aside from the way in which their ancestors had walked, who had obeyed the commandments of the LORD; they did not follow their example. 18 Whenever the LORD raised up judges for them, the LORD was with the judge, and he delivered them from the hand of their enemies all the days of the judge; for the LORD would be moved to pity by their groaning because of those who persecuted and oppressed them. 19 But whenever the judge died, they would relapse and behave worse than their ancestors, following other gods, worshiping them and bowing down to them. They would not drop any of their practices or their stubborn ways. 20 So the anger of the LORD was kindled against Israel; and he said, "Because this people have transgressed my covenant that I commanded their ancestors, and have not obeyed my voice, 21 I will no longer drive out before them any of the nations that Joshua left when he died." 22 In order to test Israel, whether or not they would take care to walk in the way of the LORD as their ancestors did, 23 the LORD had left those nations, not driving them out at once, and had not handed them over to Joshua.

5

HOME BIBLE READINGS

BACKGROUND

Judges was written to show the consequences of disobedience to God. In this regard, the Mosaic covenant forms the theological center of the book. In Deuteronomy 27 and 28, Moses clearly stated the blessings of obeying the Lord and the curses for disobeying Him. When the people came into the land, some of the tribes were commanded to stand on Mount Gerizim and pronounce the blessings for obedience, while other tribes were to stand on Mount Ebal and declare the curses (Deut. 27:12-13; Josh. 8:30-35). The first curse involved the carving of an idol (Deut. 27:15), or idolatry. One of the consequences for such behavior would be Israel's defeat by its enemies (28:25). During the time of the judges, this repeatedly happened.

The events narrated in Judges span about 350 years, from the conquest of Canaan until just before Samuel, who anointed the first king of Israel. The first of the judges in the book—Othniel—appears during the generation following Joshua. The last of the judges—Samson—was a contemporary of Samuel. During this period, Israel was oppressed from within by Canaanites and from without by the Arameans, Moabites, Midianites, Ammonites, Amalekites, Amorites, and Philistines.

The Book of Judges reveals that the Israelites began to disobey God even in the time of Joshua, and that this infidelity grew more debased over time. The people were guilty of failing to completely drive the Canaanites out of the land, of becoming idolatrous, of intermarrying with the wicked Canaanites, of not heeding the judges, and of turning away from God after the death of the judges. In fact, a four-part sequence repeatedly occurred in this phase of Israel's history: the nation's departure from God; the Lord's chastisement in the form of military defeat and subjugation; the nation's cry for deliverance; and God's raising up of liberators who led the Israelites in victory over their oppressors.

Perhaps the case of Gideon is the clearest example of the Israelites returning to idolatry right after the death of a judge. After Gideon subdued the Midianites, Israel enjoyed peace for 40 years (Judg. 8:28); but after the death of Gideon, the Israelites again began worshiping Baal. According to 8:34 the people *remembered not the LORD their God, who had delivered them out of the hands of all their enemies on every side.* Thus with the death of Gideon, a new cycle began, with the people once more bringing judgment on themselves for forsaking God for worthless idols, the most prominent of which were Baal and Ashtoreth.

Baal appears to be a general term used to describe the male gods of Canaan. The meaning of the word suggests that each individual Baal was an "owner," or lord, of a particular locality. Because these local Baals were thought to control fertility in agriculture, the Canaanites made it a priority to secure their favor. Often the Baals were portrayed as weather gods, since the timing and amount of rain were crucial to crop growth and abundance. Ashtoreth was the consort of Baal and was regarded as a goddess of fertility as well as of war. She was worshiped as Ishtar in Babylon and was the forerunner of Aphrodite, the Greek goddess of love and beauty.

The Canaanite worship of Baal and Ashtoreth included animal sacrifice, using some of the same animals that Israel sacrificed to the Lord. The worship of Baal also involved male and female temple prostitution, fertility rites using wine and oil, and in some cases human sacrifice (1 Kings 14:23-24; Jer. 19:4-5). The degrading nature of these pagan customs shows why God wanted the Canaanites destroyed so that His people would not be influenced by such evil.

NOTES ON THE PRINTED TEXT

The Book of Joshua describes the concerted efforts of the Israelite tribes to conquer the land of Canaan. Together, the Israelites managed to break the back of Canaanite resistance; but after the unifying figure of Joshua passed from the scene, it was left to the tribes to complete the conquest and settlement of the land on a tribe-by-tribe basis. The first chapter of the Book of Judges gives a sketchy report of how most of the Israelite tribes did in their warfare, and the overall picture is one of only partial success.

After Joshua's death, the people of Judah obeyed God and led the way in the war to occupy Canaan. The Simeonites joined them in routing the Canaanites and Perizzites. The tribes successfully attacked Jerusalem, fought in the hill country, the Negev to the south, and the western foothills, and also defeated Hebron (Judg. 1:1-10). Caleb promised his daughter in marriage to the man who could take the city of Debir, and Othniel led a successful attack on the city. He married Caleb's daughter Acsah, who asked for and received land with springs. Though the Judahites and Simeonites conquered the cities along the coast and in the hill country, they were unsuccessful in capturing the coastal plains and Jerusalem. Caleb was rewarded with the city of Hebron (1:12-21).

The fighting men from the tribes of Ephraim, Manasseh, Zebulun, Asher, Naphtali, and Dan were able to gain land for their clans, but at a terrible expense. One by one they compromised God's plan. They had been told to drive out the inhabitants of the land. Instead, they made treaties with some of the Canaanites, kept others as slaves, and allowed still others to remain undisturbed in the land (1:22-36). Because the Israelites failed to obey God, an angel of the Lord delivered a word of judgment, telling the Israelites that God would no longer drive out the Canaanites before them. Rather, their enemies would be thorns to them and the pagan gods would be a snare. The people responded by weeping aloud and offering sacrifices to the Lord (2:1-5).

The idolatry God condemned in the second commandment (Deut. 5:8-10) usually took one of two forms in the ancient world. It involved either worshiping God by means of forbidden images (such as the golden calf) or worshiping false gods with the use of images (idols). Early peoples in Mesopotamia worshiped hills and trees, streams, and large stones, all of which were thought to contain some form of deity. This type of idolatry is represented in the Old Testament Asherah pole (Judg. 6:25-32). Egyptians worshiped the sun, the life-giving Nile River, and many animals, such as the scarab beetle, cow, and crocodile.

Particularly vile was the religion of the Canaanites, with its sexual immorality and child sacrifice. Thus, when the Israelites conquered Canaan, God commanded His people to utterly destroy Canaanite idols (Exod. 23:24; 34:13; Num. 33:52; Deut. 7:5). This command was never completely carried out. On the contrary, the Israelites themselves often fell prey to idolatrous practices and thus invited God's judgment upon the nation.

Throughout the lifetimes of Joshua and the elders who outlived him, the Israelites served the Lord. However, the generation of Israelites who were born after Joshua did not acknowledge the Lord as the one true God. Instead, they worshiped the gods of the land's inhabitants (Judg. 2:6-15). In His mercy, the Lord used tribal chiefs called judges to rescue His people from the hand of their oppressors (2:16). To a lesser extent these individuals decided matters of law and justice. While some of the judges were corrupt, many were virtuous and honest. These leaders tried to persuade the Israelites to remain faithful to God.

Tragically, after a time of peace, the people returned to their evil ways. They committed spiritual adultery by following after other gods and bowing down to them. The previous generation of Israelites obeyed the commands of the Lord; but the next generation wanted little to do with righteousness. They cast aside the way of God for a path of idolatry and sadness (2:17). Though the Lord could have abandoned His people for their degenerate ways, He did not. Instead, He was moved with pity each time the Israelites groaned under the tyranny of their oppressors. In every instance, the Lord appointed a leader to free His people. Throughout the life of that judge, God enabled him or her to rescue and protect the Israelites from their latest foe (2:18).

As long as the latest judge lived, Israel's unfaithfulness was kept in check; but when the tribal leader died, the next generation of people became even more sinful and idolatrous than the preceding one. Rather than abandon the wicked practices of the Canaanites, God's people obstinately clung to them (2:19). The stipulations of the Mosaic covenant were intended to provide order in the lives of God's people. Indeed, the religious, social, and economic life of the nation was woven into the fabric of the law (so to speak). Yet as the Israelites venerated pagan deities, they violated the law's decrees (2:20). The people's repeated acts of rebellion compelled the Lord to back away from them. Specifically, He would no longer defeat and expel the nations left in Canaan after Joshua died (2:21). Instead, God would use these idolatrous neighbors to test the faithfulness of His people (2:22-23).

SUGGESTIONS TO TEACHERS

Philosopher George Santayana's famous phrase about those forgetting the mistakes of the past being condemned to repeat them in the future is a fair description of the Book of Judges. Time after time, God's people forgot the lessons of the past. Disobedience led to disaster. One generation turned away from God by consorting with the Canaanite deities, then suffered the consequences before finally returning to the ancestral faith. But the following generation failed to remember the lesson. Your emphasis in this week's lesson will be to help your class grow more obedient to the Lord.

1. DEADLY ATTRACTIONS: The lure of the Canaanite religion throughout Israel's history was almost irresistible. These cults promised that the adherents would have good weather for bountiful harvests and healthy offspring of their sheep and goats. The rites assuring such fertility for the barley fields and livestock always involved sexual practices and often demanded human sacrifices. Each time the Israelites allowed themselves to become mired in these pagan ways, they sank increasingly deeper into spiritual darkness and eventually experienced the judgment of the Lord.

2. DIVINE INTERVENTION: Time and time again the Israelites were led astray by their ungodly neighbors, and time and time again God allowed their enemies to afflict them. Despite the Israelites' infidelity, a message of hope emerges. Even though God's people were unfaithful, He did not abandon them. The Lord allowed the Israelites to experience not only the natural consequences of their sin, but also the joy of His mercy.

3. DISASTER AWAITS: Be sure to emphasize to the class that rebellion against God always leads to disaster. Whenever we value the things of the world (for example, wealth, power, recognition, and so on) more than the things of God, the result is frustration and disappointment. Our disobedience brings spiritual defeat and moral bankruptcy to our lives.

4. DIVINE PARDON: Let the students know that when we "own" our sin by taking personal responsibility for it, we experience the Lord's forgiveness and restoration. He wants us to examine our lives to make sure that nothing is more important to us than Him. If we discover that we value something more than the Lord, we should turn away from it immediately. When we do, we will find ourselves stunned by God's grace.

5. DISCOVER THE LIMITS: Explain that in the Bible, we find God gives us healthy boundaries for living. When we live within those limits by keeping His commands, we find benefits and health and peace.

■ **TOPIC:** Seeking Deliverance

■ **QUESTIONS:** 1. Why did God raise up judges? 2. Why did the Israelites turn away from God and worship idols? 3. How did God display compassion on His wayward people? 4. In what way did God test the commitment of His people? 5. Once a person is involved in a particular sin, why does it become increasingly more difficult to resist it?

■ **ILLUSTRATIONS:**

Protected from Harm. In 1893, the mayor of Chicago was shot and killed in his home. That murder motivated a local minister, Casimir Zeglen, to invent an early bulletproof vest. To prove the effectiveness of his invention, Zeglen himself submitted to a test in Chicago. He put on a vest of the material and an expert fired a revolver at the vest at eight paces, and not one of the bullets at all disturbed the minister.

In the spiritual realm, the evil one is always shooting his flaming arrows at believers. But without the armor of God, they are defenseless. It is only when they put on His protective armor that they can withstand Satan's attacks.

The Power of Sin. The fifteenth-century Christian writer Thomas à Kempis once said, "Sin is first a simple suggestion, then a strong imagination, then delight, then assent." Expressed differently, sin at first does not necessarily appear abhorrent to us. In fact, sin frequently intrigues us and appeals to our fallen nature. Unless we find deliverance from it through faith in Christ, we can easily fall into its death grip.

Sin's Fatal Attraction. Dave was driving to work on an unusually cold winter morning when his engine temperature gauge suddenly shot into the danger zone. He eased the car to the side of the road and shut it off. He stared blankly at the gauge, realizing he knew nothing about fixing cars. For the moment it seemed best to wait for a good Samaritan to drive by.

Thirty minutes later Dave wondered why it was that the longer he was stuck out in the cold, the better he felt. "It must be warming up outside," he decided as he snuggled down in his seat and closed his eyes. When Dave woke up, he was in a hospital emergency room, being treated for the early stages of hypothermia. He was fortunate a helpful motorist had stopped to assist him, the physician explained. Another hour and Dave might have simply frozen to death in his sleep.

"But I felt great," David exclaimed. "The warmth you felt is one of your body's warning signs," the physician replied. "When the cold becomes so pervasive that it makes you feel warm and sleepy, you're in serious danger."

Sin can be like that. When we become so used to sin—or a particular sinful environment—that we no longer recognize it as harmful, we can easily be drawn deeper into sinful actions. The solution is to look to the Lord in faith for grace to resist enticements to sin and deliverance from its evil influences.

■ **TOPIC:** Judges Bring Justice

■ **QUESTIONS:** 1. What mistake did the Israelites repeatedly make during the time of the judges? 2. Why did the idolatry of the people so anger the Lord? 3. How did God punish the Israelites when they committed idolatry? 4. How did God display His love and mercy during the time of the judges? 5. What are some things believers can do to break the destructive cycle of sin in their lives?

■ **ILLUSTRATIONS:**

Wretched Excess. Realtors state that a four-car garage is a "must" now for many of the 40-something, "gotta have it all" generation. Likewise, bakers report that the cake is the newest status symbol. Each party cake must outdo the previous party's cake. Therefore, it is important how outrageous and garish each decorated cake is made.

It is not unusual for a bakery to spend three weeks on an individual cake that will cost thousands of dollars. For instance, one man ordered a 40" by 16" three dimensional cake to replicate his metallic blue-gray sports car. The finished cake cost $2,200, according to the *New York Times*. Ironically, at the same time the homeless and hungry are being herded from the street corners of New York! In the face of such excesses, what would the Lord have said? Might He have accused the populace of unjust and inhuman treatment of others?

Modeling Care. South Bend's Center for the Homeless helps dozens of people each day. What is surprising is that young alumni and students run it from the University of Notre Dame's Center for Social Concerns.

Consider Shannon Cullinan. She developed a landscaping business that employs homeless people for eight months of training and then places them in other landscaping companies, especially as it cares for the properties in the City of South Bend, Memorial Hospital, WNDU Broadcasting, and the University properties. Then there's Drew Buscarieno. He developed a medical clinic, early childhood center, and drug and alcohol treatment center. He also developed educational facilities, job training, and care for the mentally ill.

Praised by the executive director of the National Coalition for the Homeless as a model of collaboration between university students and the local community, the center seeks to find solutions to the problems of the homeless. Here is a group of young people working to implement what God requires in their lives.

Justice and Blessing. In the *Superman* movie series, a character named Clark Kent leads a double life. In one scene, he's a mild-mannered reporter working for a large metropolitan newspaper. Then in the next scene, he's a cosmic hero who brings relief to the oppressed and the long arm of justice to villains.

Of course, in real life there is no Superman. Even so, the desire of youth for justice is worthy of commendation. They need to understand that justice comes in many forms and can be fostered by how they choose to live. For instance, when they renounce sin and display kindness to others, they are championing the cause of justice and promoting goodwill in the world. In turn, God will eternally bless His people when they conduct themselves in this way.

Rich are Richer. The number of billionaires has expanded to over 200 in the world, and they pushed their collective net worth to over $1 trillion. But the gap between the wealthiest and the rest is widening. Currently, the richest fifth of the world's population accounts for 86 percent of all private consumption. But in Africa, the average household consumes 20 percent less than it did 25 years ago. Meanwhile, natural resources as well as household purchasing power are declining.

The richest fifth of the world's people buy nine times as much meat, have access to nearly 50 times as many telephones, and use more than 80 times as many paper products and motorized vehicles than the poorest fifth. Americans spend more than $8 billion annually on cosmetics, whereas it would cost only $6 billion to provide basic education for the children in developing countries who have no schooling. Europeans spend $11 billion yearly on ice cream; about $9 billion would provide water and basic sanitation to the more than 2 billion people worldwide who lack safe water or hygienic toilets.

The Lord's message to the well-off people of the world continues to be a challenge. And His words about wanting to see justice, kindness, and humility prevail throughout the world are still true!

GOD LEADS THROUGH DEBORAH

BACKGROUND SCRIPTURE: Judges 4
DEVOTIONAL READING: Psalm 91

KEY VERSES: If thou wilt go with me, then I will go: but if thou wilt not go with me, then I will not go. And she said, I will surely go with thee. Judges 4:8-9.

KING JAMES VERSION

JUDGES 4:4 And Deborah, a prophetess, the wife of Lapidoth, she judged Israel at that time. 5 And she dwelt under the palm tree of Deborah between Ramah and Bethel in mount Ephraim: and the children of Israel came up to her for judgment. 6 And she sent and called Barak the son of Abinoam out of Kedeshnaphtali, and said unto him, Hath not the LORD God of Israel commanded, saying, Go and draw toward mount Tabor, and take with thee ten thousand men of the children of Naphtali and of the children of Zebulun? 7 And I will draw unto thee to the river Kishon Sisera, the captain of Jabin's army, with his chariots and his multitude; and I will deliver him into thine hand. 8 And Barak said unto her, If thou wilt go with me, then I will go: but if thou wilt not go with me, then I will not go. 9 And she said, I will surely go with thee: notwithstanding the journey that thou takest shall not be for thine honour; for the LORD shall sell Sisera into the hand of a woman. And Deborah arose, and went with Barak to Kedesh.

10 And Barak called Zebulun and Naphtali to Kedesh; and he went up with ten thousand men at his feet: and Deborah went up with him. . . . 12 And they shewed Sisera that Barak the son of Abinoam was gone up to mount Tabor. 13 And Sisera gathered together all his chariots, even nine hundred chariots of iron, and all the people that were with him, from Harosheth of the Gentiles unto the river of Kishon. 14 And Deborah said unto Barak, Up; for this is the day in which the LORD hath delivered Sisera into thine hand: is not the LORD gone out before thee? So Barak went down from mount Tabor, and ten thousand men after him. 15 And the LORD discomfited Sisera, and all his chariots, and all his host, with the edge of the sword before Barak; so that Sisera lighted down off his chariot, and fled away on his feet. 16 But Barak pursued after the chariots, and after the host, unto Harosheth of the Gentiles: and all the host of Sisera fell upon the edge of the sword; and there was not a man left.

NEW REVISED STANDARD VERSION

JUDGES 4:4 At that time Deborah, a prophetess, wife of Lappidoth, was judging Israel. 5 She used to sit under the palm of Deborah between Ramah and Bethel in the hill country of Ephraim; and the Israelites came up to her for judgment. 6 She sent and summoned Barak son of Abinoam from Kedesh in Naphtali, and said to him, "The LORD, the God of Israel, commands you, 'Go, take position at Mount Tabor, bringing ten thousand from the tribe of Naphtali and the tribe of Zebulun. 7 I will draw out Sisera, the general of Jabin's army, to meet you by the Wadi Kishon with his chariots and his troops; and I will give him into your hand.' " 8 Barak said to her, "If you will go with me, I will go; but if you will not go with me, I will not go." 9 And she said, "I will surely go with you; nevertheless, the road on which you are going will not lead to your glory, for the LORD will sell Sisera into the hand of a woman." Then Deborah got up and went with Barak to Kedesh. 10 Barak summoned Zebulun and Naphtali to Kedesh; and ten thousand warriors went up behind him; and Deborah went up with him. . . .

12 When Sisera was told that Barak son of Abinoam had gone up to Mount Tabor, 13 Sisera called out all his chariots, nine hundred chariots of iron, and all the troops who were with him, from Harosheth-ha-goiim to the Wadi Kishon. 14 Then Deborah said to Barak, "Up! For this is the day on which the LORD has given Sisera into your hand. The LORD is indeed going out before you." So Barak went down from Mount Tabor with ten thousand warriors following him. 15 And the LORD threw Sisera and all his chariots and all his army into a panic before Barak; Sisera got down from his chariot and fled away on foot, 16 while Barak pursued the chariots and the army to Harosheth-ha-goiim. All the army of Sisera fell by the sword; no one was left.

6

47

Monday, October 2	Psalm 91	*The God in Whom I Trust*
Tuesday, October 3	Psalm 27:1-6	*Wait for God's Guidance*
Wednesday, October 4	Judges 3:7-11	*Othniel Judges Israel*
Thursday, October 5	Hebrews 11:1-2, 32-34	*Courageous Leaders*
Friday, October 6	Judges 4:1-10	*Deborah Leads the People*
Saturday, October 7	Judges 4:12-16	*Success Assured*
Sunday, October 8	Judges 5:1-12	*Deborah's Song of Praise*

BACKGROUND

God's great act of deliverance, known as the Exodus, brought the suffering Israelites from captivity in Egypt. Under Moses, they gradually were hardened into a strong force during a 40-year sojourn in the wilderness areas of Sinai and the Transjordan. Moses passed on leadership to Joshua before dying, confident that God would fulfill His promise of bringing His people into the promised land.

Joshua's brilliant military campaign established the Israelite tribes in Canaan. But getting settled was not easy. The Israelites had been nomads since leaving Egypt, wandering with flocks from one oasis to another. It was difficult for them to deal with the sophisticated paganism of the Canaanites as well as exchange herding livestock for raising crops. The Canaanite neighbors insisted that participating in their cults brought success. The Israelites were told that the pagan gods had to be placated because they guaranteed the growth of crops and the survival of livestock. Despite the warnings of some about the need to remain faithful to God, a dismal pattern evolved in which God's people strayed from honoring Him. Consequently, disaster followed during the two centuries after Joshua's conquest.

The disasters often came at the hands of the wild desert tribes swooping through the Israelite areas. They went on a rampage of killing, robbing, burning, and enslaving. The Book of Judges is a dreary record of a series of instances where these incursions threatened to extinguish God's people. The writer and the religious leaders saw God's hand at work, punishing the people for straying into pagan ways and calling them to return to the Lord. At the same time, this seventh book in our Old Testament records that God raised up leaders in these times of crisis. They came on the scene at a time when no organized central government existed. Only a loose confederation of the tribes of the Israelite farmers linked them together in times of trouble.

In this week's lesson, we focus our attention on how a great female leader, Deborah, rallied the Israelites to rise up when they were suffering under the heel of a ruthless warlord named Sisera. Deborah is the only leader mentioned in Judges who is also called a prophet (4:4). She is also one of a select group of women in the Old Testament who are identified by that title. The others include Moses' sister Miriam (Exod. 15:20), Huldah (2 Kings 22:14), possibly Isaiah's wife (Isa. 8:3), and Noadiah (Neh. 6:14). A prophet's main duty was to be God's mouthpiece, namely, to transmit His messages to the people. The prophet believed that heralding God's declarations could bring change to a situation, as Deborah was trying to do by bringing God's message to Barak.

Deborah encouraged Barak and the Israelite warriors to take courage and oppose Sisera's mighty forces. Sisera commanded Jabin's army, which included 900 iron chariots and most likely thousands of soldiers (Judg. 4:3). According to 4:2, Jabin was a Canaanite monarch who ruled in Hazor. Before the conquest of Joshua, Hazor stood as an impressive stronghold in northern Canaan, with an estimated population of 40,000. At that time, the king of Hazor—also named Jabin—put together a coalition of kings in an effort to stop Joshua's advance. However, Joshua surprised the coalition, burned the city of Hazor, and killed Jabin (Josh. 11:1-11).

These northern Canaanites, however, recovered from their disastrous defeat. They succeeded in rebuilding Hazor on top of the ruins of the old capital and named another Jabin as their king. "Jabin" might have been a dynasty title, or possibly the Jabin in Judges 4 was a descendant of the person killed in Joshua's time. In response to the sinfulness of Israel, God allowed Hazor to regain its former prominence so as to oppress His people and bring them to repentance.

NOTES ON THE PRINTED TEXT

After its conquest of the promised land, Israel should have been in a position to grow into a godly nation that would bring others to the Lord; however, this was not what happened. Following the death of Joshua, during the time of the judges, Israel developed a consistent pattern of falling into idolatry, bring oppressed by the enemy, repenting, and then being delivered through a judge raised up by God (Judg. 2:16-19).

In Judges 4, that pattern repeats itself. After experiencing 80 years of peace through the judges Ehud and Shamgar (3:30), the Israelites again turned away from God and *did evil* (4:1) in His sight. As a result of Israel's sinfulness, God allowed a Canaanite king named Jabin to overrun the northern territories of Israel and oppress the Hebrews cruelly for 20 years. Jabin reigned in the ancient city of Hazor, once the most important city in northern Palestine (4:2). Hazor was nine miles north of the Sea of Galilee on the main trade route between Egypt and Mesopotamia. Because Israel had nothing with which to challenge the enemy, Sisera was able to terrorize the northern tribes. Finally, after two decades, the burden became too much, and the people cried out to the Lord for help (4:3).

In response to pleas for relief, God raised up Deborah to lead Israel as both a prophetess and judge (4:4). From her location just north of Jerusalem, she held court in the open air under a palm tree, as was a common practice in the Middle East (4:5). In Scripture, the palm tree is associated both with prosperity (Ps. 92:12) and leadership (Isa. 9:14). As part of her responsibilities as judge, Deborah settled disputes among the people.

Under God's direction, Deborah called for and commanded Barak to take 10,000 soldiers to an area near the Kishon River. If he took his army to the right location, God would lure Sisera into a trap and enable Barak to defeat the enemy (Judg. 4:6-7). Although Deborah promised Barak victory, he refused to obey God's command unless Deborah went with him (4:8). Perhaps Barak thought that Deborah's presence as a prophetess would ensure success or would enable him to have closer contact with the Lord for the important task. Deborah saw Barak's hesitation as a lack of faith. Although Deborah agreed to go with Barak, Deborah prophesied that the honor of killing Sisera (the opposing general) would be given to a woman, not to Barak (4:9). For a soldier of that time, to have a woman take that honor from him would have been considered a disgrace.

Despite his reluctance, Barak did obey the Lord when Deborah accompanied Barak to Kedesh. There the reluctant leader called together warriors from the tribes of Zebulun and Naphtali. Ten thousand men, along with Deborah, marched with Barak to the slopes of Mount Tabor (4:9-10). Meanwhile, a Kenite chief named Heber told Sisera that Barak and his troops had established a camp at Mount Tabor (4:11-12). The writer of Judges introduced Heber because it would be his wife, Jael, who would kill Sisera, as Deborah prophesied (see 4:18-21).

On the basis of the intelligence he received, Sisera decided to relocate his forces from Harosheth Haggoyim (more literally *Harosheth of the Gentiles*) to the Kishon River (4:13). The former was a town of Galilee that some think was located on the north bank of the Kishon River. The latter runs along a wide, shallow bed that passes through the Valley of Jezreel. During heavy rainstorms, the river quickly overflows and makes the soil of the valley miry.

On the human level, Barak's hastily gathered army had no chance against Sisera's military might; but at the opportune time, Deborah gave the command and Barak, displaying faith in God, gave up his advantageous position in the hills and descended to face the dreaded chariots in the valley (4:14). In response to Barak's trust, the Lord fought for Israel and threw the opposing army into a panic (4:15). God routed the foe by bringing a sudden downpour of rain that caused the Kishon River to flood, thereby taking away the advantage of the chariots (5:20-21). Mired in the mud, the chariots became ineffective, and the Canaanites fled the battle on foot. Perhaps the rain convinced them that the Lord was fighting for Israel.

As the Canaanites abandoned their chariots and fled from the battle scene, 4:16 says that Barak pursued the army and killed all of Sisera's troops. The vanquished military commander, however, escaped the battle and came to the tent of Jael, the wife of Heber. Because of his friendly relationship with Heber, Sisera thought he was safe with Jael. Also, the customs of hospitality usually dictated that a person tried to protect a guest from harm (see Gen. 19:8). But once Sisera was in the tent, Jael gave him milk to help him sleep and then drove a tent peg through Sisera's temple (Judg. 4:17-21). Jael's motive for killing Sisera is not mentioned in the text, although we can probably assume that for some reason she resented her husband's friendship with Israel's enemy. It is possible that Jael was an Israelite who still sided with her people.

When Barak arrived at Jael's tent, Barak discovered that he had lost the privilege of killing the opposing general, just as Deborah had prophesied (4:22). Though Barak's faith wavered at first, his name is mentioned in Hebrews 11:32. This is because Barak displayed trust in the Lord as he led his army against Sisera's forces.

SUGGESTIONS TO TEACHERS

The late great classical scholar, Frank Bourne, taught Roman history at Princeton University. He was fond of saying, "In the age of Pax Americana, there's no more important lesson we can teach young Americans than the rise and decline of Pax Romana." He always began and ended his course with the Latin words *De Nobis fabula narratur*—"Their story is our story." The same may be said about the lessons from the Old Testament. Our studies of judges and kings must be understood as examples from history that God included in His written Word to encourage us to pursue uprightness (see 1 Cor. 10:6). This week's lesson concerns the account of how a woman, Deborah, helped lead God's people to victory.

1. SCENE OF DESPAIR. The tribes of Israel had suffered 20 years of harassment and oppression. A sense of hopelessness pervaded the people. Only Deborah seemed to stand as a leader with faith.

2. SAGE IN DELIBERATION. Deborah was respected for her wisdom, which came from her trust and knowledge of the Lord. When others despaired of the situation, this great woman relied on God and proved to be the wisest leader. Deborah's single-minded devotion saved her people.

3. STRATEGY FOR DELIVERANCE. This woman who knew her Lord was the key personality for her people at that time of crisis. Point out that God chooses women as well as men to carry out His plans, and remind the class that the man or woman with trust in the Lord will be the true leader.

4. SUPPORT FOR THE DISHEARTENED. Deborah was able to get the demoralized general, Barak, to rise and rally the fighters in Israel. Deborah's faith inspired even the most timid! The person with trust in God is empowered to stand up to the most negative and disbelieving doubter!

5. SUCCESS FROM DECISIVENESS. Finally, because of Deborah's God-sent confidence, the tribes of Israel overthrew the oppressors in a battle. For us as Christians, because of the resurrection of Christ, a confidence in God's ultimate victory is given. Regardless of the circumstance, we live in hope because of the Gospel!

6. SINGLE-MINDED IN DEDICATION. Have the class look briefly at the song of Deborah (Judg. 5), which ascribes victory to the Lord. We Christians may sing with joy when we have Deborah's kind of commitment to God's work!

■ **TOPIC:** Leadership Counts!

■ **QUESTIONS:** 1. How were the Canaanites able to oppress the Israelites? 2. What roles did Deborah fulfill for Israel? 3. What was Barak's initial response to God's call? 4. How was it possible for the Israelites to route the enemy in battle? 5. Why is it important for believers to trust in God's presence during their personal struggles?

■ **ILLUSTRATIONS:**

Leader in Prison Reform. A forgotten encourager lived in England in the nineteenth century when the conditions of those in prisons were appallingly bad. Elizabeth Fry was the wife of a wealthy Quaker merchant. She already had eight of her 11 children. She had done a variety of work among the poor of London and she was serving as a minister of the Religious Society of Friends. Hers was a busy, full life. But she added Newgate Prison to her burden of concern.

Elizabeth applied for permission to visit Newgate Prison for women. She was appalled at what she saw—one male attendant and his son taking care of about 300 women and many children, all of whom were crowded into four small rooms without beds or bedding or extra clothing. There was no employment and the only recreation was to buy liquor at a taproom for which the women and children begged money from passers-by.

With the help of a London clergyman's wife and 10 Quaker women, Elizabeth Fry formed the Association for the Improvement of the Female Prisoners in Newgate. Their first task was to convince these coarse, hardened, foul-spoken women that they had come not to condemn, but to bring comfort and relief. They provided clothing, bedding, instruction in orderliness and cleanliness, and lessons from the Bible. The results were so successful that leaders from other countries came to visit Newgate and to consult with Elizabeth Fry. She was also asked to travel abroad to study conditions in other prisons and to make suggestions for improvements.

Elizabeth Fry is known today as a pioneer in prison reform, but this concern led her to ever-widening activities for the homeless, for the unemployed, and for underprivileged children. Tasks that seemed far too heavy for one woman to carry she took upon herself. She had chosen to be a follower of Jesus Christ, and to her this meant leading the way to help the captive and the poor.

Light-bearer in a Time of Darkness. Deborah was married to a man named Lappidoth, whose name in Hebrew means "light" or "lamp" or "torch." In effect, Deborah might have been called "Mrs. Light." This remarkable woman's career inspired her fellow citizens to return to their ancestral faith and to throw off the crushing oppressors. As one of Israel's judges, she shone as a lamp of justice. The faith of "Mrs. Light" served as a torch, encouraging timid and reluctant people to act bravely and faithfully. God raises up such light-bearers in times of darkness and despair!

Encourager Despite Discouragement. Few today recognize the name of Carrie Chapman Catt. Probably more than any other, this woman worked to make possible the right to vote for women in the United States. She endured ridicule and hostility. Early in her career, she was a young school teacher in Mason City, Iowa, and initiated a movement to permit women to vote in local elections. Her efforts won the praise of the illustrious Susan B. Anthony, who by then was growing old. Carrie Chapman Catt's efforts to work for women's suffrage seemed to be thwarted, however. The sudden death of her husband forced her to accept the low-paying jobs that were the only work open for widows in the late 19th century. Experiencing firsthand the powerlessness of women, this woman dedicated her life to work to give women the right to participate as full-fledged citizens in the nation.

The next years were devoted to speaking throughout the country and organizing peaceful protests. The criticism was harsh and cruel. Carrie was determined to have a Constitutional Amendment granting women suffrage in place by 1920, the 100th anniversary of the birth of her heroine, Susan B. Anthony. Gradually, Carrie began to overcome the opponents to women having the right to vote. When the House of Representatives approved a constitutional amendment in 1918, Carrie joyfully stood in the House gallery and sang the Doxology. A year later, the Senate approved the amendment. Carrie Chapman Catt then traveled throughout the nation, encouraging citizens in the states to ratify the Nineteenth Amendment. On August 26, 1920, the necessary number of states approved the amendment, and women in the United States were finally granted the right to vote, thanks to the strong leadership of this deeply committed Christian woman.

FOR YOUTH

■ TOPIC: Deborah: A Strong Leader
■ QUESTIONS: 1. What duties did Deborah perform as a judge of Israel? 2. What did the Lord command Barak to do? 3. Why did Barak at first hesitate to do what the Lord had commanded? 4. How did the Lord use Barak and his troops to defeat the enemy forces? 5. How can God's abiding presence help us overcome our personal struggles?

■ ILLUSTRATIONS:

Role Model. On September 21, 1998, Florence Griffith Joyner died of an apparent heart seizure at age 38. Her death removed one of the most positive role models for young girls. In the 1988 Olympic games in Seoul, South Korea, "FloJo" won three Olympic gold medals (the 100 meter, 200 meter, and 400 meter relay) and one silver medal (the 1600 meter relay). Known for her dazzling fingernails and speed as a runner, she devoted large amounts of time and resources to helping children, especially those in devastated neighborhoods, find and use their own talents.

"Flojo" never shrinked from taking big responsibilities such as her youth work. The commitment in time was huge. However, she willingly gave of her time and energy. Like "Flojo," Deborah never hesitated from taking on a big responsibility as well. She, too, gave large amounts of her time and energy to the cause of liberation.

Bad Example. The Spice Girls, at the peak of their popularity in 1997 and early 1998, unleashed "Girl Power," a message that girls were capable of leading and achieving great things. Many applauded that message for young ladies. Sadly, those who looked like wonderful leaders stumbled. Melanie "Scary Spice" Brown and Victoria "Posh Spice" Adams announced that they were pregnant. Although neither were wed, both claimed to be in loving and caring relationships.

In Britain, where teenage pregnancies were already Europe's highest, officials of a national school teachers association worried about copy cat pregnancies. Bill Donohue, President of the Catholic League in the United States, also sounded a similar warning, calling the Spice message "invidious and pernicious." Here is a group of women that could still make a real impact on young women, but they have chosen to be a bad example. How different they are from the heroines of the Old Testament!

Wants to Lead. She landed her open cockpit plane in Bartlesville, Oklahoma. As 67-year-old Jerrie Cobb emerged, she became a media darling interviewed by CNN, Dateline NBC, *People* magazine, CBS News, and a host of other news groups as she prepared to be honored at the Pioneer Women Museum in Ponca City. The Oklahoma native had been flying since she was 12, and had spent 35 years as a bush pilot missionary serving the Indians in Central and South America flying in medical resources, seeds, and other supplies. What few people knew was that Jerrie was also the lead woman of the Mercury 13, a group of women who endured all the grueling physical and psychological testing in the early days of the U.S. Space program.

Cobb was invited in 1960 to become part of the program. However, in 1961, NASA declared it only wanted astronauts who had been military test pilots. Since women were not allowed to fly military aircraft, gender grounded their dreams. Even though the former Soviet Union had women in its space program, America denied its women an opportunity for involvement or leadership. John Glenn went into space and Cobb went to South America. However, when Glenn agreed to fly for tests on aging in weightless conditions, Cobb returned, looking forward for the opportunity denied her in 1961, bolstered by health experts' arguments that women age differently than men.

Age and gender are never criteria to serving God. The account of Deborah shows that God used both men and women to accomplish His purpose with His people.

God Answers Samuel's Prayer

Background Scripture: 1 Samuel 7:3-13
Devotional Reading: Psalm 31:14-24

Key Verse: Samuel cried unto the LORD for Israel; and the LORD heard him. 1 Samuel 7:9.

KING JAMES VERSION

1 SAMUEL 7:3 And Samuel spake unto all the house of Israel, saying, If ye do return unto the LORD with all your hearts, then put away the strange gods and Ashtaroth from among you, and prepare your hearts unto the LORD, and serve him only: and he will deliver you out of the hand of the Philistines. 4 Then the children of Israel did put away Baalim and Ashtaroth, and served the LORD only. 5 And Samuel said, Gather all Israel to Mizpeh, and I will pray for you unto the LORD. 6 And they gathered together to Mizpeh, and drew water, and poured it out before the LORD, and fasted on that day, and said there, We have sinned against the LORD. And Samuel judged the children of Israel in Mizpeh.

7 And when the Philistines heard that the children of Israel were gathered together to Mizpeh, the lords of the Philistines went up against Israel. And when the children of Israel heard it, they were afraid of the Philistines. 8 And the children of Israel said to Samuel, Cease not to cry unto the LORD our God for us, that he will save us out of the hand of the Philistines. 9 And Samuel took a sucking lamb, and offered it for a burnt offering wholly unto the LORD: and Samuel cried unto the LORD for Israel; and the LORD heard him. 10 And as Samuel was offering up the burnt offering, the Philistines drew near to battle against Israel: but the LORD thundered with a great thunder on that day upon the Philistines, and discomfited them; and they were smitten before Israel. 11 And the men of Israel went out of Mizpeh, and pursued the Philistines, and smote them, until they came under Bethcar. 12 Then Samuel took a stone, and set it between Mizpeh and Shen, and called the name of it Ebenezer, saying, Hitherto hath the LORD helped us.

13 So the Philistines were subdued, and they came no more into the coast of Israel: and the hand of the LORD was against the Philistines all the days of Samuel.

NEW REVISED STANDARD VERSION

1 SAMUEL 7:3 Then Samuel said to all the house of Israel, "If you are returning to the LORD with all your heart, then put away the foreign gods and the Astartes from among you. Direct your heart to the LORD, and serve him only, and he will deliver you out of the hand of the Philistines." 4 So Israel put away the Baals and the Astartes, and they served the LORD only.

5 Then Samuel said, "Gather all Israel at Mizpah, and I will pray to the LORD for you." 6 So they gathered at Mizpah, and drew water and poured it out before the LORD. They fasted that day, and said, "We have sinned against the LORD." And Samuel judged the people of Israel at Mizpah.

7 When the Philistines heard that the people of Israel had gathered at Mizpah, the lords of the Philistines went up against Israel. And when the people of Israel heard of it they were afraid of the Philistines. 8 The people of Israel said to Samuel, "Do not cease to cry out to the LORD our God for us, and pray that he may save us from the hand of the Philistines." 9 So Samuel took a sucking lamb and offered it as a whole burnt offering to the LORD; Samuel cried out to the LORD for Israel, and the LORD answered him. 10 As Samuel was offering up the burnt offering, the Philistines drew near to attack Israel; but the LORD thundered with a mighty voice that day against the Philistines and threw them into confusion; and they were routed before Israel. 11 And the men of Israel went out of Mizpah and pursued the Philistines, and struck them down as far as beyond Beth-car.

12 Then Samuel took a stone and set it up between Mizpah and Jeshanah, and named it Ebenezer; for he said, "Thus far the LORD has helped us." 13 So the Philistines were subdued and did not again enter the territory of Israel; the hand of the LORD was against the Philistines all the days of Samuel.

7

Monday, October 9	Colossians 4:2-6	*Call to Prayer*
Tuesday, October 10	Psalm 31:14-24	*The Psalmist Prays*
Wednesday, October 11	1 Samuel 1:21-28	*Hannah Pays Her Vows*
Thursday, October 12	1 Samuel 2:1-11	*Hannah Prays*
Friday, October 13	1 Samuel 3:1-10	*The Lord Calls Samuel*
Saturday, October 14	1 Samuel 7:2-6	*Israel Returns to God*
Sunday, October 15	1 Samuel 7:7-13	*The Lord Helps the Hebrew People*

BACKGROUND

The 12 tribes of Israel that settled in the promised land after Joshua's campaign had no cohesive, organized way of working together. Often, when a common enemy threatened their survival, they joined forces. But during the two centuries after Joshua, they existed as somewhat independent clans without any centralized government. The judges, leaders who emerged to resolve disputes and lead those tribes uniting for common defense, sporadically headed the informal confederation of tribes.

The 40 years of oppression by the Philistines caused many Israelites to think about the need for a strong ruler who would preside over the tribes. After a disastrous defeat of the Israelite forces by the Philistines, a man named Samuel became recognized as the leader of the suffering tribal members. This outstanding personality is recognized as the human link between the time of the judges and beginning of the monarchy.

Samuel was a priest who became a prophet when he received a special call from God. While the ministry of priests was a constant in Israel's history, the work of the prophets was tailored to particular periods of crisis. The prophets were God's representatives, proclaiming His message under specific circumstances. While Abraham (Gen. 20:7) and Moses (Deut. 18:15-19) are both called prophets, as a group, prophets first appear in the biblical record during the time of Samuel. Samuel is usually referred to as the last of the significant judges and the first of the prophets.

Deuteronomy 18 makes it clear that a true prophet is always called by God (18:15, 18a), speaks for God (18:18b), derives authority from God (18:19), and cannot fail in the fulfillment of his or her predictions (18:22). Nevertheless, Israel was plagued by false prophets. Like weeds they popped up in Israel, proclaiming that their message was true, even though it was counterfeit.

In contrast, Samuel truly spoke for the Lord. Samuel was dedicated to God as a youth by his devout mother, Hannah. Samuel grew up in the temple at Shiloh under the guidance of the chief priest, Eli. Samuel's prophetic credentials were shown at the time of his dramatic call by God when he gave the dire news to Eli of his family's collapse because of the corrupt ways of the old priest's sons. Samuel took control of his people's future after the Philistines routed the Israelites in battle. Because of Samuel's unwavering service to the Lord, he was the ideal person of faith for such a profound calling.

In his old age, Samuel reluctantly conceded to the wishes of the people for a king. But he warned them that kings demand royal trappings and impose burdens on their subjects. As God's agent, Samuel privately anointed a handsome young man named Saul as the nation's first king, then later headed the public ceremony in which the people selected Saul as king by casting lots. Samuel sternly warned kings and people alike that God was meant to be held in greater allegiance than any other. When Saul failed to fulfill the command to obey the Lord, Samuel condemned Saul and foretold that Saul would be replaced by another king.

Ever heeding the leading of God, Samuel went to Bethlehem and anointed the young shepherd boy named David to be the new king. Samuel's transitional role as the last of the judges and the first of the prophets brought the Israelites from being an informal collection of tribes to an established monarchy.

NOTES ON THE PRINTED TEXT

Samuel was the last major Israelite judge in the roughly 350-year period of the judges. He appeared on the scene when Israel was disintegrating morally, spiritually, and politically. Even the priesthood, under Eli's corrupt sons, was being misused for personal gain and profit; but God responded to the needs of His people by raising up Samuel.

At this time, the Philistines were the major military threat to Israel. The Philistines, descendants of Noah's son Ham (Gen. 10:6, 14), were one of a group of migrating Sea Peoples from the Aegean Sea area. In the twelfth century B.C., the Philistines evidently left Crete and Cyprus and invaded Egypt. After the Egyptians drove them out, the Philistines settled along the southwest coast of Canaan.

Central in the religion of this seafaring people was the god Dagon (see Judg. 16:23). Some scholars believe he was depicted as part human, part fish. By Samuel's time these warlike people were well established in five cities in southwest Canaan (Gaza, Ashkelon, Ashdod, Ekron, and Gath) and were constantly pressing inland against the Israelites. The Philistines were Israel's major enemy from Samson's day until the time of David.

Since the Philistine's main cities were located in a land corridor often used by invading armies, they were eventually overrun and disappeared from the annals of history. Their one legacy was the application of their name to the land of Canaan. The region between the Mediterranean Sea and the Jordan River became known as Palestine, or "the land of the Philistines."

When Samuel was about 13 years old, the Israelites engaged the Philistines in battle at Aphek, a strategic city bordering Philistine territory on the north. The Philistines fought on to victory, slaughtering 30,000 Israelites in the process and capturing the ark (1 Sam. 4:9-11). Chapters 5:1—7:1 reveal that the Philistines took the ark to Ashdod, where God destroyed their image of Dagon. God caused tumors and plagues of rats to follow the ark wherever it went. After seven months, the Philistine diviners advised the people to return the ark—along with a guilt offering of golden likenesses of the tumors and rats—to appease the God of Israel. The Israelites eventually brought it to Kiriath Jearim, located about 10 miles west of Jerusalem. The ark could not be returned to Shiloh because that city had been completely destroyed by the Philistines (around 1050 B.C.).

As one year after another passed with the ark at Kiriath Jearim, the people of Israel longed for renewed fellowship with the Lord (7:2). The ark was kept in this city from shortly after the battle of Aphek, around 1104 B.C., until David moved it to Jerusalem in 1003 B.C., the first year of his reign over the united kingdom of Judah and Israel (see 2 Sam. 5:5; 6:1-11). The ark had been at Kiriath Jearim two decades when the events of 1 Samuel 7 took place.

Samuel addressed the nation in his first recorded act of public worship at about the age of 33. He challenged the people of Israel to demonstrate their change of heart by getting rid of all their foreign gods. If they would, then God would deliver them from the oppressive hands of the Philistines (7:3). Israel complied and abandoned worship of the Baals and Ashtoreths and the rituals associated with the veneration of these pagan gods (7:4).

After the people disposed of their idols, physically and emotionally, Samuel told them to congregate at Mizpah, where he would intercede with the Lord on their behalf. (Despite numerous references, Mizpah's location remains disputed.) There Samuel led the people in a ceremony in which water was poured out before the Lord (7:5-6). This is the only passage in Scripture where the pouring of water is said to be a sign of repentance.

The Israelites begged Samuel to continue his intercession for them so that God would save them from the Philistines (7:7-8). Samuel agreed, and after fervent prayer and the sacrifice of a lamb, the Lord answered him (7:9). How the Lord responded to Samuel prior to the battle is not known. We can only assume that the prophet clearly recognized God's voice.

The Philistines prepared to attack while Samuel was in the process of offering sacrifices for the nation. However, as the enemy approached, the Lord terrorized the Philistines in a thunderous display of divine power. The concussion of noise could have been literal thunder or simply the voice of the Lord. Buoyed by divine support, the Israelites engaged their enemies. The Philistines fled from the pursuing Israelites in panic and disarray. The Philistines were struck down and soundly defeated. So complete was the victory that the foe did not invade Israel again in Samuel's lifetime (7:10-11).

After defeating the Philistines, Samuel expressed the people's gratitude to God by erecting a stone monument between Mizpah and Shen. (The location of the latter is unknown.) Samuel called the monument *Ebenezer* (7:12), which means "stone of help." The Lord's help was so great that Israel got back all the land the Philistines had taken, broke the power of the Philistines over other neighboring peoples, and established peace with the Amorites (7:13-14). The name "Amorites" is a general designation for the original inhabitants of Canaan (see Josh. 10:5).

Throughout his life, Samuel served Israel as a circuit judge, making the rounds from Bethel to Gilgal to Mizpah to his hometown of Ramah (1 Sam. 7:15-17). This route was roughly 50 miles in circumference. As a judge, Samuel's function was primarily threefold—civil (1 Sam. 7:16; see Exod. 18:16), military (see 1 Sam. 12:11), and religious (see 7:6, 17). In his priestly capacity, Samuel erected an altar to the Lord in Ramah because the tabernacle in Shiloh had been destroyed. In whatever capacity Samuel served, worship was always his first priority.

SUGGESTIONS TO TEACHERS

Samuel's prayer had hardly fallen from his lips before God thundered His response from heaven. While such examples of God's immediate answers to prayer are exciting to read about, it is important to remember that He most often answers in a less spectacular manner and acts in ways seldom attended by such obvious displays of His supernatural power. Take a few moments during the teaching time to emphasize the following points.

1. GOD KNOWS US. We may wonder how God is able to understand our prayers when we feel so confused. But when we read the teachings of Scripture, we will discover that God knows our prayers better than we do ourselves. Even when we're not sure what the right prayers should be or the best method of prayer to use, God actively searches our hearts (Rom. 8:27), and He is able to see the motive of our prayers and respond in kind.

2. GOD IS HERE TO HELP. We know that the Bible says Jesus Christ is *the same yesterday, and to day, and for ever* (Heb. 13:8). But do we really believe that? The same God that helped Samuel thousands of years ago is the one that will help us today.

3. GOD WILL RESPOND TO OUR REQUESTS. Samuel is a good example of how we should pray. The most important attribute he displayed was a view of an awesome God who would work on behalf of anyone who was willing to trust and obey Him. It seems like the prayers God delights most in answering are the ones that begin with an acknowledgement of who He is, are filled with humble cries for help, and end with an affirmation of trust that God will always do what is right.

4. GOD IS PLEASED TO RESPOND. We sometimes forget that God hears and understands our prayers. Samuel prayed prayers that God answered—some right away, and others further down the road. Samuel learned that prayers based upon God's Word and will are prayers that particularly please the Lord. Thus, the issue is not whether God will hear and respond to our requests, but whether we are willing to trust Him to do so and pray accordingly.

■ TOPIC: Samuel Prays and God Answers

■ QUESTIONS: 1. Why did Samuel direct the Israelites to abandon their idols? 2. In what way did Samuel intercede for the Israelites? 3. What sin did the Israelites admit they were guilty of doing? 4. How did the defeat of the Philistines take place? 5. Why is it important for believers to be committed to serving only the Lord?

■ ILLUSTRATIONS:

Just in Time. A Christian woman, Joan, married an unbelieving husband, Brian (not their real names). He was a salesman who often traveled during the week, so Joan had lots of time to pray for her husband's salvation. Joan had great joy in her heart knowing that God was hearing her pleas, especially as she lifted up Brian in continuous prayer.

Joan was devastated, however, the day she received news that Brian had been instantly killed in a highway accident. Joan's faith was deeply shaken—that is, until nearly five years later, when she received a surprise visit from a young man who came looking for Brian. As it turned out, this young man, Josh, was the last person to see Joan's husband alive. Brian had picked him up as Josh was hitchhiking on a country highway. When he dropped Josh off, Brian gave him his address and said if he was ever in town to look him up.

Josh was shocked to hear Joan report that Brian had been killed only five miles beyond the place that he had last seen him. But that tragic news became less heartrending when Josh informed Joan that 10 minutes before the fatal crash, he had prayed with Brian, and that Joan's husband had repented of his sins and asked God to give him a personal relationship through faith in Jesus Christ.

God Hears and Acts. When Hope Community Fellowship sensed the time was right to move ahead on a building project, church leaders made plans to develop a monthly prayer calendar for the congregation. It was God's faithful answers to prayer that had made the project possible. The church had no desire to move forward without making prayer a priority.

Sometimes it may seem that our prayers reach no higher than the ceiling. And there are moments when we may fear that there really is no one on the other end. But Scripture assures us that God hears our prayers. He understands our deepest needs—even those we can't bring ourselves to voice.

God's faithfulness to hear our prayers is why Hope Community Fellowship lists prayer concerns in the weekly bulletin. It is why every church meeting begins and ends with prayer. And it is why some of the congregation's members believe there is no sweeter sound than someone saying, "I'll remember you in my prayers." As we learn in this week's lesson, God hears and He acts in response to our prayers.

The 'Yea, God!' Party. Not long ago I learned about a church that is planning a "Yea, God!" party to celebrate the way the Lord has answered the congregation's prayers in the past year. This local body of believers recognizes the mighty acts of God that have blessed their existence, and they are excited about giving God credit and praise for these gifts and blessings. From what I hear, this won't be a small, quiet little church service. It is going to be an all-out event. There will be a video presentation, highlighting many answered prayer requests; special music; testimonials; singing; and great food. What a wonderful way to celebrate and honor God for His mighty works among His people!

| **FOR YOUTH** | ■ TOPIC: Samuel Prays for Help |

■ **QUESTIONS:** 1. What did Samuel say that the Israelites had to do in order to return to the Lord? 2. Why was it impossible for the Israelites to serve both the Lord and the idols worshiped by the Canaanites? 3. How did the Philistines respond to the gathering of the Israelites at Mizpah? 4. How did the Lord bring about the defeat of the Philistines? 5. What are some of the conditions of our heart that make a difference in the effectiveness of our prayers?

■ **ILLUSTRATIONS:**

Pray without Ceasing. How much difference in the world could a dishwasher make, especially one who worked far removed from the hustle of daily life? Yet Brother Lawrence of the Resurrection (1605–1691) has left a permanent mark on the lives of Christians everywhere, a mark made for eternity.

This humble Carmelite monk and mystic worked in a monastery with other men in his order. His daily tasks included the routine work of kitchen help. During these countless hours laboring over the kitchen sinks—hours alone with God—Brother Lawrence began to develop his habit of communing with God.

In his later years, Brother Lawrence penned out the pathways to the discipline that had made his hours of menial labor seem so sweet. In a book entitled *The Practice of the Presence of God,* Lawrence tells about the techniques of how to keep God uppermost in the conscious and subconscious of our intellect and imagination.

This small treatise on how to incorporate prayer into every function of life has made a deep impact on the lives of many Christians. Even in the early years of your life, the meditations of Brother Lawrence can be a continual encouragement for you to always keep an ever-present God in your daily routines.

Rent Stabilized. *Guideposts* prayer volunteer Diane Williams shares about interceding on behalf of Mary, a home-healthcare aide who was unable to work due to her disability. Though Mary received a monthly check, it didn't provide enough income to pay all her bills. As she struggled to meet her payments, creditors began to pester her. things seemed to go from bad to worse when she received notification that the building where she lived was under new management and that her rent was increasing.

Diane continued to pray for Mary throughout the entire ordeal. Then one day, Mary called Diane and related her conversation with a woman in the laundry room of the apartment complex. The woman said to Mary, "I know you! You're the aide who took care of my aunt. I've always been grateful to you. How are you doing?" It was then that Mary recounted her situation, especially the mounting unpaid bills. This prompted the woman to say, "Well, you'll never have to worry about a place to live." Mary was puzzled by that statement and asked, "How can you be so sure?" And the woman replied, "I'm the owner of the new building. You can stay as long as you want. And you don't have to worry about the rent going up."

No matter how difficult your situation might seem, even at this early stage in your life, you can trust God to watch over you and provide for your needs.

Answered Prayer. In *Our Daily Bread,* well-known Christian author and speaker Josh McDowell noted that while he was in graduate school in California, his father went home to be with the Lord. Josh's mother had died years earlier, but Josh was not sure about her salvation. Soon Josh became depressed, thinking that his mother might be lost. *Was she a Christian or not?* The thought obsessed Josh. "Lord," he prayed, "somehow give me the answer so I can get back to normal. I've just got to know." It seemed like an impossible request.

Two days later, Josh drove out to the ocean. He walked to the end of a pier to be alone. There an old woman sat in a lawnchair and fished. "Where's your home originally?" she asked. "Michigan—Union City," Josh replied. "Nobody's heard of it. I tell people it's a suburb of . . ." "Battle Creek," interrupted the woman. "I had a cousin from there. Did you know the McDowell family?"

Stunned, Josh responded, "Yes, I'm Josh McDowell!" "I can't believe it," said the woman. "I'm a cousin to your mother." "Do you remember anything at all about my mother's spiritual life?" asked Josh. "Why sure—your mom and I were just girls—teenagers—when a tent revival came to town. It was the fourth night—we both went forward to accept Christ." "Praise God!" shouted Josh, startling the surrounding fishermen. He realized then that God had answered his prayer.

GOD COVENANTS WITH DAVID

BACKGROUND SCRIPTURE: 2 Samuel 7
DEVOTIONAL READING: Psalm 5

KEY VERSE: And thine house and thy kingdom shall be established for ever before thee: thy throne shall be established for ever. 2 Samuel 7:16.

KING JAMES VERSION

2 SAMUEL 7:8 Now therefore so shalt thou say unto my servant David, Thus saith the LORD of hosts, I took thee from the sheepcote, from following the sheep, to be ruler over my people, over Israel: 9 And I was with thee whithersoever thou wentest, and have cut off all thine enemies out of thy sight, and have made thee a great name, like unto the name of the great men that are in the earth. 10 Moreover I will appoint a place for my people Israel, and will plant them, that they may dwell in a place of their own, and move no more; neither shall the children of wickedness afflict them any more, as before-time, 11 And as since the time that I commanded judges to be over my people Israel, and have caused thee to rest from all thine enemies. Also the LORD telleth thee that he will make thee an house. 12 And when thy days be fulfilled, and thou shalt sleep with thy fathers, I will set up thy seed after thee, which shall proceed out of thy bowels, and I will establish his kingdom. 13 He shall build an house for my name, and I will stablish the throne of his kingdom for ever. 14 I will be his father, and he shall be my son. If he commit iniquity, I will chasten him with the rod of men, and with the stripes of the children of men: 15 But my mercy shall not depart away from him, as I took it from Saul, whom I put away before thee. 16 And thine house and thy kingdom shall be established for ever before thee: thy throne shall be established for ever. 17 According to all these words, and according to all this vision, so did Nathan speak unto David.

NEW REVISED STANDARD VERSION

2 SAMUEL 7:8 Now therefore thus you shall say to my servant David: Thus says the LORD of hosts: I took you from the pasture, from following the sheep to be prince over my people Israel; 9 and I have been with you wherever you went, and have cut off all your enemies from before you; and I will make for you a great name, like the name of the great ones of the earth. 10 And I will appoint a place for my people Israel and will plant them, so that they may live in their own place, and be disturbed no more; and evildoers shall afflict them no more, as formerly, 11 from the time that I appointed judges over my people Israel; and I will give you rest from all your enemies. Moreover the LORD declares to you that the LORD will make you a house. 12 When your days are fulfilled and you lie down with your ancestors, I will raise up your offspring after you, who shall come forth from your body, and I will establish his kingdom. 13 He shall build a house for my name, and I will establish the throne of his kingdom forever. 14 I will be a father to him, and he shall be a son to me. When he commits iniquity, I will punish him with a rod such as mortals use, with blows inflicted by human beings. 15 But I will not take my steadfast love from him, as I took it from Saul, whom I put away from before you. 16 Your house and your kingdom shall be made sure forever before me; your throne shall be established forever. 17 In accordance with all these words and with all this vision, Nathan spoke to David.

8

HOME BIBLE READINGS

BACKGROUND

First and 2 Samuel relate one of the most important developments in the history of faith, namely, the transformation of ancient Israel from a loose confederation of tribes into a monarchy. The account begins with Samuel, the last major judge of Israel, and moves to Saul, Israel's first king. God eventually rejected Saul because of his disobedience and chose David to be Israel's next king. The transition of power from Saul to David was stormy. It began with Saul persecuting David, and it ended with the death of Saul and his son Jonathan in battle.

Despite the tragic deaths of these two men, the hand of God was unmistakable in the outworking of events. He raised up David to be the next king of His people. In light of the years of decline seen in the Book of Judges, this development might appear long overdue. Nevertheless, God carried out His plans in His time and in His way. He worked through the choices of individuals and nations so that His will for His people might prevail.

Indeed, during David's reign as king, he took a divided and defeated Israel from his predecessor and built a powerful nation. Second Samuel highlights the character traits that enabled David to succeed, including his reliance on the Lord for guidance, David's sincerity, and his courage. The book also describes the tragic consequences of David's lust and pride.

It should come as no surprise that the unifying theme of 2 Samuel is the establishment of the kingdom of Israel. Throughout the narrative, there is a continuing interest in the rule of God over His people. The book emphasizes that it was the Lord who rejected Saul for his disobedience, chose David for the throne, and disciplined David for his pride. Ultimately, God was the true King of Israel. Furthermore, the key to David's successful reign was his relationship with the Lord. Through all the triumphs and tragedies of David's tenure in office, God was acting in the national and personal events of His people in order to accomplish His eternal purposes.

The writer of 2 Samuel was deeply influenced by the theology of the Book of Deuteronomy. The historical narratives in 2 Samuel reflect the belief that God blessed Israel's leaders and people when they obeyed the covenant that He had made with Moses. Conversely, God disciplined them severely when they transgressed the law. To be sure, the dominant theological idea seems to be that sin brought punishment, while repentance brought restoration. Eventually, the repeated sins of idolatry and injustice throughout the histories of Israel and Judah culminated in the ultimate punishment of exile from the promised land.

Consider the Scripture passage for this week's lesson. It does not just talk about David's reign. Instead, the writer discussed the covenant that God made with David and how it affected his reign as Israel's king. In the Lord's covenant with David, God unconditionally promised to give an eternal dynasty, an eternal throne, and an eternal kingdom to David.

NOTES ON THE PRINTED TEXT

While David was in Jerusalem's palace, he summoned Nathan the prophet to the royal court. Nathan apparently served as a private counselor to the king. David was distressed because the ark of the covenant was housed in a tent (namely, the tabernacle) while he lived in a magnificent palace (2 Sam. 7:1-2). The phrase *house of cedar* (7:2) indicates David's wealth, for cedar paneling was too expensive to be used in ordinary homes. David's palace was built from the famous cedars of Lebanon trees provided to him by King Hiram of Tyre (5:11-12).

David realized that the Lord was the one who enabled Israel to enjoy peace. Some think the king viewed his palace as a symbol of his now-established rule. Accordingly, in David's mind, housing the ark in a temple would be an appropriate symbol for God's rule over His people. Previously, after David had captured Jerusalem, he brought the tabernacle to the city (6:12-19). The inner section of the tabernacle, the Most Holy Place, housed the ark of the covenant, containing the stone tablets with the Ten Commandments, a golden pot with manna in it, and Aaron's rod (Heb. 9:4). The temple David planned to build would be an appropriate, permanent structure to house the ark.

Nathan responded by encouraging the king to pursue the noble project he had in mind (2 Sam. 7:3). The prophet reasoned that the Lord had blessed David by making his kingdom great (see 1 Chron. 14:2). However, Nathan spoke on the basis of his own understanding, for he had not consulted the Lord on the matter. Thankfully, the prophet was quick to reverse himself when ordered by the Lord. Nathan told David that up until this time in Israel's history, God had manifested His presence in the ark and its accompanying tent. Scripture repeatedly uses the image of a shepherd to depict political and spiritual leadership. Whether it is David the shepherd boy or Jesus Christ the good Shepherd (John 10:11), the idea is of leaders who love and care for their flock.

Not once did the Lord complain to Israel's leaders—the shepherds of His people— to build Him a beautiful cedar temple (2 Sam. 7:4-7). In this message to David, we learn that God did not want the king to build a sanctuary for Him. Instead, David was to focus on unifying the nation and subduing Israel's enemies. Accomplishing this task would mean the loss of many lives. God did not want the temple to be built by a warrior whose career was characterized by such bloodshed (1 Chron. 28:3). Rather than balk at the will of God, David humbly submitted to it. When the Lord called David His *servant* (2 Sam. 7:5), David joined a select group that included Abraham, Caleb, Moses, and Joshua (Gen. 26:24; Num. 14:24; Deut. 34:5; Josh. 24:29). David also made plans and collected the materials so that his son Solomon could build the temple later (1 Chron. 22:2-5; 28:2).

Nathan related that the Lord in His grace had taken David from being a shepherd boy and made him the king of Israel (2 Sam. 7:8). God had not only enabled David to subdue his enemies but would also make his name famous. In addition, the Lord used David to enable the Israelites to dwell in peace in Canaan. This had never been true since the time of the judges (7:9-11).

Second Samuel 7:11-13 records the establishment of God's covenant with David, which amplifies and confirms the promises of His covenant with Abraham (Gen. 12:1-3). Although the word *covenant* is not specifically stated in 2 Samuel 7, it is used elsewhere to describe this occasion (2 Sam. 23:5; Ps. 89:28, 34). Clearly, the issues of 2 Samuel 7 are of immense theological importance. They concern not only the first coming of the Messiah but also the Savior's eternal rule on the throne of David.

The word rendered *house* (7:11) lies at the heart of this passage. David saw his own house (or palace) and desired to build a house (or temple) for the Lord. God declared, however, that He would build a house (or dynasty) for David; and the king's son would build a house (or temple) for the Lord. In His covenant with David, God promised that the king's descendants would become a dynasty and always rule over Israel. Individual kings were subject to severe punishment (Ps. 89:30-32), but the Lord would never permanently reject the line of David from the throne (89:33-37). The New Testament reveals that God's promises to David are fulfilled in Christ. He keeps the conditions of the covenant perfectly (Heb. 4:15), serves as the Mediator of the covenant (9:15), and promised to return as the conquering King (Matt. 24:29-31).

David did not have to worry whether his kingdom would endure after his death; the Lord would make the royal throne of his son secure for all time (2 Sam. 7:13). God also pledged to establish an intimate Father-son relationship with David's descendants. When a Davidic king did wrong, the Lord would punish him just as parents discipline their rebellious children (7:14). God's punishment of David's successors would culminate in the loss of land and temple (see 1 Kings 9:6-9); yet the Lord would never withdraw His love from His covenant people. Moreover, the Davidic kings did not have to fear that God would remove His loyal love from them as He had with Saul (2 Sam. 7:15; see 1 Sam. 15:28). God's promise to establish forever the dynasty, kingdom, and throne of David would not fail (2 Sam. 7:16), being one day fully realized in the Messiah (see Jer. 33:14-26; Mic. 5:2-5).

How wonderful it must have been for Nathan to tell David all that the Lord had revealed to him in his vision (2 Sam. 7:17). Nathan, whose name means "[God] has given," proved to be a necessary and helpful gift from God to David. Nathan served as prophet, or spokesperson, to two of Israel's kings, David and Solomon. Throughout his career, Nathan displayed wisdom in his counsel and bravery in his confrontation of injustice.

SUGGESTIONS TO TEACHERS

After building a palace for himself, David felt ashamed that he allowed the sacred ark of God to remain in a tent. He dreamed of erecting a suitable temple to honor God and house the ark. When God denied him the plan to build a temple, David had to live with disappointment. But God also gave David a promise that He would remember Israel's king. This week have your class reflect on facing the challenges of (1) living with disappointment, and (2) relying on the Lord's promises to us.

1. DAVID'S DREAM AND DECISION. What finer thought than to build a beautiful temple! David's motive was noble and his plan was commendable. Sometimes, our intentions seem to fit in with what we imagine God would approve. But for various reasons, we are disappointed and not able to fulfill what we hoped to do. Some in the class may wish to share personal episodes of disappointment and how they dealt with them.

2. NATHAN'S DARING DISCLOSURE. It took courage to stand up to the king, but God's spokesman, Nathan, didn't flinch. Informed by God that David would not be permitted to erect a temple, Nathan risked David's displeasure and told him the news that God said, "No!" Going against the wishes of powerful interests and personalities is not easy or pleasant, but prophetic voices must speak up for God. The Church is called to be such a prophetic voice in these times!

3. DAVID'S DISAPPOINTMENT AND DEDICATION. To his credit, David accepted Nathan's message in which God turned down the temple building project. David's trust in God remained undiminished despite the disappointment he must have felt. A dedication to the Lord in which confidence in God continues, regardless of circumstances, is the only way to handle disappointment.

4. GOD'S DECREE AND DOMINION. God covenanted with David that He would remember David forever. God promised David that a son would eventually build the temple and continue his kingdom. David learned to accept the challenge of God's promises. For us Christians, God has spelled out His promise of His everlasting love in the person of Jesus Christ. Through the Cross and resurrection of this King, God has covenanted with us.

5. GOD'S DESIRE TO BLESS US. We may rely on God to remember us and to fulfill His plans. God may also be trusted to bless us, regardless of our current problems. Perhaps we will be blessed by seeing someone we have been teaching really grasp what God is about, or by seeing someone advance whom we helped get a job, or by seeing a positive report from a missions agency we have supported for years.

■ **TOPIC:** A Promise You Can Trust

■ **QUESTIONS:** 1. What was David's job before he became the ruler of Israel? 2. How great would David's fame be? 3. How would Israel benefit from the promise of a homeland? 4. What are some of the highpoints connected with God's promise of an enduring Davidic dynasty and kingdom? 5. How can God's eternal promises help us to deal with disappointments?

■ **ILLUSTRATIONS:**

Relying on the Promise. Arthur Ashe, the champion American tennis player, acquired AIDS through a blood transfusion at the time he underwent heart surgery. The hospital did not suspect or inspect the unit of H.I.V. contaminated blood. Ashe did not realize that he was infected with the dread virus until five years later when he suffered numbness, then growing paralysis in his playing arm. The diagnosis was a brain tumor. This stay in the hospital for surgery revealed that he had contracted AIDS from the transfusion during his heart surgery five years earlier. Released from the hospital, the seventh-ranked tennis star had to face rumors about his condition as well as face retirement from playing.

Arthur Ashe resisted the temptation to be angry at the Lord. In 1992, he addressed the students at the Niagara County Community College, and testified how in spite of his AIDS God could be trusted to keep his word.

Challenge of a Promise. Ricky Hoyt has cerebral palsy. He is confined to a wheelchair. His disability is classified technically as a spastic quadriplegic. He cannot even talk and has to communicate through a voice synthesizer. Nonetheless, Ricky Hoyt has been able to compete in over 600 sports events, including 111 triathlons, a 45-day cross country odyssey, and nearly 20 Boston Marathons. How? Because of the promise of his father and the way that promise has been kept.

Ricky's father, Dick, is a retired Lt. Colonel who has devoted himself to compete with Ricky to fulfill the dreams of his son. Rick is the heart but Dick Hoyt is the body. Together they compete. Dick pushes the wheelchair, fulfilling his promise to his boy to let him participate even in big-time marathons.

How much more does God fulfill His promises to those who trust him? David learned this.

Commitment to God's Promise. Habitat for Humanity has provided affordable housing for millions throughout the world. Few know the story of its origins. A young millionaire named Millard Fuller had amassed a fortune by the age of 29, and was able to buy anything he fancied. He discovered that his marriage had collapsed because of his greed and attention only to business. Shocked at having his wife, Linda, leave him, he began to take stock of his life.

Millard located Linda in New York and listened to her tell him that she didn't care about having him buy her things. He heard her describe how her life was barren of meaning with his kind of living. They talked and wept together. Then they knelt and prayed. That night in a hotel room in New York City, the couple promised God and each other that they would dispose of everything they had and commit themselves to helping the oppressed and homeless. The Fullers' promise has resulted in ways they never anticipated, as countless chapters of Habitat for Humanity now exist in North American communities and in many developing countries among the poorest.

FOR YOUTH	■ **TOPIC:** David's Everlasting Kingdom ■ **QUESTIONS:** 1. What role did Nathan serve in the account of God's covenant with David? 2. Where was God throughout the various

episodes of David's life? 3. What did God promise to do for David? 4. What did God promise to do for David's descendants? 5. What promises in Scripture are most precious to you? In what way do they give you hope for the future?

■ **ILLUSTRATIONS:**

Faith at Work. The renowned talk show host Larry King reported that during one of his hospital stays, he received many letters and gifts. However, the one that touched him the most was a Bible and a note sent by "Pistol" Pete Maravich, the former Louisiana State University and National Basketball Association star.

The note read: "Dear Larry, I'm so glad to hear that everything went well with your surgery. I want you to know that God was watching over you every minute, and even though I know you may question that, I also know that one day it will become evident to you . . . because He lives."

The following week, Pete Maravich died of a heart attack. Larry King says he will always remember Pete Maravich not just as a Christian, but as a caring Christian. What a wonderful legacy! What a wonderful torch to pass on!

Faith for the Next Generation? There's a quote in Tom Carter's book, *13 Crucial Questions Jesus Wants to Ask You*, that says, "To our forefathers, faith was an experience. To our fathers, faith was an inheritance. To us, faith is a convenience. To our children, faith is a nuisance."

Cost of Salvation. In his book *Be Right*, Warren Wiersbe tells how G. Campbell Morgan was trying to explain the concept of "free salvation" to a coal miner, but the man was unable to understand it. "I have to pay for it," he continually insisted. But with a flash of divine insight, Morgan asked, "How did you get down into the mine this morning?"

"Why, it was easy," the man replied. "I just got on the elevator and went down."

Then Morgan asked, "Wasn't that too easy? Didn't it cost you something?"

The man laughed. "No, it didn't cost me anything; but it must have cost the company plenty to install that elevator." Then the miner saw the truth: "It doesn't cost me anything to be saved, but it cost God the life of His Son."

Use It or Lose It. Janice took piano lessons for 12 years and developed into a promising performer. She planned to teach music someday. Then she went to college. Instead of majoring in music education as she originally intended, Janice became interested in contemporary literature and chose an English major. Extracurricular activities in the drama club and gymnastics took up her spare time. Occasionally she would sit down at the piano, but found her keyboard skills were not as sharp as they once had been.

Upon graduation, Janice moved to Chicago and found a job. She told herself that she would return to her music as soon as possible, but meanwhile she needed to earn a living. She planned to save to buy herself a piano, but a new car and vacations always consumed what she meant to set aside for the piano. New hobbies, especially golf, attracted her. Soon she devoted nearly all her weekends to sharpening her abilities as a golfer.

Then Janice met a man at a golfing party and eventually married him. When the children came, Janice quit her job for several years, reentering the work force when her last child was in junior high. Meanwhile, she sometimes remarked that she would get back to playing the piano again, but it was always "someday."

On their twentieth wedding anniversary, Janice's husband presented her with a lovely spinet piano. Delighted, Janice sat down to play. To her surprise, the years of no practice had ruined her fingering. Gripping a golf club had done something to one wrist. Her ability to sight-read the music seemed to have diminished. Her playing sounded like the clumsy efforts of a beginning piano student. Looking up at her husband, Janice smiled ruefully, "Well, the old saying is true, I guess: 'Use it or lose it.'"

Use your faith and keep progressing in Christian growth. If not, like Janice's piano playing, you lose touch with what you once loved.

God Grants Wisdom to Solomon

BACKGROUND SCRIPTURE: 1 Kings 3
DEVOTIONAL READING: Psalm 119:97-104

KEY VERSE: Behold, I have done according to thy words: lo, I have given thee a wise and an understanding heart; so that there was none like thee before thee. 1 Kings 3:12.

KING JAMES VERSION

1 KINGS 3:3 And Solomon loved the LORD, walking in the statutes of David his father: only he sacrificed and burnt incense in high places. 4 And the king went to Gibeon to sacrifice there; for that was the great high place: a thousand burnt offerings did Solomon offer upon that altar.

5 In Gibeon the LORD appeared to Solomon in a dream by night: and God said, Ask what I shall give thee. 6 And Solomon said, Thou hast shewed unto thy servant David my father great mercy, according as he walked before thee in truth, and in righteousness, and in uprightness of heart with thee; and thou hast kept for him this great kindness, that thou hast given him a son to sit on his throne, as it is this day. 7 And now, O LORD my God, thou hast made thy servant king instead of David my father: and I am but a little child: I know not how to go out or come in. 8 And thy servant is in the midst of thy people which thou hast chosen, a great people, that cannot be numbered nor counted for multitude. 9 Give therefore thy servant an understanding heart to judge thy people, that I may discern between good and bad: for who is able to judge this thy so great a people? 10 And the speech pleased the Lord, that Solomon had asked this thing. 11 And God said unto him, Because thou hast asked this thing, and hast not asked for thyself long life; neither hast asked riches for thyself, nor hast asked the life of thine enemies; but hast asked for thyself understanding to discern judgment; 12 Behold, I have done according to thy words: lo, I have given thee a wise and an understanding heart; so that there was none like thee before thee, neither after thee shall any arise like unto thee. 13 And I have also given thee that which thou hast not asked, both riches, and honour: so that there shall not be any among the kings like unto thee all thy days. 14 And if thou wilt walk in my ways, to keep my statutes and my commandments, as thy father David did walk, then I will lengthen thy days.

NEW REVISED STANDARD VERSION

1 KINGS 3:3 Solomon loved the LORD, walking in the statutes of his father David; only, he sacrificed and offered incense at the high places. 4 The king went to Gibeon to sacrifice there, for that was the principal high place; Solomon used to offer a thousand burnt offerings on that altar. 5 At Gibeon the LORD appeared to Solomon in a dream by night; and God said, "Ask what I should give you." 6 And Solomon said, "You have shown great and steadfast love to your servant my father David, because he walked before you in faithfulness, in righteousness, and in uprightness of heart toward you; and you have kept for him this great and steadfast love, and have given him a son to sit on his throne today. 7 And now, O LORD my God, you have made your servant king in place of my father David, although I am only a little child; I do not know how to go out or come in. 8 And your servant is in the midst of the people whom you have chosen, a great people, so numerous they cannot be numbered or counted. 9 Give your servant therefore an understanding mind to govern your people, able to discern between good and evil; for who can govern this your great people?"

10 It pleased the Lord that Solomon had asked this. 11 God said to him, "Because you have asked this, and have not asked for yourself long life or riches, or for the life of your enemies, but have asked for yourself understanding to discern what is right, 12 I now do according to your word. Indeed I give you a wise and discerning mind; no one like you has been before you and no one like you shall arise after you. 13 I give you also what you have not asked, both riches and honor all your life; no other king shall compare with you. 14 If you will walk in my ways, keeping my statutes and my commandments, as your father David walked, then I will lengthen your life."

9

Monday, October 23	Proverbs 1:1-7	*The Incomparable Worth of Wisdom*
Tuesday, October 24	Job 28:12-28	*Where Is Wisdom Found?*
Wednesday, October 25	Psalm 119:97-104	*Add to Wisdom Understanding*
Thursday, October 26	1 Kings 1:28-40	*Solomon Chosen to Be King*
Friday, October 27	1 Kings 3:3-9	*Solomon Requests Wisdom*
Saturday, October 28	1 Kings 3:10-15	*God Answers Solomon's Request*
Sunday, October 29	1 Kings 4:29-34	*Solomon Was Wise*

BACKGROUND

David reigned for 40 years. In his old age, he realized that he needed to groom a successor from one of his numerous sons. The Bible mentions 19 of the king's sons by name, and only four of them receive passing mention—Ammon, Absalom, Adonijah, and Solomon. Despite the lack of information regarding the rest of David's unnamed offspring, we have no reason to doubt the king's generous attitude and treatment toward each of them.

In terms of David's sons who are discussed, Ammon, the king's spoiled firstborn, raped his half-sister Tamar. Though angry over the rape, David did nothing to punish Ammon. All that is known about the king's second son is his name, Daniel. David's third son, Absalom, murdered his elder half-brother, Ammon, in retaliation for raping Tamar, Absalom's full sister. Years later, Absalom led Israel into a civil war as he attempted to usurp the throne from his father. Despite David's orders not to harm Absalom, Joab murdered him during a battle.

With David old and dying, his fourth son, Adonijah, appointed himself king. David immediately overturned Adonijah's claim and selected the younger Solomon as his actual successor. David called together key leaders to anoint Solomon, and accepted this son as co-regent. The aging king and his leaders prayed for God to bless Solomon as he had blessed David, and the elder monarch told Solomon to obey God's law and walk in God's ways. David also reminded Solomon of God's promise to bless his dynasty only as long as the rulers remained faithful to the Lord.

Solomon assumed power upon David's death, and also ruled for 40 years. Taking over the responsibilities of leading Israel was no easy task for young Solomon. Also, despite his father David's blessing, Solomon still had to wrestle the reins of power from his older brother, Adonijah. Then young Solomon had to prove to a kingdom who adored David that despite his inexperience and youth, he was the Lord's choice for the position. At the same time, Solomon had to prove himself to the various monarchs of the countries surrounding Israel. They had to know that he could protect his nation and navigate through the mine field of political intrigue and international commerce that marked the governmental climate of his age.

Solomon proved to be up to the task. He quickly consolidated his power by eliminating those threatening to cause problems, including Adonijah and Joab. The Bible also records that Solomon tolerated the presence of pagan shrines in the kingdom, and offered incense in their ceremonies. His long reign in the second third of the tenth century B.C. in a period of relative stability in the Middle East allowed Solomon to build a large empire.

Early in his rule, Solomon had a religious experience when God appeared to him in a dream. Solomon asked for the gift of wisdom to act as king of Israel, and pleased the Lord by such a request. Solomon shrewdly used that wisdom to develop trade routes to Asia Minor, Africa, Arabia, and Asia. Solomon also created administrative districts that cut across old tribal boundaries, erecting barracks, stables, and offices for the staffs of each. As a shrewd statesman, Solomon entered into alliances with neighboring realms, which were backed by marriages with princesses or others, according to political practice of that time. His efforts brought wealth and prestige, and seemed to be evidence of God's favor.

NOTES ON THE PRINTED TEXT

Many years had passed since David's sin with Bathsheba and the king's war against his son, Absalom (2 Sam. 14—18). Now much older and very weary, David was ready to pass on the reins of power to one of his sons. The question for the kingdom was which son would inherit the throne of Israel. Out of David's numerous sons, two were mentioned as being the most powerful claimants to the throne. The first was Adonijah, the son of Haggith. He was the fourth born of David's sons and the oldest surviving son of David. The second claimant was Adonijah's younger half-brother, Solomon, son of Bathsheba. Both young men had powerful allies in the royal court.

Both God and David, however, wanted Solomon to become the next king of Israel. First Kings 1 tells how Solomon thwarted Adonijah's early attempt to usurp the throne against David's wishes and became ruler of the mighty nation his father had built. David, upon hearing about Solomon's success, called his favorite son to hear his deathbed directives. David's primary instruction to Solomon was to show his loyalty to the Lord by following His commandments. If Solomon did, David assured his son that the Lord would make him prosper. Though unspoken, David implied that if Solomon and his descendants did not follow the Lord's commandments, they would fail instead of prosper (2:1-4).

By the end of his fourth year as king of Israel, Solomon had severely dealt with any internal threats to his throne. He had also begun dealing with any external threats to his kingdom by making a marriage alliance with the pharaoh of Egypt. Solomon housed his wife somewhere in the old part of Jerusalem until he could build her a palace (3:1). Moreover, at this time the Israelites offered sacrifices at the high places. These places of worship were often located on hills that were once sites to venerate

Baal. A stone sacrificial altar was usually at the center of the hilltop worship sites. Many also had large stone incense altars. Despite prohibitions against using once-pagan sites to venerate the Lord, the practice was quite common in Israel before Solomon built the temple (3:2).

To show his gratitude to God for the stability his kingdom now enjoyed, Solomon traveled to the high place near Gibeon and sacrificed a thousand burnt offerings there to the Lord (3:3-4). Though the biblical writer clearly explained that performing an offering on such high places went against God's commandments, He seemed to make allowances for it, since the temple had not yet been built (3:2). Also, while the location used to make the offerings was once used for pagan sacrifices, Solomon's attention was to thank and glorify the one, true God. The biblical writer makes a careful link between *love for the LORD* (3:3) and *walking according to the statutes.* Obedience is very important to God. As Jesus said, *If a man love me, he will keep my words* (John 14:23).

God rewarded Solomon's obedience by speaking with him through a dream. In the dream, the Lord offered to give the young monarch anything he requested (1 Kings 3:5). In response, Solomon noted that God had been exceedingly loyal to His servant David, who walked before the Lord in faithfulness, uprightness, and sincerity. God had demonstrated His steadfast love to David by allowing his son, Solomon, to sit as his successor on his throne (3:6). The new monarch was well aware that it was the sovereign Lord, the God of the patriarchs, who enabled Solomon to consolidate his power and serve in the place of his father, David. Solomon also acknowledged that he was a relatively young man and somewhat inexperienced when it came to running an entire nation (3:7).

The typical wish of Solomon's contemporaries would have included a long life, great riches, or the destruction of enemies. Instead of asking for these, Solomon requested a discerning heart so he could properly govern his kingdom. In making this remarkable request, the young Solomon—who was probably about 20-24 years old—admitted that properly ruling the 12 tribes of Israel called for more experience and knowledge than he could claim. Perhaps Solomon's first four years in power had taught him how complicated running a kingdom could be (3:8-9).

Solomon's humble request pleased the Lord (3:10). In particular, God took note of the young monarch's desire for the ability to make wise judicial decisions, rather than be given health, wealth, or even vengeance on his foes (3:11). The Lord in turn promised Solomon the wisest and most discerning heart of all time (3:12). As we learn from other portions of the Old Testament, Solomon's reputation for wisdom became renowned in the ancient world. For instance, a doubting Queen of Sheba traveled from southwest Arabia to see whether the Israelite king's reputation was warranted and returned home convinced it was.

According to 4:32, Solomon spoke some 3,000 proverbs and wrote 1,005 songs. He is also credited with scientific studies of various animals, fish, and trees. Many scholars believe that a large number of the adages in the Book of Proverbs were a part of

Solomon's thousands of wise sayings. The king probably also wrote the books of Ecclesiastes and the Song of Songs. Much of Solomon's writings, especially his proverbs, might have been lost forever if not for King Hezekiah. Solomon's wise sayings were selected, compiled, and organized by a committee of scholars appointed by Hezekiah (about 715–686 B.C.) for the purpose of reforming Israel (Prov. 25:1).

First Kings 3:13 notes that the Lord also gave Solomon what he had not requested, namely, riches and honor. The result is that David's successor was the greatest monarch of his generation. All Solomon had to do to insure receiving these blessings was to wholly follow the Lord (3:14). When Solomon awakened from his sleep, he realized the Lord had spoken to him in a dream. Then the king returned to Jerusalem, stood before the ark (or sacred chest) of the Lord's covenant, offered up burnt sacrifices to please God, presented tokens of peace as an expression of his desire for the Lord's blessing, and invited all his officials to a great banquet (3:15).

SUGGESTIONS TO TEACHERS

Wisdom is not the same as knowledge. Wisdom is not attained through university degrees. You have probably known people who had little formal education yet were blessed with wisdom in living. You have perhaps noticed these persons had the wisdom which enabled them to stand up to tasks that seemed overwhelming. Such wisdom comes from a relationship with God. This week's lesson illustrates this.

1. HOLY REQUIREMENT. David's deathbed advice to his son, Solomon, may be heeded by everyone. Solomon was wise enough to listen to his dying parent. The words about faith passed on by previous generations are never out of date! Suggest to your class that they recall words or examples of Christian commitment from parents, grandparents, or other older people, and tell about these.

2. HONEST RELIGION. Examine the way in which Solomon heeded his father's counsel. Solomon showed trust in the Lord. Using him as an example of a sincere worshiper, have the class comment on what worship should be for every believer.

3. HUMBLE REQUEST. Pay particular attention to Solomon's prayer in his dream (1 Kings 3:6-9; 2 Chronicles 1:7-10). The young king asked God for an understanding mind so that he could govern the Israelites well and know the difference between right and wrong (1 Kings 3:9). Let his request open discussion on the purpose of prayer, and the contents of praying.

4. HAPPY RESULTS. A humble and honest prayer brings God's promise of mercy and help. Solomon was young and inexperienced. He faced enormous challenges in taking over the great kingdom. He followed a father who had ruled successfully for years and had held together a far-flung empire. The task of succeeding the great king David did not overwhelm Solomon because he relied on the Lord's strength and guidance.

5. HONORABLE REPUTATION. First Chronicles 29:25 describes the respect that Solomon earned. Even today, we speak of "the wisdom of Solomon."

FOR ADULTS ■ **TOPIC:** God Answers Prayer

■ **QUESTIONS:** 1. How did Solomon show his love for the Lord? 2. What did Solomon acknowledge that the Lord had done for him? 3. Why did Solomon ask for a discerning heart? 4. What did the Lord promise to give to Solomon, in addition to wisdom? 5. How can having a discerning heart help us in our walk with the Lord Jesus?

■ **ILLUSTRATIONS:**

Missionary to Mongolia. In *Our Daily Bread,* a former missionary to Mongolia named James Gilmour related that he was once asked to treat some wounded soldiers. Although he was not a physician, he did have some knowledge of first aid, so he felt he could not refuse the request. He dressed the wounds of two of the men, but a third had a badly broken thigh bone.

The missionary had no idea what to do for such an injury. Kneeling beside the man, Gilmour asked the Lord for help. The missionary didn't know how God would answer his prayers, but he was confident that his need would be supplied. Gilmour couldn't find any books on physiology in the primitive hospital, and no physician arrived. To complicate matters, a crowd of beggars came to him asking for money. He was deeply concerned about his patient, yet his heart went out to those ragged paupers.

The missionary hurriedly gave the beggars a small gift as well as a few kind words of spiritual encouragement. A moment later Gilmour stared in amazement at one weary beggar who had remained behind. The half-starved man was little more than a living skeleton. The missionary suddenly realized that the Lord had brought him a walking lesson in anatomy! Gilmour asked the elderly person if the missionary might examine him. After carefully tracing the femur bone with his fingers to learn how to treat the soldier's broken leg, Gilmour returned to the patient and was able to set the fracture.

Years later, Gilmour related how God had provided him with a strange yet sufficient response to his earnest prayer. When we raise our petitions, we too can be certain that the Lord will help us.

Employee Evaluation. In *Guideposts,* Patrick Borders recounts an experience with his boss. Steve (not his real name) had a reputation for being disagreeable, and this situation proved to be no different. He chided Patrick for writing an unsatisfactory report and demanded that it needed to be redone by the end-of-week board meeting. The subordinate went away from that encounter feeling agitated and discouraged.

Patrick decided to spend his lunch hour at a nearby park thinking about his work situation and praying to the Lord for wisdom in how to properly handle it. Throughout the remainder of the week, Patrick rewrote the report and prayed for discernment in the process. He came to realize that his boss was stressed out from all the demands being placed on him and that this was possibly one reason why he treated others so rudely.

Patrick noted that the following Monday morning he went into Steve's office and asked how the board meeting went. In response Steve sighed, "Sometimes I don't know *what* they want." For the first time Patrick noticed the dark circles under the eyes of his boss. Patrick stated that it was "my first glimpse of the pressure Steve was under. Maybe that's what made him lash out at me."

The top-of-the-week exchange ended with Steve saying, "By the way, thanks for writing the report. Good job." Patrick could see in this circumstance how God was beginning to answer his prayers.

Hand It On. Tom Anderson was one of Scotland's most talented and best known fiddle players. Born and raised in the Shetland Islands where the fiddling tradition has been cherished for generations, Tom Anderson performed widely and won acclaim for his brilliant playing. He wrote many popular fiddle tunes, taught countless students, and led several fiddle orchestras.

In his old age, suffering from what would be his final illness, Tom Anderson called young Jacqueline Sinclair to his home. He had trained Jacqueline, a crippled girl who became a promising expert fiddler. Handing her his own treasured violin, he said to her, "You, too, have a special gift of music. I want to give you my precious fiddle. I hand it over to you. Play it well, and play it often and give joy to others." Jacqueline Sinclair prizes that instrument, and carries on the Tom Anderson legacy today as one of the premier Scottish fiddlers, teaching others and leading an orchestra.

David passed on instructions to walk in the way of the Lord as his legacy to Solomon who would take over the throne after he died. What kind of legacy are you leaving to the next generation?

FOR YOUTH

■ TOPIC: Wisdom to Rule

■ QUESTIONS: 1. What did Solomon do on the high places? 2. What happened to Solomon at Gibeon? 3. What request did Solomon make to the Lord? 4. What did God promise to do for Solomon? 5. Why is having divine wisdom an invaluable asset to have when making decisions?

■ ILLUSTRATIONS:

Carefully Considered Choice. The *Mach 3®* is a razor or "shaving system" as Gillette calls it. According to *USA Today*, it took seven years to develop at a cost of $750 million. The marketing team considered 87,000 names before making the selection. Apparently, it was a well made choice. Even at seven dollars each, it outsells other razors by 4 to 1.

If a company can appreciate a worthwhile goal, how much more can you? Resolve to follow Solomon's goal of wisdom and knowledge of the Lord.

Life's Priority. Goodwill CEO Fred Gandy (an ex-congressman and *Love Boat* star) encouraged the nation to clean out its closets and help change people's lives at the end of October in 1997. Toronto, Ohio paper boy, Adam Chesnut, asked his 50 customers to donate clothing and household items. Successful, he asked the entire town to join in the 1998 campaign, claiming he wanted to make a difference. Here is a young man who has made serving and helping others a priority in his life. You, too, must determine your priorities.

Solomon wanted to serve his Lord and the nation. This was his priority. Ignoring wealth and prestige, he asked for God to grant him wisdom so that he might serve.

Ability to Distinguish. The Commonwealth Foundation has unveiled a 63 page study that reviewed the curricula of Pennsylvania's State System of Higher Education. The study criticized the state's higher education requirements, pointing out that almost half the students graduate without taking courses in literature, history, philosophy, foreign languages, and mathematics. Instead of essential academic subjects, students trade for courses in "Star Trek and Modern Man," "Pistol 1," "Jewelry 1," "Craft Studio," and "Television Workshop." The report calls for more rigorous core courses of study instead of low-level subjects being offered.

While many students joked that they aced Star Trek 101, eventually the students must distinguish between what is superficial and ordinary and what is profound and vital. Star Trek 101 will not greatly enhance a student's post-academic life. A good composition or math course, though, might help. Solomon also had to decide between what was superficial and what would advance his life. He chose wisdom.

ELIJAH TRIUMPHS WITH GOD

BACKGROUND SCRIPTURE: 1 Kings 18:20-39
DEVOTIONAL READING: Psalm 86:8-13

KEY VERSE: When all the people saw it, they fell on their faces: and they said, The LORD, he is the God; the LORD, he is the God. 1 Kings 18:39.

KING JAMES VERSION

1 KINGS 18:20 So Ahab sent unto all the children of Israel, and gathered the prophets together unto mount Carmel.

21 And Elijah came unto all the people, and said, How long halt ye between two opinions? if the LORD be God, follow him: but if Baal, then follow him. And the people answered him not a word. 22 Then said Elijah unto the people, I, even I only, remain a prophet of the LORD; but Baal's prophets are four hundred and fifty men. 23 Let them therefore give us two bullocks; and let them choose one bullock for themselves, and cut it in pieces, and lay it on wood, and put no fire under: and I will dress the other bullock, and lay it on wood, and put no fire under: 24 And call ye on the name of your gods, and I will call on the name of the LORD: and the God that answereth by fire, let him be God. And all the people answered and said, It is well spoken. . . . 30 And Elijah said unto all the people, Come near unto me. And all the people came near unto him. And he repaired the altar of the LORD that was broken down. 31 And Elijah took twelve stones, according to the number of the tribes of the sons of Jacob, unto whom the word of the LORD came, saying, Israel shall be thy name: 32 And with the stones he built an altar in the name of the LORD: and he made a trench about the altar, as great as would contain two measures of seed. 33 And he put the wood in order, and cut the bullock in pieces, and laid him on the wood, and said, Fill four barrels with water, and pour it on the burnt sacrifice, and on the wood. 34 And he said, Do it the second time. And they did it the second time. And he said, Do it the third time. And they did it the third time. 35 And the water ran round about the altar; and he filled the trench also with water. . . . 38 Then the fire of the LORD fell, and consumed the burnt sacrifice, and the wood, and the stones, and the dust, and licked up the water that was in the trench. 39 And when all the people saw it, they fell on their faces: and they said, The LORD, he is the God; the LORD, he is the God.

NEW REVISED STANDARD VERSION

1 KINGS 18:20 So Ahab sent to all the Israelites, and assembled the prophets at Mount Carmel. 21 Elijah then came near to all the people, and said, "How long will you go limping with two different opinions? If the LORD is God, follow him; but if Baal, then follow him." The people did not answer him a word. 22 Then Elijah said to the people, "I, even I only, am left a prophet of the LORD; but Baal's prophets number four hundred fifty. 23 Let two bulls be given to us; let them choose one bull for themselves, cut it in pieces, and lay it on the wood, but put no fire to it; I will prepare the other bull and lay it on the wood, but put no fire to it. 24 Then you call on the name of your god and I will call on the name of the LORD; the god who answers by fire is indeed God." All the people answered, "Well spoken!" . . .

30 Then Elijah said to all the people, "Come closer to me"; and all the people came closer to him. First he repaired the altar of the LORD that had been thrown down; 31 Elijah took twelve stones, according to the number of the tribes of the sons of Jacob, to whom the word of the LORD came, saying, "Israel shall be your name"; 32 with the stones he built an altar in the name of the LORD. Then he made a trench around the altar, large enough to contain two measures of seed. 33 Next he put the wood in order, cut the bull in pieces, and laid it on the wood. He said, "Fill four jars with water and pour it on the burnt offering and on the wood." 34 Then he said, "Do it a second time"; and they did it a second time. Again he said, "Do it a third time"; and they did it a third time, 35 so that the water ran all around the altar, and filled the trench also with water. . . .

38 Then the fire of the LORD fell and consumed the burnt offering, the wood, the stones, and the dust, and even licked up the water that was in the trench.
39 When all the people saw it, they fell on their faces and said, "The LORD indeed is God; the LORD indeed is God."

10

HOME BIBLE READINGS

BACKGROUND

Under the direction of Jezebel, the worship of Baal had become prevalent in Israel. Jezebel had killed many of the Lord's prophets and replaced them with 450 prophets of Baal (1 Kings 18:13, 19). The word "baal" by itself means "owner" or "lord." This suggests that the god Baal was regarded as the owner of a particular region. The local Baals were thought to control rainfall as well as fertility in agriculture and animals. Because of the importance of these things to survival in Palestine, the ancient Canaanites went to extreme measures, including child sacrifice, to secure the favor of the Baals.

Elijah clearly saw the danger of Baal worship and sought ways to demonstrate the impotency of Baal. A three-year drought was intended to show that Baal did not control rain. Then, at God's direction, Elijah would prove once and for all that there was only one God. The Lord wanted the people to forsake their worship of Baal and turn back to Yahweh. The contest between rival options occurred on Mount Carmel. The Carmel range is a high ridge on the northern coast of Israel that extends inland for about 13 miles from the Mediterranean Sea, with heights ranging from 460 to 1,742 feet. Most likely, the Mount Carmel mentioned in 18:20 was the highest spot, located at the eastern end of the ridge. From there, thousands of Israelites would have an excellent view of the contest. The people could watch from the nearby gentle slopes and also hear Elijah as he spoke to them.

A simple stone altar became the centerpiece of the unfolding drama. In Old Testament times, altars were constructed for the presentation of sacrifices to God or pagan deities. These sacrifices were usually animals. In fact, the Hebrew word for "altar" literally means "place of slaughter." Nevertheless, fruit or grain were also offered for sacrifice at altars. These elevated platforms were constructed of various materials. The oldest altars either were made of mud brick or were simply mounds of dirt. These altars were most likely used by nomadic peoples who had little need for more permanent structures.

The stone altar is the most frequently mentioned type of structure in the Bible. A single massive stone could be used as an altar (Judg. 6:19-21; 1 Sam. 14:33-35), as could several stacked stones. Hebrews generally used uncut stones for their altars since to place any hewn stone on an altar symbolized defilement (Exod. 20:25). The Hebrews, however, did not always observe this restriction. In addition, early Hebrew altars were not to have steps (20:26). Some think this was to distinguish them from the Canaanite altars, which did have stairs. The Bible, however, says God did not want the nakedness of the priests to be exposed before the people.

A third type of altar mentioned in the Old Testament is the elevated platform made of bronze in the court of Solomon's temple. It measured about 30 feet in length and about 15 feet in height. It had some type of horns at the corners. A person seeking temporary asylum could grasp these horns as a measure of protection (1 Kings 1:50-51; 2:28-29). The last type of altar described in the Bible was the one made of gold. It was located just outside the holy of holies in the temple (7:48).

NOTES ON THE PRINTED TEXT

The drought was in its third year when the Lord dispatched Elijah to confront Ahab (1 Kings 18:1). The king, upon seeing Elijah, called him the troubler of Israel (18:17). In response, the prophet of God let Ahab know that it was he who had troubled Israel by forsaking the Lord (18:18). In addition, Elijah challenged Ahab to summon the people of Israel and all the prophets of Baal and Asherah for a confrontation on Mount Carmel (18:19). Ahab, no doubt frustrated by the problems caused by the long drought, agreed to Elijah's challenge and summoned the people and the prophets to Mount Carmel (18:20).

Elijah began by addressing the people gathered to see the contest. The choice he offered the audience resembled the one that Joshua had put before the people centuries earlier (Josh. 24:15). The people had to decide between the Lord and Baal. They could not *halt* (1 Kings 18:21) between the two allegiances. They could only serve the one who was truly God. Unlike during the time of Joshua (Josh. 24:16-18), the people of Elijah's day remained quiet following his declaration.

The Hebrew word translated *halt* (1 Kings 18:21) conveys the idea of limping around on two crutches; but the immediate context of this colloquial expression refers to indecision, not physical disability. Elijah used the word to highlight the indecision and ambivalence of God's people. The Israelites were attempting to hold on to both their worship of the Lord and Baal. Although the people apparently saw a benefit in this, in reality it was a vain attempt to hobble between two extremes. The people of Israel still held on to some aspects of their worship of the Lord, even though their hearts were far from Him.

Next, Elijah proposed a test to reveal whether the Lord or Baal was the true God. First, the false prophets would prepare a bull to be sacrificed. They were to cut the animal in pieces and lay it on the wood of their altar, but without setting fire to it. In the meantime, Elijah would prepare the other bull and lay it on the wood of his altar, again without setting fire to it (18:22-23). The false prophets would call on the name of their god, and Elijah would call on the name of the Lord. The god who answered by setting fire to the wood would be the true God. All the people agreed to this plan (18:24).

Elijah invited the false prophets to go first. All morning and afternoon they shouted to Baal, danced, and even injured themselves; but, perhaps to their amazement, no fire came. Of course, Baal's lack of response did not result from the god's weakness, but from the fact that he did not exist. So now it was Elijah's turn, and the stage was set for the Lord's awesome display of power (18:25-29). Elijah called for the people to come while he repaired the altar of the Lord (18:30). The prophet did not build a new one, but instead repaired the old one that had been torn down. Evidently, the Israelites had not used this altar for quite some time, and either the effects of time or some enemies had ruined it.

During this period in Israel's history, God's people existed as two separate nations— the northern and southern kingdoms. The Lord originally had intended them to be united, not divided. Elijah called attention to the covenant God had with all 12 tribes by taking 12 stones, one representing each tribe of the sons of Jacob, and building the altar with them. First Kings 18:31 makes reference to an incident involving Jacob that is recorded in Genesis 32:28. The Lord changed his name to Israel, which signified that the patriarch was under His ownership. Similarly, the descendants of Jacob were under God's ownership. They were to trust, obey, and follow Him, not false gods.

Elijah built an altar *in the name of the LORD* (1 Kings 18:32). This is significant, for many Israelites had been worshiping Baal. Elijah, through his actions, was refocusing their attention on the one true and living God. Next, Elijah made a trench around the altar. It was large enough to hold a sizeable amount of water. After digging the trench, Elijah arranged the wood on the altar. He then cut a young bull into pieces and laid those pieces on the wood (18:33). Elijah instructed the people to completely soak the animal pieces and wood resting on the altar he had made. Four large jarfuls of water were poured on the sacrifice and on the wood. This procedure was performed a second time and a third time, until the water was not only running off all sides of the altar, but even filled the trench (18:34-35). In this way Elijah ensured that nothing short of a genuine miracle would accomplish the burning up of the sacrifice and the wood on the altar.

In the sight of all the people, Elijah approached the altar he had made (18:36). This took place at the customary time when the Israelites offered the evening sacrifice, which would have been around 3:00 P.M. The prophet did not pray to Baal or any other pagan deity. Instead, he spoke to the Lord, the God of Abraham, Isaac, and Israel (Jacob). The Israelites had forgotten who was the true God of Israel. Elijah asked Yahweh to make it clear that He, not Baal, was Israel's God. In addition, Elijah prayed that the people would know he had faithfully followed and served the Lord. Elijah wanted God to validate him as His prophet, as the one who had foretold the drought and called for this contest at God's command.

Elijah asked the Lord to *hear* (18:37), or positively respond to, his request. The prophet's goal was not to make a name for himself, but for the people to repent and return to the Lord. Elijah's brief prayer stood in sharp contrast to the prophets of Baal. They had spent the entire day in a frenzy, crying out to their god. Elijah, however, confidently stood before the people and offered up a brief but powerful petition. In response, God demonstrated His awesome power. The Lord's fire not only devoured the drenched sacrifice, but also the stones of the altar and all the water in the trench (18:38). No one could accuse Elijah of faking this test.

In meeting a humanly impossible challenge, God's ultimate purpose was to turn the people back to Himself. The people recognized the divine show of might and immediately fell to worship the Lord as the only true God (18:39). At Elijah's command, the Israelites even went so far as to participate in the execution of all the prophets of Baal (18:40), a punishment required by the law for the prophets' crimes against God and Israel (see Deut. 7:2-6; 13:13-15; 17:2-5). Sadly, the effects of this day were not far reaching. Ahab remained king, and the people never completely returned to the Lord, at least not for any significant length of time.

SUGGESTIONS TO TEACHERS

The famous contest between Elijah and the hundreds of false prophets has such drama that you will find plenty of teaching material for this week's lesson. Be sure to point out that God is the central figure in this episode. He alone enabled Elijah to take a courageous stand for Him.

1. TIMIDITY. A minor character in this drama is a palace official of Ahab's named Obadiah (not the same as the writer of the Old Testament book of that name). This man tried to be faithful to the Lord but feared for his own safety if he relayed Elijah's message to the king (1 Kings 18:3-16). This response is typical of how we sometimes feel. We want to be Christians but shrink back when doing certain acts seems too threatening or costly.

2. TROUBLER. When Ahab finally met Elijah, he angrily called the prophet a troubler of Israel (18:17). By this Ahab implied that Elijah was a threat to the normal functioning of Israelite society, as seen in the severe drought and famine the nation had to endure. Ask your students who was really the nation's troubler—Ahab or Elijah? Remind the members of the class that those causing the greatest trouble for a nation are people who persist in ignoring God's ways.

3. TEST. Elijah challenged Ahab's false prophets to a contest. Let the account of the episode on Mount Carmel unfold, and allow your students to share their insights and comments. Don't let the lesson get bogged down on the details of the account, and also don't suggest that it's all right to put the Lord to the test anytime we want. The essential point is that God is supreme above all so-called gods (1 Cor. 8:4-6).

4. TESTIMONY. Elijah asked the assembled Israelites how long they would waver between two different options (1 Kings 18:21). From this we see that trying to follow the Lord and also the idols of the world is spiritually crippling. At this point, invite your students to list some "idols" that exist in the world today. Then note that nothing must ever displace God as being the Lord of their lives.

5. TAUNTS. If you have time, let some of the humor in the biblical account come to light. For instance, your students will undoubtedly chuckle when they learn about Elijah's mocking of Ahab's false prophets.

6. TRIUMPH. This week's lesson makes it clear that God is all-supreme in His authority and power. Regardless of the challenge, God will always prevail. Perhaps the greatest challenge to God's plans and power came at the Cross. But even there the Lord demonstrated conclusively that nothing—not even death itself—can thwart His loving intentions.

FOR ADULTS	■ **TOPIC:** Depending on God's Power ■ **QUESTIONS:** 1. What would a victory over Baal prove to the people of

Israel? 2. Why did Elijah go to great lengths to convince the people that the Lord was the one true God? 3. Why did Elijah refer to the Lord as the God of Abraham, Isaac, and Israel? 4. Why was the immediacy of God's response to Elijah's prayer important? 5. Why are the false gods of the world a poor substitute for the one true God?

■ **ILLUSTRATIONS:**

Overcoming the Obstacles. In 1923, Branch Rickey was a baseball coach at Ohio Wesleyan University. When the team traveled on a road trip to Indiana, a lone African American player was refused lodging in the hotel. Rickey finally prevailed on the clerk to allow the young player, Charles Thomas, to use a cot in Rickey's room.

When coach Rickey arrived in the room, he found Thomas sitting on the cot, pulling at the skin on his hands as if he could rub away the color. With tears coming down his face, Charles Thomas said, "Mr. Rickey, if I could just get this color off, I'd be as good as anybody else." This was a traumatic moment in Branch Rickey's life, and it led to his resolve to end segregation in big league baseball.

As general manager of the Brooklyn Dodgers in the 1940's, Rickey was aware that every other major league team would oppose him and that his reputation would be at stake concerning the issue of integration. In 1945, major league owners had voted 15 to 1 against the Dodgers on the issue. This vote also reflected the viewpoint of most players, coaches, umpires, sportswriters, and fans.

Rickey knew that he had little support. But being spiritually strengthened by his Christian convictions, he forged ahead that year and signed Jackie Robinson, a gifted African American baseball player. Together, these two great men destroyed the sport's color bar and ushered in a new era not only for the game but also for the entire nation.

Forward on Faith. As the Thanksgiving season approaches, we are increasingly mindful of the group of Pilgrims who landed in Plymouth on a wintry November day in 1620. Earlier, members of this brave band of Christians stepped onto a barge at Leyden, Holland, and went downstream to what is now Rotterdam. They then traveled to Southampton, England, where they transferred to a leaky old tub called the Mayflower. Only a handful—a little over a hundred of the group of Pilgrim refugees—persevered by traveling to the New World, determined by the power of God to keep their faith for themselves and others. What about the stay-at-homes in Leyden? Today, no one claims descent from the group of Separatist Englishmen who had taken up residence as refugees in Holland. Apparently they failed to persevere and eventually were simply absorbed into the Dutch culture.

Ongoing Conflict. What accounts for the enormous popularity of wrestling on television? Despite the poor acting, absurd routines, and inane conversations, wrestling remains one of the most widespread forms of entertainment available. Some claim that it is a soap opera constantly built on the battle between good and evil. Others, however, think it's a form of amusement that appeals to humanity's unspiritual nature.

In either case, you as a believer are daily confronted with the ongoing conflict between good and evil. You are not a spectator. Like the spiritual, moral, and ethical choices that the Israelites had to make, you will sometimes have to choose between whom you will serve—whether the God of Scripture or the idols of money, power, popularity, and sex (to name a few). Heed Elijah's exhortation and make your choice for God!

FOR YOUTH

■ **TOPIC:** Elijah Scores a Victory

■ **QUESTIONS:** 1. How would you describe the challenge that Elijah put before the people? 2. Why was it necessary to serve only the Lord? 3. What did Elijah do to make the test as difficult as possible for the Lord? Why? 4. How did the Lord demonstrate that He alone is God? 5. How should we respond to God's mighty demonstration of power?

■ **ILLUSTRATIONS:**

Felt Supported. In 1984, *The Karate Kid* became an immediate hit among moviegoers. It's a film about Daniel, a lonely, fatherless boy who is bullied by a gang called the Cobras. Daniel is aided by Mr. Miyagi, who teaches him karate. Through this benevolent but firm instructor, Daniel gets a new outlook on life.

In the climax, Daniel is involved in a karate match. Because he is physically abused by his archenemy in the Cobra gang, Daniel wants to quit. The odds of winning seem too great, and he doesn't believe he can possibly win. However, Mr. Miyagi offers him support and reassurance. Through Mr. Miyagi's gentle direction, Daniel finds hope and perseveres, and this enables him to finally win the match.

Think of all the youth who, like Daniel, are willing to take risks as a result of the support of others. Elijah risked action with God's help. The prophet was confident that the Lord would give him the power to prevail. Even today God can enable us to be triumphant in promoting the cause of Christ.

Mount Everest Rescue. On May 7, 2005, *Associated Press* writer Binaj Gurubacharya reported the rescue of a group of climbers who had been injured by an avalanche while attempting to scale Mount Everest. They had to wait three days before a large Russian helicopter arrived, and it had to make two trips to ferry everyone to safety. Had it not been for the power of that aircraft, the situation would have been much different for the injured climbers.

Thousands of years ago, a prophet named Elijah faced a seemingly impossible situation. Had he relied on his own strength, he would have failed in his assignment. Thankfully, he depended on the all-powerful Lord for help, and God enabled him to prevail. Even today, we who are Christians must operate in the power of God's Spirit, not our own strength. Without His abiding presence, things would be much different for us as we shun sin and promote righteousness in the world.

Toxic Crusaders. Teenagers Maria, Fabiola, and Anita were attending high school in 1999 in their Los Angeles neighborhood where most of the children are Hispanic or African American. These three girls learned that during construction of a new middle school in their community the soil and the ground water under the building were contaminated with highly toxic chemicals.

As members of a local community-based group of persons concerned about environmental health, Maria, Fabiola, and Anita called governmental agencies, passed out flyers, and went door-to-door to alert parents. The school authorities insisted that there was no danger and that the new building was safe. And despite attempts by the police to prevent the three from handing out material, the trio of toxic crusaders remained committed.

The teenagers called a community meeting, and invited school district officials, environmental agencies, and the news media. They succeeded in convincing school officials not to enroll children in the new building. Speaking for the three, Anita said, "One day, you're going to have to stand on your own two feet for something you believe in. Why not get an early start?"

JOSIAH BRINGS REFORM

BACKGROUND SCRIPTURE: 2 Kings 22—23
DEVOTIONAL READING: Psalm 103:1-18

KEY VERSE: The king stood by a pillar, and made a covenant before the LORD, . . . to perform the words of this covenant that were written in this book. And all the people stood to the covenant. 2 Kings 23:3.

KING JAMES VERSION

2 KINGS 22:8 And Hilkiah the high priest said unto Shaphan the scribe, I have found the book of the law in the house of the LORD. And Hilkiah gave the book to Shaphan, and he read it. 9 And Shaphan the scribe came to the king, and brought the king word again, and said, Thy servants have gathered the money that was found in the house, and have delivered it into the hand of them that do the work, that have the oversight of the house of the LORD. 10 And Shaphan the scribe shewed the king, saying, Hilkiah the priest hath delivered me a book. And Shaphan read it before the king. . . .

23:1 And the king sent, and they gathered unto him all the elders of Judah and of Jerusalem. 2 And the king went up into the house of the LORD, and all the men of Judah and all the inhabitants of Jerusalem with him, and the priests, and the prophets, and all the people, both small and great: and he read in their ears all the words of the book of the covenant which was found in the house of the LORD. 3 And the king stood by a pillar, and made a covenant before the LORD, to walk after the LORD, and to keep his commandments and his testimonies and his statutes with all their heart and all their soul, to perform the words of this covenant that were written in this book. And all the people stood to the covenant. . . .

21 And the king commanded all the people, saying, Keep the passover unto the LORD your God, as it is written in the book of this covenant. 22 Surely there was not holden such a passover from the days of the judges that judged Israel, nor in all the days of the kings of Israel, nor of the kings of Judah; 23 But in the eighteenth year of king Josiah, wherein this passover was holden to the LORD in Jerusalem.

NEW REVISED STANDARD VERSION

2 KINGS 22:8 The high priest Hilkiah said to Shaphan the secretary, "I have found the book of the law in the house of the LORD." When Hilkiah gave the book to Shaphan, he read it. 9 Then Shaphan the secretary came to the king, and reported to the king, "Your servants have emptied out the money that was found in the house, and have delivered it into the hand of the workers who have oversight of the house of the LORD." 10 Shaphan the secretary informed the king, "The priest Hilkiah has given me a book." Shaphan then read it aloud to the king. . . .

23:1 Then the king directed that all the elders of Judah and Jerusalem should be gathered to him. 2 The king went up to the house of the LORD, and with him went all the people of Judah, all the inhabitants of Jerusalem, the priests, the prophets, and all the people, both small and great; he read in their hearing all the words of the book of the covenant that had been found in the house of the LORD. 3 The king stood by the pillar and made a covenant before the LORD, to follow the LORD, keeping his commandments, his decrees, and his statutes, with all his heart and all his soul, to perform the words of this covenant that were written in this book. All the people joined in the covenant. . . .

21 The king commanded all the people, "Keep the passover to the LORD your God as prescribed in this book of the covenant." 22 No such passover had been kept since the days of the judges who judged Israel, even during all the days of the kings of Israel and of the kings of Judah; 23 but in the eighteenth year of King Josiah this passover was kept to the LORD in Jerusalem.

11

BACKGROUND

Josiah became king of Judah at the age of eight, following the short, two-year reign of his father Amon. King Amon followed the earlier example of Manasseh by worshiping and sacrificing to idols. Perhaps Amon's evil example caused some of his own officials to assassinate him after only a few years. Josiah, however, became one of Judah's most godly and effective kings. He reigned in Jerusalem over the kingdom of Judah for 31 years from 640 to 609 B.C. Although Josiah lived in a tumultuous period of history, this did not deter him from following the Lord with a degree of humility and devotion unmatched since the reigns of David and Solomon.

At this time, the Assyrian Empire was in decline due to external and internal factors. The once great power of the Fertile Crescent was weakened by fierce, nomadic people mounted on horses who invaded the region. Known as the Scythians, they originated in what is now southern Russia. They brought terror to the complacent Jews and may have provided the motivation for Josiah to begin his reforms and for the people to go along with the changes. The Scythians' main thrust was along the Mediterranean coast as they swept through the Philistines and were finally stopped by the Egyptians. The invaders are also credited with breaking the domination of the Assyrians over the Middle East. The last strong Assyrian king, Ashurbanipal, died about 631 B.C., and his death, coupled with the Scythian invasion, probably left the Assyrians disinterested in what went on in Judah.

It was also around this time that two other ancient world powers, Egypt and Babylon, flexed their muscles to break free of Assyrian control. Each wanted to position itself at the expense of the other as the successor to Assyria and also as the principal actor on the world stage. Small nations grabbed the opportunity to break free of the bigger powers and pursue their own destinies. For Judah, this meant getting rid of idolatry, renewing its covenant with the Lord, and extending the worship of the Lord back into the territory that once had been under the control of the northern kingdom of Israel.

Josiah's covenant with the Lord meant that there would be only one deity worshiped in Judah, for the king removed all the abominations from the country (2 Chron. 34:31-33). The reform began in 622 B.C. by removing the idols that had been placed in the Jerusalem temple. These images, representing gods such as Baal and goddesses such as Asherah (2 Kings 23:4), were of Syro-Palestinian (Canaanite) origin. The expression *host of heaven* referred to an entire pantheon of deities. Clearly, Josiah's reform was thorough.

It is significant that there were images of these various deities in the royal temple. Through the reigns of Manasseh and Amon, Josiah's predecessors, the local gods had been incorporated into Judah's royal cult. Probably both Canaanite and Assyrian deities were worshiped, for Assyria had been the ruling power over the vassal state of Judah at the time. Many of the traditional Canaanite gods had been worshiped in the northern kingdom, and an association of these deities with Israel may explain why Josiah took the cult images of Bethel for disposal. Bethel had been a site for Israel's national temple. The sanctity of the temple space in Jerusalem was retained during the reform efforts. Only priests were allowed to clean out the images. Hilkiah had been the high priest of the cult involving all these deities; but, under orders from Josiah, he removed the idols that he had served.

NOTES ON THE PRINTED TEXT

Josiah was the last godly king of Judah. He was just a boy when he ascended the throne, and for over three decades he served the Lord as Judah's monarch (2 Kings 22:1). Unlike Manasseh and Amon, Josiah did what the Lord approved, especially in following in the footsteps of his ancestor David. Throughout Josiah's reign, he did not morally deviate to the right or the left, but remained on the path of uprightness (22:2).

Right from the start, Josiah began to seek the Lord. Four years later, in the twelfth year of his reign, Josiah began to purge Judah and Jerusalem of the detestable high places, the Asherah poles, and the carved and cast images (2 Chron. 34:3). He also ordered his officials to tear down the altars of the Baals and demolish the incense altars that stood above them. Moreover, the king had the pagan objects of worship pulverized and sprinkled as dust over the tombs of those who had made idolatrous sacrifices (34:4). Josiah further defiled the pagan shrines by burning the bones of the priests on their altars (34:5). His goal was to extend his purification efforts beyond Judah and Jerusalem to the regions of the former northern kingdom of Israel (34:6-7).

Six years later, in the eighteenth year of Josiah's reign, he continued his policy of purifying the land and the temple. He dispatched Shaphan (a scribe), Maaseiah (the governor of the city), and Joah (a court secretary) to oversee the repair of the Jerusalem temple (2 Kings 22:3; 2 Chron. 34:8). This included the collection of funds and the payment of skilled laborers working on the restoration of the sanctuary (2 Kings 22:4-7; 2 Chron. 34:9-13). At some point, Hilkiah the high priest found the law scroll the Lord had given to Moses (2 Chron. 34:14). Later it is called the *book of the covenant* (2 Kings 23:2). That would indicate Hilkiah discovered a document containing Exodus 19—24. The curses Josiah heard, however, seem to have come from Leviticus and Deuteronomy. Therefore, what was likely found was either all three books or Deuteronomy, which contains a retelling of the events of the Exodus and a reiteration of God's instructions through Moses.

In any case, Hilkiah told Shaphan about the discovery and gave him the scroll. Then the scribe read its contents (2 Kings 22:8). Next, Shaphan went to the king. The scribe first reported that Josiah's instructions were being followed to the letter. In particular, the officials had melted down the silver that was being collected and stored in the temple. Then, the money was handed over to the construction foremen assigned to the Lord's temple (22:9). Shaphan next stated that Hilkah had given him an important scroll, which the king directed the scribe to read in his presence (22:10).

When Josiah heard what was written in God's Word, he tore his clothes in sorrow. The king's great concern suggests he probably heard a passage from the Mosaic law dealing with how God would judge the Israelites if they did not obey His Word. Josiah ordered the priest and his company to seek an oracle from the Lord about the future of the kingdom, including the remnant in Israel and Judah. Josiah figured out that his ancestors had disobeyed the Lord and violated His commands. They thus deserved God's righteous judgment (22:11-13).

Hilkiah and some other court officials left right away and went to talk with Huldah the prophetess. She lived in the northern part of Jerusalem (22:14). The prophetess revealed that the Lord would punish Judah, its capital, and its people in accordance with what was written in His Word. God was indignant over the fact that His people had rejected Him by offering sacrifices to foreign gods and worshiping their idols. Huldah declared that God was aware of Josiah's sorrow and humility over the disaster that awaited the people of Judah. Because the king was genuinely distressed by what he had heard, the Lord would not bring His promised judgment until after Josiah had died and was buried in peace (22:15-20).

Next, the king summoned all the leaders of Judah and Jerusalem and led them up to the temple of the Lord (23:1). The group included both civil and religious representatives, along with residents of Jerusalem and Judah. This large gathering included young and old alike. In their presence, the king read aloud all the words of the covenant scroll (23:2). Josiah positioned himself by one of two massive bronze pillars, Jakin and Boaz, in the portico at the temple entrance (see 2 Chron. 3:17). This was the usual place for royal activities that pertained to the Lord. For instance, kings were customarily crowned by the pillars (see 2 Kings 11:14).

It was at this spot that Josiah openly entered into a covenant before the Lord. This means the king made a binding agreement with God. Josiah and those with him specifically pledged to follow the Lord, that is, observe every aspect of the Mosaic law. This included God's *commandments*, *testimonies*, and *statutes* (23:3). The king, along with the people, made this promise. Josiah's hope was that by having all those in attendance participate in this ceremony, they would be stirred to confession and repentance. The king, realizing that he alone could not change the heart of the nation, hoped the people would follow his example.

Josiah's ongoing campaign against idolatry undoubtedly covered years of time (see 23:4-20), starting in the eighteenth year when the covenant was initially renewed. In that watershed eighteenth year, Josiah held a Passover celebration in accordance with what is recorded in the law of Moses (23:21). In terms of organization and attention to detail, Josiah's Passover observance surpassed all previous observances, including those held during the time of the judges and even throughout the tenures of preceding kings who ruled over the northern and southern kingdoms (23:22-23). An expanded version of this account appears in 2 Chronicles 35:1-19. That passage emphasizes that the entire nation (namely, Judah and Israel) participated in an enthusiastic and generous manner, that the Passover lambs were slaughtered exclusively by the Levites, and that all aspects of the observance adhered to the stipulations of the Mosaic law.

SUGGESTIONS TO TEACHERS

Josiah is a wonderful example of the impact a lifetime of commitment to God and His Word can have on other people. Josiah influenced an entire nation for God and gave them a new beginning of godliness and hope. If our relationship with God has weakened to a certain extent, it will take some time for us to renew it. At first the task might seem daunting. Rather than give up altogether, we should take gradual and realistic steps in renewing our relationship. At times the process will be difficult and costly in terms of what God leads us to do or stop doing. Regardless of the steps that are taken, we can rest assured that it will be well worth our time, effort, and sacrifice.

1. A HEART FOR GOD. Josiah did not suddenly become a reformer as an adult. His interest in the Lord began during his adolescent years. Josiah lived righteously and used his royal authority to promote uprightness in his realm. Your students need to realize that long-term spiritual success grows from a heart that has long been interested in God.

2. THIRST FOR GOD'S WORD. When the book of the law was found in the temple, there was never a question in Josiah's mind about whether this occurrence was a good thing. The king wanted to know what the law said and what to do about it. He was horrified to find out how far from the terms of the covenant his nation was living. We also need to respond readily to God's Word. We shouldn't look for loopholes to avoid doing what the Lord wants.

3. SHARING GOD'S WORD. Josiah did not keep God's law to himself. Instead, he eagerly shared it with everyone in his kingdom, for it concerned them. The fact that much of the message was not pleasant did not deter the young king. We need to share the truth of God's Word with others, too. Divine truth is what will change people's lives. We should take advantage of opportunities to use the Bible to help our family and friends deal with the struggles of life.

4. COMMITMENT TO GOD'S WORD. Josiah's reforms took shape when he set an example, and the nation followed it by promising to obey the Lord's covenant. By the time Josiah asked this commitment of his people, he had modeled obedience for a decade. His appeal and example had credibility. The commitment to God's Word that we model will impact our families and our friends. What we model gives credibility to the verbal appeals we make to others in our witness for Christ.

5. OBEDIENCE TO GOD'S WORD. The change in Judah that began with the covenant ceremony in the temple proved to be somewhat genuine and lasting. People in Jerusalem and around the countryside obeyed the law of the Lord day after day and year after year throughout the lifetime of King Josiah. The new beginnings that God gives to us or to those with whom we share Christ start with commitment but prove themselves real through our obedience over our lifetimes.

FOR ADULTS	■ TOPIC: Seeking Renewal ■ QUESTIONS: 1. What did the king's officials do when they found the Book of the Law? 2. What was the king's initial response upon hearing

the document's contents? 3. What was involved in renewing the covenant with the Lord? 4. What was so significant about Judah observing the Passover? 5. Why are we sometimes reluctant to renew our relationship with God?

■ **ILLUSTRATIONS:**

The First Christian Emperor. Flavius Valerius Constantinus, known as Constantine the Great, was the first Roman emperor to embrace Christianity. After he took full control over the Roman Empire in September of A.D. 324, Constantine openly proclaimed himself to be a Christian, instituting Christianity as the state religion. Previously, many of the Roman emperors, such as Nero and Caligula, had mercilessly persecuted Christians. Now, the Church could flourish without fear during Constantine's reign.

The following year, Constantine convened a council of bishops from key Christian churches in Nicea (in what is now Turkey), where they declared the divinity of Christ as a fundamental tenet of the Christian faith. Today, we recognize the statement of orthodoxy they drafted as the Nicene Creed. Thus, Constantine played a part in the Church's purifying a theology that would truly honor the Lord Jesus Christ.

Learning from the Past. Here is a set of modern proverbs about the value of experience. Which of these adages do you think Josiah would have agreed with? Which would he have argued with?

• Each generation has to find out for itself that the stove is hot.
• Education comes from reading the fine print; experience comes from not reading it.
• If at first you don't succeed, so much for skydiving.
• A good scare teaches more than good advice.
• Experience helps you recognize a mistake when you make it again.

Wholehearted Obedience. One bitter winter night a traveler on the American frontier came to a broad river that he had to cross to reach the nearest settlement. If he failed, he would freeze to death.

The traveler stepped onto the ice and thought he heard it groan. He got down on his hands and knees to distribute his weight better and started crawling across. Suddenly, the man raised his head. He heard singing coming from the wooded bank behind him. Out of the trees burst a horse-drawn sledge loaded with coal. The singing collier didn't even see the crawling traveler as he sped past him on the ice. Sheepishly, the man scrambled to his feet and hurried across the river.

Some people obey God as though they are afraid His commands can't support them. In contrast to this way of thinking, Josiah wholeheartedly obeyed God. The promises and commands of the Lord are steadfast and dependable. Thus, we can obey them with all our hearts.

FOR YOUTH

■ TOPIC: Josiah Brings Renewal
■ QUESTIONS: 1. In what way did Josiah follow the example of his ancestor David? 2. What was the general character of Josiah's reign? 3. What troubled Josiah about the words written on the scroll? 4. What religious reforms did Josiah enact? 5. What specific steps can we take to renew our relationship with God?

■ **ILLUSTRATIONS:**

Real Commitment. A college age student took a framed portrait of his girlfriend to the store to have it photocopied so that he could have one at home and one at school. When the technician took the photo from its frame, he noticed this inscription on the back: "My dearest Tom, I love you with all my heart. I love you more each passing day. I will love you forever and ever. I am yours for all eternity. Diane. *P.S. If we ever break up, I want this picture back!*"

There was no such "P.S." to Josiah's commitment to the Lord. There also must be no "P.S." to our commitment to God, especially if we want to honor Him as Josiah did.

Use Authority Responsibly. A young second lieutenant at a U.S. Army base walked over to a soft drink machine and discovered he had no change. He stopped a passing private and asked, "Do you have change for a dollar?"

"I think so. Let me take a look," the private said cheerfully.

"Soldier, that's no way to address an officer," the lieutenant barked. "We'll start over again. Do you have change for a dollar?"

The private snapped smartly to attention. "Sir! No, sir!" he shouted, did an about face, and walked briskly away.

King Josiah used his authority forcefully, but he didn't use it to show how great he was. He used his authority in the interests of others. He used authority responsibly to serve others.

Give It Your All. Years ago, Eugene Ormandy directed the Philadelphia Symphony Orchestra. One evening during a particularly energetic passage of music, Ormandy dislocated his shoulder. A pastor thought about how the conductor was putting all of himself into the music and wondered if he ever approached that sort of dedication in serving God. "Did I ever dislocate anything, even a necktie?" he asked.

If God asks you to take on a great cause for Him, like King Josiah did, give it your all. Don't be afraid to allow God to use you in great ways for His glory.

God's Instructions Are Clear. Pastor Tim, the minister in the novel *A New Song*, finds himself taking care of the three-year-old son of a hospitalized parishioner. The boy wants to watch videos, but Pastor Tim doesn't have the appropriate device. He considers buying one to pacify the toddler and wonders, "'Do we just plug it in?' He'd never been on friendly terms with high technology, which was always accompanied by manuals printed in Croatian."

When Josiah heard the law of the Lord, God's instructions were clear, not like stereo instructions and not in an unknown language. What the Lord wants from us today is also clear, especially if we read and obey His Word.

THE PEOPLE GO INTO EXILE

BACKGROUND SCRIPTURE: 2 Chronicles 36:15-21; Psalm 137
DEVOTIONAL READING: Proverbs 1:20-33

KEY VERSE: By the rivers of Babylon, there we sat down,
yea, we wept, when we remembered Zion. Psalm 137:1.

KING JAMES VERSION

2 CHRONICLES 36:15 And the LORD God of their fathers sent to them by his messengers, rising up betimes, and sending; because he had compassion on his people, and on his dwelling place: 16 But they mocked the messengers of God, and despised his words, and misused his prophets, until the wrath of the LORD arose against his people, till there was no remedy.

17 Therefore he brought upon them the king of the Chaldees, who slew their young men with the sword in the house of their sanctuary, and had no compassion upon young man or maiden, old man, or him that stooped for age: he gave them all into his hand. 18 And all the vessels of the house of God, great and small, and the treasures of the house of the LORD, and the treasures of the king, and of his princes; all these he brought to Babylon. 19 And they burnt the house of God, and brake down the wall of Jerusalem, and burnt all the palaces thereof with fire, and destroyed all the goodly vessels thereof. 20 And them that had escaped from the sword carried he away to Babylon; where they were servants to him and his sons until the reign of the kingdom of Persia: 21 To fulfil the word of the LORD by the mouth of Jeremiah, until the land had enjoyed her sabbaths: for as long as she lay desolate she kept sabbath, to fulfil threescore and ten years.

PSALM 137:1 By the rivers of Babylon, there we sat down, yea, we wept, when we remembered Zion. 2 We hanged our harps upon the willows in the midst thereof. 3 For there they that carried us away captive required of us a song; and they that wasted us required of us mirth, saying, Sing us one of the songs of Zion. 4 How shall we sing the LORD's song in a strange land? 5 If I forget thee, O Jerusalem, let my right hand forget her cunning. 6 If I do not remember thee, let my tongue cleave to the roof of my mouth; if I prefer not Jerusalem above my chief joy.

NEW REVISED STANDARD VERSION

2 CHRONICLES 36:15 The LORD, the God of their ancestors, sent persistently to them by his messengers, because he had compassion on his people and on his dwelling place; 16 but they kept mocking the messengers of God, despising his words, and scoffing at his prophets, until the wrath of the LORD against his people became so great that there was no remedy.

17 Therefore he brought up against them the king of the Chaldeans, who killed their youths with the sword in the house of their sanctuary, and had no compassion on young man or young woman, the aged or the feeble; he gave them all into his hand. 18 All the vessels of the house of God, large and small, and the treasures of the house of the LORD, and the treasures of the king and of his officials, all these he brought to Babylon. 19 They burned the house of God, broke down the wall of Jerusalem, burned all its palaces with fire, and destroyed all its precious vessels. 20 He took into exile in Babylon those who had escaped from the sword, and they became servants to him and to his sons until the establishment of the kingdom of Persia, 21 to fulfill the word of the LORD by the mouth of Jeremiah, until the land had made up for its sabbaths. All the days that it lay desolate it kept sabbath, to fulfill seventy years.

PSALM 137:1 By the rivers of Babylon—
    there we sat down and there we wept
when we remembered Zion.
2 On the willows there
    we hung up our harps.
3 For there our captors
    asked us for songs,
and our tormentors asked for mirth, saying,
    "Sing us one of the songs of Zion!"
4 How could we sing th LORD's song
    in a foreign land?
5 If I forget you, O Jerusalem,
    let my right hand wither!
6 Let my tongue cling to the roof of my mouth,
    if I do not remember you,
if I do not set Jerusalem
    above my highest joy.

12

Home Bible Readings

Background

In 605 B.C., Nebuchadnezzar invaded Judah and took hostage the sons of the leading families to insure King Jehoiakim's cooperation (2 Kings 24:1; Dan. 1:1). Daniel and his three friends, Shadrach, Meshach, and Abednego, were among the young detainees. Three years later, Jehoiakim participated in an Egypt-led rebellion against Babylon (2 Kings 24:1, 7). It took Nebuchadnezzar until early 597 B.C. to get around to dealing with the small western kingdoms who had rebelled. By the time the Babylonians reached Judah, Jehoiakim had died and been succeeded by Jehoiachin.

Nebuchadnezzar deposed Jehoiachin and replaced him with his uncle Mattaniah, whom Nebuchadnezzar renamed Zedekiah (24:8-17). At that time, Nebuchadnezzar deported thousands of people from Judah to Babylon, including Jehoiachin and his family, many soldiers, and the prophet Ezekiel (Ezek. 1:1-3). In both 605 and 597 B.C., the Babylonians plundered articles of gold and silver from the temple of the Lord (2 Chron. 36:7, 10).

The Book of Second Chronicles gives a very brief account of each of the final four kings of Judah: Jehoahaz (36:1-4), Jehoiakim (36:5-8), Jehoiachin (36:9-10), and Zedekiah (36:11-21). All of them were conquered by a foreign power. All of them were forcibly taken away by their captors. Each conqueror plundered Judah. The explanation of the spiritual failures of kings and people in the time of Zedekiah (36:14-16) applied to the whole period of spiritual apostasy.

For instance, 2 Kings 24:3 says that God's pronouncement against Judah (to remove His people from His sight) was due in part to the sins of Manasseh. He was perhaps the most wicked of Judah's kings. Consider the fact that he was guilty of shedding innocent blood. His crimes were so great that God refused to forgive Jehoiakim (24:4). Even the impressive reforms enacted by Josiah could not turn God from the fierceness of his great wrath (23:26). He decreed that Judah and Jerusalem would not escape His judgment (23:27).

During the tumultuous eight years from 605 to 597 B.C., Jeremiah consistently proclaimed the Word of the Lord. Zephaniah and Habakkuk had issued warnings, too. Sadly, though, the leadership of Judah and the mass of its population did not respond to God's prophets. Jeremiah, in particular, was well into his ministry. He had prophesied for several years before Zedekiah was even born. The 11 years of Zedekiah's reign, leading up to the fall of Jerusalem in 586 B.C., would perhaps be among the worst in Jeremiah's life.

NOTES ON THE PRINTED TEXT

Zedekiah, at the age of 21, became Judah's last king in the Old Testament period. His 11-year reign (597–586 B.C.) was an evil one in the Lord's eyes, just as Jehoiakim's reign had been (2 Chron. 36:11-12). The Judean monarch refused to humbly submit to the sovereign rule of God or to heed the voice of His prophet Jeremiah. Prophets were God's earthly representatives. They proclaimed His message under specific circumstances. While little is said about the actual way in which God revealed His word to the prophets, they were convinced that what they told the people was indeed *from the mouth of the LORD* (36:12).

In the ninth year of Zedekiah's reign, he turned to Egypt for aid as he plotted rebellion against Babylon (Ezek. 17:11-15). Zedekiah's insurrection broke an oath he had made with Nebuchadnezzar, a vow taken in God's name (2 Chron. 36:13). In Scripture, a person's name was synonymous with that individual's character. Thus, to break a solemn oath of allegiance in name of the Lord was a sin against the very character of Yahweh Himself.

Furthermore, instead of turning to God as Judah faced ever increasing danger of invasion, Zedekiah stiffened his neck and hardened his heart. The people of Israel, along with their leaders and priests, also became increasingly unfaithful. They rejected God's sovereign rule as they defiled the temple with the idolatrous religious practices of their neighbors (36:14). In His infinite mercy and because He had compassion on His people, the Lord repeatedly sent prophets such as Jeremiah and Ezekiel to warn the Israelites about coming judgment (36:15); but the people rejected every overture the Lord made to them. They mocked God's messengers, despised His warnings, and ridiculed His prophets. Since the people spurned God's remedy for their unfaithfulness, His wrath was aroused against them (36:16).

Jerusalem was a fortress city that seemed to everyone to be unconquerable (see Lam. 4:12); however, the city's greatest threat came not from outside foreign invaders, but from the contagious moral degeneracy within. As judgment upon His rebellious people's cumulative sin, God had promised that the Babylonians would conquer Judah. In the process, Jerusalem and the temple would be destroyed by fire (2 Chron. 36:17, 19). This divine judgment was carried out in three stages.

The first stage of the Babylonian conquest of Judah came in 605 B.C. Nebuchadnezzar conquered King Jehoiakim and carried part of the temple treasures, along with exiles such as Daniel, to Babylon (2 Chron. 36:6-7; Dan. 1:1-3). Then in 597 B.C., the Babylonian monarch returned a second time for more of the temple's treasures. These he transported, in company with King Jehoiachin and 10,000 of

Judah's leaders and princes, back to his kingdom in Mesopotamia (2 Kings 24:14-16). In 588 B.C., Nebuchadnezzar came yet a third time, when Zedekiah rebelled against his Babylonian overlord. For one and a half years, the Babylonian army whittled away at the city's defenses. Confident at first in their opposition to Babylon, the people began to lose courage when their ally Egypt's rescue attempt was crushed, and the other fortified cities of Judah (such as Lachish) began falling like dominoes to the Babylonians (Jer. 34:6-7).

The end of the third invasion finally came in 586 B.C. The Babylonians breached the walls, burned the city, blinded Zedekiah, and carried the king and many captives to Babylon in chains. Only a remnant of the poorest of the people was left to inhabit the rubble that was once the great city of Jerusalem (2 Kings 25:8-12). According to 2 Chronicles 36, the invaders murdered Judah's young men who were in the temple. The Babylonian king also had no mercy on the people, slaughtering both young and old, men and women, healthy and sick. The Lord delivered all of them into the hand of the enemy (36:17). Moreover, the ruler of Babylon confiscated all the utensils, whether large or small, from the Jerusalem temple, as well as the treasures found in the Lord's sanctuary and the royal palace (36:18). Then the invading army set fire to the temple, flattened the walls of Jerusalem, and burned all the palaces (36:19).

The people of Judah were held captive in Babylon until the Babylonians fell to the combined armies of the Medes and Persians in 539 B.C. (36:20). Thus, for the nearly 70 years between the first deportation in 605 and the beginning of the construction on the temple in 536 by the newly returning exiles (Dan. 9:2; Ezra 1:1), Judah received the cumulative sabbath rests God's people had failed to observe (2 Chron. 36:21; see Lev. 25:1-7; 26:34-35). The rise to power of the Medes and Persians was a providential act of God. The prophet Daniel understood this in his day, when the 70-year exile begun by the desolation of Jerusalem was nearing an end (Dan. 9:2).

Psalm 137 is a prayer of lament connected with the exile of God's people in Babylon. It is unclear whether the mournful hymn was composed and sung during the exile or immediately afterward. In either case, the writer declared his love for Jerusalem and his hope for judgment upon Judah's enemies. When the Babylonians took the Jews into exile, they were settled in a land of plains watered by rivers (such as the Tigris and Euphrates) and irrigation canals. There the exiles sat and wept as they remembered their beloved Zion, the holy city of Jerusalem (137:1).

Psalm 137:2-4 indicates that the Babylonians demanded to hear some of the joyful music of Judah. To the Jews, the demand was offensive, for their mood was the opposite of joy. Also, their music was meant to praise God. It would be wrong, they thought, to use it for entertaining Judah's conquerors. So the Jewish musicians hung their harps on tree branches as a sign that they refused to perform religious music for their captors. The psalmist vowed his continued faithfulness to Jerusalem (and therefore to Jerusalem's God). He went so far as to describe the punishments he would deserve if he broke his vow and did not consider Jerusalem his highest joy. The curses mentioned in 137:5-6 can be interpreted in different ways; but probably they mean that if the psalmist broke his vow, he should no longer be able to play the harp or to sing, which would be appropriate punishment for him.

SUGGESTIONS TO TEACHERS

This week's lesson deals with the end of a long process of spiritual and moral decay within Judah. The judgment that fell on Jerusalem at the hands of the Babylonians could have been averted. Regretfully, though, it wasn't prevented, because the people of God refused to respond to His warnings and chose (instead) to persist in their sins. The only way out of this dilemma is to repent of the sin in our lives.

1. A PROUD KING. Zedekiah led Judah into judgment, not because he was young and inexperienced, but because he would not humble himself before the prophet Jeremiah who spoke from the mouth of the Lord (2 Chron. 36:12). Spiritually arrogant people easily put their preferences in the place of God's will. It's difficult for them to repent because doing this involves admitting that they have been wrong and God has been right. Use this account to encourage spiritual humility on the part of your students.

2. A PACT-BREAKING KING. When it looked politically expedient, Zedekiah ignored a treaty made in the name of the Lord with Nebuchadnezzar. God saw this as a treacherous heart that knew no allegiance to Him. The king set an example for his people of treachery that blasphemed God's name. Remind your students that Jesus values disciples of great integrity who will keep their word (Matt. 5:33-37).

3. A PERVERSE WORSHIP. The king was not the only leader whose example led the people of Judah into divine judgment. The priests also proved unfaithful spiritual guides, and the people willingly followed them into idolatry. The priests and people even defiled the temple of the Lord with pagan worship. In all likelihood, the priests and people probably corrupted the worship of the Lord by mixing in pagan elements rather than completely abandoning Yahweh. Believers, too, have to be careful of mixing faith in Christ with dependence on contemporary idols, such as wealth, position, and power.

4. A PERSISTENT REJECTION. The Lord had been calling His people to repentance through His prophets at least since the days of Samuel (which was centuries earlier). The Lord's initial response to His people (when they disobeyed Him) was compassion. The people of God had mocked and scoffed at His prophets and despised His message for a long time before the wrath of the Lord against His people became so great that there was no remedy (2 Chron. 36:16). Encourage your students to be responsive to the warnings of the Lord when He convicts them of sin through the ministry of the Holy Spirit. They don't want to provoke God year after year until He has to discipline them more pointedly.

5. A PERVASIVE DESTRUCTION AND EXILE. When the Babylonian army captured Jerusalem, it took extreme measures against the city and exiled its inhabitants.

If God ever has to punish a Christian harshly for persistent sin, that punishment may involve exposure and shame (Mark 4:22; Luke 8:17). It may require a period of separation from the church (Matt. 18:15-17; 1 Cor. 5:3-5; 2 Thess. 3:6). It could require one to make restitution for wrongs (Luke 19:8). The most extreme chastening of God for flagrant, persistent disobedience is death (Acts 5:1-10; 1 Cor. 11:30).

FOR ADULTS	■ **TOPIC:** Making Wrong Choices ■ **QUESTIONS:** 1. How did the Lord display His mercy to His people? 2. How did God's people respond to His mercy? 3. Why did the Lord

allow the Babylonians to invade Jerusalem? 4. What was the emotional state of the exiles in Babylon? 5. How do we sometimes take God's mercy for granted?

■ **ILLUSTRATIONS:**

The Example of Leaders. So many of the last kings of Judah, including Zedekiah, set such bad examples that it is a good idea to be reminded by contrast that the examples of good leaders also are powerful. When William McKinley was 10 years old, he put his faith in Christ during a revival service at his church in Ohio. Years later when he opened his first law office in Canton, McKinley served as Sunday school superintendent for his church. After both his children died young, McKinley devoted himself to his wife Ida, who never fully recovered from those emotional blows. In 1896, McKinley campaigned for the presidency from his front porch so that he wouldn't have to leave Ida. After entering office, he broke protocol by insisting that his wife sit beside him at all state functions, for she was liable to epileptic seizures.

During his presidency, McKinley attended Metropolitan Methodist Church in Washington. D.C. On Sunday evenings he liked to gather friends and members of Congress for hymn sings in the White House. A year after being re-elected, McKinley was shot by an anarchist at the Pan American Exhibition in Buffalo, New York. He lingered eight days. The President lapsed into a coma on September 14, 1901, whispering the words to *Nearer, My God, To Thee*, his favorite hymn.

Many Americans disagreed with William McKinley's politics, but all who knew about his faith in Christ, his kindness, and his devotion to his wife were impressed by him and encouraged to be better people themselves.

Special Coffeecake? An overweight businessman decided it was time for him to get rid of a few pounds. One of the things he did to cut down on calories was change his route to the office so that he would avoid a bakery that always lured him in for amazing pasties. A week into his diet, the man arrived at work lugging a monstrous coffeecake.

"This is *special* coffeecake," the businessman announced to the office workers, who proceeded to scold him. "My mind wandered this morning, and I automatically took my old way to work. The sign in the bakery window said 'Heavenly Coffeecake,' so I thought God must want me to have one. I prayed that if I should buy a coffee cake, He would give me a parking place right in front of the store. And sure enough, on the eighth time around the block, there it was!"

How often do we perform spiritual gymnastics to convince ourselves that the sin we want to do is okay? Maybe we think our situation is an exception. Maybe we convince ourselves that God has approved our behavior or agreed to look away. Maybe we take a deep breath and plunge ahead. We realize, though, that there's no real justification for sin.

Responding to God's Discipline. In the movie *Groundhog Day*, Bill Murray plays an arrogant television weatherman named Phil from Pittsburgh who hates to go to Punxsutawney each year to cover the groundhog story. Nasty Phil finds himself in some sort of time warp in Punxsutawney, and he relives Groundhog Day over and over again. The same event happens every day. The first few times, Phil reacts with anger. Then he spends several identical days manipulating events and people for selfish ends. After a few dozen identical days, he becomes depressed.

After killing himself several times, only to wake up the next morning and begin Groundhog Day again, Phil begins to change himself. He can't change anything else. He learns foreign languages, piano playing, ice sculpture, and medicine. He starts a routine of kind acts that head off the same problems in every identical day.

Through what must have been years of repeating the same day, Phil's arrogance, selfishness, and impatience are transformed into kindness and genuine regard for others. One day he makes a true commitment of himself to another person. The next morning it is the day after Groundhog Day.

God's discipline is corrective in the lives of believers in Christ. We should respond to God's discipline by cooperating with it so that we can be changed into the person He wants us to become.

FOR YOUTH

■ TOPIC: Exile in Babylon
■ QUESTIONS: 1. How did God's people respond to the prophets He sent to them? 2. What did the Lord allow the Babylonians do to Judah and Jerusalem? 3. For how long would the land lay desolate? 4. How did the exiles respond to the harsh reality of being far away from their homeland? 5. In what ways does today's culture—or our own desires—try to turn us away from God?

■ ILLUSTRATIONS:

Don't Follow Bad Leaders. A graduate of a prestigious Ivy League university decided to invest some capital in a chicken farm. He started out with 200 chicks, but they soon died. He bought 200 more chicks, but they lasted no longer than the first batch.

In desperation, the Ivy Leaguer swallowed his pride and wrote to the Podunk School of Agriculture for advice. His letter began: "I want very much to be a successful chicken farmer. Have I been planting the chicks too deep or too close together?"

The Podunk School of Agriculture replied: "If you Ivy League people would get your heads out of the clouds, you'd realize we need a soil sample before we can answer your question."

The moral of this fictitious story is that we should be cautious about following leaders who are committed to their own agendas rather than God's Word.

Walk in the Light. The children were putting on the Christmas program for their parents at church. To show the radiance of the newborn Christ-child, a concealed electric light bulb was wired into the manger. Toward the end of the production, all of the stage lights went down so only a glow from the manger would be seen. The night of the play, the fifth-grader operating the lights got confused and turned out the manger light with the rest. A tense moment on stage ended when a first-grade shepherd said in a stage whisper audible all over the church, "Hey! You switched off Jesus."

All around you, young people are living for themselves and following bad examples set for them by selfish leaders. You either can follow Jesus by walking in the light of God's Word, or you can "switch off Jesus" (so to speak) and live like the rest of the world. The latter option was disastrous for Judah, and eventually it will be for you, too.

Consequences Are Built Into Behavior. The Indianapolis Police Department computerized its records in 1988. In the following eight years, one man was arrested 858 times for public intoxication. He was the most-arrested man in town. He couldn't stay at the rescue missions any more because he was never sober enough to check in. When the weather was bad or this man was a nuisance, an officer would pick him up and book him. One December night in 1996, the man fell down in the middle of a downtown street and went to asleep. A motorist slammed on his brakes, but he dragged the man to his death.

When the man took his first drink in high school, he never imagined he'd die under a car on a snowy street. He wasn't in his yearbook as "Most Likely to Be Most-Arrested." But he lived and died with the consequences of his choices.

GOD OFFERS RETURN AND RESTORATION

BACKGROUND SCRIPTURE: 2 Chronicles 36:22-23; Ezra 1:5-7

DEVOTIONAL READING: Jeremiah 29:10-14

KEY VERSE: All the kingdoms of the earth hath the LORD God of heaven given me; and he hath charged me to build him an house in Jerusalem. . . . Who is there among you of all his people? The LORD his God be with him, and let him go up. 2 Chronicles 36:23.

KING JAMES VERSION

2 CHRONICLES 36:22 Now in the first year of Cyrus king of Persia, that the word of the LORD spoken by the mouth of Jeremiah might be accomplished, the LORD stirred up the spirit of Cyrus king of Persia, that he made a proclamation throughout all his kingdom, and put it also in writing, saying, 23Thus saith Cyrus king of Persia, All the kingdoms of the earth hath the LORD God of heaven given me; and he hath charged me to build him an house in Jerusalem, which is in Judah. Who is there among you of all his people? The LORD his God be with him, and let him go up.

EZRA 1:5 Then rose up the chief of the fathers of Judah and Benjamin, and the priests, and the Levites, with all them whose spirit God had raised, to go up to build the house of the LORD which is in Jerusalem. 6And all they that were about them strengthened their hands with vessels of silver, with gold, with goods, and with beasts, and with precious things, beside all that was willingly offered. 7Also Cyrus the king brought forth the vessels of the house of the LORD, which Nebuchadnezzar had brought forth out of Jerusalem, and had put them in the house of his gods.

NEW REVISED STANDARD VERSION

2 CHRONICLES 36:22 In the first year of King Cyrus of Persia, in fulfillment of the word of the LORD spoken by Jeremiah, the LORD stirred up the spirit of King Cyrus of Persia so that he sent a herald throughout all his kingdom and also declared in a written edict:
23 "Thus says King Cyrus of Persia: The LORD, the God of heaven, has given me all the kingdoms of the earth, and he has charged me to build him a house at Jerusalem, which is in Judah. Whoever is among you of all his people, may the LORD his God be with him! Let him go up."

EZRA 1:5 The heads of the families of Judah and Benjamin, and the priests and the Levites—everyone whose spirit God had stirred—got ready to go up and rebuild the house of the LORD in Jerusalem. 6 All their neighbors aided them with silver vessels, with gold, with goods, with animals, and with valuable gifts, besides all that was freely offered. 7 King Cyrus himself brought out the vessels of the house of the LORD that Nebuchadnezzar had carried away from Jerusalem and placed in the house of his gods.

13

Monday, November 20	Psalm 57	*Prayer for Deliverance*
Tuesday, November 21	Isaiah 57:14-19	*God Promises to Lead and Heal*
Wednesday, November 22	Psalm 130	*God Forgives*
Thursday, November 23	Jeremiah 29:10-14	*God's Plan Revealed*
Friday, November 24	2 Chronicles 36:22-23	*King Cyrus Plans to Rebuild*
Saturday, November 25	Ezra 1	*The Exiles Return*
Sunday, November 26	Ezra 5:7b-14	*Rebuilding the Temple*

BACKGROUND

In 539 B.C., Cyrus of Persia defeated the Babylonian Empire. He then instituted a policy of allowing captive peoples to return to their homelands, live by their ancient traditions, and reestablish the worship of their respective deities. The Jewish people had been exiled in three stages, and they returned to Palestine in three stages. Zerubbabel led the first group of returnees (538 B.C.) and started to rebuild the temple (Ezra 1—6). Ezra led the second group (458 B.C.) and instituted a number of reforms (chaps. 7—10). Finally, Nehemiah led the third group (445 B.C.) and rebuilt the wall around Jerusalem (Neh. 1—6). Work on the restoration of the temple began in the reign of Cyrus (536 B.C.), extended through the time of Cambyses, and was completed in the sixth year of Darius I (516 B.C.). The reforming careers of Ezra and Nehemiah spanned the reigns of Artaxerxes Longimanus (464–424 B.C.) and Darius II (423–405 B.C.).

Cyrus the Great (or Cyrus II) founded and expanded the Persian Empire, which flourished from 539 to 331 B.C. He governed his growing kingdom through a system of provinces (called satrapies) that were ruled by governors who answered directly to him. Under his leadership, the Persians developed roads, cities, postal systems, and legal codes. Cambyses II (530–522 B.C.), the son and successor of Cyrus, added Egypt to the Persian Empire. The next ruler, Darius I (521–486 B.C.), defeated nine kings to claim all 23 Persian satrapies. This resulted in his rule extending over a vast territory nearly 3,000 miles long and 500 to 1,500 miles wide. Darius unified his empire by using an efficient gold coinage, state highways, and a more efficient postal system. In the second year of the reign of Darius, he ordered the Jewish temple at Jerusalem to be rebuilt. For the previous 14 years, the work on it had been discontinued. Darius also gave a generous subsidy that made it possible for the temple to be completed.

Ancient Jewish and the oldest Christian traditions assigned the authorship of Ezra (along with Nehemiah) to Ezra. Many contemporary scholars continue to support the view that Ezra also wrote the books of Chronicles. Included in the evidence that supports this view is the fact that the last two verses of 2 Chronicles and the first two verses of Ezra are virtually identical. Ezra may have done this to make a smooth chronological flow between the two books. Ezra was uniquely qualified to write this book, for as a scribe he would have had access to the many administrative documents contained within the royal archives of the Persian Empire. Other scholars, however, have suggested that a "Chronicler," perhaps a disciple of Ezra, brought together the memoirs of Judah's kings, Ezra, and Nehemiah to compose 1 and 2 Chronicles, Ezra, and Nehemiah.

Ezra and Nehemiah do not just record a string of historical facts about the returning exiles. Each narrative describes how God fulfilled His promises, which He had announced beforehand through His prophets. Ezra and Nehemiah indicate how the Lord brought His people back from Babylon, rebuilt the temple at Jerusalem, restored the patterns of true worship, and preserved the reassembled community from relapsing into pagan customs and idolatrous worship. The consistent message of these two books is that God works through responsible human agents to accomplish His redemptive purpose. For example, Cyrus issued his decree because the Lord had moved his spirit (Ezra 1:1). Those who returned came back because God had moved their spirits (1:5). Ezra succeeded because the hand of the Lord was upon him (7:9). Artaxerxes supported the work of rebuilding because God had put such a purpose in his spirit (7:27). Nehemiah's enemies failed because God had brought their plot to nothing (Neh. 4:15). Finally, the true motive of Nehemiah's strategy to repopulate Jerusalem was due to God putting the desire in his heart (7:5).

The extraordinary reality of God's promised restoration of His people (Jer. 27:22) is recorded in detail in Ezra and Nehemiah. The remnant did not merely return to the devastated ruins of Jerusalem. They also came back with a hope, placed in their hearts by God, to rebuild the nation both physically and spiritually. With godly determination, they rebuilt the temple. Then the Lord sent Ezra and Nehemiah to exhort them to obey His law wholeheartedly. While the people were rebuilding Jerusalem's walls, God was rebuilding their hearts so that they would truly obey and worship Him. The message for their day—as well as our own—is that the God of Israel is faithful to His promises. He will completely restore His people when they come back to Him.

Ezra and Nehemiah make it clear that God did not restore His people only one time. Rather, He repeatedly, constantly, and continually restored His people. He sent a number of prophets and leaders to teach, motivate, and guide the people into righteousness. Zerubbabel led a group of exiles to Jerusalem and began to rebuild the temple (Ezra 1—6). Next, Ezra led a second group of exiles back to Jerusalem and helped restore the people to obedience to the Mosaic law (7—10). Then, Nehemiah returned and motivated the people to rebuild the walls of Jerusalem (Neh. 1—6). Finally, Nehemiah returned a second time and exhorted the people to adhere closely to God's law (chap. 13). The pattern is clear, namely, that God continually restored His people. Despite their unfaithfulness, He accomplished His will. The returns from exile, the rebuilding of the temple, the restoration of Jerusalem's walls, the repopulation of the city, and the repeated reformation of the Israelites was clearly the work of God. In the end, His name was glorified.

NOTES ON THE PRINTED TEXT

In 586 B.C., the Lord sent King Nebuchadnezzar of Babylon to attack Jerusalem (2 Chron. 36:17). God allowed this foreign enemy to overrun the city, destroy its temple, and exile its inhabitants because His people had refused to turn from their sins. For the next 70 years, the land remained desolate, in accordance with the prophecy made by Jeremiah (36:21-22). Then, in October 539 B.C., Cyrus captured Babylon. Next, in March 538 B.C., he began his first year reigning over not only Persia, but also the old Babylonian Empire. At this time, God had Cyrus send a message throughout his kingdom announcing his decree to have the temple rebuilt. This momentous decision also meant the exiled Jews were permitted to return to their land (2 Chron. 36:23; see Ezra 1:1-2).

Note that Yahweh, *the LORD* (Ezra 1:2)—*the God of heaven*—made Cyrus the ruler of every nation in the Fertile Crescent. Additionally, the oral proclamation declared that Yahweh had chosen Cyrus to build a temple for him in the city of Jerusalem. This was a startling admission. Pagan kings were not prone to acknowledge the superiority of anyone else. Indeed, kings proved the superiority of their religions and idols by virtue of their conquests. By that logic, Israel's God was supposedly weaker than the deities of Babylon and Persia; but when God stirred the heart of Cyrus, the Lord made it clear that He is all-powerful.

As such, God would watch over His people and ensure their success in returning safely to Judah and rebuilding the temple. Cyrus called on those who lived in any place in the empire where Jewish survivors were found to help defray their relocation expenses. Most likely this was aimed at Jews who did not want to return to Judea, especially those who had been born in exile. The king ordered that the returnees be given money, supplies, and animals, as well as gifts for rebuilding the temple of God in Jerusalem (1:3-4).

The Lord had stirred the heart of Cyrus to restore the exiled Jews to their homeland. God also stirred the hearts of His people to respond to this wonderful opportunity. For instance, a number of family leaders of Judah and Benjamin made preparations to return to Jerusalem, as well as the priests and Levites. Their intent was not just to visit the holy city or establish a permanent residence there. They were also going to Jerusalem to build the temple of the Lord. In fact, God was the one who put this desire in their hearts (1:5).

All the neighbors of the Jews who were making the long journey helped the travelers. The people remaining behind gave the returnees articles made of silver and gold, along with food supplies, cattle, and valuable gifts. They also donated special gifts for the temple (1:6). Imagine how encouraged the returnees were when they received all this support from their fellow Jews. Truly the hand of God was at work among His people!

We also learn from the biblical text that King Cyrus brought out the bowls and pans that had once been in the temple of the Lord. Nebuchadnezzar had taken these articles from Jerusalem and placed them in the temple of his own god (1:7). Cyrus had Mithredeth, his chief treasurer, return the stolen items to Sheshbazzar, the new governor of Judah (1:8). There were a significant number of articles that Sheshbazzar received from Mithredath (1:9-11). The governor brought all these items along when the captives journeyed from Babylon to Jerusalem. When God stirred the heart of Cyrus, the Lord made sure that His people got more than a certificate of release and safe passage to Jerusalem. He provided for all of their needs and for the resumption of true (as opposed to idolatrous) worship in His name.

SUGGESTIONS TO TEACHERS

The Book of Ezra begins with great hope. The very thing that several generations of Jews had prayed for was about to happen. As we consider this, we realize that God does answer our prayers and He guides us. Ezra also helps us deal with the temptation to stay stuck in the past. Our lives are anchored in the present, informed by the past, and expectant of the future.

1. OUTLIVE YOUR PAST. The biblical text stresses the poignancy of the divine promise to return home. Movies, books, and plays center around the emotion associated with going home. Families today are scattered and the idea of returning may bring strong emotion, both positive and negative. Nearly everyone has things in the past we would like to forget and move beyond. Biblical faith helps people outlive their past. We are not stuck because we have a future.

2. TRUST IN GOD'S GUIDANCE. The promise to leave Babylon was clearly not just a political decision. The Jews saw it as the sovereign guidance of God, who would lead them back, just as He had led their ancestors out of Egypt. People who are in places they don't necessarily want to be in may have a tough time feeling "out of place." Ezra helps us deal with this problem. We can trust God to lead us to new places, especially places of service and obedience to Him. We may never be captive as the Jews were, but we can still trust God in everyday ways.

3. GOD USES DIFFERENT KINDS OF PEOPLE. At first glance, God's use of Cyrus, king of Persia, to be the instrument of returning His people to Jerusalem seems strange. After all, how could God use a "foreigner" and a "pagan"? We live in a widely divergent world in which variety can be God's gift to us. Yes, He used Cyrus and He can use anyone, anywhere, and at any time who is willing to be used. Part of our maturing in faith is learning to allow God to set the agenda and determine whomever He wants to be His spokesperson.

FOR ADULTS

■ **TOPIC:** Experiencing Forgiveness

■ **QUESTIONS:** 1. What momentous event occurred in the *first year of Cyrus king of Persia* (2 Chron. 36:22)? 2. Why do you think God used

Cyrus to bring about the return of His people from exile? 3. Which particular Jewish families were affected by the decree of Cyrus? 4. What help did the returnees receive to make their journey home? 5. How does God help us in small and large ways to accomplish His will?

■ ILLUSTRATIONS:

God's Will at the Dumpster. As I was leaving work, I decided to drive my garbage over to the neighborhood dumpster. Sueann (not her real name), a woman I had talked with briefly on a few occasions, was walking with her garbage in the same direction. I pulled beside her and asked if she'd like me to take her bag since I was going that way.

"Oh, no thanks, Christine" she replied. "I could use the exercise." "OK," I returned her smile and drove on. But when I stopped at the dumpster and unloaded my trash, I sensed that God was speaking to my heart: "Wait for Sueann." I was already behind schedule, but Sueann was approaching just then, so I didn't argue. "How are you doing?"

That's all it took. Sueann melted almost immediately. "Oh, not so well," she said tearfully. What ensued was a conversation about Sueann's disintegrating marriage due to her husband's alcoholism, her longing for relief, and her desire for God to be the center of her life again. She let me hug her and pray with her, and I was able to invite her to join me at my own "safe place" of community, my church.

Sueann is now seeking out godly counsel in her marriage situation and has started attending church with me. We also now pray together. This wasn't my plan; it was God's. He moved both Sueann's heart and mine to take out our garbage that day and enable her to begin to experience the wonderful forgiveness, mercy, and grace of the Lord.

The Hope of Reunion Is Strong Everywhere. Ernest Hemingway wrote a story about a father and his teenage son. In the story, the relationship had become somewhat strained, and the teenage son ran away from home. His father began a journey in search of that rebellious son. Finally, in Madrid, Spain, in a last desperate attempt to find the boy, the father put an ad in the local newspaper. The ad read: "Dear Paco, meet me in front of the newspaper office at noon. All is forgiven. I love you. Your father." The next day, in front of the newspaper office, 800 Pacos showed up. They were all seeking forgiveness. They were all seeking the love of their father.

Adversity Can Lead to Victory. On July 24, 2005, Lance Armstrong won the Tour de France for the seventh year in a row. In 1999, the first year Armstrong won, much was made about the fact that he had survived testicular cancer. The cancer had spread into his lungs and brain. Armstrong not only recovered from the cancer, but also went on to win the most prestigious race in cycling. Some said Armstrong's victory that year was hollow because some of the best competitors had to sit out the race in 1999 due to a drug scandal. Few believed he would win in the year 2000 when the best cyclists would be back and the course more mountainous. Armstrong not only returned but also won in 2000 by a whopping six minutes!

In analyzing Armstrong's amazing string of victories since then, one commentator pointed out that it was after the athlete's bout with cancer that he became a premier cyclist. After recovering from cancer, Lance was 40 pounds lighter than he had been before. While he managed to bulk up some in the recovery years, he always remained leaner than he ever had been before. This loss of weight made a difference in Armstrong's biking. It played significantly into his becoming a Tour de France winner seven times in a row.

Living with Hope, Even in the Midst of Adversity. Vaclav Havel, the Czech poet/president, spoke these words from his years of suffering oppression and persecution: "I am not an optimist, because I am not sure that everything ends well. Nor am I a pessimist, because I am not sure everything ends badly. I just carry hope in my heart. . . . Life without hope is an empty, boring, and useless life. I cannot imagine that I could strive for something if I did not carry hope in me. I am thankful to God for this gift. It is as big a gift as life itself."

FOR YOUTH	■ TOPIC: Coming Home!

■ **QUESTIONS:** 1. What prophecy was God fulfilling in the lives of His people? 2. How did God bring about the fulfillment of this prophecy? 3. What was the basic thrust of the edict Cyrus had made to the Jewish exiles? 4. How did the Jewish and non-Jewish people respond to the king's momentous decree? 5. In what ways has God recently shown Himself to be faithful to you?

■ **ILLUSTRATIONS:**
Not Seeking Personal Glory. For tae kwon do star Esther Kim, age 20, going to the Olympics has been a long-time dream. She came very close to embracing that dream at the Olympic trials, where she was scheduled to fight her best friend, Kay Poe, who was ranked number one in the world. But Poe had injured her knee in the semi-finals match and could barely stand up. Obviously, Kim could have easily defeated Poe. But she believed such a match-up would hardly be fair. In an instant, she decided to forfeit, automatically sending Poe to the Olympics.

The moment Kim made her decision, she knew it was right. "I thought, 'It's not like I'm going to be throwing my dream away. I'm just going to be handing it over to Kay.'" Kim's magnanimity was affirmed when she was given the "Citizenship through

Sports Award," which recognizes exemplary citizenship, sportsmanship, ethical conduct, and community service. In addition, the International Olympic Committee agreed to pay for her and her father (coach of Kim and Poe) to go to the Sydney Olympics.

Though some people were critical of her decision, Kim knows she made the right choice. She says, "Even though I didn't have the gold medal around me, for the first time in my life, I felt like a real champion."

God Is Still Leading People to Act Selflessly. A church gave away its building fund and received an even bigger blessing. Vaca Valley Christian Life Center in Vacaville, California, had raised $120,000 toward a multimillion-dollar sanctuary when pastor David Crone heard about the needs of another ministry. That ministry is the Los Angeles International Dream Center. The center bought the former Queen of Angels Hospital in Los Angeles and was refurbishing nine buildings as a massive center for its ministry.

Crone said he sensed God wanted the money to go to the Dream Center, not the church. He received approval from his congregation and soon was presenting a check for $120,000 to Tommy Barnett, pastor at Phoenix First Assembly of God, who was developing the center along with his son Matthew. Soon money began pouring in for Vaca Valley's building project from unexpected sources, such as a nonprofit foundation and ministries, as well as individuals. Crone and the congregation dedicated the new $1 million debt-free facility on Easter.

Another Strong Driving Force. Consider one person's journey. A man who called himself "king of prison" is leading inmates to Christ. Vladimir Kiselev, who was serving a life sentence, was known as the toughest man in his Russian prison. He was miserable, though, according to International Russian Radio/TV, a broadcast ministry to the former Soviet Union. "No one can get as low as I was at the time," he said.

Kiselev's road to freedom began when he became a Christian. Then an unusual event began to occur. He said, "I was told that I would never be a free man, but President Yeltsin pardoned me in 1995." Kiselev was told that he would never be able to have his own family, yet "today, I am married and have three darling, God-given children."

Kiselev's testimony has been broadcast to Russian prisons by IRR/TV. About 300 inmates at several prisons in central Russia have become Christians through his testimony. His follow-up work of prison ministries has also helped hundreds of people. Kiselev also visits prisons and tells inmates about "the God who fixes even an unfixable person's life. That which Satan had crushed and destroyed in 40 years of my life, God fixed and healed in seven years."

WHO IS JESUS CHRIST?

BACKGROUND SCRIPTURE: Colossians 1
DEVOTIONAL READING: Isaiah 9:2-7

KEY VERSES: Who is the image of the invisible God, the firstborn of every creature: For by him were all things created, that are in heaven, and that are in earth, visible and invisible, whether they be thrones, or dominions, or principalities, or powers. Colossians 1:15-16.

KING JAMES VERSION

COLOSSIANS 1:15 Who is the image of the invisible God, the firstborn of every creature: 16 For by him were all things created, that are in heaven, and that are in earth, visible and invisible, whether they be thrones, or dominions, or principalities, or powers: all things were created by him, and for him: 17 And he is before all things, and by him all things consist. 18 And he is the head of the body, the church: who is the beginning, the firstborn from the dead; that in all things he might have the preeminence. 19 For it pleased the Father that in him should all fulness dwell; 20 And, having made peace through the blood of his cross, by him to reconcile all things unto himself; by him, I say, whether they be things in earth, or things in heaven. 21 And you, that were sometime alienated and enemies in your mind by wicked works, yet now hath he reconciled 22 In the body of his flesh through death, to present you holy and unblameable and unreproveable in his sight: 23 If ye continue in the faith grounded and settled, and be not moved away from the hope of the gospel, which ye have heard, and which was preached to every creature which is under heaven; whereof I Paul am made a minister.

NEW REVISED STANDARD VERSION

COLOSSIANS 1:15 He is the image of the invisible God, the firstborn of all creation; 16 for in him all things in heaven and on earth were created, things visible and invisible, whether thrones or dominions or rulers or powers—all things have been created through him and for him. 17 He himself is before all things, and in him all things hold together. 18 He is the head of the body, the church; he is the beginning, the firstborn from the dead, so that he might come to have first place in everything. 19 For in him all the fullness of God was pleased to dwell, 20 and through him God was pleased to reconcile to himself all things, whether on earth or in heaven, by making peace through the blood of his cross.

21 And you who were once estranged and hostile in mind, doing evil deeds, 22 he has now reconciled in his fleshly body through death, so as to present you holy and blameless and irreproachable before him— 23 provided that you continue securely established and steadfast in the faith, without shifting from the hope promised by the gospel that you heard, which has been proclaimed to every creature under heaven. I, Paul, became a servant of this gospel.

HOME BIBLE READINGS

Monday, November 27	Luke 1:5-20	*An Angel Promises*
Tuesday, November 28	Luke 1:21-25	*Elizabeth Is with Child*
Wednesday, November 29	Luke 1:67-80	*A Father Sings His Praise*
Thursday, November 30	Matthew 3:1-6	*John Prepares the Way*
Friday, December 1	Isaiah 9:2-7	*A Son Is Promised*
Saturday, December	2 Colossians 1:9-14	*Into the Kingdom of His Son*
Sunday, December 3	Colossians 1:15-23	*Who Jesus Is*

BACKGROUND

The Letter of Paul to the Colossians is named for the city of Colosse, which is where the congregation was located. The Pauline authorship of Colossians has been universally recognized throughout church history. The apostle identified himself as the writer three different times (1:1, 23; 4:18). Furthermore, Paul closed the epistle with a handwritten greeting, which was a characteristic of several of his letters.

Colosse was located in the Roman province of Asia (modern-day Turkey) in the Lycus River Valley about 100 miles east of Ephesus. Paul evidently had not visited this Christian community. It apparently grew up under the leadership of Epaphras (1:7; 4:12) and Archippus (Col. 4:17; Philem. 2). As early as the fifth century B.C., Colosse was known as a prosperous city, but by the beginning of the Christian era, it was eclipsed by neighboring towns. Shortly after Paul sent his letter to Colosse, the cities of the Lycus Valley suffered a devastating earthquake (A.D. 61). Though Colosse was increasingly overshadowed by other nearby cities, it retained considerable importance into the next several centuries.

Colosse's population was mainly Gentile. Yet there was also a large Jewish settlement dating from the days of Antiochus the Great (223–187 B.C.). The city's mixed population of Jews and Gentiles manifested itself both in the composition of the church and in the heresy that plagued it. This erroneous doctrine combined Jewish observances (Col. 2:16) and pagan speculation (2:8). The religious frauds claimed they were adding to and improving upon the Gospel that had come from Paul.

Some of the helpful "additions" included an undue emphasis on observing religious festivals and new moon celebrations (some of which were related to astrology; 2:16), along with keeping a list of rules (vs. 20). These practices were then included within a philosophy in which angels played a leading role (vs. 18). Paul said this philosophy was based on human tradition and the elemental spiritual forces of this world (vs. 8). In other words, the rudimentary beliefs and ceremonies of human religion were nothing more than a man-made system of works-righteousness. These pagan philosophies were filled with laws and rituals that supposedly had to be observed in order to achieve divine acceptance. Far from being advanced, profound knowledge, these notions were simplistic and immature.

Paul explained to his readers that in order for them to enjoy the favor and acceptance of God, they needed to trust in Christ. He and only He could make their redemption possible. The reason is that God already accepted them by virtue of their spiritual union with Christ in His death and resurrection. The apostle stressed that while there was still a level of spiritual maturity they needed to attain (1:22-23, 28), they were already complete in Christ (2:10). Paul's letter contains teaching on several key areas of theology, including the deity of Christ (1:15-20; 2:2-10), reconciliation (1:20-23), redemption (1:13-14; 2:13-14; 3:9-11), election (3:12), forgiveness (3:13), and the nature of the church (1:18, 24-25; 2:19; 3:11, 15). The epistle serves as a bulwark against all forms of legalism (the view that saving merit is based on good works rather than God's grace) and asceticism (the view that the body must be harshly disciplined in order to earn divine favor and grow spiritually).

NOTES ON THE PRINTED TEXT

Paul's Letter to the Colossians majors on the person and work of the Messiah. In 1:15-23, Jesus' supremacy over all the cosmos is emphasized in His roles as Creator and Redeemer. The one role complements the other, for any compromise with respect to His person will lead to compromise with respect to His work, and vice versa. The reason for the apostle's emphasis on these truths is that heretical teaching in the Colossian church was promoting all sorts of theological compromises regarding who Jesus is and what He did at Calvary; but before Paul took on the heresies, he was concerned to set straight a firm understanding of the Messiah's identity.

The apostle determined this emphasis was necessary because false teachers (who had infiltrated the Gentile church at Colosse) claimed that Jesus was less than God Himself. Therefore the supremacy of the Messiah is one of the main thrusts of Paul's message to the Colossians. In the Son is seen the sum total of all the triune God's attributes, for Jesus is the *image of the invisible God* (1:15). *Image* expresses two ideas—likeness and manifestation. Jesus is the exact image of God (Heb. 1:3), like a ruler's image on a coin represents the ruler's likeness. Anyone who saw Jesus was seeing His unseen Father manifested (John 1:18; 14:9). Thus Jesus was called Immanuel—*God with us* (Matt. 1:23).

The supremacy of Christ is also conveyed in His rank as the firstborn over all creation (Col. 1:15). This does not mean Jesus had His beginning in Bethlehem's stable for, as God, He has always existed. The word rendered *firstborn* here emphasizes Jesus' priority above all creation in rank. Nothing that has been brought into existence—whether they dwell in heaven or inhabit the earth, whether we can see them or they are imperceptible to our eyes—has come into being without Christ's involvement.

Moreover, Paul stressed Christ's preeminence over the angelic realm. Within the Colossian heresy was the worship of angels. By listing their perceived hierarchy of angels (1:16), the apostle was attacking their systematic division of the angelic realm.

Since he referred to the visible as well as invisible, this hierarchy probably includes human institutions. The apostle exposed as foolish any homage to human or angelic authority because, in fact, Christ is Lord over them all.

The Son is rightfully accorded greatness, for the Father formed the creation not only through His Son but also for His Son. Without a doubt, the ultimate purpose of creation is the Messiah Himself. According to God's redemptive plan, He designed the world in such a way that it can have real meaning only in Christ. Moreover, Jesus eternally existed before the creation in time (1:17). He not only brought all things into existence, but also sustains them and enables them to fulfill their God-given function. Indeed, He upholds all things by His powerful decree (Heb. 1:3). The Messiah even occupies a place of supremacy over the church. He is the *head* (Col. 1:18) of His spiritual body as well as its *beginning*. The emphasis here is on Jesus' initiative in creating His church. He is its origin and source of life.

Beyond this, the Savior is the first person to rise from the dead. His resurrection, in turn, guarantees the future resurrection of all believers. It is no wonder that it pleased the Father to allow the Son to become first in all things. Moreover, the Father was pleased to have all His fullness dwell in His Son (1:19). In one sense this is evident through the incarnation of the Messiah; but it seems best to understand Paul as referring to the fact that the fullness of the triune God resides completely in the Savior. It is a permanent dwelling, too, not a temporary one (see 2:9).

The sad reality is that people live in rebellion against the Messiah, their Creator. Reconciliation is thus needed to repair this breech between God and humankind caused by sin. Just as the Son was the agent through whom the Father created, the Son is also the agent through whom the Father reconciles people to Himself (1:20). Behind the Greek word translated *reconcile* is the idea of exchanging hostility for friendship, with the effect being peace. This was possible through Jesus' shed blood at Calvary. The Messiah died to make peace with God possible for all who believe in Him. Furthermore, Paul declared that Jesus is the reconciler of all things. The phrase *whether they be things in earth, or things in heaven* is a further defining of *all things* just mentioned, and the apostle's way of affirming that Christ's reconciling work affects everything. Nothing is beyond the reaches of Jesus' redemptive work.

Paul next commented on the change in status for his predominately Gentile readers. The apostle noted that before trusting in Christ, they were relationally far from God, being alienated from Him due to their sin. They were His enemies in their thinking as expressed through their evil deeds (1:21). The chasm between humanity and God was seemingly infinite; but what people could not do on their own, Jesus accomplished through His physical death on the cross (1:22). The Son's atoning sacrifice was well worth the effort, for He enables believers to stand before the Father as holy, blameless, and beyond reproach. The believers' holy status refers to positional righteousness; in other words, believers in Christ are positioned before God as set apart from sin and separated to Him by virtue of Jesus' merits applied to them. The only appropriate response is for Christians to remain devoted to their Savior.

Paul referred to this unmitigated commitment as continuing *in the faith* (1:23). By this he meant the apostolic truths contained in the Gospel. The Good News he proclaimed as a minister of Christ was the basis for the believers' hope. Understandably, then, Paul wanted his readers to remain firmly rooted in the faith and ever anchored to their hope in the Lord Jesus. The true Gospel is what Paul taught while he ministered in Ephesus. Paul's servant Epaphras then took his message to Colosse and the surrounding district. Some of the citizens in that region became believers from his ministry. This is the same Gospel proclaimed universally for thousands of years. This does not mean that every single person will hear the good news about Christ, but that no group is excluded from receiving it.

SUGGESTIONS TO TEACHERS

The Lord Jesus dominates the landscape of the Scripture passages to be studied this quarter, beginning with the Letter to the Colossians. Individually and collectively these portions of God's Word serve as a reminder that the Savior needs to remain at the center of our lives. Indeed, apart from Him we can accomplish nothing of eternal value (John 15:5).

1. THE MESSIAH'S IDENTITY. Paul taught that Jesus is the visible image of the unseen God and that the Son eternally existed before the creation of the world. The Messiah is not only sovereign over all creation but also the one through whom the Father brought all things into existence. This includes all the angelic beings and human authorities. The entire universe owes its continuing existence to the Son. For these reasons He deserves our worship and service.

2. THE MESSIAH'S SOVEREIGNTY. The supremacy of Christ in our lives begins when we invite Him to become our Lord and Savior. After all, He said that He came to give us life to the full (John 10:10). No one else can give us eternal life. And we need it because we are spiritually dead in sin. There is no true life available to us, other than in Christ.

3. THE MESSIAH'S AUTHORITY. Many people today worship false gods. In contrast, the one true God has revealed Himself in His Son, the Lord Jesus. As Christ's followers, we live under His authority. Admittedly, there are times when our faith will be tested by those who ridicule us and say they don't believe in God. Yet by prayer and Scripture study, we can be better witnesses to the authority of Christ.

4. THE IMPORTANCE OF MAKING THE RIGHT CHOICE. All of us have options in life, even when it comes to the things of God. Because our eternal future is on the line, it is important that we make the right choice—indeed, the only real choice from the Lord's perspective. Encourage your students not only to receive Jesus by faith, but also to live for Him all the days of their life.

■ **TOPIC:** Seeking Reconciliation

■ **QUESTIONS:** 1. How did Paul describe the relationship between the Father and the Son? 2. What does it mean to say that the Lord Jesus is the *firstborn* (Col. 1:15, 18)? 3. How does reconciliation between God and the lost occur? 4. What did Paul tell his readers to *continue* (1:23) to do because they were reconciled to God through Christ? 5. Why is it important for us as believers to remain firm in our faith?

■ **ILLUSTRATIONS:**

Peace in Our Time? In 1938, the British Prime Minister Neville Chamberlain was hailed as bringing peace to Europe after signing a non-aggression pact with Nazi Germany. In the agreement, Adolf Hitler stated his desire never to go to war with Britain. Sadly, what appeared to be a diplomatic triumph for peace fueled Hitler's seemingly insatiable desire to seize more land. Indeed, within a year, the armies of the Third Reich invaded Poland and set off World War II. Scripture reveals that true and lasting peace can only be found through faith in Christ. Anything else is a fleeting and false substitute.

Message of Hope and Peace. Johann Sebastian Bach has struck a chord in Japan. The eighteenth-century German composer's music is conveying Christian teachings and concepts to a large and growing audience in the Asian nation, where less than one percent of the 127 million people belong to a Christian church, *First Things* magazine reported.

The nation's elite are drawn to the musical genius, and many have their first contact with Christianity through Bach's music. As many as 200 Bach choirs have started around the country in the past 10 years, and organist Masaaki Suzuki founded and conducts the Bach Collegium Japan.

Many Japanese have lost their allegiance to Buddhism and Shintoism and are attracted to the message of hope and peace they find in Bach's music. It is uncertain how many people actually have converted to Christianity.

Bridging the Gap. I once heard the story of a little girl whose parents were experiencing great difficulties in their marriage. All they seemed to have in common was their tremendous affection for their daughter Sally. One day Sally wandered into the street to play and was knocked down by a bus. While she was in a coma, she was rushed to the hospital, where physicians determined her injuries were too great to save her. Her parents hurried to the hospital, then stood helpless, watching her from either side of her bed.

Suddenly Sally's eyes opened, and she tried to smile. Then she took one arm from under the bedsheet and held it out toward her father. "Daddy," she said, "give me your hand." Turning toward her mother, Sally extended her other arm, and her mother grasped her other hand. With the daughter's last bit of strength, she drew those hands together as she died, trying one final time to bridge the gap between the two people she loved so much.

That story is a picture of the bridge Jesus built at Calvary as He extended the loving hand of God to the hand of sinful humanity. Calvary's bridge was costly to build, but without it the great gulf between God and us would never have been bridged.

<table>
<tr><td>■ FOR
■ YOUTH</td><td>■ TOPIC: Double Agent
■ QUESTIONS: 1. How is it possible for Jesus to be the firstborn over all creation? 2. In what sense do all things hold together in Christ? 3. Why</td></tr>
</table>

did Paul stress Christ's headship over the church? 4. Why is the work of the Son reconciling us to the Father important to know? 5. What difference has your faith in Christ had in your life?

■ ILLUSTRATIONS:

Secret Agent Man. In 1965, the spy series *Secret Agent* premiered. The lead character, John Drake, was a special security agent for Great Britain. His mission was to preserve world peace and create a better understanding among nations. Although he was not above punching someone silly, his trademark was to outsmart his opponents, not outshoot them.

Jesus, of course, never resorted to violence at any point during His earthly ministry. And unlike the John Drake character in the *Secret Agent* television series, the Messiah did not use morally questionable actions to bring peace between sinful people and the holy God. Instead, Jesus' death on the cross and resurrection from the dead enable the lost to be reconciled to the Lord by faith.

A Miracle from God. "Maybe 10 years ago, I heard a rumor about our pastor that could have threatened the life of the church if it had gone unaddressed," says Rick, a former member of his congregation's board of deacons. "I heard it from a friend, who had heard it from her boss. My friend said she'd get in trouble if her boss found out she'd told me. So I promised I'd keep her identity a secret. When the deacons next met, I told them the rumor, believing we would develop a response, and that would be that."

Instead, the pastor asked Rick where he had heard the rumor. "The pastor wanted to speak to the source directly. I agonized over my promise of confidentiality and the duty I owed the church. In the end, I decided that the only way healing could occur in our church would be for me to give him my friend's boss's name. Later, I called her and told her what I had done." Rick thought an apology would set things right. He was wrong. "Nothing was right after that. I'd done the unforgivable. It would have taken a miracle from God for us to be reconciled again."

Paul drew a similar conclusion about the terrible rift between humanity and God that was caused by sin. Nothing we can do can set things right and bridge that gap. It would take a miracle from God. The good news is that God agreed—and He sent His Son to die for our sake.

Saved by Grace. A Japanese gangster who became a Christian is converting other criminals. Hiroyuki Suzuki takes the Christian message to railway stations and public squares, using his notoriety to grab attention, according to the *Times of London*. He has numerous tattoos and several amputated fingers attesting to his previous allegiance to the *yakuza* organized crime organization.

Suzuki is the founder of Mission Barabbas, a group of reformed gangsters who have embraced evangelical Christianity. His ministry includes fervent preaching and singing. The *yakuza*, in contrast, includes 80,000 gang members involved in extortion rackets, prostitution, and gambling, and bloody shoot-outs on the streets are frequent.

Christianity is considered a mysterious sect by most Japanese, and only 1.5 percent of the population is Christian. But Suzuki's church in Tokyo overflows on Sundays and attracts converts by targeting his former colleagues and apprentice hoodlums. In four years, he has baptized seven members of crime syndicates and persuaded them to leave the underworld.

Suzuki dates his conversion to a point when he was deep in debt, taking drugs, and plagued by illness. He put a gun to his temple but didn't have the nerve to pull the trigger. His estranged wife had been an ardent churchgoer and, out of desperation, he sought refuge in a church.

"I told the minister I was a gangster who had done time, deserted my wife and child, and was beyond redemption. But the minister talked to me about God's love and the meaning of the cross," Suzuki told the *Times*. He returned to his family and was accepted immediately. "That made me believe in the existence of unconditional love and the fact that people can start over again."

WHAT GOD SAYS ABOUT JESUS

BACKGROUND SCRIPTURE: Hebrews 1
DEVOTIONAL READING: Luke 1:46-55

2

KEY VERSES: God, who at sundry times and in divers manners spake in time past unto the fathers by the prophets, hath in these last days spoken unto us by his Son. Hebrews 1:1-2.

KING JAMES VERSION

HEBREWS 1:1 God, who at sundry times and in divers manners spake in time past unto the fathers by the prophets, 2 Hath in these last days spoken unto us by his Son, whom he hath appointed heir of all things, by whom also he made the worlds; 3 Who being the brightness of his glory, and the express image of his person, and upholding all things by the word of his power, when he had by himself purged our sins, sat down on the right hand of the Majesty on high;

4 Being made so much better than the angels, as he hath by inheritance obtained a more excellent name than they. 5 For unto which of the angels said he at any time, Thou art my Son, this day have I begotten thee? And again, I will be to him a Father, and he shall be to me a Son? 6 And again, when he bringeth in the firstbegotten into the world, he saith, And let all the angels of God worship him. 7 And of the angels he saith, Who maketh his angels spirits, and his ministers a flame of fire. 8 But unto the Son he saith, Thy throne, O God, is for ever and ever: a sceptre of righteousness is the sceptre of thy kingdom. 9 Thou hast loved righteousness, and hated iniquity; therefore God, even thy God, hath anointed thee with the oil of gladness above thy fellows.

NEW REVISED STANDARD VERSION

HEBREWS 1:1 Long ago God spoke to our ancestors in many and various ways by the prophets, 2 but in these last days he has spoken to us by a Son, whom he appointed heir of all things, through whom he also created the worlds. 3 He is the reflection of God's glory and the exact imprint of God's very being, and he sustains all things by his powerful word. When he had made purification for sins, he sat down at the right hand of the Majesty on high, 4 having become as much superior to angels as the name he has inherited is more excellent than theirs.

5 For to which of the angels did God ever say,
"You are my Son;
    today I have begotten you"?
Or again,
"I will be his Father,
    and he will be my Son"?
6 And again, when he brings the firstborn into the world, he says,
"Let all God's angels worship him."
7 Of the angels he says,
"He makes his angels winds,
    and his servants flames of fire."
8 But of the Son he says,
"Your throne, O God, is forever and ever,
    and the righteous scepter is the scepter of your
        kingdom.
9   You have loved righteousness and hated wickedness;
    therefore God, your God, has anointed you
        with the oil of gladness beyond your companions."

BACKGROUND

Although this book is usually called "The Letter to the Hebrews," it does not read much like an epistle. Rather than a letter, we might more aptly call Hebrews "a published sermon." Most ancient letters, such as the epistles Paul wrote, began by identifying both their writers and recipients. However, the author of Hebrews did not follow that pattern. The unknown writer jumped immediately into his topic. Also, Hebrews contains few references to its readers. We may continue the tradition of calling it a letter, but it reads more like a sermon.

We have quickly alluded to a puzzling question—"Who wrote Hebrews?" Regrettably, no one knows. It might have been Paul, Apollos, Barnabas, or someone else. Thankfully, our uncertainty regarding the book's author does not dramatically affect its interpretation. The opening verses of Hebrews, as well as the epistle as a whole, are packed solid with quotations from and allusions to the Old Testament. This fact, at least indirectly, gave Hebrews its title. You can easily follow the logic behind this conclusion. The letter contains much Old Testament material. Therefore, the writer must have assumed this type of content would strongly influence his readers. Also, the readers must have been people who knew and valued the Old Testament. Therefore, the readers were likely Jews, or "Hebrews," as they are sometimes called.

Through roughly the first two-thirds of the epistle, the writer made his point—that God's people should worship Jesus, their Savior—by means of contrasts. Within these contrasts, the writer repeatedly pointed out that Jesus is superior to any other entity. In the first chapter, the author laid out two such contrasts: God's revelation in Jesus surpasses what we read in the Old Testament (1:1-3). Likewise, the stature of Jesus Himself is higher than the position angels hold (1:4—2:4).

A further survey of Hebrews brings to light similar contrasts. The content within these contrasts offers further support to the idea that this epistle was written for Jews, more specifically Jewish Christians. Each of the contrasts highlights Jesus' superiority to some person or system the Jews valued (for example, the Old Testament itself, Moses, or the temple sacrificial system). By means of these contrasts, the writer sought to prevent Jewish Christians from forsaking Jesus to return to traditional Jewish ways. The writer of Hebrews finished this first section of the book with strong words of warning: *and every transgression or disobedience [of the law] received a just recompence of reward; How shall we escape, if we neglect so great salvation* (2:2-3). You can find similar warning passages in 3:7—4:13; 5:11—6:12; 10:19-39; and 12:14-29.

What factors necessitated these warnings? Evidently readers of this book were facing persecution (see 10:32-34). Jewish Christians might have been caught in a ferocious middle ground, receiving painful exclusion, both from pagans and from non-Christian Jews. A retreat into the relative safety of Judaism might have tempted some Hebrew believers. And so the writer began this letter by reminding these Christians why they came to Jesus in the first place. The Son, the reflection of God's glory (1:3), offers a far better way.

NOTES ON THE PRINTED TEXT

The Letter to the Hebrews is directed to Christians who had faced adverse circumstances and challenges to their faith. The letter sought to strengthen believers to live wholeheartedly for Christ. Whoever penned the epistle had a keen command of Greek and a razor-sharp intellect. The author of Hebrews set his course in chapter 1 by testifying to the supremacy of Jesus Christ over all things.

Because the author was writing to an audience with decidedly Jewish roots, he set his letter against the backdrop of Jewish history. Notice the opening contrast: God speaking to the ancestors of the Jews versus God speaking to us through His Son. Long ago God's prophets declared His message in many ways and at various times (Heb. 1:1). Though their proclamations were incomplete and fragmentary, they nevertheless were inspired and authoritative. God's revelation during the period of the Old Testament closed with the last chapter of Malachi. Indeed, the prophets served God's purposes well, but at best they were His servants for a particular and limited period of time. By way of contrast, Jesus—the founder of Christianity—is far superior to the prophets of Judaism.

The writer declared that God has gone beyond the fragmentary revelation of the past to give a complete and fully adequate revelation of His Son (1:2). In particular, the writer made several statements that confirm the superiority of Christ over the prophets. Not one of these statements could be attached to even the most renowned Old Testament personality. *In these last days* refers to the messianic age, which began with the first advent of Christ. The Father sent His Son to bring His saving message to us. Jesus' superiority over the prophets is underscored by the fact that God created the universe through Him. In fact, Christ will one day inherit all things.

The Greek word translated *brightness* (1:3) can refer to radiance shining forth from an object or reflecting off an object. Either nuance is applicable to Christ, who both radiates and reflects the majesty of God. The term rendered *express image* originally referred to the die used in minting coins. The word later came to refer to the impression on coins. The writer of Hebrews was saying that Christ bears the impress of

God's nature; in other words, the Lord Jesus is the perfect revelation of the Father's will and glory.

Furthermore, the Son sustains the universe by His mighty word. The idea is not of some superhuman creature (such as the Greek god Atlas) holding up the world; rather, it is of Christ maintaining the existence of the universe and bearing it along to its God-ordained conclusion. Moreover, Christ is the one who died on the cross to atone for humankind's misdeeds. His high priestly act makes it possible for God to spiritually cleanse and forgive the believing sinner. Of course, Jesus did not remain in the grave. God raised Him from the dead and exalted Him to His right hand, the place of supreme honor. The fact that Christ is sitting down indicates His redemptive work is completed. Also, He is ministering in the true heavenly sanctuary, not an earthly copy of it. Finally, Jesus is reigning with the Father as the Lord of the universe.

In ancient times many Jews revered angels because they were supernatural creatures and because they mediated God's law at Sinai (Acts 7:38, 53). The Jews also regarded the law as God's unparalleled revelation. Admittedly, the angels of God are glorious beings, powerful, wise, and exalted; however, when all is said, they are still the servants of the Lord. In contrast, through Jesus' resurrection from the dead, the Father declared Him to be *the Son of God* (Rom. 1:4). In fact, Jesus has inherited a name—*Son*—which is far superior to any name borne by God's angels. Hebrews 1:4 could also be saying that the character and personality of the exalted Son, which is reflected in His name, is superior to that of any angel.

Christ as the Son of God is greater than the angels (1:5). The writer substantiated this truth by first quoting from Psalm 2:7. In that passage the Father declared that the anointed one was His Son. The Israelites evidently applied this verse to the descendants of David whom they coronated as king. The verse's ultimate reference, however, is to Christ. This is made clear in Acts 13:33. When God raised Jesus from the dead, He conferred great dignity on Him by declaring Him to be His Son. No angel could claim this honor.

The writer also quoted from 2 Samuel 7:14 (which is parallel to 1 Chron. 17:13). The Lord told David that He would relate to the descendants on his throne (for example, Solomon) as a father would to a son. This familial bond finds its ultimate expression in the relationship between God and Christ. The Father chose His Son to rule on His throne and serve as His official representative. No angel could claim such a relationship. In Hebrews 1:6 the quotation is doubtless from the Septuagint rendering of Deuteronomy 32:43. Angels are said to worship the Son in that day yet future, and this fact is proof of His superiority over them.

In Hebrews 1:7, the writer quoted from the Septuagint version of Psalm 104:4. This verse refers to angels as *spirits*, which reminds us that angels are created beings. God brought them into existence as His servants to carry out His will. Christ, however, is the eternal Son of God and Creator, truths that are made clear in Hebrews 1:10-12. In

1:8-9 there is a quotation from Psalm 45:6-7. Here we find one of the Bible's strongest affirmations of the deity of Christ. In these verses, the Son is addressed as God; and His royal status is alluded to in the words *throne*, *sceptre*, and *kingdom*.

As the Father's representative and co-regent, the Son rules over all creation forever. His scepter symbolizes His regal authority, which is characterized by justice and equity. Because these virtues are the basis of His unending rule, He enjoys an infinitely exalted status as King. Also, like the Father, the Son loves righteousness and hates wickedness. Because of these characteristics, the Father set His Son above everything, and anointed Him to carry out the most sacred function of all time—to bring people to salvation.

SUGGESTIONS TO TEACHERS

As the writer to the Hebrews opened his letter, he must have been thinking that the most alluring temptations his readers faced did not involve obvious evils such as murder or adultery. Instead, they were tempted to overvalue the good (such as Old Testament and angels) by elevating them to the level of the perfect (namely, God's Son). Christians today face similar temptations. Encourage your students to see the truth of the following statements.

1. ALL GOD'S GIFTS ARE VALUABLE. Just as the writer to the Hebrews valued the divine gifts of the Old Testament and the angels, so God's people today can appropriately enjoy all the good gifts God has given us. When God looked down on the world He had just made, He called it all very good.

2. BUT GOD'S GREATEST GIFT IS HIMSELF. God has given His people gifts such as natural beauty, the Scriptures, family and friends, and churches, but none of them can compare with His greatest gift—God Himself coming to earth in the form of His Son, Jesus Christ.

3. ALONG WITH HIS GIFTS, GOD GIVES A WARNING. God instructs His people to worship Him, the Giver. They become guilty of idolatry when any of even God's best gifts takes first priority in their lives.

4. WE CAN ENJOY GOD AND HIS GIFTS. The writer wanted his readers to avoid worshiping the Old Testament and the angels. He thus instructed them to obey the teaching of the Old Testament and follow the example of the angels in worshiping the one true God (Father, Son, and Holy Spirit), the giver of all good gifts. The writer knew that, when God's people worship Him alone, they can best enjoy both God and all His many gifts.

FOR ADULTS

■ **TOPIC:** Learning about God
■ **QUESTIONS:** 1. In what sense is the Son the complete and final revelation of the Father? 2. What did the writer of Hebrews mean when he

declared Jesus to be the radiance of God's glory? 3. In what ways is the Son's superior status to angels emphasized? 4. Why does Jesus merit the worship of angels? 5. What are some ways we can worship the Son, both individually and corporately?

■ ILLUSTRATIONS:

God with Skin On. The little girl's voice echoed across the hallway to the master bedroom. "Daddy, I'm scared!" The father tried his best to focus his thoughts. "Honey, don't be afraid. Daddy's right across the hall."

After a brief pause the girl said, "I'm still scared." Theologically astute, the father replied, "You don't need to be afraid. God is with you. God loves you." After a longer pause, the girl said in a quivering voice, "Daddy, I want someone with skin on." Jesus, the Son, "put skin" on the glory and the character of God the Father so that He might reveal Him to us.

Getting to Know You. For three decades, Don Kroodsma has studied the songs of birds. In fact, he is considered an expert on the biology of bird vocal behavior. It's no wonder, then, that in 2005 he wrote a book about the art and science of birdsong: *The Singing Life of Birds.*

Kroodsma is no ordinary researcher, either. To learn as much as possible about his subject, he tours the North American continent on his bicycle. In 2003, he pedaled completely across the U.S. And in 2004, he biked his way from the Atlantic shore to the Mississippi. In each case, he lugged his recording equipment with him.

Such dedication reflects the sort of attitude believers should have about their relationship with God. As the author of Hebrews explained, they learn about the Father by getting to know the Son. Indeed, becoming more knowledgeable of Christ should be their lifelong desire.

Unusual Gifts Used for God. The opening paragraph of Hebrews offered its readers a wonderful example of using the Greek language with great stylistic effect. We don't know who wrote this epistle, but we do know that he must have been a highly educated person. When the writer became a Christian, God did not ask him to leave his education and talents behind. Instead, God called him to use his thinking and writing abilities for the glory of God and the growth of the church. Perhaps you know people who offer their skills and experience to God for His use.

Joy piloted a casino boat in Baton Rouge, Louisiana, before she heard God's call on her life. Today she gives her time ministering to riverboat captains and crews. Joy knows what it's like to spend entire months away on the river. From her experience, she can minister empathetically to others who face that situation.

Barb was a computer web genius. She now gives half her time to building and maintaining a Christian website. Her site offers all kinds of information enabling Christians to minister better to nearby people of other ethnic groups.

Drifting Away. Several years before James met his future wife, Kathy, she helped lead a church youth group. One youth group trip took several leaders and teens to Atlanta. While there, everyone spent an afternoon at Stone Mountain Lake. Kathy had never sailed before but decided she would take this opportunity. She pooled money with one of the kids named Harold and rented a small sailboat. The owner gave instructions he thought were adequate.

Looking back, across many years, Kathy insists that the boat had problems and that the owner had no right to rent them a defective sailboat. Perhaps the problem lay with the boaters rather than the boat. The answer probably will never be known!

In any case, you have already figured out what happened. Out on the lake, a good breeze was blowing, but not taking Kathy in the direction she wanted. Can you imagine how the rest of the group must have laughed as they watched Kathy and Harold being towed back to shore? They had no intention of drifting away, but that's what they had done. Hebrews 2:1 exhorts us to pay greater attention to the good news about Christ, so that we do not drift away from Him, our wonderful Savior.

| **FOR YOUTH** | ■ **TOPIC:** Jesus: The Reflection of God
■ **QUESTIONS:** 1. Why did God choose to reveal Himself in progressive stages? |

sive stages? 2. Why is the Father's message through His Son clearer than His message was in Old Testament times? 3. Why did the writer of Hebrews emphasize Christ's superiority over angels? 4. Why did the writer of Hebrews quote from the Old Testament to prove the superiority of Jesus? 5. What do you think is the most compelling reason to worship Jesus?

■ **ILLUSTRATIONS:**

The Brilliant Light. Some of you have been blessed enough to observe a complete solar eclipse. During these events, the moon passes directly between the earth and the sun, blocking the sun's light. But even under these unusual circumstances, wise friends warned you not to look directly at the sun. Why? The sun still shines so brightly that even when its rays are blocked, you can be blinded by its radiance. Through the middle part of each typical sunny day, our eyes cannot distinguish the sun from its brilliance. In a similar way, we cannot separate God the Father and God the Son. Hebrews 1:3 reminds us that Jesus shines with the same brilliance of His Father.

Even Losers Have Great Value. During the 2001 season, the Seattle Mariners baseball team did not win the World Series. In fact, they did not even play in the World Series. The New York Yankees had already defeated the Mariners in the American League Championship Series. When it really counted, the Mariners did not win their last few big games. But all baseball fans recognized that the Mariners still had a great team. In fact, the 2001 Mariners won more regular season games than any team had won in several decades. One of their players, Ichiro Suzuki, won the league batting title, Rookie of the Year, and Most Valuable Player awards. And many feel that Ichiro was not even the most significant player on the team! In the end, the Mariners did not win. At least in the playoffs, they were not the best team. But, over the season, they still played very well.

The writer to the Hebrews wanted his readers to see Jesus as the ultimate winner. In value, He surpassed the Old Testament and the angels. Even so, when this writer came to chapter 11, his "Hall of Faith," he pointed out the value of the great examples from the Old Testament. Wise Christians do not neglect the Old Testament, for it offers great teaching to us all.

Twins. We have since moved across the country, but when we resided in the Midwest, we lived near Jack and Mary. They had three young children: Hannah, Helen, and Mark. I could easily distinguish Mark, for he was a boy and a bit smaller than his sisters. But the two girls were identical twins. Maybe I should have tried harder, but I never could tell the two of them apart. I miss this family, but we recently heard news that would have made living next to them even more confusing. Mary is expecting another set of twins!

You may have had similar problems with distinguishing twins you know. Even if you are not a twin, you may look similar enough to one of your siblings that other people confuse the two of you.

The first readers of Hebrews were forgetting who Jesus was. Some of them somehow thought angels more impressive than Jesus Himself. But when the writer of this letter called Jesus the exact imprint of God's very being (1:3), he helped them see that the Father and the Son are more alike than even identical twins could be.

LIGHT THAT CONQUERS

BACKGROUND SCRIPTURE: 1 John 1:1—2:6
DEVOTIONAL READING: Ephesians 5:8-14

KEY VERSE: This then is the message which we have heard of him, and declare unto you, that God is light, and in him is no darkness at all. 1 John 1:5.

3

KING JAMES VERSION

1 JOHN 1:1 That which was from the beginning, which we have heard, which we have seen with our eyes, which we have looked upon, and our hands have handled, of the Word of life; 2 (For the life was manifested, and we have seen it, and bear witness, and shew unto you that eternal life, which was with the Father, and was manifested unto us;) 3 That which we have seen and heard declare we unto you, that ye also may have fellowship with us: and truly our fellowship is with the Father, and with his Son Jesus Christ. 4 And these things write we unto you, that your joy may be full.

5 This then is the message which we have heard of him, and declare unto you, that God is light, and in him is no darkness at all. 6 If we say that we have fellowship with him, and walk in darkness, we lie, and do not the truth: 7 But if we walk in the light, as he is in the light, we have fellowship one with another, and the blood of Jesus Christ his Son cleanseth us from all sin. 8 If we say that we have no sin, we deceive ourselves, and the truth is not in us. 9 If we confess our sins, he is faithful and just to forgive us our sins, and to cleanse us from all unrighteousness. 10 If we say that we have not sinned, we make him a liar, and his word is not in us.

2:1 My little children, these things write I unto you, that ye sin not. And if any man sin, we have an advocate with the Father, Jesus Christ the righteous: 2 And he is the propitiation for our sins: and not for ours only, but also for the sins of the whole world.

3 And hereby we do know that we know him, if we keep his commandments. 4 He that saith, I know him, and keepeth not his commandments, is a liar, and the truth is not in him. 5 But whoso keepeth his word, in him verily is the love of God perfected.

NEW REVISED STANDARD VERSION

1 JOHN 1:1 We declare to you what was from the beginning, what we have heard, what we have seen with our eyes, what we have looked at and touched with our hands, concerning the word of life— 2 this life was revealed, and we have seen it and testify to it, and declare to you the eternal life that was with the Father and was revealed to us— 3 we declare to you what we have seen and heard so that you also may have fellowship with us; and truly our fellowship is with the Father and with his Son Jesus Christ. 4 We are writing these things so that our joy may be complete.

5 This is the message we have heard from him and proclaim to you, that God is light and in him there is no darkness at all. 6 If we say that we have fellowship with him while we are walking in darkness, we lie and do not do what is true; 7 but if we walk in the light as he himself is in the light, we have fellowship with one another, and the blood of Jesus his Son cleanses us from all sin. 8 If we say that we have no sin, we deceive ourselves, and the truth is not in us. 9 If we confess our sins, he who is faithful and just will forgive us our sins and cleanse us from all unrighteousness. 10 If we say that we have not sinned, we make him a liar, and his word is not in us.

2:1 My little children, I am writing these things to you so that you may not sin. But if anyone does sin, we have an advocate with the Father, Jesus Christ the righteous; 2 and he is the atoning sacrifice for our sins, and not for ours only but also for the sins of the whole world.

3 Now by this we may be sure that we know him, if we obey his commandments. 4 Whoever says, "I have come to know him," but does not obey his commandments, is a liar, and in such a person the truth does not exist; 5 but whoever obeys his word, truly in this person the love of God has reached perfection.

Monday, December 11	Matthew 1:18-25	*An Angel Speaks to Joseph*
Tuesday, December 12	2 Peter 1:16-21	*Eyewitnesses of God's Majesty*
Wednesday, December 13	2 Corinthians 4:1-6	*We Preach Jesus Christ*
Thursday, December 14	Ephesians 5:8-14	*Live as Children of Light*
Friday, December 15	1 John 1:1-4	*Jesus Is the Word of Life*
Saturday, December 16	1 John 1:5-10	*Walk in the Light*
Sunday, December 17	1 John 2:1-6	*Following Jesus*

BACKGROUND

The fourth Gospel, the Book of Revelation, and 1, 2, and 3 John are the five New Testament documents attributed to the apostle John. Knowledge and use of 1 John is attested from an early date, while 2 and 3 John were accepted as Scripture more slowly. The Johannine character of the three epistles is universally recognized, and their authorship after the fourth Gospel seems likely. For example, 1 John 1:1-5 seems to imitate John 1:1-18. The argumentative tone against the Jewish leaders that pervades much of the Gospel does not appear in the letters. Their concern was with difficulties within the Christian community.

Whereas the fourth Gospel was written to bring people to faith in the Messiah (John 20:30-31), 1 John insists that people must confess that Christ has come in the flesh (4:2). Second John 7 likewise identified as deceivers those who did not confess the incarnation of the Messiah. The letters therefore are concerned with correcting a false belief about Christ that was spreading in the churches. From this emphasis on the Incarnation, it can be assumed that the opponents held to the divinity of Christ but either denied or diminished the significance of His humanity. Their view might be an early form of Docetism (from the Greek verb *dokeo*, which means "to seem"), the heresy which emerged in the second century and which claimed that Jesus only seemed to be human. According to early church tradition, another form of heresy that John might have attacked was led by a man named Cerinthus. He contended that Christ's spirit descended on the human Jesus at His baptism but left Him before His crucifixion. John wrote that the Jesus who was baptized at the beginning of His ministry was the same person who was crucified on the cross (1 John 5:6).

The Johannine letters, therefore, provide us with a window on an early Christian church, its problems, and its developing doctrine. First John seems to be a treatise written to the Christian community where the apostle ministered. In contrast, 2 and 3 John are much briefer, about the length of a single sheet of papyrus, and they follow the conventional form of a personal letter.

Though some have argued that 1 John was written before the destruction of Jerusalem in A.D. 70, a later first-century date allows for the appearance of ideas that subsequently developed into Gnosticism, ideas that John was probably addressing in this letter. On the other hand, the epistle could not have been written later than the end of the first century, when John died. Also, the evidence of early second-century writers who knew about the letter and quoted from it demonstrates that it was penned prior to them. Thus, 1 John was written between A.D. 85 and 95, which means it postdates the fourth Gospel but predates the Book of Revelation. The tone of 1 John and especially the attitude of the apostle toward the readers suggest that he was an older person addressing a younger generation. Early church tradition says that John was living in Ephesus and writing to the churches in Asia Minor. John's letters to the congregations in the province of Asia substantiates this (see Rev. 2—3).

NOTES ON THE PRINTED TEXT

Unlike most New Testament epistles, John's first letter does not begin with a salutation and has no benediction at the end; instead, it opens with a four-verse prologue and concludes with a warning. On the basis of verifiable evidence, John established the physical reality of the Messiah's incarnation. With the Incarnation as John's foundation, his first stated objective for the letter was to cultivate fellowship between his readers and the apostles as well as between his readers and God. If this goal was accomplished, he would achieve his second objective: fulfilled joy.

First John was written primarily to combat the emerging heresy of Gnosticism, which was influencing the churches in John's day. John's pre-Gnostic opponents denied that Jesus was the Son of God who had come in the flesh. To an extent, they denied their own sinfulness and that righteous conduct was necessary to remain in good standing within the church. Apparently, the proponents of these views had once been a part of the established church in Asia Minor, but at some time made a distinct break from this fellowship (see 2:18-19). Members of this subversive group were attempting to lure the faithful away from the apostles' authoritative teachings. For this reason, John wanted to make it clear that these people were false teachers.

To accomplish his goal, the apostle began his epistle by pointing his readers to the reality of Christ's incarnation. Echoing John 1:1, the writer declared that he and others had physically encountered the incarnate Messiah (1 John 1:1). He who existed from the beginning is the same person the disciples had heard, seen, and touched. He is none other than the living Word. As John reflected on the day when the divine Word became a human being (see John 1:14), the apostle undoubtedly rejoiced. He and others had the privilege of spending time with the one who is eternal life (1 John 1:2). These disciples in turn sensed it was their calling in life to proclaim the truth about the Messiah to others. In particular, they declared that a restored relationship with God was possible through faith in the Son.

John's consistent testimony is that the Son was eternally present with the Father (and the Spirit), came from heaven to live on earth as a man, and during that time manifested His presence. The apostle bore witness to these truths so that others might come to believe and enjoy fellowship with other Christians. John explained that the basis for this was the fellowship believers had with God the Father and His Son, Jesus Christ (1:3). Thus, fellowship is the basis of spiritual joy (1:4). Both the readers' joy and that of the apostles depended on it. If John's goal of keeping these believers in fellowship with God and the apostles was realized, then his joy and that of the other apostles would reach full maturity.

False teachers had already begun to filter into the early church by the time John wrote his epistle. Some of the frauds taught that it did not matter how a person behaved as long as the person had a "spiritual" relationship with God. That contradicted what Christ taught His apostles. Jesus revealed God as *light* (1:5), namely, someone pure, holy, and totally free from sin. How could a person have fellowship with such a holy God and yet walk in darkness (1:6)? Those who claimed to have fellowship with the Lord but continued to practice sin deceived themselves. They were not truly walking with God.

In contrast, those who enjoyed genuine fellowship with the Lord walked in the light (1:7). This did not mean they were perfect or never sinned. They let the light expose sin in their lives, and they responded by turning away from sin. Those who walked in the light had fellowship with God—through the confessing and cleansing of their sins—and with other believers. John knew about false teachers who claimed they had no tendency to sin. The apostle declared they were self-deceived and did not abide in the truth of God's Word (1:8). Others asserted they never sinned. Because this contradicted what God had revealed in His Word, they made Him a liar and showed His message of truth was not in their hearts (1:10).

The proper response is to admit our tendency to sin and confess our misdeeds to God. *Confess* (1:9) means to "say the same thing," or adopt God's attitude toward the sin. Once believers forsake their wrongdoing, the Lord forgives them and cleanses them from the stain that transgression has left in their lives. God can always be trusted to pardon our sins. After all, His forgiveness is based on His justice, not on His indulgence or tolerance of sin. In turn, the basis for His justice is the sacrifice of Christ on the cross (Rom. 3:25-26).

It was John's desire that his beloved readers not transgress God's commands; but the apostle realized that on occasion all believers sin. In those moments when a moral lapse occurs, believers can look to Jesus as their divine advocate. Because He is righteous, He can represent them before the Father (1 John 2:1). As our defense attorney (in a manner of speaking), Jesus does not try to prove we are innocent; instead, He confesses our guilt for us and points to the Cross as sufficient atonement for our sins. In fact, His sacrifice was made available, not just for believers, but also for *the sins of the whole world* (2:2).

This does not mean that everyone will eventually be saved, for Scripture makes it clear that some will decisively reject the salvation that God offers (see 1 Pet. 2:7-8).

Nonetheless, Christ's offering was sufficient to cover the sins of the world, and it makes the gift of salvation available to anyone willing to receive it with a broken spirit. Living in obedience to Scripture is the proper response to God's mercy. Indeed, this is a sure indicator that we truly know the Father in a saving way (1 John 2:3). In contrast, those who revel in violating God's Word do not know Him. Despite their claims to the contrary, they are liars and devoid of the truth (2:4).

To truly know God, then, is to obey Him. As well, such upright individuals genuinely love the Lord and are assured they belong to Him (2:5). They abide in Him and the eternal life He provides through faith in Christ. God's love is perfected in the sense that the obedient believer experiences a fuller, richer expression of His love. All believers enjoy God's saving love, but obedience carries the divine love to a deeper level. This in turn enables them to love their fellow believers.

SUGGESTIONS TO TEACHERS

We learn from 1 John that a genuine relationship with God will make a difference in how a person lives. In fact, the apostle outlined for his readers what a person with a genuine relationship would be like. These identifying markers include living uprightly, obeying the Lord, and loving other believers. Plan to take a few moments to consider each of these with your students.

1. WALKING IN RIGHTEOUSNESS. This is the first of several marks of a genuine relationship with God. Broadly speaking, to walk in righteousness means to live uprightly. If we want to be followers of the Lord Jesus, we must be willing to live in a virtuous manner. That implies changing any attitude or action not in keeping with the example Christ set for us.

2. OBEYING THE LORD. Another mark of believers should be their obedience to God. If you became aware that someone had been pretending to be your friend because that person felt obligated to or was just trying to look good in front of others, the "friendship" would be meaningless. We must not have that kind of relationship with God, one propped up by legalistically obeying His commands. Our obedience, like Christ's, should come from our love for God, not from just doing what He says we should do. Then others will notice the joy we have in our relationship with Him.

3. LOVING OTHER BELIEVERS. This is a third identifying mark. Jesus stressed it in John 13:35, and showing love is a corresponding emphasis throughout 1 John. When believers demonstrate sacrificial, not self-seeking, love toward each other, they stand out in our "me-first" world. Their priority becomes giving instead of taking. They are encouraging to each other instead of berating. That kind of love should show others the depth of our relationship with God.

4. ASSESSING OURSELVES. We should ask ourselves if areas of our lives need to change to better reflect a genuine, vibrant relationship with the Lord. How is our love for fellow believers? Are we living uprightly? Do we heed the teachings of

Scripture? The answers to these questions aren't meant to condemn us, but to encourage us to press on in truth, obedience, and love.

| FOR ADULTS | ▪ **TOPIC:** Walking in the Light
▪ **QUESTIONS:** 1. What results when believers walk in the light? 2. Why are we self-deceived if we claim to be without sin? 3. In what sense is |

Jesus the atoning sacrifice for our sins? 4. Why did John equate knowing God with obeying His commands? 5. What changes would it mean in our lifestyle to live as Jesus lived, in righteousness?

▪ **ILLUSTRATIONS:**

The Invention of the Electric Light. In 1800, an English scientist named Humphry Davy created an electric battery. When he connected wires to his battery and a piece of carbon, the carbon glowed, producing light. Later, in 1860, the English physicist Sir Joseph Wilson Swan discovered that a carbon paper filament worked well, though it tended to burn up quickly. By 1877, an American named Charles Francis Brush manufactured some carbon arcs to light a public square in Cleveland, Ohio.

Around this time, the inventor Thomas Edison began experimenting with thousands of different filaments to find just the right materials to glow well and be long-lasting. Then in 1879, he discovered that a carbon filament in an oxygen-free bulb glowed but did not burn up for 40 hours. Edison eventually produced a bulb that could glow for over 1500 hours.

Undisputedly, the invention of the electric light has improved the lives of countless people around the globe. Indeed, imagine what life would be like without these marvels of technology! From a spiritual standpoint, existence would be immensely darker without the light of Christ to shine in our lives.

Death Leads to Change. On June 12, 1963, civil rights leader Medgar Evers was shot dead in the driveway of his Mississippi home. The assassination made Evers the first in a line of civil rights leaders to be cut down in the 1960s, and his murder prompted President Kennedy to ask Congress for a civil rights bill, which was signed into law by President Johnson the next year.

It took considerable pain, suffering, and loss for the light of freedom to shine brightly on underprivileged minority groups in the U.S. Similarly, the Lord Jesus had to endure the humiliation of the Cross for the light of His salvation to become a reality in our lives. We honor His redemptive work on our behalf by trusting and obeying Him.

A Beacon of Hope. In *A Pause To Ponder God's Word*, Gerald Whetstone relates that while growing up, his family "lived about a mile or so from the most photographed lighthouse in the United States, Portland Headlight, in Cape Elizabeth, Maine." In addition, Whetstone notes that this structure is "one of a series of lighthouses that guide ships into Portland harbor."

According to the author, "the lights from these beacons do more than flash a warning. They actually work together to create a stream of light down the channel for ships to follow." Whetstone also points out that "just as ships must stay in the stream of light created by those lighthouses, we must walk in the light that God gives." Jesus is that Light, an eternal beacon of hope and help to any believer in time of need.

FOR YOUTH

■ **TOPIC:** Jesus: The Light of the World

■ **QUESTIONS:** 1. In what sense had John and others seen, heard, and touched the Word of life? 2. Why did John want his readers to enjoy fellowship with the Father and the Son? 3. How does walking in darkness prevent us from fellowshipping with God? 4. Why does God want us to confess our sins to Him? 5. What does Jesus Christ, the righteous one, do on our behalf?

■ **ILLUSTRATIONS:**

Living in the Messiah's Light. This week's lesson focuses on the call to live a life that clearly reflects the Savior. Consider a teacher named LouAnn. She had just buried her father when a car crash killed one of her high-school students. The adolescent's death shocked classmates and staff. "I cried so much at his funeral," LouAnn said. "It was so empty. Neither the boy nor his family had any faith at all."

LouAnn was recruited to help counsel grieving students. Although she was still hurting, she knew her faith in God was strong enough to bring her through. She also wanted to share her eternal hope with those she counseled.

A coworker noticed the care LouAnn took with each student and asked, "Are you a Christian? I could tell by the way you talked about death." Others had encouraged students to voice their questions, but LouAnn pointed students to the One with the answers. By remaining true to her faith, she touched many lives at a crucial time of need.

A Key Performance. In June 2005, concert pianist Kit Armstrong performed Beethoven's first piano concerto with the Baltimore Symphony Orchestra. So reported correspondent Liane Hansen of National Public Radio's *Weekend Edition*. She noted that Armstrong's mature talent contrasts sharply with his diminutive stage presence. As an adolescent, he's young enough to play with the grandchildren of many members of the Baltimore Symphony. But he more than holds his own with the veteran musicians.

Perhaps at times you might wonder if you will do anything important with your life.

You may not become a concert pianist. But from an eternal perspective there are all sorts of ways you can impact your generation, especially when you walk in the light of the Lord Jesus. This means allowing His truth and love to be present in all that you think, say, and do.

Look What You Got! Making decisions in the dark can lead to some regrettable consequences. Back in the days before electricity, a tightfisted old farmer was taking his hired man to task for carrying a lighted lantern when he went to call on his best girl. "Why," he exclaimed, "when I went a-courtin' I never carried one of them things. I always went in the dark." "Yes," the hired man said wryly, "and look what you got!"

When it comes to the things of God, believers of all ages must abide in Christ, the light of the world. He is like a lamp for our feet and a light for our path (see Ps. 119:105).

THE WORD BECAME FLESH

BACKGROUND SCRIPTURE: John 1:1-34
DEVOTIONAL READING: Isaiah 53:1-6

KEY VERSE: The Word was made flesh, and dwelt among us, (and we beheld his glory, the glory as of the only begotten of the Father,) full of grace and truth. John 1:14.

KING JAMES VERSION

JOHN 1:1 In the beginning was the Word, and the Word was with God, and the Word was God. 2 The same was in the beginning with God. 3 All things were made by him; and without him was not any thing made that was made. 4 In him was life; and the life was the light of men.

5 And the light shineth in darkness; and the darkness comprehended it not. 6 There was a man sent from God, whose name was John. 7 The same came for a witness, to bear witness of the Light, that all men through him might believe. 8 He was not that Light, but was sent to bear witness of that Light. 9 That was the true Light, which lighteth every man that cometh into the world. 10 He was in the world, and the world was made by him, and the world knew him not. 11 He came unto his own, and his own received him not. 12 But as many as received him, to them gave he power to become the sons of God, even to them that believe on his name: 13 Which were born, not of blood, nor of the will of the flesh, nor of the will of man, but of God. 14 And the Word was made flesh, and dwelt among us, (and we beheld his glory, the glory as of the only begotten of the Father,) full of grace and truth.

15 John bare witness of him, and cried, saying, This was he of whom I spake, He that cometh after me is preferred before me: for he was before me. 16 And of his fulness have all we received, and grace for grace. 17 For the law was given by Moses, but grace and truth came by Jesus Christ. 18 No man hath seen God at any time; the only begotten Son, which is in the bosom of the Father, he hath declared him.

NEW REVISED STANDARD VERSION

JOHN 1:1 In the beginning was the Word, and the Word was with God, and the Word was God. 2 He was in the beginning with God. 3 All things came into being through him, and without him not one thing came into being. What has come into being 4 in him was life, and the life was the light of all people. 5 The light shines in the darkness, and the darkness did not overcome it.

6 There was a man sent from God, whose name was John. 7 He came as a witness to testify to the light, so that all might believe through him. 8 He himself was not the light, but he came to testify to the light. 9 The true light, which enlightens everyone, was coming into the world.

10 He was in the world, and the world came into being through him; yet the world did not know him. 11 He came to what was his own, and his own people did not accept him. 12 But to all who received him, who believed in his name, he gave power to become children of God, 13 who were born, not of blood or of the will of the flesh or of the will of man, but of God.

14 And the Word became flesh and lived among us, and we have seen his glory, the glory as of a father's only son, full of grace and truth. 15 (John testified to him and cried out, "This was he of whom I said, 'He who comes after me ranks ahead of me because he was before me.'") 16 From his fullness we have all received, grace upon grace. 17 The law indeed was given through Moses; grace and truth came through Jesus Christ. 18 No one has ever seen God. It is God the only Son, who is close to the Father's heart,who has made him known.

4

135

HOME BIBLE READINGS

BACKGROUND

John's Gospel is priceless both for the sinner in the process of coming to faith in the Messiah and for the believer who has walked with Him for many years. This Gospel satisfies the spiritual seeker and refreshes the Christian servant. Its fascination is immediate and enduring. Its message is simple and profound.

Though John's account of the life, work, and teachings of Jesus Christ lacks many of the features of the other three Gospels, it does include unique elements that enrich our understanding of who Jesus is and help us to appreciate the implications of His atoning work. Absent are key biographical events in Jesus' life, such as His birth, baptism, and ascension. Likewise absent are Jesus' popular parables and His interpretations of historical events. John probably excluded these because his primary intent was to defend the faith, not to present a purely chronological or historical account of the Messiah's life. The apostle chose events in Jesus' ministry that demonstrated His supernatural origin and power. If every one of them had been written down, the author supposed, the whole world would not be able to contain the number of necessary books (John 21:25). What did get recorded was sufficient to lead people to a saving knowledge of Christ.

It is clear that the fourth Gospel was written by an eyewitness of the events he described. The Gospel's details about the topography of Palestine and the towns that relate to Jesus are all on target. The author's familiarity with Jewish customs and religious practices are also dramatically evident in this Gospel. Most importantly, however, the Gospel of John provides us with unparalleled insights into Jesus Christ. It is only in this account that we hear about the marriage feast at Cana (2:1-11), the Lord's discussion with Nicodemus (3:1-21), the raising of Lazarus (11:1-44), the washing of His disciples' feet (13:1-17), and the great "I am" declarations (6:35; 8:12, 58; 9:5; 10:7, 9, 11; 11:25; 14:6; 15:5). John also gave memorable glimpses of Thomas (11:16; 14:5; 20:24-29), Andrew (1:40-41; 6:8-9; 12:22), and Philip (6:5-7; 14:8-9).

In short, the fourth Gospel stands as a living testimony of our Lord and Savior Jesus Christ. Having this record was imperative, for by the time the apostle had written his Gospel, major problems concerning doctrine had emerged. Christians needed further instruction on what to believe about the Messiah and what He had accomplished.

Heresies—especially the precursors to Gnosticism—were sprouting everywhere, and critics from many quarters outside the church were attacking the beliefs of Christians. The time was right for someone of John's stature to step in and defend the faith with the words of Christ Himself.

John clearly stated his purpose for his Gospel when he wrote, *these are written, that ye might believe that Jesus is the Christ, the Son of God; and that believing ye might have life through his name* (20:31). The apostle affirmed that Jesus was the Messiah and the Son of God. According to John, Jesus was not merely a human being, a man possessed with a type of Christ spirit, or a spirit being who merely appeared human. He was God who came in the flesh and now rules in heaven.

Throughout this Gospel, John constantly showed Jesus to be the Son of God. The apostle's presentation of Jesus' miracles, teachings, and experiences all point to the Son as the Messiah. Indeed, the fourth Gospel was intended to convince people to place their trust in the Lord Jesus as the incarnate, divine Word who had died for their sins and is coming again.

NOTES ON THE PRINTED TEXT

In John 1:1-18, we find the introduction, or Prologue, to the apostle's grand account about the promised Messiah. Here we learn that Jesus is unlike any human being who has ever walked upon the earth. Before He came to earth as a man, He eternally preexisted as a member of the Godhead, being equal to, yet distinct from, the other two members of the Trinity (1:1-2).

Note that 1:1 does not say that Jesus, the *Word*, is "a god." John clearly declared that the one who existed with God the Father (and God the Holy Spirit) before the creation of the world was in fact equal to Him in every way. In short, Jesus is God. *Word* is *logos* in the Greek. The Greek philosophers used *logos* in various ways, usually to refer to a prevailing rational principle or force that guided the universe; but to John, the *logos* was not an impersonal rational force that remained detached from humanity. The apostle used *logos* to refer to that supreme being who, although equal to God, became human and shared in the struggles and hardships of the human race.

The person we now know as Jesus created everything that exists. He is the Word who spoke all things into existence (1:3). While 1:4 is clear that we owe our physical life to Him, the meaning probably goes beyond that to include spiritual life. As the light of all humankind, Jesus shines as our ultimate hope. He alone can offer eternal life in a world filled with darkness. No matter how hard those in spiritual darkness may try, they cannot extinguish the saving light of Christ (1:5).

John the Baptist was the key person to testify that the Word was the light of the world (1:6). In so doing, John prepared the hearts of people to accept Jesus as unique. In fact, the main purpose of John's ministry was to point people to the Savior (1:7). By the time the fourth Gospel was written, some individuals held exaggerated views about John the Baptist. While not directly confronting these people, the apostle made it clear that John was simply a witness to the light (1:8).

Jesus left the glories of heaven to come to earth as a man. He came as the genuine Light, the one and only Son of the Father bringing the light of salvation to a world bound in darkness (1:9). Though Jesus was equal with God, the inhabitants of earth failed to recognize the Son as their Creator and Lord (1:10). How ironic it is that those who owed their every breath to Him refused to give Him the honor due His name.

The Greek noun rendered "world" (*kósmos*, 1:9) is an important term in the fourth Gospel. In its most basic usage, *kósmos* referred to an ornament, such as in 1 Peter 3:3, where it is used to mean the "adorning," namely, the ornamentation of jewelry and clothing. The term can also be used of the universe with its orderly ornamentation of stars and planets. Eventually *kósmos* came to refer to the earth, since (from the human perspective) that is the most important part of the universe, and also people, since they are the most significant inhabitants of the planet.

In the fourth Gospel, *world* most often refers to the majority of people and their temporal pursuits (including their goals, aspirations, values, and priorities). Since most rejected the Messiah, *the world* in this Gospel sometimes denotes humanity in opposition to Him. John's *world* is hostile to the Savior and to His followers because of their association with Him (7:7; 15:18-19); yet despite the world's hatred of God, He still loves it and gave His Son so that its people might receive eternal life (3:16).

In 1:11, John emphasized the enormous tragedy of the world's rejection of the Son. Jesus not only came to the world He created, but also to the people He had chosen, the inhabitants of Israel. Rather than welcoming Him with open arms, a majority rejected Him. The account, however, does not end there. Some received Jesus by faith and He gave them the right to become members of God's family (1:12). The good news is that we can enter God's household by grace through a spiritual rebirth. No one can earn this privilege or be born into it (1:13).

To accomplish our salvation, Jesus became human and dwelt among us (1:14). The Greek word translated *dwelt* means "pitched a tent," as though Jesus temporarily made His home with us. In the Incarnation, He accepted the limitations and conditions of humanity. Those who were close to Him, such as the apostle John, saw Jesus' divine glory and testified that He was indeed the person who had come from the Father to live as a human being.

Because John the Baptist was older than Jesus and began his ministry earlier, many naturally assumed that John was the greater of the two. People in ancient times gave the older person more respect and honor than the younger; but John reversed that custom by proclaiming that Jesus far outranked him because in reality Jesus existed as God for an eternity before He was born (1:15).

In 1:14, the apostle said that Jesus was full of grace. Then, in 1:16, John expanded on that theme, describing the Messiah as the source of all blessings. God's grace to

His people is never depleted. While Moses revealed God's justice through the law, Jesus made grace and truth available to believers to the fullest extent (1:17).

Though no one has ever seen God, Jesus is able to make God known to us because of His intimate relationship with His Father (1:18). Also, because Jesus was fully God as well as fully human, He could reveal God's nature in a way that we could understand. The Son was God's living image dwelling upon the earth. The human eye can neither detect God's spiritual nature nor survive the direct sight of all His glory; but since Jesus became a man, He was able to display God's character and speak about the Father with authority.

The Greek verb translated *hath declared him* is the same word from which we get *exegesis*, which means "to explain" or "to interpret." What could not previously be explained about the Father is now made clear in the Son. If a friend ever tells us that he or she does not understand something about God, the best thing we can do is point our friend to Jesus (see 14:8-9).

SUGGESTIONS TO TEACHERS

Imagine the scenario: you and a group of people are confined for a time in a place where no copy of the Bible is available. Let's assume that your group is in a detention camp, where you have access to paper and pencils. If your fellow prisoners asked you to write something about God, something that could be passed around in the camp, what would you state about Jesus? Use this hypothetical situation as a lesson starter. Then have your students compare what they might have written to what John wrote in his Gospel. The apostle was emphatic about letting his readers know about Jesus.

1. ENTIRETY. The eternal God and complete creation are encompassed in the opening verses of John's Gospel. What a vast view of the cosmos! Those in the class who may be science buffs or science fiction readers should become aware that the apostle's words placed Jesus into the history of the universe. Imaginary tales about spaceships, intergalactic travel, and time warps turn into puny fantasies when contrasted with John's breathtaking statements about Jesus as the Word of God existing from the very beginning.

2. ENLIGHTENMENT. Have the members of your class take note of the word *light*. It appears throughout John's writings. Light is an essential term to describe the meaning of the Messiah. Let your imagination roam as you picture what existence without light was like. Darkness brings gloomy thinking as well as gloomy living. Light, as characterized by the presence of Jesus in our lives, brings hope and even life itself.

3. EMPOWERMENT. Discuss John 1:10-13. Jesus gives to those who trust in Him for salvation the spiritual power and legal right to become children of God. In other words, Jesus' followers are reborn in a special way. Like children in a close human family, God's children may realize their intimate closeness to each other and to the living God.

4. ENFLESHMENT. Introduce the theological term *Incarnation*. What God has supremely said or promised has been disclosed in the person of Jesus. Also, the fullness of God's character and personality has been revealed in the life, death, and resurrection of Jesus. No longer do we humans have to guess what God is like. This is a central idea in this week's lesson, so devote all the class time necessary to a discussion of the concept.

5. EMPHASIS. As time permits, turn to John 20:30-31 to discuss the apostle's purpose for writing the fourth Gospel and why Scripture is so important in the lives of believers. Jesus Christ is the foundation for faith. Trusting in Him brings eternal life. Inform the students that the word *life* was important to John—and to every Christian.

FOR ADULTS

■ **TOPIC:** Receiving the Word

■ **QUESTIONS:** 1. How was it possible for the Word, who eternally existed, to become a human being in time and space? 2. What role did John the Baptist serve with respect to the Messiah? 3. What does it mean to receive Christ and how does this come about? 4. What sort of glory did John the apostle and others see in Jesus? 5. In what ways has Jesus made the Father known to you as a believer?

■ **ILLUSTRATIONS:**

Jesus—God Incarnate. When Ed and Laura decided to host a Bible study on the Gospel of John for their unbelieving friends, they were surprised to have three enthusiastic couples show up the first night. But the surprises did not end there. No sooner had they read John 1:14 than one of the husbands said, "Whoa! That can't be right."

"Why not?" Laura asked. "Well, you said Jesus is the Word, right?" the husband asked. "That's right," Laura responded. "And John 1:1 said, 'In the beginning was the Word,' right?" Ed added. The husband stated, "Well, it's not right. We haven't read the Bible before, but everybody knows Jesus was born on Christmas. How could the Bible say He existed 'in the beginning'?"

Ed and Laura looked at each other, baffled. Having grown up in Christian homes, it never occurred to them that anyone would not understand the Incarnation. The man's question gave the couple an opportunity to explain the fact that Jesus is not just God's Son, whose birth we celebrate on Christmas. As this week's lesson reminds us, Jesus is also God incarnate, the eternal Lord breaking into history in human form to change the world forever.

Like Father, Like Son. History was made in organized baseball in 1989. For the first time, a father and son played simultaneously in the major leagues. Ken Griffey, Jr., the 19-year-old son of Ken, Sr., started for the Seattle Mariners while his 39-year-old father played for the Cincinnati Reds. The physical skills of the father were evident in the son.

How often that occurs! A son resembles his father, or a daughter resembles her mother. But something far more significant is true in the life of Jesus. The very nature of His Father is shown in the Son. Just as so many of the characteristics of Ken Griffey, Sr., were evident in his son, so we see the characteristics of God when we look at Jesus.

The Father, through His Son Jesus, wanted to show us what He is like. This may be one of the reasons why Christianity grew so rapidly in its earliest years. Believers today are to be witnesses for the One who was revealed in human form.

Look Closely. One of the ways to test whether a five-dollar bill is genuine is to scrutinize the design. The numerals 2-3-9-2 are printed on the bill, but can only be found after close examination. These numbers attest that the bill is what it claims to be—an authentic five-dollar bill.

Those who may doubt that Jesus is as He claims to be should look closely at His life. They will discover that in all that He said and did is the authenticating presence of God. Jesus' life attests to the genuineness of His claims and the claims of the New Testament writers. In the person of Jesus, God presented Himself in human form, disclosing His nature once and for all. Trust this report. Believe in Jesus and live!

FOR YOUTH

■ TOPIC: Jesus: God with Us

■ QUESTIONS: 1. According to John, who is Jesus? 2. What were the differences between John the Baptist and Jesus? 3. How was Jesus' rejection on earth ironic and tragic? 4. How does a person become a member of God's family? 5. Why was Jesus so well able to reveal who God is?

■ ILLUSTRATIONS:

What He Is Like. Not long ago a controversy erupted when a doll of Egypt's Queen Nefertiti was offered for sale. The doll, with a blue caplike crown, had white skin. It had been modeled after the well-known head now in Berlin's Egyptian Museum. Protesters argued that the ancient queen was black. The question remained: What did she look like?

Mummies were examined for evidence. It was discovered that hair ranged from straight to wavy to woolly with shades of reddish brown to dark brown to black. Lips ranged from full to thin. Many mummies possessed a protrusive jaw. Noses ranged from high bridged to straight to arched and hooked. Skin colors varied from white to black. In short, Egypt was a country that was heterogeneous. Since an ancient Egyptian sculptor had fashioned the classic bust of the queen, we can trust that an accurate portrayal had been given.

John enabled his readers to see what God looked like by presenting a portrait of Jesus. As we read about the Son, we begin to see more clearly what the Father is like.

A Copy Cat! In February 2002, the BBC News service reported that researchers in Texas successfully cloned a domestic cat. The resulting kitten was appropriately named CopyCat. The work was described in the scientific journal *Nature*, which noted that this was the first time anyone had cloned a pet. According to the one of the researchers, the cloned cat appeared healthy and energetic.

Jesus is no clone. He is God the Son, the Word of God enfleshed. In the Incarnation, God is the Creator, not a genetic engineer.

Prepare the Way. When the president of the United States travels to a city or another country, an advance team of men and women have already been there weeks ahead. They work with the local law enforcement agencies to provide for the president's safety, plan his motorcade routes, and scout potential problem areas. Sections where the president will stop are swept for bombs or other dangers. This advance team anticipates problems and develops contingency plans. They do everything to prepare the way for the president.

John the Baptist was Jesus' advance party. The messenger of the Lord did everything possible to prepare the way for the Messiah, the living Word of God. What place did John prepare in your heart?

HUMILIATION AND EXALTATION

BACKGROUND SCRIPTURE: Philippians 2:1-11
DEVOTIONAL READING: 1 Peter 3:8-12

KEY VERSE: Let nothing be done through strife or vainglory; but in lowliness of mind let each esteem other better than themselves. Philippians 2:3.

KING JAMES VERSION

PHILIPPIANS 2:1 If there be therefore any consolation in Christ, if any comfort of love, if any fellowship of the Spirit, if any bowels and mercies, 2 Fulfil ye my joy, that ye be likeminded, having the same love, being of one accord, of one mind. 3 Let nothing be done through strife or vainglory; but in lowliness of mind let each esteem other better than themselves. 4 Look not every man on his own things, but every man also on the things of others. 5 Let this mind be in you, which was also in Christ Jesus: 6 Who, being in the form of God, thought it not robbery to be equal with God: 7 But made himself of no reputation, and took upon him the form of a servant, and was made in the likeness of men: 8 And being found in fashion as a man, he humbled himself, and became obedient unto death, even the death of the cross. 9 Wherefore God also hath highly exalted him, and given him a name which is above every name: 10 That at the name of Jesus every knee should bow, of things in heaven, and things in earth, and things under the earth; 11 And that every tongue should confess that Jesus Christ is Lord, to the glory of God the Father.

NEW REVISED STANDARD VERSION

PHILIPPIANS 2:1 If then there is any encouragement in Christ, any consolation from love, any sharing in the Spirit, any compassion and sympathy, 2 make my joy complete: be of the same mind, having the same love, being in full accord and of one mind. 3 Do nothing from selfish ambition or conceit, but in humility regard others as better than yourselves. 4 Let each of you look not to your own interests, but to the interests of others. 5 Let the same mind be in you that was in Christ Jesus, 6 who, though he was in the form of God,
did not regard equality with God
as something to be exploited,
7 but emptied himself,
taking the form of a slave,
being born in human likeness.
And being found in human form,
8   he humbled himself
and became obedient to the point of death—
even death on a cross.
9 Therefore God also highly exalted him
and gave him the name
that is above every name,
10 so that at the name of Jesus
every knee should bend,
in heaven and on earth and under the earth,
11 and every tongue should confess
that Jesus Christ is Lord,
to the glory of God the Father.

BACKGROUND

Philippi was an ancient town that was originally called Krenides. Krenides means "springs," which was probably a reflection of its abundant water supply. The city was renamed by King Philip II of Macedonia when he subdued it around 356 B.C. Later Philippi became a strategic Roman colony since it was situated on a major road (called the Via Egnatia) that linked Rome with the continent of Asia. This Greek city was located about 10 miles north of the Aegean Sea and was coveted for its gold mines and fertile soil.

During Paul's second missionary journey, he planted the first European church in Philippi, according to Luke's account in the Acts of the Apostles (see Acts 16:9-40). This probably occurred around A.D. 50. A few of the converts of Philippi, such as Lydia, became some of the apostle's dearest friends. The dramatic conversion of a jailer and the exorcism of a slave girl also occurred in this city. Some Bible scholars suggest that the physician Luke was from this town, since it had a prominent school of medicine and because he noted its prominence (16:12). In any case, the Philippian church always held a cherished place in Paul's heart. He came back to visit this city on his third missionary journey around A.D. 55–56; in fact, he may have passed through the city twice on this particular trip.

During the course of Paul's tumultuous career as a traveling evangelist, he was held in custody at least four times: temporarily at Philippi (about A.D. 50); once in Caesarea (about A.D. 57–59); and twice in Rome (first in about A.D. 60–62 and second in late A.D. 66 or early A.D. 67). It is most likely that Paul wrote the Letter to the Philippians during the first imprisonment in Rome while he was under house arrest (see Acts 28:14-31). Accordingly, Philippians is one of the so-called "Prison Epistles."

During the time of his first Roman imprisonment, Paul awaited trial to present his case before Emperor Nero. The apostle had been arrested back in Jerusalem, where he was wrongfully accused of inciting a riot. A mob of angry Jews tried to murder him, mistakenly thinking that Paul had defiled their temple by bringing a Gentile into their sanctuary. He was then imprisoned in Caesarea, but after a prolonged period of waiting for justice to prevail, he finally appealed to the emperor as was his right as a Roman citizen. As a result, the apostle was shipped to Rome, where he was placed under house arrest for at least two years and then apparently released. During this period of incarceration, the apostle had the freedom to entertain guests, preach the Gospel, and write. His second imprisonment in Rome's Mamertine prison was far more restrictive. In fact, this second imprisonment apparently ended with his execution.

In his Letter to the Philippians, the apostle penned some of his most penetrating insights about the divine nature of Christ. Indeed, the sacred truths revealed in this epistle came from the heart and mind of a disciple who had learned God's truths through many years of sacrificial service to Christ. After the Philippian believers sent Paul a generous gift while he was under house arrest in Rome, Paul wrote this letter to thank them for their kindness and to report on his current situation. At the same time the apostle took this opportunity to urge them to remain strong and united in their faith in Christ though many external and internal elements may have been discouraging them.

Throughout the Philippian letter, Paul's deep affection for the believers who had supported him with their prayers and financial aid is evident. Though these Macedonian Christians were being persecuted for their faith in Christ, they had neither abandoned Paul's teachings nor discarded his friendship. Such steadfast devotion to the Lord and to the apostle compelled Paul to pour out his heart to his readers, confessing his longing to be with them and his special love for them.

NOTES ON THE PRINTED TEXT

In Philippians 1:27-28, Paul talked about contending for the faith of the Gospel and not being intimidated by one's opponents. Then, in 1:29, the apostle revealed that the believers at Philippi were experiencing persecution for their faith. Amid the opposition, the apostle wanted his readers to remain firm in their devotion to Christ. Undoubtedly, the strain of being persecuted frayed emotions and created interpersonal tension among the members of the Philippian church. These sources of stress threatened to divide the congregation, which in turn would hamper its ability to resist the world's opposition. That is why Paul urged his readers to maintain an attitude of humility in which they considered the interests of others equal to their own concerns.

The apostle based his exhortation on what his readers truly enjoyed as believers. By way of example, they possessed a hope that was grounded in Christ. They were the objects of the Lord's unfailing love. There was also the closeness they felt to each other because of the Spirit as well as the affection produced in them by the Spirit (2:1). Moreover, Paul asked his readers to consider the joy he would feel at seeing them united (2:2). In particular, they were to be of the same mind, maintain the same love for each other, remain united in spirit, and have one purpose. The result would be a congregation that lived in harmony despite opposition from antagonists.

On the flip side, Paul asked his readers to avoid causes of disunity such as seeking to advance their personal agendas rather than the Savior's will. Such a concentration on selfish ambition and personal vanity would destroy their congregation. Their purpose was to advance God's kingdom, not their own (2:3). The Greek word rendered *lowliness of mind* means to be humbleminded, that is, to think rightly about one's position in life. For believers, it includes recognizing our true sinful condition and need for God's grace. Thus, humility is a continual appreciation of our dependency on the Savior and the necessity to always rely on Him. Paul reminded his readers that each of them, in humility, should be moved to treat one another as more important than themselves.

The apostle did not intend the Philippians to overlook their personal needs; but he asked that self-centeredness be replaced by a broader approach that gave equal weight to the welfare of others (2:4). It was another way of expressing Jesus' command to love our neighbors as we love ourselves (Matt. 19:19). The intense opposition in Philippi demanded a cooperative effort. Individual resistance would fail; they needed to support each other.

Having presented unselfishness and humility as the backbone of unity, Paul next pointed his readers to the greatest example of those qualities—Christ Himself—and said we as believers should strive to have the same attitude He had (2:5). Philippians 2:6-11 is considered by many Bible scholars to be an ancient Christian hymn. From the earliest days of the Church, believers sang songs expressing their devotion and faith in Christ (Col. 3:16). Most of these hymns are now lost to us, but a few are probably preserved in Paul's letters. Besides Philippians 2:6-11, parts of other possible hymns may be found in Ephesians 5:14, Colossians 1:15-20, and 1 Timothy 3:16.

We learn in Philippians 2:6 that even though Jesus existed as God, enjoying the glories of heaven, He willingly and unselfishly gave up His high position to become a servant of the very ones He created. Jesus' example cuts through the pride and self-centeredness that so often divide believers. Consider the fact that Jesus *made himself of no reputation* (2:7). The idea is that Christ set aside His heavenly privileges and instead focused on servanthood, humanity, humility, and total obedience to the Father.

In all of this, Jesus did not cease to be God while He was on earth. It was something like a monarch dressing and living as a commoner for His subjects to better know Him. He gave up the outward signs of royalty but did not cease to be King of kings. Indeed, Jesus truly became a human being and operated as a humble servant of His Father. The act of Christ becoming a human being represents the supreme example of humility. Jesus voluntarily put aside all His rights and privileges as God to assume the role of a servant. Since Jesus was sinless, recognition of His true condition did not involve sin. He did, however, demonstrate the need to depend daily on the Father for strength.

Jesus' sacrifice did not stop with Him becoming a human being. He obeyed His Father to the point of death, enduring the cruelest end imaginable so that we could enjoy eternal life. Jesus humbly died in our place, taking upon Himself the punishment we deserved and the curse that we should have borne (Phil. 2:8; see Gal. 3:13;

Heb. 12:2). Paul, however, could not end his illustration with Jesus on the cross. The place of honor that Jesus willingly forsook was given back to Him with the added glory of His triumph over sin and death. In response to His humility and obedience, the Father supremely exalted the Son to a place where His triumph will eventually be recognized by every living creature (Phil. 2:9).

The apostle emphatically tells us that every person who has ever lived will someday recognize Jesus for who He is. The *name of Jesus* (2:10) signifies the position God gave Him, not His proper name. By bowing their knees, every human being and angel will acknowledge Jesus' deity and sovereignty. Everyone will confess that Jesus is Lord—some with joyful faith, others with hopeless regret and despair (2:11).

SUGGESTIONS TO TEACHERS

Have you ever seen an advertisement for a seminar on humility? There are lots of ads about how to be successful, how to get ahead, and how to be number one. But how to be humble? Forget it. In contrast, when Paul wrote to the church at Philippi about their need to change, he did not call for a conference on management. He called for a fresh look at the suffering Savior. Until the believers took Jesus seriously, they would not discover genuine humility. The same holds true for us as Christ's followers.

1. THE EXAMPLE OF CHRIST. Jesus demonstrated humility by voluntarily relinquishing the full prerogatives of deity when He came to earth. Though Jesus did not surrender His deity, He did forego the rights of that heavenly environment. Jesus knew hunger, thirst, pain, and temptation. Then, when His executioners dragged Him to the cross, Jesus could have called down a legion of angels, but He did not do so. Instead, He humbly submitted to the will of His Father in heaven.

2. THE ATTITUDE OF BELIEVERS. Paul said our attitude toward one another should be the same that Jesus had (Phil. 2:5). This requires prayerful meditation on what Jesus did and disciplined study of His words and deeds. We confess that we cannot do it on our own. We need the Holy Spirit's empowerment. Progress is made when we look squarely at the cross. Then we will begin to grasp what it means to serve in the church with a humble attitude, one that promotes love and unity.

3. THE DECISION TO PERSEVERE. When we take seriously the high standards of the Gospel, they run smack into the world's way of thinking. That's why one of our most powerful influences on society is our decision to persevere in modeling the humble attitude displayed by Jesus. Ultimately, people cannot deny that Jesus makes a difference when they see His followers living in this way.

4. THE IMPACT OF HUMILITY ON RELATIONSHIPS. We need to understand the part humility should play in our daily relationships. When we are humble, we will pay closer attention to those around us and regularly ask God such questions as the following: How can I see this person's concerns as being as important as mine? What can I say to this person that would show God's love? How does God want me to use my time to minister to the needs of others? As we wait on the Lord, He will give us the answers and enable us to reach out in His name.

5. THE POWER OF HUMILITY ON CHURCH LIFE. Our churches would find larger responses if they were known as communities where people put the interests of others ahead of their own. Too often, it seems, the public observes more fighting than humility among God's people. Having the mind of Christ shapes the church and shakes the world.

FOR ADULTS	■ TOPIC: Keeping the Balance ■ QUESTIONS: 1. What reasons did Paul give the Philippians for pursuing oneness in the midst of being persecuted? 2. How is it possible for

believers to balance looking out for the interests of others while not neglecting their own legitimate concerns? 3. How was it possible for Jesus, who is fully God, to become fully human? 4. Why did the Father highly exalt the Son? 5. Why is it often challenging for believers to model the humble attitude of the Lord Jesus?

■ **ILLUSTRATIONS:**

Misplaced Priorities. The *Apprentice* is a nighttime television series in which a diverse group of candidates pit their wits and skills against one another to win the prize of being hired by The Trump Organization and earning a hefty six-figure salary. During one season, it's men against women. Then the next season, those with "book smarts" go up against those with "street smarts." Regardless of the venue, the competitive atmosphere remains the same. And in the end, it's not about being nice or polite. It's about remaining on top at any cost.

If believers aren't careful, they can find themselves getting sucked into this cutthroat way of living in which ambition and conceit trample sensitivity and kindness. On the one hand, the Lord does not call His people to be doormats. On the other hand, the example of Jesus reminds us that considering the needs of others is just as important as ensuring our own desires are satisfied.

The Path of Humility. Not long ago the Chinese government launched a plan to stamp out its country's notoriously bad customer service, a remnant of Communist rule. According to a report in *The New York Times*, "In China, it is common for clerks to abandon their post without notice, and to ignore—or even insult—customers who happen to come along."

To help store clerks deliver better service, the government has banned 50 of the most commonly used phrases, including these: "Buy it if you can afford it—otherwise get out of here." "Time is up—be quick." "Didn't I tell you? How come you don't get it?" "Why didn't you choose well when you bought it?"

It would be rare to hear such things from clerks in the United States. But that doesn't mean they don't want to say them. It's difficult to see others' needs as being equal to our own. If we aren't "looking out for number one," we tend to feel more like slaves than godly servants.

It doesn't have to be like that, though. In this week's Scripture passage, Paul pointed toward a better way of living through Jesus, the Creator of the universe. He demonstrated how we can live humbly among one another and bring glory to God.

Extending a Humble, Helping Hand. It was the most cluttered that David's 300-acre farm had ever looked. Fifteen combines, 24 grain trucks, and about 50 friends had converged on his land. By the end of the day, 60,000 bushels of corn would be harvested, then transported to a nearby grain elevator.

The oil company David had used for years had provided the fuel. His local bank had provided a catered lunch. Family and friends had provided the labor—and kind words of remembrance. This is how the farm community in a Midwest town mourned the unexpected death of one of its own. For a day, everyone's usual priorities had been shelved. David's widow had needed a humble, helping hand—in fact, many hands!

When was the last time you dropped everything to help someone for a day? Right now, is there someone who needs you to put his or her needs ahead of your own?

FOR YOUTH

■ TOPIC: Imitating Christ

■ QUESTIONS: 1. How can finding consolation in Christ encourage us to relate to others in a humble manner? 2. What did Paul have in mind when he enjoined his readers to be of one accord? 3. What does it mean to esteem others better than ourselves? 4. What would motivate Jesus to set aside His kingly glory to die on the cross for us? 5. In what way did the Father exalt the Son?

■ ILLUSTRATIONS:

Remember the Original. In the British Museum, a Greek writing tablet, from before the Christian era, is on display. It is the classical equivalent of a child's notebook for learning the alphabet. The instructor has written the initial line. The student has traced the second as best as he or she can by looking at the first. Every succeeding line, however, is a reproduction, not of the first line of writing, but of the last. As a result, each successive line shows a wider divergence from the original than the one before.

As we pursue holiness, it's best to keep our eye on the original—the Lord Jesus. As believers, though we are all becoming like the original, each of us still has imperfections best left unlearned by others.

Genuine Humility. A Christian pastor said, "A person who profoundly changed my life was not a preacher or the leader of a big organization. She was an office worker at the local bus company. She never married. She used her home and her slim resources to develop Christian maturity among college students. Many of them—including myself—went into ministry at home and abroad."

Few of us recognize the power of humility. But at the consummation of the age, when our life deeds are revealed, we may be surprised to learn that the major influences in God's kingdom came from humble, unselfish, loving servants. Our own lives and our churches are immeasurably enriched when we follow the mind of Christ.

Setting Aside Privileges. Jim, a Christian who started out his career as a sports reporter, thoroughly enjoyed the privileges that came with the job—passes to sports events, access to players, and things like that. Later on, he had to make a big career decision. Should he stay in the newspaper business, or should he enter Christian service? If he chose the latter, he knew he was saying good-bye to his last free pass.

Nevertheless, Jim set aside those privileges and says, "I have never regretted the decision. God more than made up for any passes I relinquished. He gave me the most satisfying work I could do in editing, writing, teaching, and preaching."

Sometimes it's hard to choose what we know to be God's will. Sometimes we're afraid God will cheat us out of something good. Do you ever consider what Jesus thought when the Father asked Him to set aside His privileges in heaven, to come to earth and take on human limitations, and to die a criminal's death for our sins? Jesus' humiliation and exaltation prove that God will never let us down. We can trust Him completely to do the very best for us.

"I AM FROM ABOVE"

BACKGROUND SCRIPTURE: John 8:31-59
DEVOTIONAL READING: John 14:23-31

KEY VERSES: If ye continue in my word, then are ye my disciples indeed;
And ye shall know the truth, and the truth shall make you free. John 8:31-32.

6

KING JAMES VERSION

JOHN 8:31 Then said Jesus to those Jews which believed on him, If ye continue in my word, then are ye my disciples indeed; 32 And ye shall know the truth, and the truth shall make you free. 33 They answered him, We be Abraham's seed, and were never in bondage to any man: how sayest thou, Ye shall be made free? 34 Jesus answered them, Verily, verily, I say unto you, Whosoever committeth sin is the servant of sin. 35 And the servant abideth not in the house for ever: but the Son abideth ever. 36 If the Son therefore shall make you free, ye shall be free indeed. 37 I know that ye are Abraham's seed; but ye seek to kill me, because my word hath no place in you.

38 I speak that which I have seen with my Father: and ye do that which ye have seen with your father. . . .

48 Then answered the Jews, and said unto him, Say we not well that thou art a Samaritan, and hast a devil? 49 Jesus answered, I have not a devil; but I honour my Father, and ye do dishonour me. 50 And I seek not mine own glory: there is one that seeketh and judgeth. 51 Verily, verily, I say unto you, If a man keep my saying, he shall never see death. 52 Then said the Jews unto him, Now we know that thou hast a devil. Abraham is dead, and the prophets; and thou sayest, If a man keep my saying, he shall never taste of death. 53 Art thou greater than our father Abraham, which is dead? and the prophets are dead: whom makest thou thyself? 54 Jesus answered, If I honour myself, my honour is nothing: it is my Father that honoureth me; of whom ye say, that he is your God: 55 Yet ye have not known him; but I know him: and if I should say, I know him not, I shall be a liar like unto you: but I know him, and keep his saying. 56 Your father Abraham rejoiced to see my day: and he saw it, and was glad. . . . 58 Jesus said unto them, Verily, verily, I say unto you, Before Abraham was, I am. 59 Then took they up stones to cast at him: but Jesus hid himself, and went out of the temple, going through the midst of them, and so passed by.

NEW REVISED STANDARD VERSION

JOHN 8:31 Then Jesus said to the Jews who had believed in him, "If you continue in my word, you are truly my disciples; 32 and you will know the truth, and the truth will make you free." 33 They answered him, "We are descendants of Abraham and have never been slaves to anyone. What do you mean by saying, 'You will be made free'?"

34 Jesus answered them, "Very truly, I tell you, everyone who commits sin is a slave to sin. 35 The slave does not have a permanent place in the household; the son has a place there forever. 36 So if the Son makes you free, you will be free indeed. 37 I know that you are descendants of Abraham; yet you look for an opportunity to kill me, because there is no place in you for my word. 38 I declare what I have seen in the Father's presence; as for you, you should do what you have heard from the Father.". . .

48 The Jews answered him, "Are we not right in saying that you are a Samaritan and have a demon?" 49 Jesus answered, "I do not have a demon; but I honor my Father, and you dishonor me. 50 Yet I do not seek my own glory; there is one who seeks it and he is the judge. 51 Very truly, I tell you, whoever keeps my word will never see death." 52 The Jews said to him, "Now we know that you have a demon. Abraham died, and so did the prophets; yet you say, 'Whoever keeps my word will never taste death.' 53 Are you greater than our father Abraham, who died? The prophets also died. Who do you claim to be?" 54 Jesus answered, "If I glorify myself, my glory is nothing. It is my Father who glorifies me, he of whom you say, 'He is our God,' 55 though you do not know him. But I know him; if I would say that I do not know him, I would be a liar like you. But I do know him and I keep his word. 56 Your ancestor Abraham rejoiced that he would see my day; he saw it and was glad." . . . 58 Jesus said to them, "Very truly, I tell you, before Abraham was, I am." 59 So they picked up stones to throw at him, but Jesus hid himself and went out of the temple.

HOME BIBLE READINGS

Monday, January 1	John 1:19-28	*A Voice in the Wilderness*
Tuesday, January 2	John 1:29-34	*Jesus Is the Lamb of God*
Wednesday, January 3	Matthew 13:11-17	*Promises Fulfilled*
Thursday, January 4	John 14:23-31	*Jesus Gives Peace*
Friday, January 5	Matthew 11:1-6	*Jesus Is the Christ*
Saturday, January 6	John 8:31-38	*Jesus Promises Freedom*
Sunday, January 7	John 8:48-59	*Jesus Speaks of Eternal Life*

BACKGROUND

Perhaps even more than the other three Gospels, the fourth one makes a strong case for the deity of Christ. The reader learns that Jesus, the Word, is God (John 1:1) who came to earth as a human being (1:14). The fourth Gospel expresses the uniqueness of the Son's relationship with the Father. The Son existed in eternity past with the Father, was sent by the Father into the world, and returned to Father after the crucifixion and resurrection events. The statements and miracles recorded in John's Gospel convincingly demonstrate that Jesus is the Messiah, the Son of God, and that He is worthy of trust and worship (20:30-31).

This observation suggests that John had both an evangelistic and apologetic purpose in writing his Gospel. The author used contrasting ideas (such as life and death, light and darkness, love and hate, and being from below and from above) to convey important truths about the person and work of Christ and to underscore the necessity of believing in Him for eternal life. John used various ways to highlight the reality of sin and our total dependence on God for salvation. The apostle made it clear that sinful people cannot come to Jesus for salvation unless the Father draws them.

John 8:21-30 (which precedes this week's Scripture passage) is a case in point. The Pharisees had alleged that Jesus was appearing as His own witness and that His testimony was false (8:13). Rather than become entrapped by their spurious charges, the Messiah declared that He would be going away. In this statement He was referring to His ascension into heaven, which would follow His crucifixion and resurrection. The unbelieving religious leaders, because they rejected the claims of Christ, would never dwell with Him there. In fact, they would die with their sins unforgiven (8:21). Jesus' statement prompted His opponents to wonder whether He would commit suicide (8:22). It did not occur to them that the civil and religious authorities would execute Him on the cross and that He would become the atoning sacrifice for the sins of the world (see 1:29).

The Messiah responded by saying that He was from heaven, whereas the religious leaders (along with all humanity) were from earth. The Savior's perspective was divine and eternal, while their viewpoint was worldly and temporal (8:23). Because He spoke on behalf of His Father and only did His Father's will, Jesus was duty bound to stress the importance of faith in Him. Undoubtedly, it troubled Him that the religious leaders would remain unbelieving and consequently die with their sins unforgiven (8:24).

Christ's immediate audience continued to be perplexed about His identity. All He said and did pointed to His status as the Messiah, but they were blinded from recognizing this due to their stony, unbelieving hearts (8:25). Much of what Jesus had to say condemned those who rejected Him; and though they charged Him with making false claims about Himself, His testimony was valid because the Father in heaven, who sent Him and whom He represented, always told the truth (8:26). Not surprisingly, the religious leaders failed to grasp that Jesus was telling them about His Father (8:27).

The Messiah, ever aware of what lay ahead, spoke about being lifted up on the cross as the Son of man. The literal fulfillment of this event would confirm to those who heard Him that He did not operate on His own authority; rather, He only declared what the Father had taught Him (8:28). Jesus was the Father's representative, and the Father was with the Son in all that He accomplished. Indeed, Jesus always did what pleased the Father, and the Father in turn would never abandon the Son (8:29). It's no wonder that many who heard these profound truths put their faith in the Messiah (8:30).

NOTES ON THE PRINTED TEXT

In John 8:30 and 8:31, two slightly different Greek phrases are both translated as *believed*. The Greek says that some believed *in Him* (8:30), while others *believed Him* (8:31). The phrase rendered *in Him* is found elsewhere in John in key passages about belief (see 3:16-17). It could mean that those referred to in 8:30 had a heart knowledge of Jesus, but the group described in 8:31 may have merely acknowledged Him intellectually.

The previous verses in John 8 focus on the validity of Jesus' testimony. After silencing His opponents, He then addressed the listeners who were placing their faith in Him. Jesus left these people little doubt as to what He expected from them. He taught that discipleship must begin with belief, but to be real it also demands obedience to Him and His teachings. Only then can a person know the truth and experience freedom (8:31-32). In contrast, possessing surface-level information can never lead to the same result, regardless of how scintillating that data might be. Furthermore, there is no spiritual freedom in possessing truth in the abstract sense. The focus in the fourth Gospel is on the person and work of Christ. Only faith in Him can deliver people from the darkness of sin.

The listeners were offended by Jesus' statement about being set free. Their proud spirit shows through in their retort that they had never been enslaved to anyone (8:33). How could they make that claim, especially considering their domination by Rome at that very moment? Perhaps it was because the Jews saw themselves as never having adopted the gods of their captors. A good example was their revolt against their Greek rulers in 167 B.C., when a statue of Zeus was erected in the temple and sacrifices were made to it. That act sparked a revolution that forced out the Greeks and gave the Jews political freedom for the next century.

The Romans kept an uneasy peace with the Jews by generally giving them the freedom to worship as they wished and allowing them to handle their own religious matters. That small sense of freedom, however, began to break down when the Roman emperor Caligula (A.D. 37–41) threatened to put a statue of himself in the temple to be worshiped. That event helped spark the Jews to an unsuccessful revolt in A.D. 70. The Romans then destroyed the Jewish temple and later built on the site their own temple dedicated to Zeus—complete with a statue of the emperor Hadrian on the former spot of the most holy place.

To support their shaky claim to liberty, Jesus' listeners also mentioned their genealogical link to Abraham (8:33). Jesus proclaimed their genealogical assertions as irrelevant, for they (along with all humanity) were enslaved to sin (8:34). Sin entices a person do what he or she would not otherwise do. Thus, no person who sins can honestly claim to be free. Likewise, no person can be a true child of Abraham if he or she is enslaved to sin's power, for slaves, unlike children, can be ejected from the household (8:35). Only by knowing the truth—as expressed in God's Son, Jesus Christ (1:14; 14:6)—can a person truly be free (8:36).

The audience's claim to be descendants of Abraham had not escaped Jesus' attention. Ironically, though, they rejected the truth He taught, and this was the reason some of them were prepared to have Him arrested and executed (8:37). While Jesus declared what He had seen in the presence of His heavenly Father, His opponents took their cues from their spiritual father, the devil (8:38; see 8:44).

By insinuating that Jesus was a Samaritan and demon-possessed (8:48), His listeners implied that He was a heretic and insane. The Savior rejected such accusations and affirmed that He honored His heavenly Father. In contrast, Jesus' detractors dishonored Him by their slanderous words; and because Jesus is God the Son, their disdainful statements about Him constituted blasphemy (8:49). Jesus' goal was not to promote Himself. His heavenly Father, though, would not only glorify Him but also judge His opponents (8:50). Those, however, who heeded Jesus' teachings had nothing to fear in this regard. Instead of unending punishment, they would enjoy eternal life (8:51).

The Savior's adversaries mistook Him to be claiming that all who obeyed His words would never physically die. The antagonists thus again claimed He was demon-possessed (8:52). They were amazed to think that Jesus might have regarded Himself as being greater than the patriarch Abraham and the Old Testament prophets, all of whom had died (8:53). Jesus responded by noting that it would be pointless for Him to glorify Himself; and He did not need to, for the God whom Jesus' detractors claimed to worship, would glorify the Son (8:54). Jesus asserted the truth that He knew the Father intimately and personally as well as heeded His commands (8:55). Moreover, Abraham, whom the listeners identified with so much, was overjoyed at the prospect of the Messiah's advent (8:56).

The audience bristled at the notion that Jesus somehow might have seen Abraham, especially since they did not enjoy such a privilege (8:57). In response, Jesus declared that before the patriarch was born, He eternally preexisted with the Father and the Spirit as the second person of the Godhead (8:58). This is one of seven "I am" statements appearing in the fourth Gospel. It points back to the divine declaration in Exodus 3:14. John 8:58 makes it clear that Jesus claimed to be God. Because His opponents rejected this assertion, they attempted to stone Him for blasphemy (8:59). Such would have been the punishment enjoined in the law (see Lev. 24:16). Whether through natural or supernatural means, Jesus somehow hid Himself and exited the temple area.

SUGGESTIONS TO TEACHERS

In this week's Scripture text, we learn about the opponents of Jesus, who asserted their status as Abraham's descendants, and who rejected Jesus' claims about His status as the Messiah. There is also the Savior's declaration of honoring His Father, knowing Him intimately, and eternally existing with Him. As we have seen, Jesus' testimony about Himself remains true and deserves our full acceptance.

1. CRITICS AND CRITERIA. Some who heard Jesus' statements of divine authority dismissed Him and His claims. These people insisted on clinging to the rational worldview of those refusing to put Christ ahead of themselves. Jesus' harshest critics are those who set themselves up as the final authorities in everything. Their criterion for evaluating the Messiah as well as everything else in life tends to be "if it feels good, do it."

2. CLAIMS AND CALLING. Devote some class time to an examination of Jesus' words in the lesson text. What were His claims? What was His calling?

3. COMMITMENT OR CAPTIVITY? Examine Jesus' words in John 8:31-38. Point out the stark contrasts. Stress the importance of being committed to the Savior, or being captured by some lesser loyalty! Note that serving anyone or anything other than the Lord Jesus ultimately brings a form of enslavement.

4. COMPLACENCY AND CONTEMPT. The authorities asserted that because they were Abraham's heirs, they had the status of being God's chosen people and could ignore Jesus' claims. The Messiah told them that the devil is the father of lies (8:44). Have your students reflect on this truth. Deceit sneaks into our speech and behavior when we regard Jesus with complacency or contempt. The devil's clever tricks can easily master us when we don't accept the truth about the Son.

5. CLOSENESS AND CONFIDENCE. Jesus' remarkable assertion of His sense of oneness with the Father must be heeded. The Savior's confidence in being the norm for what is true stems from His identity as the Son of God. We can know the truth about the Lord, about life, and about ourselves as we grow close to Jesus.

■ TOPIC: Be Free!

■ QUESTIONS: 1. What did Jesus' opponents mean when they said He was demon-possessed? 2. How could Jesus assert that He was greater than Abraham? 3. In what ways did the Son keep the Father's commands? 4. In John 8:58, what did Jesus declare about Himself? 5. How does abiding in Jesus' teachings lead to spiritual freedom?

■ ILLUSTRATIONS:

Truth Wins Out. One of the reasons why evading the truth is not a good idea is that lying does not work. Consider duplicity in politics, which tends to produce tragedy. For example, the Vietnam War led President Lyndon B. Johnson to disguise 10 billion dollars in war costs. The fibs, fudges, losses of memory, tampered records, feigned confusion, and phony definitions of words angered Americans, young and old.

President Richard M. Nixon's audacious attempt to fool millions of Americans about his role in the Watergate scandal also led to blunt outrage over his lying. Even President William Jefferson Clinton's efforts to play down his behind-the-scene liaisons angered some Americans and hampered his effectiveness to get things done. The reason behind such anger is that many citizens of all ages have a sense of right and wrong. As politicians and politics often prove, the truth eventually comes out.

Jesus told His listeners the truth about Himself. He declared that Abraham would not save them. The Savior's word and only His word would set them free.

Freedom's Light Never Snuffed Out. The Mau-Mau were a secret organization of Kikuyu tribesmen in Kenya that used terrorism in the 1950s in a rebellion against British colonial rule. During the Mau-Mau Uprising, a statue with outstretched hands held a flame. The Mau-Maus tried to extinguish the flame and actually succeeded several times. However, each time the flame was extinguished, it was reignited by Christians who braved spears and arrows to relight the flame.

There was a little boy whose hand had been cut off by the Mau-Maus for lighting the fire. When asked why he went to such extremes, the lad stated that the light of spiritual freedom must never go out or the hope of the Christians would fade away. To that child and to each of us, Jesus promised that the true light would never be overcome by darkness.

A Beacon of Freedom. Cape Cod Light House rises from the sand dunes of Truro, Massachusetts, along a stretch of coastline that has claimed hundreds of ships. As early as the late 1600s, bonfires were built as a guide and a warning to ships. These proved impractical, so the first Cape Cod Light House was built in the late 1700s. A light has been in continuous operation since then.

The light is the focal point for sailors, despite the fact that it has been rebuilt and altered. It was even moved in 1996. At that time the entire structure was raised and nudged inches a day by an ingenious system of hydraulics. Now run by the Coast Guard, this beacon of freedom sounds a warning every 12 seconds by blowing a three-second blast on its huge fog horn while the double white light rotates on a continual 300-degree beam.

The light of Christ has shined since His birth. Nothing past, present, or future, and nothing above or below, has snuffed it out. It continues to shine the light of spiritual freedom for all to see!

FOR YOUTH

■ TOPIC: Be Free!

■ QUESTIONS: 1. What sort of truth was Jesus referring to that would give believers lasting freedom? 2. What does it mean to be a slave to sin and why is this so undesirable? 3. In what ways did Jesus honor His Father in heaven? 4. How would the Father glorify His Son? 5. In what sense did Jesus exist before Abraham?

■ ILLUSTRATIONS:

Freedom in Christ. Nearly everyone is familiar with Alcatraz Island in San Francisco Bay. Although it closed in 1963, the island prison has maintained its reputation as "The Rock," an escape-proof fortress reserved for America's worst criminals. Fewer people, however, know about Marion State Penitentiary, the maximum-security facility built to take Alcatraz's place, located in the heart of southern Illinois. As one of its residents, Vic knew Marion well.

Vic, a tall, broad-chested man, was incarcerated for armed robbery. For more than 10 years, he looked out between the bars of his window at the 20-foot wall topped with barbed wire that surrounded the prison core. Between the outer wall of his cell and that unscalable barrier was a 10-foot wide stretch of grass laid with dozens of barbed-wire coils. Beyond the barbed-wire wall were numerous towers manned by armed guards. Finally, a barbed-wire metal fence rose up between the prison campus and the nearby interstate.

Vic was not going anywhere. He was trapped. Surprisingly, though, he did not feel that way. For shortly after he entered the prison, he discovered a Bible in the prison library. Curious—and utterly bored—he began to read Scripture. His life would never be the same.

Vic gave his life to Jesus behind prison walls and discovered the joy that only a relationship with God can offer. The barbed wire and steel bars mattered less with each day that Vic clung to John 8:32. At Marion Penitentiary, Vic's soul had found a freedom in Christ that put all the surrounding barriers to shame.

Freedom Takes Time. In May 1954, African Americans celebrated the Supreme Court's ruling that ended school segregation: *Brown v. Board of Education of Topeka*;

however, because of the long controversy over court-ordered busing, most of the black students remained in segregated schools until 1964.

Most African Americans agree that the inroads to political and social freedoms in this country have been long, tedious, and hard. What is signed into law may take years to become a reality in local neighborhoods.

In a similar way, Christians are given freedom to become all that God created us to be the moment we become believers. It takes time, however, for that fact to sink into our minds, touch our hearts, and become a living reality in our daily experience.

What Is True? A college junior speaking to the chaplain related how she felt forced to go along with weekend binge drinking and casual sex. She felt incapable of doing differently. When the chaplain asked what she felt were true standards, the unhappy young woman sniffed, "Truth? What's true? There isn't such a thing as a true set of values, or a true anything. Everything is relative, isn't it? Besides, how can I possibly ever know the truth about anything, anyway?"

The woman spoke for many youth in today's society who think that everything is relative and that truth can never be known. At times this cynical viewpoint can even seep into the thinking of saved adolescents. This lesson from John 8 encourages embracing an attitude that is different than the one held by the college junior.

JESUS IS AUTHORITY AND JUDGE

BACKGROUND SCRIPTURE: John 5:19-29
DEVOTIONAL READING: 2 Timothy 4:1-5

KEY VERSE: Verily, verily, I say unto you, He that heareth my word, and believeth on him that sent me, hath everlasting life, and shall not come into condemnation; but is passed from death unto life. John 5:24.

KING JAMES VERSION

JOHN 5:19 Then answered Jesus and said unto them, Verily, verily, I say unto you, The Son can do nothing of himself, but what he seeth the Father do: for what things soever he doeth, these also doeth the Son likewise.
20 For the Father loveth the Son, and sheweth him all things that himself doeth: and he will shew him greater works than these, that ye may marvel. 21 For as the Father raiseth up the dead, and quickeneth them; even so the Son quickeneth whom he will. 22 For the Father judgeth no man, but hath committed all judgment unto the Son: 23 That all men should honour the Son, even as they honour the Father. He that honoureth not the Son honoureth not the Father which hath sent him. 24 Verily, verily, I say unto you, He that heareth my word, and believeth on him that sent me, hath everlasting life, and shall not come into condemnation; but is passed from death unto life. 25 Verily, verily, I say unto you, The hour is coming, and now is, when the dead shall hear the voice of the Son of God: and they that hear shall live. 26 For as the Father hath life in himself; so hath he given to the Son to have life in himself; 27 And hath given him authority to execute judgment also, because he is the Son of man. 28 Marvel not at this: for the hour is coming, in the which all that are in the graves shall hear his voice, 29 And shall come forth; they that have done good, unto the resurrection of life; and they that have done evil, unto the resurrection of damnation.

NEW REVISED STANDARD VERSION

JOHN 5:19 Jesus said to them, "Very truly, I tell you, the Son can do nothing on his own, but only what he sees the Father doing; for whatever the Father does, the Son does likewise. 20 The Father loves the Son and shows him all that he himself is doing; and he will show him greater works than these, so that you will be astonished. 21 Indeed, just as the Father raises the dead and gives them life, so also the Son gives life to whomever he wishes. 22 The Father judges no one but has given all judgment to the Son, 23 so that all may honor the Son just as they honor the Father. Anyone who does not honor the Son does not honor the Father who sent him. 24 Very truly, I tell you, anyone who hears my word and believes him who sent me has eternal life, and does not come under judgment, but has passed from death to life.

25 "Very truly, I tell you, the hour is coming, and is now here, when the dead will hear the voice of the Son of God, and those who hear will live. 26 For just as the Father has life in himself, so he has granted the Son also to have life in himself; 27 and he has given him authority to execute judgment, because he is the Son of Man. 28 Do not be astonished at this; for the hour is coming when all who are in their graves will hear his voice 29 and will come out—those who have done good, to the resurrection of life, and those who have done evil, to the resurrection of condemnation."

7

HOME BIBLE READINGS

Monday, January 8	John 5:1-9	*Jesus Heals a Lame Man*
Tuesday, January 9	John 3:31-36	*Whom God Has Sent*
Wednesday, January 10	John 4:19-26	*I Am the Christ*
Thursday, January 11	Matthew 7:24-29	*Jesus Taught with Authority*
Friday, January 12	2 Timothy 4:1-5	*Christ Will Judge*
Saturday, January 13	John 5:19-23	*Honor the Son*
Sunday, January 14	John 5:24-30	*Jesus Speaks of Judgment*

BACKGROUND

Some think the Gospel of John is the best known book in the New Testament. It has also been important to the Church's understanding of the person of Christ. The fourth Gospel differs from the Synoptic Gospels—Matthew, Mark, and Luke. Those Gospels trace Jesus' career generally in an orderly sequence. John, however, carefully selected material so that the lost might be redeemed through faith in the Messiah (John 20:31). Certain scholars may praise the fine literary qualities of John's Gospel, but the apostle simply wanted to promote the good news of Christ. Furthermore, John wrote to induce from each reader a response to that saving message.

The fourth Gospel has been described as a drama. The opening portion is considered the prologue. Subsequently, the apostle's account introduces a series of characters, including John the Baptist, Nicodemus, and the Samaritan women at the well (to name a few). The author skillfully wove Jesus' encounters with these individuals into his Gospel, showing the Son to be the pivotal figure of the universe.

Unlike Jesus, many of His Jewish contemporaries—especially the religious leaders—would not enter Samaria because they believed that they would be defiled if they had any contact with the Samaritans. The mutual hatred between these two people groups can be traced back several hundred years. In 722 B.C. the Assyrian Empire defeated the northern kingdom of Israel and deported most of the Israelites to other parts of their empire. The Israelites who remained intermarried with foreigners. Out of these marriages came a religion that mixed the worship of Yahweh with that of other pagan deities. In 539 B.C., when the Jews returned to Jerusalem from Babylonian captivity, they encountered Samaritans who were hostile to them and their religion. By Jesus' day the Jews had cultivated and nurtured a deep hatred for the people who lived in the province of Samaria.

After Jesus' encounter with the Samaritan woman, He spent two days with His new followers in Samaria and then went to Galilee (4:43). There He was greeted enthusiastically, for the people there had witnessed the miracles He had performed in Jerusalem during the Passover Feast. In Cana, a high official approached Jesus and begged Him to go to Capernaum and heal his dying son. Jesus told the man that only a miracle would persuade him to believe. The official continued to plead and Jesus responded by telling him that his son would live. As the official was returning home, his servants met him and told him that his son was getting well. When the man learned that his son's fever broke just when Jesus made this statement to him, he and his household became believers (4:44-54).

Sometime later, Jesus performed another healing miracle at the pool of Bethesda in Jerusalem, where He enabled a lame man to walk. Since it was the Sabbath, however, some religious leaders were upset that the man who once could not walk was now carrying his mat. Because Jesus made other people well on the Sabbath and declared Himself to be equal to God, these antagonists plotted to kill Him (5:1-18). The fourth of the Ten Commandments forms the scriptural foundation for the Sabbath (see Exod. 20:8-10a). Fifteen centuries after Moses delivered God's commandments to the Israelites, the Pharisees had constructed an elaborate interpretation of this Mosaic law.

This tension between Jesus and the religious leaders is also evident in the account of the Messiah healing a blind man on the Sabbath (John 9). The Savior's actions offended the Pharisees in three ways. First, Jesus mixed His spit with mud. Though this was a simple act, the religious leaders still would have considered it work. Second, Jesus healed. According to the Pharisees, only if a person's life was at stake could medical attention be given on the Sabbath. And third, one of their obscure laws specifically forbid putting spit on a person's eyelids on God's holy day.

Despite the assertions of His antagonists, Jesus never retreated from His messianic claims. Indeed, Christ told His enemies that others had testified to His divine Sonship. First was John the Baptist, who prepared the hearts of the people for this truth. More importantly, Jesus' earthly works were evidence that God had sent Him. In fact, God the Father and the Scriptures testify concerning Jesus. If the Savior's detractors had truly believed what Moses wrote, they would have believed in Jesus—but tragically they did not (5:30-46).

NOTES ON THE PRINTED TEXT

The historical context for this week's lesson is Jesus healing an invalid at a pool in Jerusalem. The Savior's act of mercy occurred on the Sabbath, which raised the ire of the religious leaders, who believed that even this activity was wrong to do on the seventh day of the week (John 5:1-5). Because Jesus healed on the Sabbath more than once, the religious leaders harassed Him (5:16). In response to their challenges to His authority, the Son noted that He, like the Father in heaven, was always at work (5:17). Jesus' antagonists were all the more enraged by this statement because, in addition to violating their Sabbath regulations, He made Himself equal with God. Consequently, the religious leaders were much more determined to have Jesus arrested and executed (5:18).

Instead of becoming flustered by His opponents, the Son of God solemnly affirmed that He did not operate on His own initiative; rather, Jesus did only what He saw the

Father doing. Both Jesus' words and works reflected the will of the Lord (5:19). For this reason, the Father loved the Son and disclosed to Him everything He was doing (5:20). The Son's healing of an invalid on the Sabbath, in accordance with the will of the Father, was an amazing miracle; but Jesus' antagonists would hear about even more remarkable works, such as His raising Lazarus from the dead (see 11:38-53) and one day judging all humankind (5:28-30). The Son had divine authority, as did the Father, to raise the dead (5:21) and to judge humanity (5:22). In fact, the Father had left all judgment to the Son to execute.

Why would God grant to Jesus the authority to judge all humanity? The Son explained that this would force everyone to honor Him in the same way that they honored the Father (5:23). Conversely, those who refused to honor the Son were also dishonoring the Father, who commissioned and sent Him (5:24). Because Jesus is God, those who debased or slandered Him were guilty of blasphemy.

The clear message of the Gospel is that faith in Christ eternally matters. Jesus solemnly assured His audience that those who heeded His message of truth and believed in God, who sent the Savior, had eternal life. It was a present reality as well as a future hope. Because believers put their faith in the Father and the Son—both of whom existed in relational unity—they would not be eternally condemned for their sins. They could rest assured that they would not come into judgment, for they had already passed from eternal death to life (5:24). This was neither a casual decision nor a take-it-or-leave-it message. Jesus solemnly assured His audience that a time of reckoning was coming. Indeed, from the vantage point of the Lord, it was already at hand. In that day of judgment, the Son of God will summon the righteous to live eternally with Him in heaven (5:25).

Son of God is an important title that points to Jesus' status as the Messiah. Its usage also spotlights His divine commission to carry out the work of redemption. Other related emphases are the Son's obedience to the Father, intimate knowledge of and fellowship with Him, and experience of the Father's love, mercy, blessings, and protection. Jesus' divine sonship was unique to Him; that is, it exclusively applied to Him. Crucial in this regard is our response to the truth of Jesus as the Messiah, the Son of God (see 20:31). The apostle urged all readers of the fourth Gospel to put their faith in Jesus, who eternally preexisted with the Father and the Spirit, who is fully God (as they are), and who became fully human through the Incarnation (see 1:1, 14, 18).

In 5:26, Jesus explained to His listeners that just as the Father had life in Himself, so too He had granted the Son to have life in Himself. Furthermore, the Father had given the Lord Jesus authority to execute judgment over all humanity due to His status as the Son of man (5:27). Only someone who is God and had communed with the other members of the Godhead could make such claims.

Son of man is the title Jesus most commonly used to describe Himself. He wanted to teach that, as the Messiah, He combined two Old Testament roles, Son of man

(Dan. 7:13-14) and Servant of the Lord (Isa. 52:13—53:12). Daniel described a Son of man to whom God gives an eternal kingdom. Isaiah described a Servant of the Lord who suffers on behalf of others. Jesus knew that He must perform the role of the suffering Servant. This included His betrayal, rejection, crucifixion, death, and resurrection; but He also knew that eventually He would receive glory as the Son of man. As such, He would bring salvation and judgment to the human race. Jesus did these things in accordance with the will of His Father.

We can only imagine the shock and agitation Jesus' opponents felt as they heard Him make various claims about Himself. He urged them, though, not to be astonished, for assuredly a future time was coming when the Son will command the dead to rise from their graves (John 5:28). As God, the Lord Jesus has the power and authority to resurrect the dead. Two potential eternal futures await the dead. Those who have put their faith in Christ—and evidenced this by their upright lives—will be raised to spend eternity with Jesus in heaven. Oppositely, those who refused to trust in Him—as demonstrated by their wicked lives—will be condemned to eternal punishment in hell (8:29).

SUGGESTIONS TO TEACHERS

Most cult leaders pose as authoritarian figures, claiming to be the sole or real source of truth. Jesus' words to the religious leaders of His day remind us that He is the Lord of life. Likewise, He is the person who will one day judge the human race. Only the Son of God can do this, for He is the image of the invisible God. It is only when the Son is on the throne of our lives that our Father in heaven is pleased.

1. PUTTING JESUS FIRST IN OUR LIVES. Many people come to a tragic end because they make everything else but God the center of their existence. Some are wicked people, having made a god out of sensual pleasure. Others are upstanding people, yet they too have failed to put their faith in the true and living God. Whenever an occupation or anything temporal takes number one priority in life, Jesus is no longer the Lord and God of our lives.

2. MAKING JESUS THE OBJECT OF OUR WORSHIP. John admonished us not to love the things of the world, for it breeds arrogance and selfish desires (1 John 2:15-16). Let us ensure that Jesus is the object of our faith, the foundation of our hope, and the focal point for our love. Only He can help us when our plans are shattered, our health fails, or death beckons. Accordingly, encourage your students to worship only Christ.

3. WARNING THE LOST ABOUT A TIME OF JUDGMENT. Part of the Gospel message is to tell people that all stand condemned before the Lord because of their sin. Just as Jesus warned His antagonists of a coming time of judgment, so too we should alert our unsaved acquaintances of the divine punishment they face for their misdeeds. Clearly, this is an unpopular message that will probably be rejected by many people; nevertheless, those who are spiritually lost must be warned.

4. TELLING THE LOST ABOUT SALVATION IN CHRIST. It is not enough to share that the Lord will judge evildoers. We should also tell the lost about His provision of deliverance. We can emphasize how much God loves all people even though they have rebelled against Him. And we should tell them that He does not relish the idea of condemning people to an eternity of suffering.

5. REMAINING COMMITTED. Faithfully proclaiming God's message requires a high degree of commitment on our part. There will be times when we would rather avoid the responsibility altogether. As good stewards, however, we know that we need to remain unwavering in doing what the Lord wants. Some of those we talk to will refuse to listen, while others will ignore what we have to say. Regardless of how little or how much response we receive, we should not give up or slacken in our efforts.

FOR ADULTS	■ **TOPIC:** Ultimate Fairness

■ **QUESTIONS:** 1. In what sense is Jesus the Lord of life? 2. Why would the Father entrust all judgment to the Son? 3. Why is it important to accord honor to the Son, not just to the Father? 4. Why are believers in Jesus Christ not eternally condemned? 5. Why are those who reject the Son heading to a Christless eternity?

■ **ILLUSTRATIONS:**

Unparalleled Mercy. One day a man was hauled into court because he had stolen a loaf of bread. When the judge investigated the matter, he discovered that the man was unemployed and could not find work. In desperation to feed his family, the man had decided to steal a loaf of bread.

During the court proceedings, the judge said to the man, "I'm sorry I have to punish you. I have to assess a fine of 10 dollars. But I want to pay the money myself." He reached into his pocket, pulled out a 10-dollar bill, and handed it to the man. As soon as the man took the money, the judge said, "Now I also want to remit the fine." This meant the man could keep the money. "Furthermore, I instruct the bailiff to pass around a hat to everyone in this courtroom, and I fine all who are assembled here 50 cents for living in a city where a man has to steal in order to have bread to eat." After the money was collected, the judge gave it to the man.

Like the judge, God's Servant, who is our Messiah, diligently pursued His mission with unparalleled mercy.

Most Important Role. Desi Arnaz Giles is an acclaimed actor. In March 1997, he was hired to play the role of Jesus in a Passion play in Union City, New Jersey. The theater received cancellations and Giles received death threats from people who were incensed that Giles would play the role of Jesus. The reason is that Giles is African American.

At the Park Performing Arts Center, Giles and a white actor alternated in the play depicting Jesus' final days. According to the Associated Press, word spread that an African-American actor was one of the two taking the part of Jesus. Two groups canceled tickets for a performance featuring Giles, and another rescheduled for a day when the white actor was set to perform. Later, Giles received threats on his life for assuming the role.

Giles calmly went on with the part, however, calling the role "the most important one in my life. . . . I will never do anything more important than this." When asked about the possibility of being killed by racists opposed to his playing the role of Jesus, Giles showed that he was prepared to bear witness to his faith as a devout Christian. "Should someone clip me during a performance," he noted, "don't cry for me. Just rejoice, because I'm ready to go home."

Murders in Mississippi. On June 21, 2005, former Ku Klux Klan (KKK) member Edgar Ray Killen, 80, was found guilty of manslaughter in the 1964 killing of three civil rights workers. According to CNN, as Killen sat in a wheelchair with an oxygen tube attached to his nose, he showed no emotion when the verdict was read.

During the trial, prosecutors portrayed Killen as a KKK leader who recruited a mob to kill Michael Schwerner, Andrew Goodman, and James Chaney exactly 41 years earlier. The crimes triggered outrage across the country, and energized the civil rights movement. For the surviving family members of the deceased, justice was served for the murders in Mississippi that had occurred so long ago.

Sometimes the wheels of divine justice can seem as if they are advancing too slowly. Nevertheless, this week's lesson reminds us that ultimate fairness rests in the Lord Jesus and that He will one day bring about true justice for His followers.

FOR YOUTH

■ TOPIC: Justice for All

■ QUESTIONS: 1. Why did Jesus only do what He saw the Father doing? 2. Why would the Father give the Son the authority to give life to whomever He desired? 3. Why would the Father give the Son the authority to judge humankind? 4. Why did Jesus say it was just as important to honor Him as it was to honor the Father? 5. What eternal future awaits believers, and how does this differ from what unbelievers will face?

■ ILLUSTRATIONS:

Justice by Way of Reconciliation. As the death toll in Mexico's bloodstained southern state of Chiapas continued to rise in 1998, church leaders intensified their efforts toward peaceful reconciliation. So said Dean Alford in the *Christianity Today* article "Words Against Weapons: Evangelicals, Catholics Dialogue to Help Bring Peace to Violent Chiapas." Religious differences were an exacerbating part of the conflict, pitting one religious group against another. But starting in 1996, some church leaders launched a series of community-based dialogues between these Christian groups.

"When you get in a room and sit face-to-face, and each tell your stories, it's difficult to think of them as your enemy," says Ken Sehested, executive director of the Baptist Peace Fellowship of North America, which was involved in the dialogues. In order to build community, attendees serve meals and clean up the kitchen in mixed groups. Says one leader, "It's a very human thing and breaks down some barriers." Grass-roots church leaders are bringing invisible light to Chiapas as they minister together to break the bonds of religious animosity.

Learning the Secrets. The story is told of a man who wanted to learn everything about jade. He went to an old Chinese master who was reputed to be one of the world's experts in the precious stone. The aging specialist told the man that he would teach him, but the lessons would require 10 days of complete attention. The man agreed to give full attention to the master.

On the first day, the master brought out an exquisite piece of green jade. He instructed the man to examine it closely for 10 hours. The next day, the aged expert handed the man another beautiful piece of jade, and gave him the same instruction to study the piece for 10 hours. No other word was spoken. That evening, as before, the master collected the jade piece he had handed the learner in the morning. The same procedure followed the third day, the fourth, and so on.

At the end of the tenth day, the master informed the learner he had nothing more to teach him. The man was perplexed. He complained, "The expert never said a word about jade to me during any of those 10 days. On the last day, he wasted my time by handing me a fake piece of jade."

When you learn the difference between the false, unjust ways of the world and the true, just ways of the Lord Jesus, you will move from phony faith to a dynamic one. And when you know Christ so well, your life will proclaim a message of forgiveness. You will have a fresh message that those around you desperately need to know! So be sure to study the real thing.

Serving Others. Many saved teens often feel that what they do or can do to serve the Lord and others is unimportant. Since they aren't leaders or doing something that radically impacts the culture in which we live, they reason that their ministry or possible ministry isn't significant.

Bill Bennett, however, writes that in our effort to impact our culture and society, what really matters is "what we do in our daily lives—not the big statements that we broadcast to the world at large, but the small messages we send through our families and our neighborhoods and our communities." Just as the Father was with the Son in all He did for the glory of God, we can also be assured that the Lord will sustain us in the ministry to which He has called us. God will never summon us where His grace will not sustain us.

JESUS IS THE BREAD OF LIFE AND LIVING WATER

BACKGROUND SCRIPTURE: John 6:25-59; 7:37-39
DEVOTIONAL READING: Ephesians 3:14-21

KEY VERSE: I am the bread of life: he that cometh to me shall never hunger; and he that believeth on me shall never thirst. John 6:35.

KING JAMES VERSION

JOHN 6:34 Then said they unto him, Lord, evermore give us this bread. 35 And Jesus said unto them, I am the bread of life: he that cometh to me shall never hunger; and he that believeth on me shall never thirst. 36 But I said unto you, That ye also have seen me, and believe not. 37 All that the Father giveth me shall come to me; and him that cometh to me I will in no wise cast out. 38 For I came down from heaven, not to do mine own will, but the will of him that sent me. 39 And this is the Father's will which hath sent me, that of all which he hath given me I should lose nothing, but should raise it up again at the last day. 40 And this is the will of him that sent me, that every one which seeth the Son, and believeth on him, may have everlasting life: and I will raise him up at the last day. . . .

7:37 In the last day, that great day of the feast, Jesus stood and cried, saying, If any man thirst, let him come unto me, and drink. 38 He that believeth on me, as the scripture hath said, out of his belly shall flow rivers of living water. 39 (But this spake he of the Spirit, which they that believe on him should receive: for the Holy Ghost was not yet given; because that Jesus was not yet glorified.)

NEW REVISED STANDARD VERSION

JOHN 6:34 They said to him, "Sir, give us this bread always."

35 Jesus said to them, "I am the bread of life. Whoever comes to me will never be hungry, and whoever believes in me will never be thirsty. 36 But I said to you that you have seen me and yet do not believe. 37 Everything that the Father gives me will come to me, and anyone who comes to me I will never drive away; 38 for I have come down from heaven, not to do my own will, but the will of him who sent me. 39 And this is the will of him who sent me, that I should lose nothing of all that he has given me, but raise it up on the last day. 40 This is indeed the will of my Father, that all who see the Son and believe in him may have eternal life; and I will raise them up on the last day." . . .

7:37 On the last day of the festival, the great day, while Jesus was standing there, he cried out, "Let anyone who is thirsty come to me, 38 and let the one who believes in me drink. As the scripture has said, 'Out of the believer's heart shall flow rivers of living water.'" 39 Now he said this about the Spirit, which believers in him were to receive; for as yet there was no Spirit, because Jesus was not yet glorified.

8

Monday, January 15	Ephesians 3:14-21	*May Christ Dwell Within*
Tuesday, January 16	John 6:16-24	*Do Not Be Afraid*
Wednesday, January 17	John 6:25-34	*Jesus, the Heavenly Bread*
Thursday, January 18	John 6:35-40	*I Am the Bread of Life*
Friday, January 19	John 6:41-51	*Sustained by Living Bread*
Saturday, January 20	Isaiah 49:7-13	*Sing for Joy*
Sunday, January 21	John 7:37-41	*Living Water*

BACKGROUND

The context of John 6 is the Savior's feeding of 5,000 people. It also represents a major turning point in the thematic development of the fourth Gospel. Up until this time in the narrative, Jesus' ministry was primarily in Jerusalem; but now it shifts to Galilee. This change of venue brings the Son's identity into sharper relief. He is shown to be the sent one of the Father. Perhaps more than before, the distinction between and consequences of belief versus unbelief are differentiated. Those in the latter category become increasingly intense in their rejection of and hostility toward the Messiah.

An examination of 6:1-14 indicates that after leaving Jerusalem, Jesus traveled to the other side of the Sea of Galilee. It was the time when the Passover was about to be celebrated in Jerusalem. The Savior was sitting on a mountainside with His disciples when He spotted a large crowd streaming toward Him. In the episode that unfolded, Jesus miraculously fed over 5,000 people. This prompted many to wonder whether He was the prophet that Moses referred to in Deuteronomy 18:15.

Bread was essential to life in the region of Palestine. Grain was usually ground by a millstone, kneaded in a wooden bowl, and baked as circular cakes. Bread was so important to the people of the region that it was baked daily. Other foods, like fish or meat, were wrapped inside bread. Bread was also used as an eating utensil for stews and soups.

Unleavened bread was conveniently used at harvesttime when families were too busy to wait for bread to rise. When a long trip was planned, unleavened bread was practical to bring along. Bread was used in temple offerings and placed daily inside the sanctuary. It was also used to offer blessings within the Jewish family.

Wheat was the most commonly used grain in the making of bread. Barley was another grain used for bread in the region; however, barley was usually used to feed livestock. It was made into bread only for the poorest of the poor; yet Jesus made use of the barley bread donated by a young boy to feed 5,000 men and uncounted women and children. No one is recorded as complaining about being fed the cheaper bread.

Sharing bread in that culture was a sacred matter. A pious individual never ate with an unclean person, especially if one wished to observe the Pharisees' teachings about the law. In this regard, Jesus would have been expected to keep the requirements about eating, especially during Passover season; but Jesus shocked the religious elite of His day by ignoring the traditional rules about never breaking bread with anyone except respectable, law-observing Jews. The Savior did so because He was concerned with the physical needs of the people, including their hunger. Through the miracle He performed, He demonstrated that He is the only person able to satisfy the longing people have for a genuine relationship with God.

The people whom Jesus fed, in their desperation, wanted to force Him to be their king; but the kind of ruler they wanted, one who would overthrow Israel's oppressors, was not in God's plan. Thus, Jesus retreated into the hills to be alone with His Father. The disciples did not see Jesus again until evening when they were on a boat in the middle of the Sea of Galilee. As gusty winds made the waters rage, they saw Jesus approaching them. At first they were terrified because He was walking on water, but His words calmed them and together they reached Capernaum (6:15-21).

NOTES ON THE PRINTED TEXT

Apart from the Resurrection, Jesus' feeding of the 5,000 is the only miracle that is recorded in all four Gospels. John was probably familiar with some of the other accounts of this event by the other Gospel writers. As an eyewitness, though, he added a few revealing details concerning Philip and Andrew's involvement. The fact that John retold an incident that was probably already well known is an indication of the impact this miracle had on people.

The day after Jesus had performed the miracle, the people discovered that He had returned to His hometown. They in turn rushed to Capernaum to look for Him. In the ensuing exchange, Jesus noted that they were only interested in His satisfying their immediate need for food. He pointed to Himself as the true Bread from heaven, of which the manna the Israelites ate in the wilderness was a type (John 6:24-33). Put differently, the manna anticipated the perfect and everlasting nourishment that Jesus provided to those who put their faith in Him for eternal life.

Regretfully, the crowd failed to understand what Jesus meant. He referred to bread as a metaphor, whereas they thought He was speaking about literal loaves they could eat. In fact, they implored Him to give them this bread all the time (6:34). Jesus, however, remained focused on the central point, stating it more plainly in 6:35. He declared Himself to be the *bread of life*. Those who came to Him in faith would have their spiritual hunger and thirst eternally satisfied.

The crowd had the unique privilege of experiencing the words and works of Christ, particularly His feeding of over 5,000 people; nevertheless, many refused to believe in Him as the Messiah (6:36). This did not mean that everyone rejected Jesus. In fact, all whom the Father gave the Son would come to Him in faith. He in turn would welcome them, not reject them (6:37). Jesus stressed that He did not operate on His own initiative; rather, the Father had sent Him, and the Son did His Father's will (6:38). God's decree was that none of those who believed in the Son would be lost. Jesus pledged to resurrect all of them at the last day (6:39).

Jesus' mandate was clear. His purpose was to save and to raise up from the dead those who had placed their trust in Him. His ability to resurrect the dead would be the final proof of His God-given authority. Moreover, He would not abandon a single person His Father had drawn to Christ. Everyone who looks to Jesus in faith will ultimately be saved at Christ's appearing (6:40).

Jesus' feeding the large crowd fueled people's hopes that the great prophet, spoken of by Moses had come (see Deut. 18:15). Whether this prophet was to be a forerunner of the Messiah or the Messiah Himself is debated, though the Pharisees questioned John the Baptist as if the Prophet and Messiah were separate people (John 1:20-21).

The crowd saw significant signs in Jesus' ministry that He was someone worthy of being the Prophet whom Moses described. For example, Jesus miraculously fed the people a kind of Passover meal that filled 12 baskets of leftovers—symbolically, one for each of the 12 tribes (6:4, 13). Furthermore, Jesus' miracles hinted at what the people were expecting when the Messiah would come. The Savior, however, told them not to yearn for an actual feast (6:49-50), but to instead ask Him for living bread for their eternal life (6:51).

The peoples' unbelief again surfaced as they murmured among themselves their skepticism about Jesus' claim to be God's bread from heaven; and Jesus chastised the people for their grumbling. Since Jesus' statements were intolerable to most of His listeners, they rejected Him. Even some who had followed Him turned away. His closest disciples, however, did not leave. Peter, speaking for the Twelve, confessed his belief in Jesus as the Messiah. Jesus replied by telling them that He had chosen them, even the one who would betray Him (6:41-71).

After this series of events, Jesus traveled around Galilee (7:1); but when the Jewish feast of Tabernacles arrived, Jesus went to Jerusalem. Then halfway through the seven-day observance, Jesus went up to the temple courts and began teaching. He contended with the religious leaders, denied charges of being demon-possessed, and asserted that He honored the Father, who sent Him (7:2-36).

In Jesus' day, one prominent ritual the people performed included a ceremonial drawing of water. This commemorated the Lord's provision of water to the Israelites in the desert (see Num. 20:2-13). Jesus waited until the last day of the feast, which was the greatest day of the festival, to make an announcement. He cried out that whoever had spiritual thirst should come to Him and drink (John 7:37).

The Savior was inviting all to put their faith in Him. When they did, He pledged that from within them would flow rivers of living water (7:38). The exact Old Testament passage Jesus was referring to remains unclear. Perhaps He was talking about a central truth evident in several verses. For instance, there are some that associate water with the gift of the Holy Spirit at the end of the age (see Isa. 44:3; Ezek. 36:25-27).

In any case, the thrust of Jesus' promise is clear. The Spirit would be abundantly present in believers, benefiting both them and those around them (John 7:38). John noted that, prior to the day of Pentecost, the era of the Spirit had not yet arrived. Once the Son had experienced His death, resurrection, and ascension in glory to the Father, the presence and power of the Spirit would be manifested in a way not yet seen to that point in salvation history (7:39; see Acts 2:1-4).

SUGGESTIONS TO TEACHERS

A certain seminary professor who teaches students about Holy Communion insists that they must learn to bake bread before they can understand the meaning of this sacred meal. Only when they experience the joy of serving a delicious home-baked loaf and seeing the delight on the part of those receiving it, this professor says, will these students appreciate the institution of the Lord's Supper.

Perhaps you can take a cue from this teacher by actually bringing to the class a warm, fragrant, freshly baked loaf. Tortillas and pita bread are even better, since these more closely resemble what people would have eaten in Jesus' day. In any case, having each student savor the taste of freshly prepared food is a fun way of getting the lesson off to a good start! The palate immediately informs each person how Jesus is the bread of life as contrasted with the unsatisfying fillers of the world.

1. THE LUNCHBOX MIRACLE. The problem of handling the need for food for the huge audience was solved after Jesus was given a boy's lunch. Everyone received enough to eat. Sharing a simple meal of five small barley loaves of bread and two small, dried fish had a miraculous effect, as any act of sharing always does.

2. THE LIKABLE MASTER. The people present that day wanted to acclaim Jesus as their earthly king. Yet Jesus did not want mere popularity. Later, when the crowds thronged around Him again, He spoke to them about sustenance of a different type—namely, bread that would meet their deepest hunger. Jesus insisted that they accept Him on His terms as the bread of life. He expects the same response from us today. Like the folks who tried to make Him into a hero in their own image, we sometimes try to push the Lord into serving us instead of the other way around. We will always be disappointed whenever we attempt to control God.

3. THE LIVING MANNA. The Lord Jesus claimed to be the bread that gives life. No one who came to Him would ever be hungry (John 6:35). Have your students spend a few moments thinking about this assertion. Ask them to name some of the inadequate substitutes people turn to in their attempts to find nourishment for their deepest hungers. What kind of spiritual diet feeds the gnawing emptiness that some feel? Point to the fact that the Savior alone can continue to nurture a person in every stage of life.

4. THE LEARNED MURMURERS. Jesus had critics. The sneering authorities belittled His claim of being able to quench the spiritual thirst of all who come to Him in faith. But to those who believe in Him, the Son's promise of a personal relationship with the Father through the Spirit provides strength and stamina. There are still those who dismiss Jesus and His teachings. Although these critics may try to speak authoritatively about Him, only those who acknowledge Jesus' authority will be eternally satisfied in their souls.

FOR ADULTS

■ TOPIC: Lasting Results

■ QUESTIONS: 1. What did Jesus mean by declaring Himself to be the bread of life? 2. What was the will of the Father concerning those He gave to the Son? 3. What did Jesus promise to do for believers at the last day? 4. What was Jesus' intent by inviting all to come to Him and drink? 5. What is Jesus' response to all who come to Him in faith?

■ **ILLUSTRATIONS:**

The Bread That Satisfies. In the ancient refectory in San Marrco's monastery in Florence, Italy, there is a beautiful fresco. It shows St. Dominic seated at a table with a group of monks. They are shown asking a blessing over empty plates. No bread is seen on the table. The companions of Dominic are depicted with expressions of amazement on their faces. While Dominic prays, angels of God enter the room carrying the bread that means they will never hunger.

Jesus is the bread of life. Trying to feed on anything else—pleasure, money, sex, power, and so on—will never satisfy our deepest spiritual needs.

Wonder Bread. A few years ago, the humble bread loaf made a comeback. Specialty bakeries and bread-only retail stores gave rise to an incredible variety of "artisan" breads ranging from cracked wheat and cinnamon raisin to jalapeno cheese and yulakaga (a Christmas egg bread topped with mixed fruit and frosting). In addition, a flood of bread machine sales made the luxury of fresh-baked bread as easy as opening a box and pushing a button.

It is not hard to understand bread's incredible popularity. One culinary expert noted that bread is considered by many to be a soothing, comforting food. People find the smell alluring and the taste appealing. Bread, as some used to say, is the staff of life, and it is impossible to imagine life without it.

From the Israelites' dependence on manna in the wilderness to the broken bread of the Last Supper, bread has meant life and nourishment throughout Scripture. In this week's lesson, it takes on another dimension. Jesus reminded His listeners that manna fed the hungry only temporarily; yet dependence on Him would yield eternal nourishment. What human bread accomplishes for the human body, Jesus brings about for the human soul.

Mike's Hunger Pangs. Some years ago, there was a strike at Pittsburgh-based J & L Specialty Steel. One of the men from a nearby church was a supervisor at the mill on Second Avenue. Like other management personnel, he was shut in the mill, unable to leave because of the picket line, but busy turning out steel as part of a crew of supervisors and management, in spite of the strike.

The company paid these individuals handsomely for staying on in the plant. The cafeteria served free meals, and went out of its way to make them tasty. The company even arranged for movies to be brought in to entertain the crew in the plant. Everything seemed to be as comfortable as possible under the circumstances.

One day, after three weeks of confinement in the plant, a big Irish supervisor named Mike came to the man in the local congregation who worked with him. "Jack," Mike said, "I'm sick." "Then you'd better go to the infirmary," Jack said. Superintendents in the hot strip mills aren't in the soul business, and Jack was ready to dismiss Mike's complaint. But Jack saw that Mike was serious. Mike continued, "Look, I haven't been to church for weeks. I miss it. Something's wrong. I don't feel good. And I mean it!"

Mike was saying that he was hungry for the things of God. A few days later, Mike's request was honored when arrangements were made for a minister to come through the picket line to conduct worship services in the plant.

For Youth

■ TOPIC: Jesus: Life-Giving Bread and Water
■ QUESTIONS: 1. How does Jesus satisfy our deepest spiritual hunger and thirst? 2. How does Jesus respond when we come to Him in faith? 3. For what purpose did Jesus come to earth from the Father in heaven? 4. What did Jesus pledge to do for those who trusted in Him for eternal life? 5. What connection did Jesus make between streams of living water and the Holy Spirit?

■ ILLUSTRATIONS:

No Substitutes. A monarch butterfly is as beautiful as a viceroy butterfly. A bird, looking for a light lunch, might snatch either, expecting a pleasurable meal. God designed both with beautiful orange and black wings. In fact, the only major differences are the viceroy's slightly smaller size and a black stripe along its hind wings.

The viceroy would be a feathered diner's delight, but a monarch would not. Poison ingested from the milkweed plant while the monarch was a caterpillar makes the butterfly taste bitter. Once a bird eats a monarch, it won't repeat the mistake.

All around us, there are subtle counterfeits. The most dangerous are religious frauds. When Jesus declared Himself to be the true bread from heaven (John 6:32), He identified Himself as the only healthful food for the soul.

No Satisfaction. Each year, children are subjected to countless advertisements for fast food. In addition, every day nearly 1 in 10 Americans eat at a fast-food outlet.

Nutritionists note that this practice is unhealthy. Junk food simply does not satisfy nutritional needs.

In the same way, many youth take advantage of trends and fads that simply do not meet their spiritual needs. Jesus declared Himself to be the bread of life. Those who partake of Him will be eternally satisfied.

Not Forgotten. Agnes Newton Keith, and her son George, were part of the European governmental personnel rounded up by the Japanese in Sandakan, Borneo, on January 19, 1942. Agnes was separated from her husband and placed in a Japanese internment camp until September 11, 1945. There she endured an attempted rape, disease, over-work, fear, hunger, and malnutrition.

On August 24, 1945, a C-47 flew low over the camp, circled, and then dropped a torpedo-shaped object by parachute. The camp's 34 children dragged the six-foot object into the center of the camp. Its case bore the printed word *BREAD*.

Agnes was asked if the inmates raced to the canister, tore it open, and fought over the food. She replied that any such action would have horrified the community. Even though they may have felt like doing that, an equal distribution of rations was sacred. Sharing equally was the order of the day. She also noted that the parachute case meant more than food for the starving women and children. It was a reminder that they were not forgotten. That realization nourished the waning hope in their souls.

Many in the world have little to eat (such as bread), while many of us in the United States have plenty of food. Jesus makes us aware that an equal distribution of food resources needs to be implemented so that bread would be seen as sacred as it was in that camp. Sharing food is also a reminder that the rest of the world has not been for-gotten. The eternal bread of life has come for all.

"I AM THE LIGHT OF THE WORLD"

BACKGROUND SCRIPTURE: John 8:12-20; 12:44-46
DEVOTIONAL READING: Isaiah 35:3-10

KEY VERSE: Then spake Jesus again unto them, saying, I am the light of the world: he that followeth me shall not walk in darkness, but shall have the light of life. John 8:12.

KING JAMES VERSION

JOHN 8:12 Then spake Jesus again unto them, saying, I am the light of the world: he that followeth me shall not walk in darkness, but shall have the light of life. 13 The Pharisees therefore said unto him, Thou bearest record of thyself; thy record is not true. 14 Jesus answered and said unto them, Though I bear record of myself, yet my record is true: for I know whence I came, and whither I go; but ye cannot tell whence I come, and whither I go. 15 Ye judge after the flesh; I judge no man. 16 And yet if I judge, my judgment is true: for I am not alone, but I and the Father that sent me. 17 It is also written in your law, that the testimony of two men is true. 18 I am one that bear witness of myself, and the Father that sent me beareth witness of me. 19 Then said they unto him, Where is thy Father? Jesus answered, Ye neither know me, nor my Father: if ye had known me, ye should have known my Father also. 20 These words spake Jesus in the treasury, as he taught in the temple: and no man laid hands on him; for his hour was not yet come. . . .

12:44 Jesus cried and said, He that believeth on me, believeth not on me, but on him that sent me. 45 And he that seeth me seeth him that sent me. 46 I am come a light into the world, that whosoever believeth on me should not abide in darkness.

NEW REVISED STANDARD VERSION

JOHN 8:12 Again Jesus spoke to them, saying, "I am the light of the world. Whoever follows me will never walk in darkness but will have the light of life." 13 Then the Pharisees said to him, "You are testifying on your own behalf; your testimony is not valid." 14 Jesus answered, "Even if I testify on my own behalf, my testimony is valid because I know where I have come from and where I am going, but you do not know where I come from or where I am going. 15 You judge by human standards; I judge no one. 16 Yet even if I do judge, my judgment is valid; for it is not I alone who judge, but I and the Father who sent me. 17 In your law it is written that the testimony of two witnesses is valid. 18 I testify on my own behalf, and the Father who sent me testifies on my behalf." 19 Then they said to him, "Where is your Father?" Jesus answered, "You know neither me nor my Father. If you knew me, you would know my Father also." 20 He spoke these words while he was teaching in the treasury of the temple, but no one arrested him, because his hour had not yet come. . . .

12:44 Then Jesus cried aloud: "Whoever believes in me believes not in me but in him who sent me. 45 And whoever sees me sees him who sent me. 46 I have come as light into the world, so that everyone who believes in me should not remain in the darkness."

9

HOME BIBLE READINGS

Monday, January 22	Isaiah 35:3-10	*Promises for God's People*
Tuesday, January 23	Matthew 4:12-17	*Jesus Brings Light*
Wednesday, January 24	John 9:1-11	*Jesus Heals a Blind Man*
Thursday, January 25	John 9:35-41	*Who Is the Son of Man?*
Friday, January 26	Ephesians 5:15-21	*Knowing God's Will*
Saturday, January 27	John 8:12-20	*Jesus Is the World's Light*
Sunday, January 28	John 12:44-50	*I Have Come as Light*

BACKGROUND

The Feast of Tabernacles in Jerusalem of Jesus' time was a magnificent event. Tall lampstands were placed on top of the great portico of the Court of the Women. Golden bowls of oil were set on these high lampstands. Enormous wicks were made from the castoff garments of the priests. Young apprentice priests climbed ladders to light these wicks and replenish the oil supply in the golden bowls. The flaring oil wicks were so bright that every street and alley in Jerusalem was illuminated. Men carrying blazing torches danced through the streets, and the Levites played music. This dramatic light show awed everyone.

Against the backdrop of the brilliant lighting of the huge seven-pronged lampstand, Jesus boldly declared Himself to be the light of the world (John 8:12). This assertion startled His audience. First, everyone realized that Jesus set Himself as greater than the Feast of Tabernacles. Jesus also claimed to eclipse all that the religious holiday stood for. Second, Jesus was understood to equate Himself with God. The phrase *I Am* was an expression of divine authority. Throughout the Old Testament, the words *I Am* served as a cue that God would disclose something about Himself. *I Am* emphasized God's majesty and supremacy. Jesus' use of this phrase was a clear statement of His authority as the Lord God of Israel and all history. When He declared Himself to be the light of the world, He set off a furious controversy over His claims.

The Gospel of John records *I am* 29 times, 26 of these having been spoken by Jesus. The apostle wanted his readers to make no mistake about what the Messiah thought about Himself and what was the profound nature of His claims. Truly, John insisted, Jesus had the authority of the Eternal One. Those following Jesus would never walk in spiritual darkness. Every disciple of His would find Him to be the truth that brings eternal freedom.

The crowds who heard Jesus make various assertions about Himself remained divided over His true identity. Some were convinced of His divine, messianic status, while others could not get past the fact that He was from Nazareth in Galilee. The latter reasoned that the Messiah would be born of the royal line of David, in Bethlehem, the village where King David was born (7:40-43; see Ps. 89:3-4; Mic. 5:2). Regretfully, the antagonists failed to take into account that Jesus was born in Bethlehem (Luke 2:4-7).

Even though some wanted to seize Jesus, no one at this time laid a hand on Him (John 7:44). In fact, the temple guards whom the religious authorities had dispatched to arrest Jesus returned to the chief priests and Pharisees empty-handed (7:45). When the guards were questioned about this, they explained that they had never heard anyone speak as profoundly as Jesus (7:46). Aghast at such a statement, the Pharisees mockingly retorted that Jesus had deceived the guards (7:47). Perhaps the worst fear of the religious leaders was the possibility that one of their peers might succumb to Jesus' teachings (7:48). The Pharisees remarked that the crowds were duped because they did not know the Mosaic law. From the perspective of the religious leaders, the ignorant masses were under a divine curse (7:49).

At that time, a Pharisee named Nicodemus was present. He was a member of the Sanhedrin as well as the same person who had earlier met with Jesus (7:50; see 3:1-2). Nicodemus asked his peers whether it was legal to condemn anyone before that person was given a full and fair trial. How could a judgment be rendered before the full nature of the misdeeds allegedly committed were verified (7:51)? The Pharisees disdainfully stated that Nicodemus needed to search the Scriptures, for supposedly no prophet of God ever came from Galilee (7:52). This statement, however, ignored the fact that the prophet Jonah had come from that region (see 2 Kings 14:25).

NOTES ON THE PRINTED TEXT

During one heated portion of the debate between Jesus and the religious authorities, Christ announced that He is the light of the world (John 8:12). On the evening of the first day of the Feast of Tabernacles, a ceremony called the illumination of the temple took place. In that ceremony four great candelabra were lit to dispel the darkness. It was claimed that the light from these candelabra was so great that it lit up every courtyard in Jerusalem. It is little wonder that Jesus chose the Feast of Tabernacles as the setting for His message of being the light of the world.

Tragically, many of the listeners failed to rejoice in the Messiah's light, which would never burn out. This especially included Jesus' opponents, such as the Pharisees, who had physical sight, but remained in spiritual darkness. Here we see that the emphasis in 8:12 is on becoming a disciple of Jesus. Motivation for following Him can be found in the promise that believers will never stumble about in the darkness, for Jesus will be their guiding light. Despite the profound nature of Jesus' messianic claims, the Pharisees asserted that He was merely testifying about Himself and that what He said was invalid (8:13).

In Jesus' day, it was commonly understood that multiple witnesses were required for a testimony to be deemed valid. In the case of the Savior, the Pharisees considered His testimony legally unacceptable because they did not think there were any corroborating witnesses. The Son declared that the claims He made about Himself were valid and true because of His eternal preexistence with the Father and the Spirit and His eventual return to the other members of the Godhead (8:14). The Pharisees, however, were ignorant of where Jesus came from (His origin) and where He was going (His destination).

Jesus noted that His opponents made snap judgments based on outward appearances, whereas He did not pass judgment on anyone (8:15). This did not mean Christ would never judge humankind; it is just that such was reserved for a future time. In that day, the evaluation He rendered would be accurate and fair in every respect. The Son noted that He was not alone in His assessment, for He and the Father who sent Him rendered their decisions together (8:16).

Jesus directed the Pharisees to the Mosaic law, which they highly prized (and which pointed them to the Messiah). In particular, Deuteronomy 17:6 and 19:15 stated that when two or more legitimate witnesses agreed on a matter, their testimony was to be accepted as valid (John 8:17). Without equivocation, the Son declared that He was one witness and that His Father, who had sent Him to earth, was the second witness (8:18). The idea is that because Jesus had the witness of God, no other testimony was necessary, for God is always right.

Not surprisingly, the Pharisees thought the claim Jesus made was a reference to His physical father. The authorities, of course, got it all wrong. The Son was not even addressing His miraculous conception through the agency of the Holy Spirit. Jesus was talking about His intimate relationship with the Father as a member of the Trinity. For that reason, the Son declared that the Pharisees neither knew Him nor His Father (8:19). Because they refused to acknowledge the Son, they would remain ignorant of the Father, for it was through the Word that one came to know God (see 1:18; 14:9).

The apostle noted that Jesus' exchange with the Pharisees occurred near the treasury room within the temple complex (8:20). Though they wanted to have Jesus arrested and executed, this would not happen until the divinely appointed time. Two observations arise from this truth. First, Jesus had a clear sense of His mission on earth, including His passion or suffering, and He never deviated from His divinely ordained path. Second, the Father remained in full control of all that happened to His Son. Nothing took the Lord by surprise.

Even Jesus' triumphal entry into Jerusalem five days before the Passover took place in accordance with God's will (12:1, 12). Along the route a large number of people hurried to meet Jesus. These were probably Jewish pilgrims on their way to the city of God to celebrate the Passover feast. Most likely they had heard about Jesus' demonstrations of power. Indeed, they praised Him with palm branches and loud shouts, proclaiming Him to be the blessed one who saves. They also quoted Psalm 118:25 and 26 in acclaiming Him to be the Messiah, who comes in the Lord's name (John 12:13).

Regretfully, most of the Jews who came to see Jesus refused to put their faith in Him despite having witnessed the many miracles He had performed (especially the restoration of Lazarus to life; 12:17-19). In fact, the prophet Isaiah had foretold that the Jews would reject God's suffering Servant (12:37-38; see Isa. 53:1). John would not want us to think that the entire Jewish population refused to believe in Christ. In reality, many of the spiritual leaders believed. Tragically, however, they would not publicly acknowledge Jesus as the Messiah, because they were afraid of the Pharisees, who had the desire and influence to expel believers in Christ from the synagogue (John 12:42-43; see 9:22). They preferred to remain comfortable in their social standing while accepting the approval of people rather than that of God.

Jesus concluded His public ministry with one last appeal to the people to put their trust in Him. Believing in Him would be the same as believing in God, who had sent Him. Indeed, God the Father and His Son are so close that to see one is to see the other (12:44-45). As 10:30 reveals, though they are distinct persons within the Godhead, they are one in essence (along with the Holy Spirit). The members of the Trinity alike possess the fullness of the divine nature with all its perfection; in addition, they are united in redemptive purpose. Not only is Jesus one with God, but also He is the Light that dispels the darkness. Everyone is condemned to spiritual darkness except for those who receive Jesus as the spiritual light. Accordingly, Jesus beckoned the people to enter into His light and be delivered from the world's darkness (12:46).

SUGGESTIONS TO TEACHERS

Jesus' life and death demand a direct, personal response. Either we choose to accept Him into our lives or we reject Him. As this week's lesson makes clear, not everyone will choose to receive Him. Even some of those who witnessed His miracles firsthand decided they could do better without Him; but those who choose to call Him Savior and Lord are welcomed with open arms. The choice is ours.

1. JESUS REVEALED WHO HE WAS. Through His many words and works, Christ made His identity known to all who would listen. Through His teachings and power, Jesus still reveals Himself to our world today.

2. SOME REJECTED JESUS IN ANGER. Those who saw Jesus as a threat to their security and to their control of the circumstances wanted to push Him away. Later during the Passion week, they would succeed in murdering Jesus. But even that strategy could not defeat Him. Are there those in your circle of acquaintances who are resisting Jesus?

3. OTHERS RECEIVED JESUS GLADLY. The enthusiasm of Jesus' followers attracted others who joined in worshiping Him. Perhaps there are members of your class who have been quietly hanging off to the side. This Sunday might be their day for joining the crowd of disciples.

4. JESUS IS UNLIKE ANYONE ELSE. Jesus came as the humble Son of man, ready to give His life. He preaches servanthood instead of power, and sacrifice rather than glory. These truths can be hard to accept; but we know that Jesus' claims about Himself demand a response from every person. Also, we need to be open to doing everything we can to lead others to Him.

■ **TOPIC:** Overcoming Darkness

■ **QUESTIONS:** 1. What did Jesus mean when He claimed to be the Light of the world? 2. Why was Jesus' testimony on His own behalf valid, despite the opposing assertions of the religious leaders? 3. What was the nature of the relationship between the Lord Jesus and His Father in heaven? 4. Why did Jesus bring up the Mosaic law as He talked about the validity of His own testimony? 5. Why is it important to share with others that Jesus is the Light of the world?

■ **ILLUSTRATIONS:**

The True Light. In 1934, Adolph Hitler declared himself "Der Führer" ("the leader") of Germany. To garner allegiance from the young, the following song was taught to preschoolers in state-run daycare:

> Führer, my Führer, by God given to me,
> Defend and protect me as long as may be.
> Thou didst rescue Germany from her deepest need;
> I render thee thanks who dost daily me feed.
> Stay by me forever, or desperate my plight.
> Führer, my Führer, my faith, my light.
> Hail, my Führer!

At the same time, a decade-old song, "Lead Me to Calvary," was being taught to Christian schoolchildren. It glorified the true Savior and light of the world:

> King of my life, I crown Thee now,
> Thine shall the glory be;
> Lest I forget Thy thorn-crowned brow,
> Lead me to Calvary.

The Winter Solstice. The winter solstice marks the shortest day and the longest night of the year. The sun appears at its lowest point in the sky, and its noontime elevation appears to be the same for several days before and after the solstice. Following the winter solstice, the days begin to grow longer and the nights shorter.

During His earthly ministry, Jesus pushed back the frontiers of spiritual darkness. Indeed, He declared that He came as a light to shine in this dark world, so that all who put their trust in Him would no longer remain in the darkness.

In Second Place. Derrick stood center stage in his royal finery as King Lear and read loudly from his well-thumbed script, "If your diligence be not speedy, I shall be there for you." Jack stepped in front of Derrick and faced the darkened auditorium as he said, "I will not sleep, my lord, till I have delivered your letter."

"No, no, no," the director called out from the front row. "Jack, you're playing the Earl of Kent, not King Lear." "So?" asked Jack. "So don't step in front of the king to deliver your line. You're upstaging the play's central figure. You're drawing people's attention away from Lear himself," the director responded.

In theater it's crucial that minor characters not divert attention away from the more important people on stage. It misleads the audience and can potentially damage the scene. So it is with believers in their service for Christ. He is the light of the world and thus should be the focus of attention. For us as believers, it is our role to direct others' eyes to Jesus and not risk drawing attention to ourselves.

■ **FOR YOUTH** ■ TOPIC: Jesus: Our Light in the Darkness ■ QUESTIONS: 1. Why do those who follow Jesus avoiding walking in spiritual darkness? 2. Why did the Pharisees refuse to accept Jesus' testimony? 3. What was the basis for Jesus maintaining that His testimony was valid? 4. Why did many of the religious leaders not openly acknowledge their faith in Jesus? 5. How can we go from being in spiritual darkness to light?

■ **ILLUSTRATIONS:**

Isn't This a Great Job? Imagine Shaquille O'Neil—a star center for the Miami Heat basketball team—choosing you to be his personal assistant and friend during his career. And imagine him promising to share with you everything of value he acquired during his career. Your job would be to do whatever he asked of you (and, of course, being the good guy he is, he wouldn't ask you to do anything illegal or immoral).

At times O'Neil would have you drop him at the airport in one of his expensive vehicles. And there would be times when he'd want you to wash and wax those high-priced machines. But what about getting a little dirty once in a while? Even if he received the recognition and you got the dirty work, it would be a privilege just to say you personally knew him. You'd be investing time and energy in the career of a sports legend, right?

But that's not the whole picture. O'Neil would treat you as his friend, taking you out to dinner with his family and introducing you to his buddies. Who could ask for a better job? Followers of Jesus don't have to dream up a job like that—we have one. We have the privilege of serving the Lord Jesus, who is the light of the world. He has promised not only to share His inheritance but even calls us His friends.

Not without a Doubt. People theorized about the reality of atoms long before their existence could be proven in any scientific way. According to Aristotle's writings, in the fifth century B.C. the Greek philosopher Democritus suggested that apparently solid matter actually consisted of tiny, invisible particles in constant motion.

But Aristotle himself was not convinced, and the theory was ignored until 1808, when English scientist John Dalton revived the theory of atomic matter. After another 113 years, Ernest Rutherford developed the concept of atomic structure—a positively charged nucleus surrounded by negatively charged, orbiting electrons. In 1939, 26 years later, atomic theory became fact when 31-year-old John Ray Dunning split an atom for the first time at Columbia University, suggesting the possibility of self-sustaining nuclear fission.

Democritus would not have been surprised. He could not see atoms, nor could he prove their existence. Yet he believed—though Aristotle would not. Jesus declared Himself to be the light of the world. Some reject His claim and remain in spiritual darkness. It is only when we believe what He said—trusting in Him for eternal salvation—that we will have the light of life.

Our Source of Vitality. Photosynthesis is the process by which plants use the energy from sunlight to produce sugar. Without adequate light, plants eventually die. They may shed leaves, especially older ones. Flowering plants may fail to produce buds, and variegated plants may revert to solid green.

For believers the light of Christ is just as important for their eternal vitality. He guides us in the path of uprightness and steers us away from the road of the wicked. Apart from Him we will spiritually wither, but in vital union with Him, we will grow and thrive.

"I AM THE GOOD SHEPHERD"

BACKGROUND SCRIPTURE: John 10:1-18
DEVOTIONAL READING: Isaiah 40:10-14

KEY VERSE: I am the good shepherd: the good shepherd giveth his life for the sheep. John 10:11.

KING JAMES VERSION

JOHN 10:1 Verily, verily, I say unto you, He that entereth not by the door into the sheepfold, but climbeth up some other way, the same is a thief and a robber.
2 But he that entereth in by the door is the shepherd of the sheep. 3 To him the porter openeth; and the sheep hear his voice: and he calleth his own sheep by name, and leadeth them out. 4 And when he putteth forth his own sheep, he goeth before them, and the sheep follow him: for they know his voice. 5 And a stranger will they not follow, but will flee from him: for they know not the voice of strangers. . . . 7 Then said Jesus unto them again, Verily, verily, I say unto you, I am the door of the sheep. 8 All that ever came before me are thieves and robbers: but the sheep did not hear them. 9 I am the door: by me if any man enter in, he shall be saved, and shall go in and out, and find pasture. 10 The thief cometh not, but for to steal, and to kill, and to destroy: I am come that they might have life, and that they might have it more abundantly. 11 I am the good shepherd: the good shepherd giveth his life for the sheep. 12 But he that is an hireling, and not the shepherd, whose own the sheep are not, seeth the wolf coming, and leaveth the sheep, and fleeth: and the wolf catcheth them, and scattereth the sheep. 13 The hireling fleeth, because he is an hireling, and careth not for the sheep. 14 I am the good shepherd, and know my sheep, and am known of mine. 15 As the Father knoweth me, even so know I the Father: and I lay down my life for the sheep. 16 And other sheep I have, which are not of this fold: them also I must bring, and they shall hear my voice; and there shall be one fold, and one shepherd. 17 Therefore doth my Father love me, because I lay down my life, that I might take it again. 18 No man taketh it from me, but I lay it down of myself. I have power to lay it down, and I have power to take it again. This commandment have I received of my Father.

NEW REVISED STANDARD VERSION

JOHN 10:1 "Very truly, I tell you, anyone who does not enter the sheepfold by the gate but climbs in by another way is a thief and a bandit. 2 The one who enters by the gate is the shepherd of the sheep. 3 The gatekeeper opens the gate for him, and the sheep hear his voice. He calls his own sheep by name and leads them out. 4 When he has brought out all his own, he goes ahead of them, and the sheep follow him because they know his voice. 5 They will not follow a stranger, but they will run from him because they do not know the voice of strangers." . . .

7 So again Jesus said to them, "Very truly, I tell you, I am the gate for the sheep. 8 All who came before me are thieves and bandits; but the sheep did not listen to them. 9 I am the gate. Whoever enters by me will be saved, and will come in and go out and find pasture. 10 The thief comes only to steal and kill and destroy. I came that they may have life, and have it abundantly.

11 "I am the good shepherd. The good shepherd lays down his life for the sheep. 12 The hired hand, who is not the shepherd and does not own the sheep, sees the wolf coming and leaves the sheep and runs away—and the wolf snatches them and scatters them. 13 The hired hand runs away because a hired hand does not care for the sheep. 14 I am the good shepherd. I know my own and my own know me, 15 just as the Father knows me and I know the Father. And I lay down my life for the sheep. 16 I have other sheep that do not belong to this fold. I must bring them also, and they will listen to my voice. So there will be one flock, one shepherd. 17 For this reason the Father loves me, because I lay down my life in order to take it up again. 18 No one takes it from me, but I lay it down of my own accord. I have power to lay it down, and I have power to take it up again. I have received this command from my Father."

10

HOME BIBLE READINGS

Monday, January 29	Isaiah 40:10-14	*God Tends His Flock*
Tuesday, January 30	Ezekiel 34:1-6	*A Warning to False Shepherds*
Wednesday, January 31	Ezekiel 34:11-16	*I Will Shepherd My Sheep*
Thursday, February 1	Ezekiel 34:25-31	*You Are My Sheep*
Friday, February 2	John 10:1-5	*The Sheep Know their Shepherd*
Saturday, February 3	John 10:7-11	*I Am the Good Shepherd*
Sunday, February 4	John 10:12-18	*The Shepherd Suffers for the Sheep*

BACKGROUND

In Bible times, keeping sheep and goats was an important part of the economy of Israel. The flocks and herds of the people produced wool, skins, milk, and meat. City dwellers often kept a small number of animals that they grazed outside the city walls and brought home with them at night or left under guard in protected sheepfolds. Tent dwellers often had large flocks as an important part of their wealth. These flocks were cared for by family members or by shepherds hired for the job.

The necessities of the task meant that shepherds often lived apart from cities and villages. Alone or with a small group of other shepherds, they were outdoorsmen who were responsible for caring for themselves as well as their flocks. Some, the part-time hirelings, could be irresponsible in times of threat or danger.

The positive biblical pictures of a shepherd focus on those who care for the welfare of their animals. The best shepherds provided veterinary care, drove off wild animals through a variety of means, led their charges to the right kind of grassland, and lived as good stewards of their responsibilities. Perhaps these caretakers are the reason why throughout the ancient world, the concept of "shepherd" was a recognized image or title for a nation's leader.

Jesus' Jewish listeners should have readily understood the implications of His identifying Himself as a shepherd, since many of them were exposed to sheep daily. They understood the importance of herding sheep into pens and protecting them from hostile forces. They appreciated the seriousness with which shepherds assumed their role as guardians over their sheep.

Thus, when Jesus told His listeners to pay careful attention to His analogy of Himself as a shepherd, He wanted them to understand how He could be a shepherd to them. He wanted them to listen to His voice and follow His leading; and He wanted them to know to what length He would go in caring for them and how much they could mean to Him as His sheep.

John 9 forms the backdrop for Jesus' remarks about shepherds and sheep. The Messiah healed a man who had been born blind (9:1-12) and then the Pharisees investigated the incident (9:13-34). As a result of their inquiry, they called Jesus a *sinner* (9:24) whose origin was suspect (9:29). They also banished the healed man from the synagogue (9:34). John 9:35-41 clarifies the nature of Jesus' mission. While His first advent did not immediately bring about divine judgment (see 3:17; 12:47), that is the long term implication for everyone (see Heb. 9:27-28). People are forced to make a decision to either accept or reject Christ (see Matt. 13:20; Luke 11:23).

Sadly, the majority of the religious leaders of the day refused to follow Jesus. Thus, they remained spiritually blinded and condemned because of their sin. Their intent was to serve their own interests and to use their positions of leadership to exploit the masses. People became objects to promote the self-serving agendas of the leaders.

NOTES ON THE PRINTED TEXT

Jesus solemnly declared that not every spiritual leader who claimed to be honest and upright truly was (John 10:1). The Messiah used the analogy of the shepherd and his flock to convey His remarks. In that day, there were different kinds of sheepfolds. Jesus evidently was referring to a courtyard in front of a house. The compound was surrounded by a stone wall, which was often covered with briars for protection. There was usually only one entrance or door to the enclosure. This prevented the sheep from wandering out. It also kept predators from entering.

Jesus warned His listeners against thieves and robbers who were not concerned for the welfare of the sheep, but for their own self-interest. The bandits would try to sneak into the fold through some way other than through the proper entrance, that is, the gate. Who were these thieves and robbers to who Jesus referred? Since the Messiah had recently condemned the Pharisees, Jesus' listeners undoubtedly included these leaders among the thieves.

Certainly, the Pharisees had set themselves up as the shepherds of God's people, and many of them were attempting to lead the people astray by turning them against Jesus. Previously, Jesus had contrasted the Pharisees with the blind man; now He was contrasting them with Himself. But first-century A.D. Pharisees were not the only bandits Jesus was talking about. Many deceivers today are trying to lure sheep away from God's flock.

Unlike thieves and robbers, the shepherd would enter through the gate (10:2). Only the shepherds who guarded the sheep had the right to enter the fold through this doorway. The watchman knew this, and that is why he would open the gate for the shepherds (10:3). Much speculation has been written about who the watchman in this allegory represents. For instance, some believe the watchman represents leaders in the church who make sure that no one but Christ is guiding their congregations. In fact, however, there may be no symbolism necessarily intended. In any case, the sheep would know the voice of their shepherd, who would call them by their name.

Since a pen often enclosed several herds of sheep, each shepherd had a unique name for calling his sheep from among the other animals. The shepherd not only would bring them out of the pen, but also go ahead of them. A good shepherd in

Palestine would never drive his sheep from behind, but trained the animals to follow him by listening to his voice (10:4). On the other hand, if a stranger tried to call the sheep, they would panic at the sound of his voice (10:5). Jesus' listeners should have understood His parable, but most of them did not. If they were truly His sheep, they would have recognized His voice and followed Him. Their spiritual deafness prevented them from comprehending what He was trying to teach them (10:6).

Jesus resumed His discourse with another allegorical statement: *I am the door of the sheep* (10:7). Some sheep pens did not have a gate, and the shepherd himself would serve as the door by lying across the opening. This would not only keep the sheep within the fold, but would also keep potential intruders out. In addition, a good shepherd would inspect his sheep at the gate and tend to their needs and wounds. Jesus is constantly looking out for His sheep, checking for wounds and ready to heal. The Savior's primary point was that as the only gate to the fold, He is the person who determines who can enter into God's kingdom. There is no other way into God's fold except through faith in Christ (10:9).

Other people who claimed to represent God had preceded Jesus, but they were thieves and robbers (10:8). They had distorted the truth and, consciously or unconsciously, tried to take God's people from His fold. Jesus certainly was not talking about the Old Testament prophets, but about the religious leadership of His day. Furthermore, thieves would have only one thing on their minds—to get what they wanted regardless of the destruction it caused. With Jesus at the gate, however, not only is the flock protected, but also the needs of the sheep are provided for (10:10). Only in Christ is the abundant, deeply satisfying life made available.

When Jesus said He is *the good shepherd* (10:11), He portrayed Himself as the ancient Hebrews viewed God (see Jer. 23:1-3; Ezek. 34:12, 15). For example, King David began his immortal poem, *The LORD is my shepherd* (Ps. 23:1). Jesus was not only identifying Himself as God, but also distinguishing a particular characteristic of Himself as God. As the good shepherd, Jesus promised to sacrifice Himself for His sheep (John 10:11). Hired hands, however, would not risk their lives for the sheep. They would fulfill their duties of caring for the sheep not out of concern for them but for their own self-interest—that is, the wages they were paid. If a wolf threatened the sheep, the hirelings would not endanger themselves, but instead would desert the flock. Consequently, the wolf would be able to attack and disperse the sheep (10:12-13).

Once more Jesus said He is *the good shepherd* (10:14). The knowledge that Jesus has of His sheep and they of Him goes beyond mere recognition. They have an intimate familiarity with each other in the same way the heavenly Father and His Son know each other. In fact, the love and concern Jesus has for each one of His sheep is so great that He willingly laid down His life for all of us (10:15).

Jesus made it clear that His sacrificial act would include not only Jewish believers but Gentile believers as well. His current followers composed His present flock, but later Gentiles would also hear His summons to salvation and become His disciples.

When this would occur, there would not be two flocks under one shepherd—that is, a Jewish-Christian church and a Gentile-Christian church—but one united flock shepherded by the Lord Jesus (10:16).

Since perfect harmony exists between what the Father wills and what the Son does, it is only natural that the Father should love His Son; but Jesus' willingness to sacrifice His life in obedience to God's plan did not cause the Father to love Him, for that love has existed from the beginning. Rather, God's love was an expression of His approval of His Son's laying down His life—only to raise Him up from the dead (10:17). Jesus wanted it understood, however, that His death would not be forced upon Him. He would lay down His life voluntarily. Indeed, Jesus had the authority—that is, the power and the right—not only to sacrifice His life but also to take it back again. The Father Himself gave the Son this authority (10:18).

SUGGESTIONS TO TEACHERS

As the spiritual shepherd of His people, the Lord Jesus wants us to know that we can be completely dependent upon Him. He is always alert, looking after our needs. We can trust in Him to keep us safe and protected, and we can be completely dependent upon Him for the following:

1. FOR OUR PROVISION. Just as shepherds provide lush meadows for their sheep to graze and peaceful streams for them to drink from, so the Lord Jesus will provide for our needs. The Messiah has surely proven Himself to be trustworthy in meeting our needs in the past, and He can be trusted to provide our needs in the future.

2. FOR OUR GUIDANCE. As our faithful leader, the Messiah guides those of us who are His true sheep. It is interesting that Jesus called Himself *the good shepherd* (John 10:11) and not "the Good Cowboy." The work of a shepherd is done out in front of the sheep, guiding them and leading them to where they should go. The work of a cowboy is done behind the cattle, driving them and pushing them to where he wants to force them to go. Thus as our spiritual shepherd, the Lord Jesus has, in essence, paved the road before us. We need only follow Him and trust Him to guide to where we should go.

3. FOR OUR PROTECTION. Shepherds put their lives on the line to maintain their flock of sheep. To protect and rescue sheep from danger, shepherds are forced to inch out onto risky ledges and to put themselves between wild animals and their sheep. In a sense, our spiritual shepherd has done the same for us today. Jesus put His own life on the line so that our eternal lives might be rescued, and He put Himself between us and the penalty for our sin. Thus, He not only can be trusted for our protection physically, but mentally, emotionally, and spiritually, too.

4. FOR OUR CONTENTMENT. Shepherds realize that a sheep is a fearful, flighty animal that is prone to get lost or harm itself in a multitude of other ways. Therefore, shepherds seek not only to keep their sheep protected, but also to help them sense a degree of contentment in the care of the shepherd. This week's Scripture passage reminds us that that Jesus has made us His top priority. He makes it possible for us to receive and enjoy eternal life in all its fullness.

FOR ADULTS

■ TOPIC: Protection from Evil

■ QUESTIONS: 1. What sterling character qualities associated with good shepherds did Jesus spotlight for consideration? 2. Why did Jesus use the parable of the good shepherd and his flock? 3. How can Jesus be both the door (or gate) for the sheep as well as their shepherd? 4. Why would Jesus, as our good Shepherd, sacrifice Himself for us? 5. How is the love of the Father for us demonstrated in the sacrifice of His Son on the cross?

■ **ILLUSTRATIONS:**

Through the Darkest Valley. In an *Upper Room* devotional, Ellen Bergh writes how Amtrak's Coast Starlight train was filled with excited passengers, craning their necks to enjoy the Oregon scenery as the train rolled through green forests. A shining lake gleamed through the trees, and cheerful conversation filled the air.

Suddenly, the light, airy feeling was gone, like a candle blown out in a draft, as the train entered a tunnel. Expecting the sun to reappear quickly, Ellen was uncomfortable as it became even darker.

The happy sounds were a thing of the past. Everyone sat in awe of the inky blackness. The longer they traveled in the tunnel, the harder it was to remain calm without any visual cues to reassure them. Even the movement of the train seemed to fall away into pitch darkness. When they came out of the tunnel, laughter and relief filled the compartment.

"My life in Christ is like that unforgettable train ride," Ellen reflects. "Events may plunge me into darkness where I have no clues to sense the Lord's presence. Yet I can trust God is with me even when I can't see what lies ahead."

For You Are with Me. In the book, *A Window to Heaven: When Children See Life in Death*, Diane M. Komp writes how Ann and her husband were typical married baby boomers. Financially well-off, they had no time for church, and they each became busy in their respective lives. Their romance faded early, but neither wanted to give up their lifestyle. Besides, both adored their children, and their youngest son, T.J., was a special favorite of his mother.

Although the children were never sent to Sunday school and God was never mentioned in their home, one day out of the blue, T.J. said, "Mama, I love you more than anything in the world, except God. And I love Him a little bit more!" Ann was surprised but told him it was okay. *But why would he speak of God?* she wondered.

Two days later, on a bitterly cold day, while his sister was horseback riding, T.J. crossed a snow-covered creek, fell through the ice, and died. Ann remembers saying, "I hate you God!" But even then she felt herself held in loving arms.

Ann's world shattered. She remembered the Christmas gift T.J. had bought her that week. He had kept trying to give it to her before Christmas. Each time she had laughed and told him to put it away until Christmas Day. When she got home from the stables where he had died, she hurried upstairs to open it. Inside was a beautiful necklace with a cross.

Ann says that Jesus made her reach out to others rather than become lost in herself. "Helping others helped me." Ann's husband also changed, and together they became new creatures in Christ. Through her ordeal, Ann discovered a gift for spiritual hospitality, bringing healing to other parents.

By now, this young mother has reached out to help hundreds of families who have lost children in accidents. She calls her efforts T.J. Ministries, not only after her T.J., but to emphasize how she's made it since then: "Through Jesus."

| FOR YOUTH | ■ TOPIC: Whose Sheep Are You? ■ QUESTIONS: 1. In what ways does Jesus care for His spiritual flock of believers? 2. What are some ways that the goodness of Jesus' spir- |

itual leadership is evident in our lives? 3. In what sense does the Lord Jesus lead us to the green pastures of eternal life? 4. What does it mean for us to be personally known by the Savior? 5. What are some ways Jesus' followers can encourage others to become His disciples?

■ ILLUSTRATIONS:

Jesus' Care and Compassion. At the end of August, 1997, Princess Diana was killed in an automobile accident in Paris. People of all ages were stunned at her senseless death. Emotion surged and was evidenced by the thousands who brought flowers to Buckingham Palace. While Great Britain mourned, the royal family seemed aloof and uncaring. Public sentiment rose as the nation stingingly criticized Queen Elizabeth II for her seclusion and her lack of compassion. She was finally forced to speak to her nation's people.

Contrast this queen's response with that of King Jesus. Far from being indifferent and unconcerned, He got involved in the lives of people. Jesus still shows genuine care and compassion toward us as His followers. We in turn should not hold back or shy away from expressing our thankfulness to Him. He loves to hear our praise and know that we enjoy and appreciate His provision for our lives.

Praying for the Lord's Help. According to the *United Methodist News Service*, Gerald "Jay" Williams has been instrumental in freeing thousands of slaves in Sudan.

During the first semester of his freshman year at Harvard College in Cambridge, Massachusetts, he attended a gospel concert and learned about the existence of modern-day slavery. Upon hearing the stories of slaves from around the world, Jay decided that he wanted to get involved.

In September 2000, Jay traveled to the restricted country of Sudan with Christian Solidarity International (CSI), a Swiss-based group that buys slaves out of captivity. During that trip, he helped to free 4,435 slaves. Then in July 2001, Jay returned to Sudan and helped to liberate 6,706 slaves!

Jay said he met with "hundreds of slaves in tattered clothing." They were "dusty, had no shoes, and were very thin. "I almost broke down," Jay recalls. Most of these slaves were Christians who had been abducted by forces of the Islamic Khartoum government and sold to Muslims, he reported. "They said they had been praying to the Lord for help. They found strength in that."

There is a continuing need for this ministry. Money provided by CSI makes it possible for Arab Muslim "retrievers" to buy the slaves and help them return to their families. It costs about $33 to buy one person, the ministry said. The ministry also reported that tens of thousands of slaves have been freed over the past decade.

Trusting the Good Shepherd. A young man faced a critical decision. He had been active in his church as a teenager and college student. Then he was offered an attractive position at a large company after he graduated from school. But he wondered whether he should first consider Christian ministry. He feared the risks involved and the negative opinion of others.

But then the young man heard a sermon on the meaning of discipleship that changed his thinking. He decided to follow Jesus into full-time ministry, not because the business world was wrong or evil, but because he believed the Lord's will for him lay in a different area. (Many other believers, of course, have honored God by serving Him in the business world.)

Later, after more than 50 years of devoted service to Christ, the minister thought about the Messiah's faithfulness to him. This person recognized that discipleship means trusting the good Shepherd to take care of us, no matter what.

"I AM THE RESURRECTION AND THE LIFE"

BACKGROUND SCRIPTURE: John 11:1-44
DEVOTIONAL READING: Jude 17-23

KEY VERSE: I am the resurrection, and the life: he that believeth
in me, though he were dead, yet shall he live. John 11:25.

KING JAMES VERSION

JOHN 11:17 Then when Jesus came, he found that he had lain in the grave four days already. 18 Now Bethany was nigh unto Jerusalem, about fifteen furlongs off: 19 And many of the Jews came to Martha and Mary, to comfort them concerning their brother. 20 Then Martha, as soon as she heard that Jesus was coming, went and met him: but Mary sat still in the house. 21 Then said Martha unto Jesus, Lord, if thou hadst been here, my brother had not died. 22 But I know, that even now, whatsoever thou wilt ask of God, God will give it thee. 23 Jesus saith unto her, Thy brother shall rise again. 24 Martha saith unto him, I know that he shall rise again in the resurrection at the last day. 25 Jesus said unto her, I am the resurrection, and the life: he that believeth in me, though he were dead, yet shall he live: 26 And whosoever liveth and believeth in me shall never die. Believest thou this? 27 She saith unto him, Yea, Lord: I believe that thou art the Christ, the Son of God, which should come into the world.

NEW REVISED STANDARD VERSION

JOHN 11:17 When Jesus arrived, he found that Lazarus had already been in the tomb four days. 18 Now Bethany was near Jerusalem, some two miles away, 19 and many of the Jews had come to Martha and Mary to console them about their brother. 20 When Martha heard that Jesus was coming, she went and met him, while Mary stayed at home. 21 Martha said to Jesus, "Lord, if you had been here, my brother would not have died. 22 But even now I know that God will give you whatever you ask of him." 23 Jesus said to her, "Your brother will rise again." 24 Martha said to him, "I know that he will rise again in the resurrection on the last day." 25 Jesus said to her, "I am the resurrection and the life. Those who believe in me, even though they die, will live, 26 and everyone who lives and believes in me will never die. Do you believe this?" 27 She said to him, "Yes, Lord, I believe that you are the Messiah, the Son of God, the one coming into the world."

11

Monday, February 5	Jude 17-24	*Christ Offers Eternal Life*
Tuesday, February 6	Proverbs 8:22-32	*The Way of Righteousness*
Wednesday, February 7	John 11:1-7	*Jesus Delays*
Thursday, February 8	John 11:8-16	*Jesus Goes to Bethany*
Friday, February 9	John 11:17-27	*I Am the Resurrection*
Saturday, February 10	John 11:28-37	*Jesus Comforts Mary*
Sunday, February 11	John 11:38-44	*Jesus Raises Lazarus*

BACKGROUND

The *village* (Luke 10:38) where Jesus visited Mary and Martha was Bethany, located about two miles southeast of Jerusalem (John 11:1). It was on the eastern slope of the Mount of Olives, the hill outside Jerusalem where Jesus prayed and was arrested. Jesus often stayed in Bethany with the two sisters and their brother Lazarus during the Savior's travels to Jerusalem. In fact, Luke 10:38-42 records an earlier time when Jesus visited the home of the two sisters. That visit brought out some of friction between the siblings, as Mary sat at the feet of Jesus listening to Him talk while Martha busily prepared the meal. This incident notwithstanding, since Bethany was within easy walking distance to Jerusalem, the village was a good place to stay. For instance, after Jesus ministered in the holy city, He would enjoy evenings with friends in Bethany. He also spent time there in the home of Simon the leper (Matt. 26:6).

Jesus' friendship with Mary and Martha is well documented in the Gospels and was apparently familiar to John's first-century readers. John 11:5 emphasizes that Jesus loved each member of the family. Jesus' friendship with Mary, Martha, and Lazarus shows the humanity of the Lord. Although He was the Son of God, sent to die for our sins, He still experienced the same needs as we do today. Thus, it should not surprise us that Jesus had close friends who were dear to Him. In fact, we should expect that He would need such relationships outside His ministry and work.

Mary seemed to have a more emotional and devoted relationship with Jesus, as is shown when she *fell down at his feet* (11:32) after coming to Him. However, the most dramatic example of Mary's devotion to Jesus is found in the record of the dinner party Martha and Mary prepared for Jesus prior to His final entry into Jerusalem (12:1-8). Mary chose this incident to wipe the feet of Jesus using her hair and an expensive perfume. Most likely, the encounter was sufficiently well known in the church for John to refer to it before he wrote about it (see 11:2).

The cultural backdrop of that time makes Mary's action all the more significant. After walking miles on the dusty roads of Israel, travelers' feet were often caked with layers of dirt from the road. It was the host's job to assign someone to wash the visitor's feet. This was an unpleasant task and was reserved for servants and others of low stature. By washing the feet of the Lord Jesus, Mary chose to serve Him in a way that only the most humble would do.

The manner in which Mary performed the footwashing could have drawn criticism. For instance, no respectable women in Israel let their hair down in public. Usually, only immoral women unbound their hair in this fashion. By using her hair to wash Jesus' feet, Mary showed she was not concerned about what others thought regarding her service to Jesus. But what Mary did also hurt her pocketbook. The perfume she used was very expensive. John 12:5 indicates that it was worth a year's wages (perhaps $50,000 in today's currency). So Mary's devotion to Jesus was not only real but also extremely costly.

NOTES ON THE PRINTED TEXT

Lazarus, Martha, and Mary were dear friends of Jesus. Though they were not members of His traveling group, their home in Bethany was always open to Him and His disciples. When Lazarus became extremely ill, Martha and Mary sent a message to Jesus telling Him about their brother's serious condition. At the time, Jesus was in Perea, which was more than 20 miles away. They knew how much Jesus loved Lazarus and hoped that He would hurry to Bethany in time to heal him (John 11:1-3).

Jesus noted that the end of Lazarus's condition would not be death and that the Father and the Son would be glorified through the incident involving Lazarus (11:4). While Jesus loved Lazarus and his sisters, Jesus still remained where He was two more days (11:5-6). Then, at the divinely appointed time, He invited his disciples to return with Him to Judea (11:7).

When the disciples voiced concern, Jesus used veiled language to assure them of His safety (11:8-10). He then stated plainly that Lazarus not only was dead, but also that the unfolding drama would become an occasion to deepen the faith of the disciples (11:11-15). Jesus was not happy that His friend had died, but by His obeying God's plan of waiting for the right moment to raise Lazarus from the dead, the Savior's followers would witness the glory of God's power through Jesus. Of all the disciples, Thomas, who is known as the doubter, challenged the others to go with Jesus back to Judea, where death seemed imminent for all of them (11:16). This is the first time John mentioned Thomas. His comment shows his leadership and courage, even though he struggled with doubts.

After Jesus and His group arrived in Bethany, they learned that four days earlier Lazarus's body had been put into his tomb (11:17). Since a dead body decayed quickly in the hot Palestinian climate, Lazarus's family would have had his body anointed, wrapped, and laid in the family tomb soon after he had expired. The four days is significant in that Jesus would not have reached His friend while he was still alive even if He had left Perea immediately after hearing the report of Lazarus's illness. The delay was to assure, in people's minds, that the raising of Lazarus from the dead was truly a miracle.

The Jews of Jesus' day had an interesting idea about death. They thought that the soul hovered over the body for a few days after a person died. Supposedly, it was possible during this brief period of time for the body to come back to life. If a person did not revive by the fourth day, then that person was really dead. This belief may have originated from situations where people were thought to be dead but were only in a coma. Waiting a few days would make it clear whether that person was just sleeping or had really died. Since it normally took a few days for decay to become apparent, there was still a possibility for revival as long as decay was absent. Once decay set in, no revival was possible.

Since Jerusalem was no more than a few miles from Bethany (11:18), a number of Jews from the city paid their respects to Martha and Mary during their time of grief (11:19). Evidently this family had a commanding influence or were popular among the local people. The closeness between Bethany and Jerusalem indicates that news of the miracle would have circulated quickly throughout the city of God.

When the sisters of Lazarus heard that Jesus was approaching their village, Martha went out to greet Him while Mary remained in the house (11:20). On the surface, Martha's first words to Jesus appear to be a veiled rebuke (11:21). Martha, however, probably knew that Jesus could not have come in time to heal her brother of his illness. Thus, Martha's comment was more likely an expression of regret that Jesus could not have been present, a feeling the sisters had probably spoken of quite often during the past four days.

Martha's next remark might be interpreted as a sign of a remarkable faith in Jesus' power to raise people from the dead (11:22). Later, however, Martha was the one who complained when Jesus ordered the stone to be removed from the entrance to Lazarus's tomb (see 11:39). It is possible that Martha was merely noting that she still had faith in Jesus, for Martha was certain that God granted Jesus whatever request He asked (11:22).

After Jesus told Martha that her brother would rise from the dead (11:23), Martha showed that she had not thought about Jesus' bringing Lazarus back to life at that time; instead, she voiced the view of the Pharisees that God would resurrect the just at the last day (11:24). Jesus' statement may have been said to Martha and her sister many times by others to comfort them, and now it may have sounded hollow to her.

Jesus' response is incredible. He could have said that He would resurrect Lazarus; instead, Jesus said, *I am the resurrection, and the life* (11:25). His declaration is another of the great "I am" statements that spotlight His Godhood and messiahship. Jesus, in fact, is the life of the age to come, and all who put their trust in Him will experience the resurrected life. When Jesus asked Martha whether she believed what He was saying, He was actually asking her whether she believed in Him (11:26). The Savior wanted her (and all other people) to begin experiencing right now the joys of eternal life. The raising of Lazarus was intended to foster such faith in Christ; and the apostle's inclusion of this miracle in his Gospel was to encourage people down through the ages to put their trust in Jesus as the Messiah (see 20:30-31).

Regardless of her fretful nature, Martha had amazing faith in Jesus. She not only replied positively, but was also clear about what she believed—that Jesus is the Messiah, God's only divine Son, and the one who came into the world from heaven and became a man (11:27). Few, if any, could have affirmed Christ any better than Martha had. Her confession of faith parallels that voiced by Peter (see Matt. 16:16).

Jesus eventually arrived at the tomb where the body of Lazarus had been placed. As Jesus gazed at the cave before Him, He ordered the people to remove the stone that blocked its entrance (John 11:38-39). Then, in a loud voice, Jesus commanded Lazarus to leave the tomb. To the astonishment of the crowd, including Lazarus's family, Jesus' disciples, and the Jewish visitors, Lazarus obeyed. With his hands, feet, and head still bound in burial clothes, Lazarus came out of the darkness of the cave into the light of the day (11:43-44). He had returned from death by the power of God.

The people were stunned by what they had just witnessed. Jesus roused them by instructing them to remove the strips of grave clothes from Lazarus's body. By doing this they would know that Lazarus was truly alive and that his appearance was not merely a magic trick. By this amazing act of God's power, Jesus showed that He alone has authority over life and death.

SUGGESTIONS TO TEACHERS

Why did Jesus wait several days before going to Bethany? The reason is that it made the miracle of Lazarus's restoration to life all the more magnificent. As a result, many people who were with Mary and Martha put their faith in Jesus. This same account is recorded for our benefit, too, so that we might trust in Christ for salvation.

1. THE RELATIONAL FACTOR. The suspense of Jesus' raising Lazarus from the dead will help the students remain focused on the biblical text as you have them work their way through it. One option is to discuss the various intertwined human relationships. For instance, Lazarus and his sisters were quite close, and the three were dear friends of Jesus. Other relationships in the drama are Christ and His disciples as well as the many Jews who came to comfort the bereaved.

2. THE RESURRECTION FACTOR. Consider drawing attention to the reality of the emotional pain Martha must have felt and the struggle she was having as feelings of doubt and faith mixed together. Spotlight, too, the candor and openness that characterized her conversation with Jesus. Above all, make Jesus' declaration to be the resurrection and the life the high point of your teaching. Be sure to encourage the students not to miss the opportunity to put their faith in Christ, if they have not already done so.

3. THE REPORTING FACTOR. The students who have trusted in Jesus will want to share the good news about Him with others; but sometimes, through busyness or inattentiveness, opportunities pass by. Encourage your class to think about three to five people they will see this week. If the students have trouble thinking of someone, suggest that they ask God in prayer to give them guidance. Perhaps they will end up sharing Christ with an acquaintance at work or at a recreational event.

FOR ADULTS	■ **TOPIC:** Life after Death ■ **QUESTIONS:** 1. Upon Jesus' arrival at Bethany, what did the people report to Him? 2. How did others reach out to the bereaved in their time

of loss? 3. What was Martha's initial response to Jesus upon seeing Him? 4. How did Martha convey a clear and strong faith in Jesus? 5. In what sense is Jesus *the resurrection, and the life* (John 11:25) to you?

■ **ILLUSTRATIONS:**

The Sweet Scent of Life. Mint, a fragrant plant with a square stem, is found in over 3,200 varieties. Pushing its leafy foliage aside, you can examine its stem and confirm its classification. But which mint variety is it? That is trickier. Most people rely on their nose. They grab a leaf and crush it. Often its fragrance gives away its identity.

Jesus Christ, in the form of a man, was crushed. But a delicate, sweet scent still emanates from His blood-stained cross and empty tomb. By conquering death, He proved that He truly is the resurrection and the life, especially for all who put their faith in Him.

An Act of Courage and Hope. In 1982, then Vice President George Bush represented the U.S. at the funeral of former Soviet leader Leonid Brezhnev. According to Gary Thomas of *Christianity Today*, Bush was deeply moved by a silent protest carried out by Brezhnev's wife. She stood motionless by the coffin until seconds before it was closed. Then, just as the soldiers touched the lid, she performed an act of great courage and hope.

The widow reached down and made the sign of the cross on her husband's chest. There in the citadel of secular, atheistic power, the wife of the man who had run it all hoped that her husband was wrong. She believed there was another life, one best represented by the Lord Jesus, who died on the cross and rose from the dead.

What Else Is There to Do? On the day that James found himself wandering through a mall in Portland, Oregon, his life was changed. In the open court, outside the mall, he stopped to listen to a man preaching about Jesus' resurrection. The man's message was simple and to the point, and he did not accuse or berate any of his listeners. James was impressed. What was of special interest was the man himself. He appeared to be at least in his seventies. James had never seen a man that age preaching in a forum.

After the man's ending prayer, James asked him how old he was. The gentleman chuckled, "How old do you think I am?" James graciously guessed, "At least late sixties." The man laughed and said, "I turned 90 years old this last birthday!" James inquired why he was out preaching at that age.

With a tear running down his cheeks, the old man said, "I did not get saved until I was 82 years old. I never knew about the risen Lord when I was young, but I did remember one Bible verse that someone told me. The next time I heard verses from the Bible, I was 82 years old, and I believed those verses, too. I have lived almost my whole life without Jesus. So what else do you suppose I would be doing on a nice day like today?"

FOR YOUTH	■ TOPIC: Life in Christ Conquers Death ■ QUESTIONS: 1. Why did Jesus delay in coming to Bethany? 2. How do you think Mary and Martha felt over the death of Lazarus? 3. What

declaration did Jesus make about Himself? 4. What affirmation did Martha make in response? 5. How can the truth of the resurrection give us hope in times of loss?

■ ILLUSTRATIONS:

Now Is the Time. Before Janet trusted Jesus for eternal life, she felt a great deal of despair. A sense of hopelessness left her thinking it really did not matter what happened to her. In this frame of mind, she did many self-destructive things, such as consuming harmful substances and driving when she was not in control of her faculties.

When a friend kept asking Janet to come to church with her, Janet felt annoyed by the frequent invitations; but the day finally came when Janet's emptiness caused her to unexpectedly say "Yes" to her friend. At church, for the first time, Janet heard the message of eternal life. Afterward, driving home alone, she was stopped at an intersection when she received the gift of salvation through faith. She remembers weeping and having a wonderful sense of hope and a new sense of significance for life.

From this week's lesson we discover that whoever believes in Jesus can have eternal life. The disciples were given this opportunity; Mary, Martha, and Lazarus had it too; the crowds of people who surrounded Jesus and even the Pharisees were welcome to believe. The reality is that some turned away, but others who heard the message of eternal life ran toward it.

Perhaps this is the first time you have understood that whoever believes in Jesus has eternal life. If so, now is the time to accept Him as your Savior. If you have already put your faith in Him, who are those in your life right now who have yet to hear the good news and believe? Why not consider telling them about Jesus?

No Future? While some youth have little hope for the future, apparently many more are optimistic. When polled by TIME/CNN and asked what happens after death, 61 percent of Americans felt that they would go to heaven. Joni Eareckson Tada, a quadriplegic since she was 17, trusts in full body resurrection and the glorification of the body in heaven.

Consider getting together with other saved teens in your church to declare to your peers and friends the good news about Christ. The lost need to know that Jesus conquered death by rising from the dead.

He Did It for Me. One afternoon, a church youth group decided to act out the account of Jesus' trial and crucifixion. The youth leader took the role of Jesus, while the youth played the roles of Pilate, the accusers, the soldiers, and the crowds. The youthful mob shouted, "Crucify Him! Crucify Him!" Continuing their play, they led their leader toward a cross they had erected on the church lawn.

Then the one playing Jesus' role spoke. "Even though you are doing this to me, I still love you." As the youth heard those words, their drama suddenly was more than an ordinary group activity. They went silent, and a few tears appeared. Young men and women suddenly realized afresh the value of what Jesus had done for them.

Wrong Ending. Thomas Jefferson, though a great statesman, could not accept the miraculous elements in Scripture. He edited his own special version of the Bible in which all references to the supernatural were deleted. Jefferson, in editing the Gospels, confined himself solely to the moral teachings of Jesus. The closing words of Jefferson's Bible are these: "There laid they Jesus and rolled a great stone at the mouth of the sepulchre and departed." Thank God that's not the way the account really ends!

"I AM THE WAY, THE TRUTH, AND THE LIFE"

BACKGROUND SCRIPTURE: John 14:1-14
DEVOTIONAL READING: Ephesians 4:17-24

KEY VERSE: I am the way, the truth, and the life: no man cometh unto the Father, but by me. John 14:6.

KING JAMES VERSION

JOHN 14:1 Let not your heart be troubled: ye believe in God, believe also in me. 2 In my Father's house are many mansions: if it were not so, I would have told you. I go to prepare a place for you. 3 And if I go and prepare a place for you, I will come again, and receive you unto myself; that where I am, there ye may be also.

4 And whither I go ye know, and the way ye know. 5 Thomas saith unto him, Lord, we know not whither thou goest; and how can we know the way? 6 Jesus saith unto him, I am the way, the truth, and the life: no man cometh unto the Father, but by me. 7 If ye had known me, ye should have known my Father also: and from henceforth ye know him, and have seen him. 8 Philip saith unto him, Lord, shew us the Father, and it sufficeth us. 9 Jesus saith unto him, Have I been so long time with you, and yet hast thou not known me, Philip? he that hath seen me hath seen the Father; and how sayest thou then, Shew us the Father? 10 Believest thou not that I am in the Father, and the Father in me? the words that I speak unto you I speak not of myself: but the Father that dwelleth in me, he doeth the works. 11 Believe me that I am in the Father, and the Father in me: or else believe me for the very works' sake.

12 Verily, verily, I say unto you, He that believeth on me, the works that I do shall he do also; and greater works than these shall he do; because I go unto my Father. 13 And whatsoever ye shall ask in my name, that will I do, that the Father may be glorified in the Son. 14 If ye shall ask any thing in my name, I will do it.

NEW REVISED STANDARD VERSION

JOHN 14:1 "Do not let your hearts be troubled. Believe in God, believe also in me. 2 In my Father's house there are many dwelling places. If it were not so, would I have told you that I go to prepare a place for you? 3 And if I go and prepare a place for you, I will come again and will take you to myself, so that where I am, there you may be also. 4 And you know the way to the place where I am going." 5 Thomas said to him, "Lord, we do not know where you are going. How can we know the way?" 6 Jesus said to him, "I am the way, and the truth, and the life. No one comes to the Father except through me. 7 If you know me, you will know my Father also. From now on you do know him and have seen him."

8 Philip said to him, "Lord, show us the Father, and we will be satisfied." 9 Jesus said to him, "Have I been with you all this time, Philip, and you still do not know me? Whoever has seen me has seen the Father. How can you say, 'Show us the Father'? 10 Do you not believe that I am in the Father and the Father is in me? The words that I say to you I do not speak on my own; but the Father who dwells in me does his works. 11 Believe me that I am in the Father and the Father is in me; but if you do not, then believe me because of the works themselves. 12 Very truly, I tell you, the one who believes in me will also do the works that I do and, in fact, will do greater works than these, because I am going to the Father. 13 I will do whatever you ask in my name, so that the Father may be glorified in the Son. 14 If in my name you ask me for anything, I will do it."

12

HOME BIBLE READINGS

Monday, February 12	Hebrews 10:19-23	*A New and Living Way*
Tuesday, February 13	John 18:33-40	*Jesus Testifies to the Truth*
Wednesday, February 14	2 Timothy 1:8-14	*Jesus Has Brought Life*
Thursday, February 15	Ephesians 4:17-24	*Turn from Darkness*
Friday, February 16	3 John 2-8	*Walking in the Truth*
Saturday, February 17	John 14:1-7	*Jesus Is the Way*
Sunday, February 18	John 14:8-14	*The Son Reveals the Father*

BACKGROUND

After Jesus raised Lazarus from the dead, a number of Jews put their faith in Christ. The Jewish religious leaders then convened a meeting of the Sanhedrin in which they plotted Jesus' death. They feared that Jesus' activities would disturb the Romans, who would in turn strip the Jewish leaders of their authority. Knowing their intentions to arrest Him, Jesus temporarily ceased His public ministry and withdrew to a remote village with His closest disciples (John 11:45-54).

Six days before the Passover, however, Jesus and His disciples returned to Bethany (11:55-57), where He visited with Lazarus, Martha, and Mary. While they ate dinner together, Mary anointed Jesus' feet with expensive perfume. Judas Iscariot, one of Jesus' 12 disciples, protested that the money spent on the perfume could have been given to the poor. Judas didn't really care about the poor. In fact, Judas stole money from the coffers, which he was able to do because he was responsible for their money bag (12:1-8). Judas later betrayed Jesus for 30 silver coins.

Jesus rebuked Judas, saying that Mary's act was special because it honored His coming death. While Jesus' friends pondered the significance of His statement, a large crowd came to Lazarus's home to see Jesus and the one He had resurrected from the dead. Because this miracle had caused many more Jews to believe in Jesus, the chief priests decided to kill Lazarus as well (12:9-11).

All four Gospels describe Jesus' triumphal entry into Jerusalem. Although the apostle John omitted many details that the other accounts included, he provided information unique to his presentation. Only John's account mentions the crowd bringing palm branches, the disciples not comprehending the significance of the incident, and the Pharisees muttering their disapproval.

John wrote that Jesus approached Jerusalem five days before Passover (12:1, 12). Along the route, a large number of people hurried to meet Jesus. These were probably Jewish pilgrims on their way to the city of God to celebrate the Passover feast. Most likely they had heard about Jesus' demonstrations of power. Indeed, they praised Him with palm branches and loud shouts, proclaiming Him to be the blessed one who saves. In fact, they quoted Psalm 118:25 and 26 in acclaiming Him to be the Messiah, who comes in the Lord's name (John 12:13).

Jesus spent some time speaking to the crowd and then went away and secluded Himself with His disciples (12:36). The public ministry of Jesus was coming to a close, and He needed to prepare for the rejection and suffering He was about to experience. Most of the Jews who came to see Jesus refused to put their faith in Him despite having witnessed the many miracles He had performed. In fact, the prophet Isaiah had foretold that the Jews would reject the suffering Servant of God (12:37-38; see Isa. 53:1).

The Last Supper is the next event spotlighted in John's Gospel. During this final meal, Jesus demonstrated what it truly means to be a servant. Even though He was the Son of God, He humbled Himself by washing the feet of His disciples. The act was so deferential that at first Peter refused to allow the Lord to wash his feet. Jesus told Peter and the others that unless this was done, He could not accept them as one of His own. After washing their feet, Jesus explained that He had set an example for them. In particular, it was symbolic of how they were to serve one another (13:1-17).

Jesus clearly indicated that one of the Twelve would betray Him. In fact, that person was one of them who was sharing the bread they were eating. At the time, none of them knew that the betrayer was Judas Iscariot. After Satan entered Judas, Jesus told him to proceed quickly with his treachery. The others assumed that he was going about normal business for the group (13:18-30). Next, Jesus told His friends that He was about to be glorified, and that God would be glorified in Him. After instructing them to love one another in the same way He loved them, He told them He was going away. Peter exclaimed that he would follow Jesus anywhere. Peter declared that he would even die for the Messiah. Jesus sadly predicted, however, that Peter would disown Him. In fact, Peter would do so three times before the rooster crowed the next morning (13:31-38).

NOTES ON THE PRINTED TEXT

Jesus sensed the anxiety within His disciples as He spoke with them about the series of events that were soon to unfold. Thus, He urged His disciples to calm their troubled hearts. The way to do this was to put their trust in the Father as well as in the Son (John 14:1). It is remarkable that Jesus focused on comforting His followers rather than deal with His own needs. The treachery of Judas and the fickleness of the rest of the disciples did not prevent the Savior from remaining a calming presence among them.

Jesus next spoke about heaven, perhaps to further ease the minds of His followers. He referred to heaven as a large house—belonging to His Father—that has plenty of room. Though Jesus was leaving the disciples, He was going there to prepare a place for them. Jesus told the disciples that if this were not so, He would not have made this promise to them (14:2). The pledge, however, was true; and so the disciples could count on Jesus one day returning to bring them back with Him to heaven (14:3).

Throughout Jesus' public ministry He had been teaching these men what it meant to be His followers. Now He told them that they should know the way to where He was going. As they followed that way, they would end up there with Him (14:4). Thomas openly expressed his confusion, and he was probably speaking for the other 10 as well. They did not know where Jesus was going, and they did not know the way (14:5). How could they? Had not Jesus already said that where He was going, they could not come (13:33)? They were dumbfounded.

Jesus' reply to Thomas is the most profound "I am" declaration in John's Gospel. The Savior not only identified who He was, but made it clear that He is the only possible path to God (14:6). When Thomas asked Jesus the way, Jesus did not hand him a road map and give him directions. Jesus told all of them that He Himself is the way to God. In a few hours some of His followers would see Jesus hanging on a cross and would wonder how this could be true. After His resurrection they would understand that as the one who died for their sins, He is the only link between God and repentant sinners.

Despite all the lies that were charged against Jesus during His public career, His words, deeds, and character have shown Him to be the embodiment of truth. Nothing He ever taught has proved unreliable. In Him we see the truth of God in action; and what better proof of knowing that Jesus is the life than His spectacular resurrection. Indeed, only Jesus has the power over life and death.

Previously, Jesus' disciples had not fully known Him. They had seen glimpses of His true identity and had a partial understanding of who He was; but they had not fully experienced Him. If they had, they would have known that they were seeing what God the Father is like by seeing the Son. In the coming days, however, they would know Jesus and thus they would know God (14:7).

Philip asked Jesus to show the Father to the group. If Jesus would do that for them, they would be satisfied and it would end any doubts they had (14:8). Jesus was disappointed that Philip still did not understand His statement about knowing and seeing God. The disciples had spent nearly three years with Jesus. There was no need for Philip or any of them to ask Him to show them the Father. If they truly knew the Son, they would have known that to see Him was to see the Father's divine nature (14:9).

Jesus continued to describe His unity with God the Father by asking His disciples whether they believed He was in the Father and the Father was in Him. Jesus was forcing His disciples to consider what would have been outrageous to the Jewish mind—that a person could be one in essence with Yahweh (the Lord)—while expecting them to believe it. In fact, Jesus' words and works were a revelation of the triune Godhead, for the Father gave the Son the words He spoke and performed through Jesus the works He did (14:10).

Once more Jesus exhorted His disciples to believe that He is in the Father and the Father is in Him. After living with Jesus and experiencing the life He lived, they should have taken Him at His word; but even if they could not at this point, they could at least base their belief on the miraculous signs they had witnessed (14:11). Jesus was presenting faith based on miracles as second best. The best foundation of faith is Jesus' proven character, especially when a wished-for miracle did not appear.

Jesus told the disciples that those who believed in Him would do even greater things than what He had been doing (14:12). Jesus was not saying that they would possess greater powers than Him or that they would perform greater miracles. Evidently Jesus was talking about the mighty works of conversion. Whereas Jesus' ministry was primarily confined to Galilee and Judea, they would take the Gospel to distant lands; yet they could do none of this unless Jesus first returned to the Father.

According to 14:13, when we make our request known to God through Jesus' name, Jesus Himself will do it. Of course, Jesus was not providing a magical formula to be used as though one were bidding a genie to grant a wish. Nor did it mean that Jesus would always fulfill the request in the way His followers desired. Moreover, Jesus was referring to requests whose primary purpose is to glorify God, and thus are in line with God's will. Jesus' statements do not limit the power of prayer; instead, they require the petitioner to make his or her request consistent with the character of the Son and in accordance with the will of the Father (14:14). Since we pray in Jesus' name, He promised that He will do it. Thus, Jesus will be the one who is glorifying His heavenly Father. The two not only are one, but they also bring glory to each other.

SUGGESTIONS TO TEACHERS

Jesus would soon die on the cross for the sins of humanity. The news of His departure would leave the disciples unsettled and traumatized. Jesus realized this and sought to comfort His followers. He also spotlighted how important it was for them to regard Him as the only way to the Father.

1. THE NEED FOR GUIDANCE. Begin the teaching time by having the students imagine being on a hiking trip with a church group. Suddenly, they get separated from their peers and find themselves all alone. With no sense of which way to go or how to rejoin the group, they begin to feel uneasy. The only perceivable solution is for someone to come along and guide them back to their friends.

2. THE SAVIOR AS OUR GUIDE. Next, note that in the spiritual realm it's also easy to get disoriented and lost. It happens all the time to a lot of people. The only way, though, to get on track and stay on track is for us to put our faith in Jesus. Only He can guide us to the Father in heaven and make Him known to us.

3. THE BENEFIT OF JESUS LEADING US. Take a few moments to explain that when Jesus is at the center of our lives, we benefit from the divine truth and life He brings. He also enables us to be more effective in our Christian service. With Jesus as our guide, we can do great things for God, things that will bring Him honor and last for eternity. Also, with Jesus as the focal point of our praying, we are sure to make requests that are in harmony with the will of God. We can rest assured that such petitions are certain to be answered.

■ **TOPIC:** A Guide for Life

■ **QUESTIONS:** 1. Why would trusting in the Lord Jesus have calmed the troubled hearts of the disciples? 2. In what sense was Jesus going to prepare a place for His disciples? 3. In what sense is Jesus the way? 4. How is it possible to find truth and life in Jesus? 5. How does the Godhead work together to answer our prayers?

■ **ILLUSTRATIONS:**

Jesus Guides Us. Recently, when I typed the word *map* in my favorite internet search engine, I obtained thousands of listings to help me look for locations, get directions, and so on. One typical website claims users can not only find addresses and phone numbers, but also obtain directory listings for airports, hotels, post offices, restaurants, and schools (to name a few items).

In the spiritual realm, there is no substitute for the Lord Jesus in navigating through life. At times we might feel directionless. In those moments, Christ is present to guide us. On other occasions, we might struggle with depression or anxiety. In those seemingly dark times, the Savior will comfort us with His abiding presence and love.

My Way? On December 30, 1958, in Hollywood, California, Frank Sinatra did a recording of the hit song "My Way." In fact, it quickly became one of his signature tunes. Through each of the stanzas, Sinatra croons the refrain "I did it my way." Allegedly, every moment in life—with its pivotal decisions and key turning points—is characterized by this self-focused mindset.

We who are Jesus' followers have a different view of existence. On the one hand, life should be lived to the fullest extent possible. But in contrast to the world's way of thinking, existence is not about standing tall on our own, taking life's blows, and claiming we did things on our own terms. Instead, we humbly admit that we often get sidetracked and quagmired by the folly of our sin. And it is only by turning to the Savior in faith and relying fully on Him that we find the true and lasting way that leads to eternal life.

Jesus Is the Only Way. In Hinduism, a guru is a personal religious guide, spiritual teacher, or psychic master. Some believe that gurus point the way to a deeper God-consciousness within each person. It is also claimed that gurus are agents of enlightenment who show others how to attain a state of absolute blessedness. Supposedly, gurus have mystical insight into the soul of their followers.

For Christians, Jesus is the only way to God, the only source of divine truth, and the only one through whom they can receive eternal life (John 14:6). Christ's followers realize that apart from Him no one can go to the Father. In fact, it is only through knowing the Son that anyone can truly know the Father (14:7).

Spiritual Sight through Christ. For people who are blind and visually impaired, daily tasks that others don't even think about can be a real challenge. That's why at its inception, the concept of a dog guide was revolutionary. The seeing-eye dog has helped to enhance the independence, dignity, and self-confidence of people who are blind by enabling them to travel safely and independently.

In the spiritual realm, we are all born blind. Left on our own, we would stumble about in the darkness of sin. Thankfully, the Father has sent His Son to help us remain on the right course. Only He can show us how to pursue holiness and help us avoid the pitfalls of sin.

FOR YOUTH

■ TOPIC: Jesus Is the Way

■ QUESTIONS: 1. How did Jesus comfort His troubled disciples? 2. How can Jesus be the way, the truth, and the life? 3. What is the best way to get to know the Father in heaven? 4. What sort of greater works does Jesus accomplish through His disciples? 5. What role does Jesus serve in ensuring that our prayers are answered?

■ **ILLUSTRATIONS:**

Jesus, Our Traveling Companion. David and Christine had never traveled overseas before. Now they were actually making plans for 10 days in western Europe, with stops in France, Belgium, Switzerland, and Germany.

David was earnestly listening to some French language tapes, trying to memorize key phrases, when the doorbell rang. It was a special-delivery letter from his Uncle Gabe, a missionary stationed just outside Paris. "Instead of just stopping by on your way through," Gabe wrote, "why don't you and Christine stay with us? We can give you the grand tour, help with the language, and make sure nobody takes advantage of you."

David smiled in relief as he turned off the French language tape and went to share the news with his wife. Suddenly he knew the whole trip was going to be better than they had thought. With Gabe and his family as their companions, they were certain to have a great time. And even though David thought he might still try out some of his French, Gabe would be there to make sure he did not get snails when he wanted steak.

As this week's lesson points out, Jesus knew how beneficial it can be to have a traveling companion, someone to help us make sense of what we are experiencing, empower us to try new things, console us when things do not work out, and lead us on the most productive path. As the way, the truth, and the life (John 14:6), Jesus is our lifelong friend. Apart from Him, we cannot do God's will (see 15:5).

Jesus, Our Spiritual Rudder. A rudder is a device attached to the stern of a boat or ship so that it can be steered effectively in various directions. Rudders are most commonly flat in shape and attached to the sternpost in an upright position. The apparatus is also hinged at its forward edge so that it can direct the water flowing past it in such a way as to cause the vessel to be redirected from its original course. In large ships, hydraulic, steam, or electrical equipment is used to turn the rudder.

In a metaphorical sense, Jesus is our spiritual rudder. When we get off course, He redirects us. Regardless of the situation, we can rely on Him to steer us in paths of righteousness. Even when we encounter enticements to sin, we can lean on Him to pull us through the ordeal.

Jesus, Our Spiritual Compass. A Global Positioning System (GPS) uses satellites to help people navigate through unfamiliar territory. The GPS is extremely accurate in letting users know their precise location and the direction in which they should head to reach their destination. The system remains effective even in the worst weather conditions.

Just as military and civilian users rely on the GPS to help them get from one locale to the next, so too Jesus is the believers' spiritual "compass" pointing them to God. In addition, the Son is the only pathway to the Father. Moreover, divine truth and eternal life can only be found in the Savior. Indeed, He alone is the hope of every human being, whether young or old.

"I AM THE TRUE VINE"

BACKGROUND SCRIPTURE: John 15:1-17

DEVOTIONAL READING: Psalm 1

KEY VERSE: I am the vine, ye are the branches: He that abideth in me, and I in him, the same bringeth forth much fruit: for without me ye can do nothing. John 15:5.

KING JAMES VERSION

JOHN 15:1 I am the true vine, and my Father is the husbandman. 2 Every branch in me that beareth not fruit he taketh away: and every branch that beareth fruit, he purgeth it, that it may bring forth more fruit. 3 Now ye are clean through the word which I have spoken unto you. 4 Abide in me, and I in you. As the branch cannot bear fruit of itself, except it abide in the vine; no more can ye, except ye abide in me. 5 I am the vine, ye are the branches: He that abideth in me, and I in him, the same bringeth forth much fruit: for without me ye can do nothing. 6 If a man abide not in me, he is cast forth as a branch, and is withered; and men gather them, and cast them into the fire, and they are burned. 7 If ye abide in me, and my words abide in you, ye shall ask what ye will, and it shall be done unto you. 8 Herein is my Father glorified, that ye bear much fruit; so shall ye be my disciples.

9 As the Father hath loved me, so have I loved you: continue ye in my love. 10 If ye keep my commandments, ye shall abide in my love; even as I have kept my Father's commandments, and abide in his love. 11 These things have I spoken unto you, that my joy might remain in you, and that your joy might be full. 12 This is my commandment, That ye love one another, as I have loved you. 13 Greater love hath no man than this, that a man lay down his life for his friends. 14 Ye are my friends, if ye do whatsoever I command you. 15 Henceforth I call you not servants; for the servant knoweth not what his lord doeth: but I have called you friends; for all things that I have heard of my Father I have made known unto you. 16 Ye have not chosen me, but I have chosen you, and ordained you, that ye should go and bring forth fruit, and that your fruit should remain: that whatsoever ye shall ask of the Father in my name, he may give it you. 17 These things I command you, that ye love one another.

NEW REVISED STANDARD VERSION

JOHN 15:1 "I am the true vine, and my Father is the vinegrower. 2 He removes every branch in me that bears no fruit. Every branch that bears fruit he prunes to make it bear more fruit. 3 You have already been cleansed by the word that I have spoken to you. 4 Abide in me as I abide in you. Just as the branch cannot bear fruit by itself unless it abides in the vine, neither can you unless you abide in me. 5 I am the vine, you are the branches. Those who abide in me and I in them bear much fruit, because apart from me you can do nothing. 6 Whoever does not abide in me is thrown away like a branch and withers; such branches are gathered, thrown into the fire, and burned. 7 If you abide in me, and my words abide in you, ask for whatever you wish, and it will be done for you. 8 My Father is glorified by this, that you bear much fruit and become my disciples. 9 As the Father has loved me, so I have loved you; abide in my love. 10 If you keep my commandments, you will abide in my love, just as I have kept my Father's commandments and abide in his love. 11 I have said these things to you so that my joy may be in you, and that your joy may be complete.

12 "This is my commandment, that you love one another as I have loved you. 13 No one has greater love than this, to lay down one's life for one's friends. 14 You are my friends if you do what I command you. 15 I do not call you servants any longer, because the servant does not know what the master is doing; but I have called you friends, because I have made known to you everything that I have heard from my Father. 16 You did not choose me but I chose you. And I appointed you to go and bear fruit, fruit that will last, so that the Father will give you whatever you ask him in my name. 17 I am giving you these commands so that you may love one another.

13

HOME BIBLE READINGS

Monday, February 19	Matthew 13:18-33	*How the Word Grows*
Tuesday, February 20	John 17:13-19	*Jesus Prays for His Followers*
Wednesday, February 21	1 John 2:24-29	*Abide in Christ*
Thursday, February 22	2 John 7-11	*Continue in Christ's Teachings*
Friday, February 23	Psalm 1	*The Blessed*
Saturday, February 24	John 15:1-8	*I Am the True Vine*
Sunday, February 25	John 15:9-17	*Love One Another*

BACKGROUND

This week's lesson continues what is called "the Upper Room Discourse." Jesus addressed His closest followers in what He knew would be the closing hours of His earthly ministry. Jesus was aware of their flaws and weaknesses. Judas had already deserted the Savior. Now in the final minutes of His time with the remaining disciples, the Lord Jesus chose a symbol to describe His identity and their time with Him: the vine.

In the time of Christ, the cultivation and harvest of grapes was a prominent part of Israel's economy. Grape plants grew best under certain conditions and in particular locations. For example, they required plenty of sunshine, ample amounts of water, and fertile, well-drained soil. Gently rolling plains and the slopes of hills were ideal spots for grape plants to grow.

The cultivation of grapes was a hard and painstaking job. For instance, farmers had to gently place vines that had fallen to the ground back into position. They also had to constantly repair trellises and poles supporting the vines and regularly pull the weeds. In addition, a number of things could diminish the quantity and quality of the harvest obtained from a grape plant. Along with heavy rains and strong winds, the intrusion of wild animals and careless people could severely damage a plant's delicate vines. If farmers did not regularly prune healthy branches and remove dead ones, the plant would not produce a good crop of fruit. The grapes that grew on the plants needed to sufficiently ripen before the farmers could pick them. Otherwise, if they prematurely harvested the fruit, it would taste quite sour.

When Jesus used the imagery of the vine and vineyard, He knew that in several places in the Old Testament, Israel is referred to as a vineyard. For example, in Isaiah 5:4 we read that God desired His vineyard (Israel) to bring forth grapes (righteousness); instead, the people brought forth wild grapes (unrighteousness). As a nation ready for exile, Israel's behavior was not pleasing to God. The Father, whom Jesus called the *husbandman* (John 15:1), planted the true vine by sending His Son to dwell among us. Unlike the nation of Israel, the Lord Jesus lived a life of fruitfulness that was pleasing to the Father. For instance, Christ voluntarily offered up His life as the acceptable sacrifice for the sins of the world.

In referring to Himself as the vine of the grape plant, Jesus was stating that He supplied the needs of His people—the branches growing from the vine. Their relationship with Christ supplied whatever they required to live and bear fruit for the kingdom of God. It's not clear to whom Jesus was referring as the unfruitful branches (15:2). Some think He was talking about people who had formerly embraced Him by faith but no longer did so. Others believe the branches represent people who were never really saved. In both cases, the judgment being faced is eternal separation from God. A third group asserts that Jesus was talking about persistently wayward believers whom God removes from active ministry.

NOTES ON THE PRINTED TEXT

Perhaps the Lord Jesus motioned toward a nearby plant when He spoke of Himself as the *true vine* (John 15:1). This is the last of the seven great "I am" statements, all of which in some way point to Jesus' divinity (see 6:35, 48; 8:12; 10:7, 9; 10:11, 14; 11:25; 14:6). In this case the Savior referred to Himself as the only true source of life and power through which God, as the farmer, brings forth fruit for the divine kingdom.

In the same way a gardener prunes a grapevine in order for the plant to yield the maximum number of grapes, our Father removes and discards deadwood and trims productive branches. The Father is vitally concerned with our fruitfulness and will carefully clip away anything that drains our spiritual resources (15:2). We who are in Christ are already clean (15:3); yet God continues to work in our lives, cutting away sin and empowering us to be like the Messiah. Jesus calls us to abide in Him as He abides in us. As we remain in Him, His life will flow through us, and we will continue to bear fruit. Apart from the life-giving resources of the vine, no branch can bear fruit of itself. In the same way, Christians are wholly dependent upon God when it comes to being productive (15:4).

Although there is a mutual indwelling between Christ and His followers, we must not be confused about our distinctive roles. Jesus is the vine and we are the branches (15:5). Though we abide in Him and He in us, we still can accomplish nothing apart from Him. In fact, if a branch is not attached to the vine, it will be thrown away. Like a severed branch, those who are not in Christ will be cast into the fire and burned (15:6). This is a reference to judgment by the Lord.

The concept of fruitful and unfruitful branches can be illustrated by two of Jesus' disciples. Christ chose Judas as a follower. Possibly because of the latter's ability as a businessperson, he was given the job as treasurer for the group (12:6; 13:29); but Judas's abilities helped lead to his downfall because of his greed. Though Judas was associated with Jesus, heard His teaching, and witnessed His works, Judas did not have an abiding spiritual union with Jesus; rather than bearing fruit, Judas's life ended in destruction. In fact, 15:6 could read, "He is like *the* branch that is thrown away and withers," perhaps making a specific reference to Judas.

Christ also chose Peter to be one of His disciples. Jesus taught him the same truths and gave him the same opportunities to witness that He had given Judas. Peter did not begin his life as a disciple with great success, but after some pruning (such as his denial of Christ and reinstatement later), Peter bore much fruit. He found the key to a productive life in a living relationship with Christ.

In 15:7, Jesus returned to the subject of prayer. Again, He promised to give the believer whatever is asked. There are, however, certain conditions. First, we must abide in Him. When we live in oneness with Christ, our desires will be in line with God's will. Second, we must remain obedient to Jesus' teachings. When we are faithful in these ways, we will pray for the things God wants, and He will give them to us. Moreover, when we show that we are Christ's followers by the fruit we bear, we bring glory to God the Father. Since fruitfulness is evidence that God is at work in Christ's disciples, the abundance of that fruit brings honor to God (15:8). Because He is the gardener, that fruit is His property—it does not belong to the branches.

Jesus shared important truths with His friends because He loved them deeply. In fact, Jesus' love for His disciples is as great as God's love for Him. Jesus told His friends to continue in His love by keeping His commands. In the same way Jesus has stayed in the Father's love by remaining obedient to His will (15:9-10). Obeying Christ is not a burden; in fact, it is the only thing that brings lasting joy (15:11). Jesus was not talking here about a life of pleasure or one filled with unending happy moments. The joy Christ provides is independent of circumstances because it stems from a dynamic, ever-growing relationship with the Lord—something that can never be taken away from us.

Jesus summed up His teachings with one commandment: His followers are to love one another as He has loved them (15:12). This kind of love is demonstrated by a willingness to lay down one's life for that friend (15:13). Indeed, Jesus did this very thing for us when He voluntarily subjected Himself to death, even death on the cross. Jesus set the example of the type of sacrificial love we should demonstrate toward our fellow believers in Christ.

Jesus considers His followers His friends (15:14), not His servants (or "slaves," which the original Greek word implies in 15:15). Normally, servants are not in on their master's intentions or plans; instead, they must obey instructions without question. Jesus, however, treats us like friends in that He discloses to us everything His heavenly Father has revealed to Him. By taking His disciples into His confidence, Jesus elevated His relationship with believers to a far more intimate level. In this type of relationship we can obey Him out of love rather than compulsion.

Like other disciples who attached themselves to a particular teacher or rabbi, Jesus' followers may have thought they had chosen Jesus to be their Master. The Savior, however, made it clear that He had selected them to be His disciples. Furthermore,

Jesus had appointed His disciples to specific tasks that would bear fruit that had eternal value. While performing these tasks, we can ask for and receive the things we need in order to accomplish God's work (15:16). At this point Jesus once more commanded His friends to love one another (15:17). He knew they needed each other's love because of the intense suffering that lay ahead for them.

SUGGESTIONS TO TEACHERS

Jesus used the vine and its branches to illustrate the close union that He would have with His disciples. As grapevine branches cannot produce fruit apart from the main vine, so followers of Jesus cannot bear fruit for Him if they exist apart from Him. This great symbol of the vine brings out the following points.

1. THE POWER OF THE VINE. The source of our spiritual vitality is Jesus Christ. As branches are dependent on the vine for nourishment and growth, we are dependent on the Savior. Otherwise, our faith eventually withers. Jesus' warning in John 15:5 clearly reminds us that those who claim they can be connected to the Messiah without being part of His redeemed community are like severed branches.

2. THE PURPOSE OF THE BRANCH. The only reason for the existence of a branch is to be productive. The section of a grape vine not bearing fruit merely takes strength away from other parts of the vine. That section is pruned and thrown away. Our usefulness to the Lord Jesus is characterized by our sharing of the love He has poured on us.

3. THE PREEMINENCE OF LOVE. Jesus boldly told those in the upper room that He was giving them a new commandment. In fact, some have dubbed this the "11th commandment." The Savior's directive instructs us to love one another, just as He has loved us (15:12). During the teaching time, take a few moments to talk about what love is, according to Jesus. Help the class distinguish between the mushy notions of "love" in popular culture and how love is described in the Word of God.

4. THE PROMOTION OF SERVANT TO FRIEND. Jesus stated that He regarded His followers not as mere servants but as friends (15:15). *Friend* is a word weighted with deep meaning. A servant merely carries out orders. A friend wants to do everything in the best interests of his or her colleagues. One friend trusts the other friend and is likewise trusted. Friends enjoy an openness with each other and cherish the times in each other's company. All of these ways of a friend are meant to be practiced and enjoyed in the relationship we have in our friendship with the Messiah.

5. THE PROCESS OF CHOOSING. Throughout the years, the subject of God choosing us has been a sore spot for some. It is assumed that the Lord somehow is playing favorites in selecting a few to be special buddies, while rejecting others. However, nothing in this week's Scripture passage implies this. God did not choose us because we were nicer or smarter or holier than any others. Instead, the Lord brought us to salvation because He does not want any to perish to a Christless eternity (2 Pet. 3:9). In short, God does not play favorites!

■ **QUESTIONS:** 1. What do the vine and branches symbolize? 2. What is the job of the farmer? 3. What are the benefits of remaining in Christ? 4. What are the characteristics of Jesus' love for us? 5. How is the Father glorified when we bear spiritual fruit as disciples of the Lord Jesus?

■ **ILLUSTRATIONS:**

Keep in Touch! Jim had lost touch with Herb (not their real names). Back in the 1960s, they had worked closely together in the civil rights movement. Herb had been a promising young seminary graduate. In particular, he was a gifted speaker, and was actively involved in civic affairs. His energy and intelligence had propelled him to a position of leadership.

Herb's peers were convinced that he would be recognized as one of the outstanding church leaders of the late 20th century. Then Herb moved to the West Coast. His former friends—such as Jim—gradually lost touch with him. It was learned through other sources that Herb was doing some heavy drinking, and had a series of church jobs, followed by a campus assignment. Then he dropped out of both the church world and work world. His wife told Jim in a letter that Herb had left her. Herb married again, then divorced that woman also. Others reported that Herb suffered some health problems related to emotional stress.

Twenty years later, Jim unexpectedly ran into Herb. But this was a different person. This Herb was a tired, burned-out old man. He admitted that he had dropped out of the Church altogether. He felt disillusioned by church people and hadn't been active for years. With a tone of resignation, he sighed, "I'm even out of touch with God, I guess."

All of us grow tired of trying to touch the needs of sufferers around us. But when we persist in allowing the risen One to be in touch with us through His enlivening presence, we will be given the stamina to keep in touch with the world of suffering people.

Jesus commands His followers to bear fruit. Indeed, John 15:1-17 opens and closes by repeating that the vine and the branches exist for the purpose of bearing fruit, or being productive for others. Herb tried to bear fruit without staying in touch with the Lord Jesus and His followers. Regretfully, Herb wound up a broken man.

Keep in touch with the risen Christ and with the Church. With these connections, you'll find yourself able to minister to the needs of the people around you, without getting burned out.

The Winning Team. Many people still remember Vince Lombardi. Lee Iacocca, once one of the most powerful men in the car industry, asked the legendary football coach what it takes to make a winning team. This was Lombardi's answer:

> There are a lot of coaches with good ball clubs who know the fundamentals and have plenty of discipline but still don't know the game. Then you come

to the third ingredient: if you're going to play together as a team, you've got to care for one another. You've got to love each other. Each player has to be thinking about the next guy and saying to himself, "If I don't block that man, Paul is going to get his legs broken. I have to do my job well in order that he can do his." The difference between mediocrity and greatness is the feeling these guys have for each other.

In a healthy church, each believer learns to care for others. As we take seriously Jesus' command to love one another, we contribute to a winning team.

Remaining Connected to Christ. As I tidied up our yard one day, my son noticed several dead branches on an otherwise lush bush. As he parted the vibrant, green branches that surrounded them, I saw telltale brown leaves. Winds from an early spring storm had buffeted these branches so hard that they had fractured. They were still attached to the bush but were completely withered. In their brokenness they could not receive life-sustaining nutrients.

Storms come. We expect them. But we cannot be certain when one will hit and how much damage it will cause. In the Christian community, just as in my yard, there are vibrant branches. But if strong winds sever their connection to the Savior, they will wither. That's why all believers are wise to remain joined to Christ. It's the only way to survive and thrive spiritually in this world.

FOR YOUTH

■ TOPIC: Connected to the Vine

■ QUESTIONS: 1. Why was the figure of the vine so important to Israel? 2. In what way is Jesus the true vine? 3. How and why does God spiritually prune us as branches on the vine of the Savior? 4. What does it mean to abide in the Lord Jesus? 5. How does remaining joined to Christ by faith help us bear fruit?

■ ILLUSTRATIONS:

The Key to Fruitful Living. Legend tells us that John Chapman (nicknamed "Johnny Appleseed") traveled widely in the Ohio River valley in the early part of the 19th century, planting apple seeds. The popular image of Chapman is of a wandering farmer simply casting handfuls of seeds along his path as he walked. However, for his work to succeed, Chapman not only had to plant, but also to tend his trees.

It is similar with those tending vineyards. Pruning and training are the methods the vine grower uses to keep the vine in order and to ensure a fairly large quantity of fruit. The vines that yield to the vine grower's actions will be the ones that produce the most and best fruit.

This is Jesus' goal for every believer: that we would so closely abide in Him that we rely on His nurture and nourishment as much as we do His pruning and training. After all, apart from Him we can do nothing.

Bear Fruit. A 17-year-old named Ben came to church. His parents were getting a divorce and he had spent Saturday night talking with his friends. Although they all said that they felt sorry for him or said that they knew what he was going through, not one had a satisfactory answer for his needs. He drifted into church, and after worship spoke with the pastor.

The minister asked Ben if he believed in Jesus Christ, and, if so, whether they could pray together. Ben replied that he had never accepted Jesus as Savior. In fact, before the morning sermon, the teen had never heard about trusting in the Messiah. "How's that?" asked the pastor. "Because no one ever told me about Jesus," said Ben.

If that does not make all young people squirm, it should. One who is spiritually attached to Jesus and draws his or her nourishment from Him must bear fruit. Those like Ben in this world must come to know the Vine through each of you.

Joined to Jesus. One hot summer when I was a teenager, a friend invited me to pick fruit with him at a nearby orchard. We had been busily harvesting fruit at one peach tree when I noticed that a limb had been severed from the trunk. The limb still had fruit on it, but the peaches were beginning to rot and shrivel up. Because the limb had separated from the tree, it was no longer able to produce good fruit.

In a spiritual sense, Jesus is like the trunk of the peach tree, and we are like the limbs growing from it. If we want to grow and thrive as believers, we must remain intimately connected to the Savior.

Restricted Freedom? In the fall of 1996, Pittsburgh joined other metropolitan areas in passing a teen curfew ordinance. Young people had to be off city streets from 10 P.M. until 6 A.M. on weekends. The idea behind the curfew was to save adolescent lives and keep them out of trouble by getting them off the streets at night. Special provisions were made for working teens or those who were in the company of their parents.

As county commissioners expected, many youth balked and complained at what they perceived as restrictions to their freedom. However, commissioners were adamant. A loss of some freedom was worth the cost of helping the youth.

Jesus made it clear that His followers were to bear fruit. A branch must be vigorously pruned in order to keep it productive. In the same manner, to produce spiritually mature young people, some things must be pruned away for the maintenance of spiritual health.

THE LIGHT OF LOVE

BACKGROUND SCRIPTURE: 1 John 2:7-17
DEVOTIONAL READING: 1 Peter 4:1-11

KEY VERSE: He that loveth his brother abideth in the light, and there is none occasion of stumbling in him. 1 John 2:10.

KING JAMES VERSION

1 JOHN 2:7 Brethren, I write no new commandment unto you, but an old commandment which ye had from the beginning. The old commandment is the word which ye have heard from the beginning. 8 Again, a new commandment I write unto you, which thing is true in him and in you: because the darkness is past, and the true light now shineth. 9 He that saith he is in the light, and hateth his brother, is in darkness even until now. 10 He that loveth his brother abideth in the light, and there is none occasion of stumbling in him. 11 But he that hateth his brother is in darkness, and walketh in darkness, and knoweth not whither he goeth, because that darkness hath blinded his eyes. . . .

15 Love not the world, neither the things that are in the world. If any man love the world, the love of the Father is not in him. 16 For all that is in the world, the lust of the flesh, and the lust of the eyes, and the pride of life, is not of the Father, but is of the world. 17 And the world passeth away, and the lust thereof: but he that doeth the will of God abideth for ever.

NEW REVISED STANDARD VERSION

1 JOHN 2:7 Beloved, I am writing you no new commandment, but an old commandment that you have had from the beginning; the old commandment is the word that you have heard. 8 Yet I am writing you a new commandment that is true in him and in you, because the darkness is passing away and the true light is already shining. 9 Whoever says, "I am in the light," while hating a brother or sister, is still in the darkness. 10 Whoever loves a brother or sister lives in the light, and in such a person there is no cause for stumbling. 11 But whoever hates another believer is in the darkness, walks in the darkness, and does not know the way to go, because the darkness has brought on blindness. . . .

15 Do not love the world or the things in the world. The love of the Father is not in those who love the world; 16 for all that is in the world—the desire of the flesh, the desire of the eyes, the pride in riches—comes not from the Father but from the world. 17 And the world and its desire are passing away, but those who do the will of God live forever.

Monday, February 26	2 Peter 1:5-11	*Partakers of the Divine Nature*
Tuesday, February 27	Romans 12:9-21	*Living in Love*
Wednesday, February 28	Romans 13:8-14	*Fulfilling the Law in Love*
Thursday, March 1	Galatians 5:13-26	*Serve with Love*
Friday, March 2	1 Peter 4:1-11	*Love Deeply*
Saturday, March 3	1 John 2:7-11	*Called to Live in Love*
Sunday, March 4	1 John 2:12-17	*Live for God*

BACKGROUND

Neither the Epistles of John nor the Gospel of John identify their author. Church fathers as early as Irenaeus in the second century attributed them to John the beloved disciple of Jesus, the son of Zebedee, and the brother of James. The earliest citations of John's works are found in writings from western Asia Minor around Ephesus, where the apostle John ministered in the later years of his life. John's authorship of these books has been universally accepted into the modern era, and even many critical scholars find the evidence compelling.

First John reflects a date of composition late in the first century, probably between A.D. 85 and 95. John addressed his readers from the perspective of an elderly man, calling them little children (2:1). In 2 and 3 John, the apostle referred to himself as *the elder* (2 John 1; 3 John 1). The false teaching addressed in John's epistles also reflects ideas characteristic of a later date rather than an earlier one in the apostolic period.

In John's day, Ephesus was an ancient city that prided itself as the cultural center of the province of Asia. That culture was thoroughly Hellenistic and included many forms of revived paganism that tried to bring together different strands of religious thought, old and new, eastern and western. John's letters reflect a struggle between the truth of God's Word and some heretical teachings within the churches around Ephesus that threatened to divide the congregations.

The proponents of the heretical teachings seem to have agreed that *God is light* (1 John 1:5). They accepted Christ as a heavenly being, but denied His humanity (4:2). They believed the Gospel freed them from the presence of *sin* (1:8). They assumed they were free from any further practice of sin (1:10). They did not make a connection between their belief and their behavior. They were neither gracious nor loving (3:14-17). They were involved in missionary activity to expand their sect (2 John 10). The new sect had been a part of the church around Ephesus. By the time John wrote his first letter, the heretics had separated from the church and had begun rivaling it (1 John 2:19). The apostle summoned the members of the church to resist the sect that wanted to divorce faith and life. One must walk in the light; one must live in love; and to abide in God one must obey His commands.

This last statement reminds us that throughout John's Gospel and his letters, the apostle often used the metaphor of light and darkness in order to contrast the ways of God with the ways of the world. The concept of light and darkness had great significance in Hebrew culture. In Scripture, the words "lamp," "light," and "life" are often used as synonyms. In the Book of Job, for example, Bildad said of the depraved, *the light of the wicked shall be put out, and the spark of his fire shall not shine. The light shall be dark in his tabernacle, and his candle shall be put out with him* (Job 18:5-6). In the teachings of Jesus, being cast into outer darkness was symbolic of the coming judgment of the unrighteous (Matt. 8:12; 22:13; 25:30).

According to John, the only place where genuine fellowship with God may be found is in the light—that is, a lifestyle that remains fully accountable to the truth of God's Word. This type of authentic living makes genuine fellowship with other believers possible. Furthermore, in addition to producing true fellowship, walking in the light keeps us cleansed from sin (1 John 1:7). As believers walk in the light, the Holy Spirit discloses their sins. Though at times painful, living with an openness to this uncovering work of the Holy Spirit is the best way to keep short accounts with God.

NOTES ON THE PRINTED TEXT

First John 2:3-6 underscores the importance of obeying God's commands. Perhaps in light of this, some of John's readers may have wondered whether there were commands they might not know about. After all, religious frauds claimed to have a secret saving knowledge. Thus, John's readers may have been struggling with doubts. John made it clear to his dear friends that he was not presenting some new requirement or obligation, but an old command that they had had since the Gospel was first proclaimed (2:7).

The command that John had in mind was apparently to *walk, even as [Jesus] walked* (2:6) and its natural corollary, to love one another (2:10). Whatever the false teachers were telling John's readers, he wanted one thing understood. Their obligation was not to some new idea or teaching, but to the message they had heard from the beginning of their Christian experience. The Greeks had two different words for "new." One referred to something that was new in regard to time, that is, something that recently had come into existence. The other word, the one used in 2:7, referred to something that was new in regard to quality. Because of Jesus' example, the command to love was something new in character.

When Christ first gave the command to love one another, He called it new (2:8; see John 13:34). The apostle presented it again as if it were still new. The commandment to love was first realized in Christ and then in His followers. John made reference to this fact in terms of the true light of the Messiah already shining brightly. Because the apostle saw the victory of light over darkness as something previously begun, he urged his readers to hold fast to what they had already heard and not be influenced by the teaching of their opponents.

The commandment to love others did not belong to the old era that was passing away. It belonged to the new era of righteousness that was introduced by the Savior's incarnation and made possible by His atoning work on the cross. It follows that any professing Christian who claims to follow Jesus but harbors hatred toward others is still living in the old era of darkness (1 John 2:9).

Believers who demonstrate genuine love for others are living in the light of the new era in Christ. And because of this, there is nothing in them that would cause others to stumble (2:10). Professing believers, however, who nurse grudges and cultivate bitterness, remain spiritually darkened. These people lose their bearings as they stumble around in the dark (2:11).

In the prologue of his epistle, John gave his readers two reasons for writing to them (see 1:1-4). The first was to foster fellowship between his Christian readers and the apostles, then ultimately with God Himself. The second objective was to make the apostle's joy complete. In the remainder of chapter 2, John expanded upon these objectives by detailing how he wanted to see them fulfilled. The warnings and admonitions John gave in 1:5—2:11 might lead one to believe that the apostle was dissatisfied in some way with the spiritual state of his readers. First John 2:12-14 suggests just the opposite. John commended his readers for their relational knowledge of God and their reliance upon the Lord for victory in spiritual warfare.

While the spiritual state of John's readers was healthy, the apostle still felt compelled to warn them about the dangers of getting too intimate with the world. Regardless of the maturity of their faith or the depth of their commitment to Christ, the possibility of stumbling into sin was always present. In 2:12-14, John reminded his readers about the benefits they enjoyed as children of God. Their sins were forgiven, they knew the true God, and they had been victorious in the spiritual battle over Satan. Then in 2:15-17, the apostle encouraged believers to take the high road mandated by their divine calling. He commanded his readers not to love the world or anything in it.

The Greek word for *world* (2:15) here is *cosmos*. It refers to the secular, ungodly, humanistic system under Satan's control. At every turn this system opposes God and actively seeks to subvert His plan of salvation for humankind. For this reason, John wanted it understood that one cannot love that world and all that it has to offer and love God at the same time (see Jas. 4:4). A clear choice had to be made—love God and hate the world or love the world and hate God. The two options are mutually exclusive.

John explained that everything in the world has its origin in the world's system, not from the Father. In describing what the world has to offer, John specifically named three things. First is *the lust of the flesh* (1 John 2:16). The Greek word *epithumia*, translated *lust* here, almost always signifies the sinful desires that come from within the human heart. This craving represents a self-centered, short-term perspective. It is exemplified in the demand to have one's wants satisfied immediately.

The second thing John identified as having its origin in the world is *the lust of the eyes*. This speaks of the temptations that assault believers from the outside. Jesus called the eye *the light of the body* (Matt. 6:22). If the eyes were good, in the moral sense, then the body and the spirit would remain clean. If the eyes were bad, in the same moral sense, then body and spirit would be tainted by sin. Allowing the eyes to dwell upon an object of desire, whether it be a person or a thing, will eventually lead to sinful attitudes and actions.

The third item in John's list of worldly offerings involved boasting about what one has and does (1 John 2:16). The meaning here, while difficult to be precise, seems to refer to the arrogance that can come with success. Ultimately, all of our talents and abilities come from God, so there is never anything to boast about when it comes to what we have accomplished with our skills. The only appropriate response to the blessings in our lives is gratitude, not gratuitous boasting.

In John's view, a believer should have nothing to do with any of these worldly values. In fact, according to the apostle, it is only logical to reject the world and cling to God. The empty values and hollow promises of the world are even now in the process of passing away. Obedience to God and His will, on the other hand, leads to everlasting life (2:17). How foolish it is to remain on a sinking ship when God has tossed a lifeline within the grasp of every human being.

SUGGESTIONS TO TEACHERS

We have to recognize the incompatibility of the darkness of the world and God's light. We need to remind ourselves that fellowship with the world leads to judgment, while fellowship with the Father and His Son leads to eternal life. We also need to remind ourselves that, when we live as children of God, we will receive the same treatment from the children of the world that Jesus did.

1. WALK IN THE LIGHT. God radiates glory, purity, and truth into the lives of His spiritual children. We need to live our lives in God's light and allow His light to transform us. If we avoid His light in favor of the darkness of the world, our fellowship with the Father and His Son will be interrupted. If we open our lives every day to God's light, it will expose our sins and we will experience the daily cleansing from our sins by Christ's blood.

2. CONFESS YOUR SINS. God's light will make our sins hateful to us, but we will sin. When we do, Jesus Christ defends us to the Father on the basis of His blood shed to appease God's wrath and wash away our guilt. We acknowledge the reality of our sins and our responsibility for them through the act of confession to God and to the people we hurt. If we conceal our sins, deny our sins, or ignore our sins, we walk out of God's light into the darkness of the world. This breaks our fellowship with the Father and His Son.

3. OBEY GOD'S WORD. In the theology of the apostle John, to know God, to abide in God, and to love God are all synonymous expressions for obeying God. We who say we know and love the Father and the Son ought to walk just as He walked (1 John 2:6). We know the Father because the Son has shown Him to us (John 1:18; 14:8-11). The example and commands of Jesus provide the blueprint for our obedience of God (14:21).

4. LOVE NOT THE WORLD. No one can serve two masters (Matt. 6:24). The devil works through the allures of the *world* (1 John 5:19) to draw believers away from fellowship with God into fellowship with the world. We are not ignorant of the devil's schemes (2 Cor. 2:11). He uses selfishness, greed, and vain status seeking to appeal to our sinful natures and seduce us from fellowship with the Father and His Son.

FOR ADULTS

■ **TOPIC:** Love Is Light

■ **QUESTIONS:** 1. What new aspect about the command to love did John convey to his readers? 2. How is it possible for believers to remain in the light of the Lord Jesus? 3. What differentiates the various lusts mentioned in 1 John 2:16? 4. What connection is there between the world and its lusts? 5. How can we abide forever?

■ **ILLUSTRATIONS:**

What the World Needs Now. In 1965, Jackie DeShannon wrote and performed the top ten single "What the World Needs Now Is Love." The chorus for this popular song stated that love is "the only thing that there's just too little of" and that "sweet love" is "not just for some but for everyone."

Few people would claim that DeShannon's sentiments don't apply today. In an era in which people tend to live for themselves and take advantage of others to satisfy their own greedy desires, the world needs a special kind of love. It's not the sort, though, that remains confined to our hearts. We need the love of Christ, a practical love that seeks the benefit of others, a caring love that is active and sincere.

Scripture teaches that the light of the Father's love has shown brightly in His Son. When Jesus became Incarnate, He came as a gift from the Creator. God knew we needed help, and Jesus Christ was His answer. Through Him, let us shine the light of God's redemptive love to a world that is lost in sin.

What Does Love Look Like? On August 29, 2005, Hurricane Katrina slammed into the Gulf Coast region of the United States. In the aftermath of the storm, New Orleans was flooded, forcing its population to evacuate. Entire coastal towns in Louisiana, Mississippi, and Alabama were wiped out. And many lives were lost both during and after the storm.

In the midst of one of the worst natural disasters in United States history, the whole nation was mobilized into action. Both civilian and private organizations shifted personnel and resources to the devastated region. Entire families were relocated to far flung places throughout the country. People not directly affected by the storm opened their homes and lives to complete strangers so that they might have a roof over their heads, clothes on their backs, and food in their stomachs.

This massive and sustained relief effort demonstrated in a concrete way what love looks like. And it's the type of compassion that John had in mind when he penned his first letter. Such kindness takes into account the needs of others. It's willing to say no to one's personal desires so that others can be helped. Surely God smiles on such endeavors, especially when they are made in the name of Christian love!

The Way of the World. Some time ago, a newspaper in Tacoma, Washington, carried the story of Tattoo, the basset hound. Tattoo didn't intend to go for an evening run, but when his owner shut his leash in the car door and took off with Tattoo still outside the vehicle, he had no choice.

A motorcycle officer named Terry Filbert noticed a passing vehicle with something that appeared to be dragging behind it. As he passed the vehicle, he saw the object was a basset hound on a leash.

"He was picking them up and putting them down as fast as he could," said Filbert. He chased the car to a stop, and Tattoo was rescued, but not before the dog reached a speed of 20 to 25 miles per hour, and rolled over several times. The dog was fine but asked not to go out for an evening walk for a long time.

If you befriend the world, it will take you for a ride that wears you out and rolls you over. And, if you aren't rescued by the Savior (through faith in Him), your life will end in eternal darkness.

FOR YOUTH

■ TOPIC: Turn on Your Heart Light

■ QUESTIONS: 1. What did John mean by stating that the commandment to love was both old and new? 2. What does it mean to abide in the light? 3. In what sense has the darkness blinded those who hate other Christians? 4. Why did John urge believers not to love the world? 5. Why is it important to abide in the Lord?

■ ILLUSTRATIONS:

Come into the Light—Now! Nearly 200 years ago, Charles Finney was the best-known American evangelist. Once, during a series of meetings in Rochester, New York, Finney had a strange experience. The chief justice of the supreme court of New York sat in one of the upper balconies of the church. As he listened to Finney preach, he thought, *That man is speaking the truth. I ought to make a public confession of Jesus Christ.*

Another voice in his head told him he was an important person who didn't need the humiliation of going forward like an ordinary sinner. The attorney knew he would talk himself out of doing what he should if he sat there very long. So he left his seat, went down the stairs, and headed down the aisle—all while Finney kept preaching away. The judge stepped onto the platform, tugged on the evangelist's sleeve and announced, "If you will call for decisions for Christ now, I am ready to come."

Now is the time for us to come into the light and experience the new life that the Lord Jesus offers.

Walk This Way. Back in the late 1980s, Meryl Streep starred in *Ironweed*. She played a ragged derelict who died in a cheap motel room. For more than half an hour before that scene was filmed, Streep hugged a bag of ice cubes in an attempt to discover what it was like to be a cold, clammy corpse. When the cameras came on, she just lay there as Jack Nicholson's character cried and shook her limp body.

Streep lay there for take after take and in between takes, too. One of the crew members got scared and went to the director and said, "What's going on? She's not breathing!" When the director looked at her, he saw no signs of life, but he kept the camera rolling. After the scene was done and cameras were off, Meryl Streep still didn't move. It took 10 minutes for her to emerge from the semi-conscious state she had sunk into. The director was amazed and said, "Now that's acting! That is an actress!"

Meryl Streep identified so closely with death that she took on its character. The challenge of the Christian life is to identify so totally with Jesus that we take on His character. The great difference is that we are identifying with the abundant life and light that Jesus offers, not the death and darkness of sin.

There's Always a Catch. A high-spirited cowpoke was riding his horse into town one day when he spied a hunched over, old farm-hand plodding along on a mule. Deciding to have a little fun, the cowboy drew his six-shooter and ordered the old man down off his mule. "Dance, clodbuster!" the cowpoke shouted and started firing bullets into the ground near the old man's feet. The cowboy roared with laughter as the old guy shuffled and hopped.

Then the unamused field-hand sauntered to his mule and pulled a shotgun from under his pack. The cowboy's revolver was now empty. "Did you ever kiss a mule long and hard on the mouth?" the old man drawled. The suddenly subdued cowboy said, "No, but I've always wanted to."

Sometimes the world offers selfish, greedy, status-seeking actions that seem like such a good idea at the time. But they don't last. In the end, there's a price to pay for embracing the darkness of sin. That's why, before it's too late, we need to turn our hearts to the warmth and joy found in the light of Christ.

THE TEST OF LOVE

BACKGROUND SCRIPTURE: 1 John 3:1-24
DEVOTIONAL READING: 1 Corinthians 13

2

KEY VERSE: Beloved, now are we the sons of God,
and it doth not yet appear what we shall be. 1 John 3:2.

KING JAMES VERSION

1 JOHN 3:11 For this is the message that ye heard from the beginning, that we should love one another. 12 Not as Cain, who was of that wicked one, and slew his brother. And wherefore slew he him? Because his own works were evil, and his brother's righteous. 13 Marvel not, my brethren, if the world hate you.

14 We know that we have passed from death unto life, because we love the brethren. He that loveth not his brother abideth in death. 15 Whosoever hateth his brother is a murderer: and ye know that no murderer hath eternal life abiding in him. 16 Hereby perceive we the love of God, because he laid down his life for us: and we ought to lay down our lives for the brethren. 17 But whoso hath this world's good, and seeth his brother have need, and shutteth up his bowels of compassion from him, how dwelleth the love of God in him? 18 My little children, let us not love in word, neither in tongue; but in deed and in truth. 19 And hereby we know that we are of the truth, and shall assure our hearts before him.

20 For if our heart condemn us, God is greater than our heart, and knoweth all things. 21 Beloved, if our heart condemn us not, then have we confidence toward God. 22 And whatsoever we ask, we receive of him, because we keep his commandments, and do those things that are pleasing in his sight.

23 And this is his commandment, That we should believe on the name of his Son Jesus Christ, and love one another, as he gave us commandment. 24 And he that keepeth his commandments dwelleth in him, and he in him. And hereby we know that he abideth in us, by the Spirit which he hath given us.

NEW REVISED STANDARD VERSION

1 JOHN 3:11 For this is the message you have heard from the beginning, that we should love one another. 12 We must not be like Cain who was from the evil one and murdered his brother. And why did he murder him? Because his own deeds were evil and his brother's righteous. 13 Do not be astonished, brothers and sisters, that the world hates you. 14 We know that we have passed from death to life because we love one another. Whoever does not love abides in death. 15 All who hate a brother or sister are murderers, and you know that murderers do not have eternal life abiding in them. 16 We know love by this, that he laid down his life for us—and we ought to lay down our lives for one another. 17 How does God's love abide in anyone who has the world's goods and sees a brother or sister in need and yet refuses help?

18 Little children, let us love, not in word or speech, but in truth and action. 19 And by this we will know that we are from the truth and will reassure our hearts before him 20 whenever our hearts condemn us; for God is greater than our hearts, and he knows everything. 21 Beloved, if our hearts do not condemn us, we have boldness before God; 22 and we receive from him whatever we ask, because we obey his commandments and do what pleases him.

23 And this is his commandment, that we should believe in the name of his Son Jesus Christ and love one another, just as he has commanded us. 24 All who obey his commandments abide in him, and he abides in them. And by this we know that he abides in us, by the Spirit that he has given us.

HOME BIBLE READINGS

Monday, March 5	1 Corinthians 13	*Love Is Eternal*
Tuesday, March 6	John 13:31-35	*Jesus Commands Us to Love*
Wednesday, March 7	Mark 12:38-44	*A Widow's Gift of Love*
Thursday, March 8	1 John 3:1-5	*God Loves Us*
Friday, March 9	1 John 3:6-10	*Avoid the Wrong*
Saturday, March 10	1 John 3:11-15	*Evidence of New Life*
Sunday, March 11	1 John 3:16-24	*Love as Christ Loves*

BACKGROUND

The information in 1 John 3:1-10 provides a basis for understanding what the apostle wrote in 3:11-24. In chapter 2, John explained how the new birth should show itself in godly conduct. In chapter 3, he focused on the love of God that makes the new birth possible and on the life of purity that should follow. A life cleansed from continual sin is made possible only through Christ, who Himself is the supreme example of moral purity. The apostle stated two reasons why believers should be pure. The first is based on God's past work for His children, that is, Christ's work on the cross. The second is related to a future work, that is, Christ's eventual return.

John was astonished at the magnitude of the heavenly Father's love. God's compassion is so great that it actually enables some to become His spiritual children (3:1). Regrettably, since the world will not acknowledge Christ, it is not going to acknowledge those who belong to Him. This knowledge is spiritually discerned and therefore unavailable to those who do not possess the Spirit of God (see 1 Cor. 2:14). For those who follow Jesus, recognition and glorification must wait for His return. When Jesus appears, believers will be transformed into the likeness of Christ (1 John 3:2). When that happens, the full reflection of God's glory will radiate from every Christian.

In hope of the Messiah's return, every believer has the responsibility to live an increasingly purified life, just as Jesus is pure (3:3). To a certain extent, the idea of purification here is like ceremonial cleansing often associated with the Passover (see John 11:55). But the word also signifies cleansing on the inside as well (see Heb. 10:19-23). The Savior represents the measure of righteous perfection that every believer should strive to attain—by the power of the Holy Spirit.

From a discussion of purity in the believer's life, John turned to its opposite—sin. Everyone who commits sin is a lawbreaker, because in fact, sin is lawlessness (3:4). By *transgression,* John meant a departure from any of God's standards. The term was intended to be as inclusive as possible so as to encompass all manner of sin. In 3:4-6, John addressed the ingrained, overt, deliberately insensitive sin in the lives of unbelievers. This uncaring attitude cannot be the experience of believers, suggested John, because those who abide in Christ do not keep practicing sin as a way of life. To do so indicates that one has neither seen nor known Christ (3:6) and is not born of God.

The seriousness of sin was highlighted by the fact that Jesus came in order to *take away our sins* (3:5). The Lord entered the world to exterminate sin in the lives of those who would accept Him (see John 1:29; Heb. 9:28). The apostle warned his spiritual children not to let anyone lead them astray on this issue. Righteousness results from doing what is right, not from the acquisition of some special, secret knowledge (as the antichrists were teaching). Righteous acts spring from a Christlike character and reveal a redeemed nature. Again, John set forth Jesus as the perfect example of what he was saying (3:7).

Next, John noted that those who sin habitually and without concern show that they are *of the devil* (3:8). The idea is that to practice sin in any form is to participate in Satan's work and oppose the intentions of Christ, who came expressly to destroy the devil's work. In contrast, those born of God do not habitually and flauntingly sin (3:9). The apostle's point is clear. A righteous God produces righteous children, while an unrighteous devil produces unholy children. Another characteristic of God's offspring is love for other members of the Body of Christ (3:10). The display of love, to put it simply, is righteousness with feet and hands. It is righteousness put into practice.

NOTES ON THE PRINTED TEXT

John's message to his readers was not something new, but what they had heard from the beginning of their Christian experience. God's children are expected to *love one another* (1 John 3:11). Before explaining exactly what Christian love was, the apostle first revealed what it was not. He did this with an illustration from the dawn of human existence. It is the account of the first murder in history.

John pointed out that by murdering his brother, Cain demonstrated that he was a child of Satan, the *wicked one* (3:12). The reason for the murderous act, John explained, was Cain's jealousy and resentment toward Abel's righteousness as compared with his own lack of godliness (see Gen. 4:2-8). Why God accepted Abel's offering rather than Cain's is not directly stated in Genesis 4. First John 3:12 suggests that it was the attitude of the two men's hearts rather than the nature of their offerings that made the difference.

Since the world displays the evil qualities Cain possessed and acted upon, believers should not be surprised that the world hates them (3:13). Christians should expect the wicked to treat the righteous just as wicked Cain treated his righteous brother. Jesus Himself warned His followers that they should expect the world to hate them because it hated Him first (see John 15:18-19, 25). John's point is clear. The world's hatred of Christians is normal. The hatred of one Christian for another, however, is not.

In 3:14, the apostle connected love to life and hatred to death. The test that one has experienced the new life in Christ is an ever-deepening love for other believers. God's children naturally have a desire to meet together for prayer and fellowship. An unbelieving world wants no part of such activity. Thus, to harbor hatred for believers suggests a closer intimacy with the world than with Christ.

Is it possible for one who genuinely belongs to God to hate another believer and to actually commit murder (3:15)? Tragically, the answer is yes. John was saying that the Christian who hates another believer is in essence living in fellowship with the world rather than in intimate fellowship with God. John's statement that no murderers have eternal life residing in them may refer to abiding in Christ. In the apostle's thinking, Jesus Himself is eternal life (see John 14:6; 1 John 1:2; 5:20). Thus, the believer who hates—who has committed murder in his or her heart—is not abiding in Christ's way of life. As long as a murderous spirit is present in that person's heart, Christ cannot be at home there.

John contrasted genuine Christian love with hatred. The sheer starkness of the contrast is clearly seen when the sacrificial death of Christ is set against the murderous act of Cain (1 John 3:16). John wanted his readers to understand that the heart of true Christian love is not self-serving, but self-sacrificing. And the supreme example of self-sacrifice was Jesus' death on the cross on behalf of a rebellious human race. While sinful Cain murdered righteous Abel, a righteous Christ died for a sinful human race.

John warned his readers not to be like Cain. Instead, as we follow the example of Christ, we should be ready and willing to lay down our lives for our fellow believers. Self-sacrificing love is the responsibility of every Christian. While few are called to sacrifice their lives for others, every believer can give sacrificially of their material resources (3:17). Christian love should motivate God's children to have pity, a deeply felt emotional response of concern for a brother or sister in need of the basic necessities of life—such as food, clothing, and shelter. The love of God demands it. Christians who refuse to be moved by the needs of others reveal an absence of divine love in their hearts. John warned his readers that mere verbal expressions of love with no actions were useless in the face of need (3:18).

A great sense of failure or inadequacy may result if a believer compares his or her faith in action to the high standard set by Jesus. Believers' consciences may condemn them in this regard, even though they have been performing the tangible acts of love to which John referred. The practicing Christian may have an oversensitive spirit to his or her own inadequacies, when that person should be resting in the sufficiency of God's grace. The guilty conscience in this instance ought to find repose in the knowledge that an all-compassionate God is aware of its acts of faith (3:19-20).

As a consequence of performing deeds of love, believers can find peace for their unsettled consciences and confidently approach the throne of God in prayer. And as they draw near to God, they can have confidence that their prayers will be answered (3:21-22). John did, however, state that the praying Christian must keep God's commands and do the things that please Him. Obeying the Lord requires an ongoing attitude of submission to His will. And doing what pleases God speaks of requests that are also subjected to His will. Thus, the one requesting and the request itself must be subordinated to the divine will. In connection with this is the supreme command. Believers are directed to trust in Christ and unconditionally love one another (3:23).

The claim to abide in Christ (3:24) must be proven by a believer's fidelity to three foundational commands: (1) believe in Christ; (2) love one another (3:23); and (3) live righteously (see 3:7-10). Expressed differently, abiding in Christ must be accompanied by a confession that Jesus is the Son of God and Savior of the world. Also, one's life is characterized by unconditional love for other believers and the practice of personal holiness.

How can the believer know that Christ abides within him or her (3:24)? Assurance comes from the indwelling Spirit. The Holy Spirit prompts the confession and acknowledgment concerning the person of Christ (see 2:20, 27; 4:1-6). The Spirit is also the one who enables the believer to fulfill God's will, to live righteously, and to love fellow Christians (see Gal. 5:16, 22-23). Thus, the crucial evidence of Jesus' abiding in us and we in Him is the work of the Holy Spirit, whom Christ Himself gave us. The Holy Spirit, as John proceeded to show, is both the Spirit of faith and the Spirit of love (see 1 John 4:1-16). Moreover, the Spirit of God makes the two-part command given in 3:23 a reality in the believers' life.

SUGGESTIONS TO TEACHERS

It's easy to claim that we are loving people, but it is much harder to show by our actions. What is the incentive for us to be compassionate, sensitive, and kind to others, even when they have mistreated us? The answer is the Father's love for us in His Son. Jesus' self-sacrificing love, as demonstrated at Calvary, is the reason why we can be vessels of mercy to those around us.

1. THE COST OF LOVE. The love Jesus had while He was on earth cost Him humiliation, torture, and death for our sake. As His followers, our love for others will mean no less. We likely will never writhe in pain on a cross, but there will be times, if we choose to love as Christ loves, when our hearts will be cruelly, carelessly, and mistakenly crushed by others—even by other believers.

2. THE TENACITY OF LOVE. The natural reaction to pain is either to strike back or to permanently retreat for protection. But neither of these reactions is anything like God's love or the love He calls us to have for one another. Love makes itself vulnerable to the pain, endures it, and seeks reconciliation in hope of a meaningful relationship.

3. THE FOUNDATIONAL NATURE OF LOVE. It is through our meaningful relationships—relationships based on love, full of grace and truth—that we best reflect God's love and draw others to Him. Love is the bottom line when it comes to practicing our profession of faith in the Lord Jesus.

4. THE DISPLAY OF LOVE. Each day we have opportunities to demonstrate God's love. And each time an opportunity presents itself, we have a choice to make. The decision to love, however, is not always easy to make. We must focus on the love God has demonstrated to us. In remembering His love, we find the courage and strength, despite our emotions, to act in loving ways toward others.

FOR ADULTS

■ **TOPIC:** Striving for Pure Love

■ **QUESTIONS:** 1. How does our unconditional love for our fellow believers verify our passage from death to life? 2. Why would one of Jesus' followers close his or her heart to someone in need? 3. What does it mean to demonstrate Christ's love through one's actions? 4. How can believers, as compassionate followers of Jesus, have confidence before God? 5. How can we know that the Father abides in us?

■ **ILLUSTRATIONS:**

The Spotlight of Love. Across the African continent, AIDS (Acquired Immune Deficiency Syndrome) is attacking adults in their prime and robbing the very young and the very old of caretakers and breadwinners. To bring attention to this catastrophe, a cable channel premiered a new documentary called *Tracking the Monster*. It began airing in the summer of 2005.

In one episode, correspondent Ed Gordon talked with recording artist India Arie and actress Ashley Judd. These two had teamed up to highlight the plight of the 38 million Africans suffering from AIDS. They told Gordon about their journey to some of the hardest-hit regions of the continent to witness first-hand what's being done to help the infected and those who struggle to survive after they're gone. This is a contemporary example of how the spotlight of love can be used to bring compassion and relief to so many suffering people.

Undying Love. He owned a small-town newspaper, which was published once a week. He was an excellent writer and journalist. His wife was a dedicated schoolteacher, greatly admired by her students and respected by their parents. The years passed, and the time for retirement came. The owner sold his newspaper, and his wife retired from the schoolroom. They returned to live in the town where they were born.

Less than a year after the couple moved to their new home, the wife began to show tell-tale signs of Alzheimer's disease. To the dismay of her husband, it progressed rapidly. His devotion to her was such that he adjusted, almost daily, to her mental deterioration.

Eventually, it was necessary for the husband to place his wife in a convalescent center. He stayed with her. When it became necessary, he fed her every meal, bite by bite. His adult children tried to persuade him to move home and visit with his wife less often. But he refused, reminding them about the marriage vows he and their mother had taken. For more than 50 years they had deeply enjoyed each other's company. He held her hand

and wept softly as she slipped away one day. Only a few months later, he also died. The story of the undying love of this couple became a legend in that small town.

Out-of-the-Ordinary Love. Sharon had a hard time finding a church for her mother, Pearle. They needed a wheelchair-accessible sanctuary and people not put off by Pearle's dementia. One Sunday, they entered a church with wide aisles and room at the back for those in wheelchairs. *Great,* Sharon thought, *but what about the people?* Her answer came during the sermon.

The pastor used the word "home" and a man who also had dementia stood up and began to sing "Home on the Range." The pastor stopped preaching, invited everyone to stand, and led them in a chorus of the song. Afterward, they sat down and the service went on without a hitch. *This,* Sharon thought, *is a church that helps people feel the pure love of God.* The lives of believers are to be filled with such examples of out-of-the-ordinary love.

FOR YOUTH

■ **TOPIC:** Love in Action
■ **QUESTIONS:** 1. Why is it important for believers to be compassionate and kind to each other? 2. Why would John compare hatred to murder? 3. Why is God's love equated with helping others in need? 4. How can the love of God calm our sometimes fearful hearts? 5. What has God commanded us to do?

■ **ILLUSTRATIONS:**

Loved Ones Remembered. The Philadelphia Foundation noted that in 2005, a group of eighth-graders took on a monumental assignment as part of the *Gun Violence Film Project*. They memorialized 35 school-aged children killed by gun violence over the past 12 months in the Strawberry Mansion section of Philadelphia. For their year-long assignment, the students set out to record the memories and impressions of the surviving parents and grandparents of teenagers who were slain.

In the project, grieving adults were grouped with interviewers who were usually no older than their lost son or daughter. As the victims' personalities and recollections were detailed, the same basic theme was often repeated. There was a desire for a beloved child or grandchild to be remembered and a wonder at what might have been. This is just one way out of many that young people like yourself are showing love in action.

An Appeal for Common Courtesy. The young woman had grown up observing the courteous way in which her father treated her mother. He never failed to go around to the passenger side of the car and open the door for her. She had never heard him raise his voice at her mother even when they were having a disagreement. He bought her flowers at the appropriate time, and never forgot her birthday or their wedding anniversary.

Time came for the young woman's first date. The suitor drove up to the front of her home. She watched discreetly from a window. He did not get out of his car for a few moments. Then he lightly tapped on his horn. After awhile, he sounded two long blasts on the horn. Eventually, he came to the door and was barely able to conceal his impatience because she had not responded to his car horn.

The young woman's parents knew the boy's mother and father, and they knew he was basically a good person. Obviously he had not witnessed, or been taught, common courtesy. When the two youths left for the date, the boy asked the girl why she had not come out of the house. She gave him a lesson in common courtesy that she had learned through observation. Because he thought so highly of her, he listened carefully. On the next date, he was a true gentleman. He came to the door and went inside for a brief visit with her parents. He opened the car door for her to get in and was there to help her get out. He became one of the most chivalrous young men in his high school!

What Love Is Not. According to Mandalit del Barco of *National Public Radio*, it was on a red-hot August night in 1965 that the Watts neighborhood of Los Angeles exploded with racial frustration. Six days later, 34 people were dead, hundreds more injured, and a wide swath of south-central Los Angeles was scarred with burned-out buildings and looted stores.

Del Barco noted that despite the passage of over four decades, many area residents still remember those days. For instance, Alice Harris—known as "Sweet Alice" to her neighbors—has lived in Watts for almost 50 years. She says things haven't changed much at all. She noted that "everybody is tense," that there are "no jobs, zero tolerance in the housing projects," and that "people are scared of the police."

Regrettably, in the absence of the self-giving, self-sacrificing love of Christ, it's hard for communities ravaged by violence and poverty to be transformed. Maybe God is calling you to put love into action by supporting community-based relief efforts in troubled areas such as Watts.

THE SOURCE OF LOVE

BACKGROUND SCRIPTURE: 1 John 4:7-21
DEVOTIONAL READING: John 21:15-19

KEY VERSE: We love him, because he first loved us. 1 John 4:19.

3

KING JAMES VERSION

1 JOHN 4:7 Beloved, let us love one another: for love is of God; and every one that loveth is born of God, and knoweth God. 8 He that loveth not knoweth not God; for God is love. 9 In this was manifested the love of God toward us, because that God sent his only begotten Son into the world, that we might live through him. 10 Herein is love, not that we loved God, but that he loved us, and sent his Son to be the propitiation for our sins. 11 Beloved, if God so loved us, we ought also to love one another. 12 No man hath seen God at any time. If we love one another, God dwelleth in us, and his love is perfected in us. 13 Hereby know we that we dwell in him, and he in us, because he hath given us of his Spirit.

14 And we have seen and do testify that the Father sent the Son to be the Saviour of the world. 15 Whosoever shall confess that Jesus is the Son of God, God dwelleth in him, and he in God. 16 And we have known and believed the love that God hath to us. God is love; and he that dwelleth in love dwelleth in God, and God in him.

17 Herein is our love made perfect, that we may have boldness in the day of judgment: because as he is, so are we in this world. 18 There is no fear in love; but perfect love casteth out fear: because fear hath torment. He that feareth is not made perfect in love. 19 We love him, because he first loved us. 20 If a man say, I love God, and hateth his brother, he is a liar: for he that loveth not his brother whom he hath seen, how can he love God whom he hath not seen? 21 And this commandment have we from him, That he who loveth God love his brother also.

NEW REVISED STANDARD VERSION

1 JOHN 4:7 Beloved, let us love one another, because love is from God; everyone who loves is born of God and knows God. 8 Whoever does not love does not know God, for God is love. 9 God's love was revealed among us in this way: God sent his only Son into the world so that we might live through him. 10 In this is love, not that we loved God but that he loved us and sent his Son to be the atoning sacrifice for our sins. 11 Beloved, since God loved us so much, we also ought to love one another. 12 No one has ever seen God; if we love one another, God lives in us, and his love is perfected in us.

13 By this we know that we abide in him and he in us, because he has given us of his Spirit. 14 And we have seen and do testify that the Father has sent his Son as the Savior of the world. 15 God abides in those who confess that Jesus is the Son of God, and they abide in God. 16 So we have known and believe the love that God has for us.

God is love, and those who abide in love abide in God, and God abides in them. 17 Love has been perfected among us in this: that we may have boldness on the day of judgment, because as he is, so are we in this world. 18 There is no fear in love, but perfect love casts out fear; for fear has to do with punishment, and whoever fears has not reached perfection in love. 19 We love because he first loved us. 20 Those who say, "I love God," and hate their brothers or sisters, are liars; for those who do not love a brother or sister whom they have seen, cannot love God whom they have not seen. 21 The commandment we have from him is this: those who love God must love their brothers and sisters also.

BACKGROUND

At the end of 1 John 3, the apostle explained that the evidence of Christ's abiding in believers and of believers abiding in Christ is the work of the Holy Spirit. But how can Christians tell the difference between the work of God's Spirit in their lives and the activity of false spirits? In 4:1-6, John explained how the spirits could be tested to determine their true character and origin.

The apostle's discussion on testing the spirits contains three elements: (1) a command to test the spirits (4:1a); (2) the reason for testing the spirits (4:1b); and (3) an explanation of how to test the spirits (4:2-3a). John first commanded his readers not to indiscriminately accept what every spirit had to say, but to put them to the test to determine if what they proclaimed was from God (4:1a). This testing was necessary because many false prophets and teachers were spreading lies among the people. Apparently some of John's readers were accepting any teaching from anyone claiming a degree of spiritual authority.

By definition, a prophet always speaks on behalf of some spirit. In Scripture, a true prophet speaks for the Spirit of God, who is also the Spirit of truth (4:6b). False prophets, on the other hand, speak for the *spirit of antichrist* (4:3b), who is the *spirit of error* (vs. 6b). In short, every prophet is inspired by a spirit, and every spirit is animated either by God or by Satan. Before any spirit should be accepted, its origin must be determined. The reference to false prophets going out *into the world* (4:1) may identify false teachers in general who were engaged in a type of missionary endeavor (4:3b). But it could also refer back to the antichrists mentioned in 2:18-19. These may have once been church attenders who left the fellowship of true believers.

Next, John turned to the matter of how to discern the spirits and how to recognize the Spirit of God (4:2). The litmus test was the messengers' beliefs about the incarnation of Christ. If a teacher acknowledged that the Messiah had come in the flesh, then this person could be considered a true prophet of God. A denial of this essential doctrine unmasked the spirit of the antichrist, which John had earlier warned his readers about (2:18-27; see 2 John 7). The apostle assured his readers that they were capable of living in victory over the religious frauds who threatened their spiritual community. The reason for their victory, he explained, was because the Spirit of God who was within them was greater than the spirit of darkness who was in the world (1 John 4:4).

In all of life's spiritual struggles, reliance on God is the only resource for overcoming the enemy. The Holy Spirit, the one who indwells every believer (see Rom. 8:9; 1 John 3:24; 4:13), is infinitely more powerful than Satan. While Satan, *the prince of this world* (John 12:31), may be an imposing foe for mere mortals, he is no match for the power of God. Though he would like us to believe otherwise, Satan is not God's opposite. The devil is merely a created being—intensely powerful, but always on a leash (in a manner of speaking) held by God.

John explained to his readers that because the antichrists were from the world and naturally spoke from a worldly point of view, unbelievers paid close attention to what they had to say (1 John 4:5). It should come as no surprise that when the prince of this world speaks, the ungodly find his words appealing. Those who are from God, on the other hand, listen to and apply the apostles' teaching, not the false doctrines of the antichrists. Since Pentecost, the teaching of the apostles has been the standard by which the Spirit of truth can be distinguished from the spirit of falsehood (4:6).

NOTES ON THE PRINTED TEXT

John exhorted his dear friends to *love one another* (1 John 4:7). Just as believing in Christ's incarnation identifies one as being from God, so too does genuine love, because such compassion originates with God. Love is not a natural thing or a learned behavior. Its origin is from God. Thus, all who practice Christian love show that they have been born of God and that they have an intimate relationship with Him. Next, John noted that if love is not present in an individual, then that person cannot possibly have an intimate knowledge of God. Though the phrase "born of God" is not present in 4:8, John was likely talking about someone who has not accepted Christ, and is thus incapable of demonstrating divine, unconditional love.

The Lord abundantly demonstrated the reality of His love by sending His cherished Son to die on behalf of sinful humanity (4:9). Here we see that real love has nothing to do with humanity's love for God. The initiative was all on God's side. He was the one who first reached out to us in love when He sent the Lord Jesus to earth to die on the cross as the *propitiation for our sins* (4:10). His atoning sacrifice appeased God's wrath and satisfied His demands for justice in connection with our transgressions.

Any expression of Christian love is only a response to the love the Father first showed us. Since God loved us so much that He sent His Son to die for us, then we are morally obligated to *love one another* (4:11). Expressed differently, since Christ loved us sacrificially, it is our duty to love each other the same way. It is true that God has never been seen by any human being in all of His essential character. However, as Christians express mutual love, the invisible God manifests Himself through their acts of caring and tenderness (4:12).

The exact meaning of the statement that God's *love is perfected in us* is disputed among commentators. Most likely, the apostle was emphasizing that the love God has for us is not an abstract theological truth. Instead, it is manifested in our love for others. Indeed, as we reach out to others with kindness and compassion, God's love in us is completed or brought to full expression.

In 4:13, John continued his discussion about the mutual abiding of a believer and Christ. For proof that this mutual abiding is in effect, one has to look for the work of the Holy Spirit in that believer's life. Obedience to the two-part command to believe in the Lord Jesus and love one another is a direct result of the Spirit's work within a believer's heart (see Rom. 5:5; 1 John 3:24; 4:2). Thus, a Christian's Spirit-prompted obedience is the real evidence that a believer and God abide in one another.

The apostle had just told his readers that if we love each other, then the invisible God lives in us and His love is perfected in us (1 John 4:12). As a result of this experience, according to John, we manifest and affirm the apostolic truth that the Father sent His Son as the Savior of the world (4:14). In practical terms, while God is invisible to the eye, He becomes visible in a spiritual sense when His indwelling presence is evident in the mutual love between believers.

In light of what John just said, he told his readers that anyone who acknowledged that Jesus is the Son of God was indwelled by God and in turn dwells in God (4:15). Here again is a test or evidence of mutual indwelling. Life-changing belief in the deity of Christ suggests obedience to Him and surrender to His will. This is essential for the mutual indwelling to become a reality.

In 4:16, the apostle stated that the Christian community had come to know and believe the love that God has for His children. This truth can be a source of great joy for every believer. As Christians live in a community of mutual love with other believers, it results in an intimate experience of God's love and a renewed faith in that love. As before, John reaffirmed the truth that everyone who abides in love experiences intimate fellowship with God.

The love that has been perfected among God's children is the very love that the Father, who is love, reproduced in His children by placing His Spirit in them (4:17). If this love is brought to full expression in the believer's life on earth, it will produce a confidence to approach the judgment seat of Christ without shame or regret. The basis for this confidence is the believer's present likeness to Christ, and in this particular case, a likeness in His love. In ancient Greek literature, the judgment seat, or "bema," usually referred to a seat or throne set up in a public place. From this seat judgment and other official business was conducted. Paul used the word "bema" when he referred to the judgment seat of Christ (see 2 Cor. 5:10). It is likely that John had in mind that same type of assessment in 1 John 4:17.

As was the apostle's habit, he followed the positive aspect of this spiritual truth with its negative counterpart. Fear is the opposite of confidence before Christ at His coming (4:18). If a believer anticipates the judgment seat of Christ with dread of some impending punishment, love has not been made complete in that Christian's heart. The full flowering of God's love is incompatible with fear. Perfected love expels anxiety from the heart.

The catalyst for loving other believers (and for having confidence at Christ's return) is the love God first showed for us (4:19). Christians who love other believers also love God. The real proof that a Christian loves God, in John's estimation, is the love he or she demonstrates to fellow believers (4:20). A Christian's love for other believers (who are visible) demonstrates his or her love for God (who is invisible).

While it is an easy thing to proclaim "I love God," John pointed out that genuine piety is demonstrated by Christian love. The one who claims to love God while hating other believers, said John (in his typical bluntness), is a liar. These people are also commandment breakers, because God had established that whoever loves Him is also morally obligated to love other believers (4:21). Here the two objects of Christian love are joined together. Love for God cannot be separated from love for our brothers and sisters in Christ.

SUGGESTIONS TO TEACHERS

God is love, so those who belong to Him should love Him and others. Love is also the believer's natural response to what the Father did for us in the sacrifice of His Son. And since no one actually sees God, the best way to know Him is through the love shown by His children.

1. A MATTER OF FAITH. Our experience of God's love begins through faith in Christ. It is at that time that the Lord forgives our sins and restores our relationship to Him. We also inherit the privilege and responsibility of loving others with that same kind of love. John explained that key principle in his first epistle.

2. A MATTER OF LIFE AND DEATH. The presence of Christlike love indicates the presence of the life of God in a person. The absence of such love indicates the presence of death in a person. Anyone who hates others is condemned as a murderer by Jesus' teaching in the Sermon on the Mount (Matt. 5:21-22). Sacrificial love is not optional for a child of God. It should not be regarded as something extraordinary. Sacrificial love should be the norm.

3. A MATTER OF KNOWING GOD. Sacrificial love is a normal character trait of God. It is not a normal character trait of human beings. People learn to love sacrificially when they share in the life of God through spiritual rebirth. Jesus modeled this sacrificial love when He died on the cross as the atoning sacrifice for our sins. As we comprehend the love of Jesus and the love of His Father, we will be changed by love so that we can love sacrificially as well.

4. A MATTER OF SHOWING GOD. A small part of the world once glimpsed God by seeing the love of His incarnate Son. Now God wants the whole world to see Him through the sacrificial love His adopted children show to one another. God is spirit and invisible to human sight. His abiding presence can be seen through our Spirit-empowered lives of love. The testimony of eyewitnesses has set in motion a fellowship between God and those of us who have never seen Him. His love makes Him real to us, and our love makes Him real to one another.

<table>
<tr><td>■ TOPIC: Showing Divine Love</td></tr>
</table>

FOR ADULTS	■ TOPIC: Showing Divine Love

FOR ADULTS

■ TOPIC: Showing Divine Love

■ QUESTIONS: 1. What is meant by the declaration that *God is love* (1 John 4:8)? 2. How did God take the initiative in showing His love for us? 3. Why is it important to affirm that *Jesus is the Son of God* (4:15)? 4. How is it possible for perfect love to cast out all fear (4:18)? 5. How can claims of love for God be contradicted?

■ ILLUSTRATIONS:

Building with Love. An older carpenter prepared to retire. He told the contractor for whom he worked about his plans to stop building and to enjoy a more leisurely life with his wife and extended family. He would miss the paycheck, but he needed to retire. They could get by.

The contractor was sorry to see his good worker go and asked whether he would build just one more house as a personal favor. The carpenter agreed, but in time it was easy to see that his heart wasn't in his work. He grew careless and took shortcuts on quality. It was an unfortunate way to end his career. When the carpenter finished the house, the contractor handed him the front-door key. "This is your house," the contractor said. "It's my gift to you in appreciation for all your dedicated work."

If the carpenter had known he was building his own house, he would have done it all so differently. We build our lives every day by the way we express God's love to those around us. Our love should be like the love of Jesus—only the highest quality—so that our lives will be like His, too.

Love Sacrifices for Others. During the Great Depression of the 1930s, thousands of displaced people wound up in tent cities in California where they had gone searching for nonexistent jobs. One day, a man and woman worked their way through one of these tent cities inviting boys and girls to go to Sunday school. They invited a 10-year-old girl whose father was an alcoholic and whose older sisters were prostitutes. The girl herself was likely headed toward prostitution. But this couple came the next Sunday and took the ragged little girl to church. After church, they took her home with them and fed her. Week after week they showed her love. Eventually, the girl came to know Christ as Savior.

Three of that girl's sons served as pastors. As the twenty-first century moves along, three of her grandchildren pastor churches. Other descendants teach Sunday school and lead worship as musicians. The nameless couple in California invested a lot of time in a ragged child many would have ignored. Who knows whether this couple's sacrifice seemed great or small at the time? They loved a neglected child and changed the course of one branch of a family tree.

Hate Kills. When Elizabeth Barrett married the famous poet, Robert Browning, her parents were so upset that they disowned her. She and her husband settled far from England in Florence, Italy. Elizabeth loved her mother and father and pursued reconciliation with them. Several times a month she wrote expressive, loving letters.

After 10 years of no response, a package came from Elizabeth's parents. It was a happy moment for her as she opened it. Inside she found all of the letters she had sent— unopened. Like her husband, Elizabeth Barrett Browning was a poet. Her letters seeking reconciliation were eloquent. But her parents never read them. What must have happened in the soul of Elizabeth when she felt the full impact of her parents' cruelty and rejection? Did it feel like death?

FOR YOUTH

■ TOPIC: Blessed by Love

■ QUESTIONS: 1. Why is it so important for believers to love one another? 2. How is the Father's love revealed in His Son? 3. How can we know that we abide in God and that He abides in us? 4. How can we have boldness in the day of judgment? 5. What is the reason we are to love others?

■ **ILLUSTRATIONS:**

Laying Down Your Life. Author and lecturer Leo Buscaglia was once asked to judge a contest to identify and reward the most caring child in the area. Buscaglia selected a four-year-old child, whose next-door neighbor was an elderly gentleman who had recently lost his wife. Upon seeing the man cry, the little boy went into the old gentleman's yard, climbed onto his lap, and just sat there. When his mother asked him what he had said to the neighbor, the little boy said, "Nothing. I just helped him cry" (Jack Canfield and Mark Victor Hansen, *A 3rd Serving of Chicken Soup for the Soul*).

Christlike love probably makes more little sacrifices than big ones. Sometimes we miss the most important acts of love because we think love must make dramatic sacrifices. Love pays attention to who needs what and tries to help.

Love One Another. After an accident in which she lost her arm, a girl named Jamie refused to go to school or church for an entire year. Finally, the young teen thought she could face her peers. In preparation, her mother called her Sunday school teacher and asked that he not call attention to Jamie. The teacher promised, but when he got sick one Sunday and had to call a substitute, he forgot to tell the second teacher. At the conclusion of the lesson that day, which was about inviting friends to church, the substitute led the class in doing the hand motions to the familiar children's poem:

Here's the church.
Here's the steeple.
Open the doors.
See all the people.

Jamie's eyes filled with tears. A 13-year-old boy realized how she must be feeling. He knelt beside her. With one hand apiece, they made the church, steeple, and people. Jamie laughed, and the boy felt like a hero. What was heroic was recognizing Jamie's pain—when no one else noticed—and carrying it with her for a few minutes.

Love Gives Life. During their second month of nursing school, the students walked into a class and faced a pop quiz. Most nurses-in-training breezed through the early questions. Then one by one they reacted in confusion to the last item on the quiz. It read: "What is the first name of the woman who cleans this building?" The students thought this was some kind of joke. They had seen the cleaning woman. She was tall, dark-haired, and in her 50s, but how could they know her name? Most left the last item blank when they handed in their quiz papers.

At the end of class, one brave student asked if the last question would count toward the quiz grade. "Absolutely!" said the professor. "In your careers you will meet many people. All are significant. They deserve your attention and care, even if all you do is smile and say hello." By day's end all the students knew that the cleaning lady was named Dorothy.

The nurses-in-training learned a lesson in humility. The cleaning lady felt as though she were the most important person in the school. Love lifted her from obscurity to first-name friendship with everyone.

THE WAY TO LOVE

BACKGROUND SCRIPTURE: 1 John 5:1-12
DEVOTIONAL READING: John 17:1-5

KEY VERSE: And this is the record, that God hath given to us eternal life, and this life is in his Son. 1 John 5:11.

4

KING JAMES VERSION

1 JOHN 5:1 Whosoever believeth that Jesus is the Christ is born of God: and every one that loveth him that begat loveth him also that is begotten of him. 2 By this we know that we love the children of God, when we love God, and keep his commandments. 3 For this is the love of God, that we keep his commandments: and his commandments are not grievous. 4 For whatsoever is born of God overcometh the world: and this is the victory that overcometh the world, even our faith. 5 Who is he that overcometh the world, but he that believeth that Jesus is the Son of God?

6 This is he that came by water and blood, even Jesus Christ; not by water only, but by water and blood. And it is the Spirit that beareth witness, because the Spirit is truth. 7 For there are three that bear record in heaven, the Father, the Word, and the Holy Ghost: and these three are one. 8 And there are three that bear witness in earth, the Spirit, and the water, and the blood: and these three agree in one. 9 If we receive the witness of men, the witness of God is greater: for this is the witness of God which he hath testified of his Son.

10 He that believeth on the Son of God hath the witness in himself: he that believeth not God hath made him a liar; because he believeth not the record that God gave of his Son. 11 And this is the record, that God hath given to us eternal life, and this life is in his Son. 12 He that hath the Son hath life; and he that hath not the Son of God hath not life.

NEW REVISED STANDARD VERSION

1 JOHN 5:1 Everyone who believes that Jesus is the Christ has been born of God, and everyone who loves the parent loves the child. 2 By this we know that we love the children of God, when we love God and obey his commandments. 3 For the love of God is this, that we obey his commandments. And his commandments are not burdensome, 4 for whatever is born of God conquers the world. And this is the victory that conquers the world, our faith. 5 Who is it that conquers the world but the one who believes that Jesus is the Son of God?

6 This is the one who came by water and blood, Jesus Christ, not with the water only but with the water and the blood. And the Spirit is the one that testifies, for the Spirit is the truth. 7 There are three that testify: 8 the Spirit and the water and the blood, and these three agree. 9 If we receive human testimony, the testimony of God is greater; for this is the testimony of God that he has testified to his Son. 10 Those who believe in the Son of God have the testimony in their hearts. Those who do not believe in God have made him a liar by not believing in the testimony that God has given concerning his Son. 11 And this is the testimony: God gave us eternal life, and this life is in his Son. 12 Whoever has the Son has life; whoever does not have the Son of God does not have life.

Monday, March 19	Mark 1:16-20	*Jesus Calls Disciples*
Tuesday, March 20	John 3:16-21	*God's Love Saves Creation*
Wednesday, March 21	John 17:1-5	*Jesus Seeks the Father*
Thursday, March 22	Romans 8:9-17	*We Belong to God*
Friday, March 23	Galatians 4:1-7	*We Are God's Heirs*
Saturday, March 24	1 John 5:1-6	*Love God's Children*
Sunday, March 25	1 John 5:7-13	*God Gives Eternal Life*

BACKGROUND

While 1 John has traditionally been regarded as a letter, it lacks key distinguishing features of an epistle (for example, a salutation, introductory greeting, and final greeting). Nevertheless, the apostle addressed his readers as *my little children* (2:1). He seemed to be writing to a specific group of people with whom he had a close relationship. Thus, in its basic purposes of admonition and instruction, 1 John is similar to most of the New Testament letters.

This epistle does not yield naturally to a structural outline. All the same, one is discernable. The prologue (1:1-4) introduces the incarnate Word of Life, Jesus Christ. This is followed by material dealing with walking in the light as God's children (1:5—2:27), practicing righteousness as God's children (2:28—4:6), and showing unconditional love as God's children (4:7—5:12). The letter ends with the epilogue (5:13-21).

The language of this letter is not difficult or technical, but the ideas expressed are profound. For example, the writer said that God has been revealed in Christ in order to communicate eternal life to those who believe. God is light, truth, and love. Each of these characteristics is the subject of some meditation, but always in connection with the development of corresponding virtues in believers. The ideals of purity and love that are held out to the reader are gifts of God, communicated from His self-revelation in Christ. At the same time, these ideals are real for believers when they are lived out. This reality is possible through being born again and through the forgiveness of sin.

As an eyewitness of the events of Jesus' ministry, death, and resurrection, John bore testimony to all he saw so that his readers could enjoy fellowship with the Father, the Son, and the community of believers in Jesus (1 John 1:1-3). This week's lesson text develops the concept of "testimony" introduced in 1:2. Indeed, John supplied several witnesses in keeping with Old Testament laws of evidence. Two of John's witnesses, *water and blood* (5:6) in the life of Jesus, strike modern readers as odd.

In sorting out this issue, it is clarifying to note that the Old Testament law required two or three witnesses to establish the judicial certainty of a matter. In fact, it was only on the evidence of two or three witnesses that a charge could be sustained (Deut. 19:15). This principle was especially important in capitol cases. Specifically, the law mandated that a person could not be put to death on the evidence of only one witness (17:6). Thus, when the witnesses who testified against Jesus at His trial could not provide a unified testimony (Mark 14:55-59), He should have been released on the basis of the Mosaic law. Furthermore, Paul prescribed this standard in the Church for handling charges against elders. The apostle said that an accusation against an elder was never to be accepted, except on the evidence offered by two or three credible witnesses (1 Tim. 5:19).

With respect to the person and work of the Messiah, John presented three witnesses: *the Spirit, and the water, and the blood* (1 John 5:8). There are various ways to understand this verse. Some equate the water and the blood with two ordinances: baptism and the Lord's Supper. Others connect the passage with the spear thrust into the side of Jesus and the blood and water that came out of the wound (John 19:34-35). Another view finds a link to Christ's birth in the *water* (1 John 5:6) and to His death in the *blood*. The most widely held view makes the water and the blood references to Christ's baptism and death. Support for this notion is found in the fact that Jesus began His earthly ministry with His baptism, and He ended it with His crucifixion.

John insisted that the witness of Jesus' baptism and death testified to different conclusions than those proposed by the false teachers the apostle was combating. Jesus had recognized His redemptive mission long before His baptism (Luke 2:41-52). At His baptism, the descending Spirit and the Father's voice from heaven did not mark the arrival of the Son in human flesh, but the beginning of the road to the cross (3:21-22). On the cross, the Son of God shed His blood for the sins of the world (Mark 15:39). Until Jesus returns, the Spirit of God will continue to testify through the water and the blood in the Christian observances of baptism and the Lord's Supper.

NOTES ON THE PRINTED TEXT

Throughout 1 John, the apostle used three primary tests of genuine faith: obedience to God, love for other Christians, and a correct belief in God's Son. In 5:1-5, John used all three of these as evidences of the new birth. This approach was one of the ways the apostle undermined the efforts of false teachers who denied that Jesus is the Christ, the long-awaited Jewish Messiah. John did not back down from emphasizing that recognizing Jesus as the Christ showed that believers were truly born again (5:1). Because such a commitment resulted from a new birth, it was evidence of regeneration.

The new birth also brought love for the Father as well as for His other children. John wrote at a time when members of a family were closely affiliated under the father's headship. Therefore, the apostle could use the family to illustrate that anyone who loves God the Father will surely love His children. Similarly, we cannot love our fellow believers without loving the Father in the process.

The way that we show our love for the Father is through obedience to Him (5:2). Regrettably, when people who are not Christians think about God's demands, they equate them with regulations like those of the scribes and Pharisees, something that is truly difficult and overwhelming (5:3). The new birth, however, changes a believer's perspective and gives that person the strength through the Spirit to obey God's commands. As the Lord Jesus Himself said, *my yoke is easy, and my burden is light* (Matt. 11:30).

Keeping God's commands is possible because of the believers' victory, in Christ, over the world's sinful pattern of life (1 John 5:4). These are the same individuals who affirm by faith that Jesus is the Son of God (5:5). The latter title points to Jesus' status as the Messiah and highlights His divine commission to carry out the work of redemption. As the Son of God, Jesus overcame the world, defeating sin and death by His sinless life, atoning sacrifice, and triumphant resurrection. Faith in Him enables believers to share in His victory and experience personal triumph over sin. Through faith, believers can obey the Father's commands in a way that is a joyful victory celebration.

While believing in the deity of Jesus opens the door for triumph over sin, the extent of our triumph depends on our willingness to claim what is ours by faith. The evil forces of the world cannot prevail against confidence in the one who overcame the world. Expressed differently, our faith gives us access to the victory that Jesus obtained while He was on the earth. Because of that, we can battle our sinful impulses and obey the commands of the Father.

Our faith is the entryway to our salvation because it accepts the witness of God's Spirit regarding His Son (1 John 5:6). John's statement about the Spirit, the water, and the blood was apparently intended to refute any teaching that made a distinction between Jesus of Nazareth and the Christ of faith. Thus, the apostle made the point that the Messiah did not come by water only (at the time of Jesus' baptism), but the Messiah was also crucified on the cross, shedding His blood for the sins of the world.

The triune God affirms the aforementioned testimony. Heaven is the dwelling place of the Godhead, and it is from there that the Father, the Word, and the Holy Spirit uniformly declare that Jesus is the Messiah, the Son of God (5:7). Together, these heavenly witnesses—in agreement with the Spirit, the water, and the blood (5:8)—establish the identity of the divine Word. The Spirit opens our eyes to the historical witness of Christ while also providing a confirmation through experience of the truth.

The issue, then, is what people do with that testimony concerning the Lord Jesus. John maintained that since we accept human testimony that is confirmed by witnesses, how much more should we accept divine witnesses? If the agreement of three witnesses on earth is enough to establish a case in human courts, then certainly the agreement of three with God as their source should be more than sufficient to establish the identity of Jesus (5:9). How does the Spirit bear witness? He does so inwardly and supernaturally as He opens our eyes and ears to perceive what God teaches (1 Cor. 2:12). It does not matter if the testimony of people is not available. The Spirit is an undying witness who confirms the proclamations and teachings about Jesus as truth and accompanies every true declaration of Jesus' message with spiritual effectiveness.

Saving faith in Christ is the purpose of the testimony regarding the Son. Whoever believes the evidence has the Father's own witness in his or her heart. Indeed, faith itself is God's gift to the believer. Thus, anyone not receiving this testimony makes God out to be a liar since He has confirmed Jesus' identity (5:10). Rejecting the Son contradicts the testimony of the Father regarding Jesus, namely, that eternal life is in the Son (5:11). This is the heart of the Christian faith. Christianity is not a philosophy or religious system or merely a set of beliefs. It is a relationship with the Lord Jesus. Salvation can only come in the context of that personal relationship. Accordingly, to believe in the Son is to be truly born again. Likewise, to reject the Son is to be eternally lost (5:12).

SUGGESTIONS TO TEACHERS

A confident life is one of fellowship with the Father, the Son, and God's people (1 John 1:1-3). In the last chapter of his first epistle, the apostle summarized the qualities a person needs to respond to God, the evidence a person should accept, and the attitudes that characterize eternal life in fellowship with God.

1. THE BELIEVER'S TRIUMPH THROUGH FAITH. Faith in Christ includes an understanding of who He is and a complete reliance upon Him for salvation and an overcoming lifestyle. Through this kind of faith, believers experience victory over the sinful influences of this world. If we place our confidence in anything other than Christ to overcome sin, we will be disappointed, for only He has defeated sin. He alone offers the power we need to gain freedom from sin and escape the threat of sinful influences.

2. THE BELIEVER'S VICTORY IN CHRIST. John declared that our faith is the victory that overcomes the sinful influences of the world. And then, as if to test his readers' comprehension of that statement, the apostle asked who overcomes the world. The answer is that only those who believe that Jesus is God's Son are victorious. No other agent or formula defeats the sinful influences we face. Only Jesus faced them all and overcame them all. It is only when we acknowledge our own helplessness and place our confidence in the sufficiency of Christ's victory that we experience victory over sin.

3. THE BELIEVER'S DEPENDENCE ON CHRIST. We may try other means, such as willpower, accountability, support groups, human thought or philosophy, rituals or routines, aversion techniques, or shame and guilt. We may even find that some of these things offer limited success in helping us curb certain behaviors or keep them in check temporarily. But it is only through faith in Christ that we can be sensitive to His will, our mind can comprehend His Word, and our actions can become joyful acts of worship.

4. THE BELIEVER'S NEED FOR CHRIST. If we believe in and rely on anything but Jesus' victory to overcome sin, our efforts are doomed. It is a good idea, then, for us to examine ourselves periodically to be sure that our faith is not misplaced (2 Cor. 13:5).

What a relief it is to know that the hard part of overcoming sinful influences has been done for us by Jesus' life, death, and resurrection. To remain in His victory, we need only to depend on the Father's provision for us in His Son.

| **FOR ADULTS** | ■ **TOPIC:** The Way to Love and Life |

■ **QUESTIONS:** 1. What tests of faith did John mention to his readers? 2. How is faith in Christ the key to overcoming sinful impulses? 3. What is the testimony concerning the Messiah? 4. What is the result of rejecting this testimony concerning the Messiah? 5. What does it mean to have the Son?

■ **ILLUSTRATIONS:**

Love's Cost-Benefit Analysis. "We become vulnerable when we love people and go out of our way to help them," declared wealthy industrialist Charles Schwab after winning a nuisance lawsuit at age 70. Given permission by the judge to speak to the audience, he made the following statement: "I'd like to say here in a court of law, and speaking as an old man, that nine-tenths of my troubles are traceable to my being kind to others. Look, you young people, if you want to steer away from trouble, be hard-boiled. Be quick with a good loud 'no' to anyone and everyone. If you follow this rule, you will seldom be bothered as you tread life's pathway. Except you'll have no friends, you'll be lonely, and you won't have any fun!" Schwab's point is that love may bring heartache, but it's worth it! God's point is that love costs, but it pays eternal dividends.

Keep Your First Love. Jerome, the sixth-century translator of the Latin Vulgate, related that the apostle John, when he became old, used to go among the churches around Ephesus, everywhere repeating the words, "Little children, love one another." John's disciples, wearied by the constant repetition, asked him why he always said this. "Because," the apostle replied, "it is the Lord's commandment; and if it only be fulfilled, it is enough." John knew that the greatest truth was most apt to be forgotten because it often gets taken for granted.

The Gift of Love. Jane, a longstanding member of her community church, told me about a young couple who visited the congregation the previous December. They sat a few pews in front of Jane during the worship service. She learned they were new to the area and were not doing well financially. Jane noticed that the young mother was wearing only a light outer garment and shivering as she listened to the sermon.

Jane began to wonder why this person was not wearing a warm coat. Suddenly, a thought popped into Jane's head—*Give her yours.* During that Sunday service, Jane wore a long black coat, which was one of the nicest garments she owned. Giving it up didn't seem to matter, though, especially as she saw the young mother tightly clasping her arms around her torso for the remainder of the service.

When church had ended, Jane took the opportunity to ask the young mother what she thought of the area. The visitor stated that she and her loved ones had just moved from Florida and were unable at that time to buy the right clothes for the colder climate in which they now lived. Jane could not resist the desire to give her coat to the young mother. "Here, please take my coat," Jane offered as she removed the garment and placed it around the visitor.

A few weeks later, the visiting family changed churches, and Jane lost contact with them. It wasn't until the following winter that she received a card from the woman to whom she had given her coat. The young mother wrote, "You have no idea how much your gift of love meant to me. Now I plan to share it with someone else who needs it."

Obedience Builds Character. In the eleventh century, King Henry III of Bavaria grew tired of court life and the pressures of being a monarch. He made application to Prior Richard at a local monastery, asking to be accepted as a contemplative and spend the rest of his life in the monastery. "Your Majesty," said Prior Richard, "do you understand that the pledge here is one of obedience? That will be hard because you have been a king."

"I understand," said Henry. "The rest of my life I will be obedient to you, as Christ leads you."

"Then I will tell you what to do," said Prior Richard. "Go back to your throne and serve faithfully in the place where God has put you."

When King Henry died, a statement was written: "The King learned to rule by being obedient." When we tire of our roles and responsibilities, it helps to remember that God has planted us in a certain place and told us to be a good accountant or teacher or mother or father. Christ expects us to be faithful where He puts us, and when Jesus returns, we'll rule together with Him.

FOR YOUTH

■ **TOPIC:** Live Forever in Love

■ **QUESTIONS:** 1. Who are those who have been born of God? 2. How can we know that we truly love the children of God? 3. What does the Spirit testify concerning the Son? 4. How can believers have assurance of salvation? 5. Wherein can the lost find eternal life?

■ **ILLUSTRATIONS:**

Share God's Life. The article "What Good Is a Tree?" in *Reader's Digest* says that when the roots of trees begin to mingle, a strange fungus grows among them. This fungus facilitates an interaction among the roots of the trees—even between trees of dissimilar species. A whole forest may be linked together. If one tree has access to water, another to nutrients, and a third to sunlight, the trees have the means to share with one another. Love certainly isn't a fungus, but it has the ability to link God's people together and disperse the life of God among them.

Love Me Tender. In the nineteenth century, British Prime Minister William Gladstone announced in the House of Commons the death of Princess Alice, daughter of Queen Victoria. Gladstone related how Princess Alice's small daughter had become gravely ill with diphtheria. The physicians had told the princess not to kiss her daughter at the peril of her own health. As her child struggled to breathe, princess Alice had taken the little one into her arms to keep her from choking to death. Rasping and wheezing, the child begged, "Momma, kiss me!" Alice kissed her daughter. She contracted diphtheria and some days later she died, and the prime minister made his announcement.

Real love forgets self. Real love forgets danger. Real love doesn't count the cost.

Routine Obedience. The preacher said, "We think giving our all to the Lord is like taking a thousand dollar bill and laying it on the table. 'Here's my life, Lord. I'm giving it all.'"

"But the reality for most of us is that God sends us to the bank and has us cash in the thousand dollar bill for quarters. We go through life putting out 25 cents here and 50 cents there. We listen to the neighbor kid's troubles instead of saying, 'Get lost.' We go to a committee meeting instead of doing what we want to do. We give a cup of water to a shaky old man in a nursing home instead of hanging out with our friends. Usually, giving our life to Christ isn't glorious. It's done in all those little acts of love, 25 cents at a time. It would be easy to go out in a flash of glory; it's harder to live the Christian life little by little over the long haul."

The preacher is right.

Unwavering Commitment. The most famous and best-loved athlete Scotland ever produced was Eric Liddell. He was an internationally known rugby player and an Olympic gold medallist. The story of his refusal to run in the preliminary heats of the 100-meter dash at the Paris Olympics in 1924 (when they were held on Sunday) was told in the movie entitled *Chariots of Fire*.

Liddell was a man who had an unswerving commitment to love the Lord and keep His commandments. While the race put him into a conflict with his fellow citizens, the leaders of his nation, the International Olympic Committee, his friends, and others, Liddell would not deviate from his stand.

Like Liddell, you will often be torn by conflicting allegiances to family, peers, and others. But like Liddell, you too can stand up to the world by relying on God's power. He will give you the strength to do what is right.

CHRIST IS OUR KING

BACKGROUND SCRIPTURE: Revelation 1:1-8; Luke 19:28-40
DEVOTIONAL READING: Psalm 118:21-28

KEY VERSE: Blessed be the King that cometh in the name of the Lord: peace in heaven, and glory in the highest. Luke 19:38.

5

KING JAMES VERSION

REVELATION 1:8 I am Alpha and Omega, the beginning and the ending, saith the Lord, which is, and which was, and which is to come, the Almighty. . . .

LUKE 19:28 And when he had thus spoken, he went before, ascending up to Jerusalem. 29 And it came to pass, when he was come nigh to Bethphage and Bethany, at the mount called the mount of Olives, he sent two of his disciples, 30 Saying, Go ye into the village over against you; in the which at your entering ye shall find a colt tied, whereon yet never man sat: loose him, and bring him hither. 31 And if any man ask you, Why do ye loose him? thus shall ye say unto him, Because the Lord hath need of him. 32 And they that were sent went their way, and found even as he had said unto them. 33 And as they were loosing the colt, the owners thereof said unto them, Why loose ye the colt? 34 And they said, The Lord hath need of him. 35 And they brought him to Jesus: and they cast their garments upon the colt, and they set Jesus thereon. 36 And as he went, they spread their clothes in the way. 37 And when he was come nigh, even now at the descent of the mount of Olives, the whole multitude of the disciples began to rejoice and praise God with a loud voice for all the mighty works that they had seen; 38 Saying, Blessed be the King that cometh in the name of the Lord: peace in heaven, and glory in the highest.

NEW REVISED STANDARD VERSION

REVELATION 1:8 "I am the Alpha and the Omega," says the Lord God, who is and who was and who is to come, the Almighty. . . .

LUKE 19:28 After he had said this, he went on ahead, going up to Jerusalem.

29 When he had come near Bethphage and Bethany, at the place called the Mount of Olives, he sent two of the disciples, 30 saying, "Go into the village ahead of you, and as you enter it you will find tied there a colt that has never been ridden. Untie it and bring it here. 31 If anyone asks you, 'Why are you untying it?' just say this, 'The Lord needs it.'" 32 So those who were sent departed and found it as he had told them. 33 As they were untying the colt, its owners asked them, "Why are you untying the colt?" 34 They said, "The Lord needs it." 35 Then they brought it to Jesus; and after throwing their cloaks on the colt, they set Jesus on it. 36 As he rode along, people kept spreading their cloaks on the road. 37 As he was now approaching the path down from the Mount of Olives, the whole multitude of the disciples began to praise God joyfully with a loud voice for all the deeds of power that they had seen, 38 saying,

"Blessed is the king
    who comes in the name of the Lord!
Peace in heaven,
    and glory in the highest heaven!"

247

Home Bible Readings

Background

In the verses preceding this week's lesson text, we learn that Jesus' disciples could not understand His predictions about His suffering, death, and resurrection (Luke 18:31-34). But the Savior continued toward His destiny in Jerusalem. Near Jericho a blind man's insistent shouts brought Jesus to him, and he was healed (18:35-43). Another man, Zacchaeus, despised because he was a chief tax collector, was honored to have Jesus visit his home. He gave away half his wealth and promised to more than right his past wrongs. Jesus said salvation had come to his house (19:1-9).

Zacchaeus lived in Jericho, only 18 miles from Jerusalem. It seemed the closer Jesus got to the holy city, the more expectations grew that He would announce Himself as Israel's king and set up His kingdom there. To combat this misconception, Jesus told a parable implying that the nature and timing of the Kingdom are quite different from what most Jews anticipated (19:10-27).

Some elements in Jesus' parable have symbolic applications. A man of noble birth went to a distant country to be appointed king; similarly, after the Ascension, Jesus would be gone for some time before returning as King. Before he left, the man entrusted his servants with an assignment; similarly, Jesus would leave His followers with a task—to tell the Good News and make disciples. Some opponents did not want the nobleman to rule over them; similarly, many would oppose Jesus' reign. The nobleman returned to his own people; similarly, Jesus will someday return to His followers. The servants who faithfully invested the money their master entrusted to them were rewarded, while those wicked men who opposed his authority were put to death. Similarly, Jesus' return will be a time of both reward and judgment.

One element of Jesus' parable may have been based on an actual event His listeners would have recognized. When Herod the Great died in 4 B.C., he left part of his kingdom, Judea, to his son Archelaus. But Herod's authority existed only because Rome permitted it. So Archelaus traveled to the capitol to gain endorsement as a client king—one who ruled over territory officially belonging to Rome. His request for the throne was opposed by people, who sent their own delegation to Rome to argue against it. But eventually, Archelaus was granted rulership.

In Jesus' parable, 10 servants are each given a mina, which was a unit of weight equal to about one and one-quarter pounds. In other words, they received that amount of a precious metal, probably gold or silver. They were told to put this money to work (19:13). The parable of the minas suggests that the Kingdom was not going to be set up in its fullness immediately. But in the process, the parable teaches some other ideas as well: the Kingdom will definitely come and no one can stop it (19:14-15a); Christ's servants are to be productively involved as they wait for His return (19:13, 15b); faithfulness will be rewarded at Christ's return (19:16-19); and sloth and disobedience will be punished (19:20-24).

The inactive servant was not an enemy of the king. Yet he did not have a healthy relationship with his master. This servant was too afraid of his master to serve well. As a result, he was unable to give a profit back to his master. The master took away the little the unfaithful servant had and gave it to the one who already had 10 minas (19:24-25). This may seem unfair, but the principle it illustrates is an essential element of living under Christ's reign. If we use the abilities and resources Jesus entrusts to us, we will gain even more. But if we neglect our abilities, we will lose them (19:26-27).

NOTES ON THE PRINTED TEXT

In Revelation 1:7, John described the second coming of Christ, which is a major theme of the book. Then, in 1:8, the Lord declared that He is the *Alpha and Omega*. These are the first and last letters of the Greek alphabet. Put another way, the Lord is the beginning and the end of all things. God is sovereign over all that takes place in human history. Moreover, His lordship encompasses the past, the present, and the future. This remained true even during Jesus' time of ministry on earth. Not even His trial and crucifixion could snuff out the saving light of His eternal presence and power (John 1:5).

Part of this week's lesson text concerns the Messiah's triumphal entry into Jerusalem. During this episode, Jesus knew what would happen to Him in the holy city. He had already told His disciples three times what was coming, the third time in detail just a few days earlier (Luke 18:31-34). The confrontation between Jesus and the religious leaders would lead to the Savior's arrest and crucifixion, but first He must enter Jerusalem with all the symbolism associated with the Messiah.

Jesus' last week of earthly ministry began with a highly visible event. To the cheers of an adoring crowd, and to the dismay of His critics, Jesus rode triumphantly on a donkey. Luke 18:35 and 19:1 imply that Jesus and His disciples were approaching Jerusalem on Passover week from the east. They had just made the 18-mile journey from Jericho to Jerusalem, apparently in the company of many other pilgrims headed for the temple to celebrate Passover (19:28). On this road, there were two villages outside the holy city. Bethphage was about half a mile from Jerusalem, while Bethany was less than two miles away (19:29). Both villages lay on the eastern side of the Mount of Olives, a high, two-mile-long ridge, generously capped with many olive trees.

From Bethany, Jesus sent two disciples on ahead to Bethphage to fetch a young donkey. Matthew 21:2 mentions two animals in Jesus' triumphal entry, *an ass tied, and a colt with her.* The other three Gospels refer only to the colt. Some modern skeptical commentators have said this means that Matthew misread the prophecy from Zechariah 9:9 and thought two animals should be present, not one. Thus, Matthew invented one. However, this is a misinterpretation of the commentators, not Matthew's mistake.

Zechariah 9:9 says that the Messiah would come riding on a donkey colt, an unbroken *foal*, which had never been ridden (Mark 11:2). Unused animals were often taken for religious purposes (Num. 19:2; 1 Sam. 6:7-8). Jesus rode the young colt, but the colt's mother could also have been taken along as a steadying influence, leading the way as the colt followed (Matt. 21:7). Therefore, the mention of two animals is more likely an eyewitness detail from Matthew. The other Gospel writers simply mentioned the actual animal that Jesus rode.

It is not clear whether Jesus had arranged with someone to provide the colt or whether He knew about the animal supernaturally. At any rate, the colt was an appropriate choice. According to Jewish belief, the fact that it had never been ridden before made it especially suitable for religious purposes (Luke 19:30). Also, everything occurred just as Jesus had said. The disciples found the donkey; its owners questioned them; and they told about the Lord's need (19:31-34).

When the two disciples Jesus had dispatched returned with the colt, they spread their cloaks (or outer garments) on the animal and then Jesus sat on it (19:35). The news traveled swiftly that Jesus was arriving for the Passover celebration. And a large crowd of Passover pilgrims went out from Jerusalem to meet Him. Many in the crowd were spreading their cloaks on the road (19:36), which was considered a display of honor to royalty (2 Kings 9:13). Other people were cutting palm branches off the trees and spreading them on the road (Matt. 21:8; John 12:13).

As Jesus approached the road leading down from the Mount of Olives, those who were traveling with Him and those who had come out to meet Him joined in praising God (Luke 19:37). They began to joyfully laud Jesus for all the miracles they had seen Him do. As the multitudes shouted the words of Psalm 118:25-26, they acknowledged the blessing of God on the Davidic King, who came in the name of the Lord. Peace and glory throughout the created realm and even to the farthest reaches of heaven were the result of the Messiah's redemptive work (Luke 19:38).

According to Matthew 21:9, Mark 11:9, and John 12:13, the crowds also shouted *Hosanna.* This term comes from Psalm 118:25 and means "O, save" or "Save, we pray." This psalm was originally sung in connection with the observance of the Feast of Tabernacles, accompanied by the waving of palm branches. By the New Testament era, both activities were practiced at other feasts as well. *Hosanna* was a shout of joy and had become closely associated with Israel's messianic hope.

According to Matthew 21:9, the crowd that welcomed Jesus into Jerusalem not only shouted *Hosanna* but also identified Him as the *son of David*. It is highly unlikely that those announcing the coming kingdom of David understood the suffering and death that the Messiah must endure in the coming week. The kingdom they were looking for was an immediate, earthly realm free from Roman dominion. God had chosen David to be the first of many successive kings of Israel (2 Sam. 7:8-16). But the dynastic rule was broken when Jehoiakim died and his son Jehoiachin was carried away in exile to Babylon (2 Kings 24:15; 25:27-29; Jer. 36:30). Later, the prophets said that God would one day restore David's dynasty (Ezek. 37:24-25; Amos 9:11).

Luke 19:39 reveals that there were some Pharisees in the crowd, and the religious leaders did not miss the meaning of the shouts. They recognized that Jesus was being acclaimed as the Messiah. Angrily, the Pharisees insisted that He halt what they believed were the extravagant claims of His followers. Their unbelief is all the more amazing when we realize that Jesus' entry into Jerusalem occurred not long after the miracle of Lazarus being raised from the dead. Some of the people in the crowd in the city of Jerusalem had witnessed Jesus' calling Lazarus from the tomb (John 12:12-18).

Besides raising Lazarus, Jesus had done many other things to upset a number of the religious leaders. However, when they saw Him ride like royalty into Jerusalem, on a colt, in fulfillment of prophecy, they realized the symbolism of what He had done. He could have become king any time He pleased. Even if He did not, His popularity among the people was in danger of surpassing the Pharisees'. Jesus refused to put a damper on His disciples' enthusiasm. It was necessary and right for them to praise God. Indeed, the day was so momentous that even if people kept silent, inanimate objects would proclaim God's praises and hail the Messiah (Luke 19:40).

SUGGESTIONS TO TEACHERS

The account of Jesus entering Jerusalem on a donkey may be so familiar to your students that they might think they don't have to pay attention to the lesson. Consequently, you will want to present this material in a way that seems fresh, interesting, and relevant. Consider discussing the following points with them.

1. PROVIDING THE MESSIAH'S ASSIGNMENT. Mention the compliance of the two disciples who obeyed Jesus. They readily went and obtained what He wanted for His grand entrance. How willing are we to carry out His commands?

2. PRESENTING THE MESSIAH'S ANNOUNCEMENT. Jesus' coming to Jerusalem on the back of a donkey amid the shouts of the crowds was His public announcement of His identity as the promised Messiah. Explain to the class that Jesus did not accidentally stumble into being arrested and crucified. Also emphasize that He was not merely another worshiper. Rather, He was presenting Himself as the King-Deliverer of Israel.

3. PRAISING THE MESSIAH'S ARRIVAL. The people on the streets immediately recognized the symbolism of the entrance and responded accordingly. How do we show our awareness of Jesus' rule in our lives? Is our religion merely a Palm Sunday show, or is our recognition of Christ's lordship evident in our spending, our use of spare time, and our efforts to promote justice in society?

4. PREPARING FOR THE MESSIAH'S DEATH. Note that Jesus' followers were hoping He would use the great national celebration of Passover to claim His place as King of the Jews. And the religious leaders were hoping to find an opportunity to kill Him. Knowing the danger, Jesus could have stayed away. Yet He decided to enter Jerusalem—but on His own terms. His courage and commitment to the Father is one more reason why we can acclaim Jesus as our Savior and Lord.

FOR ADULTS	■ **TOPIC:** Yielding to Christ's Lordship ■ **QUESTIONS:** 1. What truth about the Lord is disclosed in Revelation 1:8? 2. What was the significance of the colt on which Jesus' rode?

3. Who were the people shouting praises to Jesus? 4. In what sense is Jesus the King? 5. Why were the religious leaders upset with the declarations coming from the crowd?

■ **ILLUSTRATIONS:**

Powerful Symbol. Waving palm branches during Jesus' entry into Jerusalem had immense political meaning. Like a flag is to moderns, so palm branches were a symbol of nationalism to people in Judea. The Jews, while living under Roman occupation forces, regarded palm branches as a way of expressing their long-suppressed traditions of freedom.

Palm branches reminded the people of the great revolt by the Jewish hero, Simon Maccabeus, against the cruel Antioches Epiphanes IV, who had desecrated the temple and tried to stamp out Judaism. In 142 B.C., Simon Maccabeus drove out the occupation army. (The Jewish festival of Hanukkah celebrates this victory.) When Maccabeus paraded down the Mount of Olives in his victory procession, the grateful people threw down palm branches to welcome the national liberator. From then on, palm branches stood as the symbol of liberation by a great national hero. The coins carried the likeness of the palm branches. Like firecrackers and red-white-and-blue bunting on July 4th for Americans, palm branches symbolized national pride and freedom for those in Jerusalem the day that Jesus rode into the city on a donkey.

When Jesus arrived, some people evidently mistook Him for the national liberator in the mold of Simon Maccabeus. They looked to Jesus to bark commands and rally troops. They thought He would be another powerful generalissimo who would bring victory of the occupiers. How mistaken they were!

Missing the Real Event. The story is told of the boy from the country who came to town many years ago to see the circus. He had never seen one before, and was excited at the prospect of watching the clowns, elephants, lions, and tigers. The boy got up early and drove his horse and wagon to town in time for the big parade. Standing at the curb, he clapped enthusiastically as the steam calliope tooted and the stream of gaudily painted circus wagons rumbled by.

The boy shrieked with delight at the clowns and acrobats, and he grew wide-eyed with wonder at the sight of the wild animals in their cages. He laughed at the shuffling lines of elephants and watched the jugglers with wonder. When the parade reached its end, the boy rushed up to the last man in the procession and handed him his money, and then the boy went back home. The lad didn't discover until later that he hadn't seen the circus but had merely watched the parade. He missed the acts under the big top and merely caught sight of the procession leading to the performance.

Some church members are a bit like that boy. They watch the Palm Sunday procession, but they never go any further. They enjoy a brief emotional experience but miss the real action of the cross and the empty tomb. They enjoy the pageantry and watch the parade briefly, but they never participate in the meaning of the resurrection. Sadly, they never get beyond Palm Sunday's events.

The Cheering Stopped. When World War I ended, American President Woodrow Wilson was a hero across western Europe. The American forces had swung the battle to the Allies. Everyone felt optimistic. Maybe the nations had truly fought their last war and the world had been made safe for democracy. Everyone loved Wilson for his part in the flow of events.

After the war, when Wilson first visited Paris, London, and Rome, cheering crowds greeted him everywhere. Their enthusiasm lasted about a year. Then it gradually stopped. Europeans forgot what Wilson had done and focused their attention on resuming all facets of normal life. Back in Washington, D.C., the U.S. Senate vetoed Wilson's plan for an international peace organization, the League of Nations.

During the last days of his presidency, Wilson's health began to fail. His party lost the next national election. Within a short time, Wilson went from world hero to a broken man. How quickly the crowds turned on him! Jesus did not break under the strain, but He faced the same pattern. Crowds that welcomed Him as He entered Jerusalem deserted Him as He moved toward the end.

FOR YOUTH

■ TOPIC: Blessed Is the King!

■ QUESTIONS: 1. What was significant about the way Jesus' entered Jerusalem? 2. Why was Jesus' riding on a colt consistent with His character? 3. How did the crowd respond to Jesus' entry into Jerusalem? 4. Why would Jesus choose this time to enter Jerusalem in a royal way? 5. Why did Jesus choose to accept the praises of the crowds?

■ ILLUSTRATIONS:

Understand the Excitement. On Sunday, January 25, 1998, the Denver Broncos defeated the highly favored Green Bay Packers 31-24 to win Super Bowl XXXII. The win gave the AFC its first victory over an NFC team in 13 long years. It also gave quarterback John Elway and the Denver team their first Super Bowl win in four tries. The city of Denver celebrated wildly. Some fans, fueled by too much alcohol consumption, destroyed property in their exuberance.

While people in society expect and accept the wild joy and excitement of a football team winning the Superbowl, they have difficulty understanding how the entire city of Jerusalem could be thrown into turmoil over Jesus' arrival. They fail to understand that Jesus is no ordinary person. He is the King and Messiah!

Unwanted Royalty. On November 10, 1997, Australians voted for 76 elected delegates to a constitutional convention to be held in 1998. One surprise was that over 50 percent of all Australians supported key governmental figures in wanting the Queen of England to bow out as Australia's head of state, in removing her face from Australian currency, and in deleting any reference to Australia as part of the British crown. The governor-general would replace the queen and become the country's president.

In Jerusalem, key religious and governmental leaders wanted Jesus out of the picture. He was a King nobody wanted around. But without the finesse and political correctness demonstrated by the Australian politicians, these leaders pulled the strings and made backroom deals to have Jesus discredited and murdered.

No Compromise. The Mel Gibson movie called *Braveheart* was set in thirteenth-century Scotland. It focuses on a common man, William Wallace, who tried to unite all the independent clans to fight off the English army. Wallace needed the help of Robert the Bruce, the leader of the most powerful clan. But Bruce refused to help. Why? Bruce summarized his thought in these lines: "Wallace is an uncompromising man. Uncompromising men are admirable. But only a compromising man can be king."

Jesus refused to compromise. Thus, the authorities murdered Him. But in an even greater way than William Wallace, Jesus ultimately won the victory.

Concern for Wealth. Why does the typical young person head off to college? One survey found that, 30 years ago, Kathy, a typical young woman, went to college to gain wealth in knowledge and personal development. Today, a similar survey shows the priority has shifted. Hannah, today's typical college student, prefers the green type of wealth. She wants an education, not as an end in itself, but as a means to a big house and bank account. Greed kept the religious leaders from the true worship of the Son of God. It's still true that the love of money is a root of all sorts of evil.

CHRIST IS RISEN

BACKGROUND SCRIPTURE: Revelation 1:9-20; John 20:1-18; 30-31
DEVOTIONAL READING: Romans 14:7-12

KEY VERSES: And he laid his right hand upon me, saying unto me, Fear not; I am the first and the last: I am he that liveth, and was dead; and, behold, I am alive for evermore. Revelation 1:17-18.

KING JAMES VERSION

REVELATION 1:12 And I turned to see the voice that spake with me. . . . 17 And when I saw him, I fell at his feet as dead. And he laid his right hand upon me, saying unto me, Fear not; I am the first and the last: 18 I am he that liveth, and was dead; and, behold, I am alive for evermore, Amen; and have the keys of hell and of death. . . .

JOHN 20:11 But Mary stood without at the sepulchre weeping: and as she wept, she stooped down, and looked into the sepulchre, 12 And seeth two angels in white sitting, the one at the head, and the other at the feet, where the body of Jesus had lain. 13 And they say unto her, Woman, why weepest thou? She saith unto them, Because they have taken away my Lord, and I know not where they have laid him. 14 And when she had thus said, she turned herself back, and saw Jesus standing, and knew not that it was Jesus. 15 Jesus saith unto her, Woman, why weepest thou? whom seekest thou? She, supposing him to be the gardener, saith unto him, Sir, if thou have borne him hence, tell me where thou hast laid him, and I will take him away. 16 Jesus saith unto her, Mary. She turned herself, and saith unto him, Rabboni; which is to say, Master. . . .

30 And many other signs truly did Jesus in the presence of his disciples, which are not written in this book: 31 But these are written, that ye might believe that Jesus is the Christ, the Son of God; and that believing ye might have life through his name.

NEW REVISED STANDARD VERSION

REVELATION 1:12 Then I turned to see whose voice it was that spoke to me. . . .

17 When I saw him, I fell at his feet as though dead. But he placed his right hand on me, saying, "Do not be afraid; I am the first and the last, 18 and the living one. I was dead, and see, I am alive forever and ever; and I have the keys of Death and of Hades. . . .

JOHN 20:11 But Mary stood weeping outside the tomb. As she wept, she bent over to look into the tomb; 12 and she saw two angels in white, sitting where the body of Jesus had been lying, one at the head and the other at the feet. 13 They said to her, "Woman, why are you weeping?" She said to them, "They have taken away my Lord, and I do not know where they have laid him." 14 When she had said this, she turned around and saw Jesus standing there, but she did not know that it was Jesus. 15 Jesus said to her, "Woman, why are you weeping? Whom are you looking for?" Supposing him to be the gardener, she said to him, "Sir, if you have carried him away, tell me where you have laid him, and I will take him away." 16 Jesus said to her, "Mary!" She turned and said to him in Hebrew, "Rabbouni!" (which means Teacher). . . .

30 Now Jesus did many other signs in the presence of his disciples, which are not written in this book. 31 But these are written so that you may come to believe that Jesus is the Messiah, the Son of God, and that through believing you may have life in his name.

6

Monday, April 2	Luke 22:7-23	*This Is My Body*
Tuesday, April 3	Romans 14:7-12	*Jesus Is Lord of All*
Wednesday, April 4	John 20:1-9	*Mary Finds an Empty Tomb*
Thursday, April 5	John 20:10-18	*Jesus Appears to Mary*
Friday, April 6	John 20:19-23	*Jesus Appears to His Disciples*
Saturday, April 7	John 20:24-31	*Jesus Appears to Thomas*
Sunday, April 8	Revelation 1:9-12, 17-18	*Jesus, the First and Last*

BACKGROUND

The Savior's crucifixion is the historical prelude to His resurrection from the dead. After the crowd outside the Praetorium insisted on Barabbas's release, Pilate ordered his soldiers to flog Jesus. They pressed a crown of thorns on Jesus' head and wrapped a purple robe around Him. Then they mocked Him and smacked Him in the face (John 19:1-3).

Perhaps Pilate thought this harsh treatment of Jesus would elicit the crowd's sympathy for Him. No such compassion was demonstrated, however. After telling the people once more that he found Jesus innocent of any charge, and after parading Him before them in ridiculous attire, Pilate presented Jesus to them (19:4-5). Pilate soon became disgusted with the heartless attitude of the Jewish officials. He told them to crucify Jesus themselves. Yet they argued that their law required that He be executed since He professed to be God's Son (19:6-7).

Pilate withdrew once more and asked Jesus to reveal His origin. Jesus' silence infuriated Pilate, who reminded this peasant that as governor he possessed the authority to free Him or sentence Him to die on the cross (19:8-10). Pilate's comment failed to impress Jesus, however. He told Pilate any authority he had over Him was granted by God. While Pilate had the power to sentence Jesus to death, Caiaphas had delivered Him to the Roman governor. Therefore, Caiaphas was guilty of a worse sin (19:11).

When Pilate sought some way of letting Jesus go, the Jewish rulers warned him loudly that such an act would be treason to Caesar (19:12). Faced with this implied threat, Pilate ordered Jesus to stand before His accusers while the governor sat on the judgment seat (19:13). It was Friday morning of the Passover week when Pilate pointed to Jesus and contemptuously said to the crowd, *Behold your King!* (19:14).

The people had turned into a mob thirsty for blood. They repeatedly yelled for Jesus to be crucified. Pilate asked them whether they really wanted him to do this. Ironically, the chief priests who had condemned Jesus for blasphemy proclaimed Caesar to be their only king. Thus, having exhausted all attempts to free Jesus, Pilate finally yielded to their demands and commanded his soldiers to take Jesus away to be crucified (19:15-16).

The details of Jesus' crucifixion are recorded in 19:17-27, His death is discussed in

19:28-37, and His burial is the focal point of 19:38-42. Joseph of Arimathea, a wealthy and prominent member of the Sanhedrin (see Matt. 27:57; Mark 15:43), was instrumental in arranging for the Messiah's burial. Though Joseph had kept his faith in Jesus a secret because he was afraid of his colleagues, he had not consented to the council's decision to condemn Jesus (see Luke 23:50-51). Now that Jesus had been executed, Joseph openly expressed his devotion to the Savior by boldly seeking Pilate's permission to allow him to bury Jesus in Joseph's own tomb (John 19:38; see Matt. 27:60).

After Pilate gave his consent, Joseph and Nicodemus took the body of Jesus away. Nicodemus was another member of the Jewish ruling council and the Pharisee who had come to Jesus at night to inquire about the kingdom of God (see John 3:1-15). The two retrieved Jesus from the cross and prepared His body for burial. Nicodemus had brought about 75 pounds of myrrh and aloes, and together they dabbed strips of linen with the spices and wrapped Jesus' body with the cloths in keeping with the proper burial customs of the Jews (19:39-40).

Joseph and Nicodemus took Jesus' body to a new tomb that was empty of any other corpses. John also mentioned that the tomb was in a garden, which is another indication that Jesus was not buried in a public cemetery. The tomb was apparently close to the execution site. This was fortunate since sundown, which was fast approaching, would mark the beginning of the Passover sabbath (19:41-42).

NOTES ON THE PRINTED TEXT

When John turned around to see who was speaking to him, he saw seven golden *candlesticks* (Rev. 1:12), or lampstands. The lampstands used in the Jerusalem temple typically had a sturdy base, a central shaft, three branches on each side, and bowls on top of each branch as well as on top of the central shaft (for a total of seven bowls). Presumably, the lampstands of John's vision were similar. The apostle also saw Christ standing among the lampstands (1:13), which verse 1:20 says represented the seven churches. (These are first mentioned in 1:11.) Jesus was there to walk among His followers in times of hardship, to guide them in times of uncertainty, and to discipline them in times of moral laxity.

As John stood before the Messiah, the apostle dropped to his knees as though he were dead (1:17). Isaiah, Ezekiel, and Daniel had similar responses when suddenly exposed to the glorified presence of God (see Isa. 6:5; Ezek. 1:28; Dan. 8:17). This was not the same experience John had when he leaned against Jesus at the Last Supper, some 60 years previous. Here now was his closest friend—exalted, honored, and glorified. The Savior touched John, perhaps both to strengthen him physically and comfort him emotionally.

Christ told John not to be afraid, for He is *the first and the last* (Rev. 1:17). This is a divine title that appears elsewhere in Scripture in reference to the Lord (see Isa. 41:4;

44:6; 48:12). It means essentially the same thing as the title the *Alpha and Omega* (Rev. 1:8). At the time John wrote Revelation, the Roman government was pressuring believers to renounce Christ and declare the emperor to be their lord. Jesus' words to John underscored why it was wrong to do so. All human authorities are mortal and limited, whereas Christ is immortal and infinite in power. The gods of Rome were lifeless, whereas Christ is the one who lives (1:18). This means that His essential nature is characterized by life.

Not even the grave could hold the Savior. Though He died on the cross and was buried in a tomb, Jesus rose from the dead and now lives forevermore. His victory through the Resurrection enabled Him to control the keys of death and hell (or Hades, the place of the dead). In ancient times, keys were symbols of authority. Also, death and Hades were considered places where people were bound and held captive. The Son wanted His followers to know that He alone had the power and the authority to free them from the shackles of death and give them eternal life.

These truths are illustrated in the account found in John 20 of Jesus' resurrection. In ancient times, the Sabbath lasted from 6 P.M. on Friday until 6 P.M. on Saturday. Thus, Sunday would mark the first day of the following week. Very early on Sunday morning, before the sun had dawned, Mary Magdalene ventured to the tomb in which Jesus had been buried (20:1).

When Mary saw that the stone had been rolled away from the entrance to the tomb, she ran to tell Peter and John the news. They in turn ran back to the tomb to verify that it was indeed empty (20:2-9). Meanwhile, after Peter and John had returned to their homes (20:10), Mary stood outside the tomb and wept. Mary was distraught over the unexplained disappearance of the Lord's body and possibly also that He had been crucified. As Mary wept, she bent down and looked into the tomb (20:11). To her amazement, she saw two angels in white sitting where the body of Jesus previously had been lying. One angel was at the spot where Jesus' head had rested, while the other angel was at the place where Jesus' feet had been (20:12).

The angels referred to Mary as *Woman* (20:13), which was a polite form of address in ancient times. The heavenly visitors asked her why she was weeping. Mary explained her concern that she did not know where certain unidentified robbers had taken the body of the Savior. At that moment, Mary sensed the presence of another person. She turned and saw a man standing outside the tomb with her, but she did not realize the person was Jesus (20:14). Either there was something different about the risen Lord that prevented not only Mary but also other of His friends from immediately recognizing Him (see Luke 24:13-31; John 21:4), or they were supernaturally prevented from recognizing Him until the time was right. Mary thought that He was the gardener (John 20:15).

Jesus first addressed Mary as *Woman* as the angels had done. Moreover, like the angels, Jesus asked Mary why she was weeping, but also inquired as to whom she was seeking. Previously, she had thought that Jesus' enemies might have stolen His body, but now she hoped that this man, whom she assumed was responsible for the upkeep of this private cemetery, might have moved the body. Mary did not answer Jesus' questions, but implored Him to reveal the whereabouts of the Savior's body if He had carried it away. Mary promised to return the body to the tomb herself.

Once, Jesus had described Himself as the good Shepherd. He said that when He calls His sheep by their name, they will know His voice (see 10:3). Something like this must have occurred here with Mary, for she recognized the Lord when she heard Him say her name. Her immediate response was to turn toward Jesus again, but this time to exclaim *Rabboni* (20:16). John translated this Aramaic title of respect to mean *Master*, but it can also carry overtones of "Teacher" and "my dear Lord."

Excitedly, Mary tried to hold Jesus, but He stopped her. It was not that Jesus forbade Mary to touch Him at all. Rather, the phrase *Touch me not* (20:17) conveys the idea of "do not cling to Me." Mary wanted to clutch on to the Lord she thought she had lost, but He had an ascension for Himself and an assignment for her. Mary was to return to the other disciples with the great news of Christ's victory over death. Mary could not run fast enough (20:18).

This is just one of the accounts John included in his Gospel. He noted that many miracles were not recorded in his narrative about Jesus' public ministry. What the apostle did write, however, was sufficient to convince readers that Jesus is the Messiah and the Son of God and that by believing in Him they might have eternal life (20:30-31).

SUGGESTIONS TO TEACHERS

God shone His light into the darkness of death on Easter morning. Because of Jesus' victory over death, believers need not fear their own deaths. And when those they love are taken from them, they can know that this life is not an end, but a beginning.

1. THE ULTIMATE SUFFERING. In His suffering, Jesus the victim identified with us. Although He was the Son of God, He laid aside His privileges and, as the Son of man, experienced our human condition. He felt the loneliness of rejection, the humiliation of ridicule, and the excruciating physical pain of crucifixion. In taking our sins upon Himself on the cross, He experienced the ultimate suffering—total separation from God. That separation is something those who believe in the Lord Jesus will never have to experience.

2. A NEW BEGINNING. After giving up His own life, Jesus was buried. From all outward appearances, the movement He had begun died with Him. The disciples were in hiding, fearful for their lives. It seemed as if the religious leaders had won and Satan had been victorious. But the last chapter had not been written. When Christ rose from the dead, the tables were turned (so to speak). He became the victor and Satan the loser. What had seemed like the end was really a new beginning.

3. AN OPPORTUNITY FOR VICTORY. Jesus' resurrection is a promise of our own resurrection and victory over sin, suffering, and death. Though our ultimate victory will be realized when we one day join Christ in heaven, we can, like the first disciples, also be victors here on earth. The moment Mary Magdalene heard Jesus call her name and she responded to Him, she shared in His victory. By focusing on the Son, Mary's despair turned to joy, and so can ours.

FOR ADULTS

■ **TOPIC:** Discovering Resurrection

■ **QUESTIONS:** 1. Why did John respond as he did at the sight of the glorious Lord? 2. In what sense does the Son have the keys of hell and death? 3. Why was Mary Magdalene initially weeping outside the tomb? 4. What was the nature of the exchange between Mary and the two angels? 5. What caused Mary to recognize the risen Lord?

■ **ILLUSTRATIONS:**

The Power in a Seed. In a cemetery in Hanover, Germany, there is a grave where huge slabs of granite and marble are cemented together and fastened with heavy steel clasps. It belongs to a woman who did not believe in the resurrection of the dead. Yet strangely, she directed in her will that her grave be made so secure that, if there were a resurrection, it would not include her.

On the marker were inscribed these words: "This burial place must never be opened." In time, a seed covered over by the stones began to grow. Slowly it pushed its way through the soil and out from beneath them. As the trunk enlarged, the great slabs were gradually shifted so that the steel clasps were wrenched from their sockets. A tiny seed had become a tree that had pushed aside the massive stones.

The power seen at the Resurrection is the same power that can change a hardened heart toward God. The power seen at the Resurrection is the same power that will raise those who die in Christ to eternal life with Him.

The Only Answer. Some of the hardest questions in life all have the same answer: What is it that gives a widow courage as she stands beside a fresh grave? What is the ultimate hope of the amputee, the abused, or the burn victim? How can the parents of a brain-damaged or physically handicapped child keep from living their lives totally depressed? Where do the thoughts of a young couple go when they finally recover from the grief of losing their newborn child? How about when a family receives the news that their dad was killed in a terrorist attack? How about when a son or daughter dies due to an overdose? What is the final answer to pain, mourning, senility, insanity, terminal diseases, sudden calamities, and fatal accidents? By now, hopefully, you have guessed the correct answer: the hope of our coming resurrection!

Alive! Not long ago, one of the oldest members in our congregation passed away. At the funeral, our pastor refused to speak about Mabel in the past tense with phrases such as "she was" or "she had been." He pointed out that she is in heaven and that she is in the presence of the Lord and that she is alive! Our pastor reminded us of the Scripture that assures us that when we are absent from our earthly bodies we are present with the Lord (2 Cor. 5:8).

Though I had always believed this truth, I had never thought of speaking about a deceased person in the present tense. This added a whole new dynamic for me in thinking about our loved ones who have already left this life here on earth. How exciting it is to think about them as being alive right now. In addition, as believers, we all have that same assurance that death is not the final chapter for us. It is the new beginning that we all are waiting for and believing in.

<table>
<tr><td>

FOR YOUTH

</td><td>

■ **TOPIC:** Alive Forever!

■ **QUESTIONS:** 1. Why could John (along with all believers) discontinue being afraid?

</td></tr>
</table>

2. What did Mary do as she stood weeping outside the tomb? 3. What explanation did Mary give to the angels? 4. What was Mary's response when she recognized the risen Lord? 5. Why did Jesus tell Mary not to touch Him?

■ **ILLUSTRATIONS:**

Lives Again. Her remains were excavated by the Association for the Preservation of Virginia Antiquities, the group that owns the Jamestown site. She was discovered in the fall of 1998 by Jamie May as part of an ongoing archaeological dig at the historical site.

This first lady was Mistress Forrest, the wife of Thomas Forrest. She had come to Jamestown in October 1608 from England. She was accompanied by her maid, Anne Burras. Mistress Forrest died shortly after arriving and was buried naked in an elaborate pinewood coffin. (In those days clothing was considered too valuable to bury with the dead.)

The remains of Mistress Forrest were taken to the Smithsonian Institution for careful examination. Painstaking analysis determined her diet to have been wheat rather than corn. It was also discovered that she was a Caucasian, four feet eight inches tall, and about 35 years old (quite old for that time!). Even her facial features were reconstructed using modern technology. But despite this, Mistress Forrest remains a lifeless mass.

Centuries earlier, others trooped to a burial site to look at the remains of someone who had meant so much to them. His life and words had been indelibly inscribed into their lives. However, instead of gazing at a corpse, they met the risen Lord. They discovered that He lives forevermore!

Put Things Right. On August 10, 1944, John McConnan was an aviator on a B-24 Liberator, guiding the plane back from a bombing raid over the German-held oil fields in Ploesti, Romania. The plane was hit by antiaircraft fire that severed the tail. Four men parachuted out and were captured by the Germans. McConnan and five others rode the plane down and were killed in what is today Albania. When the war ended and the Iron Curtain descended, there was no word of McConnan's body. This bothered James McConnan, John's younger brother.

When the Iron Curtain was lifted, James contacted Albanian journalists and enlisted help in searching for his brother's remains. James finally learned that the B-24 had crashed into a farmhouse and killed the entire family in Goraj, Albania. Villagers had buried two of the crewmen in an unmarked grave. Responding to James' request, members of the U.S. Army's Memorial Affairs Activity in Europe spoke with villagers, who directed them to the graves in 1995.

In April of 1998, James McConnan traveled to Albania to meet with men from the U.S. Army's Central Identification Laboratory. The group recovered the remains of the two servicemen. On March 5, 1999, the remains were positively identified as those of John McConnan and Wayne O. Shaffner. The remains were to be returned to the families for burial.

John McConnan was reburied on May 15, 1999, because a brother refused to rest until the fallen aviator was given a decent burial. James admitted, "It doesn't solve any problems and it doesn't make anything really different, but it puts it right."

Almost two millennia ago some women also wanted to put things right. They went out knowing that their simple embalming chores would not change recent events, but at least it would give their friend a decent burial. However, early that Sunday morning they discovered that Jesus was alive! No longer would He be just a memory. Now He was present among them!

Empty! What is the biggest difference between the world's great religions? Look at the founders of each one. You can find the tomb of Muhammed in Saudi Arabia, and his body is there. You can find the tomb of Buddha in India, and his body is there. Look for the tomb of Jesus in Jerusalem, and even if you were certain of the site, you would find it empty. That He is alive today makes the difference in each one of our lives. It reminds us of the old hymn that begins, "I serve a risen Savior. He's in the world today." No other religion can dare make that claim.

GOD IS WORTHY OF PRAISE

BACKGROUND SCRIPTURE: Revelation 4:1-11

DEVOTIONAL READING: Psalm 111

KEY VERSE: Thou art worthy, O Lord, to receive glory and honour and power: for thou hast created all things, and for thy pleasure they are and were created. Revelation 4:11.

KING JAMES VERSION

REVELATION 4:1 After this I looked, and, behold, a door was opened in heaven: and the first voice which I heard was as it were of a trumpet talking with me; which said, Come up hither, and I will shew thee things which must be hereafter. 2 And immediately I was in the spirit: and, behold, a throne was set in heaven, and one sat on the throne. 3 And he that sat was to look upon like a jasper and a sardine stone: and there was a rainbow round about the throne, in sight like unto an emerald. 4 And round about the throne were four and twenty seats: and upon the seats I saw four and twenty elders sitting, clothed in white raiment; and they had on their heads crowns of gold. 5 And out of the throne proceeded lightnings and thunderings and voices: and there were seven lamps of fire burning before the throne, which are the seven Spirits of God. 6 And before the throne there was a sea of glass like unto crystal: and in the midst of the throne, and round about the throne, were four beasts full of eyes before and behind. 7 And the first beast was like a lion, and the second beast like a calf, and the third beast had a face as a man, and the fourth beast was like a flying eagle.

8 And the four beasts had each of them six wings about him; and they were full of eyes within: and they rest not day and night, saying, Holy, holy, holy, Lord God Almighty, which was, and is, and is to come. 9 And when those beasts give glory and honour and thanks to him that sat on the throne, who liveth for ever and ever, 10 The four and twenty elders fall down before him that sat on the throne, and worship him that liveth for ever and ever, and cast their crowns before the throne, saying, 11 Thou art worthy, O Lord, to receive glory and honour and power: for thou hast created all things, and for thy pleasure they are and were created.

NEW REVISED STANDARD VERSION

REVELATION 4:1 After this I looked, and there in heaven a door stood open! And the first voice, which I had heard speaking to me like a trumpet, said, "Come up here, and I will show you what must take place after this." 2 At once I was in the spirit, and there in heaven stood a throne, with one seated on the throne! 3 And the one seated there looks like jasper and carnelian, and around the throne is a rainbow that looks like an emerald. 4 Around the throne are twenty-four thrones, and seated on the thrones are twenty-four elders, dressed in white robes, with golden crowns on their heads. 5 Coming from the throne are flashes of lightning, and rumblings and peals of thunder, and in front of the throne burn seven flaming torches, which are the seven spirits of God; 6 and in front of the throne there is something like a sea of glass, like crystal.

Around the throne, and on each side of the throne, are four living creatures, full of eyes in front and behind: 7 the first living creature like a lion, the second living creature like an ox, the third living creature with a face like a human face, and the fourth living creature like a flying eagle. 8 And the four living creatures, each of them with six wings, are full of eyes all around and inside. Day and night without ceasing they sing,

"Holy, holy, holy,
the Lord God the Almighty,
who was and is and is to come."

9 And whenever the living creatures give glory and honor and thanks to the one who is seated on the throne, who lives forever and ever, 10 the twenty-four elders fall before the one who is seated on the throne and worship the one who lives forever and ever; they cast their crowns before the throne, singing,

11 "You are worthy, our Lord and God,
to receive glory and honor and power,
for you created all things,
and by your will they existed and were created."

HOME BIBLE READINGS

Monday, April 9	Psalm 145:8-12	*Praise to a Gracious God*
Tuesday, April 10	Psalm 111	*Great Is Our God*
Wednesday, April 11	Ephesians 3:7-13	*God's Eternal Purpose*
Thursday, April 12	Jeremiah 10:6-10	*None Is like God*
Friday, April 13	Ephesians 4:25—5:2	*Live a Life of Love*
Saturday, April 14	Revelation 2:1-7	*Endure Hardships*
Sunday, April 15	Revelation 4	*God Is Worthy of Praise*

BACKGROUND

Our awareness of Jesus' exhortations to the seven churches located in Asia Minor helps us to better appreciate the heavenly scene recorded in Revelation 4. Beginning with the church in Ephesus, Christ said He would let those who remained faithful to Him eat from the life-giving tree in God's wonderful garden (2:7). Scripture first mentions the tree of life in Genesis 2:9. In Revelation, it symbolizes the believers' access to God's life-giving blessings (see 22:2, 14). The *paradise of God* (2:7) refers to the eternal place of peace and rest in the Lord's presence. We who have trusted in Christ and remained faithful to Him will enjoy unending peace with the Father in the eternal state.

Next, Jesus told the Smyrnean Christians to remain faithful to Him, even to the point of death. God would reward such faithfulness with a crown that would endure forever. As before, Christ again challenged His people to heed His message. Those who refused to compromise their faith, even though it resulted in their martyrdom, were overcomers (2:11). They had the assurance that they would never experience eternal separation from God. They might have to taste a violent physical death, but certainly not the second death—that is, being banned from the living God forever.

Then Jesus pledged that those at Pergamum who did not compromise with worldliness would receive the hidden manna to eat. This promise was particularly fitting for believers tempted to join in festivities in which food sacrificed to idols was eaten (2:17). Christ also promised to give overcomers *a white stone*. Jesus said He would write a new name on the white stone, a name known only to the recipient of the object. Our new name will indicate that we remained loyal to Christ despite the opposition we encountered to our faith.

Next, the Messiah urged the faithful believers at Thyatira to refrain from immorality. He also promised not to add further burdens on them. Jesus exhorted them to hold firmly to the teaching they had received from Him. He would eventually return for them and bring them to their heavenly home. In the meantime, they were to stand their ground and resist every new thrust of the enemy (2:25).

Concerning the church in Sardis, Christ described the majority of the believers as wearing clothes that had been soiled by evil deeds. He also described a minority of believers as wearing white garments, which symbolized virtue and integrity. Because they had remained faithful to Him, He would allow them to be clothed in righteousness and enjoy the sweet fellowship of His presence (3:4).

Next, the Redeemer promised the church in Philadelphia that He would make those who were victorious, pillars in the heavenly temple of His God. This metaphor symbolizes permanence and stability. Jesus was saying that the faithful will have an enduring place in the Lord's heavenly sanctuary. Jesus' words look forward to the new Jerusalem, where God will allow His people to dwell in His presence (3:12; see 21:2-3).

Finally, Jesus censured the pitiful spiritual condition of the Laodicean Christians. Because He loved them, He promised to discipline them if they did not renew their zeal and repent (3:19). At the door of the Laodicean assembly Christ stood and knocked. If the church as a whole ignored the Savior's gentle call, there might be certain individuals who would hear and heed Him. Intimate fellowship with the Messiah would be the experience of all who welcomed Him. Together they would enjoy a leisurely time of feasting in His presence (3:20). Jesus promised those who were victorious that in the coming age they would take their place beside Him on His throne. He will graciously allow them to share in His future reign. This is a message worth heeding (3:21-22).

NOTES ON THE PRINTED TEXT

Chapters 4 and 5 of Revelation form a gateway to the rest of the book. In chapter 4, the Father appears in a scene of worship as the King of heaven and earth. Then in chapter 5, innumerable angels sing hymns of praise to Christ. In John's vision, he saw a door standing open in heaven, and this allowed him to enter into the celestial realm. The apostle heard the penetrating voice of Christ directing him to come up to heaven and receive special revelation concerning the future (4:1). Some think the Messiah's invitation is a symbolic reference to the rapture of the church. More likely, John's experience parallels that of other believers in Scripture—for example, when Moses went up to Mount Sinai, or when Paul was caught up to heaven to receive special revelations from God (see Exod. 19:3, 20; 2 Cor. 12:2).

The phrase *which must be hereafter* (Rev. 4:1) may be an indication that chapters 6 through 20 concern the final great conflict between God and the forces of evil. Satan and his demonic cohorts will neither immediately nor voluntarily surrender to Christ. Nevertheless, Jesus will be victorious in His mission of defeating the devil and condemning him to the lake of fire. The Spirit immediately took control of John, perhaps by putting him in a trance. The apostle found himself standing before a throne in heaven, and he saw the Lord sitting on it. In ancient times thrones were symbols of power, sovereignty, and majesty. The throne of God radiated His glorious presence (4:2; see 1 Kings 22:19; Ezek. 1:26-28).

In Revelation 4, John did not describe the details of God's appearance. This reminds us that His greatness and glory are beyond our ability to comprehend. First Timothy 6:16 says that the Lord dwells in such blazing glory that no human can approach Him. As the eternal and holy God, He neither had been nor could be seen by the naked eye. Perhaps this is why John described his vision of the Lord by referring to the appearance of precious stones. The apostle first mentioned jasper and sardine (or carnelian). Jasper is usually green or clear, while carnelian is usually deep red or reddish-white. John also described seeing the glow of an emerald (light green) encircling God's throne like a rainbow. The picture is one of a transparent jewel radiating the splendor of God (Rev. 4:3).

In ancient times, a king would permit lesser rulers (such as tribal judges) to sit on thrones next to his. In John's vision, he saw 24 thrones surrounding God's royal seat, and 24 elders were on these thrones. They wore white clothes, which represent purity and uprightness. They also wore gold crowns, which symbolize honor, splendor, and victory (4:4). These elders may have been exalted angels who served God in His heavenly court, or they could have been glorified saints in heaven. Some think the number 24 is a symbolic reference to the 12 tribes of Israel in the Old Testament and the 12 apostles in the New Testament. This suggests that all the redeemed of all time (both before and after Christ's death and resurrection) are represented before God's throne and worship Him in His heavenly sanctuary.

John saw flashes of lightning and roars of thunder coming from God's throne. These storm phenomena symbolized the power and majesty of the Lord. Seven lampstands with burning flames—which represented the seven spirits of God—stood in front of the throne (4:5). The lampstands symbolized the perfection, completeness, and fullness of the Holy Spirit. He worked through the redeemed in their various churches to shine the light of the Gospel to a lost world. In front of God's throne, John also saw something that looked like a sea made of glass. It was clear and sparkling like crystal (4:6a). In New Testament times, glass was a rare item, and crystal-clear glass was virtually impossible to find. The celestial ocean in John's vision may symbolize the purity and magnificence of God.

Next, the apostle saw four living creatures in the center around God's throne. The eyes covering the front and back of each creature may symbolize their unceasing watchfulness (4:6b). It is possible that these entities were representations of God's attributes or symbols of the natural order of creation. More likely, they were angels, perhaps similar to the cherubim of Ezekiel 1 and 10 or the seraphim of Isaiah 6. The four living creatures guarded the throne of God, proclaimed His holiness, and led others in worship.

It is possible that these angelic beings portrayed various aspects of divine majesty. For instance, the first creature had the form of a lion, possibly symbolizing either mobility or majesty. The second creature had the form of calf or ox, perhaps representing either strength or faithfulness. The third creature had a human face, possibly symbolizing wisdom. And the fourth creature had the form of an eagle with its wings spread out as though in flight, perhaps signifying either speed or control (Rev. 4:7; see Ezek. 1:5-10).

Each of the living creatures had six wings, and their bodies (including the underside of their wings) were covered with eyes, which is suggestive of alertness and intelligence. Day after day and night after night, these angelic beings praised the Lord. Their threefold repetition of the word *holy* (Rev. 4:8) underscored the truth that God is absolutely sinless. Their refrain also stressed that He is the almighty Ruler of the universe. Further, they emphasized that He is not bound by the limitations of time.

John saw that the living creatures never stopped praising, honoring, and thanking the Lord. The apostle also noticed that the 24 elders prostrated themselves before God's throne and placed their crowns at the base of His royal seat. These were fitting acts of worship to give to the one who controls all time and all people (4:9-10). Whereas the living creatures praised God for His holiness, the elders lauded Him for His creative acts (4:11). He not only brought all things into existence, but also sustains them. The idea is not of some superhuman creature (such as the Greek god Atlas) holding up the world. Rather, it is of God maintaining the existence of the universe and bearing it along to its divinely ordained conclusion.

SUGGESTIONS TO TEACHERS

God is so faithful and consistent in providing for our needs that we tend to forget He is present. We arrogantly think we have control over what happens to us. We imagine that we are self-sufficient and can survive solely by means of our wit and strength. We know, however, from this week's lesson that our lives are in God's hands. He is to be praised for the marvelous world He created and for the wonderful life He gives to us.

1. WE OWE EVERYTHING TO GOD. The Lord is worthy of our praise because He created us and because He lovingly sustains us. This week's Scripture passage helps us to see that the mercy, or loyal love, of the Lord is everlasting. Consequently, we can count on His enduring compassion and grace to be there when we need it. This is a marvelous reason to give Him thanks.

2. OUR GOD IS ABSOLUTELY HOLY. This week's lesson text draws attention to the infinite glory and uniqueness of the Lord over any other entity in the universe. Indeed, there is not a trace of sin within Him. For this reason He deserves our praise.

3. OUR GOD IS AWESOME IN POWER. We should not be surprised by the truth that God, our Creator and Sustainer, performed great wonders when He brought the world into existence. This is the same God who sustained His people in the Old Testament. For instance, He watched over the Israelites from the time they left Egypt to the time they settled in the promised land. And down through the centuries, people of faith have trusted in the same God to uphold them during their darkest moments. For these and countless other reasons, we should give unending thanks to the Lord of heaven, our Creator.

FOR ADULTS

■ **TOPIC:** Worshiping God Alone

■ **QUESTIONS:** 1. How did John describe the glory of the sovereign Lord? 2. Who were the 24 elders that John saw? 3. What was the significance of the seven lamps of fire? 4. What did the four living creatures unceasingly proclaim? 5. Why did the four elders throw their crowns before the throne?

■ **ILLUSTRATIONS:**

Charles's Choice. Charles was a promising young lawyer in Adams, New York. One day he decided to buy a Bible because his law texts frequently quoted from it. At first he didn't show anyone he was reading the Bible and hid it among his law books. But the more he read, the more convicted he became of the need to serve Christ instead of pursuing a law career.

On October 10, 1821, Charles made his choice. He accepted Christ as his Savior and told people that he had been given "a retainer from the Lord Jesus Christ to plead His cause." That same day Charles brought 24 people in town to know the Lord, including another lawyer and a distiller. Later Charles would preach revivals in New York City, Boston, and Philadelphia, with as many as 50,000 people converted in one week in Boston. It has been claimed that in his lifetime, the great American evangelist Charles Finney influenced over a half-million people to worship God through Christ, assuring them it was the wisest choice in life they would ever make.

Our lives are filled with choices, too, some of which are more pivotal than others. When the Lord Jesus is at the center of our decision-making and the sole object of our worship, we will make the right choices, those that count both for time and eternity.

Why God Gives Us Choices. Madeleine L'Engle notes the following in her book entitled *Walking on Water*: "The problem of pain, of war, and the horror of war, of poverty, and disease is always confronting us. But a God who allows no pain, no grief, also allows no choice. There is little unfairness in a colony of ants, but also there is little freedom. We human beings have been given . . . this ability to make choices, to help write our own story, is what makes us human . . . even when we make the wrong choices, abusing our freedom and the freedom of others."

Consider the following. If God gave you 70 years of life, you would spend:

• 24 years sleeping
• 14 years working,
• 8 years in amusement,

- 6 years at the dinner table,
- 5 years in transportation,
- 4 years in conversation,
- 3 years in education, and
- 3 years reading.

If you went to church every Sunday and prayed to the Lord five minutes every morning and night, you would be giving God five months of your life in worship. That's only five months out of 70 years!

Rich toward God. The Marquis de Lafayette was a French general and politician who was extremely rich and fit into the highest French social class. He assisted George Washington in the American Revolution, and then he returned to France and resumed his life as the master of several estates.

In 1783, the harvest was a poor one, but the workers of Lafayette's farms still somehow managed to fill his barns with wheat. "The bad harvest has raised the price of wheat," said one of his workers. "This is the time to sell." Lafayette thought about all the hungry peasants in the surrounding villages. Then he said, "No. This is the time to give."

Lafayette had an opportunity to store up treasures for himself, but decided instead to offer his wealth to the poor. This act did not impoverish him, but instead made him rich—rich toward God. Such generosity is good planning for anyone who wants to store up treasures in heaven and worship God, not money (see Matt. 6:19-24).

 FOR YOUTH

■ **TOPIC:** Sing Praise!
■ **QUESTIONS:** 1. What did the voice from heaven command John to do? 2. Who was the person seated on the throne? 3. What did the throne in heaven look like? 4. What sorts of creatures were around the throne? 5. To whom was worship given?

■ **ILLUSTRATIONS:**

O Worship the King. Sir Robert Grant was acquainted with kings. His father was a member of the British Parliament and later became chairman of the East India Company. Following in his father's footsteps, young Grant was elected to Parliament and then also became a director of the East India Company. In 1834, he was appointed governor of Bombay, and in that position he became greatly loved. A medical college in India was named in his honor.

Late in his life, Grant wrote a hymn based on Psalm 104. The progression of titles for God in the last line of that hymn—"O Worship the King"—is interesting. We know

God first as our Maker. Then, even before our conversion, He is our Defender. We know Him then as Redeemer, and finally, as we walk day by day with Him, we know Him also as Friend.

> Frail children of dust, and feeble as frail,
> In Thee do we trust, nor find Thee to fail;
> Thy mercies how tender, how firm to the end,
> Our Maker, Defender, Redeemer, and Friend.

From "I" to God. In Donald Deffner's opinion, one of the most dramatic and world-renowned shifts from "I" to God is the conversion of C. S. Lewis. This little man, who held the chair of Medieval and Renaissance Literature at Cambridge, sat in his study without typewriter or secretary and penned the great masterpieces that made him perhaps the most broadly read Christian writer of the twentieth century. C. S. Lewis was once an agnostic, but was *Surprised By Joy*—the title of a book in which he tells about "The Shape of My Early Life" as Christ replaced the "I" in his life.

C. S. Lewis describes the exchange between self-will and God's will in *Beyond Personality*. His words are a challenge to us to put God first in our lives and make Him the sole object of our praise:

> Christ says, "Give me all. I don't want so much of your money and so much of your work—I want you. I have not come to torment your natural self, but to kill it. No half-measures are any good. I don't want to cut off a branch here and there, I want to have the whole tree down. I don't want to drill the tooth, or crown it, stop it, but to have it out. Hand over the whole natural self instead. In fact I will give you myself, my own will shall become yours."

God's Awesome Power. On May 18, 1980, Mount Saint Helens in the Cascade Range of Washington state exploded with what is probably the most visible indication of the power of nature that the modern world has ever seen. At 8:32 A.M., the explosion ripped 1,300 feet off the mountain, with a force of 10 million tons of TNT, or roughly equal to 500 atom bombs. Sixty people were killed, most by a blast of 300-degree heat traveling at 200 miles an hour. Some were killed as far as 16 miles away.

The blast also leveled 150-foot Douglas firs as far as 17 miles away. A total of 3.2 billion board-feet of lumber were destroyed, enough to build 200,000 three-bedroom homes. This incident is just a small reminder of the awesome power of God, the one to whom we sing praise.

CHRIST IS WORTHY TO REDEEM

BACKGROUND SCRIPTURE: Revelation 5:1-14
DEVOTIONAL READING: Psalm 107:1-9

KEY VERSE: And every creature which is in heaven, and on the earth, and under
the earth, and such as are in the sea, and all that are in them, heard I saying,
Blessing, and honour, and glory, and power, be unto him that sitteth upon
the throne, and unto the Lamb for ever and ever. Revelation 5:13.

KING JAMES VERSION

REVELATION 5:1 And I saw in the right hand of him that sat on the throne a book written within and on the backside, sealed with seven seals. 2 And I saw a strong angel proclaiming with a loud voice, Who is worthy to open the book, and to loose the seals thereof? 3 And no man in heaven, nor in earth, neither under the earth, was able to open the book, neither to look thereon. 4 And I wept much, because no man was found worthy to open and to read the book, neither to look thereon. 5 And one of the elders saith unto me, Weep not: behold, the Lion of the tribe of Juda, the Root of David, hath prevailed to open the book, and to loose the seven seals thereof. . . .

11 And I beheld, and I heard the voice of many angels round about the throne and the beasts and the elders: and the number of them was ten thousand times ten thousand, and thousands of thousands; 12 Saying with a loud voice, Worthy is the Lamb that was slain to receive power, and riches, and wisdom, and strength, and honour, and glory, and blessing. 13 And every creature which is in heaven, and on the earth, and under the earth, and such as are in the sea, and all that are in them, heard I saying, Blessing, and honour, and glory, and power, be unto him that sitteth upon the throne, and unto the Lamb for ever and ever. 14 And the four beasts said, Amen. And the four and twenty elders fell down and worshipped him that liveth for ever and ever.

NEW REVISED STANDARD VERSION

REVELATION 5:1 Then I saw in the right hand of the one seated on the throne a scroll written on the inside and on the back, sealed with seven seals; 2 and I saw a mighty angel proclaiming with a loud voice, "Who is worthy to open the scroll and break its seals?" 3 And no one in heaven or on earth or under the earth was able to open the scroll or to look into it. 4 And I began to weep bitterly because no one was found worthy to open the scroll or to look into it. 5 Then one of the elders said to me, "Do not weep. See, the Lion of the tribe of Judah, the Root of David, has conquered, so that he can open the scroll and its seven seals." . . .

11 Then I looked, and I heard the voice of many angels surrounding the throne and the living creatures and the elders; they numbered myriads of myriads and thousands of thousands, 12 singing with full voice,

"Worthy is the Lamb that was slaughtered
to receive power and wealth and wisdom and might
and honor and glory and blessing!"

13 Then I heard every creature in heaven and on earth and under the earth and in the sea, and all that is in them, singing,

"To the one seated on the throne and to the Lamb
be blessing and honor and glory and might
forever and ever!"

14 And the four living creatures said, "Amen!" And the elders fell down and worshiped.

Monday, April 16	Psalm 107:1-9	*Thanks for Redemption*
Tuesday, April 17	Hebrews 9:11-15	*Serving the Living God*
Wednesday, April 18	1 Peter 1:13-21	*Life in Exile*
Thursday, April 19	Psalm 40:1-5	*Praise for Redemption*
Friday, April 20	Philippians 1:3-11	*That Your Love May Overflow*
Saturday, April 21	Revelation 5:1-5	*The Scroll Is Opened*
Sunday, April 22	Revelation 5:11-14	*Worthy Is the Lamb*

BACKGROUND

A lot of mystery surrounds the Book of Revelation. Perhaps no other book of the Bible is more difficult to interpret than this one. Its abundant figures and intriguing symbols have stimulated many different explanations about the book's message. And certainly the unusual imagery of the book has caused numerous disagreements among interpreters.

There are four main groups who take different approaches to interpreting Revelation. First, there are those who hold the "finished" view, believing the prophecies of Revelation have already been fulfilled. Second, some hold the "continuing to happen" view, believing these prophecies have been and are continuing to be fulfilled. Third, there are those who hold the "yet to happen" view, believing the prophecies will be primarily fulfilled at the end of time. Finally, some hold the "allegorical" view, believing these prophecies represent ageless truths with no definite time of fulfillment.

The "finished" camp is otherwise known as preterists. This group believes the prophecies of Revelation have already been fulfilled in earlier history. They maintain that the destruction of Jerusalem and the temple in A.D. 70 and the fall of the Roman Empire are pivotal events in understanding the book. This group thinks the seven churches mentioned in Revelation 1—3 were actual congregations that existed during the time of the apostle John. They believe chapters 4—19 symbolize conditions contemporary to John's time, while chapters 20—22 represent heaven and the victory of good over evil.

The "continuing to happen" camp is otherwise known as historicists. This group thinks Revelation 6—18 offers a general chronological (or recurring) outline of the course of church history from the first century (6:1) until the return of Christ (19:11). Thus, the prophecy in Revelation has been and is in the process of being fulfilled. Like the first group, this one thinks the seven churches mentioned in chapters 1—3 were actual congregations that existed during the time of John. They regard chapters 4—19 as symbolizing the events of history, and they say that chapters 20—22 deal with the final judgment and the eternal state.

The "yet to happen" camp is otherwise known as futurists. This group thinks most of the prophecies of Revelation will occur in a period of final crisis just before the return of Christ. Many in this group think the seven churches mentioned in chapters 1—3 were real congregations that existed during the time of John. Others, however, believe the seven churches symbolize seven stages of church history. This group generally thinks chapters 4—19 concern a time of future tribulation. They maintain that God will judge an apostate church as well as Antichrist and his followers. Those who hold this view say that the time of judgment will end with the return of Christ.

The "allegorical" camp is otherwise known as idealists. This group thinks the symbols and prophecies of Revelation represent principles of spiritual war, not specific events in history. They maintain that the principles are operative throughout church history and may be repeated in numerous ways. Like the first and second groups, this one thinks the seven churches mentioned in chapters 1—3 were real congregations that existed during the time of John. However, they regard chapters 4—19 as symbolizing the conflict of good and evil, while chapters 20—22 represent the triumph of good.

In stepping back from these views, it is helpful to acknowledge that the imagery in Revelation is colorful, intense, and capable of being understood in a variety of ways. That is why some believers prefer to use a combination of approaches when interpreting the book. And despite the mystery surrounding Revelation, this book is still primarily characterized by hope. The writer declared that the Messiah will one day return to vindicate the righteous and judge the wicked and unbelieving. Revelation is also known for its warnings. Throughout this spectacular vision, Jesus calls believers to commit themselves to live in righteousness and integrity by the power of the Holy Spirit. Moreover, He admonishes the wicked to turn away from their sin and trust Him for their salvation.

NOTES ON THE PRINTED TEXT

As the apostle John looked, he saw the sovereign Lord sitting on His heavenly throne. And He held a *book* (Rev. 5:1), or scroll, in His right hand. This roll made out of papyrus or leather had writing on the inside and outside, and it was sealed in seven places. In ancient times, scrolls usually had writing on only one side and were sealed in one place. The writing on the front and back indicates that the decrees of God recorded on the scroll were extensive. The number seven, representing completion or perfection, indicates how thoroughly the contents of the scroll were sealed for secrecy.

There are a variety of views about the contents of the sealed scroll that John mentioned. Most likely, it contained God's plan for the future. Probably the document told how things will ultimately end for all people—judgment for those who reject God and eternal life for those who trust in Him. Unless the seals of the scroll were broken, the future would not take place. In the vision, these seals are opened in Revelation 6.

John saw a mighty angel issue a call for someone to come forward and break the seals, revealing the scroll's contents. Interestingly, the angel did not ask who was able, influential, or powerful enough. He asked who was *worthy* (5:2) to perform the task. Only someone who was morally perfect could do so. No one in all of God's creation responded to the angel's summons (5:3). This is only one of many places in Revelation where angels are mentioned. These celestial beings serve an important role not only in this book but also throughout the rest of Scripture.

Drawing on the many biblical references to angels, we can piece together a partial description of them. Angels are supernatural beings whom God created before He created humans. Angels possess some divine characteristics, such as spiritual forms, and some human characteristics, such as limited knowledge. Angels normally live in heaven, but God sometimes uses them on earth as mediators between Himself and people. When angels appear on earth, they look like humans. God has sent angels to people to announce, to warn, to guide and instruct, to guard and defend, to minister, and to assist in judgment.

John was so caught up in the drama unfolding before him that he wept repeatedly when no one came forward to open the scroll (5:4). Apparently, the apostle sensed the urgent significance of the document. In the midst of John's anguish, one of the 24 elders seated around the throne told him to stop weeping. Lamenting was unnecessary, for there was someone who had the virtue and authority to bring history to its final conclusion (5:5).

The elder revealed the one who was worthy to take the scroll from God's hand and open its seals—*the Lion of the tribe of JudaH, the Root of David.* Both of these metaphors are familiar Old Testament titles, and together summed up Israel's hope for the coming Messiah (see Gen. 49:9-10; Isa. 11:1, 10; Jer. 23:5). God's people called Judah—the founder of the tribe—a lion, and now the elder applied the name to the greatest of all the members of Judah. The lion represented power and victory, and these were typified in the risen Christ. The word translated *Root* (Rev. 5:5) describes a shoot or sprout out of the main stem. As the *Root of David*, Jesus is identified as the Messiah who sprang from the house and lineage of David.

When John looked, he did not see a mighty lion, but instead a Lamb that looked as if it had once been killed (5:6). This unexpected image portrays sacrificial death, thus linking the Messiah to the Old Testament Passover lamb (see Exod. 12:5-6; Isa. 53:7). A lamb is a gentle animal, and so suggests someone who is approachable. Also, a lamb was a sacrificial animal, and so suggests salvation and forgiveness. As we go through various hardships, these truths can be a source of great comfort to us.

This Lamb, who bore the marks of death, also possessed the symbols of divine power and abundant knowledge. The seven horns may represent perfect power, and the seven eyes indicate the Lamb's perfect knowledge. John explained further that the seven eyes were the seven Spirits of God sent out into all the earth (Rev. 5:6). This is a reference to the perfection of the Spirit. His basic ministry is to exalt Christ and make Him alive and real to all who trust in Him.

John watched as the Lamb came forward and took the scroll from God's hand. By allowing this action, the Father authorized His Son to carry out His plan for the world (5:7). When the Lamb took the scroll, the four living creatures and the 24 elders around the throne fell down in worship before Him. They played harps, or lyres, the instruments used to accompany the singing of psalms. Their golden bowls full of incense were symbolic of the prayers of the Lord's holy people, which were probably petitions for the full and final realization of the kingdom of God (5:8).

John heard the singing of countless angels around the throne of God, along with the voices of the living creatures and the elders (5:11). The heavenly choir praised the Lamb for His worthiness. It was fitting for Him to receive glory, power, and praise for who He is and what He has done. He is the Son of God, the one who died on the cross so that those who trust in Him might become His servants in His unending kingdom (5:12).

John next heard every creature in heaven, on earth, under the earth, and in the sea sing hymns in adoration to the Father and the Son. The idea in 5:13 is that every creature in the universe united their voices to give unending praise to the Father and the Son (the Lamb). The four living creatures affirmed their praise by declaring *Amen* (5:14), and the 24 elders responded appropriately by prostrating themselves in worship before the throne.

SUGGESTIONS TO TEACHERS

In John's vision of the heavenly throne room, all honor, praise, and worship are given to Jesus, the Lamb who was slain. Why is He worthy of praise? The reasons He is praised in heaven are the same reasons why we should praise Him now with our own songs of celebration.

1. JESUS DIED FOR US. Though He did not have to, Jesus willingly died on the cross for the sake of those in every tribe, language, people, and nation who would put their trust in Him (Rev. 5:9). The Greek verb rendered *slain*, which was used to describe His death, reminds us just how much Jesus suffered for us. Whenever we think we have suffered too much ourselves, we should remember His suffering.

2. JESUS SAVED US. Jesus died for a purpose. His death was not an accident of history. His blood *redeemed* (5:9) us from the slavery into which sin has put us. We cannot save ourselves. We have been purchased with a price, Jesus' blood. Any time we think we are worthy of praise, we must remember who we are without Christ.

3. JESUS ADOPTED US. God loved us so much that He brought us who have trusted in Christ into His kingdom. One day we *will reign on the earth* (5:10) with Jesus. But what does that mean for us today? It means that Jesus has overcome the world (John 16:33), so we can as well. The more we live for Him, the more His kingdom will come and His will be done, on earth *as it is in heaven* (Matt. 6:10). As an echo of the praise Jesus receives in heaven, we should sing the old hymn of grace and praise—and mean what it says: "Were the whole realm of nature mine, that were a present far too small; love so amazing, so divine, demands my soul, my life, my all."

<table>
<tr><td>

FOR ADULTS

</td><td>

■ TOPIC: Redeemable

■ QUESTIONS: 1. What was distinctive about the scroll John saw? 2. Why was the Lamb worthy to open the scroll? 3. In what way is Jesus

</td></tr>
</table>

the Root of David? 4. Who did John see around the throne of God? 5. What did the heavenly creatures ascribe to the Lord God?

■ **ILLUSTRATIONS:**

Who Is the Redeemer? Is Jesus more worthy of worship than any of the other great teachers and philosophers of history? Frederick Buechner, in his book entitled *Now and Then*, compares the teachings of Buddha and Christ.

"Buddha sits enthroned beneath the Bo tree in the lotus position. His lips are faintly parted in the smile of one who has passed beyond every power in earth or heaven to touch him. 'He who loves fifty has fifty woes, he who loves ten has ten woes, he who loves none has no woes,' he has said. His eyes are closed.

"Christ, on the other hand, stands in the garden of Gethsemane, angular, beleaguered. His face is lost in shadows so that you can't even see his lips, and before all the powers in earth or heaven he is powerless. 'This is my commandment, that you love one another as I have loved you,' he has said. His eyes are also closed."

Beneath his tree Buddha is shutting out the world and its suffering, while Christ is taking the world and its people into His heart and loving them. In fact, He died to redeem all people—including you. As Revelation 5:9 says, by Jesus' blood He purchased for God, people from every walk of life. Jesus alone is worthy of our worship.

Only Jesus. An anonymous author made this striking comparison: "Socrates taught for 40 years, Plato for 50, Aristotle for 40, and Jesus for only 3. Yet the influence of Christ's 3-year ministry infinitely transcends the impact left by the combined 130 years of teaching from these men who were among the greatest philosophers of all antiquity. Jesus painted no pictures; yet some of the finest paintings of Raphael, Michelangelo, and Leonardo da Vinci received their inspiration from Him. Jesus wrote no poetry; but Dante, Milton, and scores of the world's greatest poets were inspired by Him. Jesus composed no music; still Haydn, Handel, Beethoven, Bach, and Mendelssohn reached their highest perfection of melody in the hymns, symphonies, and oratorios they composed in His praise. Every sphere of human greatness has been enriched by this humble Carpenter of Nazareth.

"His unique contribution is the salvation of the soul! Philosophy could not accomplish that. Nor art. Nor literature. Nor music. Only Jesus Christ can break the enslaving chains of sin and Satan. Jesus alone can speak peace to the human heart, strengthen the weak, and give life to those who are spiritually dead."

What's Wrong with Me? Sue's grandparents had only daughters. Then, when their first grandchild—Sue's older brother—was born, he became the apple of their eye. So when Sue came along 4 years later—a girl—they were less than excited.

Once, when Sue was about six, her family was visiting. For no apparent reason, her grandmother had a present for Sue's brother. It was one of those huge antique car models complete with working doors, because they knew he loved to put models together. Naturally, Sue assumed she would get a present too, so she asked where her present was. It was obvious, even to a six year old, that her grandmother hadn't even thought about giving one to Sue.

The grandmother left the room for a few minutes and returned with a box of pink tissues, saying "This is for you." Sue was devastated, but having been taught to always say thank you, she did. Then, Sue thought to herself, *What was so wrong with me that I didn't get a present?* Although her mother tried to make up for this by getting Sue a doll she had been wanting, the damage was done. Sue never forgot the feeling of not being worthy of a special gift.

So often we do this to Jesus. We will give our time and money to sports, shopping, or other things, leaving little for Him. Whether we realize it or not, what we end up giving Him shows how much we think He is worth.

FOR YOUTH

■ **TOPIC:** Praise the Worthy One!
■ **QUESTIONS:** 1. Who was worthy to open the seven-sealed scroll? 2. In what sense is Jesus the Lion of the tribe of Judah? 3. What did the many worshipers declare concerning the Lamb? 4. What did the four living creatures shout? 5. What did the elders do in response?

■ **ILLUSTRATIONS:**
Keeping Our Minds on Worship. We were members at a church where the youth helped the adults worship better each Sunday. The youth made a group decision to sit up front each week, so they would be more accountable in paying attention to the service and message. However, a more important thing happened. After a few weeks, they found themselves actually worshiping.

When I had a conversation with one of the girls, Kara, she told me that it was very powerful how they found the words in the songs to have more meaning, and the message to really speak to their hearts. They had put themselves in a position where they had fewer distractions, and they were less tempted to talk to each other, pass notes, or fall asleep. They actually felt like the Lord was present with them during worship.

Kara said she was amazed that, when she took the focus off herself and her friends, she began to realize more of who Jesus is and what He had done in her life. Kara also knew others in the youth group who were beginning to feel the same way.

This made a big impact on the adults in our church. The youths' example helped us all to see the need to focus on Jesus, and not something else during times of worship. Their behavior challenged us to not write out our grocery lists or think about where we were eating lunch when church was over. We were on our way as a church community to take seriously the task of being a kingdom and priests who served our God (Rev. 5:10).

Who's All Wet? In the years 1014–1035, a Danish king named Canute ruled over England. King Canute grew tired of hearing his servants flatter him with extravagant praises about his greatness, power, and invincibility. He decided to give his people an object lesson. He ordered his throne to be set down on the seashore, where he commanded the waves not to come in and soak him. No matter how forcefully he ordered the tide not to come in, however, his order was not obeyed. Soon the waves lapped around his throne.

One historian says that King Canute never wore his crown again, but hung it on a statue of the crucified Christ. Now his people understood who was really worthy of praise and worship.

Who Gets the Praise? In Anne Graham Lotz's book entitled *The Vision of His Glory*, she says, "If Jesus alone is worthy of all praise—and He is!—why do we seek praise for ourselves? Why are we offended when others don't give us credit for what we have done?"

Lotz goes on to tell a true story about a person who spoke dynamically for one hour and 45 minutes—about herself! When she finished, those present applauded politely (and thankfully) as she went to her seat. When the master of ceremonies stepped to the microphone, she gestured for the audience to stand for the closing prayer. The woman did not see this and she thought the audience was giving her a standing ovation! Quickly she stepped back up to the microphone to thank them!

We are all guilty of doing something like this, even if it is on a smaller scale. We want the praise and attention for ourselves, when in fact, we simply don't deserve it without recognizing who gave it to us. We need to remember that whether we achieve our goals on the athletic field or in the classroom, the one who makes it possible for us to accomplish these things is the Lord Jesus.

CHRIST IS OUR PROTECTION

BACKGROUND SCRIPTURE: Revelation 7:1-17
DEVOTIONAL READING: Psalm 121

KEY VERSE: These are they which came out of great tribulation, and have washed their robes, and made them white in the blood of the Lamb. Revelation 7:14.

KING JAMES VERSION

REVELATION 7:1 And after these things I saw four angels standing on the four corners of the earth, holding the four winds of the earth, that the wind should not blow on the earth, nor on the sea, nor on any tree. 2 And I saw another angel ascending from the east, having the seal of the living God: and he cried with a loud voice to the four angels, to whom it was given to hurt the earth and the sea, 3 Saying, Hurt not the earth, neither the sea, nor the trees, till we have sealed the servants of our God in their foreheads. . . . 9 After this I beheld, and, lo, a great multitude, which no man could number, of all nations, and kindreds, and people, and tongues, stood before the throne, and before the Lamb, clothed with white robes, and palms in their hands. . . .

13 And one of the elders answered, saying unto me, What are these which are arrayed in white robes? and whence came they? 14 And I said unto him, Sir, thou knowest. And he said to me, These are they which came out of great tribulation, and have washed their robes, and made them white in the blood of the Lamb.
15 Therefore are they before the throne of God, and serve him day and night in his temple: and he that sitteth on the throne shall dwell among them. 16 They shall hunger no more, neither thirst any more; neither shall the sun light on them, nor any heat. 17 For the Lamb which is in the midst of the throne shall feed them, and shall lead them unto living fountains of waters: and God shall wipe away all tears from their eyes.

NEW REVISED STANDARD VERSION

REVELATION 7:1 After this I saw four angels standing at the four corners of the earth, holding back the four winds of the earth so that no wind could blow on earth or sea or against any tree. 2 I saw another angel ascending from the rising of the sun, having the seal of the living God, and he called with a loud voice to the four angels who had been given power to damage earth and sea, 3 saying, "Do not damage the earth or the sea or the trees, until we have marked the servants of our God with a seal on their foreheads." . . .

9 After this I looked, and there was a great multitude that no one could count, from every nation, from all tribes and peoples and languages, standing before the throne and before the Lamb, robed in white, with palm branches in their hands. . . .

13 Then one of the elders addressed me, saying, "Who are these, robed in white, and where have they come from?" 14 I said to him, "Sir, you are the one that knows." Then he said to me, "These are they who have come out of the great ordeal; they have washed their robes and made them white in the blood of the Lamb.

15 For this reason they are before the throne of God,
and worship him day and night within his temple,
and the one who is seated on the throne will shelter them.

16 They will hunger no more, and thirst no more;
the sun will not strike them,
nor any scorching heat;

17 for the Lamb at the center of the throne will be their shepherd,
and he will guide them to springs of the water of life,
and God will wipe away every tear from their eyes."

9

HOME BIBLE READINGS

BACKGROUND

Our Scripture passage begins with the words *And after these things* (Rev. 7:1). This refers back to the events recorded in chapter 6. John remembered seeing the Lamb break four seals and unleash judgments in the form of four horsemen, who brought war, famine, disease, and death to the earth. When the fifth seal was broken, it revealed those who had been martyred for the faith and are awaiting vengeance on the enemies of God (6:1-11).

According to 6:12, after Christ opened the sixth seal, a severe earthquake occurred. As John looked, he saw a number of other cosmic disturbances take place. For instance, the sun became as dark as black sackcloth. (This was a rough, dark-colored fabric made from goat or camel hair and worn in times of trouble or sorrow.) The apostle also noted that the moon turned as red as blood and the stars fell to earth like unripe figs shaken loose by a windstorm. The sky also rolled up like a scroll and disappeared, and all the mountains and islands of the earth were dislodged from their places (6:13-14). These cosmic disturbances are predicted elsewhere in the Old Testament, and anticipate the return of Christ (see Isa. 13:10; 34:4; Joel 2:30-31). In the New Testament, the coming of the Son of Man soon follows extraordinary phenomena involving the sun, moon, and stars (see Luke 21:25-27).

Specifically, in Jesus' Olivet Discourse, He described the signs that would signal the approach of the end times (Matt. 24; Mark 13). His prediction of distant events closely parallels the seal judgments of Revelation 6. Jesus said the last days would be characterized by false messiahs, wars, famines, plagues, earthquakes, and death (Matt. 24:4-8, 23-28; Mark 13:5-8, 21-23). As the time of the end drew near, there would also be unimaginable suffering and anguish (Matt. 24:9-22; Mark 13:9-20). In the midst of all this calamity, the Messiah would return in great power and glory (Matt. 24:29-30; Mark 13:24-26).

With respect to the divine judgment the apostle John witnessed in his vision of the end of the age, all the people of the earth reel in fear. Kings and slaves, rich and poor, soldiers and civilians, all make desperate attempts to hide themselves from God. The mention of seven types of people in Revelation 6:15 suggests that the scope of His judgment is comprehensive. Perhaps at one time the people of the world felt safe from harm as they lived in rebellion against God. In the midst of the Lamb's judgment, however, not even the mountains and rocks of the earth are able to shield them from His wrath. Apart from God's grace, no one survives this time of judgment (6:16-17).

The wrath shown by the Father and the Son is a familiar phenomenon appearing throughout Scripture. Previous occurrences of God's wrath serve as a reminder that He will one day judge the wicked for all their evil deeds. Sadly, many will try to avoid the Lord, rather than abandon their sin and turn to Him in faith (see Rom. 1:18; 2 Thess. 2:5-10).

NOTES ON THE PRINTED TEXT

In John's vision he saw four angels, and each one was standing on one of the earth's four corners (Rev. 7:1). This reference does not suggest an outdated view of the shape of the globe. Rather, the expression was used in John's day in a way similar to how we might refer to the four points of the compass. The identity of the four angels is not clear. Some say they are the four living creatures mentioned in chapters 4 through 6, while others think they are four previously unidentified celestial beings. In either case, they function as God's agents of destruction.

The angels held back the four winds of judgment from blowing across the globe. As a result, not a leaf rustled in the trees, and the sea became as smooth as glass. The mention of four winds is reminiscent of similar expressions found in the Old Testament. For instance, in Jeremiah 49:36 four winds are used to symbolize military might, and in Ezekiel 37:9 four winds are used to represent every region of the globe (see also Dan. 8:8).

John saw another angel coming from the east. The phrase *ascending from the east* in Revelation 7:2 might also be rendered "ascending from the rising of the sun." This suggests that the sun's rays were beaming behind the angel as it made its journey skyward. The angel held *the seal of the living God.* In ancient times people placed a seal on a scroll or document to identify and protect its contents. When the Lord placed His seal on His servants, He identified them as His own and guaranteed their protection as the time of distress continued.

God gave the four angels power to harm the lands and seas of the earth. He prevented them from doing so, however, until His angels placed a seal on the foreheads of His servants (7:3). The Lord's ability to bring the judgments to a halt tells us that He is ultimately in control. Things cannot get out of hand. The Lord is able to accomplish His purposes even in the midst of what seems to be chaos.

In Ezekiel 9:4, it is suggested that God's mark of ownership and protection was the Hebrew letter *taw*, which looks like the English letter "X." Revelation 3:12, 14:1, and 22:4 suggest that God's name is the imprint He places on the foreheads of His servants. God's seal is the exact opposite of the mark of the beast mentioned in Revelation 13:16. These imprints place the people of the world in two distinct categories—those who are owned by the Lord and those who cooperate with Satan—both in action and attitude.

God placed His seal on the foreheads of 144,000 people from all the tribes of Israel (7:4-8). These saints could be a select group of people from the literal 12 tribes of Israel. Or they could be a specific number of believers whom God will in some way shield from a final period of distress. Others say the group is a symbolic number for the fullness of the people of God; that is, the Lord will bring *all* His followers safely to Himself. He will protect them either by removing them from the earth (this is called the Rapture) or by giving them strength they need to endure persecution and remain loyal to Him.

We can only imagine how stirred John was as he saw in heaven a vast crowd that was too large to count. Certainly the depth of their unity far exceeded any earthly counterpart. This throng was made up of people from every nation, tribe, people, and language, and they all stood before the throne of God and before the Lamb (7:9). Many ideas have been suggested regarding the identity of this host of believers. They could be the saved of all the ages, only Gentile believers, or martyrs killed during a final period of great distress, to name three common views. While the earth is about to feel the full force of God's wrath, these saints are standing before His throne, a place of safety and security. The Lord has accepted and honored them as His true servants.

The long white robes worn by the saints in heaven represent the purity, righteousness, and glory of Christ. The palm branches they carry represent total victory and unending joy. Everything about the scene points to the acceptance of these believers before God. They are celebrating triumph in a place of honor in the sacred presence of the Lord and the Lamb.

These truths are reflected in the chorus that the multitude in heaven shouted before the throne. They acknowledged that salvation comes only from God the Father and the Lamb, His Son (7:10). John noted that all the angels who stood around God's throne knelt in front of it with their faces to the ground. And the elders and the four living creatures knelt there with the angels. Together they worshiped God and sang a chorus of praise to Him (7:11).

Amen (7:12) introduces the sevenfold doxology, and *Amen* closes it. The heavenly choir first used the term to register their approval of the cry of the multitude, and they shout *Amen* at the end to affirm the reliability of each quality of God. The angels, elders, and four living creatures ascribe seven different attributes to God. Each term in the doxology is accented in the original language by the definite article "the"—in other words, *the* blessing, *the* glory, *the* wisdom, and so forth. The idea is that God is perfect in every way, and thus He deserves unlimited praise from His creatures.

When one of the elders asked John about the multitude (7:13), he humbly admitted that he did not know the answer. Based on the elder's response, some identify the *great tribulation* (7:14) with a final period of persecution shortly before the return of

Christ. Others, however, note that believers have endured affliction and grief throughout history, so that the entire church age can be seen as a time of tribulation. Perhaps John intended to comfort both first-century Christians as well as God's people living during a time of final crisis. The mention of *the blood of the Lamb* tells us that the people in this vast throng, like all believers, have been saved on the basis of Christ's sacrifice. The disputed identity of this group does not alter the hope we see here.

The elder revealed that the glorified state will include service for God in His heavenly sanctuary. Scripture does not tell us what that service will entail, but surely it will involve worship. Moreover, *dwell among* (7:15)—which can be rendered as "spread his tent over"—indicates that God will shelter and protect His people with His presence. The believers who have endured hardship will find rest and relief from their pain.

In the Lord's presence, Jesus' followers will experience joy, peace, and comfort (7:16). Furthermore, Christ will lead them to the waters of life (7:17). The imagery is that of a shepherd guiding his sheep to a freshwater spring in the desert. God will wipe away all tears from their eyes. In heaven, they will never experience pain, suffering, sickness, or death. In some way, the Lord will cause their past never to bring them remorse in the coming age. Those facing almost certain death at the hands of Roman authorities could take heart at this vivid glimpse of the glory that awaited them. And a vast number of Christians throughout history have also received courage to face life's trials by meditating on these words.

SUGGESTIONS TO TEACHERS

What will heaven be like? Will we just be sitting on clouds all day playing harps and singing? We do not have all the answers to our questions that we wish we did, but the Book of Revelation tells us what rewards believers will find when they reach paradise. Three stand out in this week's lesson.

1. NO MORE SEPARATION FROM GOD. Revelation pictures believers standing by the throne of God, worshiping Him *day and night in his temple* (7:15). There will be no barriers in heaven between God and His people, and no separation between believers due to nations, tribes, or languages. While we cannot exactly have that now, remind your students that we can see some of the glory of God reflected in our own lives when we faithfully serve Him, and we should work toward breaking down those barriers that separate believers here on earth.

2. NO MORE HUNGER OR THIRST. All our basic physical needs will disappear in heaven. We will no longer be hungry or tired or thirsty. As the Good Shepherd who leads His sheep to the greenest pasture, Jesus will guide us to the *living fountains of waters* (7:17), where we will not want. While physical needs may be paramount in our lives today, they will be nonexistent in heaven.

3. NO MORE SUFFERING. The Scripture that has comforted millions of believers who have lost loved ones tells us that one day *God shall wipe away all tears* (7:17).

The suffering of this life, and our heart-breaking separation from other believers who have died, will end in heaven one day. While it is sometimes hard for us to remember, our life today is only temporary. The everlasting joys of eternity are really just around the corner.

<table>
<tr><td>
FOR ADULTS
</td><td>
■ **TOPIC:** Source of Security

■ **QUESTIONS:** 1. Why were the four angels holding back the four winds of the earth? 2. What were these angels told not to damage? 3. What
</td></tr>
</table>

sorts of people made up the great multitude John saw? 4. What is the great tribulation mentioned in Revelation 7:14? 5. Why will the great multitude in heaven hunger no more?

■ **ILLUSTRATIONS:**

No More Weeping. "God, where were you in Paris?" asked a church leader named Josef Homeyer, his voice quavering with emotion as he addressed 350 people at a worship service in Hanover, Germany, after a Concorde airliner burst into flames and crashed outside Paris on July 25, 2000, killing 113 people, most of them German tourists, Reuters reported. "Why have you deserted us? Our hearts are heavy."

Homeyer then reminded the mourners of the assurance of the resurrection. After him, a church leader named Horst Hirschler reminded the audience of a similar tragic incident two years earlier, when a high-speed train crashed near Hanover, taking the lives of more than 100 people. One minute vacationers were happily looking forward to the time of their lives, and the next minute they were faced with death, the pastor said. "What a tragic transformation."

The only real consolation is that even the Son of God had asked His Father in heaven, "Why hast thou forsaken me" before He died on the cross, Hirschler said. He assured his audience that Jesus Christ is with those who are feeling desperate and who mourn over the loss of their loved ones. "You will never fall deeper than into God's hand."

Enduring Hope in God's Promises. Victor Hugo, in his story "Ninety-Three," tells of a ship caught in a dangerous storm on the high seas. At the height of the storm, the frightened sailors heard a terrible crashing noise below the deck. They knew at once that this new noise came from a cannon, part of the ship's cargo, that had broken loose. It was moving back and forth with the swaying of the ship, crashing into the side of the ship with terrible impact. Knowing that it could cause the ship to sink, two brave sailors volunteered to make the dangerous attempt to retie the loose cannon. They knew the danger of a shipwreck from the cannon was greater than the fury of the storm.

That is like human life. Storms of life may blow about us, but it is not these exterior storms that pose the gravest danger. It is the terrible corruption that can exist within us that can overwhelm us. The furious storm outside may be overwhelming but what is going on inside can pose the greater threat to our lives. Our only hope lies in conquering that wild enemy. Trusting God and being assured of His promises of heavenly glory are our only hope of stilling the tempest that can harm our souls and cripple our lives.

Former Things Shall Not Be Remembered. A couple of years ago, Pastor Jeff Wallace discovered an incident at the parsonage that left his daughter, Gracie, in tears. Jeff had left a little lavender-colored ceramic planter out on the deck. But this little planter was special. It had "Baby" molded into the side, and when he wound it up, a music box inside played a lullaby.

Some dear friends of Jeff had given this planter to him 11 years before just after Gracie was born. It must have been the rising and falling of the temperatures over several seasons that somehow shattered that little treasure into multiple pieces. Gracie glared at the pieces in her hands, tears streaming from her eyes at her sense of the loss.

We all feel saddened when an earthly treasure is taken from us. But the assurance of future glory in heaven can go a long way toward helping us through a trying situation.

FOR YOUTH

■ **TOPIC:** Perfect Security

■ **QUESTIONS:** 1. Where were the four angels standing? 2. Who brought the seal of God, and what did he say? 3. Where did the great multitude come from? 4. What was the multitude wearing? 5. What will believers be doing or experiencing in heaven?

■ **ILLUSTRATIONS:**

Blessed Assurance. Fanny Crosby (1820–1915) was one of the most prolific hymnists in history. Though blinded at six weeks of age, she wrote over 8,000 hymns. About her blindness, she said, "It seemed intended by the blessed providence of God that I should be blind all my life, and thank Him for the dispensation. If perfect earthly sight were offered me tomorrow I would not accept it. I might not have sung hymns to the praise of God if I had been distracted by the beautiful and interesting things about me."

In her lifetime, Fanny Crosby was one of the best known women in the United States. To this day, the vast majority of American hymnals contain her work. When she died, her tombstone carried the words, "Aunt Fanny" and "Blessed assurance, Jesus is mine. Oh, what a foretaste of glory divine." Such thoughts remind us of the joys of heaven, as foretold in Revelation 7:15-17.

Ready to Die. In her book, *I Heard the Owl Call My Name*, Margaret Craven tells the story of a cleric's visit to a young minister serving a tribe of Native Americans in

British Columbia. The cleric knew and loved this tribe, and enjoyed their feasting and dancing. At the end of his visit he tried to describe his feelings to the minister.

"Always when I leave the village," the cleric said slowly, "I try to define what it means to me, why it sends me back to the world refreshed and confident. Always I fail. It is so simple, it is difficult. When I try to put it into words, it comes out one of those unctuous, over-pious platitudes at which clerics are expected to excel."

They both laughed.

"But when I reach here and see the great scar where the inlet side [of the river] shows its bones, for a moment I know."

The minister asked, "What, my lord?"

"That for me it has always been easier here, where only the fundamentals count, to learn what every man must learn in this world."

"And that, my lord?"

"Enough of the meaning of life to be ready to die."

THE FINAL BANQUET

BACKGROUND SCRIPTURE: Revelation 19:1-21
DEVOTIONAL READING: Psalm 148:1-14

KEY VERSE: Alleluia: for the Lord God omnipotent reigneth. Revelation 19:6.

KING JAMES VERSION

REVELATION 19:5 And a voice came out of the throne, saying, Praise our God, all ye his servants, and ye that fear him, both small and great. 6 And I heard as it were the voice of a great multitude, and as the voice of many waters, and as the voice of mighty thunderings, saying, Alleluia: for the Lord God omnipotent reigneth. 7 Let us be glad and rejoice, and give honour to him: for the marriage of the Lamb is come, and his wife hath made herself ready. 8 And to her was granted that she should be arrayed in fine linen, clean and white: for the fine linen is the righteousness of saints. 9 And he saith unto me, Write, Blessed are they which are called unto the marriage supper of the Lamb. And he saith unto me, These are the true sayings of God. 10 And I fell at his feet to worship him. And he said unto me, See thou do it not: I am thy fellowservant, and of thy brethren that have the testimony of Jesus: worship God: for the testimony of Jesus is the spirit of prophecy.

NEW REVISED STANDARD VERSION

REVELATION 19:5 And from the throne came a voice saying,
"Praise our God,
    all you his servants,
and all who fear him,
    small and great."
6 Then I heard what seemed to be the voice of a great multitude, like the sound of many waters and like the sound of mighty thunderpeals, crying out,
"Hallelujah!
For the Lord our God
    the Almighty reigns.
7 Let us rejoice and exult
    and give him the glory,
for the marriage of the Lamb has come,
    and his bride has made herself ready;
8 to her it has been granted to be clothed
    with fine linen, bright and pure"—
for the fine linen is the righteous deeds of the saints.
9 And the angel said to me, "Write this: Blessed are those who are invited to the marriage supper of the Lamb." And he said to me, "These are true words of God." 10 Then I fell down at his feet to worship him, but he said to me, "You must not do that! I am a fellow servant with you and your comrades who hold the testimony of Jesus. Worship God! For the testimony of Jesus is the spirit of prophecy."

10

HOME BIBLE READINGS

Monday, April 30	Matthew 22:1-14	*Parable of the Wedding Banquet*
Tuesday, May 1	Revelation 15:1-5	*The Song of the Lamb*
Wednesday, May 2	Revelation 11:15-19	*He Will Reign Forever*
Thursday, May 3	Psalm 148:1-6	*The Heavens Praise*
Friday, May 4	Psalm 148:7-14	*The Earth Praises*
Saturday, May 5	Revelation 19:1-5	*Hallelujah!*
Sunday, May 6	Revelation 19:6-10	*Give God Glory*

BACKGROUND

The triumph of the Lamb, which is the key theme of Revelation 19, has as its backdrop the fall of Babylon, which is the focus of chapters 17 and 18. Some think that Babylon is a code name for either Jerusalem or Rome. In John's day, the latter was the epitome of opposition to God and His people. Others maintain that some notorious ancient city—possibly Babylon, Rome, Tyre, or Jerusalem—will be rebuilt in the end times as the capitol of a great world empire headed up by a literal Antichrist. Still others think that Babylon is used metaphorically to represent the corrupt political, commercial, social, and religious system of the world. Regardless of how literal or figurative Babylon is understood to be, the name remains a fitting label for all that is corrupt within humankind and counterfeit to the Lamb.

In chapter 17, John provided an in-depth look at the depraved character of civilized humanity apart from Christ, and this serves as the reason the Lamb had to judge Babylon. A legal context predominates this portion of Revelation. Indeed, the scene is of a universal courtroom in which a lawsuit is brought forward. The followers of Christ are the plaintiffs, Babylon is the defendant, and the Lamb is the Judge. The indictment is the exploitation and murder of the innocent in the interest of power and idolatry. In light of all the evidence that is presented, Babylon is found guilty and the Judge pronounces the sentence against Babylon.

These observations suggest that throughout history unregenerate humanity has been in rebellion against the Messiah. This understanding of events is highlighted in 17:12-14. An interpreting angel revealed to John that the 10 horns of the scarlet beast represented 10 kings who had not yet risen to power (see Dan. 7:7, 24). For a brief moment they rule with the beast, and agree to give their power and authority to it. Together the beast and these rulers wage war against Christ (see Rev. 16:12-16; 19:17-21). Nevertheless, He crushes their insurrection, for He is the supreme Lord and sovereign King. The uniform message throughout Revelation is that the divine Messiah's triumph vindicates the faith of His followers, whom He had called, chosen, and enabled to remain loyal to Him.

Chapter 18 gives more explicit and detailed information concerning the demise of the harlot, who is called Babylon the Great in 17:5. The mournful chant that appears in 18:2-3 draws heavily upon the language of the Old Testament to herald the fall of Babylon (see Isa. 21:9; Jer. 51:6-10). Moreover, in the verses that follow, John adopted expressions typically found in ancient funeral lamentations to add realism to what he saw. In the first dirge (Rev. 18:9-10), the *monarchs* of the world mourned as they saw the smoke rising from Babylon's charred remains. In the second dirge (18:11-17a), the *merchants* of the world wept over the fact that they could no longer buy the exotic and lavish items Babylon once offered. In the third dirge (18:17b-19), the *mariners* of the world cried out in despair over the ruin of Babylon.

In 18:20, John shifted his attention from the forces of evil to those that were good. Everyone in heaven was called to rejoice with Christ's followers—the saints, prophets, and apostles—over the downfall of Babylon, for that evil system had persecuted and murdered countless believers. The Lamb's people were not deriving grim satisfaction over the judgment of the wicked. Rather, the saints praised God for vindicating their faith and bringing justice to pass.

Revelation 18:21-24 records a doom song of Babylon. At the second advent (see 19:11-21), Christ utterly destroys this once powerful entity so that it never rises again. No music, workers, machinery, light, or happiness is found in Babylon anymore. The Messiah breaks her spell over the world and repays her for her murderous treatment of His people (see Ezek. 24:7; Rev. 6:10; 17:6; 19:2).

NOTES ON THE PRINTED TEXT

In John's vision, he remembered hearing a vast crowd in heaven shouting *Alleluia* (Rev. 19:1). This word is derived from the Hebrew verb *hâlal*, which means "to be boastful" or "to praise." The Hebrews joined the word *Yah*, which is the shorted form of Yahweh (the covenant name of the Lord) to the verb *hâlal*. The combined phrase biblically meant "Praise the Lord!"

The celestial throng praised God for His salvation. This includes more than just Christ's deliverance of believers from sin and all its dire consequences. Salvation here denotes Jesus' final victory over the principalities of this world that crucified Him and murdered His followers. The heavenly choir declared that glory and power belonged to God alone, for His judgment of the wicked was honest and fair. This is seen in the way He punished the filthy prostitute. As a lover of iniquity, she had corrupted humanity with her shameful deeds. And as an enemy of righteousness, she had murdered believers. Thus, it was right for the Lord to make her pay for her crimes (19:2).

John once again heard the throng in heaven praise God for overthrowing Babylon. They noted that the smoke from her charred body will never stop rising (19:3). It is possible that these worshipers are an angelic host. They could also be the saved of all ages or martyrs killed during a final period of great distress. Regardless of the crowd's exact identity, their example underscores the importance of giving praise to God for His love.

As God sat on His throne, the 24 elders and the four living creatures prostrated themselves before Him in worship. They complemented this action by shouting, *Amen; Alleluia* (19:4). A voice from the throne then commanded all God's servants to give praise to the Lord. The worshipers are not limited to one group. All believers from every social class and economic level joined together in revering God (19:5). This reminds us that no one is more spiritually elite than others in the divine kingdom.

John next heard what sounded like the shout of a huge crowd, the roar of mighty ocean waves, and the crash of loud thunder all mixed together (19:6). A vast multitude praised God for being the sovereign and all-powerful King. He deserved unending praise because His triumph over evil set the stage for the wedding of the Lamb. Indeed, the Savior's bride had made herself ready for this momentous event (19:7).

Scripture teaches that the church—which consists of all true believers—is the bride of Christ (see 2 Cor. 11:2; Eph. 5:25-32). In a sense, the church right now is betrothed to Jesus and awaits the day when He will claim her as His bride. At His return, He will join Himself to His people in intimacy, love, and joy. Throughout the centuries, the Savior's bride has been preparing herself for the day when she will meet her Lord. In contrast to the gaudy clothing worn by the prostitute (see Rev. 17:4; 18:16), Jesus' bride is wearing a wedding dress made of pure and fine linen. This garment symbolizes the upright deeds believers have done in the Messiah's power and for His glory (19:8; see Eph. 2:10; Phil. 2:13).

At the command of an angel, John wrote that God's blessing rests on all whom He invites to the wedding feast of the Lamb. What the Lord has pledged is true and will surely take place (Rev. 19:9). The Near Eastern marriage banquet is a fitting symbol of the celebration that will occur when Jesus consummates His union with the church. This joyous feast stands in sharp contrast to the carnage noted in 19:17-18. While eternal rewards await the righteous, unending loss awaits the wicked.

Perhaps feeling overwhelmed by what he heard and saw, John knelt at the feet of the angel and began to worship him. But the angel stopped him, explaining that he was a servant of God, as were John and his fellow Christians. They not only believed the witness Jesus bore in His life and death but also told others about their faith in the Savior (19:10). The angel urged John to worship God, who is the source of all genuine revelation. The prophecies of Scripture, in turn, ultimately concern the Messiah. Of course, the message He declared is the essence of prophetic truth. Angels, on the other hand, are God's servants whom He sends to help believers (see Heb. 1:14).

The Christ-centered emphasis of Revelation 19:10 should not be overlooked. The focus of the last book of Scripture is ultimately on the Messiah. This emphasis is found in 19:11-21, where the Lamb returns as the divine King. His glorious presence, ability to judge, and sovereignty to rule are stressed in the descriptions John provided of Him.

We learn that Christ's eyes were like flames of fire, a description that symbolized His great power and wisdom. Jesus wore many crowns on His head, after the manner of ancient kings who wore multiple crowns to represent their authority over many nations (19:12). Moreover, the apostle saw a name written on Christ that only He knew. While interpretations vary regarding what John meant, surely it indicates that there is much about the Messiah we are not able to understand. His nature and person are so exalted that they transcend our full comprehension.

In his vision, John saw the Lamb clothed with a robe that had been dipped in blood. The mention of blood may refer to Jesus' sacrificial death. Another possibility is that John was talking about the blood shed by Christ's enemies, whom He will slay in battle (19:13). The Father will give the victorious Redeemer a designation that sums up all that He is, namely, *The Word of God.* To His followers, the Messiah is above all else, the revelation of the one who is eternal.

Christ will not return alone. Behind Him will be the armies of heaven clothed in white and riding upon white horses. These armies will be angels, believers, or a combination of both (19:14). Their Lord has a sharp sword proceeding out of His mouth. This sword possibly is a reference to the Gospel. It certainly is a symbol of the conqueror's might to defeat those who refuse to accept God's truth (19:15). The Messiah will rule the nations with an iron scepter and trample His enemies as in a winepress, causing their lifeblood to pour out. This image calls to mind people trampling grapes to make them into wine. The winepress is a symbol of the wrath of God (see Isa. 63:3).

On Christ's robe and on His thigh is written the name *KING OF KINGS, AND LORD OF LORDS* (Rev. 19:16). This title sums up who Jesus is in relation to the rest of the universe. In a civilization where there was an emperor and many lesser kings and lords, John wanted his readers to know that there is one who is the most powerful of all. Every human ruler is subservient to Him. And one day the Messiah's kingship will be fully exercised.

SUGGESTIONS TO TEACHERS

John called on the saints to endure and resist becoming one with the world. He also recorded how much God longed for those who are caught in the world's snares to come over to His side. These people are not only the enemies of God and Christians, but also the captives of Satan and his schemes. They are "prisoners of war" (POWs) in a cosmic struggle between good and evil, prisoners that all Christians can help release and repatriate to the "good" side. Why should we call them POWs? This acronym describes their current condition.

1. POWERLESS. Without the power of the Holy Spirit in their lives, the unsaved remain Satan's prisoners. Can they receive God's power and be released? Certainly, but we must help them, by explaining the Gospel to them and by showing them how wonderful a regenerated life in Christ can be.

2. OPPRESSED. What keeps people as slaves to Satan? Paul said they have a disobedient spirit that keeps them following the desires of the flesh, rather than the Holy Spirit (Eph. 2:2-3). The unsaved are oppressed by the desire to always serve themselves and do whatever their hearts desire. Leading them to trust in Christ can lift that burden from their lives and bring them into a relationship with the one who bears our burdens for us.

3. WITHOUT HOPE. People with no hope have nothing to live for except today. They do not see a future outside the fence of Satan's confinement. They need Christians who will show them that there is an eternal side to life, and that a grand and glorious future awaits those who will be with the Lord forever. Whether or not they realize it, in this life they are making eternal choices, and we need to help them see the right choices to make.

FOR ADULTS	■ **TOPIC:** Finding Community ■ **QUESTIONS:** 1. Why were the saints of heaven directed to give praise

to God? 2. In what sense did the sovereign Lord reign? 3. To what does the marriage of the Lamb refer? 4. What did the fine linen worn by the saints represent? 5. Whom was John exhorted to worship and why?

■ **ILLUSTRATIONS:**

Part of the Family. Being close to Christ, and Him to you, is something like living in a small town. My spouse and I lived in town of about 3,000 people for over 12 years. The town was basically a mile square, with one stoplight on Main Street. Just like the joke says, we really didn't need to use our turn signal while driving because everyone knew where we were going. And if I forgot to use my seatbelt, the children I taught at school would tell me about it the next day. If we missed Sunday morning church, we would receive a call that afternoon, asking if we were OK.

This kind of closeness helped us feel like we belonged there. We were members of the family, and our actions were noticed by everyone. Christ wants us to belong to Him, and be part of His spiritual family. He wants our lives to reflect Him now, and He wants us to be among those who are blessed at the end of time.

How Can I Find God? There is an ancient tale about a young man who was seeking God. He went to an old sage for help. "How can I find God?" he asked the wise man. The sage took him to a nearby river. They waded out into the deep water. Soon the water was up just under their chins. Suddenly, the old man seized the young man by the neck and pushed him under the water. He held the young man there until the young man was fighting for his life.

Finally, the old man released his grip and allowed the young man to surface. Coughing water from his lungs and still gasping for air, the young man asked the old man indignantly, "What did that have to do with my finding God?"

The old man asked him quietly, "While you were under the water, what did you want more than anything else?" The young man thought for a minute and then answered, "I wanted air. I wanted air more than anything else." The old man replied, "When you want God as much as you wanted air, you will find Him."

Those who have found God know how strong the desire is to want more of Him. He becomes as much a part of our lives as the air that we breathe. A relationship this close helps develop feelings of belonging to Him and the community of the redeemed.

Life Is like a Deck Chair. In a *Peanuts* comic strip, there was a conversation between Lucy and Charlie Brown. Lucy said that life is like a deck chair. Some place it so they can see where they are going; some place it so they can see where they have been; and some place it so they can see where they are at present. Charlie Brown's reply: "I can't even get mine unfolded."

Do you need help unfolding your "deck chair" and placing it where you belong? In other words, have you found your purpose and direction in life? When we put our lives in God's hands, we may not know everything that will happen to us in this life, but we can be assured that He will stay beside us now and that we will be with Him throughout eternity.

 FOR YOUTH

■ TOPIC: A Great Party!

■ QUESTIONS: 1. What did the voice from the throne declare? 2. Why were the saints exhorted to rejoice? 3. What was the wedding of the Lamb? 4. What did the angel instruct John to write? 5. What is the ultimate focus of biblical prophecy?

■ **ILLUSTRATIONS:**

Found Feline. In July 1994, Carol Ann Timmel carefully placed her beloved cat, Tabitha, in a special pet carrier provided by the airliner for the flight from New York to Los Angeles. But when Timmel arrived in Los Angeles and tried to pick up her cat, she could not find the animal. The airline staff could not explain how Tabitha could be missing.

Timmel then filed a lawsuit to force the airliner to conduct a thorough search, but finally dropped it when the company agreed to ground the plane for 24 hours. Meanwhile, 12 days had elapsed. The aircraft had flown from New York to Los Angeles, New York to San Juan, Puerto Rico, and New York to Miami. Newspapers picked up the story of Timmel's determined effort to find her pet, and some ran a daily "Cat Watch" with photos of Tabitha.

Finally, 12 days and 12,000 miles after Tabitha had gotten lost in the belly of a jumbo jet, the high-flying cat was found. After being retrieved from a hiding place in the drop ceiling of the jet's cargo area, Tabitha emerged into the arms of its joyful owner. The pet had been without food or water for the entire time and lost two pounds, though was otherwise fine.

The airline president estimated the company had invested 100 staff hours in fruit-less searches for Tabitha, but recognized Timmel's love for her cat and backed her tire-less effort to find the animal. Everyone celebrated finding Tabitha! God is even more determined to bring us back to Him. And the celebration in heaven is far more joyous when we are reconciled to Him through Christ.

A Reason to Rejoice. In May 1998, Robert Ballard found the *USS Yorktown*. Ballard, who 10 years before had discovered the lost ocean liner, *Titanic*, had been searching for the *Yorktown*, a World War II aircraft carrier that sank 56 years earlier after a Japanese torpedo attack.

The expedition was the largest and most technologically challenging undersea search ever mounted by the United States Navy and the National Geographic Society. For several weeks while aboard the research vessel *Laney Chouset*, Ballard and his crew crisscrossed 300 square miles of the Pacific ocean north of Midway Island. They watched and waited as a towed mapping device and an underwater drone scanned the ocean bottom miles below. The wreckage was finally discovered 16,650 feet down, which is nearly one mile further down than the wreckage of the *Titanic*.

If people will go to such extremes to find an old sunken aircraft carrier, imagine the extent to which God has gone to seek and save us! Though lost, we can be found and reconciled to Him by trusting in Christ. Now that is a reason to rejoice!

Revolution Ending. In years gone by, adolescents lived for the next wild party on their calendar. But these days, the so-called "sexual revolution" seems to be slowing, and perhaps, even ending. Mark Judge of *Insight* magazine cites surveys (including one of 200,000 teens done by *USA Today*) that demonstrates a "decline" in sexual activity among teens. Literally thousands more young people are saying no to premar-ital sex, are waiting for marriage, and are returning to more traditional dating and courtship patterns.

A growing tide of problems, such as sexually transmitted diseases, AIDS, divorce, and a culture saturated with sex, plus a more affirmative effort by churches, has led a younger generation to adopt a different perspective on physical intimacy. As a follow-er of Christ, you will want to consider what the Bible teaches about this. Let your love for God and commitment to His Word be demonstrated by your efforts to remain chaste.

OUR NEW HOME

BACKGROUND SCRIPTURE: Revelation 21:1-8
DEVOTIONAL READING: 2 Peter 3:10-18

KEY VERSE: Behold, the tabernacle of God is with men, and he will dwell with them, and they shall be his people, and God himself shall be with them, and be their God. Revelation 21:3.

KING JAMES VERSION

REVELATION 21:1 And I saw a new heaven and a new earth: for the first heaven and the first earth were passed away; and there was no more sea. 2 And I John saw the holy city, new Jerusalem, coming down from God out of heaven, prepared as a bride adorned for her husband. 3 And I heard a great voice out of heaven saying, Behold, the tabernacle of God is with men, and he will dwell with them, and they shall be his people, and God himself shall be with them, and be their God. 4 And God shall wipe away all tears from their eyes; and there shall be no more death, neither sorrow, nor crying, neither shall there be any more pain: for the former things are passed away. 5 And he that sat upon the throne said, Behold, I make all things new. And he said unto me, Write: for these words are true and faithful. 6 And he said unto me, It is done. I am Alpha and Omega, the beginning and the end. I will give unto him that is athirst of the fountain of the water of life freely. 7 He that overcometh shall inherit all things; and I will be his God, and he shall be my son. 8 But the fearful, and unbelieving, and the abominable, and murderers, and whoremongers, and sorcerers, and idolaters, and all liars, shall have their part in the lake which burneth with fire and brimstone: which is the second death.

NEW REVISED STANDARD VERSION

REVELATION 21:1 Then I saw a new heaven and a new earth; for the first heaven and the first earth had passed away, and the sea was no more. 2 And I saw the holy city, the new Jerusalem, coming down out of heaven from God, prepared as a bride adorned for her husband. 3 And I heard a loud voice from the throne saying,

"See, the home of God is among mortals.
He will dwell with them as their God;
they will be his peoples,
and God himself will be with them;
4 he will wipe every tear from their eyes.
Death will be no more;
mourning and crying and pain will be no more,
for the first things have passed away."

5 And the one who was seated on the throne said, "See, I am making all things new." Also he said, "Write this, for these words are trustworthy and true." 6 Then he said to me, "It is done! I am the Alpha and the Omega, the beginning and the end. To the thirsty I will give water as a gift from the spring of the water of life. 7 Those who conquer will inherit these things, and I will be their God and they will be my children. 8 But as for the cowardly, the faithless, the polluted, the murderers, the fornicators, the sorcerers, the idolaters, and all liars, their place will be in the lake that burns with fire and sulfur, which is the second death."

11

Monday, May 7	Philippians 3:17-21	*Our Citizenship Is in Heaven*
Tuesday, May 8	1 Corinthians 15:20-28	*The Coming of the Kingdom*
Wednesday, May 9	2 Corinthians 5:1-10	*Our Heavenly Dwelling*
Thursday, May 10	Hebrews 11:10-16	*Longing for a New Home*
Friday, May 11	2 Peter 3:10-18	*The Day of the Lord*
Saturday, May 12	Isaiah 65:17-19, 23-25	*New Heavens and a New Earth*
Sunday, May 13	Revelation 21:1-8	*God Will Dwell among Us*

BACKGROUND

The events highlighted in Revelation 20 form the prelude to the new heaven and new earth John recounted in chapter 21. The apostle saw an angel descend from heaven holding both the key to the Abyss and a heavy chain. The angel grabbed Satan, bound him, threw him into the bottomless pit, and then shut and locked the pit's entrance. This will prevent the devil from further deceiving the nations for a thousand years. Afterward, he will be released for a short while (21:1-3).

There are two ways to understand the binding of Satan. Some think this refers to the results of Christ's death and resurrection that has already restricted the devil's power to deceive (see John 12:31; Col. 2:15). Others associate Satan's binding with the beginning of an extraordinary future age of peace and prosperity (see 1 Thess. 2:18-19; 1 Pet. 5:8-10). There are also differences concerning the reference to 1,000 years in Revelation 20:2. Some think John referred to a literal period of 1,000 years in which Christ will reign on earth. Others think the apostle was speaking metaphorically about an indefinite interval in which Christ rules from either heaven or earth.

John did not identify the occupants on the thrones mentioned in 20:4. While they could be angels, they are most likely believers—whether the 12 apostles, the resurrected martyrs from a final period of distress, or the redeemed throughout history. God allows these people to exercise judgment and rule with Christ (see Matt. 19:28; 1 Cor. 6:2-3; Rev. 3:21). Moreover, John saw the souls of believers who had died remaining loyal to Christ. Despite the abuse they received from the forces of darkness, they refused to give up. God will vindicate their faith when He raises them from the dead and allows them to reign with Christ.

John called this the first resurrection (Rev. 20:5). According to some, John referred to a bodily resurrection of all believers. When Christ returns, He will raise them from the dead and allow them to reign with Him in His kingdom (Luke 14:14; John 5:29; 1 Cor. 15:51-57; 1 Thess. 4:13-18). According to others, John referred to a spiritual resurrection of believers. It takes place either at the moment of regeneration or when one goes to be with Christ at the time of bodily death (John 5:24-25; 2 Cor. 5:8; Phil. 1:23). John explained that God did not resurrect the remainder of the dead until the end of the 1000-year period. It's not clear whether this group is restricted to the wicked or includes both saved and unsaved people. In either case, the participants in the first resurrection are blessed and holy, for they are immune to the *second death* (Rev. 20:6)—namely, eternal separation from God (see 20:14). They will serve as priests of the Father and the Son, and they will reign with Christ in His kingdom.

When the thousand years end, Satan will be released from his prison. Despite the long passage of time, wickedness and rebellion will still characterize the devil and unregenerate humanity. Satan tricks the world's nations to join him in a final assault against God and His people. John probably had in mind the language of Ezekiel 38—39 when he said that Gog and Magog symbolize a vast evil horde under Satan's control (Rev. 20:7-8).

It's unclear whether the apostle was referring to a virtual or figurative battle when he described the forces of evil surrounding the beloved community of God's redeemed. There is no doubt about the outcome, however. Fire from heaven devours the attacking armies. Then Satan will be placed in the lake of burning sulfur, where he—along with the beast and the false prophet—will spend eternity in torment (20:9-10). Unlike human victories, Christ's triumph does not end on the battlefield but before the pure and holy throne of God. Earth and heaven will flee from the Lord's presence, yet there will be no place they can hide (20:11). Some think it's at this time that God will destroy the present heaven and earth and replace them with a new heaven and earth.

John saw the dead, both small and great, standing before God. No great reputation or noteworthy lifestyle will exempt anyone. Similarly, there is no human life so humble or insignificant that God will overlook it. It is not clear who will actually stand before God's throne. Some say the judgment involves only unbelievers, while others maintain that both saved and unsaved will appear before God. Either way, God's judgment will be fair and impartial. Only those who have trusted in Christ will be saved from eternal condemnation.

John saw God open several books that contain a record of the deeds of every human being. The Lord will judge all people according to their works. This did not mean that salvation is based on good deeds, but that God keeps a record of what people do in this life. Then God will open *the book of life* (20:12), which records the names of those who trusted in Christ for salvation. The Lord will deliver from judgment only those whose names appear in this book. For those who spurn Christ, all that remains is for God to condemn them.

John saw the sea giving up the dead who were in it, and death and Hades (the realm of the dead) also giving up their dead. The idea is that no one will escape judgment. God will cast death and Hades into the eternal lake of fire. John called this the second death because it is the final state of everlasting torment (20:13-14). The documents detailing humanity's deeds will be a sobering witness that cannot be refuted. God will banish forever from His presence those who do not have their names listed in the Lamb's book of life. No unsaved person will escape this fate (20:15).

NOTES ON THE PRINTED TEXT

Revelation 21 shifts the focus from time to eternity, especially with respect to the new creation that awaits believers. John related that he saw *a new heaven and a new earth* (21:1). These are total replacements for their old counterparts, which God had destroyed. He evidently did this to eliminate any corrupting presence or influence of sin (see 2 Pet. 3:7, 10-13).

God will do away with the vast and mysterious seas. In the Old Testament, the sea was a symbol for the agitation and restlessness associated with evil (see Isa. 57:20; Jer. 49:23). In Revelation, the sea is the source of the satanic beast and the burial site for the dead (see Rev. 13:1; 20:13). In the eternal state, there can be no real or symbolic place for this seething cauldron of wickedness. What John saw is consistent with Isaiah's reference to the new heaven and a new earth (Isa. 65:17). The apostle, however, was not thinking merely of a world free of sin and hardness of heart. John's vision was a creation new in all its qualities.

The apostle's attention next turned to the holy city—the new Jerusalem—which God sent down out of heaven (Rev. 21:2). The Lord magnificently adorned the new Jerusalem (the bride) for her husband (the groom). The implication here is that the city surpassed the beauty of everything else God had made. Some think the new Jerusalem will be a literal city where God's people dwell for all eternity. Others think the holy city is a symbol of the Christian community in heaven. In either case, it is clear that a new world is coming, and it will be glorious beyond imagination.

The adornment of the new Jerusalem as a bride for her husband points back to the marriage of the church to the Redeemer (19:7-9). As before, the focus is on believers having intimate fellowship with the Messiah throughout eternity. For the followers of Jesus, eternal life does not begin when we die and go to heaven. It starts here and now. The Savior wants us to enjoy to the fullest extent the new vistas of joy, satisfaction, and fruitfulness that the presence of His indwelling Holy Spirit makes possible.

A loud voice from the heavenly throne revealed that in the eternal state God will permanently dwell (or tabernacle) among the redeemed of all ages. They will be His people, and He will be their God (21:3). The voice also disclosed that five scourges of human existence will not exist in the eternal state—tears, death, sorrow, crying, and pain. The new order of things will eliminate all these forms of sadness (21:4).

The sovereign Lord, while seated on His holy throne, declared that He was doing away with the old order and making everything new. The apostle John was told to write down what God had said, for His words were true and trustworthy (21:5). Next, the Lord declared that everything was finished. As the *Alpha and Omega, the beginning and the end* (21:6), God is all-powerful and eternal. He embraces all things and transcends all time and space.

The Lord promised to give water from the life-giving fountain to everyone who was thirsty. This promise is a vivid reminder of the refreshment and satisfaction believers will enjoy in heaven. In the eternal state, God will satisfy the yearnings of the soul. This assurance is grounded in the Lord's own nature. Those who overcome in this life will receive an eternal inheritance and an eternal relationship. They will be the eternal children of the eternal God (21:7).

Life for the redeemed in heaven will be characterized by virtue and purity. It should come as no surprise, then, that the Lord will ban from heaven all who are characterized by the vices listed in 21:8. These include those who spurn the Messiah in cowardice as well as those who refuse to believe in Him. Also mentioned are the corrupt, the murderers, the immoral, the sorcerers, the idolaters, and the liars. The habitually wretched actions of these people will be irrefutable evidence that they are not saved (see Matt. 7:21-23). Their consignment to the eternal lake of fire is a just end to a life characterized by the abominations of the world.

SUGGESTIONS TO TEACHERS

What will increase the sales of almost any product on the market? Add to the product's name the words "New and Improved!" People seem to be fascinated by new things, so John's vision of a new heaven, a new earth, and a new Jerusalem probably intrigues us. There are at least three reasons for our fascination, and these three reasons can also help us rethink our Christian lives on this side of eternity:

1. NEW THINGS ARE UNTARNISHED. The *new heaven* (Rev. 21:1) and the *new earth* that are coming will only faintly resemble what exists now. None of the problems that are here now will be found in eternity. In much the same way, Paul said, when we trust in Christ for salvation, we become new persons. We are not the same anymore, for our old life is gone, having been replaced by a new life (2 Cor. 5:17). God wants to always be at work in our lives through the Holy Spirit, creating in us new people who are genuinely transformed (Rom. 12:2).

2. NEW THINGS ARE FRESH. New life in springtime brings fresh leaves and plants, not a recoloring or reworking of what was there last year. The old fall leaves, for example, do not suddenly change color and reattach themselves to the branches. Thus, a plant always has new opportunities to grow and flourish. Similarly, people should always grow in Christ, continually looking for new opportunities to serve Him and to be more like Him.

3. NEW THINGS ARE UNCLUTTERED. Though the Holy Spirit makes us new creations in Christ, it's hard to be a completely new person in Him because we carry with us the "clutter" of what we once were or are still trying not to be. Thankfully, in the new heaven and new earth, the past will not even be a memory. The slate will be wiped clean. Though we have a start on that process now, we can only fully complete it with Christ in eternity, for when we leave this earth to be with Him, we will "leave our baggage at the terminal before departing."

<table>
<tr>
<td>

FOR ADULTS

</td>
<td>

■ **TOPIC:** The Eternal Home

■ **QUESTIONS:** 1. What is the new heaven and the new earth? 2. Why did John describe the new Jerusalem as a bride? 3. With respect to the eter-

</td>
</tr>
</table>

nal state, in what sense will the former things have passed away? 4. What does it mean that God will make all things new in the eternal state? 5. How does the final end differ for those who trust in Christ and those who reject Him?

■ **ILLUSTRATIONS:**

Evacuees Get New Homes. The *Reuters* news service reported that the destruction caused by Hurricane Katrina on August 29, 2005, required relocating thousands of evacuees to the Astrodome in Houston, Texas. From there, the displaced citizens were moved to apartment complexes throughout the city. Others were moved to new accommodations in Colorado, Florida, New York, and Massachusetts (to name a few states).

John Walsh, deputy chief of staff for the mayor of Houston, told *Reuters*, "It's a tremendous chance and opportunity." And Guy Rankin, head of the Katrina Housing Task Force, said most of the evacuees from devastated New Orleans seeking the apartments would become permanent residents in Houston. That view was echoed by many of the people who temporarily occupied the Astrodome and Reliant Center. For instance, Michael Williams, a chef who was evacuated from the New Orleans' Superdome, said, "We're planning on staying out here."

That willingness to begin afresh, despite the tragedies of the past, reflects the attitude believers should have as they anticipate spending eternity with their Lord in heaven. They long for a better country, that is, a heavenly one (see Heb. 11:16).

Home Where I Belong. My spouse and I were settled into our lives in western Kansas. We thought we had found our "hometown." We had lots of friends and ministry opportunities that made us feel wanted and loved. However, we both felt God calling us into full-time ministry. For us that meant we had to move away to a large city in another state to attend seminary. We left our nice home to live in a small two-bedroom apartment on the seminary campus. We left friends who knew all of our strengths and weaknesses to be with people we did not know. We left good-paying jobs with lots of benefits to work five part-time jobs between us with no benefits.

Even with all of the losses, we found a wonderful new home. God blessed us with new friends, wonderful professors, and exciting challenges. God always provided for our needs—even if it was at the last minute! God also helped us grow spiritually in ways we never had imagined. We both felt we had finally come home to a place we had always needed to be.

I think we experienced just a small taste of what our new home in the eternal city will be like. Although everything will be new, we will feel like we have come home to the place where we belong.

Let's Go to Your House. Tom was elderly, and for many years he had enjoyed taking long walks with the Lord each evening. On these walks, he would talk about all kinds of things with the Lord, especially about many of the important times in Tom's life, such as when he met his wife, the birth of his children, and other special events.

One day, while Tom was out walking with the Lord for an especially long time, Tom sensed the Lord conveying to him, "We are closer to My house than we are to yours. Why don't you just come home with Me?" Tom was glad to go.

I think that is the way God would like for all of us to view His house. In Revelation 21:7, the Lord said He will be our God and we will be His children. Going to heaven is going home to be part of the everlasting family of God.

The Definition of Heaven. Robert Capon, author of *The Parables of the Kingdom*, says, "'Heaven' or 'heavenly' in the New Testament bear little relation to the meanings we have so unscripturally attached to them. For us, heaven is an unearthly, humanly irrelevant condition in which bed-sheeted, paper-winged spirits sit on clouds and play tinkly music until their pipe-cleaner halos drop off from boredom. But in Scripture, it is a city with boys and girls playing in the streets; it is buildings . . . that use amethysts for cinder blocks and pearls as big as the Ritz for gates; and indoors, it is a dinner party to end all dinner parties at the marriage supper of the Lamb. It is, in short, earth wedded, not earth jilted. It is the world as the irremovable apple of God's eyes.'"

This new city that God is creating for us will be more than we could ever hope for or imagine. God is eagerly awaiting the time when all believers will be gathered together at His table, having come to His house to stay.

■ **TOPIC:** A Fresh Start

■ **QUESTIONS:** 1. What happened to the first heaven and the first earth? 2. What is the new Jerusalem the apostle John saw? 3. Why will God want to dwell among His people in the eternal state? 4. In the eternal state, what will God do with death? 5. What will be the final end for those who reject Christ?

■ **ILLUSTRATIONS:**

Leaving the Old Behind. During my growing up years, my family moved around a lot because of my dad's job. I was in six different school systems by the time I graduated from high school. While going to someplace new was scary and hard on me, my mom always tried to help my brothers and me see the good things that could come from all things being new. She told us it was our golden opportunity to change a bad habit or attitude we did not like about ourselves. No one would know all of our past faults, and the new people would not be able to throw our past mistakes up in our face.

I especially remember one move during my middle school years. I went from a school with about 300 students to one with over 900 students. I decided I was going to be more outgoing and not as shy in this new school. It was fun to create a "new world" for myself. I was still true to myself—with the same likes, dislikes, and morals, for example—but I was "allowed" to talk more freely in class and to be more adventurous. I even tried out for the school play and joined several clubs!

As we look ahead to the new world God will create for believers in heaven, we can be excited to know that all old things will pass away. No one will care about the past mistakes and failures in our lives if our name is written in the Lamb's book of life.

A Happy Ending. Katie was offered the opportunity to select a dog for her birthday present. At the pet store, she was shown a number of puppies. From them, she picked the one whose tail was wagging furiously. When Katie was asked why she chose that particular dog, she said, "I wanted the one with the happy ending."

Everyone will share in the ultimate "happy ending," if they make the choice now to follow the living Christ as Lord and Savior. Revelation promises us that a new world is coming for all believers and what a happy "beginning" it will be!

What Will Heaven Be Like? Billy Graham once said, "Just as there is a mystery to hell, so there is a mystery to heaven. Yet I believe the Bible teaches that heaven is a literal place. Is it one of the stars? I don't know. I can't even speculate. The Bible doesn't inform us. I believe that out there in space where there are one thousand million galaxies, each a hundred thousand light years or more in diameter, God can find some place to put us in heaven. I'm not worried about where it is. I know it is going to be where Jesus is. Christians don't have to go around discouraged and despondent, with their shoulders bent. Think about it—the joy, the peace, the sense of forgiveness that He gives you, and then heaven, too."

GOD IN OUR MIDST

BACKGROUND SCRIPTURE: Revelation 21:9—22:5
DEVOTIONAL READING: Ephesians 1:15-23

KEY VERSE: And there shall be no night there; and they need no candle, neither light of the sun; for the Lord God giveth them light: and they shall reign for ever and ever. Revelation 22:5.

KING JAMES VERSION

REVELATION 21:9 And there came unto me one of the seven angels which had the seven vials full of the seven last plagues, and talked with me, saying, Come hither, I will shew thee the bride, the Lamb's wife.
10 And he carried me away in the spirit to a great and high mountain, and shewed me that great city, the holy Jerusalem, descending out of heaven from God. . .

22 And I saw no temple therein: for the Lord God Almighty and the Lamb are the temple of it. 23 And the city had no need of the sun, neither of the moon, to shine in it: for the glory of God did lighten it, and the Lamb is the light thereof. 24 And the nations of them which are saved shall walk in the light of it: and the kings of the earth do bring their glory and honour into it. 25 And the gates of it shall not be shut at all by day: for there shall be no night there. 26 And they shall bring the glory and honour of the nations into it. 27 And there shall in no wise enter into it any thing that defileth, neither whatsoever worketh abomination, or maketh a lie: but they which are written in the Lamb's book of life.

22:1 And he shewed me a pure river of water of life, clear as crystal, proceeding out of the throne of God and of the Lamb. 2 In the midst of the street of it, and on either side of the river, was there the tree of life, which bare twelve manner of fruits, and yielded her fruit every month: and the leaves of the tree were for the healing of the nations. 3 And there shall be no more curse: but the throne of God and of the Lamb shall be in it; and his servants shall serve him: 4 And they shall see his face; and his name shall be in their foreheads. 5 And there shall be no night there; and they need no candle, neither light of the sun; for the Lord God giveth them light: and they shall reign for ever and ever.

NEW REVISED STANDARD VERSION

REVELATION 21:9 Then one of the seven angels who had the seven bowls full of the seven last plagues came and said to me, "Come, I will show you the bride, the wife of the Lamb." 10 And in the spirit he carried me away to a great, high mountain and showed me the holy city Jerusalem coming down out of heaven from God. . . .

22 I saw no temple in the city, for its temple is the Lord God the Almighty and the Lamb. 23 And the city has no need of sun or moon to shine on it, for the glory of God is its light, and its lamp is the Lamb. 24 The nations will walk by its light, and the kings of the earth will bring their glory into it. 25 Its gates will never be shut by day—and there will be no night there. 26 People will bring into it the glory and the honor of the nations. 27 But nothing unclean will enter it, nor anyone who practices abomination or falsehood, but only those who are written in the Lamb's book of life.

22:1 Then the angel showed me the river of the water of life, bright as crystal, flowing from the throne of God and of the Lamb 2 through the middle of the street of the city. On either side of the river is the tree of life with its twelve kinds of fruit, producing its fruit each month; and the leaves of the tree are for the healing of the nations. 3 Nothing accursed will be found there any more. But the throne of God and of the Lamb will be in it, and his servants will worship him; 4 they will see his face, and his name will be on their foreheads. 5 And there will be no more night; they need no light of lamp or sun, for the Lord God will be their light, and they will reign forever and ever.

12

303

BACKGROUND

In Revelation 21:9, the new Jerusalem is referred to as the bride, the wife of the Lamb. An awareness of ancient Near Eastern wedding customs helps to clarify what John wrote. In Bible times, the wedding ceremony usually took place after dark at the bride's house. Prior to the event, the groom and his friends would form a procession and walk to the home of the bride. After the couple was officially married, the procession would return to the home of the groom or his father.

As the procession journeyed along a planned route, friends of the groom would join the group and participate in singing, playing musical instruments, and dancing. The bride would wear an ornate dress, expensive jewelry (if she could afford it), and a veil over her face. The groom typically hung a garland of flowers around his neck. Once the procession arrived at its destination, a lavish feast, lasting up to seven days, would begin. Friends would sing love ballads for the couple and share stories about them. Everyone would consume food and drink in generous quantities. At the end of the first day's festivities, the bride and groom would be escorted to their private wedding chamber.

In John's vision of the new Jerusalem, the city is holy and perfect down to the last detail. And an itemized description of this virtuous place is given in 21:11-21. The apostle noted that the eternal abode of the redeemed was filled with the glory of God and its radiance was like an extremely precious jewel. Indeed, the holy city was crystal clear like a prized jasper stone (21:11). In Bible times, jasper tended to be mostly reddish in hue, though stones have been found that are green, brown, blue, yellow, and white in color. The new Jerusalem sparkling like a gem suggests that it radiated the majesty of the Lord.

The holy city had a massive, high wall with 12 gates. On the latter were the names of the 12 tribes of the nation of Israel, and there were 12 angels stationed at the gates (21:12). In terms of distribution, the east, north, south, and west sides of this magnificent abode each had three gates (21:13). Moreover, the wall of the new Jerusalem had 12 foundation stones, and on them were inscribed the 12 names of the 12 apostles of the Lamb (21:14). Incidentally, all the dimensions of the holy city are multiples of 12, which symbolically designates the fullness of God's people. Also, the Lamb is very prominent in the new Jerusalem, along with the Father and the Spirit.

The angel who was talking with John held a golden measuring rod, which he used to calculate the dimensions of the holy city, along with its gates and walls (21:15). The length, width, and height of the new Jerusalem were equal (about 1,400 miles), making it a perfect, gigantic cube (21:16). The wall was about 200 feet thick (or high; 21:17) and made of jasper. The pristine city was pure gold, like transparent glass (21:18), while its foundation stones were inlaid with 12 gems (21:19-20). And each of the 12 gates was made from just one pearl. The main street of the new Jerusalem was pure gold, as transparent as glass (21:21). The splendor and opulence of the city reflected the beauty and majesty of God. The believers' eternal home was characterized by awesomeness and durability.

Notes on the Printed Text

Revelation 15 spotlights seven angels emerging from the tabernacle in heaven. One of the four living creatures gave each of them a gold vial or bowl filled with the wrath of God (15:5-8). These represent the final judgments God brings on evildoers whose hearts remain hardened against Him to the end. One of these seven angels invited John to see the bride, the wife of the Lamb (21:9). Suddenly, the apostle found himself being transported in the spirit (or by the Spirit) to a huge, majestic mountain. From there John could see the holy city—the new Jerusalem—descending out of heaven from God (21:10).

Abraham was someone who looked forward to living in this celestial abode. Even when the patriarch arrived in Canaan—the land God promised to Abraham's descendants—he had to live as a resident alien, not as the land's owner (Heb. 11:9). The reason the patriarch could accept this arrangement was that through his faith he anticipated living in an eternal city designed and built by God Himself (11:10). This truth is all the more incredible when we realize that Abraham, like other Old Testament saints before him, accepted God's promise by faith even though His promise was not clearly visible. All of them recognized that the complete fulfillment of God's promise was heavenly, not earthly. They saw themselves as earthly pilgrims whose ultimate citizenship was in God's hands (11:13).

The author of the letter noted that these saints of old were looking for a country of their own (11:14). If they had been looking for an earthly country, they would have returned to their original homelands (11:15). For example, Abraham could have gone back to Ur. But they were not anticipating an earthly home; they were looking for a heavenly home, and with such people God was pleased. The Lord rewarded them for their faith in Him and His promise by preparing for them a heavenly home where they could dwell forever (11:16).

Although the heroes of faith did not receive the fulfillment of God's promise during their earthly lives, they did receive God's commendation because they lived by faith (11:39). And this is the reason God planned something better for them. In fact, the author of Hebrews said that they would be included in the promise the Lord made to him and his readers (11:40). Also included in God's promise are believers throughout all generations, including us, who have placed our faith in God and His promise of eternal life. Through the Son, the Father has begun delivering on His promises. True faith—saving faith—is unwavering trust in Jesus. All believers are citizens of the same kingdom of God. In Christ are the better things that even the ancient heroes of faith looked forward to, such as the new Jerusalem of the eternal state.

Unlike the Jerusalem of Bible times, the new Jerusalem that John saw will have no temple within it (Rev. 21:22). The reason is that *the Lord God Almighty and the Lamb* are the city's temple. Similarly, the new Jerusalem will have no need for the sun or the moon, for *the glory of God* (21:23) illuminates the city and *the Lamb* is the city's source of light. All *the nations* (21:24) will walk in the light of the new Jerusalem. Likewise, *the kings of the earth* will bring their glory and honor to the city. The new Jerusalem will truly be the center of life for the redeemed in eternity. It will be such a safe and secure haven that during the day its gates will never *be shut* (21:25). Even night, with all the fears and uncertainties connected with it, will be eliminated.

John stated that in this pure and holy city, all the nations will bring their glory and honor (21:26). Here, redeemed humanity in all its cultural diversity will live together in peace. This is possible because nothing ritually unclean will be allowed in the new Jerusalem. God will also ban from the holy city anyone who does what is detestable or practices falsehood. The inhabitants will only be the saints, namely, those whose names are recorded in *the Lamb's book of life* (21:27).

The angel that John mentioned in Revelation 21:9 next showed him a pure, crystal-clear river whose waters gave life. The river flowed from God's throne down the middle of the holy city's main thoroughfare (22:1). The river and its water are a symbol of the fullness of eternal life that proceeds from the presence of God. To those living in the hot and dry climate of Palestine, this scene would be a vivid image of God's ability to satisfy a person's spiritual thirst (see John 4:7-14; Rev. 22:17).

In Revelation 22:1, John mentioned *the throne of God and of the Lamb*. The apostle's repeated reference to the Messiah suggests that John did not want us to miss the significance of the Lamb in the eternal state. In this vision of the future, God and the Lamb are joint owners of the heavenly throne. Also, the imperial role of the Father and the Son has become a functional unity. The fact that they share one single throne underscores the full divinity of the Son and His equality with the Father and the Spirit.

John noted that a tree of life grew on each side of the river. Some think the Greek word rendered *tree* (22:2) should be taken in a collective sense to refer to an orchard lining both sides of the riverbank. In either case, the tree bears 12 different kinds of fruit, with a new crop appearing each month of the year. The fruit gives life, and the leaves are used as medicine to heal the nations. The presence of healing leaves does not mean there will be illness in heaven. Rather, the leaves symbolize the health and vigor that believers will enjoy in eternity (see Ezek. 47:12).

A tree of life first existed in the Garden of Eden, and it must have been lush. After Adam and Eve sinned, God did not allow them to eat the fruit of the tree. In eternity, however, the Lord will allow the redeemed to partake fully of eternal life, which is symbolized by the tree with its fresh, abundant fruit (see Gen. 2:9; 3:22). Moreover, after the Fall, God placed everything under sin's curse. In the eternal state, however, He will remove the curse of sin and all its effects. Similarly, God will ban from the new Jerusalem anyone who is accursed because of wickedness (Rev. 22:3; see Gen. 3:14-19; Rev. 22:15).

In the new creation, the Father and the Son will be seated on their thrones, and the redeemed will worship and serve them continually. In a way that is unclear to us this side of eternity, believers will somehow see the face of God, and His name will be imprinted on their foreheads (Rev. 22:4). Expressed differently, God will establish unbroken communion with His people, and He will claim them as His own.

The end of history will be better than the beginning, for a radiant city will replace the Garden of Eden, and the light of God's glory will drive out all darkness. There will be no idleness or boredom in the eternal state, for the Lord will give His people ruling responsibilities (22:5). Revelation assures us of God's final purposes. The book should also increase our longing for communion with God.

SUGGESTIONS TO TEACHERS

Throughout human history, people have failed in their attempts to create utopian communities. God, however, will ensure that the situation is far different in the eternal state for believers. They will dwell in the new Jerusalem and enjoy the beauty of the Lord. Moreover, those who are victorious in this life will enjoy unbroken fellowship with the Lord of glory. Believers today can draw the following from this prophecy of hope.

1. THINGS WILL GET BETTER FOR US. Whatever pain, sorrow, or hurts that we have to face right now are merely tests of our endurance and perseverance. Our sole task is to keep our eyes on the Lord and listen to Him through His Word as He provides direction and protection for our individual lives. If we endure and persevere in our faith, we have the sure and certain hope of being rewarded—of being the recipients of God's ultimate and fantastic promises!

2. THINGS WILL GET BETTER FOR OUR CHILDREN. Past generations of people have been quite concerned about "making things better" for future generations. Much of this concern has been directed toward efforts at making future generations better physically, mentally, emotionally, and (especially) financially. God puts back in the hearts of His people the desire for their children to be better off spiritually. And if this is a concern of our present generation, God promises that He will bless future generations of our children with eternal peace.

3. THINGS WILL GET BETTER FOR GOD'S PEOPLE. The supreme hope for the culmination of the future kingdom of God is that His people will be better off because the effects of sin will be eliminated. God's grace will overrule all wickedness and His goodness and righteousness will create an atmosphere of peace and prosperity, where all the spiritual members of His family will be blessed.

FOR ADULTS	■ **TOPIC:** Living in Our New Home ■ **QUESTIONS:** 1. How was John able to catch a glimpse of the new Jerusalem? 2. Why won't the new Jerusalem have any temple? 3. What

will people bring into the new Jerusalem? 4. In the new Jerusalem, what prominence is given to the Lamb? 5. What will God's servants do in the new Jerusalem?

■ **ILLUSTRATIONS:**

The Beginning and the End. In John's description of the great heavenly city, he referred to the tree of life, first mentioned in Genesis 2:9 (Rev. 22:2). Many themes introduced in Genesis find their fulfillment in Revelation. For instance, God created the sun (Gen. 1:14-18), but in the eternal state it will no longer be needed (Rev. 21:23; 22:5). Sin long ago entered the human race (Gen. 3:1-7), and is banished in the end (Rev. 21:8, 27; 22:15). Whereas before people tried to hide from God (Gen. 3:8), in the eternal state the redeemed enjoy intimacy with Him (Rev. 21:3; 22:4).

The Ultimate Master Builder. For over two decades, *This Old House* has televised home improvement stories. Each week, a group of experts—including a master carpenter, a general contractor, a heating and plumbing specialist, and a landscaper—share their tips and tricks on how to do home remodeling and renovation. Watching the crew perform their "magic" on a run-down house is both educational and entertaining.

In the grand scheme of things, our Lord is the ultimate master builder. After all, He commanded all that we know into existence. And one day He will remake the universe—along with everything in it—so that our eternal dwelling place is infinitely pure and pristine. He will leave nothing undone and spare no expense (in a manner of speaking) so that we can live in our new home with Him for eternity.

Seeing the Big Picture. Three people were part of a construction crew working on a large building project. A passerby asked each, "What are you doing?" "I'm mixing mortar," one said. Another said, "I'm helping put up this big stone wall." The third person responded, "I'm building a cathedral to the glory of God."

Those on the construction crew could just as well have been working in a factory, managing a retail store, or doing any one of a variety of jobs. Most people work to earn a living so they can provide for themselves and their families, and be successful. However, these reasons should not be the only ones for why Christians work. Like the third person in our story, we need to see that what gives work eternal value is not the product or service, but doing the job faithfully to the glory of the Lord. In the eternal state, as we dwell with the Lord in the new Jerusalem, the honor we sought to bring Him in this life will endure through endless ages to come.

Extreme Makeover. The television series by this name showcases everyday people who undergo a series of cosmetic procedures and supposedly have their lives changed forever. The 2005 season included two sisters who struggled with cleft palettes and underwent nearly 40 surgeries; a colorful bull rider who had his teeth knocked out and wanted to be transformed into an urban cowboy; and a female rock musician who spent her days hiding behind her shocking stage appearance. These and other participants recuperated at the "Makeover Mansion," a luxurious residence tucked away in the Hollywood Hills, complete with stunning views, a swimming pool, fully equipped home gym, and plasma televisions.

This primetime version of a new start on life is a far cry from what we find revealed in Scripture. God doesn't promise to revamp our dying physical bodies. And we aren't going to be deposited in lavish manor that will eventually decay and fall apart. What the Lord has in store for us is far better and will be everlasting.

FOR YOUTH

■ TOPIC: Home, but Not Alone!
■ QUESTIONS: 1. Why is the new Jerusalem called the bride, the wife of the Lamb (Rev. 21:9)? 2. What will be the source of light in the holy city? 3. What role do the Father and the Son serve in the new Jerusalem? 4. Who will stream into the holy city? 5. In the eternal state, why will there be no more need for the light of the sun?

■ **ILLUSTRATIONS:**
Worthless Digging. In the spring of 1608, the settlers at Jamestown, Virginia, hardly bothered to concern themselves about anything except digging gold. They neglected to plant crops or erect buildings for winter or prepare for cold, but applied themselves frantically to washing the precious metal. In fact, the colonists would not even have survived the summer of 1608 if it had not been for the native residents who fed them.

After working all spring, the newcomers loaded their valuable cargo on board a ship for England. They smugly told themselves they were rich. To their chagrin, their gold turned out to be worthless iron pyrite, sometimes known as "fool's gold." The Jamestown settlers had wasted all their time and energies for fool's gold!

God wants us to invest our lives for time and eternity. This happens when we live for the Lord and make His kingdom our primary concern (see Matt. 6:33). It means we don't store up treasures here on earth, where they can be eaten by moths and get rusty, and where thieves can break in and steal. Instead, we store our treasures in heaven, where they will be eternally safe (see 6:19-20). And in our celestial dwelling place, we will enjoy the close presence of our Lord, who will shield us from all harm.

All Alone. John Wayne Riley, 15, and Billy Ray Grimes, Jr., 12, ran away from their Hamilton, Ohio, homes 25 miles northwest of Cincinnati. They jumped a train on November 23, 1998. Momentarily, life seemed exciting and good as the slow train rolled up the tracks. Later, the two switched to another train.

Unknown to the adolescents, the train that they had boarded was heading for the Miller Brewing Company in Trenton. Somehow, the boxcar's door slammed shut and locked, trapping the two boys. During their eight days of isolation, the two survived by drinking the drops of stale beer left in the mostly empty bottles. Finally, a brewery employee, taking inventory in the rail yard, heard the boys pounding on the boxcar's side and freed them.

Imagine how scary it would feel to be completely alone like that. In the eternal state, believers will not have to fear being abandoned and forgotten. They will be in the company of the Lord, the saints of all the ages, and the angels of heaven!

Traditional Family Gone. The "traditional family image"—where Mom is a "homemaker" and Dad is "the bread winner" and the two live in a first marriage for both within a union that produces children—is gone. Now, only 10 percent of the families in the United States fit that mold, says Danielle Lichter, Director of Penn State University's Population Institute. The traditional family has been replaced by single parent families.

Whatever the type of family in which you reside, God and the people in that family are what is important. Houses, possessions, cars—all these are unimportant. The relationships between the people in the family are what is important. And in heaven the members of God's spiritual family will dwell with Him and one another for endless ages.

CHRIST WILL RETURN

BACKGROUND SCRIPTURE: Revelation 22:6-21
DEVOTIONAL READING: John 16:17-24

KEY VERSE: He which testifieth these things saith, Surely I come quickly. Amen. Even so, come, Lord Jesus. Revelation 22:20.

KING JAMES VERSION

REVELATION 22:6 And he said unto me, These sayings are faithful and true: and the Lord God of the holy prophets sent his angel to shew unto his servants the things which must shortly be done. 7 Behold, I come quickly: blessed is he that keepeth the sayings of the prophecy of this book. 8 And I John saw these things, and heard them. And when I had heard and seen, I fell down to worship before the feet of the angel which shewed me these things. 9 Then saith he unto me, See thou do it not: for I am thy fellowservant, and of thy brethren the prophets, and of them which keep the sayings of this book: worship God. 10 And he saith unto me, Seal not the sayings of the prophecy of this book: for the time is at hand. . . . 12 And, behold, I come quickly; and my reward is with me, to give every man according as his work shall be. 13 I am Alpha and Omega, the beginning and the end, the first and the last. . . . 16 I Jesus have sent mine angel to testify unto you these things in the churches. I am the root and the offspring of David, and the bright and morning star. 17 And the Spirit and the bride say, Come. And let him that heareth say, Come. And let him that is athirst come. And whosoever will, let him take the water of life freely. 18 For I testify unto every man that heareth the words of the prophecy of this book, If any man shall add unto these things, God shall add unto him the plagues that are written in this book: 19 And if any man shall take away from the words of the book of this prophecy, God shall take away his part out of the book of life, and out of the holy city, and from the things which are written in this book.

20 He which testifieth these things saith, Surely I come quickly. Amen. Even so, come, Lord Jesus. 21 The grace of our Lord Jesus Christ be with you all. Amen.

NEW REVISED STANDARD VERSION

REVELATION 22:6 And he said to me, "These words are trustworthy and true, for the Lord, the God of the spirits of the prophets, has sent his angel to show his servants what must soon take place."

7 "See, I am coming soon! Blessed is the one who keeps the words of the prophecy of this book."

8 I, John, am the one who heard and saw these things. And when I heard and saw them, I fell down to worship at the feet of the angel who showed them to me; 9 but he said to me, "You must not do that! I am a fellow servant with you and your comrades the prophets, and with those who keep the words of this book. Worship God!"

10 And he said to me, "Do not seal up the words of the prophecy of this book, for the time is near." . . .

12 "See, I am coming soon; my reward is with me, to repay according to everyone's work. 13 I am the Alpha and the Omega, the first and the last, the beginning and the end." . . .

16 "It is I, Jesus, who sent my angel to you with this testimony for the churches. I am the root and the descendant of David, the bright morning star."

17 The Spirit and the bride say, "Come."
And let everyone who hears say, "Come."
And let everyone who is thirsty come.
Let anyone who wishes take the water of life as a gift.

18 I warn everyone who hears the words of the prophecy of this book: if anyone adds to them, God will add to that person the plagues described in this book; 19 if anyone takes away from the words of the book of this prophecy, God will take away that person's share in the tree of life and in the holy city, which are described in this book.

20 The one who testifies to these things says, "Surely I am coming soon."

Amen. Come, Lord Jesus!

21 The grace of the Lord Jesus be with all the saints. Amen.

13

Monday, May 21	John 16:17-24	*Pain Becomes Joy*
Tuesday, May 22	John 16:25-33	*Jesus Overcomes*
Wednesday, May 23	Ephesians 4:1-6	*One Body, One Spirit*
Thursday, May 24	Colossians 3:12-17	*May Christ Rule Your Hearts*
Friday, May 25	Revelation 22:6-11	*Worship God*
Saturday, May 26	Revelation 22:12-16	*The Reward for Faithfulness*
Sunday, May 27	Revelation 22:17-21	*The Invitation*

BACKGROUND

The New Testament writers used three Greek words when referring to the second coming of Christ. *Parousia* carries the ideas of "presence" and "coming," especially the official visit of a person of high rank (for example, a king or emperor). The word implies personal presence and excited states (1 Thess. 4:15; 2 Thess. 2:8). *Apokalypsis* means "revelation" or "disclosure." In connection with end-time events, it refers to the unveiling of Christ at His second coming. This may suggest the suddenness of His return (1 Cor. 1:7; 2 Thess. 1:7; 1 Pet. 4:13). *Epiphaneia* means "appearing" or "appearance" and refers to a visible manifestation of a hidden divinity. In Titus 2:13, Christ's *appearing* is said to be *glorious*. This idea of divine glory is taken one step further in 2 Thessalonians 2:8, where *epiphaneia* is translated *brightness*.

Taken together, the three words tell us that Jesus' second coming will involve His personal presence, His unveiling, and His appearing in power and glory. From Acts 1:11, we learn that the Savior will return in His resurrection body. And Matthew 24:30 reveals that His second advent will be glorious and visible to the whole world. At His appearing, none will doubt that He is Lord. Indeed, as Revelation 1:7 indicates, people will mourn either because of the judgment that is about to fall on them or because of the sins they have committed.

The parable of the sheep and the goats is especially informative. Jesus noted that He will come in *glory* (Matt. 25:31), or divine splendor, no longer simply appearing as an ordinary man. Second, He will bring with Him *all the holy angels,* who will no doubt serve as His assistants. Third, He will rule in splendor. Once Jesus is seated on His glorious throne, all the nations will be gathered before Him, and He will separate the people one from another (25:32). The purpose of the judgment will be to divide the righteous from the wicked. Only God can do that with perfect justice. As the shepherd of judgment, Christ will put the *sheep* (25:33) on His right and the *goats* on His left. The remainder of Jesus' parable describes what He will do with the sheep, or the righteous, and the goats, or the wicked, once He has them separated—first the sheep (25:34-40), then the goats (25:41-45).

The Savior will address those on His right side as *blessed of my Father* (25:34).

They will be favored by God in the blessing they will receive as an inheritance from Him, namely, the kingdom of heaven. All along, it has been a part of God's plan to bless the righteous with His kingdom. Upon Christ's return, it will be time for the plan's fulfillment. The righteous inherit the Kingdom because of how they have treated Jesus. They will have met His needs for food, drink, shelter, clothing, nursing, and visitation in prison (25:35-36). Jesus said that the righteous will ask Him when they did such things for Him (25:37-39), and He will explain that service done for His needy brothers and sisters is the same as service done for Him (25:40).

Next, Christ will tell the ones on His left to depart. Instead of being blessed by the Father, these people will be cursed. Moreover, instead of inheriting the Kingdom prepared for the righteous, these people will be consigned to the eternal fire (hell) prepared for Satan and the demons (25:41). This happens because they did not meet Jesus' needs. They will have been presented with the same opportunities to give Him food and drink and the rest, but they will have chosen not to do so (25:42-43). The wicked will ask when they refused to help the Lord (25:44). And Christ will explain that by refusing to serve His needy followers, they chose not to serve Him (25:45).

Matthew 25:46 reveals that the wicked go away to eternal punishment and the righteous to eternal life. The parable does not mean that one's eternal state is based upon good works. The New Testament is clear that faith in Christ (or its absence) determines our eternal destiny. But we can take away from this parable the ideas that Jesus rewards service done to Him, that real faith is expressed in works, and that He counts service done to His people as service done to Him. This is all the more reason to live in a pure and blameless manner—one characterized by compassion for others—while we wait for the return of the Savior (2 Pet. 3:14).

NOTES ON THE PRINTED TEXT

If John had any doubts concerning the vision he had received, the interpreting angel dispelled them with words of reassurance. He declared that God's prophecies about the future—for instance, the overthrow of evil and the joys awaiting believers in the eternal state—were true, trustworthy, and certain to take place at the divinely appointed time (Rev. 22:6). God promises to bless those who heed the message of Revelation. One prominent aspect of this message is the return of Christ at the end of the age. The certainty of His appearing comforts us in times of hardship and motivates us to be obedient and faithful in times of temptation (22:7).

John was an eyewitness to the visions recorded in Revelation, and he faithfully wrote down what he saw so that we could read and obey these unveiled mysteries. Every portion of Revelation is designed to shift our focus from ourselves to God. That is why, when John fell down to worship at the feet of the angel (22:8), the celestial being urged the apostle to revere the Lord. Indeed, all who serve God and declare His prophetic truths should make Him the recipient of their homage and praise (22:9).

In Daniel 12:4, we learn that an angel commanded Daniel to seal, or close up, the vision he had received so that it would remain confidential. In contrast, an angel told the apostle John not to keep secret the prophecies he had received. The message he recorded was relevant not only for first-century Christians but also for believers today. As we study and apply the truths of Revelation, we will be better prepared for Christ's return (Rev. 22:10). We are encouraged to serve the Lord Jesus out of love and with deep devotion. And we discover that by His grace we can resist any temptation to compromise our faith (22:11).

As John wrote, he and other believers faced intense persecution. Also, throughout history Christians have endured abuse from enemies of the faith. Jesus' promise that He is coming soon has been a source of comfort for His followers down through the centuries (22:12). In turn, people can respond either positively or negatively to the message of this book. A proper response includes repenting of sin, seeking to live uprightly, and desiring to become more like Christ. An improper response includes remaining entrenched in the world's evil system and taking God lightly. In either case, the Lord Jesus will repay according to what each of us has done. Ultimately, the way people live is an indicator of whether they are regenerate or unregenerate.

No one can determine when Christ will return. Yet we know that when His appearing does occur, it will take place quickly. We can rest assured of His second advent, for Jesus, as the *Alpha and Omega* (22:13), is sovereign over all that takes place in history. Furthermore, as *the beginning and the end, the first and the last,* His lordship encompasses the past, the present, and the future.

The Lord Jesus assured His followers that what is recorded in Revelation is true and can be trusted. He could guarantee what He had declared, for He is the Messiah who came from the house and lineage of David. As the *bright and morning star* (22:16), He ensures that a new day of salvation will dawn. With such promises awaiting fulfillment, it is no wonder that God's Spirit and His people (*the bride,* 22:17) extend an invitation for everyone to come to the Messiah in faith and experience the joys of salvation. All are welcome to drink from the water of eternal life, which the Savior offers free of charge.

Revelation—like the rest of Scripture—is to be distinguished from mere human words. The message of the book is so important that God promises to judge those who might distort what it says (22:18). For instance, this could occur if someone either adds things to or omits things from Revelation (22:19). This warning should prompt us to handle Scripture with care and respect, and to heed what it discloses (see Deut. 4:2; 12:32).

To be sure, God's will is that everyone will hear and heed what Revelation has to say. By turning to Christ in faith (and thereby longing for His return), they will have a share in the tree of life (namely, salvation) and in the holy city (namely, the new Jerusalem), both of which Revelation describes (Rev. 22:19). The good news is that

Jesus will one day return. With John and all believers, we can affirm the certainty of this promise (22:20). Moreover, it is comforting to know that when the Redeemer appears, we will be able to face Him with joy and gladness. John fittingly ended these grand truths with a benediction of the Messiah's abundant grace for God's people (22:21; see 1 John 2:28).

SUGGESTIONS TO TEACHERS

According to Hebrews 1:2, we are living in the *last days.* In other words, with the first advent of Christ, the messianic age has dawned. And at His second advent, the full flowering of His Kingdom will occur. While we should not be preoccupied with how and when end-time events will take place (1 Thess. 5:1), we certainly need to be ready at all times for Jesus' second coming, whenever it may be (5:6). How can we be ready? Some of the same things we do to get prepared for a trip apply to being ready for Jesus' return.

1. BE FISCALLY READY. We look at our finances before a trip to be certain we have the money we need and have made the proper financial arrangements. In a similar way, we are to give to God that which is His to support His work here until Jesus comes. After all, Christ taught that where our treasure is, that's where our heart will be too (Matt. 6:21).

2. BE PHYSICALLY READY. For a trip there is usually the physical preparation of packing. While we cannot "pack" for our trip to heaven, physically we should always be aware of who we are and what we are doing in light of Jesus' return. In other words, if the Savior came today, would there be things we do now that we would not want Him to find us doing? Are we being His witnesses to those around us, or would they never guess we are Christians by our words and actions?

3. BE EMOTIONALLY READY. Trips can be emotional experiences, something we are either "up" for or not. As Christians, would our emotions at this time say, "This world is not my home," or "I am both in the world and of the world. I'm too tied to things here to even think about leaving"?

4. BE SPIRITUALLY READY. It is wise to pray before a trip, asking God to watch over our travels. Of course, we first need salvation through our Lord Jesus Christ for our final, heavenly trip (1 Thess. 5:9). But beyond that, is our life characterized right now by faith, love, and hope? Imagine creating a mental record of "spiritual" things we should all be doing every day as we wait for Jesus to return. That can become our checklist to help us get ready for the Messiah when He appears.

FOR ADULTS

■ TOPIC: The Ultimate Happy Ending

■ QUESTIONS: 1. In what sense are those who heed Revelation blessed by God? 2. Why did John fall down to worship the angel? 3. Why did

Jesus emphasize the truth of His second coming? 4. In what sense is Jesus the root and offspring of David? 5. Why is it fitting that Revelation ends with the mention of the Savior's grace?

■ ILLUSTRATIONS:

Fiction versus Reality. Most fairy tales end by saying "and they lived happily ever after." For instance, the prince and princess marry and ride off into the sunset to begin their new life together as husband and wife—a life full of promise, romance, and above all, love. Of course, reality tends to be far different. At first, most couples are clueless about how to make their marriage succeed. And many marital unions tragically end in divorce.

The situation is vastly different between Christ and His church. Without a doubt, there is a "happily ever after." In this case, the bride—the wife of the Lamb (Rev. 21:9)—will live and reign with the Savior in heaven throughout eternity. Even though lifetime dreams have a way of being shattered, the ultimate happy ending for believers is certain to come to pass. Moreover, nothing in the entire universe can prevent almighty God from fulfilling His promises to His people.

Wait and Watch. The Lord has given special commendation to those who not only *wait* for His return, but also earnestly *watch* for Him. The difference between these terms can be illustrated by the story of a fishing vessel returning home after many days at sea. As they neared the shore, the sailors eagerly watched the dock where a group of their loved ones had gathered. The skipper looked through his binoculars and identified some of the wives he saw waiting there.

One man became concerned because his wife was not on the dock. Later, he left the boat sadly and trudged up the hill to his home. As he opened the door, his wife ran to meet him saying, "I have been waiting for you!" Quietly, he replied, "Yes, but the other men's wives were watching for them." While this man's wife obviously loved him, she had not been actively watching for his homecoming as he had hoped. That is what happens when we fail to be ready for Jesus to return at any time; this is not a good time to be "surprised."

Ready or Not. The wreckage of the luxury liner, *Titanic,* thought to have been "unsinkable," now rests 13,120 feet down on the Atlantic Ocean floor. In its day, the *Titanic* was the world's largest ship, weighing over 46 tons, being 882 feet long, and rising 11 stories high. The vessel employed a crew and staff of almost 1,000 and could carry nearly 2,500 passengers. The ship was ready for its passengers with a complete gymnasium, heated pool, squash court, and the first miniature golf course.

Even for all the elegant and luxurious extras this ship had, it still lacked some basic equipment needed for survival if something "unthinkable" happened. It was short the needed number of lifeboats for all of its passengers and crew, and on its first voyage it was short a simple pair of binoculars needed for the lookouts to spot icebergs. On its first trip, the ship received at least seven warnings about dangerous icebergs in its path. However, the captain and others were more concerned with getting to America in record time instead of watching out for the safety of the ship and its passengers.

The night of April 14, 1912, the "unthinkable" happened to the "unsinkable." Near midnight, the great *Titanic* struck an iceberg, ripping a 300 foot hole through 5 of its 16 watertight compartments. It sank in 2 1/2 hours, killing 1,513 people.

Sometimes we act as if Jesus is never coming back, despite the knowledge that He is. The *Titanic* supplies a lesson for us all. If the people in charge would have been more watchful and more diligent in doing the right things, many lives would have been saved, and possibly the entire ship would have made it to its destination on time. Jesus wants us to be ready and expectantly waiting for what He will bring us today or tomorrow.

Now Instead of Later. President John F. Kennedy once said, "The time to repair the roof is when the sun is shining." My grandfather said somewhat the same thing when he told me, "The time to shut the barn door is not after the cow is already gone." The time to get ready for Jesus to come is not when He has returned. Now is the time to get ready for Jesus. We all need to be doing things every day to help us prepare to meet Him, whether that meeting is at the Second Coming or when we die. Don't put off reading your Bible, or praying, or talking to someone who is lonely, or sharing the Gospel with someone who is lost. Every day we can be getting ready to meet Jesus, in small and big ways.

FOR YOUTH

■ **TOPIC:** He's Back!

■ **QUESTIONS:** 1. What did Jesus promise believers? 2. What did the angel urge John to do? 3. What will be the basis for the eternal reward Jesus will give to believers? 4. What invitation did the Spirit and the people of God extend to all individuals? 5. What warning appears at the end of Revelation?

■ **ILLUSTRATIONS:**

Real Appreciation. In 1975, the television series, *Welcome Back, Kotter,* debuted. The situation comedy was about Gabe Kotter, who returned to his Brooklyn-based alma-mater, James Buchanan High School, to teach a collection of misfits called the Sweathogs. The Sweathogs were a group of supposedly unteachable, under-achieving, and incorrigible students. Gabe, who at one time was a Sweathog himself, tried to reach out to these adolescents by relating his own experiences to them.

In contrast to these unruly students, who never seemed to fully appreciate the return of Gabe, believers will be overjoyed at the second coming of the Messiah. In fact, their entire lives are played out against the backdrop of this blessed hope. As a saved teen, the prospect of Jesus' return can give you courage to remain faithful to Him even when your peers pressure you to do otherwise.

I Can Sleep. A young man applied for a job as a farmhand. When the farmer asked for his qualifications, the young man said, "I can sleep when the wind blows." This puzzled the farmer, but he took a liking to the young man and hired him. A few days later, the farmer and his wife were awakened in the night by a violent storm. They quickly began to check things out to see if all was secure. They found that the shutters of the farmhouse had been securely fastened. A good supply of logs had been set next to the fireplace. The farm implements had been safely placed in the storage shed. The tractor had been moved into the garage. The barn had been properly locked. All was well. Even the animals were calm. It was then that the farmer grasped the meaning of the young man's words: "I can sleep when the wind blows." Because the farmhand had performed his work loyally and faithfully when the skies were clear, he was prepared for the storm when it broke. Consequently, when the wind blew, he had no fear. He was able to sleep in peace.

This is your life. You need to live it in order to be ready to meet your daily responsibilities and obligations. And as a Christian, one of your responsibilities is to be ready to meet Jesus. Do those things that the Lord asks of you so that you too may sleep in peace.

"Fish" for Life. A young boy stood idly on a bridge watching some fishermen. Seeing one of them with a basket full of fish, he said, "If I had a catch like that, I'd be happy."

"I'll give you that many fish if you do a small favor for me," said the fisherman. "I need you to tend this line a while. I've got some business down the street."

The young boy gladly accepted the offer. After the man left, the trout and bass continued snapping greedily at the baited hook. Soon the boy forgot everything else, and was excitedly pulling in a large number of fish. When the fisherman returned, he said to the young boy, "I'll keep my promise to you by giving you everything you've caught. And I hope you've learned a lesson. You mustn't waste time daydreaming and merely wishing for things. Instead, get busy and cast in a line for yourself."

This young boy made the most of his time, not realizing that he was really going to benefit the most from the amount of energy he put into catching the fish. He could have just as easily put out only enough effort to catch one or two fish. It's your life. What you get out of it depends greatly on what you put into it. As you think about being prepared for the second coming of Christ, "fish" as if your heavenly reward depends on it.

AMOS CHALLENGES INJUSTICE

BACKGROUND SCRIPTURE: Amos 5:10-15, 21-24; 8:4-12; 2 Kings 13:23-25
DEVOTIONAL READING: 1 Peter 4:1-11

KEY VERSE: But let judgment run down as waters,
and righteousness as a mighty stream. Amos 5:24.

KING JAMES VERSION

AMOS 5:10 They hate him that rebuketh in the gate, and they abhor him that speaketh uprightly.

11 Forasmuch therefore as your treading is upon the poor, and ye take from him burdens of wheat: ye have built houses of hewn stone, but ye shall not dwell in them; ye have planted pleasant vineyards, but ye shall not drink wine of them. 12 For I know your manifold transgressions and your mighty sins: they afflict the just, they take a bribe, and they turn aside the poor in the gate from their right. 13 Therefore the prudent shall keep silence in that time; for it is an evil time. 14 Seek good, and not evil, that ye may live: and so the LORD, the God of hosts, shall be with you, as ye have spoken. 15 Hate the evil, and love the good, and establish judgment in the gate: it may be that the LORD God of hosts will be gracious unto the remnant of Joseph. . . .

21 I hate, I despise your feast days, and I will not smell in your solemn assemblies. 22 Though ye offer me burnt offerings and your meat offerings, I will not accept them: neither will I regard the peace offerings of your fat beasts. 23 Take thou away from me the noise of thy songs; for I will not hear the melody of thy viols. 24 But let judgment run down as waters, and righteousness as a mighty stream.

NEW REVISED STANDARD VERSION

AMOS 5:10 They hate the one who reproves in the gate,
and they abhor the one who speaks the truth.
11 Therefore because you trample on the poor
and take from them levies of grain,
you have built houses of hewn stone,
but you shall not live in them;
you have planted pleasant vineyards,
but you shall not drink their wine.
12 For I know how many are your transgressions,
and how great are your sins—
you who afflict the righteous, who take a bribe,
and push aside the needy in the gate.
13 Therefore the prudent will keep silent in such a time;
for it is an evil time.
14 Seek good and not evil,
that you may live;
and so the LORD, the God of hosts, will be with you,
just as you have said.
15 Hate evil and love good,
and establish justice in the gate;
it may be that the LORD, the God of hosts,
will be gracious to the remnant of Joseph. . . .
21 I hate, I despise your festivals,
and I take no delight in your solemn assemblies.
22 Even though you offer me your burnt offerings and
grain offerings,
I will not accept them;
and the offerings of well-being of your fatted animals
I will not look upon.
23 Take away from me the noise of your songs;
I will not listen to the melody of your harps.
24 But let justice roll down like waters,
and righteousness like an ever-flowing stream.

Monday, May 28	Psalm 82:1-8	*A Plea for Justice*
Tuesday, May 29	Isaiah 59:9-15	*Where Is Justice and Truth?*
Wednesday, May 30	Jeremiah 22:1-5	*Do What Is Just*
Thursday, May 31	Amos 3:1-10	*God Admonishes Israel*
Friday, June 1	Amos 8:4-8	*Protect the Poor*
Saturday, June 2	Amos 5:10-15	*Seek Good, Not Evil*
Sunday, June 3	Amos 5:20-25	*Let Justice Roll Down*

BACKGROUND

The dozen prophetic books at the end of the Old Testament have been grouped together since at least 200 years before the Messiah's first advent. In combination, they are sometimes called the Book of the Twelve. They are also called the Minor Prophets, not because they are minor in importance, but because they are minor in size. The Major Prophets—Isaiah, Jeremiah, and Ezekiel—are much bigger books.

We begin this quarter by focusing on the Book of Amos. This spokesperson for God declared that he was not one of the professional prophets. He also noted that he had never trained to be one. Instead, he was a shepherd by occupation, and he took care of sycamore-fig trees (7:14). Such truths notwithstanding, the Lord called Amos away from his flock and commissioned him to prophesy to the people in Israel (7:15). Amos was a resident of Tekoa, a village 10 miles south of Jerusalem (1:1). He usually lived in Judah, but ministered in Israel.

The prophecies recorded in Amos date from two years before a prominent earthquake, when Uzziah was king of Judah and Jeroboam II was king of Israel. We don't know when that particular earthquake took place. But Uzziah reigned from about 792 to 740 B.C. and Jeroboam II reigned from about 793 to 753 B.C. Probably the prophecies in this book were delivered around 760 B.C.

Unlike many of the prophets, Amos spoke out during a time of peace and a booming economy. That may have made his job harder, for people seem to care less about God's will when things are going well. The governments of Judah and Israel were well established, and these nations had few outside threats to distract them. Egypt and Assyria were weak at this time, and Syria was in turmoil. That period of peace, however, led to moral laxity that compelled Amos to speak out. The people in power were exploiting the poor and ignoring justice. Furthermore, the people viewed their prosperity as a sign of God's approval on them.

After the introductory heading recorded in 1:1, Amos announced his main theme: judgment. In 1:2, we read that the Lord roared like a lion from Zion and thundered like a storm from Jerusalem. These loud noises were signs of God's displeasure. He would pounce like a lion upon the Israelites and crash like a storm upon them because of their sins. At the sound of the Lord's voice, the pastures of the shepherds mourned.

Also, the top of the Carmel mountain range withered. Mount Carmel, located in Israel, was known for its rich vegetation. When God judged Israel, He would have the effect of a devastating drought on the land.

Starting with the main body of his prophecies, Amos used a clever tactic to capture his audience's attention. He did not set in immediately to declare their guilt. Instead, he began by delivering oracles (prophecies) of judgment against some of the Israelites' neighbors: the Syrians, Philistines, Phoenicians, Edomites, Ammonites, Moabites, and Judahites (1:3—2:3).

All eight of the judgments against nations recorded in chapters 1 and 2 of Amos begin with the phrase, *For three transgressions of [some place], and for four, I will not turn away the punishment thereof* (1:3, 6, 9, 11, 13; 2:1, 4, 6). This numerical formula is similar to others used in Hebrew poetry (for example, see Job 5:19; Prov. 6:16; Mic. 5:5). It signifies an unspecified number. The nations were guilty of a multitude of sins; therefore, God would judge them.

Amos's Israelite listeners probably would have been happy to think that those others were going to get what they deserved. But the smile on the Israelites' faces must have faded as Amos began to shine his spotlight closer and closer to Israel itself. In the end, he would show that Israel was as surely destined for judgment as were the other nations (Amos 2:4-16).

The passages coming after Amos's opening oracle against Israel confirm God's plan to judge the northern kingdom. God reminded the Israelites that He had revealed His plan of judgment to them (3:1-10), presumably through the prophets. He reaffirmed His plan to judge Israel harshly (3:11-15). In Amos 4, the Lord declared that He would overthrow the Israelites because they persisted in sinning, refusing to take advantage of opportunities to repent. God offered a lament for Israel (5:1-3) and called on the Israelites to change their ways (5:4-9). If the people refused to do so, there was coming a time of sadness in Israel (5:16-17).

NOTES ON THE PRINTED TEXT

The judgment of the Lord on His people was warranted. For instance, the rich and powerful hated those who advocated on behalf of the just in the city gates (which were comparable to our courts of law today). Even those who told the truth in such proceedings were abhorred (Amos 5:10).

This was not the extent of the injustices. According to 5:11, the government trampled the poor by levying an excessive agricultural tax on their scant crops. Meanwhile, the wealthy built lavish mansions out of hewn stone. But the Lord in His justice would not allow the wicked rich to occupy these dwellings. They would not even be able to enjoy the fruit produced by the lush vineyards they had planted. This privilege would go to others.

A seemingly endless list of transgressions and sins could be compiled against the leaders and people of the northern kingdom of Israel. Amos 5:12 mentions those who oppressed the righteous, accepted bribes, and prevented the poor from getting a fair trial in court. The *just* were not righteous in the sense of being blameless or sinless. These poor people were *right* in their cause. In other words, they were honest, upright individuals being unjustly treated by powerful people, such as judges and creditors.

In such evil times, even the prudent sensed it was better to play it safe and keep quiet (5:13). But these self-protection tactics did not reflect God's will. He wanted good, not evil, to be promoted. This led to life, not death, and was favored by God (5:14). By hating evil, loving good, and establishing justice in the land, those in positions of authority would demonstrate that they were serious about living as an upright remnant in God's sight (5:15).

The Israelites believed *the day of the LORD* (5:20) would be a positive event, something to eagerly anticipate in the future. Generally, the phrase referred to a time when the Israelites would be fully restored to the promised land after a time of exile (Hos. 2:16-23; Amos 9:11-15). However, Amos's description of that day in 5:20 does not involve hope and restoration. His reference to a dark and mournful day would have been a terrifying concept to the Israelites.

At nightfall, when the door of a home was secured, an oil lamp was lit. Only total poverty would prevent a villager from keeping a lamp burning throughout the night hours. No Israelite would have considered sleeping in the dark, as Westerners do. In the teachings of Jesus, being cast into outer darkness (a place completely devoid of light) was symbolic of the coming judgment of the unrighteous (Matt. 8:12; 22:13; 25:30). In Amos 5:20, the imagery signified both coming judgment and a total state of hopelessness that came from an inability to change the picture of doom.

This would have devastated Amos's audience, especially if he delivered this prophecy at the annual autumn festival in Bethel, which may have been called *the day of the feast of the LORD* (Hos. 9:5). Amos would be telling the prosperous Israelites that they had focused so much on the wonderful, future day of the Lord that they had ignored the current injustices in their nation.

On top of everything else, the unrighteousness of Israel made all of the people's religious observances loathsome in God's sight. He absolutely despised their feast days and could not stand the stench associated with their solemn assemblies (Amos 5:21). Even their various offerings—whether burnt, meat, or peace offerings—were odious to the Lord. Thus, He refused to accept them (5:22). Each of the elements of Israel's worship was mentioned with strong verbs of condemnation. The worship of the Israelites was so hypocritical, in fact, that the Lord did not even want to hear the *noise* (5:23) of their shallow songs of praise.

The Hebrew word translated *viols* can also refer to harps or lutes. It was a portable, wooden-framed instrument having eight or ten strings made of stretched sheep gut. Whether the strings were plucked with the fingers or a plectrum (pick), is unknown.

The instrument was used at festivals (Isa. 5:12), at prophetic utterances (1 Chron. 25:1), and to alter moods (1 Sam. 16:23).

Amos, of course, was not condemning worship itself. The problem was that the people of Israel performed empty religious rituals on the heels of injustice and their oppression of the poor. Their music was like a choir singing that had lost the knowledge of who they are singing to.

What God required of His people was an unrelenting devotion to justice and an unending commitment to righteousness. The image in Amos 5:24 is of justice (in their relationships with one another) and righteousness (in their relationship with God) flowing continually through the land like a mighty river. These qualities were not to be found sporadically, like the intermittent streams that flowed through the desert wadis (ravines) of Israel only after a rare thunderstorm. If justice and righteousness did not inundate the land (so to speak), not even the remnant of Israel could hope to survive the coming day of the Lord.

SUGGESTIONS TO TEACHERS

When is worship a sham? When is it real? What should we look for when we worship? Is worship mostly well-rehearsed choral music, beautiful liturgies, and eloquent speakers? These are the kinds of questions raised by the material you will cover in this week's lesson.

1. DELUDING HUMAN ATTAINMENTS. Form and rituals without repentance and concern for the hurting count for nothing with God. Amos warned that worship in Israel was spiritually empty because the people failed to back their elaborate words to God with acts that promoted peace and justice. From this we see that social concerns go hand-in-hand with prayer and personal piety.

2. DEFAMING GOD'S GLORY. Take a few moments to consider Amos 5:4-6, where the prophet accused Israel of trifling with their Creator. Sometimes in our worship, we act as if the all-powerful Lord can be manipulated to do our bidding. Amos (as well as the rest of Scripture) emphasizes that people can never control God. We are meant to serve the Lord, not the other way around.

3. DECLARING GOD'S INTENTION. Next, focus the attention of your students on 5:14-15, *Seek good, and not evil, that ye may live . . . Hate the evil, and love the good, and establish judgment* (or "justice"). Why are these virtues lacking among believers today, and how can the church reemphasize them? Give specifics.

4. DENOUNCING VAIN WORSHIP. Amos dealt sternly with those blithely longing for the day of the Lord because they thought God would rescue them and make everything pleasant. Instead, Amos stated that it would be a time of reckoning for Israel. Have your students consider the implications of 1 Peter 4:17, which says, *For the time is come that judgment must begin at the house of God: and if it first begin at us, what shall the end be of them that obey not the gospel of God?*

5. DEMANDING JUSTICE AND RIGHTEOUSNESS. End the lesson time by discussing Amos 5:21-24. Be sure to stress that worship without justice and righteousness is empty.

<table>
<tr><td>

FOR ADULTS

</td><td>

■ **TOPIC:** Committed to Doing Right

■ **QUESTIONS:** 1. How had the wicked rich deprived the poor of justice in the courts? 2. Why were the Israelites facing divine judgment

</td></tr>
</table>

rather than mercy? 3. Why was the Lord dismissive of Israel's offerings and festivals? 4. Why would God refuse to listen to the worship music offered by His people? 5. Why did the Israelites allow themselves to replace justice with injustice?

■ **ILLUSTRATIONS:**

Tuning Fork Truth. An old music teacher once showed his minister a tuning fork hanging on a cord. Striking the tuning fork and listening to the hum for a moment, the teacher said, "That is the good word. That is G, and no matter how the weather may change or what may happen in human affairs, it remains G." Continuing, he pointed out that refusing to listen to the correct note and trying to do the performance in another key would result in discordant music. As a musician, he knew the consequences of not obeying the basic tenets of harmony. The same is true with God's spiritual and moral requirements!

Costly Consequences. An East coast high school soccer team had an outstanding season a few years ago. With exceptionally talented players, it moved to the state playoffs. The team won their first two tournament games and were poised to move on to the championship. Then two star starting players, a goalie and a halfback, were arrested and charged with having alcohol in their possession and drinking in a car on the Saturday night before the semifinals.

Both players, who had known the rules about not using alcohol, were immediately suspended from the team. Hampered by not having these two key players, the soccer team lost 3-1, despite good performances by substitute players. The team coach voiced the feelings of disappointment that everyone else felt: "Some kids made the team their priority, and some didn't. And it's obvious who the ones are who didn't."

Money as Servant, Not Master. William Jennings Bryant, the well-known political figure early in the twentieth century, was never mistaken for being a social philosopher. Yet he did have a fitting response to those who worshiped the idol of financial gain. "Money is to be the servant of people," he once stated, "and I protest against all theories that enthrone money and debase humankind."

Mistaken Religion. Doris, a teacher of second graders in a parochial school, had a bright idea one day as an assignment for the children in her religion class. She told them to take paper and crayons and make a picture to show what they would do if they were to spend a day with Jesus. The kids eagerly went to work, and Doris felt pleased that valuable spiritual lessons were being learned. Then one tyke approached her carrying her nearly-finished drawing and asked, "Teacher, how do you spell Bloomingdales?"

Garbage Problems. In one day, a typical American creates nearly four and a half pounds of garbage. And in one year, we produce a total of 217 million tons of garbage, up from 88 million tons only 40 years ago. Much of our trash is food waste. The report of our prodigious amount of throwaway stuff at a time when hunger and malnutrition are widespread in certain areas of the world, including the United States, should disturb us. The Old Testament prophets thundered against such a wasteful lifestyle in which some had plenty while others had little or nothing. Our offerings of prayer and worship are empty if we do not show concern for the hungry, poor, and oppressed.

FOR YOUTH

■ **TOPIC:** God Has High Expectations

■ **QUESTIONS:** 1. Why did some prominent Israelites detest those who told the truth? 2. Why would God prevent the wicked rich from enjoying their mansions and vineyards? 3. Under what condition could the Israelites anticipate God's mercy? 4. What was God's attitude toward Israel's religious festivals? 5. How could the Israelites foster the practice of fairness within their society?

■ **ILLUSTRATIONS:**

Only a Show. Melvin Adams, who retired from the Harlem Globetrotters in 2000, described his mother waking him each Sunday to go to church. He went with his mother, but sat in the back of the church in the last pew. Instead of an open Bible on his lap, he held an open copy of *Sports Illustrated,* which he read. Outwardly, Melvin looked religious and committed, but his worship participation was only a show. Not until much later in his life did he finally make a commitment to Christ.

Like Adams, many people are mechanical in their worship participation. They may sit in church, but their minds are somewhere else. Their worship is phony, for they make empty offerings of praise to God. Amos called his listeners to make their offerings to Lord genuine and wholehearted.

End of Time. A *Peanuts* cartoon strip pictured an upset Peppermint Patty. She had heard that the end of the world was near. Trembling, she asked her friend, Marcie, "What if the world ends tonight?" Marcie responded, "I promise there'll be a tomorrow, sir. In fact, it is already tomorrow in Australia."

Many youth now, as well as in Amos's time, reflect Marcie's belief. They assume that the end will be a wonderful time when God will bless His people. Yes, this is true for believers. But the prophet also said that the end would be a time of judgment for those who have not committed themselves in faith to the Lord. All lives will undergo scrutiny.

More Commitment? One happy and surprising note is that the number of American teenagers attending worship has risen. In 1975, the number on an average weekend was 47 percent. In 2005, the number had risen to 55 percent. Another significant sign is the increase in volunteer service. Perhaps some youth are finally making more than empty offerings to the Lord. They are trying to offer genuine worship and truly work for justice and righteousness in the world.

Bad Decision's Consequences. The battle of Midway abruptly changed the course of World War II in the Pacific. Up to that point, the Japanese had experienced nothing but victory. But on the morning of June 3, 1942, the situation dramatically changed. The Americans followed up a Japanese air attack on Midway Island with one of their own from the island and from aircraft carriers.

Admiral Nagumo had four aircraft carriers (the *Akagi*, *Kaga*, *Soryu*, and *Hiryu*, which were all Pearl Harbor veterans), two battleships, two cruisers, several destroyers, and a few support craft. Nagumo used his fleet to beat back every American plane. The admiral then received word that an additional attack would be necessary to invade Midway. However, Nagumo also received surprising information about the presence of additional American ships, including an aircraft carrier.

This news caught the admiral by surprise and prompted him to hesitate in making a decision. His own airborne planes needed to land and refuel. Others sat ready on the aircraft carrier decks. A colleague named Admiral Yamaguchi advised that an immediate air attack be launched on the American fleet, and other officers agreed with this advice.

But Nagumo ignored the counsel of the other admirals and ordered that the flight decks be cleared of all aircraft. Thus, fully loaded planes, laden with bombs and torpedoes, were moved below in the hanger bay as the returning planes were landed and readied for a second attack.

Meanwhile planes from the American aircraft carrier, *Yorktown*, flew over the Japanese armada and found the flight decks of the four enemy aircraft carriers crowded with planes that were ready to be launched and loaded with fuel and explosives. The American pilots immediately decided to attack. By day's end, all four of the Japanese carriers and a heavy cruiser lay at the bottom of the Pacific Ocean.

The American victory occurred because a Japanese admiral ignored the wise advice of his subordinates. Similarly, the failure of believers to obey God is sometimes due to their refusal to listen to the wise council of their friends in the faith.

HOSEA PREACHES GOD'S ACCUSATION AGAINST ISRAEL

2

BACKGROUND SCRIPTURE: Hosea 4:1-4; 7:1-2; 12:7-9; 14:1-3; 2 Kings 15:8-10
DEVOTIONAL READING: Hosea 14

KEY VERSE: There is no truth, nor mercy, nor knowledge of God in the land. Hosea 4:1.

KING JAMES VERSION

HOSEA 4:1 Hear the word of the LORD, ye children of Israel: for the LORD hath a controversy with the inhabitants of the land, because there is no truth, nor mercy, nor knowledge of God in the land. 2 By swearing, and lying, and killing, and stealing, and committing adultery, they break out, and blood toucheth blood. 3 Therefore shall the land mourn, and every one that dwelleth therein shall languish, with the beasts of the field, and with the fowls of heaven; yea, the fishes of the sea also shall be taken away. 4 Yet let no man strive, nor reprove another: for thy people are as they that strive with the priest. . . .

7:1 When I would have healed Israel, then the iniquity of Ephraim was discovered, and the wickedness of Samaria: for they commit falsehood; and the thief cometh in, and the troop of robbers spoileth without. 2 And they consider not in their hearts that I remember all their wickedness: now their own doings have beset them about; they are before my face. . . .

12:8 And Ephraim said, Yet I am become rich, I have found me out substance: in all my labours they shall find none iniquity in me that were sin. 9 And I that am the LORD thy God from the land of Egypt will yet make thee to dwell in tabernacles, as in the days of the solemn feast.

NEW REVISED STANDARD VERSION

HOSEA 4:1 Hear the word of the LORD, O people of Israel;
for the LORD has an indictment against the
inhabitants of the land.
There is no faithfulness or loyalty,
and no knowledge of God in the land.
2 Swearing, lying, and murder,
and stealing and adultery break out;
bloodshed follows bloodshed.
3 Therefore the land mourns,
and all who live in it languish;
together with the wild animals
and the birds of the air,
even the fish of the sea are perishing.
4 Yet let no one contend,
and let none accuse,
for with you is my contention, O priest. . . .
7:1 When I would heal Israel,
the corruption of Ephraim is revealed,
and the wicked deeds of Samaria;
for they deal falsely,
the thief breaks in,
and the bandits raid outside.
2 But they do not consider
that I remember all their wickedness.
Now their deeds surround them,
they are before my face. . . .
12:8 Ephraim has said, "Ah, I am rich,
I have gained wealth for myself;
in all of my gain
no offense has been found in me
that would be sin."
9 I am the LORD your God
from the land of Egypt;
I will make you live in tents again,
as in the days of the appointed festival.

HOME BIBLE READINGS

BACKGROUND

Hosea, the son of Beeri, came from the northern kingdom of Israel. His messages were primarily directed at Israel, but in some cases they encompassed Judah as well. The heading for the Book of Hosea (1:1) loosely dates the prophet's ministry by the reigns of one king of Israel and four kings of Judah. This suggests that Hosea may have compiled the book in Judah after Israel's fall to the Assyrians. Hosea's ministry probably extended from about 760 to 715 B.C.

God told Hosea to marry a woman named Gomer who was characterized by harlotry (1:2). Her marital infidelity became a picture of Israel's unfaithfulness to God. Hosea eventually rejected his wife for her disloyalty, and this rejection is evident in the names the prophet gave to their three children. Jezreel, which means "sown (or scattered) by God" (1:4-5), pictured the fall of the northern kingdom and the scattering of its people into captivity. Loruhamah, which means "without compassion" (1:6), pictured the extent of God's wrath toward His unfaithful people. In fact, He allowed the Assyrians to conquer the nation in 722 B.C. Loammi, which means "not my people" (1:8-9), pictured the break in the covenant relationship between God and Israel.

In Hosea 1:10—2:1, the theme suddenly changes from judgment to blessing. The blessing would involve population growth, a relationship to God, and reunification of the northern and southern kingdoms. These promises were perhaps partly fulfilled when Jews returned to Judah from Babylonian exile beginning about 538 B.C. However, most conservative commentators believe the final fulfillment comes later. Some commentators believe these promises are fulfilled in the Christian church. Other commentators believe they are yet to be fulfilled in Jewish history.

Some details in these verses deserve special comment. The promise that the Israelites would be as numerous as the sand on the seashore (1:10) was a repetition of a promise originally made to Abraham (Gen. 22:17). The apostle Paul applied the promise of divine adoption (Hos. 1:10) to the inclusion of Gentiles in the Christian church (Rom. 9:26). The *one head* (Hos. 1:11) under whom *the children of Judah and the children of Israel* would be reunited is probably the Messiah, Jesus of Nazareth. The reference to God's people coming up *out of the land* is probably a reference to a return from exile. The names of Hosea and Gomer's children are used in all three of these verses as contrasts to promised blessing.

In 2:2, Hosea told the faithful remnant of God's people to rebuke their unfaithful peers for abandoning their relationship with the Lord. Because the nation refused to turn from her evil ways, she would suffer the calamities mentioned in 2:3-13. The Lord was just in doing this because His people attributed their prosperity to false gods. This would signify God's temporary rejection of His chosen people. When this period of chastisement ended, the Israelites would repent of their sin and be restored in their relationship with God.

When the Messiah returned to earth, God would speak to Israel's heart and bring her back to the promised land (2:14-15). In that day, the Lord would change the name of the valley of Achor, which means "valley of trouble," into *door of hope.* At the end of the age, God would pour out His favor on His chosen people. They would recognize Him as their husband and would abandon their idolatrous ways (2:16-17). In the future day of restoration, Israel would live in safety from wild beasts and people (2:18). She would be faithful to God (2:19-22), return to the promised land, experience His compassion, and be His people (2:22-23).

The Lord commanded Hosea to love Gomer by restoring her as his wife (3:1). The prophet bought her for the equivalent of 30 shekels of silver (3:2). Hosea's love continued to picture God's affection for unfaithful Israel. Hosea kept Gomer in seclusion for *many days* (3:3), which pictured the long period of time in exile that Israel would be without monarchy, sacrifice, or holy vest (3:4). Hosea 3:5 reveals that this time of exile would eventually end, and that God would permit Israel to return to Canaan. She would be faithful to the Lord and desire the establishment of the kingdom promised to David. Like the restored Israel of the coming messianic age, we should make every effort to be faithful to God. Likewise, our deepest desire should be the establishment of His kingdom (Matt. 6:10).

NOTES ON THE PRINTED TEXT

Sadness is woven throughout the fabric of the Book of Hosea. The parallel between Gomer's adultery and Israel's betrayal of God graphically teaches the meaning of forgiveness and enduring love in the face of sorrow. Hosea, whose name means "salvation," tried to rescue his wife from prostitution. In like manner, God desired that His people repent of their adultery. But that was not to be the case. Hosea described Israel's idolatry and wickedness, resulting in judgment, captivity, and deportation by the Assyrians. However, God's unchanging love offered hope. Hosea later told about the remnant who would be restored to God and their homeland.

Such divine mercy is all the more incredible against the backdrop of Israel's many sins. In 4:1, the Lord acted like a modern-day prosecutor to bring a list of charges against Israel, the defendant. He had blessed His people by rescuing them from Egypt and enabling them to conquer and settle the promised land. But despite all that, the

Israelites still persisted in violating the stipulations of the Mosaic covenant. In particular, the people were guilty of being unfaithful and unloving, both to Him and to their fellow human beings. In addition, there was no acknowledgment of God throughout the land. The Hebrew word rendered *knowledge* does not refer to intellectual awareness, but to recognition of God's authority as the covenant Lord of Israel.

Hosea 4:2 continues to catalogue the nation's sins. The Israelites had violated the third of the Ten Commandments by invoking God's name in pronouncing a curse on others (see Exod. 20:7). When the people lied, they broke the ninth commandment (see 20:16). Murder went against the sixth commandment (see 20:13). Stealing was an infraction of the eighth commandment (see 20:15). Finally, adultery broke the seventh commandment (see 20:14). From the divine perspective, Israel's sins knew no limits. All ethical boundaries had been breached, with one sin of violence leading to murder. In fact, the cascade of crimes was unrelenting, as if one transgression followed another so closely that they appeared to be touching (Hos. 4:2).

This was a lamentable circumstance for the Israelites. It was as if the land mourned and everyone who dwelt within it languished. Evidently, God sent a drought to punish the Israelites. Because the land was parched, all who depended on it—the wild animals of the field, the birds in the sky, and the fish in the sea—were perishing (4:3). The temptation in such a dire situation would be for leaders and people alike to foist the blame for their iniquities onto others. But the Lord forbid this from happening (4:4). He held people accountable for their own crimes. God compared the Israelites to people with a complaint against the priests. According to Deuteronomy 17:12, contempt against a priest was a capital crime.

In Hosea 7, God's charges against His people continue to be enumerated. It is not as if the Lord did not care. He repeatedly sought to heal Israel. But then the sins of Ephraim and the crimes of Samaria were exposed. The idea is that the transgressions of the people were exceedingly great. In 7:1, *Israel* refers to the northern kingdom (in contrast to the southern kingdom of Judah). *Ephraim* denotes the most influential tribe in the northern kingdom. *Samaria* was the capitol city of the northern kingdom. Generally speaking, each of these terms collectively refers to the Israelites. The people were guilty of committing fraud. For example, thieves broke into houses and gangs of bandits raided people in the streets. These crimes reflect the ethical bankruptcy of the nation.

The Israelites mistakenly thought that they could commit their crimes and get away with it. Supposedly, the Lord was not watching or did not really care what occurred in the promised land among His covenant people. Hosea 7:2, however, declares that God was fully aware of their transgressions, and He never forgot any of them. These were not trivial matters, either. God's people were suffocating under the crushing weight of their iniquities. Their transgressions surrounded them and inundated them like a flood. The only way out was for them to turn to the Lord in repentance and faith.

That was not likely to happen, though. According to 12:7, Israel's merchants used dishonest business practices to increase their wealth. The people incorrectly assumed that their ill-gotten riches were a sign of God's blessing and favor. Based on this faulty premise, the Israelites smugly imagined that God's prophets would not convict them of iniquity or sin (12:8). But nothing could be further from the truth.

The sovereign Lord had every right to discipline His wayward people. After all, He had been their God ever since He freed them from slavery in Egypt (12:9). The verse relates a future when the Israelites would be forced to exchange their comfortable homes for flimsy huts like those they used during the feast of tabernacles (Lev. 23:42-43). Hosea 12:9, then, is a glimpse of conditions during the Assyrian captivity. Such would be the heavy price God's covenant people would have to pay for centuries of wallowing in sin.

SUGGESTIONS TO TEACHERS

How would you describe God's love to someone who asked what that compassion is like? Perhaps as a Christian you might talk about the Cross. But could you come up with some other illustration of the sacrificial and undeserved caring of God (which we see in Jesus laying down His life)? Hosea's experience is a superb example of God's love.

1. MARRIAGE SHOWING GOD'S CONCERN. Hosea's heartbreaking experience of having his beloved wife, Gomer, leave him and turn into a harlot provided the scenario for Hosea's messages. This prophet realized that God felt the same hurt and heartache toward His wayward and unfaithful people. Remind your students that the Lord is not aloof or dispassionate. His emotional involvement with us is greater than we realize.

2. MESSAGE STATING THE NATION'S CONDITION. Have your students note the names Hosea gave to his three children and the significance of each of these names. This prophet wanted to make as public a statement as possible about the transgressions of God's people. While we would not saddle our children with such names, we should be willing to go public with our understanding of how God wants His people to live.

3. MISERY SURFACING FROM ISRAEL'S AFFAIR. Hosea compared Israel's unfaithfulness to God with Gomer's infidelity to the prophet. The hurt and harm of her behavior was deep and destructive. Even more hurtful and harmful was Israel's insistence on her "affairs" with idols.

What are some of the false gods of our time that we are inclined to run off with? Power? Success? Popularity? Violence? Greed? Pleasure? When any of these (or others) become more interesting and absorbing than the Lord, we have become unfaithful to Him. Talk with your students about the importance of maintaining unwavering commitments, especially to the Lord.

4. MEMORY SUMMONING PEOPLE'S RETURN. Allow sufficient lesson time to get across Hosea's message of God's astonishing mercy. Despite broken vows, God refuses to forget us and give us up as His beloved people. In these days when many despair about the Church or see no hope for the future, encourage your students to note Hosea's words of promise.

FOR ADULTS	■ **TOPIC:** God's Indictment of Israel

■ **QUESTIONS:** 1. Why did the Lord bring a covenant lawsuit against His people? 2. How was it possible for the Israelites to have lost a true knowledge of God? 3. Why did the people of the northern kingdom practice fraud and resort to thievery? 4. In what sense had the Israelites become surrounded by their sins? 5. Why would God's people think that their wealth would absolve them of their iniquities?

■ **ILLUSTRATIONS:**

A Call to Faithfulness. Jesse was an avid hunter. He loved the fall season each year, when the big Northern geese began to fly south over the harvested fields of Washington wheat. It was his favorite kind of hunting. However, today wasn't the same as most of his hunting days. Jesse's mind was preoccupied with thoughts of infidelity.

Jesse and Robin had been married for 12 years, and though she was a loyal and loving wife, Jesse was growing weary of his commitment. He knew what he was thinking about was wrong. The Bible referred to it as *vain . . . imaginations* (Rom. 1:21). But Jesse wasn't sure it was as bad as all the sermons he had heard. There were two women that Jesse couldn't get out of his thoughts. One was a coworker who had made her intentions clear. The other was the flirtatious wife of an occasional hunting partner.

Suddenly, Jesse heard the sound of geese, but it was a sound from ground level. A few yards away, two Canadian "honkers" were waddling toward the pond. One goose dragged an obviously broken wing, while the other goose seemed to stand watch over its companion. Jesse remembered how geese mate for life, and if one is shot or injured, the other goose seemed to stand watch over its partner. Under his breath, he whispered quietly to the healthy bird, "You must be quite a specimen to stay with this one, when you could be off doing what you want."

Jesse immediately realized he had just heard the answer to a question that he had never thought to ask—about the importance of his own faithfulness in his relationship with his wife and God.

Permanent Vows. Gomer, Hosea's wife, was unfaithful to her marriage vows. The heartbreaking experience served as a way for Hosea to tell God's people how they were not keeping their vows to the Lord.

Vows to a marriage partner, like our vows to the Lord, are meant to be kept. With almost half of all marriages in the United States failing and ending, we are called to remember that the commitment to one's spouse is modeled on God's commitment to us through Christ. God has vowed to stay with us, caringly, faithfully, and permanently. In turn, we as husbands and wives give our word to the Lord, to one another, and to the public that we will remain together caringly, faithfully, and permanently.

Tragically, many enter into the marriage relationship along the lines indicated in a recent cartoon in *The Wall Street Journal*. A prospective bride and groom are shown standing before a pastor, with the husband-to-be asking, "Do you have a ceremony less drastic than marriage?"

Prophet-Like Poem. A church newsletter carried this poem, which tells of the way we all break our vows to the Lord.

> I think that I shall never see
> A church that's all it ought to be;
> A church whose members never stray
> Beyond the straight and narrow way.
> A church that has no empty pews,
> Whose pastor never has the blues,
> A church whose deacons always deak
> And none is proud and all are meek;
> Where gossips never peddle lies,
> Or make complaints or criticize.
> Where all are always sweet and kind
> And to all others' faults are blind.
> Such perfect churches there may be,
> But none of them are known to me.
> But still we'll work and pray and plan
> To make our own the best we can.

FOR YOUTH
■ TOPIC: Living Up to God's Higher Expectation
■ QUESTIONS: 1. What charge did the Lord bring against Israel? 2. What sorts of iniquities did the Israelites commit? 3. Who did God say were responsible for these crimes? 4. How extensive was God's awareness of His people's sins? 5. What was the nature of Ephraim's boasting?

■ ILLUSTRATIONS:
Long Term Consequences. Voluminous research has documented the effects of marital infidelity and divorce on children. A team of psychologists from Catholic

University of Milan, Italy, compared 160 teens from intact homes with solid marriages with a similar number of those young people from homes with broken marriages. Those from the shattered homes had a higher level of distrust of other people, were fearful of a marital commitment, less confident of themselves, more suspicious of others in general, and more likely to engage in premarital and extramarital sexual relationships.

God calls for faithful commitment to Himself and to one's spouse and family. The long-term consequences for those who are in committed relationships with God and their families are a healthier and more emotionally stable world.

Key to Happiness. Most people generally assume that being single and living the carefree life of a young swinger is truly happy. There appear to be no responsibilities or duties except to oneself.

Numerous studies, however, have demonstrated that faithfully married people live happier lives than those who are single. Most recently, Wayne State sociologists Steven Stack and J. Ross Eshleman studied 18,000 adults in 17 industrialized countries including Japan, Canada, Australia, and Europe, and they concluded that couples living in faithful marriages were happier than couples who were cohabiting together, and much happier than singles.

Gomer never understood that being committed to her spouse (Hosea) could have led to happiness. Gomer thought that satisfaction came outside the bounds of marriage. This led her to a variety of relationships with other men in the impossible quest to find joy. Ultimately, she never did realize that the key to happiness lay in being loyal to her spouse.

Weakened Institution. If the family is the main institution of American life, what is the shape of our nation? Consider that 30 percent of American children grow up in a single-parent home. The single parent is just as likely to have never married (35%) as divorced (37%). According to the latest U.S. Census Bureau statistics in "Marital Status and Living Arrangements," the number of unmarried couples living together, almost 4 million, is 7 times more than the figure from a decade earlier. Small wonder that some youth fear that the basic institution of society—marriage—is crumbling.

God calls for faithful commitments between a husband and a wife. This was the model that Hosea tried to demonstrate through his relationship with Gomer.

ISAIAH CALLS FOR TRUE WORSHIP

BACKGROUND SCRIPTURE: Isaiah 1:10-20; 2 Kings 15:32-35
DEVOTIONAL READING: Isaiah 58:6-12

KEY VERSE: Seek judgment, relieve the oppressed. Isaiah 1:17.

KING JAMES VERSION

ISAIAH 1:10 Hear the word of the LORD, ye rulers of Sodom; give ear unto the law of our God, ye people of Gomorrah. 11 To what purpose is the multitude of your sacrifices unto me? saith the LORD: I am full of the burnt offerings of rams, and the fat of fed beasts; and I delight not in the blood of bullocks, or of lambs, or of he goats. . . . 14 Your new moons and your appointed feasts my soul hateth: they are a trouble unto me; I am weary to bear them. 15 And when ye spread forth your hands, I will hide mine eyes from you: yea, when ye make many prayers, I will not hear: your hands are full of blood.

16 Wash you, make you clean; put away the evil of your doings from before mine eyes; cease to do evil; 17 Learn to do well; seek judgment, relieve the oppressed, judge the fatherless, plead for the widow. 18 Come now, and let us reason together, saith the LORD: though your sins be as scarlet, they shall be as white as snow: though they be red like crimson, they shall be as wool. 19 If ye be willing and obedient, ye shall eat the good of the land: 20 But if ye refuse and rebel, ye shall be devoured with the sword: for the mouth of the LORD hath spoken it.

NEW REVISED STANDARD VERSION

ISAIAH 1:10 Hear the word of the LORD,
    you rulers of Sodom!
Listen to the teaching of our God,
    you people of Gomorrah!
11 What to me is the multitude of your sacrifices?
    says the LORD;
I have had enough of burnt offerings of rams
    and the fat of fed beasts;
I do not delight in the blood of bulls,
    or of lambs, or of goats. . . .
14 Your new moons and your appointed festivals
    my soul hates;
they have become a burden to me,
    I am weary of bearing them.
15 When you stretch out your hands,
    I will hide my eyes from you;
even though you make many prayers,
    I will not listen;
    your hands are full of blood.
16 Wash yourselves; make yourselves clean;
    remove the evil of your doings
    from before my eyes;
cease to do evil,
17 learn to do good;
seek justice,
    rescue the oppressed,
defend the orphan,
    plead for the widow.
18 Come now, let us argue it out,
    says the LORD:
though your sins are like scarlet,
    they shall be like snow;
though they are red like crimson,
    they shall become like wool.
19 If you are willing and obedient,
    you shall eat the good of the land;
20 but if you refuse and rebel,
    you shall be devoured by the sword;
    for the mouth of the LORD has spoken.

Monday, June 11	Psalm 65:1-8	*Praise for God's Goodness*
Tuesday, June 12	2 Kings 15:32-36	*Doing Right in God's Sight*
Wednesday, June 13	Isaiah 6:1-8	*Here Am I; Send Me*
Thursday, June 14	Isaiah 58:6-12	*The Fast that Pleases God*
Friday, June 15	Isaiah 40:1-5	*Comfort for God's People*
Saturday, June 16	Isaiah 1:10-14	*Not Desiring Sacrifices*
Sunday, June 17	Isaiah 1:15-20	*Learn to Do Good*

BACKGROUND

Verse 1 of chapter 1 is the heading for Isaiah. It reveals basic information about the book. Isaiah, whose name means "the Lord saves," was born and reared in Jerusalem in days of prosperity. It seems that Isaiah's family was an affluent one and that he was well educated. Jewish tradition holds that Isaiah's father, Amoz, was a brother of King Amaziah. If so, then Isaiah was a grandson of King Joash and a first cousin of King Uzziah. Certainly Isaiah spent much time in the company of royalty. He even gave advice on foreign affairs to King Hezekiah.

According to 8:3, Isaiah was married to a *prophetess*. This word may mean that she carried on a prophetic ministry of her own, or it may simply mean that she was the wife of a prophet. She and Isaiah had two sons, whose names were symbolic (Isa. 7:3; 8:3). Isaiah received his call to ministry in the year of King Uzziah's death, that is, 740 B.C. Isaiah's ministry continued through the reigns of *Uzziah, Jotham, Ahaz, and Hezekiah.* These four men were consecutive *kings of Judah* whose combined reigns stretched from 792 to 686 B.C. According to tradition, Isaiah was martyred during King Manasseh's reign (697–642 B.C.) by being sawed in half inside a hollow log. Possibly Hebrews 11:37 refers to this event.

The Book of Isaiah is a compilation of history, predictions, warnings, and promises relayed from God, through Isaiah, to the people of Judah. That Isaiah wrote the book is confirmed by the appearance of his name an additional 15 times throughout the book. Apparently the revelation that God gave Isaiah came, at least partly, in visual form. Throughout his long ministry, Isaiah preached about God's righteousness, warned about judgment for sin, and proclaimed God's love and forgiveness. Isaiah also prophesied the glory that awaits those who remain faithful to God. Among Christians, the Book of Isaiah is one of the best-loved books in the Old Testament. The primary reason for this is that Isaiah contains more prophecies of the Messiah, Jesus, than any other Old Testament book. John 12:41 says that Isaiah saw Jesus' glory and spoke about Him.

We don't know for sure how the prophecies of chapter 1 fit into the period of Isaiah's ministry. The same is true for many of the prophecies in the book. Yet, even without knowing the precise historical context or date for certain parts of the book, we can gain useful spiritual insight from those parts. The first chapter of Isaiah takes the form of a lawsuit against the people of Judah. The Lord indicted the people because they violated the Mosaic covenant. This covenant (or agreement), containing God's commandments, had been made with the nation at Mount Sinai, following the Exodus. In Deuteronomy, God promised great blessings if the nation would live in obedience to the covenant. God also warned that if the nation disobeyed His commands, it would experience the punishments listed in the covenant (Deut. 28:15-68)—including exile.

In this courtroom scene, Isaiah called upon heaven and earth to act as witnesses to the accusations leveled against the nation (Isa. 1:2; see Deut. 30:19; 31:28). The whole universe was to bear witness that God's judgments are just. The Lord charged Judah with rebelling against Him. The word for *rebelled* (Isa. 1:2) was often used among the ancients in reference to a subordinate state's violation of a treaty with a dominant nation. In Isaiah 1, the word points to Judah's blatant violation of God's covenant. Even dumb animals like oxen and donkeys find their way to their masters and homes. But the people of Judah, as if they were more ignorant than beasts of burden, stubbornly refused to go back to their heavenly Master (1:3). Judah was also indicted as a *sinful nation* (1:4).

In 1:5-6, wayward Judah is compared to a beaten body with external wounds—head to foot—and internal wounds—in the heart. Externally (or politically), Judah was beset on all sides by hostile enemies. These enemies inflicted *wounds* by seizing some of Judah's territory. Internally (or spiritually), Judah was spiritually destitute. Judah's whole "body" was in a state of ruin, and this was due to the nation's rebellion against God. This beaten body is further described in terms of the land being *desolate* (1:7), *burned*, and *overthrown* (vs. 7). In Isaiah's time, Judah suffered attacks from Israel, Syria, Edom, Philistia, and Assyria.

The *daughter of Zion* (meaning Jerusalem; 1:8) is described as *a cottage in a vineyard* and *a lodge in a garden of cucumbers.* These temporary structures were lightweight sun shelters for people who guarded the crops against thieves. After the crops were harvested, the structures were abandoned. Similarly, Jerusalem was deserted. Also, it was like a *besieged city.* The survival of some of the people of Judah was God's gracious provision to prevent the nation's complete disappearance (1:9). If it were not for this group of survivors, Judah would have been utterly destroyed for its sin—just as the cities of Sodom and Gomorrah had been destroyed long before (Gen. 18:16—19:29).

NOTES ON THE PRINTED TEXT

Despite the blessings the Israelites had enjoyed under David and Solomon and the loving chastisements that they had later experienced, God's chosen people still failed to remain in a vital relationship with the Lord. Isaiah's mission was to warn that because of their affront to and rejection of God, His faithful promise of consequentially tragic judgment was sure and imminent. Isaiah likened both the rulers and the people of Judah to the evil cities of Sodom and Gomorrah. Because these cities were horribly evil, they had been destroyed. Judah, too, was ripe for judgment because of sin. Isaiah therefore urged the nation to listen to God's Word (Isa. 1:10).

One of Isaiah's most important messages was that religious rituals are meaningless if the worshipers' life is not brought into conformity with God's righteous standards. For instance, the people of Judah were hypocrites and their rituals were shams. They offered plenty of sacrifices—the burnt offering of rams, the fat of well-fed beasts, and the blood of bulls, lambs, and goats—but it was almost as if they were trying to bribe God to spare them the punishment they knew they deserved (1:11). The purely legalistic performance of rituals, festivals, offerings, and incense burning had become unbearable to God. In fact, He saw these seemingly pious acts for the hypocrisy they represented (1:12-13). Isaiah 1:14 specifically mentions Judah's New Moon festivals as well as other appointed feasts. The former occurred monthly, following the lunar cycle.

Massive offerings and the blasting of trumpets characterized the New Moon festival. The purpose was to celebrate Israel's unity and to commemorate God's covenants. But because of Judah's rebellion, God now hated these feast days. They were like a heavy burden that He was tired of carrying. Even the prayers of His people were odious to Him, regardless of the manner in which the petitions were made or the number of times they were offered (1:15a). Isaiah was not saying that rituals were wrong in themselves. Rather, he was speaking out against going through the motions of religion, which might make people feel better, but their hearts remained festering with the filth of unrepentance.

During Isaiah's lifetime, social injustice was widespread in Judah. Examples of the injustice Isaiah and his contemporary, Micah, condemned were the making of unjust laws to deprive the poor and needy of their rights (Isa. 10:1-2) and the use of fraud as a means to seize property (Mic. 2:1-2). As always, social injustice in that time and place took the form of victimization of the weak by the strong. According to Isaiah, God's people not only should avoid victimizing others, but should also actively take the part of those who are victimized. The reference, though, in Isaiah 1:15b to the hands of the people of Judah being full of blood indicates how far removed they were in their practice from the divine ideal. In particular, God's people had on their hands the blood of those whom they mistreated.

Isaiah 1:16 contains an exhortation for the people of Judah to wash and cleanse themselves. They were also to remove their evil deeds from God's sight. The Lord's call to repentance was to transcend mere emotion, being demonstrated in concrete action within the socio-economic realm. If the people responded accordingly, God would forgive them. The people of Judah were not left directionless about the Lord's expectations. God commanded them to stop doing wrong and learn to do right. They were to pursue justice by rebuking the oppressor and consoling the oppressed (1:17).

After making His case for Judah's guilt, the Lord urged them to join Him in considering their options for the future. If they repented, they would experience His forgiveness and renewed blessing. But if they persisted in sin, they would endure His judgment. *Come now, and let us reason together* (1:18) translates a common phrase used among ancient people in reference to arguing a legal case in a courtroom. The idea seems to be that as a result of the argument that had been presented in God's court, the defendants (the guilty people of Judah) were to realize their error, turn from sin, and receive cleansing from God.

The sins of the people were said to be like scarlet (a red dye) and as red as crimson (a red cloth). In other words, their iniquities were like bloodstains on their souls. But if they turned away from sin and turned toward God, their sins would be cleansed and spiritually they would be as white as snow or wool. Judah was now presented with a choice. Heeding the covenant would restore blessing to the land (1:19). But insurrection would bring judgment in the form of military defeat (1:20). This section closes with the solemn words that the mouth of the Lord had spoken. By this statement, Judah was assured that Isaiah's pronouncements would surely come to pass.

SUGGESTIONS TO TEACHERS

Guilt has never been a popular concept, and it probably has never been less acceptable to people than it is today. In fact, many go so far as to cynically think that having any standards at all is what leads to trouble. Supposedly, if you do not have any standards, you do not break them. This week's lesson from Isaiah 1 is a strong corrective to such warped thinking.

1. RECOGNIZING SIN IN OUR LIVES. Like the Israelites, we can easily allow arrogance and pride to poison our attitudes. The new gods of secular thought seduce us away, and even for the believer they can gradually replace what had been godly ways of thinking. How readily do we worship the idols of secular reasoning and materialism over God's inspired Word? When we do find ourselves struggling with any of these sins, we need to take to heart the message of Isaiah presented in this week's lesson.

2. DEALING WITH SIN IN OUR LIVES. We cannot relate to God unless we first admit that we are sinful. Our iniquities are like deep, bloody stains that we cannot remove from our souls. The only way to find cleansing from sin's defilement is to trust in the same Messiah whom Isaiah anticipated. Redemption for God's people comes when they believe in His Son, Jesus Christ. Only God can cleanse that soul, making it spiritually white as snow.

3. EXPERIENCING GOD'S FORGIVENESS. This is an important step along the path of becoming increasingly holy. We can feel rather good about how our spiritual life is going when we compare ourselves to those around us. But when we step into the presence of a holy God, our self-righteousness suddenly appears to us as filthy rags. We suddenly get things into perspective.

4. CONSIDERING GOD'S HOLINESS. Doing this can be a purifying experience. It helps us see ourselves as individuals who are stained by sin. It also helps us to see our need for God's cleansing, be attentive to His invitation to become spiritually reborn in Christ, and live for the Savior in humble adoration. God does not want us to look at ourselves in comparison to our neighbor. He wants us to remain in His presence, where we will remember the truth about ourselves and about His grace. Thereby being humbled and enthused, we then long to worship God and be made worthy of serving Him.

FOR ADULTS

■ **TOPIC:** True Worship!

■ **QUESTIONS:** 1. What was it about Sodom and Gomorrah that made them the epitome of sin? 2. What had gone wrong with the multitude of the people's sacrifices to the Lord? 3. What was burdensome to God about the festivals His people observed? 4. What sorts of wrongs had God's people committed? 5. What would the result be if the people of Judah continued to rebel against God?

■ **ILLUSTRATIONS:**

Disappointment. May was a 46-year-old mother of three children when she was diagnosed with gastric cancer. An operation followed, but failed to remove all of the cancer. Chemotherapy next followed with periodic days of hospitalization. Still, the hardest problem was not the nausea or the pain. Rather, it was seeing the apparent indifference of her three children.

Two high schoolers and a middle schooler would walk by the dining room where May's bed had been set up and would perhaps say, "Hi," and acknowledge her presence, before moving on to their own rooms. She confided in her pastor the hurt and sadness of seeing years of love and devotion to them forgotten so quickly when the illness appeared. They seemed not to notice her feelings of pain and disappointment towards them.

Long before this woman vocalized her feelings, the prophet Isaiah voiced God's disappointment with His people. Rather than shower Him with true worship, they spurned His love.

Pushing Away. Isaiah and the rest of the Old Testament prophets frequently reminded their hearers that they were rejecting the true worship of God. The words of the Lord's spokespersons should also warn us not to reject Him. But sometimes we view their warnings as being irrelevant.

Perhaps the Dutch can help us in this regard. They use the Dutch word *afstofen* to translate the term "reject." In Dutch, *afstofen* means "to push away," as in pushing away a boat from a pier. The seafaring Dutch immediately understood the meaning of the prophets' warning against "pushing away" from the Lord. The image of refusing to be tied fast in a trusting relationship with God suggested to this nation of mariners that they, like their oceangoing vessels, would be in peril if they pushed away from the pier instead of being permitted to establish a safe and firm mooring.

Sadie's Loss. A woman named Sadie served as a housemother for many years in a school for missionaries' children in the Philippines. Sadie loved books. She had brought a large collection of beautiful volumes with her when she came from the United States to the Philippines. Though she initially loaned out a few to some favored children, Sadie preferred to hoard her prized library in a footlocker under her bed. She seldom bothered to open the footlocker or to take out any of her treasured volumes. For years, her books remained in the footlocker under her bed.

One night, Sadie thought she heard a faint gnawing noise. After searching everywhere in the room, she finally discovered that the sounds were coming from the footlocker under her bed. She opened the locker, and to her dismay, she found nothing but an enormous pile of dust. Termites had devoured all the precious books in her treasured library!

God's judgment is somewhat like that. Just as Sadie had hoarded her expensive books rather than share them (or even use them), so too God's people in Isaiah's day had refused to share or show His mercy to others. Such a miserly attitude led to their eternal loss, not gain.

FOR YOUTH

■ TOPIC: The Heart of Worship

■ QUESTIONS: 1. Why did some prominent Israelites detest those who told the truth? 2. Why would God prevent the wicked rich from enjoying their mansions and vineyards? 3. Under what condition could the Israelites anticipate God's mercy? 4. What was God's attitude toward Israel's religious festivals? 5. How could the Israelites foster the practice of fairness within their society?

■ ILLUSTRATIONS:

Heartfelt Worship. Old Miss Snell was as mean as she was aged, according to the kids. True, the elderly woman had a sharp tongue for children she felt were misbehaving in the church. Many a young child was rebuked for running or wearing what she thought was inappropriate clothing, or speaking too loudly, or not paying attention, or eating outside the lounge or the fellowship hall, or committing a host of other transgressions known only to Miss Snell.

More than one youngster heard Miss Snell lecture that the church was God's home, and that it was to be treated with respect. While most of the children listened grudgingly, they also came to respect the Sunday school teacher's opinion. They learned from her that just as the temple was used as a special place to worship God, so too the church could be a special place for the children and for all Christians to gather together and revere the Lord in heartfelt worship.

Competing Loyalties. Nine-year-old John Rosemond's bike broke. Because it could not be repaired, he asked his stepfather to buy him a new one. Several days later, at the bike shop, John looked over the rows of shiny new bikes and made his selection. When he showed it to his stepfather, he was told that he was in the wrong section and that he did not need a new bike. A used one would be fine.

When John protested, his stepfather took him outside and showed him the family car, which was purchased a few months earlier. "Do you know what year's model this is?" the stepfather asked. John learned that even though his parents could have bought a new car, they chose not to so that some of their income could be used in charitable ways. Their loyalty was in helping others, not in merely gratifying their own desires. John's stepfather was trying to teach him the same lesson about the choices he made.

Like John and his family, you need to decide where you want your loyalties to be. Will they reside with you, or will you offer your loyalty to God and His people? If you chose the first option, this will lead to an inflated sense of your own importance, intolerance of others, and a lack of charity.

Childhood Guilt. When I was a child, I once took a plastic toy and threw it across the room. Instead of landing on the couch, it went through a large picture-frame window behind the sofa. I remember the glass shattering and pieces of it flying everywhere. I was alone for the moment, so of course I dashed out of the room while there were no witnesses to testify.

It did not take long for my mother to respond. She called all of the kids before her and sternly asked who had done it. For what seemed like decades of silence, no one said anything. Finally, I broke down. My arm began to rise. It seemed the only reasonable response. I pointed my finger at my little sister and said, "I saw her do it!"

Why did I lie? We have all been there. We cannot stand the thought of facing the consequences of our sinful actions. Of course the irony was that my lie was by far an even greater wrong. And my ensuing guilt was the more terrible consequence. Truth did eventually come out. With it also came the forgiveness and restoration that is found through faith in Christ.

ISAIAH INVITES US TO GOD'S FEAST

BACKGROUND SCRIPTURE: Isaiah 55:1-11
DEVOTIONAL READING: 2 Corinthians 9:10-15

4

KEY VERSE: Seek ye the LORD while he may be found, call ye upon him while he is near. Isaiah 55:6

KING JAMES VERSION

ISAIAH 55:1 Ho, every one that thirsteth, come ye to the waters, and he that hath no money; come ye, buy, and eat; yea, come, buy wine and milk without money and without price. 2 Wherefore do ye spend money for that which is not bread? and your labour for that which satisfieth not? hearken diligently unto me, and eat ye that which is good, and let your soul delight itself in fatness. 3 Incline your ear, and come unto me: hear, and your soul shall live. . . .

6 Seek ye the LORD while he may be found, call ye upon him while he is near: 7 Let the wicked forsake his way, and the unrighteous man his thoughts: and let him return unto the LORD, and he will have mercy upon him; and to our God, for he will abundantly pardon. 8 For my thoughts are not your thoughts, neither are your ways my ways, saith the LORD. 9 For as the heavens are higher than the earth, so are my ways higher than your ways, and my thoughts than your thoughts. 10 For as the rain cometh down, and the snow from heaven, and returneth not thither, but watereth the earth, and maketh it bring forth and bud, that it may give seed to the sower, and bread to the eater: 11 So shall my word be that goeth forth out of my mouth: it shall not return unto me void, but it shall accomplish that which I please, and it shall prosper in the thing whereto I sent it.

NEW REVISED STANDARD VERSION

ISAIAH 55:1 Ho, everyone who thirsts,
    come to the waters;
and you that have no money,
    come, buy and eat!
Come, buy wine and milk
    without money and without price.

2 Why do you spend your money for that which is not
        bread,
    and your labor for that which does not satisfy?
Listen carefully to me, and eat what is good,
    and delight yourselves in rich food.
3 Incline your ear, and come to me;
    listen, so that you may live.
I will make with you an everlasting covenant,
    my steadfast, sure love for David. . . .
6 Seek the LORD while he may be found,
    call upon him while he is near;
7 let the wicked forsake their way,
    and the unrighteous their thoughts;
let them return to the LORD, that he may have mercy
        on them,
    and to our God, for he will abundantly pardon.
8 For my thoughts are not your thoughts,
    nor are your ways my ways, says the LORD.
9 For as the heavens are higher than the earth,
    so are my ways higher than your ways
    and my thoughts than your thoughts.
10 For as the rain and the snow come down from
        heaven,
    and do not return there until they have watered
        the earth,
making it bring forth and sprout,
    giving seed to the sower and bread to the eater,
11 so shall my word be that goes out from my mouth;
    it shall not return to me empty,
but it shall accomplish that which I purpose,
    and succeed in the thing for which I sent it.

343

HOME BIBLE READINGS

BACKGROUND

Until the late eighteenth century, Isaiah's full authorship of the book went virtually unchallenged. At that time, however, some scholars began to argue that Isaiah wrote only chapters 1 through 39. They said this because, to them, chapters 40 to 66 seemed to have a different writing style and a different theology. Those scholars also pointed out that chapters 40 to 66 deal with events that happened later than Isaiah's time, such as the Babylonian Captivity and Cyrus's role in Judah's restoration. And operating under the assumption that predictive prophecy is impossible, they concluded that another author (or authors) must have written this section of Isaiah some 150 years after Isaiah's time.

Although many scholars today continue to argue that more than one person wrote the Book of Isaiah, most conservative scholars maintain the position that Isaiah wrote all 66 chapters of the book. These scholars rebut the critics with evidence along several lines. The conservative scholars argue that the difference in writing style between the two parts of the book is not so great as once assumed. They point out that almost 50 unusual phrases and sentences appear in both sections of the book. For example, Isaiah's title for God—*the Holy One of Israel*—appears 12 times in chapters 1 to 39 and 14 times in chapters 40 to 66. This title occurs only six other times in the rest of the Old Testament. Furthermore, these scholars remind us that Isaiah had a long career—about 50 years. Some variations in his writing style are therefore to be expected.

As for supposed theological differences between the earlier and later parts of the book, most conservative scholars say they don't exist. The subjects of the two parts are different, but theologically the parts are in perfect agreement. These scholars argue that Isaiah was indeed speaking predictively in the prophecies contained in the later chapters. In fact, as they point out, a central theme of Isaiah 40—48 is that the Lord demonstrates He alone is God by announcing in advance those events He will bring to pass. Finally, the 21 references to Isaiah in the New Testament establish the unity of the book. For instance, John quoted from Isaiah 53:1 and then from Isaiah 6:10, attributing both verses to Isaiah (John 12:38-41). Passages from the later section of the book are quoted as Isaiah's by Luke (Luke 3:4-6), Matthew (Matt. 8:17), and Paul (Rom. 10:16, 20).

When Isaiah began his ministry in 740 B.C., the northern kingdom of Israel was near collapse due to political, spiritual, and military deterioration. Things were going from bad to worse. In 723 B.C., the weakened northern kingdom finally fell to the Assyrian Empire, which had been expanding steadily for the past century and a half. The southern kingdom, Judah, was heading for a similar fate. Under the leadership of wicked King Ahaz, Judah was ripe for a fall. The nation had become corrupt socially, politically, and religiously. It was during this time that Isaiah delivered his messages to the people of Judah.

Isaiah called Judah to repent of idolatry and moral degeneracy. But then, failing to turn the nation Godward, Isaiah informed the people of Judah that their rebellion would lead to captivity at the hands of the Babylonians. Isaiah also predicted that, following the captivity, God would restore His people. God's foretelling all this in advance (through Isaiah) was intended to highlight His sovereignty in contrast to the powerlessness of false gods. Moreover, Isaiah foretold the ministry of the Servant of the Lord, who would redeem not only Judah, but also the whole world. About 700 years later, the "suffering Servant"—Jesus Christ—died for sinners as prophesied by Isaiah.

NOTES ON THE PRINTED TEXT

The messages recorded in Isaiah were addressed to God's people as they approached a great turning point in their history. Eighteen years after the prophet began his ministry, Assyria would conquer and exile the northern kingdom of Israel (722 B.C.). And 136 years later, Babylon would defeat and deport the southern kingdom of Judah (586 B.C.). What is the reason for these tragic turns in history? Throughout his book, Isaiah's words burn with God's denunciation of the sins into which His people had fallen. Even so, all of Isaiah's messages of doom are lined with a shining hope. The prophet not only graphically pictured the chastisements the Israelites would experience, but also glowingly depicted the blessings of the future millennial kingdom.

Isaiah 54 would be a case in point. It describes the splendor of Judah at the time of the exiles' return from captivity in Babylon. In 54:11-17, the restored nation is compared to a city of righteousness and security. God pledged to rebuild the city with precious stones, to teach Israel's children, and to establish justice in the land. In the messianic age, the Lord will protect His people from enemies and give them the victory.

In chapter 55, God called His people to move from the comfort and relative prosperity of Babylon to half-ruined Jerusalem. It begins with the summons found in 55:1 to *come . . . to the waters*. The offer of life-giving water was made possible through the offering of the suffering Servant, who is vividly pictured in Isaiah 53. That chapter points to the sacrifice of the Messiah. He made redemption possible by bearing the iniquities not only of the Jews in exile, but of the entire human race. Isaiah 55, then, invites everyone to partake of God's salvation and enjoy the glories He has prepared for His people.

The call in 55:1 echoes that of a water vendor, who was part of the commercial scene in water-scarce Near Eastern countries. The vendor would call out to attract attention to his precious commodity as he walked the streets. Isaiah, however, was not speaking about physical refreshment, but about spiritual refreshment, and offered wine and milk besides the water. God not only wants to give us life, but He also wants us to thrive—to have abundant life. Milk implies healthy nourishment for growth and strength. God wants us to grow spiritually strong. Wine implies celebration, joy, and abundance. God wants our spiritual life to overflow with the joy of our salvation.

The thirsty were invited, those who acknowledged their need for something more satisfying than the world's empty promises. God's grace makes all that He offers in Christ, free gifts. We cannot purchase our salvation. The sacrifice of God's Servant has paid the cost (53:5-9). Receiving the gifts depends only upon a sense of need and a readiness to accept the offered blessings.

In 55:2, the Lord asked the exiles why they would waste their money on what was not really bread or labor hard for what did not really satisfy. If they heeded Him, they would find nourishment for their souls. In 55:3, the prophet again invited the exiles to come near and pay attention. If they listened to Him, they would live. The focus here is on covenantal blessing. For the exiles, it primarily meant material prosperity and national security. The benefits are those connected with the everlasting covenant God made with David (2 Sam. 7:11-13). In that covenant, God promised David that his line would continue forever, culminating in the coming of the Messiah. Furthermore, the people would enjoy the unfailing love promised to David. Human love can fail, but God's sure mercies never fail.

We should listen to God and respond immediately when He calls us because we have no guarantees. Our lives could end at any time and we may not be able to perceive God's call at a later time. Also, Jesus could return and the opportunity to repent would be over. Indeed, every moment is an opportunity to enjoy a relationship with God.

Isaiah 55:1 and 3 are echoed in 55:6, but with more urgency. Sinners are implored to seek the Lord while He may be found. This implies that God cannot be found at times while people remain unrepentant. Now, while the people had the opportunity, was the time to return to the Lord (see 2 Cor. 6:2). The Hebrew term rendered *seek* (Isa. 55:6) should not be limited to sacrifice, prayer, or even a combination of the two. The basic meaning of the word is to "tread," implying the action of stepping toward God or coming to Him. The true seeker wants to establish a close relationship with God and runs away from the world toward Him. Isaiah 55:6 does not imply a local God who moves from place to place. He is everywhere present and always willing to receive a repentant sinner. However, we may not always sense His calling or be emotionally ready to respond.

Although Isaiah referred to the wicked and the unrighteous in 55:7, he was not addressing two types of individuals, but aspects of life: *ways* and *thoughts*. The truly repentant person will turn completely to God for mercy and forgiveness, both of which are freely given. From this verse we see that we must change both our behavior and our thoughts, for outward changes without inward changes are meaningless. We may be able to fool ourselves and others, but not God. He sees what others cannot, and He judges us by our thoughts and actions.

God's ways and thoughts are as high above those of wicked people as the heavens are above the earth (55:8). Just as the full height of the heavens cannot be measured or fully understood, so God's will is so far above us that we cannot fully grasp it (55:9). We only understand and follow a portion of what God desires of us and makes known to us. Isaiah 55:10 shows the endless cycle of nature and summarizes the whole food-producing process. The emphasis, however, is not on the cycle, but on the rain and snow completing the intention for which they were sent. In a sense, they complete God's purpose for nature.

Likewise, God's word is guaranteed effective for its intended purpose. That His purpose will be fulfilled is as certain as the endless cycle of rain and harvest. What God speaks will always be accomplished (55:11). The word that goes out from God is not magical and possesses no power of its own. However, because the word belongs to the Lord, it always fulfills its purpose. Whether it is the promise to return the exiles to their homeland or redeem all who trust in the Messiah, the divine promise achieves all God intends.

SUGGESTIONS TO TEACHERS

God offers to quench our spiritual thirst by giving us what we long for—the drink of salvation through His grace. By seeking Him and turning from sin, we respond to His good purposes and experience the refreshment of divine forgiveness and salvation.

1. OFFERING SALVATION. We discover in the Book of Isaiah that even before the Messiah and the New Testament, salvation was being preached to humankind. God called people to receive His gift of restored relationship with Him. This timeless message is as urgent and relevant for us today as it was for those who first heard Isaiah's message.

2. EXPERIENCING SALVATION. Though we may have experienced salvation and begun our relationship with God, in one sense we are continuing to be saved from sin even after our initial encounter with God's saving grace. Someone has said we have been saved (in our initial conversion experience); we are being saved (in our continued relationship with God); and we will be saved (when our relationship with Him is completely restored in His presence).

3. GUARDING AGAINST SIN. For both the saved and the unsaved, sin is a constant threat to our ongoing relationship with God. For the unsaved, sin can be a distraction from seeking God and accepting His salvation. For the saved, sin can stifle our relationship with Him.

Even if we have already experienced salvation and have a relationship with God, we must continue to be on our guard against sin. The Lord urges us to always turn away from sin and turn to Him in faith. When we drink heavily from the life-saving water found in the Messiah, our relationship with the Lord will be vibrant and flourishing, rather than parched and lifeless.

4. MAKING GOD A PRIORITY. Like our relationships with others, our relationship with God must be nurtured and maintained to stay healthy and thrive. If we are not careful, we may get sidetracked and deceived by sin. We may neglect spending time with the Lord and lose the closeness we need with Him. Then we will not experience all the good things God intends for us as His children.

| **FOR ADULTS** | ■ **TOPIC:** Finding Satisfaction ■ **QUESTIONS:** 1. Why would God extend an invitation to His wayward people to come to Him in faith? 2. In what sense is God's covenant with |

His people everlasting? 3. What sometimes prevents God's people from seeking Him, even though He is always present? 4. How is it possible for the Lord to freely pardon sinners? 5. Why is the decree of God so effective in accomplishing His will?

■ **ILLUSTRATIONS:**

Dealing with Life's Storms. "It was enough to make me pray to God," said one man who survived Hurricane Mitch's devastating passage through Honduras in 1998. As winds of more than 150 miles per hour raged overhead, he and his family had huddled in their basement. Three days later, they came up to find their home gone and their village destroyed by floodwaters and mudslides. A disaster like that might lead even an atheist to consider prayer.

Prayers, though, can bring peace in the midst of much more than everyday crises— the bills we may not know how to pay, the work that isn't going so well, difficult relationships, and painful losses. In this week's Scripture passage, we learn that cultivating a vibrant relationship with God—for instance, through prayer and thanksgiving— is the best way to find true and lasting satisfaction in the midst of life's most harrowing storms.

Rejoicing in Christ. A little over a year ago, the Lord called home a dear, 95-year-old relative of mine. What do I fondly remember about her? Sometimes, it is the little things, like her love of desserts (for instance, "Grandma, would you like apple, peach, or pecan pie?" "A little of each . . . no, not that little!" she'd respond with a smile.)

Even more, I remember her time-tested faith in the Lord. Because her "old stories" were new to me, I could listen for hours to the faith lessons she had learned.

What was it like to have an adult child killed in a gruesome car-truck accident? What goes through your mind when a son is determined to marry outside of your faith? How do you dig down to your deepest reserves when a spouse is in the process of dying for years? This elderly saint would answer that it was prayer and thanksgiving. Through these two spiritual activities, we can surrender our anxieties to God and find true peace of mind.

How You Look at It. In a comic strip is a picture of a little bird lying on the ground, with its wings and beak all spiraled out before it. The caption reads, "Worms are hard to find this time of year, the high winds make it hard to fly, and it's predicted we will have an early, long winter."

The next box shows a picture of a little bird dancing and singing along. The caption reads, "I've been able to find one worm every day, just enough to feed my little chicks. The high winds have made it easier for me to teach them how to fly, and we are just going south a little earlier to escape the cold winds. Isn't life great!"

The two little birds had the same problems, but one allowed its concerns to drag it down. The other saw its problems from a more positive point of view. As the reading from this week's Scripture passage emphasizes, the way we look at things can mean the difference between satisfaction and disappointment.

FOR YOUTH

■ **TOPIC:** The Promise Is Real
■ **QUESTIONS:** 1. Why are the blessings of God offered to His people free of charge? 2. What sorts of changes in the lives of His people did the Lord stress? 3. Why do we not see and understand things the way God does? 4. How can we come to a clearer understanding of the will of God? 5. What does God promise will happen when His decree is spoken?

■ **ILLUSTRATIONS:**

Encouragement from the Savior's Promises. Many of the people who came to America's shores in the 17th century knew firsthand the reality of the Savior's promises and how that proved to be a source of strength for them. They observed a discipline of honoring His promises as they lived out each day.

Family devotions each morning and evening were the centerpiece of the settlers' lives. These believers called themselves Puritans because they wanted to purify the Christian Church, especially in England, and insisted that the family was a "little church" and "the nursery of the Church." Worship among family members was considered the foundation for both the church life and for a godly society.

With the encouragement they drew from the Savior's promises, they set out to be "a city upon a hill," to use Governor John Winthrop's words. The Puritan head of a household served as a "priest" presiding over his "little church" during morning and evening Scripture readings, prayers, psalm singing, and giving thanks at meals. The Scriptures were read chapter by chapter through entire books of the Bible, with family members often taking turns reading the passages aloud. The table graces were usually offered both before and after each meal.

What a contrast this lifestyle is to our often casual approach to personal or family worship! How we see the promises of Christ relating to our everyday lives can make all the difference in the world.

False Advertising. The order placed on the company's web site was simple enough, but when the package arrived it did not contain what the customer had wanted. In this case, what was promised in the advertisement proved to be false.

When God spoke to His disobedient people, He made a real promise, one that He had the power to fulfill. Isaiah compared God's offer to a free shopping spree at the mall. The prophet also likened God's invitation to a rich banquet. What was the catch? The people had to come to the Lord in repentance and faith.

Sadly, many youth refuse to turn to the Lord. In fact, they want nothing to do with God. Thankfully, there are some adolescents like yourself who want what the Lord has to offer. Through faith in His Son, you can find sublime delights and eternal satisfaction.

A New Remedy. In *The Healing of Persons*, Paul Tournier describes an incident involving a Christian physician who had heard from an old friend suffering from Parkinson's disease. The man wrote a curt note in which he told the physician, "Come only if you have some new remedy. I've had enough of doctors who say they cannot cure me."

The physician decided to accept the challenge. After arriving at his friend's home and greeting him, he promptly said, "I brought you a new remedy—Jesus Christ!" At first skeptical, the friend still listened, and then he gradually started to soften. It took several more visits before the man began to show a remarkable change in the way he thought and spoke. Finally, he trusted in Christ for salvation, and his soul was healed of sin and its accompanying bitterness. This was a far greater miracle according to many who knew him.

This week's Scripture passage reveals that everyone carries sin's symptoms of rebellion, self-centeredness, and bitterness. And yet the various healings or interventions that most people seek for their lives have nothing to do with the cause. Every person is born with a disease called *sin* that is incurable by any human means.

There is only one cure for the terrible ailment of sin—faith in Christ. Isaiah was given a glimpse of this truth centuries before the time of the Messiah. For those of us who have accepted the one life-giving remedy in Christ's atonement, the healing is undeniable.

MICAH ANNOUNCES GOD'S REQUIREMENTS

BACKGROUND SCRIPTURE: Micah 2:1-4; 3:1-5, 8-12; 6:6-8
DEVOTIONAL READING: Hebrews 12:6-12

KEY VERSE: He hath shewed thee, O man, what is good; and what doth the LORD require of thee, but to do justly, and to love mercy, and to walk humbly with thy God? Micah 6:8.

5

KING JAMES VERSION

MICAH 3:1 And I said, Hear, I pray you, O heads of Jacob, and ye princes of the house of Israel; Is it not for you to know judgment? 2 Who hate the good, and love the evil; who pluck off their skin from off them, and their flesh from off their bones; 3 Who also eat the flesh of my people, and flay their skin from off them; and they break their bones, and chop them in pieces, as for the pot, and as flesh within the caldron. 4 Then shall they cry unto the LORD, but he will not hear them: he will even hide his face from them at that time, as they have behaved themselves ill in their doings. . . .

6:6 Wherewith shall I come before the LORD, and bow myself before the high God? shall I come before him with burnt offerings, with calves of a year old? 7 Will the LORD be pleased with thousands of rams, or with ten thousands of rivers of oil? shall I give my firstborn for my transgression, the fruit of my body for the sin of my soul? 8 He hath shewed thee, O man, what is good; and what doth the LORD require of thee, but to do justly, and to love mercy, and to walk humbly with thy God?

NEW REVISED STANDARD VERSION

MICAH 3:1 And I said:
Listen, you heads of Jacob
    and rulers of the house of Israel!
Should you not know justice?—
2   you who hate the good and love the evil,
who tear the skin off my people,
    and the flesh off their bones;
3 who eat the flesh of my people,
    flay their skin off them,
break their bones in pieces,
    and chop them up like meat in a kettle,
    like flesh in a caldron.
4 Then they will cry to the LORD,
    but he will not answer them;
he will hide his face from them at that time,
    because they have acted wickedly. . . .
6:6 "With what shall I come before the LORD,
    and bow myself before God on high?
Shall I come before him with burnt offerings,
    with calves a year old?
7 Will the LORD be pleased with thousands of rams,
    with ten thousands of rivers of oil?
Shall I give my firstborn for my transgression,
    the fruit of my body for the sin of my soul?"
8 He has told you, O mortal, what is good;
    and what does the LORD require of you
but to do justice, and to love kindness,
    and to walk humbly with your God?"

HOME BIBLE READINGS

BACKGROUND

Micah was from the town of Moresheth Gath (Mic. 1:1, 14), which was located in the foothills of Judah about 20 miles southwest of Jerusalem. Though Micah was a resident of the country and removed from the national policies of Judah, God nonetheless called him to proclaim a message of judgment to the rulers and inhabitants of Jerusalem.

Micah's prophetic ministry overlapped the reigns of Jotham (750–735 B.C.), Ahaz (735–715 B.C.), and Hezekiah (715–686 B.C.). The prophet's indictments of social injustices and religious corruption were particularly suited to the reign of Ahaz. The northern kingdom of Israel fell during the ministry of Micah, and this explains why the prophet dated his messages with only the mention of Judean kings. It also explains why he principally directed his comments to the southern kingdom, where he lived.

The economic prosperity and the absence of international crises, which had marked the days of Jeroboam II (793–753 B.C.), were slipping away. It was a time when Syria and Israel invaded Judah and in which Assyria overthrew Syria and Israel (during the reign of Ahaz). When Hezekiah withdrew his allegiance from Assyria, this prompted Sennacherib to besiege Jerusalem, though it proved unsuccessful due to the Lord's gracious intervention.

Instead of growing closer to God out of gratitude for His blessings, Judah and Israel had slipped into moral bankruptcy. Those who became wealthy during this time ruthlessly exploited the poor. Consequently, Micah predicted the fall of both Samaria and Jerusalem, focusing more on the Babylonian captivity of the southern kingdom and the eventual restoration of its people.

Micah 1:2 constitutes an introduction to the prophecy that follows. God called the people of the world to listen to a witness against them. The meaning seems to be this: As the people of the world would see the way God judged His own people—the Israelites and Judahites—because of disobedience, the nations would see the way God would treat them unless they turned to Him.

Micah 1:3-4 draws attention to a visitation of the Lord. In this visitation, He descends from heaven and uses the high places as His stepping-stones. Under His feet, the mountains melt and the valleys split apart. All of this is symbolism for the way

God would send judgment on His rebellious people. According to 1:5, the purpose for the judgment would be to punish the sins of Israel (*Jacob*) and Judah. People from both nations had violated God's covenant by worshiping other gods. The mention of the two capitols in 1:5 may mean either (1) that false worship was going on in both cities or (2) that the political leadership of both nations was involved in the sin of idolatry. Perhaps both were true.

For Israel's transgression, God would utterly destroy the city of Samaria (1:6-7a). In particular, God would destroy the city's idols and all that went along with idol worship. Possibly in this passage, God was foretelling what would happen when the Assyrians captured Samaria. However, at that time the city was not seriously damaged. (It was destroyed 600 years later, then rebuilt.) The second half of 1:7 is not entirely clear. It may mean that Samaria's conquerors would destroy Israel's idols, which had been paid for by pagan religious prostitution, and then the conquerors would reuse the precious metal for idols of their own. Or perhaps it means that the metal from idols was used by the Assyrian invaders as payment for prostitutes.

It was not an easy thing for Micah to tell about the destruction of Samaria (1:6-7). The thought of it affected him deeply. He vowed to display signs of mourning publicly (1:8). Undoubtedly, Micah grieved for the Israelites' sake. But he grieved more because of what the destruction of Samaria meant for his own people, the Judahites. Samaria's destruction showed that God was willing to turn His wrath upon His covenant people if they persisted in sinning against Him. Thus, the judgment (*wound*, 1:9) upon Samaria threatened Jerusalem, too. As a matter of fact, the Assyrians all but overtook Jerusalem in 701 B.C., the way they overtook Samaria about 22 years earlier.

While Micah foretold that Jerusalem would be threatened with judgment, he predicted that other cities of Judah would actually be judged (1:10-16). This accurately describes what happened in 701 B.C. The Bible and Assyrian records agree that the Assyrian emperor, Sennacherib, captured dozens of cities in Judah but failed to capture Jerusalem. Most of the cities in 1:10-16 (all except the first) were in Judah and targets of the Assyrian invasion. Micah chose to mention most of these cities (all except the last) because of what their names mean or sound like. In other words, these verses contain a series of puns in which a city's name is linked with the rest of the prophecy related to it.

NOTES ON THE PRINTED TEXT

In Micah 2 and 3, the prophet began his report on Judah, the southern kingdom. He detailed how social injustice, government corruption, and dishonest trade practices were all in the course of a normal business day. Micah analyzed the great social, political, and spiritual contrasts in his country: rich versus poor, big landowners versus small farmers, the urban business class versus the country folks, and false prophets versus the Lord God.

Beginning in 3:1, Micah summoned the heads of Jacob and the princes of the house of Israel to hear and heed what he had to say on behalf of the Lord. (In this context *Jacob* and *Israel* are synonyms for all 12 tribes.) God had established them as the governing authority over His people (see Rom. 13:1). Thus, they should have known the difference between justice and injustice, enforcing the former and eliminating the latter. Tragically, they did neither.

The nation's leaders perverted justice by hating what is right and loving what is wrong (Mic. 3:2). They were like cannibals in their inhumane treatment of ordinary citizens. Micah accused the corrupt rulers of metaphorically tearing the skin off God's people and ripping the flesh from their bones. In this grisly depiction, the wicked rich ate the people's flesh and broke their bones in pieces. The princes and nobles alike sliced the people up like meat for the pot and their flesh for the cauldron (3:3).

Perhaps at the time that Micah prophesied, the leaders of God's people enjoyed power and prestige. However, this would not last. Micah foretold that a day of calamity was soon to come. But just as the evil rulers had turned a deaf ear to their fellow citizens, so too the Lord would be unresponsive to the wicked when they cried out for help in their moment of need. Because of the unjust things they had done, God would disregard them (3:4).

The harsh tone of Micah's messages shows how upset he was with Israel and Judah. Things were so bad that he may have literally walked around barefoot and naked through Jerusalem (as Isaiah did) to call attention to the sins of the nation (Mic. 1:8; see Isa. 20:2). This prophet from the country was not so backward that he did not know sin when he saw it. His declarations include a (dirty) laundry list of iniquities he found among the priests, judges, and leaders.

Wealthy landowners carried out evil plans conceived at night in bed (Mic. 2:1), cheated families out of homes and land (2:2, 8), took over lovely residences belonging to women (2:9), swindled orphans out of their inheritances (2:9), and loved prophets who promised them strong liquor on which to get drunk (2:11). False prophets foretold security for anyone who gave them food, and disaster for those who refused to feed them (3:5). They taught and preached only for money (3:11) and told fortunes and practiced witchcraft (5:12).

Businesspersons used dishonest scales (6:11), hated justice and twisted the truth (6:12), and made cruelty, murder, and crime their way of life (3:9-10; 7:3). Driven by personal motives, unethical judges and politicians demanded and accepted bribes (3:11; 7:3). Micah warned people not to trust their neighbors and friends. It seemed as if no one was loyal to God and not one person did what was right. The times were so wicked that looking for righteous people was like looking for fruit when it was out of season (7:1-2).

The image in Micah 6 is that of God bringing His people to court and presenting

His case against their sinfulness (6:1-2). One major area where the Lord saw abuse was in His system of sacrifices. What good is an atonement offering when the sinner says, "I plan to continue doing wrong, but this sacrifice might suspend God's punishment"?

The dishonesty and injustice in daily life carried over into a hypocritical relationship with God. When confronted with their guilt, people took a circuitous path to avoid going directly to the Lord. Bypassing repentance, they wanted to buy off the Holy One with extravagant sacrificial gifts. But the most high God would not be satisfied by large, expensive sacrifices given by those who were unjust, corrupt, or rich. The quantity and quality of the sacrifice did not make a difference. Micah 6:6 mentions burnt offerings and year-old calves. And 6:7 specifies thousands of rams and ten thousand rivers filled with olive oil. Neither these nor the offering of one's firstborn child would erase one's transgression or wipe away one's sin.

Micah's famous call is recorded in 6:8. The Lord defined what He considered to morally upright and what He required of those whom He considered *good*. For Him, piety was lived out in daily encounters with others. To act justly means to treat others with honesty, integrity, and equity. To love mercy implies being loyal to God and kind to others. This is not done impulsively, but rather as a consistent part of our lives. To walk humbly with God signifies being circumspect in what we say and modest in our demeanor. We willingly choose to follow the Lord and submit to His will.

SUGGESTIONS TO TEACHERS

Many persons are cynical about their leaders. The scandalous behavior and the unscrupulous practices of certain government and religious officials have caused confusion and disillusionment, especially among the younger generation. Some media personalities' lack of values has also had a corrupting effect. Some of your students may be wondering what is right and what is wrong, and also how God wants them to act. This week's lesson will help address these important issues.

1. CONTENTION WITH CIVIL LEADERS. Micah said that the practices of corrupt rulers and government officials were reprehensible. Their greed and callous disregard for the needs of the underclass was devastating the poor and hungry. The impoverished were like helpless lambs in the midst of cunning and savage beasts. This reminds us that those in government have a responsibility to look after the hurting and forgotten in society.

2. CONDEMNATION OF RELIGIOUS LEADERS. Micah referred to corrupt prophets and priests, and his words remind us as "God's people" that we carry a heavy burden of duty to the impoverished living around us. Your congregation may already be doing noble service through a food pantry or participation in housing programs for the poor. Are there other areas that should be addressed? Also, how do you overcome "compassion fatigue"?

3. CONSEQUENCES OF DISOBEDIENCE. Like all prophets, Micah warned his hearers that their heartless lack of concern for those suffering in society would result in the destruction and end of their comfortable way of life. How do Micah's pronouncements apply to our society?

4. CONTROVERSY WITH THE COVENANTED COMMUNITY. Micah, like Hosea, told how deeply disappointed God was with His faithless nation. The disobedient had deliberately broken the sacred relationship between God and His people, and this in turn immensely grieved the Lord. How do your students think God feels toward the church in general and toward their congregation in particular?

5. CONCENTRATION ON GOD'S REQUIREMENT. Be sure to focus at length on Micah 6:8, especially discussing what it means to *do justly, and to love mercy, and to walk humbly* before God. You might even want to save the largest part of the lesson time to discuss this key verse. Why not encourage your students to commit this verse to memory?

FOR ADULTS	■ **TOPIC:** Doing the Right Thing

■ **QUESTIONS:** 1. How could the nation's leaders have hated what is right and loved what is wrong? 2. What sorts of injustices were the leaders guilty of committing? 3. Why would the Lord not respond to the nation's leaders in their time of distress? 4. How had the leaders made a sham of worshiping before the Lord? 5. What did the Lord require of His people?

■ **ILLUSTRATIONS:**

Divine Expectations. It was on the night of his 40th birthday that Randy stole away from the festivities for some private time with the Lord. As was Randy's custom when he turned 20, and again when he turned 30, he prayed and read his Bible and asked the Holy Spirit to give him illumination for the next decade. Each time God brought a Scripture verse to Randy's attention that would be a special guide for the next 10 years.

For Randy's 40th birthday, the verse was Micah 6:8. Randy found it to be a simple declaration of what God was asking him to work on in his next decade. Randy hadn't been overtly guilty of transgressing this verse in the past, but he knew that God was leading him to walk in a greater depth of what this Scripture admonished.

Halfway through his 40s now, the following is what Randy has learned. First, to act justly means that we will never knowingly or purposefully allow any advantage to come to us through manipulation or deceit. Every benefit and opportunity that Randy now receives, he makes sure it comes as a result of the service he renders to others, and never at their expense.

Second, Randy discovered that to be a lover of mercy, one must first be the recipient of mercy. He found himself in experiences where God's mercy was freely given to him on a personal level. Showing mercy to others seemed much easier now. Third, humility seems to be the natural by-product of choosing to obey this life-calling of justice and mercy. Randy often finds himself overwhelmed by this grace of God.

The Weed of Envy. "Envy is wanting what another person has and feeling badly that I don't have it. Envy is disliking God's goodness to someone else and dismissing God's goodness to me. Envy is desire plus resentment. Envy is anti-community," asserts John Ortberg in *Love Beyond Reason: Moving God's Love from Your Head to Your Heart.*

An envious heart is incapable of showing justice, mercy, and humility. It is too pre-occupied. Have you witnessed the results of envy? Envy frequently makes its way into criminal acts. But on a private level, envy is damaging too. Its seed of discontentment quickly grows into the weed of resentment. This weed can choke relationships—even among Christians.

So how does a believer eradicate this weed? Extermination begins with developing a right attitude toward God and the blessings He, in His wisdom, bestows.

The Trinity of Tabernacle and Temple. The wilderness tabernacle and the Jerusalem temple both had three main areas where priestly service was conducted. The outer courts were for the general sacrificial cleansing of the people for their oft-committed sins. It held the brazen altar and the laver filled with water.

The Holy Place was the location where the general priestly services to the Lord were performed. This spot had the table of showbread, the golden lampstand, and the altar of incense. The innermost area was called the Most Holy Place and was only to be entered by the high priest as he made special petitions for the people's sin on the day of Atonement.

These three areas made up the tabernacle and temple. Each place had its function. They were meant to be kept together to achieve the role of the temple ceremonies. Similarly, Micah makes it clear that justice, mercy, and humility are three characteristics meant to be performed together to bring about the healthy relationship between God and one another that makes for a blessed community.

FOR YOUTH

■ TOPIC: What Does God Want, Anyway?

■ QUESTIONS: 1. How is it possible to have a genuine knowledge of right from wrong? 2. In what sense did the nation's leaders rip the flesh from the bones of God's people? 3. Why would God hide His face from the nation's leaders in the day of calamity? 4. How did the people of God try to atone for their sins? 5. What does it mean to act justly and love mercy?

■ ILLUSTRATIONS:

Modeling Care. South Bend's Center for the Homeless helps dozens of people each day. What is surprising is that young alumni and students run it from the University of Notre Dame's Center for Social Concerns.

Consider Shannon Cullinan. She developed a landscaping business that employs homeless people for eight months of training and then places them in other landscaping companies, especially as it cares for the properties in the City of South Bend, Memorial Hospital, WNDU Broadcasting, and the University properties. Then there's Drew Buscarieno. He developed a medical clinic, early childhood center, and drug and alcohol treatment center. He also developed educational facilities, job training, and care for the mentally ill.

Praised by the executive director of the National Coalition for the Homeless as a model of collaboration between university students and the local community, the center seeks to find solutions to the problems of the homeless. Here is a group of young people working to implement what God requires in their lives.

Divine Moral Standards. The father regularly taught his son to do what is right. One day, while they worked together with some other men, the language became exceedingly profane. When the lad joined in the talk, his father reminded him that such language was inappropriate.

God expected Israel and Judah to live up to His high moral standards. Instead, the rulers, priests, false prophets, and people wallowed in the ways of their corrupt neighbors, allowed immorality and injustice to prevail, and hypocritically worshiped the Lord.

It's perilously easy for us who are Christians to go through the motions of worship, prayer, and other religious activities. We forget that God wants us to grow in our love for Him, to mature in our spiritual wisdom and understanding, and to become more like Jesus in our thoughts and actions. The Book of Micah helps us to see how dangerous it is to pretend we're walking with God when we're not.

Chicago Boy's Response. Alex Kotlowitz of *The Wall Street Journal* did a study of two boys growing up in the "jects" (the public housing projects) in Chicago. He reported that one mother commented on his proposal to write about her children. She said, "There are no children here."

These women (who usually are single and head the household) watch their children caught in the despair and violence of the community. Understandably, these kids know little about normal childhood. When Kotlowitz asked one 10-year old what he wanted to be when he grew up, the youngster replied, "If I grow up, I'd like to be a bus driver." (Please note, he said "if," not "when.") Why not consider what your Sunday school class can do to help out disadvantaged youth such as this.

Zephaniah Announces God's Justice

Background Scripture: Zephaniah 3:1-13; 2 Chronicles 34:1-3
Devotional Reading: Psalm 27:7-14

Key Verse: My determination is to gather the nations, that I may assemble the kingdoms, to pour upon them mine indignation, even all my fierce anger: for all the earth shall be devoured. Zephaniah 3:8.

KING JAMES VERSION

ZEPHANIAH 3:1 Woe to her that is filthy and polluted, to the oppressing city! 2 She obeyed not the voice; she received not correction; she trusted not in the LORD; she drew not near to her God. 3 Her princes within her are roaring lions; her judges are evening wolves; they gnaw not the bones till the morrow. 4 Her prophets are light and treacherous persons: her priests have polluted the sanctuary, they have done violence to the law. 5 The just LORD is in the midst thereof; he will not do iniquity: every morning doth he bring his judgment to light, he faileth not; but the unjust knoweth no shame. . . .

8 Therefore wait ye upon me, saith the LORD, until the day that I rise up to the prey: for my determination is to gather the nations, that I may assemble the kingdoms, to pour upon them mine indignation, even all my fierce anger: for all the earth shall be devoured with the fire of my jealousy. 9 For then will I turn to the people a pure language, that they may all call upon the name of the LORD, to serve him with one consent.

NEW REVISED STANDARD VERSION

ZEPHANIAH 3:1 Ah, soiled, defiled,
oppressing city!
2 It has listened to no voice;
it has accepted no correction.
It has not trusted in the LORD;
it has not drawn near to its God.
3 The officials within it
are roaring lions;
its judges are evening wolves
that leave nothing until the morning.
4 Its prophets are reckless,
faithless persons;
its priests have profaned what is sacred,
they have done violence to the law.
5 The LORD within it is righteous;
he does no wrong.
Every morning he renders his judgment,
each dawn without fail;
but the unjust knows no shame. . . .
8 Therefore wait for me, says the LORD,
for the day when I arise as a witness.
For my decision is to gather nations,
to assemble kingdoms,
to pour out upon them my indignation,
all the heat of my anger;
for in the fire of my passion
all the earth shall be consumed.
9 At that time I will change the speech of the peoples
to a pure speech,
that all of them may call on the name of the LORD
and serve him with one accord.

6

359

HOME BIBLE READINGS

BACKGROUND

The prophet, Zephaniah, stood in a unique relationship to his contemporary, Josiah, king of Judah. Both were descendants of Hezekiah, one of Judah's most godly kings. Several generations stood between Zephaniah and Hezekiah (Zeph. 1:1); two stood between Josiah and Hezekiah, namely, kings Manasseh and Amon. King Amon had been unaffected by the late but sincere repentance of Manasseh. Amon had returned to the worst excesses of his father and had been assassinated by dissatisfied nobles after a reign of just two years (2 Chron. 33:21-25).

Josiah ascended to the throne of Judah in 640 B.C., when he was eight years old (34:1). When the king was 20 years old, he launched a campaign to eradicate idolatry in Judah and in northern Canaan, which had been ruled by the Israelites before the Assyrian conquest and deportation of the population (34:3-7). When Josiah was 26 years old, he began an extensive renovation of the neglected temple of the Lord in Jerusalem (34:8).

Zephaniah probably prophesied early in the reign of Josiah before the king's reforms were generally successful. Zephaniah's messages may have served as part of the impetus for those reforms. The prophet addressed Judah and Jerusalem when idolatry was rampant (Zeph. 1:4-6, 9) and before the leadership of the nation had been purified (1:8; 3:3-4). Assyria was still viewed as the great world power (2:13-15). Thus, Zephaniah's prophecies were most likely made when the emperor Ashurbanipal died and Assyria began a rapid decline.

Zephaniah was an older contemporary of Nahum and Jeremiah. Nahum predicted the terrible destruction of the Assyrian capitol Nineveh, which occurred in 612 B.C. Jeremiah's ministry began in 626 B.C., the fourteenth year of Josiah's rule, and continued until some time after 586 B.C. when Jerusalem was destroyed by Babylon. Jeremiah admired King Josiah (2 Chron. 35:25; Jer. 22:15-16). It's likely that Jeremiah regularly visited Josiah's court as he did those of later wicked kings. Zephaniah also showed familiarity with the court of Judah (Zeph. 1:8; 3:3). The older prophet may have been acquainted with the younger Jeremiah at the outset of the latter's ministry.

The dominant theme of Zephaniah's prophecy is *the day of the LORD* (1:7, 14, 18), often referred to as *that day* (1:9, 15; 3:11, 16) or *the day* (1:8; 3:8). The day of the Lord is both a time of great judgment and a time of restoration. Usually, Old Testament prophets emphasized one of those dimensions and mentioned the other, but

Zephaniah held them in balance—first, stressing judgment (1:2—3:8) and then, highlighting the blessing of the remnant (3:9-20). Through His servant Zephaniah, the Lord jolted Judah's proud leaders with the message of judgment (3:11) and encouraged all humble people with a message of hope (3:12).

NOTES ON THE PRINTED TEXT

The focal point of Zephaniah's message is the day of the Lord, in which a foreign enemy, functioning as God's agent of judgment, would inflict severe calamity upon Jerusalem (Zeph. 1:7-18). Amazingly, despite Zephaniah's pronouncements of judgment, there was spiritual complacency among the people (see 1:12). The apathy of the wicked led them to believe God was likewise complacent. Supposedly, He would neither prosper nor punish His people, regardless of how they chose to live. Nothing could be further from the truth. Zephaniah depicted the Lord as using clay oil lamps to search for people in Jerusalem's darkest corners. The goal was to find and punish those entrenched in their sin.

God's prophet was not indifferent to the waywardness of his fellow citizens. Indeed, he urged them to repent and seek the Lord so that they might be spared from His anger (2:3). Zephaniah noted that the coming destruction would include the people of Philistia, Moab, Ammon, Cush, and Assyria (2:4-15). He then turned his attention to the future of Jerusalem.

The immoral conditions of Judah's capitol are shocking. Before Manasseh died, he repented of his evil ways, threw out the idols, and restored the true worship of God (2 Chron. 33:14-17). However, these efforts were too little, too late to overcome the many years of wickedness he had encouraged among God's people. In fact, Manasseh's son, Amon, worshiped and sacrificed to all the idols his father had made. He refused to repent, and then, after being king just two years, his own officials assassinated him. Next, they made his son, Josiah, the next king (33:21-25).

Throughout these years, two factions jousted for supremacy in Jerusalem—those who remained faithful to God and those who followed idolatrous practices. The masses in the middle simply followed whatever party was in power at the time. They could be swayed according to the circumstances and the examples of the kings, either for true worship under someone like Hezekiah or idolatry under someone like Manasseh.

Zephaniah indicted Jerusalem for being filthy and stained by its social violence. The rich and powerful oppressed the poor and weak. The city was marked by rebellion against God. It was polluted by the idolatrous worship of Baal, the stars, and Malcham (or Molech; see Zeph. 1:4-5). There were no restraints, once God's laws had been abandoned (3:1). Zephaniah followed the common practice of personalizing cities. Jerusalem became *she* (3:1-2) and *her*. The prophet made four specific charges against the corrupt and lawless capitol: (1) disobedience, (2) refusing divine correction, (3) distrust of the Lord, and (4) refusal to draw near to God.

Zephaniah described four classes of leaders in Judah who were failing in their responsibilities of leading the people. One group was the *princes* (3:3), namely, the royal officials and members of the king's family. They were motivated by greed rather than seeking justice for the people. Another group was the *judges*. These civil magistrates and rulers behaved as predatory beasts rather than protectors of justice.

A third group was the *prophets* (3:4). This class of official spokespersons did not include God's prophets like Zephaniah and Jeremiah. The false spokespersons were arrogant and unfaithful to the Lord, whom they claimed to represent. They did not speak the truth. The fourth group was the *priests*, including all the other religious leaders besides the prophets. They were guilty of profaning God's sanctuary and violating His law.

The king, his officials, the priests, and the prophets were all caught in Zephaniah's indictment. Their lawlessness grew out of their failure to trust and obey God. Of course, they would not worship the Lord if they did not trust in Him. Though the Lord was still the God of His people, they had rejected Him. They lacked personal faith in and commitment to Him. Without these spiritual foundation stones, the city was certain to fall, for the personal relationship between God and His people had been severed.

Zephaniah compared Jerusalem's corrupt princes to roaring lions hunting for their victims and consuming everything they found. Also, their judges were like ravenous wolves that prowled at night and completely devoured their prey by morning (3:3). Both groups ravaged the possessions of vulnerable people so badly that nothing was left. They looked out for themselves and forsook the public welfare. Among the leaders in this outrage were the members of the royal family, who took advantage of their privileged positions to rob and cheat the poor (1:8).

Jerusalem's false prophets were characterized as proud and arrogant (3:4). Instead of leading people to God and urging them to the true worship of Him, they made pronouncements according to the wishes of the rich and powerful cliques. We know from the books of Jeremiah and Ezekiel that they were people of great influence. God said the declarations of the false prophets were void of truth. He condemned them for preaching peace when there was no peace (Jer. 5:12; 6:14). The Lord accused them of lying in His name and said they were prophesying false visions, worthless predictions, and the delusions of their own mind (14:14).

With respect to the priests, instead of leading people to faith, repentance, and forgiveness, they presided over bogus and idolatrous ceremonies in the temple (Zeph. 3:4). Though they did not totally abandon the worship of God, they permitted and encouraged the veneration of idols. In this way they insulted God's holiness, defamed His character, and broke His laws.

Zephaniah 3:5 is like a breath of fresh air. Zephaniah contrasted the wickedness of Jerusalem with the righteousness, justice, and faithfulness of the Lord. He continued to manifest His presence in the city, and He was innocent of wrongdoing, for He dealt fairly with His people. With the dawn of each day, His justice grew more evident. All who did evil, though, remained shameless in their misdeeds.

Zephaniah 3:6-7 reveals that God destroyed the surrounding nations as a warning to the people of Jerusalem, yet they eagerly sinned. Undoubtedly, this circumstance dispirited the righteous remnant. God encouraged them to wait patiently for Him to vindicate their faith. The Lord assured those who remained true to Him that a time was coming when He would judge all those who were evil, whether in Jerusalem or elsewhere. In that day, God would rise up (in a manner of speaking) to attack and plunder His enemies. It is also possible that in 3:8, the Lord used a legal metaphor to depict Himself as testifying against the iniquities of the wicked.

God had decided to assemble the world's nations and kingdoms to unleash on them His righteous indignation. He could do this as the Holy One of Israel. Human rulers can be petty and fickle, but the Lord remains just as He zealously manifests His holiness throughout His creation. Indeed, one day the entire earth will be consumed by God's fiery wrath.

Starting with 3:9, Zephaniah looked to a day of future blessing and restoration. God, by purifying the lips of all people, will enable them to offer Him unsullied praise. They will call upon Him for deliverance. And a family of nations will serve Him with united hearts. These worshipers will come even from the areas beyond the Nile River (3:10). The faithful remnant was to wait for the day of the Lord when God will purify His people and remove the arrogant from Jerusalem (3:11). He will leave a faithful remnant in the holy city (3:12). Unlike the princes, judges, prophets, and priests of Zephaniah's day, the faithful remnant will be virtuous and upright (3:13).

SUGGESTIONS TO TEACHERS

Zephaniah's prophecy faced the darkest sin of Judah with stark realism and looked to the future of the restored remnant with triumphant hope. Studying his prophecy today can motivate Christians to shake off any spiritual complacency or cynicism and to obey the Lord with renewed fervor and humility.

1. THE PERIL OF COMPLACENCY. The leaders of Jerusalem had become used to power. They no longer believed God would intervene in their lives to reward or punish. This complacent attitude set in motion processes of moral and spiritual decay in their lives. Christians today live in a culture that encourages us to keep our beliefs to ourselves and not to act or talk as though our faith matters much. We also live in a materially prosperous society that measures security in terms of insurance and retirement accounts, rather than dependence on God's presence and power. Spiritual complacency is a danger for us all.

2. THE PERIL OF AUTONOMY. The leaders of Jerusalem became detached from any sense that the Lord was active in their lives to deal with their sin and bless their uprightness. They lived as though they were accountable to no one but themselves. No one could teach them. No one could correct them. They avoided intimate contact with God. When Christians become complacent about their Lord and their faith, they can begin to act autonomously, too. We can ignore the positive teachings of Scripture, turn a deaf ear to God's Word that would correct sin in our lives, and avoid honest, intimate moments with our Lord. Every time a poll reports that the behavior of Christians doesn't differ from that of the unbelieving population, we see evidence of Christians living as they wish rather than as God desires.

3. THE PERIL OF IGNORING GOD. Zephaniah reported that the complacent, autonomous secular rulers of Judah had become greedy oppressors of the populace. The spiritual leaders had led the people astray and defiled what was holy. Neither group of leaders thought it mattered what they did, but they were wrong. They had ignored God, but that didn't mean He was non-existent or that He wasn't active. His presence was available at the temple every morning to receive worship and dispense justice, even if the leaders didn't come to bow down before Him and serve as His agents of justice. God still waits for His people to worship Him and do His will in the world. When we go our own way, though, we invite God's displeasure as surely as the leaders of Jerusalem did.

4. THE PROMISE OF A PURE FUTURE. Zephaniah predicted that the day of the Lord would remove the haughty leaders who had no time for God and leave the humble people who desired to know the Lord and obey Him. The application of this prophecy to Christian people is that haughty attitudes need to be judged by God and replaced by humble ones. Complacency needs to give way to eagerness, autonomy to dependence, and ignorance to acknowledgement. Then our lives will know God's pleasure and blessing.

FOR ADULTS

■ TOPIC: Getting Ready for Judgment

■ QUESTIONS: 1. Why would Jerusalem and its officials refuse to draw near to God? 2. How had the leaders, prophets, and priests become corrupted? 3. What would motivate the upright to wait on the Lord? 4. How could almighty God, who is just, pour out His fierce anger on the nations and peoples of the world? 5. How would the Lord get His wayward people to serve Him once again?

■ ILLUSTRATIONS:

Justice for Those Who Take Advantage of Others. A physician was chatting with an attorney at a party when a woman came up and interrupted their conversation. She had a pain in her leg and wanted some medical advice from the physician. He told her what to do and stood with a puzzled look on his face as she walked away. Turning back to his attorney friend, the physician asked, "Do I have a right to send that woman a bill for professional services?" "Certainly," the lawyer replied. So the next day in the physician's outgoing mail was a bill to the woman. And in the physician's incoming mail was a larger bill from the attorney!

The complacent leaders of Jerusalem thought they could oppress others and get away with it. Justice often arrives unexpectedly in time and form.

Ignoring God. In the heyday of nineteenth century immigration to New York, a newly arrived Irish minister found himself looking for a room in the Bowery. He was nibbling gumdrops and checking ads in windows and doorways when he felt a gun in his ribs. An Irish brogue rasped, "All right mister, gimme all your money!" The minister reached for his wallet, but by then the robber had seen his Bible. "Forgive me, pastor, I didn't know you were a minister," the thief muttered. "That's all right, son," the minister replied. "Repent of your sin. Here, have a gumdrop." "Oh, no thank you, pastor. I don't eat candy during the Easter season."

What's wrong with this picture? The thief had no relationship with God or love for Him. He was doing as he pleased in violation of God's law. Observing Easter made his confused conscience feel better. But it didn't get him anywhere with God.

When the Innocent Suffer. It's not fair when powerful people oppress the poor. We don't know why God lets suffering come to innocent people, but we do know He will be with them through that pain. Vance Havner said the following: "God uses broken things. It takes broken soil to produce a crop, broken clouds to give rain, broken grain to give bread, broken bread to give strength. It is the broken alabaster box that gives forth perfume. It is Peter, weeping bitterly, who returns to greater power than ever."

Pray for the oppressed, especially that God will make something good result from their pain.

FOR YOUTH

■ **TOPIC:** Think about It!

■ **QUESTIONS:** 1. In what sense were Jerusalem and its inhabitants polluted? 2. What did Zephaniah imply by calling Jerusalem's leaders roaring lions and evening wolves? 3. In light of God's righteousness, why would the wicked continue in their shameful acts? 4. Why would the Lord pour out His wrath on the nations? 5. What does it mean to call on the name of the Lord?

■ **ILLUSTRATIONS:**

Abuse of Power. A lady wanted a parrot that talked to keep her company. The pet shop owner told the woman he had a talking parrot, but it had been owned by a bartender. Occasionally the bird swore. The lady bought the parrot anyway and soon had it saying, "Praise the Lord!"

One day, the lady forgot to feed and water the bird. When she got home from work that evening, the bird was swearing like a sailor. The lady grabbed the bird from the cage and stuffed the startled parrot into the freezer. After a few minutes the lady took the shivering bird from the freezer and put it back in its cage, and lectured it about using foul language.

The parrot did really well for about six months. Then, the lady went to work again without feeding or watering the bird. When the lady came home, the bird was cussing up a blue streak. Back in the freezer the parrot went! However, this time the woman left it there for 30 minutes. The parrot was nearly dead when the lady pulled it out and warmed it with a hair dryer. When the parrot could move again, the lady asked it, "Are you going to swear any more?" "No ma'am," the parrot promised. After a pause the parrot went on, "Can I ask you a question?" "Yes," the lady replied. "I thought I knew all the bad words there were. Just what did that turkey in the freezer say?"

The parrot thought its owner was a terrible tyrant because the bird misunderstood the presence of a frozen turkey in the woman's freezer. But abuse of power is common in the world on the part of people who ignore God's Word and the love of Christ.

A Changed Life Can Surprise People. Tony Campolo told about a man who needed to change. Everyday he came home sweaty and smelly from the factory, dragged in the back door, grabbed something from the fridge, and plopped in front of the television until supper. His wife was ready to leave him.

So one day the man showered and shaved at the plant and put on fresh clothes. He stopped at a florist and picked up roses. He went to the front door instead of the back and rang the bell. When his wife opened the door, he bowed and held out the flowers. The startled woman burst into tears. Between sobs she said, "This is terrible. First, Billy broke his leg. Then your mother's coming for three weeks. The washer broke down. And now you've come home drunk!"

Sudden, major change in someone can be a shock to people. That's not bad, however. Just think how much that woman was going to enjoy her changed husband in the days ahead.

Changed to Make a Difference. Miss Jones, long-time reclusive resident in a small town, died, and the editor of the weekly newspaper couldn't come up with anything to say about her in an obituary. He met the mortician at the diner and found out he had nothing for the tombstone.

Miss Jones apparently had never been anywhere or done anything. The editor decided to pass the obituary item to a reporter. When he got back to the paper, no one was in the office but the sports writer. The editor gave him the assignment. The following Thursday, the obituary of Miss Jones read as follows: "Here lie the bones of Nancy Jones. For her, life held no terrors. She lived by herself. She died by herself—no hits, no runs, no errors."

Life has to mean more than that. God gives us physical life through birth and eternal life through faith in Jesus Christ. He makes us more and more like His Son so that we will live in a way that matters to Him and others. Live to make a difference.

Habakkuk Announces the Doom of the Unrighteous

BACKGROUND SCRIPTURE: Habakkuk 2:1-20; 2 Kings 23:35-37
DEVOTIONAL READING: Psalm 37:27-34

KEY VERSE: For the earth shall be filled with the knowledge of the glory of the LORD, as the waters cover the sea. Habakkuk 2:14.

KING JAMES VERSION

HABAKKUK 2:6 Shall not all these take up a parable against him, and a taunting proverb against him, and say, Woe to him that increaseth that which is not his! how long? and to him that ladeth himself with thick clay! 7 Shall they not rise up suddenly that shall bite thee, and awake that shall vex thee, and thou shalt be for booties unto them? 8 Because thou hast spoiled many nations, all the remnant of the people shall spoil thee; because of men's blood, and for the violence of the land, of the city, and of all that dwell therein. 9 Woe to him that coveteth an evil covetousness to his house, that he may set his nest on high, that he may be delivered from the power of evil! 10 Thou hast consulted shame to thy house by cutting off many people, and hast sinned against thy soul. 11 For the stone shall cry out of the wall, and the beam out of the timber shall answer it. 12 Woe to him that buildeth a town with blood, and stablisheth a city by iniquity! 13 Behold, is it not of the LORD of hosts that the people shall labour in the very fire, and the people shall weary themselves for very vanity? 14 For the earth shall be filled with the knowledge of the glory of the LORD, as the waters cover the sea.

NEW REVISED STANDARD VERSION

HABAKKUK 2:6 Shall not everyone taunt such people and, with mocking riddles, say about them,
"Alas for you who heap up what is not your own!"
How long will you load yourselves with goods taken in pledge?
7 Will not your own creditors suddenly rise,
and those who make you tremble wake up?
Then you will be booty for them.
8 Because you have plundered many nations,
all that survive of the peoples shall plunder you—
because of human bloodshed, and violence to the earth,
to cities and all who live in them.
9 "Alas for you who get evil gain for your houses,
setting your nest on high
to be safe from the reach of harm!"
10 You have devised shame for your house
by cutting off many peoples;
you have forfeited your life.
11 The very stones will cry out from the wall,
and the plaster will respond from the woodwork.
12 "Alas for you who build a town by bloodshed,
and found a city on iniquity!"
13 Is it not from the LORD of hosts
that peoples labor only to feed the flames,
and nations weary themselves for nothing?
14 But the earth will be filled
with the knowledge of the glory of the LORD,
as the waters cover the sea.

7

Monday, July 9	Psalm 37:27-34	*The Lord Loves Justice*
Tuesday, July 10	2 Kings 23:31-37	*Judah Becomes Egypt's Vassel*
Wednesday, July 11	Habakkuk 1:12-17	*Habakkuk's Complaint*
Thursday, July 12	Habakkuk 2:1-5	*The Lord Answers*
Friday, July 13	Habakkuk 2:6-14	*Woes Reported*
Saturday, July 14	Habakkuk 2:15-20	*The Lord Will Act*
Sunday, July 15	Habakkuk 3:13-19	*The Lord Is Our Strength*

BACKGROUND

Habakkuk was a prophet of Judah who lived in the seventh century B.C. In his day, the civil and religious leaders of the nation were corrupt. Such conditions especially prevailed following the death of King Josiah (609 B.C.) and during the reign of King Jehoiakim (609–597 B.C.).

Habakkuk predicted that the Babylonians would come against Jerusalem. This occurred when Nebuchadnezzar invaded Judah in 605 B.C. and took the civil and religious leaders into captivity. In order for Habakkuk's prophecy to have any credibility, it must be dated prior to the time when it was fulfilled. When the text of Habakkuk is compared with the period in which it was written, it proves to be the reliable product of a Judean prophet who lived during the time preceding Babylon's destruction of Judah. All things considered, Habakkuk probably wrote his book around 607 B.C.

The book begins with the Hebrew word rendered *burden* (1:1), which means "oracle" and refers to a message that is serious in tone. Habakkuk's prophecy was an announcement of judgment on Judah and her enemies. This message was difficult for God's representative to hear and even more difficult for him to deliver. The announcement of judgment is revealed in God's answers to the probing questions Habakkuk asked.

The prophet began by inquiring whether God was just in permitting the wicked to prevail in Judah. Habakkuk had asked the Lord several times to deliver the people of Judah from ruthless exploitation at the hands of their political and religious leaders. God appeared not to have heard Habakkuk's prayer because no action was forthcoming (1:2). He questioned why God made him view the sin and suffering in Judah. Habakkuk saw robbery and bloodshed as well as strife and contention among members of the Judean nation (1:3). The result seems to be that God's law was ineffective and justice was perverted. This permitted the wicked to prevail over the righteous in Judah (1:4).

The prophet wondered how a just and holy God could allow such inequities to occur. In answer to Habakkuk's complaint, the Lord told him and the people of Judah to look among the nations for His chastening instrument upon them (1:5). God would use as His instrument the Babylonians, who were known for their ruthlessness and speed in conquering other nations. The Babylonians would conquer Judah and possess her dwelling places (1:6).

The Babylonians were to be feared, for they were a law to themselves and took no thought of God's law (1:7). Their cavalrymen speedily conquered their prey (1:8). Like an advancing desert wind, the enemy could not be stopped. Their policy was to take numerous prisoners into captivity (1:9). The Babylonians laughed mockingly at the political and military leaders of other nations. The invaders also scoffed at the fortresses of others and built earthen ramps to conquer them (1:10). Then, the Babylonians would move on to other conquests. God would hold them guilty because they worshiped their own strength. Although the Lord used them as His chastening instrument, He would still hold them responsible for their excessively cruel actions against Judah (1:11).

The Babylonians made three raids on Judah. In the first two, which occurred in 605 and 597 B.C. (respectively), primarily the nobility were taken captive. The political and religious leaders complained about the invasions, and in fact were the first whom God judged. Nevertheless, there was a faithful remnant among them, including Daniel, Shadrach, Meshach, and Abednego (Daniel 1:1-7).

Habakkuk referred to the Lord as being eternal and holy, and Habakkuk affirmed his belief that Judah would not completely perish. Yet the Lord was using the Babylonians to judge and punish others (Hab. 1:12). The prophet knew that God could not tolerate sin and wrongdoing. That is why Habakkuk wondered how the Lord could sit by in silence as the wicked conquered people who were more righteous than themselves (1:13).

The prophet noted that the people God put on earth were similar to fish or other creatures of the sea without a leader (1:14). The enemy would come along and capture them with hooks and nets (1:15). This catch made the wicked so elated that they offered sacrifices to their fishing nets, for they thought their equipment made them rich and enabled them to enjoy sumptuous food (1:16). Habakkuk wondered whether God would allow this evil nation, Babylon, to continue to haul in its nets and destroy other nations without showing mercy (1:17).

NOTES ON THE PRINTED TEXT

The Lord did not ignore Habakkuk's probing questions. Instead, He graciously responded. He told His spokesman to record on tablets the revelation he was about to receive. The Hebrew word rendered *tables* (Hab. 2:2) refers to slabs of dressed wood, stone, or clay that were used for writing. Habakkuk was to clearly inscribe the message on a tablet, such as a herald would run with to give a message to others. This is perhaps a poetic way to speak of the importance of preserving or passing on the information. The Lord revealed that the vision awaited a future time of fulfillment. This is a reference to the demise of the Chaldean Empire in 539 B.C. It is true that more than six decades would pass before the predicted events would take place. Nevertheless, God's people were to patiently wait for the prophecy's fulfillment. In the divinely appointed time, He would honor His word (2:3).

The Lord told Habakkuk and the people of Judah that they—unlike the king of Babylon—were not to be puffed up. The righteous were to live by their faith. Habakkuk 2:4 refers to all true followers of God, namely, those who conform their lives to His holy standard. This verse can also be translated, "The righteous will live by his faithfulness." This implies that believers should remain unwavering in their loyalty to God. They can do so knowing that one day the Lord will right all wrongs. The Bible promises that the wicked will be judged and that the righteous will be eternally blessed. There are several places in the New Testament where Habakkuk 2:4 is quoted. This reminds us that faith, not good works, is the perspective for a person's right relationship with God. Those who are genuinely saved, trust and obey the Lord regardless of the circumstances (Eph. 2:8-10). They remain loyal to Him even when life seems unfair.

Ancient history reports that the Babylonians were a dreaded people. Their brutality and arrogance were epitomized by their king. He was not only filled with pride, but also harbored evil aspirations of conquering and destroying other people (Hab. 2:5). The Lord revealed to Habakkuk that this haughty ruler would one day meet his demise. The Lord used five oracles to disclose how Babylon would be destroyed. Each taunt song consisted of three verses in which a series of indictments were brought against the wicked. In the first *woe* (2:6), it is revealed that Babylon's victims would ridicule the mighty foe with a *parable* and scorn it with a *taunting proverb*. These enigmatic sayings and riddles would expose the folly of Babylon's ways and the ultimate demise that awaited this empire of evil.

The Babylonian rulers were guilty of stockpiling what belonged to others and seizing wealth from people through extortion. The wicked oppressors forced conquered nations to pay onerous sums of tribute. This resulted in treasured items and human hostages being taken as a pledge to guarantee compliance with the conquerors' demands. Understandably, the downtrodden masses wondered how long such atrocities would continue.

Habakkuk 2:7 indicates a reversal of roles. Those who were debtors to the Babylonians would rise up suddenly and attack them. In other words, the creditors would wake up and terrify their former tormentors. In effect, the predator would become the prey. The Lord would allow this in judgment for the crimes the Babylonians committed. The survivors of the nations they robbed would one day plunder them. This would be the appropriate outcome for the tormentors having murdered countless people in their march to power. Indeed, the Babylonians wiped out entire regions, cities, and their inhabitants (2:8), so voracious was their appetite for what belonged to others.

The evil Babylonian empire did not just exploit surrounding nations. The oppressors also did whatever they could to exalt themselves. They built their dynasty (or *house*; 2:9) by unjust means. The wicked rich were convinced that becoming the superpower of the day would ensure their survival. It would be like a bird of prey building its nest in a spot so high that other predators could not reach it. But no matter how inaccessible such a place might seem, the Babylonians would not escape the clutches of disaster. Over the course of their existence, the Babylonians were guilty of using schemes and ploys to get what they wanted. In the process, they brought many countries and cultures to ruin. The tormentors, though, brought shame to their own empire and would self-destruct. They took the lives of others and would forfeit their own existence in recompense (2:10).

Habakkuk 2:11 personifies Babylon's victims as the materials used to build the dynastic house of the oppressors. But the victims would not remain silent about the wealth extorted from them. Stones in the walls would cry out and the beams of the rafters would echo a corresponding reply. They would serve as witnesses in a law court against the all the iniquities committed by the Babylonians. The cumulative weight of the evidence would condemn them for their imperialistic ways.

Calamity awaited the Babylonians for using the slaughter of the innocent to build one city after another. Far too many towns were established by means of iniquity (2:12). God would not allow such injustices to go unnoticed and unanswered. The Lord of heaven's armies decreed that everything Babylon exhaustingly labored to accomplish would end up being fuel for the fire of His judgment. The more the oppressors wearied themselves to achieve their vaunted goals, the more in vain it would be. In the day of reckoning, their attainments would be reduced to ashes (2:13).

In ancient Israel, the Lord's glory—His visible presence and power—filled the tabernacle and temple. This was one way He made Himself known to His people and gave them an opportunity to honor Him throughout the course of their daily activities. Imagine God's glory not only filling a sanctuary but also the entire planet! Just as the waters cover the sea, so one day earth will be inundated with the knowledge of the Lord's glory (2:14). Then all races, nations, and people will recognize His sovereign majesty and presence.

SUGGESTIONS TO TEACHERS

Habakkuk addressed some classical spiritual problems. How can God be just if He lets the unrighteous get away with their sins? How can God be loving if He lets the bullies of the world beat up on the little people? Habakkuk thought he could win an argument with God, only to find out that he had no idea how all-encompassing God's plan was for His people and the world.

1. STARK CONTRASTS. The sobering message of this week's lesson reminds us that the lifestyle and priorities of Christians should contrast with that of unbelievers. Jesus taught His followers to be lights in the darkness and beacons of hope in a night of despair. There is evidence that our Lord's desire for His people is being realized. Here and there, Christians are making a significant impact in race relations, in the political arena, and in ministering to the world's downtrodden.

2. TRAGIC COMPROMISES. Regrettably, there are also indications that believers are yielding to the world's pressures to conform. The values around us are seldom adopted all at once. The first stage may be reluctance to speak out against a practice Christians know to be wrong. In time, though, the activity is treated as insignificant, and eventually Christians may embrace it without reservation.

3. IMPORTANT CHOICES. By pressuring us to take the shape of the world around us, unbelievers keep us from being the positive moral influence Jesus intended. The Lord, however, calls us to live according to His values. We need to place our lifestyles and priorities under the focus of His Word and see what is reflected before the Lord and the world. If we are true to the teachings of Scripture, we will please our Lord and draw others to Him. But if we live in a way that contradicts the Word of God, then we need to change our lifestyles. Ultimately, those who rebel against the Lord will experience His judgment.

4. SOBERING CONCLUSIONS. Point out that although Habakkuk's message was primarily directed to people in a specific category—the wicked Babylonians—he expected God's faithful remnant to heed the warnings. Indeed, messages of God's judgment still apply to us today. All of us must come to grips with any behavior that might offend the Lord.

FOR ADULTS	■ **TOPIC:** A Reason to Hope

■ **QUESTIONS:** 1. In what ways had Babylon plundered other nations? 2. Why had the Babylonians ravaged lands and cities? 3. How would the Babylonian's schemes bring shame to them? 4. Why would Babylon's victims testify against them? 5. What had the Lord of hosts decreed concerning the exhausting labor of the nations?

■ **ILLUSTRATIONS:**

Surefooted Faith. Experts say that the number one cause of marital distress and division is money problems. For Bruce and Charlotte, that could have been the case—but it wasn't. Instead of letting their financial woes overtake an otherwise wonderful life together, they learned to commit their struggles to the Lord. Indeed, He was the basis for them having hope.

Thus, while the couple seemed to barely squeak by year after year, they not only stayed together, but they also grew closer to one another and to God. Financial pressures seemed to be a part of their life's burden. But through regular prayer, it was a burden that could be endured. Though they were lower-income by government standards, they felt rich by kingdom standards.

Kidnapped—but Still Blessed. While a missionary in Beirut, Lebanon, Benjamin Weir was kidnapped by Shiite Moslems. For 16 months he was blindfolded most of the time and his hands manacled. This is his report on one of the early days of captivity:

I lifted my blindfold and began examining the room. What was here that could bring me close to the sustaining presence of God? I let my imagination have total freedom. Looking up, I examined an electric wire hanging from the ceiling. The bulb and socket had been removed so that it ended in an arc with three wires exposed. To me, those wires seemed like three fingers. I could see a hand and an arm reaching downward—like the Sistine Chapel in Rome, Michelangelo's fresco of God reaching out His hand and finger toward Adam. Here God was reaching toward me, reminding me, saying, "You're alive. You are mine; I've made you and called you into being for a divine purpose."

By the end of the day, Weir was humming the hymn, "Count Your Blessings." He counted (among other things) his health, life, food, mattress, pillow, blanket, wife, family, faith, prayer, Jesus, the Holy Spirit, the Father's love—33 things in all. In the process of reviewing these blessings, he found that his feelings of fear and helplessness were replaced by hope.

Guilty! In his book *Whatever Became of Sin?*, Karl Menninger tells about a stern-faced man who stood on a city street corner and watched pedestrians hurry by. Every few minutes, the man would lift one arm and solemnly point to an individual and exclaim, "Guilty!" An observer said the effect on people was eerie. They would hesitate, glance at the man, and hurry off.

In a sense, we need to be like that stern-faced man. However, instead of pointing at other people, we need to point out the attitudes and priorities in our own lives that conflict with God's values. We need to admit our guilt and change our ways. We need to examine ourselves as candidly as the stern-faced man judged some of the people who passed by him. With God's help, all these things are possible.

FOR YOUTH

■ **TOPIC:** Reason to Hope

■ **QUESTIONS:** 1. Why would Babylon be subjected to taunts? 2. By what means did the Babylonians make themselves wealthy? 3. How did the Babylonians think they could escape the clutches of disaster? 4. Why had the Babylonians resorted to bloodshed and injustice? 5. How would the labor of the wicked become fuel for the fire of God's judgment?

■ **ILLUSTRATIONS:**

Whom Do You Trust? At the west end of Constitution Avenue in Washington, D.C., screened from the street by a grove of elm and holly trees, sits a bronze statue of Albert Einstein. Einstein's figure is 21 feet tall. He's seated on a three-step base of white granite. The physicist is depicted in a baggy sweater, wrinkled corduroy trousers, and sandals. His shock of hair is in familiar disarray.

At Einstein's feet is a map of the universe—a 28-foot square slab of granite in which 2,700 small metal studs are embedded. Each stud represents the location in the sky of a planet, major star, or familiar celestial body at noon on April 22, 1979—the time the memorial was dedicated.

The expression on the face of Einstein's statue is a mixture of wisdom, peace, and wonder. The face reflects the serenity of a man who believed a divine mind had conceived the universe he spent his life trying to understand. He would tell his colleagues who believed in a random universe, "God does not play dice."

Einstein was not a Christian. He put his confidence in an impersonal deity. You can go beyond Einstein by putting your trust and hope in the personal God of the Bible, Jesus Christ, to bring you safely through any difficulty of life.

Faith Knows God Has the Answers. A *Time* magazine reporter asked Russian-born novelist Ayn Rand, "Ms. Rand, in a sentence, what's wrong with the modern world?"

The novelist replied, "Never before has the world been clamoring so desperately for answers to crucial problems, and never before has the world been so fanatically committed to the belief that no answers are possible. To paraphrase the Bible, the modern attitude is 'Father, forgive us for we know not what we are doing and please don't tell us.'"

Rand didn't get it in one sentence, but she did capture an important concept. When things fall apart, we need to look to God for explanation, for refuge, and for hope. If we don't, we will be full of despair.

Who Loves You? An old man died, leaving one child—a son—as his sole survivor. The father had been hard to know. The son remembered a respectful but formal relationship. Suddenly, he was alone in his father's house looking through all the items kept in all the places a child never looks when his or her parents are alive.

The big stuff was easy to deal with—property, life insurance, and bank accounts. It was the personal stuff that was hard to handle. Finally, the son came to the bureau drawers in the bedroom. Here were carefully sorted socks. There were several small boxes and a cigar tin. One box held military insignia, another tie tacks and foreign coins. This one had miscellaneous keys. That one held his mother's wedding ring and a lock of her hair.

In the cigar tin was a yellowed index card wrapped in tissue paper. Tiny teeth were glued to the card. A date was jotted under each tooth in his father's neat handwriting. His father had been the tooth fairy. The son always assumed it was his mother.

God loves you in ways you've never imagined. He isn't distant and uncaring, though you may think so. He has been looking out for you all your life. You can depend on Him to keep doing so forever. He isn't going to leave you an orphan, like the son in the story. Be sure your relationship with your heavenly Father is closer than the relationship in the story. *God wants it that way.*

JEREMIAH ANNOUNCES THE CONSEQUENCES OF DISOBEDIENCE

BACKGROUND SCRIPTURE: Jeremiah 7:11-15; 2 Kings 23:36-37
DEVOTIONAL READING: 2 Chronicles 7:11-16

KEY VERSES: Because ye have done all these works, . . .
I will cast you out of my sight. Jeremiah 7:13, 15.

KING JAMES VERSION

JEREMIAH 7:11 Is this house, which is called by my name, become a den of robbers in your eyes? Behold, even I have seen it, saith the LORD. 12 But go ye now unto my place which was in Shiloh, where I set my name at the first, and see what I did to it for the wickedness of my people Israel. 13 And now, because ye have done all these works, saith the LORD, and I spake unto you, rising up early and speaking, but ye heard not; and I called you, but ye answered not; 14 Therefore will I do unto this house, which is called by my name, wherein ye trust, and unto the place which I gave to you and to your fathers, as I have done to Shiloh. 15 And I will cast you out of my sight, as I have cast out all your brethren, even the whole seed of Ephraim.

2 KINGS 23:36 Jehoiakim was twenty and five years old when he began to reign; and he reigned eleven years in Jerusalem. And his mother's name was Zebudah, the daughter of Pedaiah of Rumah. 37 And he did that which was evil in the sight of the LORD, according to all that his fathers had done.

NEW REVISED STANDARD VERSION

JEREMIAH 7:11 Has this house, which is called by my name, become a den of robbers in your sight? You know, I too am watching, says the LORD. 12 Go now to my place that was in Shiloh, where I made my name dwell at first, and see what I did to it for the wickedness of my people Israel. 13 And now, because you have done all these things, says the LORD, and when I spoke to you persistently, you did not listen, and when I called you, you did not answer, 14 therefore I will do to the house that is called by my name, in which you trust, and to the place that I gave to you and to your ancestors, just what I did to Shiloh. 15 And I will cast you out of my sight, just as I cast out all your kinsfolk, all the offspring of Ephraim.

2 KINGS 23:36 Jehoiakim was twenty-five years old when he began to reign; he reigned eleven years in Jerusalem. His mother's name was Zebidah daughter of Pedaiah of Rumah. 37 He did what was evil in the sight of the LORD, just as all his ancestors had done.

8

Monday, July 16	Hebrews 2:1-4	*Pay Greater Attention*
Tuesday, July 17	2 Chronicles 7:11-16	*Forgiveness Is Possible*
Wednesday, July 18	1 Kings 9:1-9	*Choices of Consequences*
Thursday, July 19	Jeremiah 19:1-6	*Disaster Is Coming*
Friday, July 20	Jeremiah 26:1-6	*Downfall Threatened*
Saturday, July 21	Jeremiah 7:1-7	*Amend Your Ways*
Sunday, July 22	Jeremiah 7:8-15	*Judgment of the Wicked*

BACKGROUND

The collection of messages in Jeremiah 7–10 is commonly called "The Temple Address," since the prophet delivered these messages at the sanctuary in Jerusalem. Chapter 26 describes the probable historical events surrounding these prophecies. King Josiah's reforms died when he did, and the idolatry of the Canaanites rapidly reemerged in Judah during the early reign of Josiah's son, Jehoiakim. Both Jeremiah 7 and 26 warn that the temple in Jerusalem might come to the same end as the tabernacle at Shiloh centuries before (7:12-15; 26:4-6).

With the temple of God in their midst, the people of Judah felt safe and secure enough to live morally depraved lives and to treat the disadvantaged in inhumane ways (7:9). But as a dire warning to the Judahites and to reveal the fallacy of their belief that God's presence was itself insurance against disaster, Jeremiah pointed to the sad end of Shiloh, the city where the nation had first located its tabernacle (7:10-15; see Josh. 18:1; Judg. 18:31; 1 Sam. 1:3; 4:3-4).

After David captured Jerusalem and made it the capitol of his kingdom, he eventually moved the ark from Shiloh to the holy city. Shiloh thereafter lost its importance and the nation abandoned it as the center of worship. Psalm 78:56-61, however, gives the ultimate reason for Shiloh's decline. Asaph stated that because of the Israelites' idolatry and rebellion, *[God] forsook the tabernacle of Shiloh, the tent which he placed among men* (78:60).

Scripture does not give a specific account of Shiloh's fall. Nevertheless, it is clear that after the Philistines captured the ark of the covenant during Samuel's judgeship of Israel (1 Sam. 4:1–7:1), the enemy destroyed Shiloh around 1050 B.C. The fact that the nation's priests were operating out of Nob during the reign of Saul (22:11) confirms that the Philistines had destroyed Shiloh. The essence of Jeremiah's warning to the people of Judah is clear. The prophet declared that what God had done to Shiloh, He would certainly do to Jerusalem.

NOTES ON THE PRINTED TEXT

Late in 609 or early in 608 B.C., the Lord instructed Jeremiah to deliver a warning to the worshipers at the temple. Following God's directions, Jeremiah positioned himself at a prominent gate of the sanctuary—perhaps the New Gate (see 26:10)—where he could address the people of Judah who came through these gates to worship the Lord (7:2-3). Though the people of Judah attended temple activities, their religion was nothing but insincere ritual. Today, we would say that Jeremiah's message was for professing believers—for people who join churches, attend at least occasionally, and who probably are offended if anyone suggests that they are living hypocritically.

Jeremiah challenged the people to live in a manner that was consistent with their apparent worship. The prophet urged them to change their ways and start living uprightly, if they had any hope of remaining in the promised land. He warned that trusting in the temple would not keep the people safe and that those who taught otherwise were false prophets (7:4). Simply chanting the phrase *the temple of the* LORD was believed to ward off destruction. Surely God would not allow His own sanctuary to be destroyed—or so the people believed. This delusion is held today by those who feel that God's judgment "can't happen here." It is similar to the idea that becoming a professing Christian is a safeguard against the troubles that afflict humanity in general.

A century earlier (701 B.C.), the Lord had delivered Jerusalem from the invading armies of Assyria, which Sennacherib had commanded (see 2 Chron. 34:8-13). In Jeremiah's time, the "temple theology" of the false prophets concluded that none of Judah's enemies could touch the sanctuary—or, for that matter, the people who worshiped there. The Lord declared that such talk was *lying words* (Jer. 7:4, 8). The only thing that would protect Jerusalem was the people's obedience to its covenant with God. They were to honor the Lord with righteousness and justice, and end all bloodshed, idolatry, and oppression of the powerless. Honoring God with their actions would be the only security they needed to continue living in their land (7:5-7). Anything less was worthless (7:8).

Instead of pursuing justice, the inhabitants of Judah brazenly violated one command after another. For instance, they were guilty of theft, murder, adultery, and lying. These were not the qualities God wanted to see in His people. Rather, He desired them to be just, fair, kind, and virtuous (7:9). The Lord declared that His people were guilty of burning incense to Baal. This was an absurd practice, for this and other pagan deities had never done anything beneficial for the Judahites.

Baal was an ordinary Hebrew word for "owner," and therefore "lord" or "master." It was also a common term for husband (Deut. 21:13; 2 Sam. 11:26; Prov. 31:11, 23, 28) and was sometimes applied that way to the Lord Himself (Isa. 54:5; Jer. 3:14). However, the most frequent use of Baal in the Old Testament is as the name of the chief deity of the Canaanites. The ancient people of Palestine considered Baal to be the owner of those who followed him.

Instead of being a loving husband, however, Baal was more like an abusive spouse. To appease him, the prophets of this pagan deity had a practice of cutting themselves to draw blood (1 Kings 18:28). False prophets taught that Baal would reward anyone who pleased him with sacrifices and gifts. Meanwhile, Baal made no ethical claims on anyone. For example, he didn't care how cruel, greedy, or immoral people were as long as they offered regular sacrifices to him. By contrast, the Lord—the God of Abraham, Isaac, and Jacob—demanded mercy and justice even more than sacrifice.

Tragically, after the people of Judah wantonly disregarded the covenant, they trotted off to the temple, offered their sacrifices, and breathed a sigh of relief as they said, *We are delivered* (Jer. 7:10). We can imagine the Lord asking incredulously, "Safe for what? Safe to do all these abominations?" There are several reasons why the temple was so important to the Judahites. The sanctuary was a symbol of God's holiness, His covenant relationship with His people, and His willingness to forgive their sins. The Lord used the temple to centralize worship at Jerusalem. In the temple God's people could spend time in prayer. Finally, its design, furniture, and customs were object lessons that prepared the people for the Messiah.

The Lord asked a question that Jesus would pick up centuries later when He cleansed the temple: *Is this house, which is called by my name, become a den of robbers in your eyes?* (7:11; see Mark 11:17). Like robbers who lie, cheat, and steal before running back to their hideout, the people of Judah committed acts of injustice, only to return to the temple. And though they came to the Lord's house, their worship never seemed to affect their day-to-day behavior. The people's externals of worship could never make up for the lack of integrity and a growing relationship with God. Jeremiah's contemporaries needed to practice the quality of justice before the temple and the worship conducted there could mean anything.

To compel the people of Judah to consider that judgment could fall on Jerusalem and its temple, the Lord asked them to remember what had happened at Shiloh (Jer. 7:12). The prophet declared that what God had done to Shiloh, He would certainly do to Jerusalem. When Jeremiah stood at the temple gate and warned the people that the sanctuary would not magically save them from judgment, the structure had been standing in Jerusalem for about 350 years. During those centuries, the Lord had repeatedly called to His people through the prophets (7:13). The persistent refusal of the Judahites to listen to God's warnings left Jerusalem vulnerable to the same kind of destruction Shiloh had experienced more than 400 years earlier (7:14).

The people's sin also made their nation and capitol vulnerable to the same awful end that came to the northern kingdom of Israel, which Jeremiah called *Ephraim* (7:15) after the dominant tribe of Israel. More than a century before Jeremiah delivered his prophecy in the temple, the Assyrians had destroyed the northern kingdom and removed the people from the land (722 B.C.). Likewise, in 586 B.C., the Lord would use the Babylonians to drive out the people of Judah.

For 23 years, Jeremiah had labored as God's prophet (Jer. 25:3). Seventeen of those years had been during Josiah's reign. The prophet continued through three months of Jehoahaz's brief tenure and six years into Jehoiakim's rule. Josiah was the last of the godly kings of Judah. His rule extended from 640–609 B.C. Despite all the nationwide religious reforms he enacted, it did not abate the Lord's fierce anger for all the idolatry, iniquity, and immorality committed during the long reign of Manasseh (697–642 B.C.; 2 Kings 23:26). Just as God had spurned Israel, so too He would reject Judah. He would banish the people from His presence and allow the holy city and temple to be destroyed (23:27).

Before that happened, though, Josiah died at Megiddo while engaging the Egyptians in battle (23:29). Then the people of Judah installed his son, Jehoahaz, as the next king (23:30). His reign, however, lasted only three months (23:31). The Egyptians deposed him and instead made his brother, Jehoiakim (also known as Eliakim), the monarch of Judah (23:34). He in turn paid a heavy tribute of silver and gold to Pharaoh Necho (23:35). Jehoiakim became Judah's king at the age of 25 and his reign in Jerusalem lasted 11 years (from 609–598 B.C.). According to 23:36, his mother's name was Zebudah. She was the daughter of Pedaiah and came from Rumah, a town some think may have been located in Galilee.

Like his ancestors, Jehoiakim did evil before the Lord (23:37). For example, he used compulsory, uncompensated labor to build a luxurious palace while practicing other injustices (Jer. 22:13-17). Jeremiah's announcement of judgment notes the eventual demise of Jehoiakim, who would neither be lamented nor buried with royal honors (22:18-19).

SUGGESTIONS TO TEACHERS

Jeremiah 7:14 reveals that the leaders and people of Judah placed their trust in the Jerusalem temple to shield them from divine judgment. Even today believers can misplace their trust. The three primary ways are undue confidence in circumstances, other people, or ourselves.

1. THE PROBLEM OF EVIL. With so much evil and injustice in the world, it is sometimes hard for us to discern how God is working through various circumstances. Like people in ancient times, we might feel upset or discouraged by the crime and hatred all around us. God's answer to us is the same as He would have given back then. He wants us to be patient and place our confidence exclusively in Him. We can trust Him to bring about His perfect justice in His time.

2. THE WISE PLANS OF GOD. All of us go through times when life seems bleak and hopeless. If we had to rely solely on ourselves, our circumstances, or others, we would surely lose hope. The way to prevent this from happening is to continue to rely on the Lord. We can rest assured that He is directing all things according to His wise plans. We also know that He will never let us down, regardless of how difficult our times might be.

3. THE SUPREME POWER OF GOD. It is not always easy for us to be patient when we see a multitude of wrongs taking place all around us. We should remember that God is in full control and that His timing, not ours, is perfect. If we find the sinful activities of the world abhorrent, He does even more. As the sovereign and just Lord, He cannot allow iniquity to go unpunished forever. At the right moment, He will deal with all who have rebelled. Until then, we need to continue to trust Him fully, even when we cannot figure out why He has allowed certain events to take place.

4. THE FOCAL POINT OF FAITH. The world is filled with egotistical, self-satisfied people who place all their confidence in themselves. We know from this week's lesson that ultimately such individuals will fail. This reminds us that we must trust in God for temporal and eternal matters. We are saved through faith in Christ, and we live each day by continuing to trust in Him.

FOR ADULTS	■ **TOPIC:** Your Actions, Your Consequences ■ **QUESTIONS:** 1. Why did the Lord, through Jeremiah, mention the town of Shiloh? 2. How did God repeatedly try to speak to the way-

ward people of Judah? 3. Why did the rulers and people of Judah place so much trust in the temple? 4. Why did God plan to exile His people to Babylon? 5. What was the divine conclusion on the nature of Jehoiakim's reign as king of Judah?

■ **ILLUSTRATIONS:**

Living with the Consequences. The Yankees let Babe Ruth go in 1934. Ruth accepted that his playing days were over. He wanted to manage. Then something awful happened. No one took him seriously. Manage? How could Babe Ruth manage a baseball team when he'd never even been able to manage himself?

The Babe had jumped straight from an orphanage to the big leagues. He had scoffed at discipline, eaten hotdogs by the dozen, drank like a fish, and womanized without restraint. Everybody looked the other way while he was the Sultan of Swat, but when he wanted to be taken seriously as a leader of others, they just looked away. It broke the Babe's heart to live with the consequences of his self-indulgence.

Habits Are Hard to Break. A successful businessman escaped to his lake house every weekend like clockwork. To save time, he flew to a small airport near his retreat. It dawned on him that he could save even more time by fitting his plane with pontoons and landing on his lake. That Friday, he and his wife headed for the lake. Mentally he was already fishing as he made his approach to the airport. His wife's scream brought him to reality. "You can't land here! You've got the pontoons on!"

The man jerked his plane out of its approach. With trembling hands, he flew to the lake, touched down, and taxied right to his dock. He looked at his wife, laughed sheepishly, and said, "Old habits die hard." Then he opened his door and hopped out into five feet of water.

This man's wife must have felt like Jeremiah warning Judah. Her husband was so habituated to one way of doing things that he had a hard time acting differently, even when he wanted to. We have to beware of letting any sin become a part of our way of living. It may become a hard thing to break away from.

At the Crossroads. One of Robert Frost's most famous poems is "The Road Not Taken." Here's part of it:

> Two roads diverged in a yellow wood,
> And sorry I could not travel both
> And be one traveler, long I stood
> And looked down one as far as I could
> To where it bent in the undergrowth;
> Then took the other. . . .
> Two roads diverged in a wood, and I—
> I took the one less traveled by,
> And that has made all the difference.

If only Judah had chosen the way "less traveled by," the nation would not have faced the judgment of conquest and captivity. Judah ignored the ancient paths in favor of the road of rebellion. Make godly choices at the crossroads of your life.

 FOR YOUTH

■ TOPIC: What Goes Around, Comes Around
■ QUESTIONS: 1. How had the Jerusalem temple been misused?
2. How did the Lord previously respond to the wickedness committed at Shiloh? 3. Why did the people of Judah refuse to repent? 4. How would God judge the Judahites? 5. What characterized Jehoiakim's reign?

■ ILLUSTRATIONS:

Truth and Consequences. The young man had grown up in a Bible-believing church but wanted some "freedom." Soon he found himself experimenting with drugs and alcohol with his new "friends." He knew it was wrong, and he expected God to strike him down with a lightning bolt. But nothing dramatic happened. He dropped most contact with his parents and took a cheap apartment in a nasty part of town.

Then the young man moved in with a girl. She was pretty and willing and made him feel important. But he didn't love her and resented her hints that they should marry. Now the young man really thought God was going to get him. He interpreted most comments from his family as criticisms. He grew increasingly angry and suspicious.

Then the girl got pregnant, and the young man wondered whether she did it on purpose to trap him. He married her for the baby's sake, but now he hated her. They moved to a bigger apartment and started going in debt. The young man drank more, missed work more, and eventually got fired. The only good thing he could see in it all was that God hadn't struck him down. But then one day it occurred to him that his judgment was built into his sin. *He was living the consequences of his disobedience.*

Getting Right with God. The young soldier was tasting World War II combat for the first time in a bloody battle in the Italian mountains. He dived into a foxhole just ahead of some bullets and began deepening the shallow pit. As he frantically scraped with his helmet, he unearthed something shiny. It was a metal cross, lost by a former foxhole occupant.

A second man hurtled in beside the frightened soldier as another round of artillery screamed overhead. After the explosions, the soldier noticed his companion was a chaplain. Holding out the cross, the soldier gasped, "Am I glad to see you! How do you work this thing?"

When circumstances are going bad, help from God can look pretty attractive. If a person doesn't have a relationship with God through faith in Jesus Christ, figuring out how to connect with the Lord can seem puzzling. It's best to come to faith in Jesus and walk with Him in obedience all along so there's no need to try to figure out how to get in touch with Him when life feels overwhelming.

Choosing the Right Path. Elizabeth was a teen-aged girl from a wealthy family when the Germans started bombing London in 1940. She could have moved to one of their country homes and waited out the war riding horses and visiting her rich friends. But Elizabeth had seen Winston Churchill with his cigar clamped in his mouth striding through London in defiance of danger from the air.

Elizabeth made a choice. She pulled on dungarees, rolled up the bottoms, and drove a truck through debris-littered streets—one more teenager supporting the war effort. Only Elizabeth wasn't just one more teenager. Her father was George VI, king of England. Elizabeth's choice marked her. She earned the respect of the British people. *And she's never lost it.*

The choices you make now will shape your life for decades to come, even as Elizabeth's did. Choose the ancient paths, the good way. Heed the warnings of God's Word and walk in His ways.

Jeremiah Invites Jews in Babylon to Trust God

Background Scripture: Jeremiah 29:1-14
Devotional Reading: Psalm 145:13b-21

Key Verse: For I know the thoughts that I think toward you, saith the LORD, thoughts of peace, and not of evil, to give you an expected end. Jeremiah 29:11.

KING JAMES VERSION

JEREMIAH 29:1 Now these are the words of the letter that Jeremiah the prophet sent from Jerusalem unto the residue of the elders which were carried away captives, and to the priests, and to the prophets, and to all the people whom Nebuchadnezzar had carried away captive from Jerusalem to Babylon; 2 (After that Jeconiah the king, and the queen, and the eunuchs, the princes of Judah and Jerusalem, and the carpenters, and the smiths, were departed from Jerusalem;) 3 By the hand of Elasah the son of Shaphan, and Gemariah the son of Hilkiah, (whom Zedekiah king of Judah sent unto Babylon to Nebuchadnezzar king of Babylon) saying, 4 Thus saith the LORD of hosts, the God of Israel, unto all that are carried away captives, whom I have caused to be carried away from Jerusalem unto Babylon; 5 Build ye houses, and dwell in them; and plant gardens, and eat the fruit of them; 6 Take ye wives, and beget sons and daughters; and take wives for your sons, and give your daughters to husbands, that they may bear sons and daughters; that ye may be increased there, and not diminished. 7 And seek the peace of the city whither I have caused you to be carried away captives, and pray unto the LORD for it: for in the peace thereof shall ye have peace.

8 For thus saith the LORD of hosts, the God of Israel; Let not your prophets and your diviners, that be in the midst of you, deceive you, neither hearken to your dreams which ye cause to be dreamed. 9 For they prophesy falsely unto you in my name: I have not sent them, saith the LORD. 10 For thus saith the LORD, That after seventy years be accomplished at Babylon I will visit you, and perform my good word toward you, in causing you to return to this place. 11 For I know the thoughts that I think toward you, saith the LORD, thoughts of peace, and not of evil, to give you an expected end. 12 Then shall ye call upon me, and ye shall go and pray unto me, and I will hearken unto you. 13 And ye shall seek me, and find me, when ye shall search for me with all your heart. 14 And I will be found of you, saith the LORD: and I will turn away your captivity, and I will gather you from all the nations, and from all the places whither I have driven you, saith the LORD; and I will bring you again into the place whence I caused you to be carried away captive.

NEW REVISED STANDARD VERSION

JEREMIAH 29:1 These are the words of the letter that the prophet Jeremiah sent from Jerusalem to the remaining elders among the exiles, and to the priests, the prophets, and all the people, whom Nebuchadnezzar had taken into exile from Jerusalem to Babylon. 2 This was after King Jeconiah, and the queen mother, the court officials, the leaders of Judah and Jerusalem, the artisans, and the smiths had departed from Jerusalem. 3 The letter was sent by the hand of Elasah son of Shaphan and Gemariah son of Hilkiah, whom King Zedekiah of Judah sent to Babylon to King Nebuchadnezzar of Babylon. It said:
4 Thus says the LORD of hosts, the God of Israel, to all the exiles whom I have sent into exile from Jerusalem to Babylon: 5 Build houses and live in them; plant gardens and eat what they produce. 6 Take wives and have sons and daughters; take wives for your sons, and give your daughters in marriage, that they may bear sons and daughters; multiply there, and do not decrease. 7 But seek the welfare of the city where I have sent you into exile, and pray to the LORD on its behalf, for in its welfare you will find your welfare. 8 For thus says the LORD of hosts, the God of Israel: Do not let the prophets and the diviners who are among you deceive you, and do not listen to the dreams that they dream, 9 for it is a lie that they are prophesying to you in my name; I did not send them, says the LORD.

10 For thus says the LORD: Only when Babylon's seventy years are completed will I visit you, and I will fulfill to you my promise and bring you back to this place. 11 For surely I know the plans I have for you, says the LORD, plans for your welfare and not for harm, to give you a future with hope. 12 Then when you call upon me and come and pray to me, I will hear you. 13 When you search for me, you will find me; if you seek me with all your heart, 14 I will let you find me, says the LORD, and I will restore your fortunes and gather you from all the nations and all the places where I have driven you, says the LORD, and I will bring you back to the place from which I sent you into exile.

9

HOME BIBLE READINGS

Monday, July 23	Psalm 145:13b-21	*The Goodness of the Lord*
Tuesday, July 24	Jeremiah 30:18-22	*God Restores*
Wednesday, July 25	Jeremiah 31:1-9	*Loved with an Everlasting Love*
Thursday, July 26	Jeremiah 31:10-14	*Shepherd of the Flock*
Friday, July 27	Jeremiah 31:33-37	*They Shall Be My People*
Saturday, July 28	Jeremiah 29:1-9	*Jeremiah Writes the Exiles*
Sunday, July 29	Jeremiah 29:10-14	*God's Good Plans*

BACKGROUND

In Jeremiah 27, we learn that 13 years after the events of chapters 25—26 (595 B.C.), Jeremiah began to wear a wooden yoke on his neck as an object lesson: everyone needed to prepare themselves to submit to the yoke of Babylon. To reinforce his graphic display of servitude, the prophet sent messages to the kings of surrounding nations. King Zedekiah and the priests and people of Judah received the same message. Jeremiah further warned them not to believe the lies of the false prophets who promised an early deliverance from the interference of Babylon.

Jeremiah continued to wear the wooden yoke as a remainder of the coming Babylonian rule. Then, during the summer of 593 B.C., Hananiah, one of the false prophets, challenged Jeremiah's message of submission to Babylon (28:1-2). The imposter confronted him in the temple courtyard before a large crowd of priests and people. Hananiah was from Gibeon, a city located about five miles northwest of Jerusalem. Like Jeremiah's hometown of Anathoth, Gibeon was designated for the homes of priests and Levites. Hananiah, like Jeremiah, may have come from a priestly family.

Hananiah began his false prophecy with the same formula Jeremiah had used: *Thus speaketh the LORD of hosts, the God of Israel* (28:2; see also 27:4). Hananiah predicted that the Lord would break the yoke of Babylonian dominance from Judah's neck. Then the fraud gave three specific details: this turn of events would take place within two years; all the sacred temple furnishings would be returned; and King Jehoiachin, whom Nebuchadnezzar had deported in 597 B.C. along with 10,000 Judahites (2 Kings 24:14), would come home with the other exiles (Jer. 28:3-4).

As Jeremiah stood in front of all the priests and people at the temple, he gave his "amen" to what Hananiah had predicted. Jeremiah wished that the Lord would return all the temple objects and deportees taken to Babylon (28:5-6). However, it would require an unusual ability to accurately predict peace. Jeremiah declared that any prophet who made such a prediction should be suspect until the prophecy was fulfilled (28:7-9). Hananiah spoke lies to the people. Though his deceitful words were popular, they brought false hope to the people. In contrast, Jeremiah spoke the truth, even though it was unpopular.

Having mimicked the pattern of Jeremiah's prophetic words, Hananiah now imitated his use of an object lesson. He took the yoke from Jeremiah's neck and smashed it, repeating his claim that the Lord would deliver Judah from Babylon within two years. Jeremiah had no immediate response from the Lord, so he said nothing and went on his way (28:10-11). A short time later, the Lord gave Jeremiah a response to Hananiah. The wooden yoke Hananiah had broken would be replaced with a more uncomfortable yoke of iron (28:12-13). This yoke would be placed upon the shoulders of Judah by Nebuchadnezzar, king of Babylon. His power would be so extensive that even the wild animals of the desert would submit to him (28:14). The difference between the wooden yoke and the iron yoke may have illustrated the difference between submitting voluntarily to a dominant power and being forced to surrender to slavery.

The Lord had a personal word of judgment for the false prophet, Hananiah. Jeremiah told him that because Hananiah had encouraged the people to believe lies and feel secure when they needed to repent, he would die within the year. Jeremiah's prophecy was true, for Hananiah died two months later (28:15-17). God had previously outlined the signs of a true prophet (Deut. 18:20-22). This person's predictions always came true, and his words never contradicted previous revelation from God. Jeremiah was such a prophet.

NOTES ON THE PRINTED TEXT

Jeremiah wrote a letter to encourage the exiles in Babylon. The prophet directed the correspondence to the surviving elders, priests, prophets, and all the other Judahites whom Nebuchadnezzar had deported from Jerusalem to Babylon (Jer. 29:1). This forced removal occurred in 597 B.C. At that time, Jeconiah (or Jehoiachin, the son of Jehoiakim), was taken to Babylon. Other deportees included the queen mother (Nehushta; see 2 Kings 24:8; Jer. 13:18), the *eunuchs* (Jer. 29:2) or palace officials, the princes of Judah and Jerusalem, and various craftsmen (such as carpenters and metal workers). Ezekiel was in this group.

Elasah the son of Shaphan (29:3) was one of the letter's couriers. He possibly was the brother of Ahikam, who backed Jeremiah when the priests and prophets in Jerusalem wanted to kill God's spokesperson for declaring that the city and its temple would be destroyed (see 26:24). *Gemariah the son of Hilkiah* (29:3) was the other letter courier. He may have been a son or grandson of the high priest who found the book of the law during the reign of Josiah (see 2 Kings 22:3-4, 8, 10). The courier is different from another individual named Gemariah, who was one of several officials seeking to preserve the first scroll of Jeremiah's prophecies (see Jer. 36:10-12, 25).

In ancient times, it was customary for a vassal such as Zedekiah to send couriers to an overlord such as Nebuchadnezzar (29:3). It is unclear whether the incident under consideration occurred before or after those recorded in chapter 28. According to 51:59, Zedekiah himself traveled to Babylon in the same year mentioned in 28:1. Perhaps several items were on the king's agenda when he made the trip, including bringing tribute from Judah, affirming the vassal's allegiance to Babylon, and delivering the letter recorded in 29:4-23.

Israel's God declared Himself to be the sovereign Lord of heaven's armies. In the final analysis, it was He who sent His people into exile (see 29:14). Of course, Nebuchadnezzar was God's agent or servant in bringing His will to pass (see 25:9; 27:6, 20; 29:1). In light of this, the Lord directed the exiles to adjust to life in Babylon. They were to build houses and dwell in them. Also, they were to plant gardens and eat what they produced (29:5). Moreover, the exiles were to marry Jewish women (see Deut. 7:3), start families, and increase in number (Jer. 29:6). Part of settling down in Babylon included promoting peace and working hard for the prosperity of the cities in which the exiles lived. They were to pray to the Lord for this to happen. Ultimately, the vitality of the cities would enable the Jews to thrive in captivity (29:7).

The deportees from Judah were forced by their captors to settle southeast of Babylon between the Tigris and Euphrates Rivers. Nippur was the largest city in the area. Ezekiel identified a community of Jewish captives at Telabib along the Chebar River (Ezek. 1:1; 3:15). This was a navigable canal that exited the Euphrates in Babylon and rejoined it many miles downstream.

Little is known about the life of the exiles in Babylon, though an anonymous psalmist remembered at least one time of sadness during the initial portion of the captivity (Ps. 137:1). Years later, when the Jews were permitted to return to their homeland, many chose to stay in Babylon (Ezra 1:5-6). Those who were young enough to travel the distance to Judah had been born and raised in Babylon. They had never seen Judah. Many of them would have been reluctant to leave familiar surroundings to travel to a strange place that had yet to recover from the ravages of a bygone war.

The Lord exhorted the exiles not to be deceived by false prophets in their midst who claimed they could use divination to predict the future (Jer. 29:8). The exiles were also not to accept as true the dreams they elicited from the charlatans. God declared He had not sent these fraudulent messengers, who prophesied lies in His name (that is, by His authority) to the Jews in captivity (29:9).

Though the captivity would not be brief, it would not last indefinitely. The Lord promised that after His people had been in exile in Babylon for 70 years, He would release them from captivity (29:10). He would also restore them to their homeland (see 25:11-12). In 539 B.C., almost 50 years after Nebuchadnezzar captured Jerusalem and deported Jews to Babylon, the Persian king, Cyrus, conquered the Babylonian Empire. Even though Persian governors ruled the provinces of his empire, Cyrus gave the people in each province much control over their own affairs. He also encouraged them to keep their native customs and to practice their ancestral religions. Exiled peoples like the Jews had the option to stay where they were or return to their native land.

In 538 B.C., Cyrus issued a decree allowing the Jews to return to Judah to rebuild the temple. The next year, the king appointed Sheshbazzar as the governor of Judah and returned the temple treasures taken by Nebuchadnezzar. Sheshbazzar led a group of exiles back to Judah (Ezra 1). In 458 B.C., with royal authority to revive Jewish religious practices (7:1-10), Ezra the priest escorted a second group back to the land. Then under Nehemiah, cupbearer to the Persian king Artaxerxes I, another group of Jews returned to Judah in 445 B.C. to repair the walls of Jerusalem (Neh. 1—2).

Whether it was the Jews' time of captivity in Babylon or their eventual return to their homeland, God's plan for them included peace, not evil. He wanted them to prosper, not be harmed. Because He is the sovereign Lord, He would ensure their future was filled with hope, not despair (Jer. 29:11). Indeed, as far back as the time of Moses, it was revealed that prosperity would follow the captivity of God's people (see Deut. 30:1-5). During their time of exile, they were to repent and pray for God to forgive them and restore them to their homeland (see 1 Kings 8:46-51). This perspective forms the backdrop of Daniel's prayer on behalf of the exiles (see Dan. 9:1-19).

Likewise, in Jeremiah 29:12, the Lord encouraged the Jews in captivity to call out to Him in prayer. They could do so with the assurance that He would hear and heed their requests. However, they were not to be disingenuous or indifferent in their petitions. God wanted His people to repent of their sins, seek Him wholeheartedly, and experience His pardon (29:13). If the exiles approached the Lord's throne of grace with such a humble attitude (see Heb. 4:16), He would be with them and accept their worship. Also, regardless of where God had banished them, He would bring them back to the promised land. Just as He had initiated their captivity, so He would spearhead their return from exile (Jer. 29:14). The oracle of the Lord would surely be fulfilled. Nothing could thwart it from coming to pass.

SUGGESTIONS TO TEACHERS

In Jeremiah's letter to the exiles, he urged them not to be deceived by false prophets and diviners (Jer. 29:8-9). Even today, many false prophets have gone out into the world (1 John 4:1). This means we should not believe everything we hear just because people claim their words are inspired by God.

1. BE DISCERNING. First Thessalonians 5:21 says, *Prove all things; hold fast to that which is good.* The idea is that we should put everything we hear to the test and accept only that which is in agreement with Scripture. Most Christians are somewhat able to discern truth from error, but all of us should be striving to become even more discerning, for ideas really matter.

2. DO A REALITY CHECK. There are several ways we can test to see whether a message proclaimed in the Lord's name truly came from Him. For instance, we can check to see if the words being declared match what God has said in the Bible. If the two do not agree, we are to accept what Scripture says and reject the false message. We can also check to see how committed the person speaking in the name of the Lord is to the body of Christ. For example, some people say they speak for God, but have no real involvement in any local church.

3. EXAMINE THE PERSON'S LIFE AND MINISTRY. Another way to evaluate speakers is to examine their lifestyle. Those who say their messages are from God are lying if they participate in ungodly or immoral practices. This does not mean that all true followers of Christ are absolutely pure in their behavior. Nevertheless, their lives are not to be characterized by sordid conduct. Moreover, we can check out the fruit of the ministries of those who claim to be speaking for the Lord. It is one thing to make pretentious declarations. It is another thing to see one's life used significantly by God.

4. KNOW GOD'S WORD. To become more discerning of false messages, we can diligently study God's Word. The better we know what Scripture has to say, the more perceptive we will be of false messages. We can also attend a Bible study that is investigating the false teachings of various non-Christian religious organizations. Moreover, this can be an interesting way of learning about the experiences others have had with those who are proclaiming false messages in God's name.

FOR ADULTS

■ TOPIC: Getting through the Pain

■ QUESTIONS: 1. Why did Jeremiah write a letter to the Babylonian exiles? 2. Who delivered Jeremiah's letter? 3. How difficult would it have been for the exiles in Babylon to get on with their lives? 4. What deceptive messages were the exiles receiving from false prophets? 5. When did God intend to restore His people to their native land?

■ ILLUSTRATIONS:

The Touch of the Master's Hand. Pierre Auguste Renoir pioneered impressionist techniques in French painting late in the nineteenth century. As Renoir's fame spread, so did the number of Renoir forgeries. The painter was understandably upset by the proliferation of these imitations, but after a time he came to accept their existence.

As a favor to collectors he liked who were stuck with one of these fakes, Renoir occasionally touched up a canvas and signed it so the collector could display or resell it as an original. Angry friends urged him to take legal action against the forgers, but Renoir could see no benefit in the litigation. He preferred repairing paintings to punishing forgers.

Like Renoir, the Lord has no desire to bring judgment on people. Instead, He prefers to rescue the ruined canvases of sinful lives. Only when all opportunities to repent have been rejected will the unrepentant "forgeries" be exposed for punishment.

Bad Habits Are Hard to Break. In the motion picture, *Charade*, Cary Grant and Audrey Hepburn search for a treasure hidden in plain view by Hepburn's mysterious husband, who is thrown from a train as the opening credits roll. Everyone —good guys and bad guys—combs through the handful of personal effects Charles left on the train.

A child innocently pursuing his hobby discovers that the three stamps on Charles's unmailed letter to his wife are the most rare specimens in the world. Every villain and hero in the movie had handled that letter. They had all looked at the stamps, but no one really "saw" them. They couldn't break the habit of ignoring the envelope while focusing on the letter inside it.

The people of Judah had become habitual idolaters. Jeremiah's messages from the Lord made no sense to them. Thus, the people made the same spiritually disastrous errors over and over because these were ingrained in the way they lived every day. When we let sinful thinking or behaving become our normal way of responding in an area of life, we will have trouble recognizing the true value of God's Word. It will seem irrelevant.

Hear the Word of the Lord. Something strange and wonderful happened in England at the start of the seventeenth century when James I was king. It took place a century earlier in Germany. Private and public morality improved markedly. Marriages and families flourished. Crime dropped. People were talking about God and salvation.

The Bible had appeared in everyday languages. The King James Bible in English (A.D. 1611) recreated the phenomenon experienced in northern German states when Luther's Bible came out in the people's native language (A.D. 1534). English kings and German princes controlled the pulpits, but they had no control over the Word of God read in the homes of peasants, artisans, and merchants.

Be sure it is the Word of God you listen to as you make the major decisions of your life. Lots of voices clamor for your attention. Don't let them drown out or distort the message of the Lord.

FOR YOUTH

■ **TOPIC:** Have I Got a Plan for You!
■ **QUESTIONS:** 1. Whom had Nebuchadnezzar deported to Babylon? 2. What circumstances brought about the Jewish Captivity? 3. What did Jeremiah encourage the exiles to do? 4. What promise did the Lord make about the duration of the Captivity? 5. How might the promise of a future return to their homeland have encouraged the exiles in Babylon?

■ **ILLUSTRATIONS:**

Which Are You? We can rejoice in the fact that we have instructions written down for us in the Bible. But God also comes to us to build a relationship with us. This difference is described well in the following analogy by a Christian college professor:

"There are two ways that I can tell you how to get from wherever you are to the school where I teach. I can give you a map that charts out the route for you to take. With such a map, you might or might not get there, depending on how good you are at reading maps and whether roads are closed. The other option I can offer is to get into your car, sit beside you, and direct you as we go along."

Are you a map reader or a companion of God? The Lord is eager to come into our lives, interact with us, and make known His plan for us.

A God-Focused Life. In the Mount Hope Cemetery in Hiawatha, Kansas, there is a strange memorial to a farmer and his wife. An orphan by the name of John M. Davis married a young woman whose family he disliked intensely. Davis decided early on that he would leave nothing of his governing fortune to his wife's family.

In 1930, when Mrs. Davis died, John began commissioning the work of stone masons to construct a giant mausoleum with statuary commemorating different periods of their life together. The lifelike poses of Mr. and Mrs. Davis were hewn from Kansas granite and were extraordinarily expensive.

However, John Davis left no money for the upkeep of the expansive work after his death in 1974 at the age of 92. Because of the weight of this huge monolith, today the tomb is sinking into the earth and becoming an eyesore. Local residents refer to it as "the old man's folly." What a reminder this is that a self-focused life is not God's plan. He wants our lives to be focused on Him.

A New Relationship. Brian grew up in a minister's home. Though his parents were loving and had thoroughly grounded him in the essentials of the Christian faith, Brian found himself looking for answers in his sophomore year of college. His answers came through a lovely girl named Anne.

Brian had met Anne in one of his English classes at the university. True, she was bright and attractive, but what interested Brian most was her spirituality. Brian had never seen a peer with such an "active" relationship with God. Brian knew that though he had heard and learned about God as a child, Brian never had come close to experiencing the kind of relationship with the Lord that he could see at work in Anne's life. The more Brian saw of this, the more he wished that he, too, could have that kind of experience.

When Brian turned 20, after the surprise birthday party that his college friends threw for him, he was invited to a bigger party yet. This time the festivities took place in heaven as the angels of God rejoiced in the heartfelt prayer that Brian uttered as he asked God to begin a lifelong relationship with him.

LAMENTATIONS URGES HOPE IN GOD

BACKGROUND SCRIPTURE: 2 Kings 25:1-2, 5-7; Lamentations 3:25-33, 55-58
DEVOTIONAL READING: Psalm 23

KEY VERSE: It is good that a man should both hope and quietly wait for the salvation of the LORD. Lamentations 3:26.

KING JAMES VERSION

LAMENTATIONS 3:25 The LORD is good unto them that wait for him, to the soul that seeketh him. 26 It is good that a man should both hope and quietly wait for the salvation of the LORD. 27 It is good for a man that he bear the yoke in his youth. 28 He sitteth alone and keepeth silence, because he hath borne it upon him. 29 He putteth his mouth in the dust; if so be there may be hope. 30 He giveth his cheek to him that smiteth him: he is filled full with reproach. 31 For the Lord will not cast off for ever: 32 But though he cause grief, yet will he have compassion according to the multitude of his mercies. 33 For he doth not afflict willingly nor grieve the children of men. . . .

55 I called upon thy name, O LORD, out of the low dungeon. 56 Thou hast heard my voice: hide not thine ear at my breathing, at my cry. 57 Thou drewest near in the day that I called upon thee: thou saidst, Fear not. 58 O Lord, thou hast pleaded the causes of my soul; thou hast redeemed my life.

NEW REVISED STANDARD VERSION

LAMENTATIONS 3:25 The LORD is good to those
    who wait for him,
    to the soul that seeks him.
26 It is good that one should wait quietly
    for the salvation of the LORD.
27 It is good for one to bear
    the yoke in youth,
28 to sit alone in silence
    when the Lord has imposed it,
29 to put one's mouth to the dust
    (there may yet be hope),
30 to give one's cheek to the smiter,
    and be filled with insults.
31 For the Lord will not
    reject forever.
32 Although he causes grief, he will have compassion
    according to the abundance of his steadfast love;
33 for he does not willingly afflict
    or grieve anyone. . . .
55 I called on your name, O LORD,
    from the depths of the pit;
56 you heard my plea, "Do not close your ear
    to my cry for help, but give me relief!"
57 You came near when I called on you;
    you said, "Do not fear!"
58 You have taken up my cause, O Lord,
    you have redeemed my life.

10

HOME BIBLE READINGS

Monday, July 30	Isaiah 30:15-19	*Promise of Deliverance*
Tuesday, July 31	2 Kings 25:1-2, 5-7	*Jerusalem Destroyed*
Wednesday, August 1	Psalm 33:12-22	*God Is Our Hope*
Thursday, August 2	Psalm 130	*My Soul Waits*
Friday, August 3	Lamentations 3:19-24	*God Is Faithful*
Saturday, August 4	Lamentations 3:25-33	*Wait for the Lord*
Sunday, August 5	Lamentations 3:55-59	*God Hears My Plea*

BACKGROUND

Jeremiah began Lamentations by noting that Jerusalem's streets, though once bustling with activity, were now silent. None of the city's former lovers were there to offer comfort. Her friends (former allies) had betrayed her and were now her enemies (1:1-2). God allowed Judah to be led away into captivity. Her enemies had chased her down, afflicted her, and enslaved her. The roads to Jerusalem—once filled with joyous crowds on their way to celebrate temple festivals—were characterized by mourning (1:3-7).

God's people had defiled themselves with immorality. Consequently, He allowed them to be humiliated by their adversaries. All they could do now was hide their faces in shame. Everyone in the city groaned while searching for food. They even traded their valuables for barely enough scraps to stay alive (1:8-11). There are times when God must deal with His us in extreme ways, especially when we refuse to respond to His preliminary chastenings. He might allow difficult circumstances—even tragedies—into our lives so that we might understand how much we need Him.

Continuing to be personified in Jeremiah's first lament, Jerusalem pleaded with those who witnessed God's discipline upon her to have regard for her plight. This is followed by a cry to the Lord for vindication before her enemies. In her suffering she called for divine retribution against the wickedness of those enemies who rejoiced over her calamity (1:12-22).

Jeremiah noted that the Lord's anger hung over Jerusalem like a dark cloud. In His righteous indignation, God allowed the Babylonians to destroy Judah's homes, fortified cities, and even the temple. He was like an enemy who bent His bow against His people (2:1-4). On the surface, it appeared that Babylon was the sole agent of destruction. But Jeremiah declared that God ultimately brought about the destruction of Judah's forts and palaces. The Lord was the one who blotted out all memory of the holy festivals and sabbath days. Not even Jerusalem's walls and ramparts could withstand the siege. Her kings and princes were exiled to distant lands, and her prophets received no more visions from God (2:5-9).

The leaders of Jerusalem sat on the ground in silence, and the young women lowered their heads in shame. Even Jeremiah wept over the demise of his country and beloved city (2:10-11). Indeed, Jerusalem's devastation was beyond comparison. While the city's enemies mocked the people in their fallen condition, it was God who had brought this judgment upon Jerusalem for her sin. In anguish, Jeremiah called upon the Lord to consider the wretched scenes of cannibalism, annihilation, and death (2:12-22).

Jeremiah said that he had personally seen the afflictions that resulted from God's judgments. The prophet felt as if he were alone in a dark place, and that God caused him numerous physical and spiritual afflictions (3:1-6). Moreover, Jeremiah felt walled in and unable to escape. Though he cried for relief, the Lord seemed as if He refused to listen. In one instance, God seemed to have blocked Jeremiah's path with a high stone wall. In another instance, the Lord seemed like a bear or lion who waited to attack and maul the prophet (3:7-11).

Jeremiah depicted God as bending His bow and shooting His arrows deep into the prophet's heart. Meanwhile, Jeremiah's own people laughed at him. Whatever peace and prosperity Jeremiah once knew were gone. Everything he had hoped for from the Lord appeared to be lost (3:12-18). With the exception of 3:18, the name of the Lord is omitted in this section. Perhaps this is an indication of the prophet's feelings of abandonment by God. As Jeremiah saw the impoverished and homeless condition of Jerusalem's inhabitants, it was like bitter poison that left him feeling emotionally depressed (3:19-20).

Despite the intense misery, though, hope remained (3:21). God's unfailing love was the reason the Babylonians had not completely wiped out the Judahites (3:22). God's great compassion was renewed every morning, so abundant was His faithfulness to the survivors (3:23). Jeremiah put his hope in the Lord, for He alone was the prophet's eternal *portion* (3:24). This expression is based on Numbers 18:20, in which Aaron was denied a share in the land but was told instead that God Himself was his priestly inheritance. Since Jeremiah had made the Lord the focal point of his existence, it is no wonder that the prophet was able to wait for Him.

NOTES ON THE PRINTED TEXT

We learn from Lamentations that Jeremiah depended completely on the Lord, for He was all that the prophet really needed to live. Each day, as Jeremiah leaned on God (3:25), he experienced a renewed appreciation for the Lord's goodness. The idea here is of trusting in the grace and kindness of God. He is the object of the believers' hope, the one whom they wait for and seek wholeheartedly. The result is a life characterized by obedience.

The longing of the survivors centered in one day experiencing the salvation of the Lord (3:26). From a temporal standpoint, this meant being freed from captivity in Babylon and restored to the promised land. From an eternal standpoint, God's salvation would result in the righteous remnant experiencing unbroken fellowship with Him in heaven (see Rev. 21:7, 22; 22:3-5). Jeremiah stated that it was good for those who were younger to bear the yoke of God's discipline. The historical context indicates that the prophet was referring to the agony and humiliation of languishing under the subjugation of the Babylonians. This was especially evident in the deportation of Jerusalem's inhabitants.

Both the Assyrians and Babylonians used the phrase *bear the yoke* (Lam. 3:27) as a metaphor for submission. They made vassal nations as subservient to them as yoked beasts of burden were to their masters. In the case of the Jews, their exile in Babylon would last for 70 years. For those who were middle-aged and older, the burden of exile would seem intolerable. In contrast, those in their youth who submitted to this yoke of discipline had hope. Despite the tragedy of Jerusalem's fall and the temple's destruction, they faced the prospect of living until the divinely appointed return to their native land.

Regardless of the age of the survivors during their time of extended suffering, it was almighty God who had permitted it to happen. Because He was disciplining His people, they were wise to sit alone in silence (3:28). The solitude would give the righteous remnant an opportunity to learn from the mistakes their predecessors had made, reform their ways, and avert future judgment. Jeremiah also proposed that his fellow Jews lie face down in the dust of the ground. Being in such a state of abject humility had teaching value, for God's people would abandon their folly and begin to revere Him once again. The adoption of this wise course of action would keep alive the hope that the Lord might grace His people one more time with His favor (3:29; see Prov. 1:7; 9:10).

Under different circumstances, it would be ill-advisable for one group to permit another group to strike them freely on the cheek. But for the survivors of the Babylonian conquest, repeated attempts to thwart the enemy had utterly failed. On three separate occasions, Babylon had invaded Judah, with the third incursion leading to the nation's destruction. It was in that context that Jeremiah exhorted his peers to offer their cheek to their captors (see Jesus' remarks in Matt. 5:39 and Luke 6:29). The better part of wisdom was for God's people at this time and under these conditions to accept the insults of their enemies. The reproaches the Babylonians heaped on Judah were part of the yoke of discipline God wanted the upright to bear while in captivity (Lam. 3:30).

God was calling His people to wait for Him and seek Him with their entire hearts (3:25). With so little of the world's goods and pleasures to distract them, the survivors could more readily focus their attention on God. He had disciplined His wayward people, allowed them to be crushed by their enemies, and even let their place of worship be demolished. Such realities notwithstanding, God would never ultimately forsake His people. His covenant promises to the patriarchs would one day be fulfilled (3:31). The grief that the Lord brought on His people was neither arbitrary nor whimsical. It was intentional and would one day come to an end. The compassion the Lord had shown was based on the abundance of His *mercies* (3:32). The Hebrew word translated *mercies* is *hesed,* which refers to the loyal love of God. The Lord's compassion for the righteous remnant would never fail because He would remain faithful to His covenant promises.

Lamentations 3:33 underscores an important truth, namely, that it is not the Lord's delight to bring affliction to humankind. Similarly, He does not take pleasure in causing any human being to experience grief. Only the wicked are filled with glee over the suffering of others. When God allows sorrow to enter into the lives of His people, it is so that they might be weaned from their sinful ways and driven to Him in faith. Hopefully, as they draw near to God, their desire to sin will be tempered and their interest in spiritual things will be enhanced.

Even in his afflictions, Jeremiah realized that the God he served was neither vindictive nor unjust in His condemnation of sin. Instead, the Lord sought the repentance and return of His people so that He might forgive their sins and restore them to Himself (3:55). In this light, Jeremiah could lead the survivors in a prayer for deliverance and vindication. Even though he and his fellow citizens had suffered afflictions because of God's wrath, the Lord was always present when the prophet called on His name from the dungeon of despair and from the pit of gloom.

Jeremiah's plea on behalf of the survivors was that the Lord would not close His ears (so to speak) to the cries of His people for help (3:56). God responded by drawing near to the righteous remnant and encouraging them to jettison fear (3:57). In the court of divine justice, the Lord would take up His people's case and champion their cause. As the righteous Judge, He would one day redeem His people by releasing them from captivity (3:58).

SUGGESTIONS TO TEACHERS

Lamentations deals specifically with a nation grieving because it had experienced judgment for its sin, and struggling to find a basis for a hopeful future in the love and compassion of God. You may have students in your class trying to come to terms with the consequences of sinful behavior, but it's more likely that they will apply the message of hope found in Lamentations to griefs that have arisen out of ordinary circumstances in their life.

1. SEVERE JUDGMENT. Jerusalem acknowledged that her sins had provoked the wrath of God to the point that the Lord sent fire, bondage, and desolation as agents of His judgment. Judah had known that sin could bring judgment, but she had never imagined how devastating judgment could be. Remind your students that the consequences of sin are typically built into the behavior itself. We know that we risk reputation and respect, perhaps even family and career, when we gossip, lie, cheat, steal, commit adultery, or abuse drugs. Experiencing sin's consequence usually is much worse than imagining it.

2. SUPREME SORROW. Jerusalem was reduced to weeping and wailing that could not be consoled because of her loss at the hands of Babylon. The city's extreme sorrow brought her to realize that she had to repent and turn to the Lord again. Encourage your class members to recognize the value of godly sorrow as an emotion that God can use to turn us from sin to righteousness (2 Cor. 7:10-11). Also, be sure to caution your students not to interpret every difficulty of life as a judgment for sin. After all, Judah and Jerusalem experienced devastation one time after centuries of provoking the Lord to wrath.

3. STEADFAST LOVE. Even in the midst of the debris and carnage of a recent war zone, Jeremiah realized that the love of the Lord was the permanent thing. Even the devastation all around the city would not last forever. Encourage your students to reflect on the character of God when facing hard times, such as depression, divorce, illness, death, unemployment, loneliness, and age-related limitations. The steadfast love of God can pull us through dark places that seem everlasting but eventually will end.

4. SURE HOPE. Jeremiah hoped in God Himself, not just in some abstract characteristic of God. The prophet realized that he still had a covenant relationship with the Lord that let him call God his *portion* (Lam. 3:24). Your students can also hope in the Lord as long as they have a personal relationship with Him through faith in Christ as their Savior from sin. All believers can hope in the daily mercies of God and affirm *great is thy faithfulness* (3:23).

FOR ADULTS

■ TOPIC: Maintaining Hope!

■ QUESTIONS: 1. What does it mean to seek the Lord? 2. What eternal good can result from submitting to God's discipline? 3. In what sense does God's love never fail? 4. What is the divine intent behind earthly affliction? 5. What does it mean to call on the name of the Lord?

■ ILLUSTRATIONS:

True Beliefs Show During Hard Times. In 1921, Evan O'Neill Kane had already practiced surgery for 40 years. He was chief of surgery at a prominent New York City hospital that bore his name, Kane Summit Hospital. For some time, Kane had toyed with the idea of performing many common surgeries under local anesthesia. He wanted to experiment with an appendectomy, but months passed and he couldn't find a volunteer willing to take the risk.

Then one gray February day, a brave soul came forward. He was wheeled into surgery where Kane prepped him, administered a local anesthetic, deftly opened his abdomen, and removed the troublesome appendix. All the while, the patient was fully alert but feeling no pain, which was a good thing since Kane was removing *his own* appendix.

Many Christians profess to trust God's faithfulness, steadfast love, and tender mercies to see them through any trial of life. That is easy to say, but much more difficult to do. We know our professed faith is genuine when we have relied on God's faithfulness, love, and mercy during an emergency.

Which Way Will You Go? C. S. Lewis once observed, "Every road into Jerusalem is also a road out of Jerusalem." He meant that every circumstance in life is intended by God to lead people to Him, but no circumstances of life are one-way streets. People can travel away from God on the very paths meant to take them to Him.

Jeremiah described the horrors of the destruction of Jerusalem and grieved over the plight of his people. Then the prophet drew near to God along the path of his people's sorrow. This reminds us that now is the time to turn away from sin and return to the Lord in wholehearted devotion. The longer we wait to do what is right, the harder it might be for us to abandon our sinful ways.

Suffering Deepens Appreciation. Helen Keller once attended a concert given by a leading Christian vocalist. Keller could neither see nor hear him, but she had devised ways of perceiving beauty. Keller and her companion met the singer at his dressing room. Through her companion, Keller asked the musician to sing the final number of his concert there in the tiny room.

Miss Keller stood with her face inches from the singer and placed the fingers of one hand on his lips and the fingers of the other hand on his larynx. The man sang once more at full volume and with the same range of expression, "Were You There When They Crucified My Lord?" When the last vibrations of his voice stilled, a tear ran down Helen Keller's cheek and she whispered indistinctly, "I was there."

FOR YOUTH

■ TOPIC: Despair and Hope
■ QUESTIONS: 1. What is meant by the concept of bearing the yoke in one's youth? 2. Why should believers submit to the Lord? 3. Why should believers hope in the Lord? 4. Why should believers pray to the Lord? 5. How can the presence of God in the believer's life dispel all fear?

■ ILLUSTRATIONS:

Trust God When Things Look Bad. An American man and an Irish woman who had been pen pals since childhood finally realized they had fallen in love. John scraped together enough money to fly to Dublin where Maureen was to meet him wearing a green scarf, a green hat, and a green carnation.

John stepped from the plane and scanned the crowd in the terminal. When he spotted the green scarf, green hat, and green carnation on the homeliest woman he had ever seen, his heart sank. But Maureen was John's dearest friend, so he approached her with a smile to give her a hug.

"Hey! Get away from me," the homely woman cried out when John embraced her. "Is this airport full of crazy people today? That girl over there just paid me 20 pounds to wear all this green."

The prettiest girl John had ever seen stepped forward and held out her hand. "I'm so pleased that you came, John. Please forgive my little trick. I'm just so tired of shallow men who only care about my looks."

How tired God must get of people who claim to love Him as long as their lives are going well but who desert Him as soon as anything ugly happens to them. Trust the Lord's love and mercy in the bad times, and you'll find out how true a friend He can be.

Choose Hope. Back in the days of the Cold War, Woody Allen observed, "Civilization stands at the crossroads. Down one road is despondency and despair, and down the other is total annihilation. Let us pray that we choose the right road."

Jeremiah could have said, "Civilization is at a dead end. We went down the road of total annihilation and ended up at despondency and despair. It's all the same." But the prophet didn't say that. Instead, he stopped looking at his dark circumstances and faced the bright sun of God's love and compassion. There, Jeremiah found hope. Always turn your face to God and choose hope.

Taste and See That the Lord Is Good. Years ago, an atheist was touring the country giving lectures about the folly of religion. At the end of his presentation, the atheist always challenged the audience to pose any questions they wanted, and he would take the opportunity to overpower any who dared oppose his conclusions.

In one audience the town drunk was present. He had recently come to faith in Christ at the local rescue mission and was enjoying his sobriety and his walk with the Lord. When the atheist issued his usual challenge, the former drunk ambled to the podium, took out an orange, peeled it, and started to eat. The audience laughed and hooted, figuring the guy was drunk again. The speaker was unsure what to do.

Finally the rescue mission convert smiled at the atheist and asked, "Was my orange sweet or sour?"

The flustered lecturer bellowed, "You idiot, how would I know? I never tasted the orange. You tell me."

"Well, how can you know anything about Jesus when you never tried Him neither?" asked the former drunk.

Many people might say that it makes no sense to trust God when life falls apart. But the people who do trust Him at the worst moments discover that He tastes sweet indeed!

EZEKIEL PREACHES ABOUT INDIVIDUAL RESPONSIBILITY

BACKGROUND SCRIPTURE: Ezekiel 18
DEVOTIONAL READING: Psalm 18:20-24

KEY VERSE: For I have no pleasure in the death of him that dieth, saith the Lord GOD: wherefore turn yourselves, and live ye. Ezekiel 18:32.

KING JAMES VERSION

EZEKIEL 18:4 Behold, all souls are mine; as the soul of the father, so also the soul of the son is mine: the soul that sinneth, it shall die. . . .

20 The soul that sinneth, it shall die. The son shall not bear the iniquity of the father, neither shall the father bear the iniquity of the son: the righteousness of the righteous shall be upon him, and the wickedness of the wicked shall be upon him.

21 But if the wicked will turn from all his sins that he hath committed, and keep all my statutes, and do that which is lawful and right, he shall surely live, he shall not die. 22 All his transgressions that he hath committed, they shall not be mentioned unto him: in his righteousness that he hath done he shall live. 23 Have I any pleasure at all that the wicked should die? saith the Lord GOD: and not that he should return from his ways, and live? . . .

30 Therefore I will judge you, O house of Israel, every one according to his ways, saith the Lord GOD. Repent, and turn yourselves from all your transgressions; so iniquity shall not be your ruin. 31 Cast away from you all your transgressions, whereby ye have transgressed; and make you a new heart and a new spirit: for why will ye die, O house of Israel? 32 For I have no pleasure in the death of him that dieth, saith the Lord GOD: wherefore turn yourselves, and live ye.

NEW REVISED STANDARD VERSION

EZEKIEL 18:4 Know that all lives are mine; the life of the parent as well as the life of the child is mine: it is only the person who sins that shall die. . . .

20 The person who sins shall die. A child shall not suffer for the iniquity of a parent, nor a parent suffer for the iniquity of a child; the righteousness of the righteous shall be his own, and the wickedness of the wicked shall be his own.

21 But if the wicked turn away from all their sins that they have committed and keep all my statutes and do what is lawful and right, they shall surely live; they shall not die. 22 None of the transgressions that they have committed shall be remembered against them; for the righteousness that they have done they shall live. 23 Have I any pleasure in the death of the wicked, says the Lord GOD, and not rather that they should turn from their ways and live? . . .

30 Therefore I will judge you, O house of Israel, all of you according to your ways, says the Lord GOD. Repent and turn from all your transgressions; otherwise iniquity will be your ruin. 31 Cast away from you all the transgressions that you have committed against me, and get yourselves a new heart and a new spirit! Why will you die, O house of Israel? 32 For I have no pleasure in the death of anyone, says the Lord GOD. Turn, then, and live.

BACKGROUND

Ezekiel was 30 years old in 593 B.C. when God called him into prophetic ministry (Ezek. 1:1) by means of an astonishing vision of Himself and four cherubim (1:4—3:15). We learn that Ezekiel was a priest (1:3), but he never really had an opportunity to serve in the temple because he had been deported from Jerusalem to Babylon with thousands of others in 597 B.C. (2 Kings 24:14) when he was 25 years old (Ezek. 1:2). Thirty was a significant age for Old Testament priests (Num. 4:3) and may explain why God called Ezekiel at that time in his life. His ministry lasted until 571 B.C. (Ezek. 29:17).

Ezekiel lived in Tel-abib, a community of exiles from Judah, on the River Chebar, a major irrigation channel that diverted water from the Euphrates River into farmland southeast of the city of Babylon (Ezek. 3:15). He was prominent among the exiles, as shown by the respect afforded him by the community elders (8:1; 14:1; 20:1). Ezekiel was married (24:18) and owned a home (3:24). His wife died on the day that Jerusalem fell to the Babylonians, as a sign to the exiles that the temple had been desecrated (24:18-21).

Ezekiel ministered in Babylon to the exiles from Judah while Jeremiah was prophesying in Jerusalem. Neither mentioned the other in their preserved messages. Nevertheless, both had harsh words for the evil shepherds who led God's people astray politically (Jer. 23:1-8; Ezek. 34:1-10) and false prophets who led them astray spiritually (Jer. 23:9-40; Ezek. 13). Both Jeremiah and Ezekiel referred to misuse of the proverb about parents eating sour grapes and children having their teeth set on edge (Jer. 31:29; Ezek. 18:2). Both prophets emphasized personal responsibility for sin and righteousness (Jer. 26:3; 31:30; 35:15; Ezek. 18). And both anticipated a new covenant that would be inward and personal (Jer. 31:31-34; Ezek. 34:25-31).

The Lord used Ezekiel to urge the exiles to heed the stipulations of the Mosaic covenant and seek after God. Through the prophet's teaching, he stressed the holiness and transcendence of God, His grace and mercy toward the righteous remnant, His sovereignty, and individual accountability for transgressions committed. Ezekiel revealed that God pledged to preserve a remnant of His people through whom He would fulfill His promises.

The Book of Ezekiel begins with the call of the prophet (chaps. 1—3), moves to messages about judgment on Judah for her sins (chaps. 4—24), then announces judgment on the nations surrounding Judah (chaps. 25—32), and concludes with messages of hope for the exiles (chaps. 33—48). Chapter 18 is one in a series of prophetic answers to imagined objections by Judah to Ezekiel's message of judgment (chaps. 12—19). In chapter 18, the prophet addressed the objection that it wasn't fair for God to judge the present generation for the sins His people had committed over many generations.

NOTES ON THE PRINTED TEXT

From 593–586 B.C., Ezekiel warned the exiles that Jerusalem would be destroyed and that there was no hope of an immediate return. The news of Jerusalem's fall in 586 B.C. dashed the false hopes of an immediate deliverance for the exiles. From this point on, Ezekiel's prophecies related Israel's future restoration to its homeland and the final blessings of the divine kingdom.

In 18:1-2, we learn about a popular proverb in use among the Jews. They went around quoting the maxim so they could excuse themselves of responsibility. The proverb meant that because of the sins of previous generations, the present one was suffering. According to this logic, one generation could blame their troubles on the misdeeds of previous generations. Even more distressing was the fact that the adage, as it was improperly applied by the exiles, asserted that God was punishing their generation for the transgressions their ancestors had committed. In other words, God allegedly was unfair in the way He treated His people. The Lord, however, declared that He was punishing the exiles for their own sins.

Since there was no one greater than the sovereign Lord, He swore by His own life when He revealed His will. It was His desire that the Jews no longer use the proverb about intergenerational responsibility, for it represented a perverted view of how He executed justice (18:3). In 18:4, God declared that every living entity belonged to Him, including the parent and the child. As the Lord of life, He had the right to execute judgment as He desired. It was His unchanging will that guilt would not be transferred from one generation to the next. Only the person who sinned would die for his or her sins.

To illustrate what He meant by the principle that the one who sins will die, God presented hypothetical situations. He talked about a man (18:5-9), his son (18:10-13), and his grandson (18:14-18). These examples show that people are held responsible for their own sin, and that guilt is not transferred across generations. From these verses we see that God does not allow people to fault others for their behavior. No matter how hard we try to shift the blame to others, we cannot escape the fact that one day we will have to answer to the Lord for all we have done. This is a strong incentive for us to freely admit when we have done something wrong.

In their confused thinking, some of the Jews asserted that upright children should be punished for the wrongdoings of their ungodly parents (18:19). However, the Lord rejected this mistaken notion. He made it clear that only those who persisted in sin and rebellion would be put to death. To underscore this vital truth, the Lord declared that children would not suffer for the sins of their parents. Likewise, parents would not suffer for the sins of their children. More generally speaking, good people would be rewarded for what they did, and evil people would be punished for what they did (18:20).

The Lord commented on the wicked who abandoned their sinful ways, kept all His statutes, and carried out justice and righteousness. God declared that they would certainly live. Although they might physically die, the Lord would give them a future in His kingdom. Ezekiel 18:22 reveals that none of the transgressions the repentant had committed would be held against them. In other words, God would forgive all their previous offenses, especially because they had abandoned their evil deeds and embraced the truth and ways of the Lord. In making these points to the exiled Jews, the Lord wanted them to recognize their unjust acts. He also wanted them to abandon their wickedness and return to Him in devotion. If they did, He promised them life (both physical and eternal), not death, and joy, not sorrow.

The sovereign Lord declared that He did not like to see wicked people die. It was not a source of pleasure for Him. Instead, it delighted Him when they turned from their sin, trusted in the Messiah, and obeyed the laws (18:23). In contrast, God was displeased when formerly upright people turned to sinful ways and started acting like the wicked. The disgusting things they did would negate all their good deeds, and they would experience death because of their sins (18:24). In the case of those who were formerly wicked, it was God's grace that prevented them from dying before they repented. And in the case of those who were formerly upright, it would be God's mercy that would spare them. In either situation, the Lord's desire was for all people to abandon their rebellious acts and trust in His Son for eternal life. That ancient truth is still applicable today.

The people of Ezekiel's day were suffering from the consequences of a history of rebellion against God. With a cloud of pessimism hanging over their heads (so to speak), they found it easier to blame their ancestors for sin than to take personal responsibility for their own offenses. They also found it convenient to charge God with injustice. The Lord responded that His people were unjust in their ways, especially since they were distorted in their thinking about how God dealt with the righteous and unrighteous (18:25).

God refuted the charge of being unjust by reasserting the truth of individual responsibility. If the upright started doing evil, they faced the sentence of death, for they rebelled against the Lord (18:26). In contrast, if evil people started doing right (by abandoning their wickedness and heeding the law), God would spare them (18:27). He would pardon them because they decided to forsake the path of corruption (18:28).

Clearly, then, heredity was not a factor in one's eternal future. Rather, it was personal choices each individual made. Those who repented of their sin and turned to the Lord in faith would live, while those who spurned Him for what is depraved would die physically and ultimately eternally. Thus, the people's indictment of God was baseless. They (not He) were guilty of unfairness in their thinking and iniquity in their actions (18:29).

The Lord informed the house of Israel that He would judge each person for what he or she had done. God exhorted all of them to turn from their transgressions and not let themselves be destroyed by iniquity (18:30). They were commanded to put their rebellious attitudes and ways behind them and exchange these for a new heart and a new spirit (18:31). Taking this action would enable the exiles to think pure thoughts and remain faithful to God. It would also prevent the sovereign Lord from putting people to death because of their sins. After all, He did not delight in condemning a person. He wanted all people to turn away from the precipice of destruction and live by trusting in and obeying Him (18:32).

SUGGESTIONS TO TEACHERS

Even today God calls us to live according to His values. We need to place our lifestyles and priorities under the focus of His Word and see what is reflected before Him and the world. If we are true to His teachings, then we will please our Lord and draw others to Him. If we are not true, then we need to change our lifestyles, or like the people of Ezekiel's day, we will incur His displeasure.

1. A NEW HONESTY. God does not accept blame shifting for anyone's sin. He would not let the exiles in Babylon blame their ancestors for the judgment they were facing. He wanted them to know that He responds to individuals on the basis of their own behavior, not that of their parents or children. Urge your students to examine their lives to see whether they tend to blame their past or their situation for their mistakes or sin. God understands the influences that affect people, but He doesn't accept excuses for sin.

2. A NEW ACCOUNTABILITY. Ezekiel taught that even in a family—the most closely-knit human social unit—each individual must account for his or her actions before God. Ezekiel was not downplaying the importance of family relationships. Instead, he was emphasizing personal accountability. Help your students explore the significance of that truth for themselves. Adults are not responsible before God for the mistakes of their children. Also, young people are not limited in God's eyes by the failures of their parents.

3. A NEW START. Ezekiel taught that a person's spiritual condition can change. It isn't determined by one's parents and it isn't locked in by one's past or present behavior. A great sinner can turn from his or her sin, commit to obeying God, and enjoy the eternal life that God gives. Ezekiel viewed repentance primarily from this perspective. You can expand on the idea of repenting of one's sins by relating it to faith in the sacrificial death of Jesus as the payment for those sins.

4. A NEW EQUITY. The exiles from Judah who were living in Babylon, accused

God of unfairness for punishing them, for they believed their ancestors were the ones who had provoked Him to act. God asserted that they were the unfair ones for refusing to accept responsibility for their own wicked actions. In the case of those who were formerly wicked, it was only God's grace that prevented them from dying before they repented. And in the case of those who were formerly upright, it would only be God's mercy that would spare them. In either situation, the Lord's desire was for all people to abandon their rebellious acts and trust in His Son for eternal life.

5. A NEW HEART. Ezekiel pointed out that effective repentance and renewed living depended on *a new heart and a new spirit* (Ezek. 18:31). Both Ezekiel and Jeremiah anticipated a future era when God would relate to His people in a new way, one that would change people's motivation and ability to live by God's standards. We are living in that era now with the advent of the Messiah.

FOR ADULTS

■ **TOPIC:** Personal Consequences of Sin!

■ **QUESTIONS:** 1. What was it about the false proverb that disturbed God? 2. How did God pledge to deal with righteous and wicked people? 3. What did God say would happen to those who continued in sin? 4. Why do you think God exhorted His people to abandon their rebellious ways? 5. How are others negatively affected when we refuse to accept personal responsibility for our misdeeds?

■ **ILLUSTRATIONS:**

Who's to Blame? A 19-year-old boy from a small Midwest town wrote his parents a note that said, "I'm out of control." Then he killed himself because he couldn't pay his gambling debts. Three East coast high schoolers were arrested for running a $6500-a-week sports betting operation. A 16-year-old paid off his gambling debts by turning his girlfriend into a prostitute. The Director of the Harvard Medical School Center for Addiction Studies said, "We will face in the next decade more problems with youth gambling than we'll face with drug use."

All of these young people were manipulated by adults to start gambling. Maybe their parents gambled, too. But no matter how much one can explain their behavior and understand what influenced it, one can't remove the responsibility each person had for what he or she did. That's because God holds each individual accountable for his or her actions.

Be All That You Can Be. Shug Jordan used to coach football at Auburn. The story goes that he sent a former player out to scout high school teams. The young man asked the old coach, "What kind of player are you looking for?" "Well, Mike," Coach Jordan said, "you know there's that fellow, you knock him down, and he stays down." Mike said, "We don't want him, do we, Coach?"

"No, that's right. Then there's that fellow, you knock him down and he gets up, but you knock him down again and he stays down." "We don't want him either, do we, coach?" "No. But, Mike, there's a fellow, you knock him down and he gets up. Knock him down, he gets up. Knock him down, he gets up. Knock him down, he gets up." "That's the guy we want, isn't it, Coach?" Shug Jordan answered, "No, we don't want him either. I want you to find the guy who's knocking everybody down. That's the guy we want!"

Through the Book of Ezekiel we learn that God wants His people to follow all His ways with total commitment. In other words, we should not be half-hearted Christians. Rather, God wants us to "be all we can be" (as the slogan says) for Christ.

Why Would Anyone Argue with God? The people of Ezekiel's day accused God of being unfair when He held them accountable for their sins. They were like the naval officer who realized his lifelong ambition when he was given command of a battle-ship. One stormy night, as the powerful vessel sailed toward a harbor, the lookout spotted a strange light rapidly closing with them.

Immediately the captain ordered his signalman to flash the message, "Alter your course ten degrees to port." Almost instantly the reply came, "Alter your course ten degrees to port."

Determined to take a back seat to no one, the officer sent this message: "Alter course ten degrees. I am a highly decorated captain." Back came the reply: "Alter your course ten degrees. I am a third class seaman."

Infuriated, the captain grabbed the signal lamp and flashed, "Alter course. I'm a battleship." Back came: "Alter your course. I'm a lighthouse."

The moral of this story is that we shouldn't argue with God, for He knows where the "rocks" are (metaphorically speaking). He doesn't want anybody to end up spiri-tually shipwrecked. Also, He wants everyone to trust in the Messiah. Of course, they have to heed His warnings about death and life and do what He says.

FOR YOUTH

■ TOPIC: Turn and Live!

■ QUESTIONS: 1. What was the nature of the proverb being quoted by the Jewish exiles in Babylon? 2. Why was it wrong for God's people to accuse Him of unfairness? 3. In what ways were the exiles the ones guilty of unfair-ness? 4. What awaited the wicked if they repented of their sin? 5. Why did God so strongly urge the wicked to repent?

■ ILLUSTRATIONS:

Sometimes You Have to Be Firm. A rough and tumble sort of fellow experienced a dramatic conversion and was eager to serve the Lord. He kept pestering his pastor for something to do around the church to show his love for Christ. The pastor had no idea what this man could do. In desperation the pastor gave the zealous convert a list of 10 names and said, "These are members who seldom attend services. Some are prominent people in the community. Contact them any way you can and try to get them to be more faithful. Use the church stationary to write letters if you want, but get them back in church!"

About three weeks later, a letter arrived from a well-known physician whose name was on the list. In the envelope was a check for $50,000 and this note: "Dear Pastor, enclosed is my check to make up for missed offerings. I'm sorry about my frequent absence from worship. I assure you I will be much more regular in the future. Sincerely, P. T. Kruser, M.D.

"P.S. Would you kindly tell your secretary there is only one 't' in 'dirty' and no 'c' in 'skunk.'"

Ezekiel spoke harsh words to the exiles in Babylon to get their spiritual attention. Sometimes it takes a bit of a jolt before we realize God means business when He calls us to turn from our sins and live uprightly.

Truth Is Like Light. When he was 12 years old, Robert Louis Stevenson already showed the love of language that would make him a master storyteller. He was looking out his upstairs bedroom window late one winter evening and watching the lamplighter kindle one streetlight after another. Stevenson's governess came into his room and asked the frail little boy what he was doing. He replied, "I'm watching a man cut holes in the darkness."

There was a lot of spiritual darkness in the villages of Babylon where the exiles from Judah lived during Ezekiel's time. Hopefully, God's message about individual responsibility "cut many holes in their darkness" (so to speak).

A New Spirit. You might suppose that the most important day in renowned novelist John Grisham's life was when he sold his first book or graduated from law school. Instead, he says it was one Sunday when he was eight years old. The Grishams were in Arkansas where John's father worked construction seven days a week. His mother always scrubbed her kids and took them to the local church for Sunday school and worship.

Grisham told an interviewer, "I came under conviction when I was in the third grade, and I talked with my mother. I told her, 'I don't understand this, but I need to talk to you.' We talked and she led me to Jesus. The following Sunday I made a public confirmation of my faith. In one sense, it was not terribly eventful for an eight-year-old, but it was the most important event in my life."

With the Spirit of God abiding within us, we are able to live for the Lord. Regardless of who we are or what we do (even writing award-winning novels), our lives can be transformed by the power of God through faith in the Messiah.

Zechariah Calls for a Return to God

BACKGROUND SCRIPTURE: Zechariah 1:1-6; 7:8-14; 8:16-17, 20-21, 23
DEVOTIONAL READING: Isaiah 12

KEY VERSE: Thus saith the LORD of hosts; Turn ye unto me, saith the LORD of hosts, and I will turn unto you, saith the LORD of hosts. Zechariah 1:3.

KING JAMES VERSION

ZECHARIAH 1:1 In the eighth month, in the second year of Darius, came the word of the LORD unto Zechariah, the son of Berechiah, the son of Iddo the prophet, saying, 2 The LORD hath been sore displeased with your fathers. 3 Therefore say thou unto them, Thus saith the LORD of hosts; Turn ye unto me, saith the LORD of hosts, and I will turn unto you, saith the LORD of hosts. 4 Be ye not as your fathers, unto whom the former prophets have cried, saying, Thus saith the LORD of hosts; Turn ye now from your evil ways, and from your evil doings: but they did not hear, nor hearken unto me, saith the LORD. 5 Your fathers, where are they? and the prophets, do they live for ever? 6 But my words and my statutes, which I commanded my servants the prophets, did they not take hold of your fathers? and they returned and said, Like as the LORD of hosts thought to do unto us, according to our ways, and according to our doings, so hath he dealt with us. . . .

7:8 And the word of the LORD came unto Zechariah, saying, 9 Thus speaketh the LORD of hosts, saying, Execute true judgment, and shew mercy and compassions every man to his brother: 10 And oppress not the widow, nor the fatherless, the stranger, nor the poor; and let none of you imagine evil against his brother in your heart. 11 But they refused to hearken, and pulled away the shoulder, and stopped their ears, that they should not hear. 12 Yea, they made their hearts as an adamant stone, lest they should hear the law, and the words which the LORD of hosts hath sent in his spirit by the former prophets: therefore came a great wrath from the LORD of hosts. 13 Therefore it is come to pass, that as he cried, and they would not hear; so they cried, and I would not hear, saith the LORD of hosts: 14 But I scattered them with a whirlwind among all the nations whom they knew not. Thus the land was desolate after them, that no man passed through nor returned: for they laid the pleasant land desolate.

NEW REVISED STANDARD VERSION

ZECHARIAH 1:1 In the eighth month, in the second year of Darius, the word of the LORD came to the prophet Zechariah son of Berechiah son of Iddo, saying: 2 The LORD was very angry with your ancestors. 3 Therefore say to them, Thus says the LORD of hosts: Return to me, says the LORD of hosts, and I will return to you, says the LORD of hosts. 4 Do not be like your ancestors, to whom the former prophets proclaimed, "Thus says the LORD of hosts, Return from your evil ways and from your evil deeds." But they did not hear or heed me, says the LORD. 5 Your ancestors, where are they? And the prophets, do they live forever? 6 But my words and my statutes, which I commanded my servants the prophets, did they not overtake your ancestors? So they repented and said, "The LORD of hosts has dealt with us according to our ways and deeds, just as he planned to do." . . .

7:8 The word of the LORD came to Zechariah, saying: 9 Thus says the LORD of hosts: Render true judgments, show kindness and mercy to one another; 10 do not oppress the widow, the orphan, the alien, or the poor; and do not devise evil in your hearts against one another. 11 But they refused to listen, and turned a stubborn shoulder, and stopped their ears in order not to hear. 12 They made their hearts adamant in order not to hear the law and the words that the LORD of hosts had sent by his spirit through the former prophets. Therefore great wrath came from the LORD of hosts. 13 Just as, when I called, they would not hear, so, when they called, I would not hear, says the LORD of hosts, 14 and I scattered them with a whirlwind among all the nations that they had not known. Thus the land they left was desolate, so that no one went to and fro, and a pleasant land was made desolate.

12

407

Monday, August 13	James 4:6-10	*How to Return to God*
Tuesday, August 14	Psalm 103:8-18	*God's Everlasting Love*
Wednesday, August 15	Isaiah 12	*God Is My Salvation*
Thursday, August 16	Zechariah 1:1-6	*Return to God*
Friday, August 17	Zechariah 7:8-14	*The People Refuse God*
Saturday, August 18	Zechariah 8:1-8	*Divine Deliverance for God's People*
Sunday, August 19	Zechariah 8:14-17, 20-23	*Seek the Lord*

BACKGROUND

Zechariah, like his contemporary, Haggai, encouraged the people of Israel to again start to rebuild the temple in Jerusalem. The project had initially begun in 536 B.C., but it was interrupted until about 520 B.C. because of Samaritan opposition and indifference on the part of many of the Jews. Through the ministry of Zechariah and Haggai, the building of the temple was begun again and was completed in 516 B.C.

Zechariah's ministry began in October–November 520 B.C. (Zech. 1:1). The last date the prophet mentioned is December 7, 518 B.C. (7:1). However, conservative scholars generally agree that his ministry did not end until sometime between 480 and 470 B.C. This would account for the difference in style of Zechariah's writing between the first eight chapters and the last six chapters.

Zechariah was a relatively young man when he began his ministry (2:4). He was also the son and grandson of priests, his grandfather's name being Iddo (1:1; see Nehemiah 12:4). Therefore, Zechariah ministered as both a priest and a prophet as he encouraged his people to complete the rebuilding of the Jerusalem temple.

Despite the similarities in the historical backgrounds of Haggai and Zechariah, their ministries differed in emphasis. Haggai's work centered on the rebuilding of the temple, while Zechariah's was largely designed to encourage God's people about the welfare of Jerusalem and its long-term future. Zechariah challenged the returning exiles to turn to the Lord, to be cleansed from their sins, and to experience again the Lord's blessings.

The book contains a variety of literary forms. The visions of the first part (chaps. 1—8) are similar to the visions of Ezekiel and Daniel, in part because later prophecy in Israel employed more visions. The visions of the horsemen (Zech. 1:7-11), the four chariots (6:1-8), and the woman in the basket (5:5-11) might be viewed as apocalyptic (or revelatory). This is also true of chapter 14, which contains a description of a climactic battle against Jerusalem, in which the Lord comes as a victorious warrior to rescue His people from their enemies.

A major concept in Zechariah is the term rendered *Zion*. In fact, Zechariah referred to Zion eight times in his prophecy. The name *Zion* initially referred to the fortified hilltop of Jerusalem before the Israelites occupied the town. The hill was located between the Tyropoeon and Kidron valleys. After David captured the stronghold of Zion (2 Sam. 5:6-9), he changed its name to the City of David. The name *Zion* eventually became a synonym for Jerusalem.

The biblical writers used *Zion* in a number of ways. Isaiah used the term to refer to the entire nation of Israel (Isa. 1:27). Amos called the capital of Judah *Zion* (Amos 6:1). Writers often used *Zion* to describe Solomon's temple (Ps. 132:13). The most common use of the term *Zion* is to describe the city of God in the age to come. The name is often used to refer to the Jerusalem that will come down from heaven (Isa. 60:14; Heb. 12:22; Rev. 14:1). Theologically, the term *Zion* refers to the dwelling place of God. That is why the Hebrews believed *Zion* was impenetrable and unconquerable. This led to a false sense of security that ultimately contributed to the fall of Jerusalem.

NOTES ON THE PRINTED TEXT

The Book of Zechariah begins by identifying its author and the historical context of his ministry (1:1). Zechariah, whose name means "God remembers," was born in Babylon and returned to Jerusalem with Zerubbabel and Joshua in 538 B.C. He took over the leadership of the family from Iddo, his grandfather (see Neh. 12:4, 16). Zechariah's father, Berechiah, died early or for some other reason was not able to carry on the leadership of the family.

Zechariah was a young man when he began his ministry (2:4). He was also a member of a priestly family. Therefore, Zechariah ministered as both a priest and a prophet as he encouraged God's people to complete the rebuilding of the Jerusalem temple. This explains his vital interest in the spiritual well-being of the Jews.

In 1:2, Zechariah stated that the Lord was very angry with the ancestors of His people. The verse suggests a long and controlled indignation and emphasizes God's displeasure with the preexilic Jews. Their sin and idolatry resulted in the destruction of the temple in 586 B.C. and their captivity in Babylon. Zechariah's listeners were well aware that the Exile was a direct result of God's wrath against their ancestors, and they needed to be only briefly reminded of the past. The people of Zechariah's day could change their course and go in the opposite direction from that of their predecessors (1:3). Although they had, to some extent, returned to the Lord, they were encouraged to do more.

The urgency of the command is demonstrated by the repeated use of the title LORD *of hosts.* The phrase emphasizes God's majestic sovereignty. This was a key concept in the post-exilic world of towering human empires and rulers. If the Jews returned to God, He promised to return to them. Isaiah, Jeremiah, and Ezekiel warned the preexilic Jews to turn away from their wickedness and evil behavior, but these ancestors refused to listen to God speaking through the prophets (1:4). Their defiance was the primary reason for the Exile in Babylon. As 2 Chronicles 36:16 explains, they mocked God's messengers, despised His warnings, and ridiculed His prophets. The Lord's anger against His people burned so intensely that there was no one who could prevent His judgment.

Zechariah used rhetorical questions to emphasize the results of the earlier disobedience and to note that the ancestors and prophets of the Jews had died a long time ago. The abruptness of these questions suggests an unexpected end of life. The prophet did not have to elaborate on the calamities that came upon them, for the events were fresh in everyone's memory. While the lives of the prophets and people were temporary (Zech. 1:5), God's Word remained active and powerful (1:6). His words lived on to be fulfilled, as was shown by how they caught up with the earlier generation of Jews. The Hebrew word rendered *take hold of* is a hunting term and implies that the Word of God pursued, caught, and put to death the evildoers.

Zechariah clearly implied the messages heralded by the earlier prophets were the inspired words of God (see 2 Pet. 1:20-21). Although the people chose to ignore them, God's warnings were fulfilled exactly as given by His messengers. Apparently, some of the Jews' ancestors did repent, either before or after the Exile began (Zech. 1:6). This again shows the triumph of God's Word as some of the people eventually recognized its truth. Zechariah hoped that his listeners would respond immediately to his call for repentance and not wait until it was too late.

In 7:8-10, the prophet emphasized the spiritual renewal of the people. And he did so in response to a question posed by representatives from Bethel (7:1-3). This town once served as a center of worship for the northern kingdom. Former residents of Bethel were among the first captives to return from Babylon (see Ezra 2:28). Apparently, this remnant quickly rebuilt the city and were eager to obey the Lord. The people of Bethel sent representatives to inquire of Zechariah. They wondered whether they should continue the discipline of fasting as they had done in Babylon (Zech. 7:3). God called into question the motives of those whose worship had become empty and meaningless. They were fasting and feasting with little thought of their relationship with the Lord (7:4-7).

In contrast to the shallow attitude shown in the fasting, Zechariah proclaimed the essence of God's former message to His people (7:8). With four commands he summed up the teaching of the earlier prophets. The admonition to *execute true judgment* (7:9) involved more than just rendering fair sentences in a judicial court. It also meant protecting all individuals in a society from inequities and partiality. Related to that, the prophet told the people to show tender love and loyalty in their relationships with each other. The earlier prophets frequently denounced oppression.

In 7:10, Zechariah selected some of the common victims of persecution to illustrate his point. The widow, fatherless, strangers, and poor were all in a position where they could easily be wronged. God made it clear that any infringements upon their rights would bring His wrath. Not only did the prophets command the people not to oppress each other, but they also told them not to even contemplate the idea of harming someone else. True fasting could not take place if the Jews were treating others unjustly, failing to show love to each other, oppressing the weak, or even just considering an action that would harm someone else.

Although the Lord issued decrees repeatedly through His prophets, the preexilic Jews refused to take God's message seriously. Pulling away the shoulder was akin to stubbornly turning away one's back, while stopping the ears spoke to impairing one's ability to hear and heed the divine injunctions (7:11). Zechariah's message to the people was clear: Do not imitate the behavior of your obstinate ancestors, or you may suffer a similar end. The prophet accused the former generations of hardening themselves against the Lord and refusing to listen to Him (7:12). Despite the effort of the Spirit of the almighty Lord in speaking directly through His prophets to the people, their hearts were as hard as a rock, and so God's Word did not penetrate their souls. As a result, the Lord was angry at them.

Because the people refused the Lord's repeated calls for repentance, He would not listen to them when they cried for help in the midst of their distress (7:13). Jeremiah warned the people of this dire consequence of their disobedience (see Jer. 11:11-14). The Lord's anger resulted in the exile of His wayward people among all the nations (Zech. 7:14). This was one of the curses for breaking God's covenant with them (see Deut. 28:64-68). The unbelief and sin of the preexilic Jews brought captivity for Judah. None of them crossed through or returned to the once fruitful land, which was now left desolate behind them.

SUGGESTIONS TO TEACHERS

Like Haggai the prophet, Zechariah encouraged the people to return to the Lord and finish building the temple. The book that bears his name used a mixture of exhortation, prophetic visions, and judgment oracles to get its message across. Several messianic prophecies come from Zechariah, including the Messiah's coming on a donkey (9:9), His betrayal for 30 pieces of silver (11:12), and the striking of the shepherd (13:7).

1. A SUMMONS TO BE VIRTUOUS. Many of the conditions in post-exilic Judah during Zechariah's time are also present in our world today. And this is why we need the message Zechariah preached to his generation. The words of God through this prophet call us back to moral values and ethical guidelines.

2. A SUMMONS TO BE UPRIGHT. God chose Zechariah to denounce sin, and the prophet did so with candor. He was not afraid to condemn the superficial religion and oppression of the poor prevalent in his day. God has also called us to advance the cause of truth and goodness as well as justice and righteousness in the world. He also wants us to act compassionately to stop injustice and to help care for those in need.

3. A SUMMONS TO BE SOCIALLY CONSCIOUS. Instead of spending so much time on our wants and even our needs, we should evaluate our walk with Christ and determine whether we are aware of God's concerns for social issues. If we do not, we may find ourselves in the same spiritual condition as Zechariah's listeners.

4. A SUMMONS TO RETURN TO GOD. The people of Zechariah's day related to God in a perfunctory manner. Our devotion to God becomes formal and lifeless when we merely go through the motions of worship. Rather than love God and the people He created, we busy ourselves in a flurry of religious activities. The solution is to unclutter our minds of everyday concerns and chores and refocus our attention on God's concerns for social issues.

FOR ADULTS

■ **TOPIC:** Call for Repentance

■ **QUESTIONS:** 1. Why had the Lord been angry with the ancestors of the exiles? 2. Why did the Lord exhort His people to return to Him? 3. Why did the preexilic Jews balk at heeding the Lord's decrees? 4. Why had God's people failed to administer justice to the disadvantaged? 5. Why had God's people stubbornly refused to pay attention to His prophets?

■ **ILLUSTRATIONS:**

How Shall We Respond? "Too many of us play at Christianity. We wear salvation as a kind of convention badge admitting us into the circle of the elect, but rarely stop to focus our whole lives seriously on God's claims upon us." That was the analysis of Christian author, editor, and minister, A.W. Tozer (1897–1963), several generations ago. Those words are just as incisive today.

What does Tozer say we should do instead? "Throw yourself out recklessly upon God. Give up everything and prepare yourself to surrender even unto death all of your ambitions, plans, and possessions," he exhorted. In the lives of Christians you know, how might the surrender that Tozer advocated look? Would all them respond favorably to a divine summons to repent?

Called to Commitment. The Calvary Chapel association has caught the essence of Jesus' call to His original disciples by training lay persons to live out their Christian commitment. Founded in 1965 by Chuck Smith, Calvary Chapel now claims over 600 congregations in the United States and another hundred worldwide, including the former Soviet bloc. Chuck Smith and his fellow pastors stress strong lay leadership, and they plant new churches by sending these lay people as a small core from parent churches. The leadership often quote the following slogan: GOD DOES NOT CALL THE QUALIFIED; HE QUALIFIES THE CALLED. Are those in your class aware of the truth of this saying?

What Kind of Commitment? The Roper Center for Public Opinion Research at the University of Connecticut publishes a journal entitled *Public Perspective*. In it the Center shows the results of careful polls carried out by George Gallup. A couple of years ago, one survey indicated what Gallup called "gaps" in the religious affairs of Americans. For instance, "the ethics gap" showed the disturbing difference between what people said and what they did.

Gallup also identified what he labeled "the knowledge gap." He pointed out the huge difference between what persons in this country claim to believe and their appalling lack of the most basic knowledge about their faith.

The third was "the church gap." Gallup found that Americans tended to view their faith mostly as a matter between themselves and the Lord, and not tied to or affected by any congregation or religious institution. They were not influenced by the church or any form of organized religion, and saw no need to be committed to any faith community.

Gallup summed up his report by suggesting that Americans want the fruits of faith but few of its obligations. Of the list of 19 social values tested in the polls, "following God's will" ranked low on the list, coming after "happiness, satisfaction, and a sense of accomplishment."

What Kind of Service? "I'm in the Lord's service, too," the man announced loudly, trying to impress a saintly visiting missionary. The man's wife, who knew the bigmouth better than anyone else, chimed in, "Yeah, the secret service." Is your commitment to Christ evident to those closest to you?

FOR YOUTH

■ TOPIC: Grow Up, Take Responsibility, and Speak the Truth
■ QUESTIONS: 1. Why did the Lord, through Zechariah, urge the people to be virtuous? 2. Why did the ancestors of God's people refuse to heed the warnings of the prophets? 3. How did the people of Zechariah's day respond to his prophetic declarations? 4. Why did the Lord want His people to be kind and merciful to others? 5. What could God's people do to avoid experiencing desolation?

■ ILLUSTRATIONS:

Willing to Take Responsibility. In October 2005, *OPB News* correspondent, Colin Fogarty, told the story of a 17-year-old teen named Stanley Waters. The resident of Portland, Oregon, lives in a neighborhood where "drugs and gangs are never far away." And in his short life, he's attended almost a dozen different schools while being "shuffled from one relative to another with his siblings."

In addition, Stanley is "exceptionally polite, clean cut, clearly smart" and a whiz at the piano. Because of his innate ability, he is able to master a complex musical score "by hearing a piece just a few times." Stanley's mother—a recovering drug addict—says his "hours and hours at the piano has been a means of emotional escape for him."

Here's an adolescent who has survived and thrived in a less-than-ideal situation. Indeed, his tough life circumstances have not prevented him from acting in a mature, responsible manner. He really is an inspiration for today's youth!

Speaking the Truth. When the skyscrapers of New York City were hit by terrorists on September 11, 2001, it radically affected the American psyche. Hijacked commercial jetliners filled with passengers plunged into the top floors of both towers of the World Trade Center in lower Manhattan, destroying both of the buildings and killing thousands.

In the months that followed, the drop-off in air-travel was extreme, creating desperate financial conditions for many airlines. It also created desperate psychological conditions for many, including Jared Millens. Giving motivational and inspirational messages to others was Jared's life work, but it necessitated a significant amount of air travel. Now, he found himself in need of that inspiration and motivation.

Jared had been a Christian most of his life. He came from a home with godly parents, and his own family was deeply committed to the Savior. After the initial shock of the bombing attacks, Jared and his wife and children sat down together and talked about the fears of accident and destruction. Jared was comforted by the statements of truth given by his youngest daughter. She said, "Daddy, don't forget the verse that says, 'Greater is He who is in us, than he who is in the world.'"

A Declaration of Encouragement. The movie *The Hiding Place* shows how Corrie ten Boom and her sister Betsie were sent by the Nazis to a women's work camp for their part in helping to hide Jews in their father's home. In one scene, after Corrie's sister had died, the women of the camp were all standing at roll call on a bitter cold December day. This particular morning, Corrie's name was called, and she was told to step forward, presumably to be taken away and put to death.

But before leaving her place in the lineup, Corrie handed her tiny New Testament to the woman next to her, encouraging her in her newfound faith. Then, as Corrie made her way forward, she turned to the rest of the women, and in a voice husky with emotion, declared, "God is with you!"

God, not the Nazis, would prevail in their hearts and lives. God, not the Nazis, held their days, hours, and months in His hand. And God, not the Nazis, could give them eternal salvation.

MALACHI DESCRIBES GOD'S JUST JUDGMENT

BACKGROUND SCRIPTURE: Malachi 2:17—4:3
DEVOTIONAL READING: Psalm 34:11-22

KEY VERSES: Behold, I will send my messenger, and he shall prepare the way before me: and the LORD, whom ye seek, shall suddenly come to his temple. . . . But who may abide the day of his coming? and who shall stand when he appeareth? Malachi 3:1-2.

KING JAMES VERSION

MALACHI 2:17 Ye have wearied the LORD with your words. Yet ye say, Wherein have we wearied him? When ye say, Every one that doeth evil is good in the sight of the LORD, and he delighteth in them; or, Where is the God of judgment?

3:1 Behold, I will send my messenger, and he shall prepare the way before me: and the Lord, whom ye seek, shall suddenly come to his temple, even the messenger of the covenant, whom ye delight in: behold, he shall come, saith the LORD of hosts. 2 But who may abide the day of his coming? and who shall stand when he appeareth? for he is like a refiner's fire, and like fullers' soap: 3 And he shall sit as a refiner and purifier of silver: and he shall purify the sons of Levi, and purge them as gold and silver, that they may offer unto the LORD an offering in righteousness. 4 Then shall the offering of Judah and Jerusalem be pleasant unto the LORD, as in the days of old, and as in former years.
5 And I will come near to you to judgment; and I will be a swift witness against the sorcerers, and against the adulterers, and against false swearers, and against those that oppress the hireling in his wages, the widow, and the fatherless, and that turn aside the stranger from his right, and fear not me, saith the LORD of hosts. . . .

4:1 For, behold, the day cometh, that shall burn as an oven; and all the proud, yea, and all that do wickedly, shall be stubble: and the day that cometh shall burn them up, saith the LORD of hosts, that it shall leave them neither root nor branch.

NEW REVISED STANDARD VERSION

MALACHI 2:17 You have wearied the LORD with your words. Yet you say, "How have we wearied him?" By saying, "All who do evil are good in the sight of the LORD, and he delights in them." Or by asking, "Where is the God of justice?"

3:1 See, I am sending my messenger to prepare the way before me, and the Lord whom you seek will suddenly come to his temple. The messenger of the covenant in whom you delight—indeed, he is coming, says the LORD of hosts. 2 But who can endure the day of his coming, and who can stand when he appears?
For he is like a refiner's fire and like fullers' soap; 3 he will sit as a refiner and purifier of silver, and he will purify the descendants of Levi and refine them like gold and silver, until they present offerings to the LORD in righteousness. 4 Then the offering of Judah and Jerusalem will be pleasing to the LORD as in the days of old and as in former years.

5 Then I will draw near to you for judgment; I will be swift to bear witness against the sorcerers, against the adulterers, against those who swear falsely, against those who oppress the hired workers in their wages, the widow and the orphan, against those who thrust aside the alien, and do not fear me, says the LORD of hosts. . . .

4:1 See, the day is coming, burning like an oven, when all the arrogant and all evildoers will be stubble; the day that comes shall burn them up, says the LORD of hosts, so that it will leave them neither root nor branch.

13

Monday, August 20	Psalm 34:11-22	*God's Concern for the People*
Tuesday, August 21 1	1 Corinthians 3:10-15	*Our Works Are Tested*
Wednesday, August 22	1 Corinthians 4:1-5	*God Judges Our Hearts*
Thursday, August 23	Malachi 2:17—3:7	*God Will Judge*
Friday, August 24	Malachi 3:8-12	*Will Anyone Rob God?*
Saturday, August 25	Malachi 3:13-18	*Choosing between Good and Evil*
Sunday, August 26	Malachi 4:1-6	*The Day of the Lord*

BACKGROUND

As with many of the prophets, we know little about Malachi's personal circumstances. His ministry evidently took place after Nehemiah's first stint as governor but before his second return to Judah. (Nehemiah was governor of Judah in the fifth century B.C.) This is based on the fact that the conditions described in the Book of Malachi (for example, the presence of mixed marriages, oppression of the poor, sabbath violations, problems with tithing, and economic hardship) closely match conditions mentioned by Nehemiah (Neh. 13; Mal. 1:6; 2:14-16; 3:5-11). The Book of Malachi therefore was written between 450–400 B.C. This would make it the last message from God to Israel until the time of Christ, a period that lasted over four centuries.

Malachi's message was directed toward the second generation of those who returned from captivity. The Hebrew word rendered *burden* (1:1) indicates his oracle was one of condemnation and judgment. God brought a number charges against the priests and people of the restored community. Each time they questioned the veracity of an accusation He made, God responded by validating His point.

In the first charge, God stated His love for Israel. But when the people questioned His love, He asserted that it was true (1:2). Did not the Lord's choice of Jacob (the ancestor of the Israelites) over Esau (the ancestor of the Edomites) verify His love for Israel? Did He not destroy the nation of Edom (1:3)? God also promised that Edom, which historically remained hostile toward Israel, would be destroyed every time she tried to rebuild (1:4). Thus, Israel would see God's love and praise Him (1:5).

In the second charge, God indicted the priests. Rather than honoring the Lord's name, they despised it. Of course, they questioned the validity of this accusation (1:6). The fact that the priests offered unclean sacrifices was sufficient proof (1:7-8). In contrast to what God desired, the priests offered what was blind, lame, and sick. God argued that the ruler of Persia would not look favorably on those who did not give him what was pleasing. Therefore, why should the Lord, the heavenly ruler, be treated worse than an earthly ruler (1:8-9)?

Tragically, the priests made no attempt to stop offering unacceptable sacrifices (1:10). They kept the doors of the temple open and continued to offer polluted sacrifices. God declared that one day even the Gentiles will honor His name and offer Him what is pleasing (1:11). The priests, however, continually defiled God's name with their words and actions. They spoke disrespectfully of the Lord's altar and its food. They also complained that their service at the altar was a troublesome burden. God, the great king, censured them for offering blemished animals instead of the acceptable ones they had (1:12-14).

God again addressed the unfaithful priests (2:1). He commanded them to honor His name, or else He would turn their blessings into a curse (2:2-3). This warning would signal to them that the Lord intended to keep His covenant with the priesthood of Levi (2:4). God blessed Levi because he revered Him, spoke the truth, lived in intimate fellowship with God, and was His messenger before the people (2:5-7). The unfaithful priests, however, did not have intimate fellowship with God and did not speak the truth to the people (2:8-9).

God's people had debased the covenant of their ancestors by marrying pagan women. The wives of such unholy unions often influenced the Israelites to worship false gods. That is why God loathed such marriages (2:10-11). The prophet asked God to deal forthrightly with the offenders and their supporters (2:12). Others were divorcing their Israelite wives. God, of course, abhorred this display of marital unfaithfulness (2:13-14). He had created the man to become one with his wife, to have children, and to encourage the children to walk with God (2:15). That is why He directed His people to ensure that marital infidelity never occurred (2:16).

NOTES ON THE PRINTED TEXT

God accused His people of wearing Him out with their words. The cynical had asserted that God was pleased with evil and did not care about justice (Mal. 2:17). Their suffering in the Exile caused them to think that God favored the cause of the wicked, who seemed to enjoy prosperity while breaking God's moral law. They reasoned that if God was holy, He certainly would have judged them by now.

This questioning of God's justice showed that the people no longer feared Him or believed in His power to judge evil in the world. Their attitude resulted from a lack of faith in God's Word as well as a blindness to what was happening around them. They skipped over the Lord's message of judgment for sinners and did not see the emptiness and disastrous end of those they envied.

The question of God's justice had special significance in the Old Testament because the Lord had promised to reward Israel's obedience with material prosperity (Deut. 28:1-14). The promise, however, applied to the entire nation and was therefore difficult to carry out in a context in which wickedness and righteousness were found together among the people.

In response to the questioning of His justice, the Lord promised to send His messenger, who would prepare the way before Him. In Hebrew, the phrase rendered *my messenger* (Mal. 3:1) is *malaki*, which is the same form as the prophet's name. However, in this verse the messenger is an end-time figure who was about to come.

According to 4:5, *Elijah the prophet* is the messenger. The New Testament identified this person as John the Baptist (Matt. 11:10; Mark 1:2) because he came in the power and authority of Elijah (Matt. 11:14; 17:11-12; Luke 1:17). Thus, John could be a separate personality from Elijah and yet fulfill the promise. John's work is described as preparing the way before the Lord. In ancient times, Eastern kings sent men before them in their travels to remove barriers from their path. John's purpose was to remove opposition to the Lord by preaching a message of repentance to sinners.

A second view states that John did not completely fulfill the prophecy. John himself denied that he was Elijah (John 1:21). The mention of the day of the Lord in connection with Elijah in Malachi 3:5 also shows that this prophecy is still future, since that day has not yet come. Accordingly, some have identified the two witnesses in Revelation 11:1-14 as Moses and Elijah.

A third view equates the *messenger of the covenant* (Mal. 3:1) with the Lord Himself. Along with the other cases, this messenger enforces God's covenant with His people, who were guilty of violating that solemn agreement. Concerning the Messiah, He came to the temple as a baby and then most notably during the last week before His crucifixion. Even in their sin, the Jews of the postexilic community desired deliverance through the Messiah. But as Malachi proceeded to point out, the people were not ready for the Redeemer's coming.

Along with vindication for the righteous, the coming of the Lord ultimately meant judgment for the wicked. The covenant-breaking Jews, as well as the wicked of all other nations, would find the day of the Lord to be a terrible time of punishment. Although the people of the postexilic community expressed a desire for it, none of them would be able to endure it in their present state.

The Lord's judgment at His coming is compared with two purifying agents: fire for metals and soap for clothing (3:2). With respect to the refiner's fire, people in ancient times used intense heat to melt metal. This allowed the dross, which floated to the top, to be scooped off. Both metaphors indicated that God's intention would not be to destroy the nation, but to purify it. His purpose would be to purge out the wickedness in Judah.

In 3:3, the Lord is represented as a smelter who watches both the intensity of the fire and the metal being purified of its dross. The Messiah would cleanse the entire nation, beginning with the Levites. Above all else, God was concerned about the holiness of His people. Once the refining process was complete, God would have an acceptable priesthood to carry out the sacred temple ministry. Because the offerings and gifts would be given from hearts right in the sight of God, they would be acceptable before Him. As in the past, probably the days of Moses and Phinehas, the sacrificial worship of the priests would be pleasing to the Lord (3:4).

Besides purifying the Levites, God would judge sinful people when He came (3:5). Sorcerers are the first addressed in the list of wicked behavior. Magical arts prevailed in Judah in post-captivity days, perhaps due to the influence of the foreign wives. Adulterers included those who divorced their Jewish wives so they could marry idolatrous women. Those who swore falsely were perjurers. For instance, while under oath in a court of law, they gave fradulent testimony. They also broke promises they had vowed to keep.

Malachi's concern for social justice comes out clearly in the last half of his list. Those who treated their servants unfairly in regard to wages are included along with the adulterers, those who oppressed the weak in society (such as the widow and the orphan), and those who deprived immigrants and resident aliens of justice. All these examples of evil behavior are traced to one source: a lack of reverence and respect for the Lord.

The mention of God's judgment upon the wicked in 3:16 led the prophet into a discussion of the day of the Lord in chapter 4. This day, so prominent in Old Testament prophecy, refers to the time when God's wrath will be poured out on the rebellious human race. Fire, a symbol of God's judgment, will be the means of destruction upon the earth, just as water was in the days of Noah (4:1). Like stubble that lasts only for moments when thrown into a blazing furnace, the wicked will be completely destroyed. None of them will escape this judgment. The arrogant who were envied by the Jews are specifically mentioned as being totally consumed in God's furnace. How much better it is to fear the Lord and be spared His wrath!

SUGGESTIONS TO TEACHERS

In our day, when "tolerance" seems to be the highest virtue, many feel it does not matter what you believe or what you do. Malachi disagrees. Only through faithfulness to the true God can we leave off messing around with things that don't matter and connect ourselves with what God really wants to do in human history.

1. SOME DON'T KNOW HOW MUCH DANGER THEY ARE IN. Many in Malachi's day looked forward to the Messiah's coming, little suspecting that His coming might mean judgment for them. Likewise, many of our friends and neighbors (and even we ourselves?) take the possibility of judgment too lightly.

2. GOD WANTS TRUE WORSHIP. Some are "high church"; some are "low church." Some are "charismatic"; some are not. What matters more than these kinds of distinctions is that we worship God honestly and openly, with contrite hearts, purified through faith in the Christ of Scripture.

3. GOD IS AWARE OF EACH BELIEVER. None of us need ever think that God is so busy with great world events that He overlooks a single believing heart. Do you truly believe in Jesus, God's Son? Are you trying to live a holy life? Take comfort: *God knows.*

4. THE DESTINIES OF THE WICKED AND OF THE RIGHTEOUS DRAS-TICALLY DIVERGE. Though many in our day refuse to believe it, there is a time of reckoning coming. Destruction awaits those who live for themselves instead of for God, while joy awaits the forgiven.

5. JESUS CHRIST IS AT THE CENTER OF JUDGMENT. For each person, the Lord Christ is either Savior or Judge. His coming forces each one to choose, and what we decide to do with Him determines what will occur when we stand before His throne.

FOR ADULTS

■ TOPIC: Living Responsibly in the Community of Faith

■ QUESTIONS: 1. How had the people of God wearied Him with their words? 2. What is the identity of the messenger the Lord promised to send? 3. What similes did God use to describe His messenger? 4. What did the Lord promise to do to evildoers in the day of reckoning? 5. What will the day of the Lord be like?

■ **ILLUSTRATIONS:**

Different Destinies. Tom lay seriously ill in the intensive care unit of the hospital after having major surgery. Although a good family man, he had not been a faithful, practicing Christian. Did he understand the different destinies that confronted him? He heard the pastor's words about God's love and forgiveness in Christ. How hard it was to be sure whether he understood his need to admit his sins and receive Christ.

Sadly, many people are like Tom. They do not reach out to God early in life, even though they have a religious upbringing. God is not a major factor in their lives. They do not realize that the choice they make in this life will determine their future in the next.

Malachi made different destinies clear in his powerful images of judgment and blessing. How much better it is to turn to God as our loving Father than to receive His just condemnation in the end. Our lives will be filled with His eternal blessings when we choose to live responsibly in the community of faith.

Responsible Christianity. At the height of the 1960s social revolution, Francis A. Schaeffer dared to write a book called *the God who is there*. (For emphasis, he capitalized only the word "God" in its title.) In a culture proclaiming, "God is dead" and "God is irrelevant," the God who is there" stood apart. He still does.

In an attempt to clear the intellectual haze permeating the 1960s culture, Schaeffer reminded his Christian contemporaries that "there are two aspects of lostness," namely, "present and future." Schaeffer noted that before trusting in the Messiah, he was spiritually dead. It was only through receiving Christ by faith that Schaeffer passed from "death to life." He stressed that it is the responsibility of Christians to tell people that "the present death" they know is "moral death and not just metaphysical lostness" with which they wrestle.

Clearly, there are differences between believers and unbelievers. And to blur those distinctions is to slash at the heart of the Gospel. All is not well with a person's soul until it is grafted onto the Savior through faith. As Schaeffer emphasized, it is irresponsible to water down the Gospel in order to make it palatable to our culture. To dilute it is to alter its meaning and void it of its power.

Decisions that Make a Difference. Once again, a legal technicality had rescued Cheryl—she was free to go. The prosecutor threw down his notepad in disgust as Cheryl smirked at him on her way out of the courtroom. It was another loss for justice and another step toward darkness for Cheryl.

The young woman had been in courtrooms since childhood, first for custody hearings, but soon for a variety of crimes. Cheryl was a "habitual offender" who knew how to play the system, and she was rarely convicted. Among the crowd of unsavory characters she ran with, she was affectionately known as "Cheryl: Princess of Thieves."

Three years later, the same prosecutor again had his grip on Cheryl. She was sentenced to two years in jail. While serving her time, Cheryl was gloriously saved. She said it was the persistent witness of a volunteer chaplain who had made the difference.

When Cheryl got out of jail, she went right back to her old crowd, but with a calling from God to win them for Christ. Cheryl took her responsibility seriously. She shared the Good News with them, and the results were extraordinary. Her unconditional love was her pulpit, and her changed life was her message.

FOR YOUTH

■ **TOPIC:** Here Comes the Son
■ **QUESTIONS:** 1. What did the Lord say His messenger would do for Him? 2. Why would God refine the Levites like gold and silver (Mal. 3:3)? 3. What promises did the Lord make to the upright remnant? 4. How would God bring about the purification of His people? 5. What would the day of the Lord be like for the unrighteous?

■ **ILLUSTRATIONS:**
Differing Values. Jim's best friend and fellow athlete went for a drive one night. Earl seemed like a good guy who went to church. Despite the fact that they were both under the legal drinking age, Earl took a six-pack of beer in his car and urged Jim to drink a can with him. Jim refused. From then on they drifted apart, Earl into a rather typical pattern of short-term jobs and drinking and Jim into the ministry.

Of course, that one decision did not determine how they would live their lives. But it does illustrate the different choices you as a young person will have to make, not just about drinking but also about sexual practices, using drugs, cheating in class, and so on. As you seek to live responsibly for the Lord, you will want others to see that your Christian values differ sharply from the world's.

In Malachi's day, God's people thought the unbelievers were enjoying the good life while they suffered. Many of them decided to join the evildoers. Malachi told God's people to repent, especially if they wished to be spared divine judgment and receive the Lord's blessings when the Savior appeared.

Here Comes the Son! In the summer of 1969, the Beatles recorded "Here Comes the Sun" at the Abbey Road Studios in London. The song is about the change of seasons from a "long cold lonely winter" to the feel-good days of summer. The song celebrates the arrival of warmer, brighter moments in which ice melts away and smiles return to the faces of people.

At the Savior's first advent, the brilliant light of His presence dispersed the dark, gloomy shadow of the evil one. Hope replaced despair and salvation pushed aside enslavement to sin. Jesus truly is *the bright and morning star* (Rev. 22:16), whom all believers long to see at His second advent.

Surprising Rescue. Jeffrey Bils and Stacey Singer reported in the *Chicago Tribune* that on Friday, August 16, 1996, a group of nine children and three adults were enjoying the animals of the Tropic World exhibit at Brookfield Zoo in Chicago. They walked to the large gorilla pit where seven western lowland gorillas live in an environment that resembles their native home, with flowing water, trees, and grass.

Then, what every mother fears actually happened. Somehow, as the group viewed the gorillas from the highest point overlooking the pen, a three-year-old boy climbed up the railing without his mother seeing him. He then tumbled over the railing and fell some 24 feet to the concrete floor of the gorilla pit. As he fell, his face struck the wall, and when he landed, he lay completely still.

At the sight of the toddler left at the mercy of gorillas, the crowd immediately began screaming and calling for help. One gorilla, named Binti-Jua, quickly moved toward the boy. She reached down with one arm and picked him up. With him in one arm and her own baby gorilla on her back, she carried the boy some 40 feet to the door where the zookeepers enter.

When another gorilla moved toward her, Binti-Jua turned away, shielding the boy. Then she gently laid him down at the door of the gorilla pit and waited with him until zookeepers arrived to take him away. Meanwhile, other staff sprayed water at the other gorillas to keep them away. The boy was rushed to the hospital in critical condition, but he soon recovered and returned home.

The fact that the gorilla Binti-Jua saved rather than mauled the little boy was a surprising outcome to a menacing situation. Like Binti-Jua, many things we fear are actually used by God to rescue us. Our Lord is the God of surprising outcomes, the God who sends astonishing deliverance.

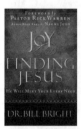
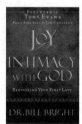

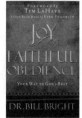

The Word at Work...
Around the World

What would you do if you wanted to share God's love with children on the streets of your city? That's the dilemma David C. Cook faced in 1870s Chicago. His answer was to create literature that would capture children's hearts.

Out of those humble beginnings grew a worldwide ministry that has used literature to proclaim God's love and disciple generation after generation. Cook Communications Ministries is committed to personal discipleship—to helping people of all ages learn God's Word, embrace his salvation, walk in his ways, and minister in his name.

Opportunities—and Crisis

We live in a land of plenty—including plenty of Christian literature! But what about the rest of the world? Jesus commanded, "Go and make disciples of all nations" (Matt. 28:19) and we want to obey this commandment. But how does a publishing organization "go" into all the world?

There are five times as many Christians around the world as there are in North America. Christian workers in many of these countries have no more than a New Testament, or perhaps a single shared copy of the Bible, from which to learn and teach.

We are committed to sharing what God has given us with such Christians.

A vital part of Cook Communications Ministries is our international outreach, Cook Communications Ministries International (CCMI). Your purchase of this book, and of other books and Christian-growth products from Cook, enables CCMI to provide Bibles and Christian literature to people in more than 150 languages in 65 countries.

Cook Communications Ministries is a not-for-profit, self-supporting organization. Revenues from sales of our books, Bible curriculum, and other church and home products not only fund our U.S. ministry, but also fund our CCMI ministry around the world. One hundred percent of donations to CCMI go to our international literature programs.

CCMI reaches out internationally in three ways:

· Our premier International Christian Publishing Institute (ICPI) trains leaders from nationally led publishing houses around the world to develop evangelism and discipleship materials to transform lives in their countries.

· We provide literature for pastors, evangelists, and Christian workers in their national language. We provide study helps for pastors and lay leaders in many parts of the world, such as China, India, Cuba, Iran, and Vietnam.

· We reach people at risk—refugees, AIDS victims, street children, and famine victims—with God's Word. CCMI puts literature that shares the Good News into the hands of people at spiritual risk—people who might die before they hear the name of Jesus and are transformed by his love.

Word Power—God's Power

Faith Kidz, RiverOak, Honor, Life Journey, Victor, NexGen — every time you purchase a book produced by Cook Communications Ministries, you not only meet a vital personal need in your life or in the life of someone you love, but you're also a part of ministering to José in Colombia, Humberto in Chile, Gousa in India, or Lidiane in Brazil. You help make it possible for a pastor in China, a child in Peru, or a mother in West Africa to enjoy a life-changing book. And because you helped, children and adults around the world are learning God's Word and walking in his ways.

Thank you for your partnership in helping to disciple the world. May God bless you with the power of his Word in your life.

For more information about our international ministries, visit www.ccmi.org.